APPLIED DEVELOPMENTAL SCIENCE

The SAGE Program on Applied Developmental Science

Consulting Editor
Richard M. Lerner

The field of Applied Developmental Science has advanced the use of cutting-edge developmental systems models of human development, fostered strength-based approaches to understanding and promoting positive development across the life span, and served as a frame for collaborations among researchers and practitioners, including policymakers, seeking to enhance the life chances of diverse young people, their families, and communities. The **SAGE Program on Applied Developmental Science** both integrates and extends this scholarship by publishing innovative and cutting-edge contributions.

APPLIED DEVELOPMENTAL SCIENCE

An Advanced Textbook

Editors

Richard M. Lerner ◆ Francine Jacobs ◆ Donald Wertlieb

Tufts University

SAGE Publications
Thousand Oaks ▪ London ▪ New Delhi

Copyright © 2005 by Sage Publications, Inc.

For information:

Sage Publications, Inc.
2455 Teller Road
Thousand Oaks, California 91320
E-mail: order@sagepub.com

Sage Publications Ltd.
1 Oliver's Yard
55 City Road
London EC1Y 1SP
United Kingdom

Sage Publications India Pvt. Ltd.
B-42, Panchsheel Enclave
Post Box 4109
New Delhi 110 017 India

Printed in the United States of America

Library of Congress Cataloging-in-Publication data

Applied developmental science : an advanced textbook / editors
Richard M. Lerner, Francine Jacobs, Donald Wertlieb.
    p. cm. — (The Sage program on applied developmental science)
Includes bibliographical references and index.
ISBN 1-4129-1570-8 (pbk. : alk. paper)
    1. Child development. 2. Adolescence. I. Lerner, Richard M.
II. Jacobs, Francine. III. Wertlieb, Donald. IV. Series.
HQ767.9.H345 2005
305.231—dc22

2004024940

05   06   07   08   09   10   9   8   7   6   5   4   3   2   1

Acquiring Editor:	Jim Brace-Thompson
Editorial Assistant:	Karen Ehrmann
Production Editor:	Sanford Robinson
Typesetter:	C&M Digitals (P) Ltd.
Indexer:	Teri Greenberg
Cover Designer:	Michelle Kenny

Contents

Section III: Strengthening Policies and Programs   247

Section IV: Enhancing Service Systems   399

Preface

In the last decades of the twentieth century and in the first years of the present one, the nations of the world experienced a myriad of social problems, some old, some new, but all affecting the lives of vulnerable children, adolescents, adults, families, and communities. Many scholars and practitioners sought to address these issues through preventing their occurrence. Others—a growing proportion—sought to supplement if not supplant prevention with promotion, with attempts to enhance human development by focusing on the strengths of people and the assets of their communities.

With either prevention or promotion approaches to improving the life chances of children, families, and communities, but especially in regard to promotion, scholars have combined dynamic, developmental systems theories of human development with a range of quantitative and qualitative methodologies to address—through research and policy and program applications—the continuing and the contemporary issues affecting the lives of individuals, families, and communities. Together, these issues speak to the need to establish, maintain, and enhance civil society.

This work has reflected and furthered growing interest in *applied developmental science* (ADS). Indeed, over the last two decades, increasing numbers of developmental scientists from diverse disciplines have come to identify themselves professionally as *applied* developmental scientists as partners in building civil society. Joining under this umbrella are colleagues from allied disciplines and specialties in the biological, psychological, social, and behavioral sciences and the helping professions, all sharing the goals and the vision found in ADS, that is, in the use of scientific knowledge about human development to improve the life chances of the diverse infants, children, adolescents, adults, families, and communities of the world.

In order to both reflect the state of these arts and sciences pertinent to applied developmental science and to extend further the burgeoning vision within scholarship and program and policy applications relevant to enhancing positive development among children, their families, and their communities, we edited in 2003 the *Handbook of Applied Developmental Science: Promoting Positive Child, Adolescent, and Family Development Through Research, Policies, and Programs,* a four-volume work encompassing about 100 chapters (Lerner, Jacobs, and Wertlieb, 2003). The vision we sought to further in the *Handbook* is predicated on a belief that infants, children, adolescents, and families have significant strengths and capacities for healthy lives, and that all people possess individual and ecological assets that can be actualized to create their well-being. Such well-being involves having a healthy start in life, living in a safe environment, receiving an education that results in marketable skills, having the opportunity to participate in community life, and living free from prejudice and discrimination. Well-being is marked by individuals who manifest caring and compassion, competence, confidence, positive connections to others, and character. Such individuals, and the families and communities that support them, may be said to be thriving.

Owing to the favorable response to the *Handbook* by scholars, practitioners, policymakers, and students, the present textbook was developed to represent the essential theoretical ideas, research areas, and lessons from practice found across the four volumes. *Applied Developmental Science: An Advanced Textbook* was organized by selecting, in collaboration with members of the audience using the *Handbook,* a set of chapters from the four volumes that reflect the breadth of applied developmental science and, as well, depth of scholarship in a select but representative sample of the work ongoing in this field. The goal in organizing this text was, therefore, to inform graduate students about the foundational ideas in applied developmental science, to provide them with several key instantiations of the research-program and policy perspectives in the field, and to convey the positive vision of human strength, and the potential for promotion of healthy development across thelife span, that marks all facets of the application of developmental science (and that was present across all volumes of the *Handbook*).

It is useful here to comment more fully about the positive, strength-based conception of human behavior inherent in the field of applied developmental science.

THE POSITIVE HUMAN DEVELOPMENT PERSPECTIVE

The positive psychology movement engaging many contemporary scholars, for example, in the January 2000 issue of the *American Psychologist,* edited by Seligman and Csikszentmihalyi, is one instance of the positive human development perspective. However, the positive psychology movement is but one example of a much broader paradigm shift in the field of human development, one that has decades-long roots in developmental science and in the profession of youth development program practice.

For too long, traditions in the behavioral sciences and the helping professions have focused on the negative aspects of human behavior and development; for example, risk, disorders, pathology, and people's problems, deficits, and weaknesses. Positive psychology, as well as the independent but conceptually consonant ideas that have arisen under the labels of "positive youth development," "child well-being," "community youth development," "developmental assets," and "thriving," replace these deficit-oriented approaches by articulating the power of strength-based approaches.

Accordingly, the contributions of colleagues involved in the area of positive psychology are consistent with the now more than decade-long commitment of organizations such as the National 4-H Council and the International Youth Foundation to the promotion of community youth development or to positive infant, child, and adolescent development. This latter work represents commitments of the practitioner and philanthropic communities, respectively, to the growing stress on enhancing the positive features and well-being of the world's young people. Similarly, this emphasis is reflected in the work of Search Institute, which seeks to facilitate the alignment of the individual and ecological assets of communities in order to promote thriving among infants, children, and adolescents. The accomplishments of these groups as well as scores of other contributors to applied developmental science are presented in the *Handbook*. The work of many of these organizations are represented in *Applied Developmental Science: An Advanced Textbook*.

The growing interest in the promotion of positive development offers scholars, practitioners, and policymakers a new and exciting range of theoretical ideas, data sets, programming strategies, evaluation methods, and policy options. However, no graduate textbook has organized this scholarship in a manner that, within one semester, graduate students could access. The *Handbook* was aimed at being comprehensive in its treatment of applied developmental science orientations to programs and policies for children, adolescents, and families. In turn, this textbook provides a specification of the foundation of the field, some of its current and key instantiations of state-of-the-art research and programs dimensions, and some predictions about where the field will be headed during the first decades of the twenty-first century.

We see the publication of *Applied Developmental Science: An Advanced Textbook* as a particularly timely event, given the character of the challenges facing infants, children, adolescents, and families at the dawn of this new millennium and the importance of training a new cohort of scholars and practitioners with the vision and methodological tools needed for the application of developmental science to the promotion of positive human development.

Such training, we believe, is vital for both science and society. Each year, as the world's repository of natural resources declines, its population of children increases by 100 million. How, in the year 2020, will the more than one billion additional children be fed, clothed, and housed? How will their energy needs will be met? How will the world's economies grow the hundreds of millions of jobs required so that these young people are able to contribute effectively and productively to their own well-being and to the well-being of their families and communities? Finally, how will we manage to reduce the marginalization of young people that still occurs—in the United States and around the globe—so that all young people may thrive as engaged citizens of a single, interconnected, civil society. The chapters in *Applied Developmental Science: An Advanced Textbook* offer analyses and proposals for addressing some of these concerns and for building our global civil society.

If we aspire not only to prevent problems of behavior and development in the world's infants, children, and adolescents but also to promote positive life outcomes and to further social justice and civil society, the scope and complexity of the science that informs application must be greatly enhanced. While the challenge for policy and programs is enormous, no less of a challenge exists for science. This challenge is especially true in relation to the now predominant theoretical and empirical approaches to understanding human life; that is, those perspectives framed by developmental systems models. These approaches conceptualize and study human behavior and development as a process involving integrated and changing **relations** among the biological, psychological, spiritual, social, cultural, physical, ecological, and historical variables comprising human life. The agenda for the application of developmental science that is framed by such models is to conduct scholarly activities in a manner and with timeliness that provide the highest quality scholarship with a content and an ethical sensibility that efficiently and effectively meet diverse and complex community needs.

As illustrated by the contributions in *Applied Developmental Science: An Advanced Textbook,* key items in this agenda include the following:

- Developing change- and context-sensitive measures of child well-being or thriving, and of the individual and community assets that promote positive development among diverse infants, children, and adolescents
- Designing and implementing program evaluations that (a) identify program effects when they occur, (b) improve the day-to-day quality of a program, and (c) empower program participants and other stakeholders to bring to scale and sustain effective programs
- Serving the community through the use of such tools of "outreach scholarship" as needs assessment, asset mapping, issues identification, technical assistance, consultation, continuing education and training, demonstration research, and participatory action research
- Leveraging the resources of higher education institutions to engage proactively in partnerships with community institutions, involving, for instance, (a) community-collaborative research, program design, implementation, and evaluation; (b) joint economic development, business/industry partnerships, and neighborhood revitalization; and (c) undergraduate service learning and graduate/professional training within the context of collaborations with the not-for-profit/non-governmental organization (NGO) sector and the governmental sector of the community

- Engaging policymakers and funders through dissemination about (a) the effectiveness of community programs promoting child well-being; (b) the impact of current policies on child well-being and positive development; and (c) the potential of possible policy innovations for enhancing child well-being and positive development

In short, there is a vast and interrelated set of research, program, and policy actions that are being taken by the individuals and institutions involved in the process of fostering generations of healthy children. In civil society, all citizens are part of this collaborative network. Existing institutional, professional, and youth-serving organizational groups are developing innovative ideas and bold action agendas to address the challenges faced by today's and tomorrow's children. In addition, new concepts are being articulated and new and promising individual and collective efforts are being created and honed to address these challenges. It is useful to describe how *Applied Developmental Science: An Advanced Textbook* conveys this exciting and important work.

AN OVERVIEW OF THE TEXT

Applied Developmental Science: An Advanced Textbook is divided into four sections that reflect the range of scholarship and application included in the *Handbook*. The first section of the text, "Foundations of Applied Developmental Science," provides an introduction to the historical development of applied developmental science and to the current theoretical, methodological, and substantive architecture of the scientific and professional efforts to develop policies and programs that promote positive child, adolescent, and family development. The chapters in this section serve as a conceptual frame for the organization of the entire text, and underscore a central theme in current scholarship and application: the need to develop policies and programs that appropriately treat the bidirectional (or, in other terms, reciprocal, dynamic, or systemic) **relations** among diverse individuals and their diverse contexts.

In addition, this section underscores another level of relation that is central in understanding the distinct developmental trajectories involved in diverse and mutually influential person $\leftarrow \rightarrow$ context relations. This level is the bidirectional linkage that exists between theory and application involved in the promotion of positive infant, child, and adolescent development.

Accordingly, the second section of the text focuses on "Enhancing Individual $\leftarrow \rightarrow$ Context Relations" through enacting work that integrates theory and application. The focus in the chapters in this section is on the relations children and adolescents have with their families and schools and, in turn, the importance of studying the child $\leftarrow \rightarrow$ context relation within a ecological system that ranges from the community level to culture and history, and includes policies, programs, and service systems aimed at both prevention and the promotion of positive human development.

The final two sections of the text discuss these instances of contextual support of human development. Chapters in the third section of the text, "Strengthening Policies and Programs," focus on issues pertinent to capitalizing on the human developmental system both to address (a) the risks to healthy development that exist across the first two decades in the lives of infants, children, and adolescents; and, in turn, (b) the opportunities that exists to use the assets of infants, children, adolescents, and their communities to promote positive development. These opportunities are discussed in regard to promoting positive infant, child, and adolescent, and family development through the ways in which (a) programs are designed and implemented; and (b) public policies are engaged to create, bring to scale, and sustain an effective child and family agenda.

The chapters in the last section of the text, "Enhancing Service Systems," discuss the ways in which public child- and family-serving systems may foster healthy development. These systems range from those that focus on individuals and families, to those that seek to alter the educational, living environments, and economic contexts (e.g., through welfare reform or philanthropy) of human development. The chapters illustrate well that the design, implementation, and evaluation of infant-, child-, adolescent-, and family-serving programs and policies occur in many settings and involve the actions of numerous agents and institutions of civil society.

In sum, across the sections and chapters of *Developmental Science: An Advanced Textbook* readers are provided with the information to understand the theoretical and methodological foundations of applied developmental science; to understand why and how research derived from the strength-based, positive human development approach may enhance the individual $\leftarrow \rightarrow$ context relation; to draw conclusions about the character of current child and family programs and policies, and in some cases, the strength of the research base that supports particular initiatives; and to understand the role of and challenges to service systems aimed at improving the lives of individual, families, and communities. Necessarily, then, the figure/ground of the discussions across the text shift, as each contributor—apart from the specific focus of his or her work—considers the breadth of the dynamic, developmental system, and of the actions and institutions within it, to promote positive human development.

ACKNOWLEDGMENTS

There are numerous people to thank in regard to the preparation of *Applied Developmental Science: An Advanced Textbook*. First and foremost we are indebted to the contributors to the text and, of course, to the larger

Handbook from which their chapters were drawn. Their scholarship and dedication to excellence and social relevance in developmental science and its application enabled this work to be produced and serve as a model of how scholarship may both contribute to knowledge and the positive development of people across their life spans.

Our colleagues and students at Tufts University and at the Eliot-Pearson Department of Child Development were great resources to us in the development of this volume. We thank Jennifer Davison, Managing Editor, and Katherine Connery, Assistant Editor, within the Editorial Office of the Institute for Applied Research in Youth Development, for their expert editorial support and guidance. James Brace-Thompson, our editor at Sage Publications, was a constant source of excellent advice, encouragement, and collegial support, and we are pleased to acknowledge our gratitude to him.

Finally, we deeply appreciate the love and support given to us by our families during our work on *Applied Developmental Science: An Advanced Textbook*. They remain our most cherished developmental assets and we gratefully dedicate this book to them.

—R. M. L.
—F. J.
—D. W.

REFERENCES

Lerner, R. M., Jacobs, F., & Wertlieb, D. (Eds.). (2003). *Applying developmental science for youth and families: Historical and theoretical foundations.* Volume 1 of *Handbook of applied developmental science: Promoting positive child, adolescent, and family development through research, policies, and programs.* Editors: Richard M. Lerner, Francine Jacobs, and Donald Wertlieb. Thousand Oaks, CA: Sage.

Jacobs, F., Wertlieb, D., & Lerner, R. M. (Eds.). (2003). *Enhancing the life chances of youth and families: Public service systems and public policy perspectives.* Volume 2 of *Handbook of applied developmental science: Promoting positive child, adolescent, and family development through research, policies, and programs.* Editors: Richard M. Lerner, Francine Jacobs, and Donald Wertlieb. Thousand Oaks, CA: Sage.

Wertlieb, D., Jacobs, F., & Lerner, R. M. (Eds.). (2003). *Promoting positive youth and family development: Community systems, citizenship, and civil society.* Volume 3 of *Handbook of applied developmental science: Promoting positive child, adolescent, and family development through research, policies, and programs.* Editors: Richard M. Lerner, Francine Jacobs, and Donald Wertlieb. Thousand Oaks, CA: Sage.

Lerner, R. M., Wertlieb, D., & Jacobs, F. (Eds.). (2003). *Adding value to youth and family development: The engaged university and professional and academic outreach.* Volume 4 of *Handbook of applied developmental science: Promoting positive child, adolescent, and family development through research, policies, and programs.* Editors: Richard M. Lerner, Francine Jacobs, and Donald Wertlieb. Thousand Oaks, CA: Sage.

Section I

FOUNDATIONS OF APPLIED DEVELOPMENTAL SCIENCE

CHAPTER 1

Historical and Theoretical Bases of Applied Developmental Science

RICHARD M. LERNER
DONALD WERTLIEB
FRANCINE JACOBS

The latter part of the 20th century was marked by public anxiety about myriad social problems, some old, some new, but all affecting the lives of vulnerable children, adolescents, adults, families, and communities (Fisher & Murray, 1996; Lerner, 1995; Lerner & Galambos, 1998; Lerner, Sparks, & McCubbin, 1999). For instance, in America, a set of problems of historically unprecedented scope and severity involved interrelated issues of economic development, environmental quality, health and health care delivery, poverty, crime, violence, drug and alcohol abuse, unsafe sex, and school failure.

Indeed, in the last years of the 20th century and the first years of the present one, across the United States and in other nations, infants, children, adolescents, and the adults who care for them continued to die from the effects of these social problems (Dryfoos, 1990; Hamburg, 1992; Hernandez, 1993; Huston, 1991; Lerner, 1995; Lerner & Fisher, 1994; Schorr, 1988, 1997). And if people were not dying, their prospects for future success were being reduced by civil unrest and ethnic conflict, by famine, by environmental challenges (e.g., involving water quality and solid-waste management), by school under-achievement and dropping out, by teenage pregnancy and parenting, by lack of job opportunities and preparedness, by prolonged welfare dependency, by challenges to their health (e.g., lack of immunization, inadequate screening for disabilities, insufficient prenatal care, and lack of sufficient infant and childhood medical services), and by the sequelae of persistent and pervasive poverty (Dryfoos, 1990; Huston, 1991; Huston, McLoyd, & Garcia Coll, 1994; Lerner, 1995; Lerner et al., 1999; Lerner &

Fisher, 1994). These issues challenge the resources and the future viability of civil society in America and throughout the world (Lerner, Fisher, & Weinberg, 2000a, 2000b).

The potential role of scientific knowledge about human development in addressing these issues of individuals, families, communities, and civil society has resulted in growing interest and activity in what has been termed *applied developmental science (ADS)*. Indeed, over the last two decades, increasing numbers of developmental scientists from diverse disciplines have come to identify themselves professionally as *applied developmental scientists*. Joining under this umbrella are colleagues from allied disciplines and specialties in the biological, psychological, social, and behavioral sciences and the helping professions, all sharing common goals and visions captured in some of the more formal definitions of the ADS field.

In many ways, ADS is "old wine in a new bottle"; that is, significant historical antecedents to the burgeoning field are evident today (Wertlieb, 2003). It is useful here to provide a brief overview of this history, focusing most on the events over the last quarter of a century that have given shape to contemporary ADS.

APPLIED DEVELOPMENTAL SCIENCE: A BRIEF HISTORY

ADS has its roots in numerous fields concerned with human development, for example, home economics/family and consumer sciences (Meszaros, 2003; Nickols, 2002), human ecology (Bronfenbrenner & Morris, 1998), comparative psychology (Tobach, 1994), and developmental psychology (Wertlieb, 2003). Using the latter

field as a sample case, we may note that several extensive histories of developmental psychology have been published and most include references to the ebb and flow of interest and priority for what might be termed the *applied, practical,* or *societally oriented issues* central to ADS. Especially relevant are discussions offered by Bronfenbrenner, Kessel, Kessen, and White (1986); Cairns (1998); Davidson and Benjamin (1987); Hetherington (1998); McCall (1996); McCall and Groark (2000); Sears (1975); Siegel and White (1982); Parke, Ornstein, Reiser, and Zahn-Waxler (1994), Zigler (1998); and Zigler and Finn-Stevenson (1992, 1999). Hetherington (1998) frames her analysis by accenting her use of the term "developmental science . . . to emphasize both the scientific and multidisciplinary foundations of the study of development and the recognition that development is not confined to childhood but extends across the life span" (p. 93), an emphasis that is lost or diluted in the too-limiting term *child psychology*. Hetherington interprets and extends Sears's (1975) classic analysis, reaffirming that "unlike many areas in psychology [with their histories documented by Boring (1950) and Koch & Leary (1985)], developmental science originated from the need to solve practical problems and evolved from pressure to improve the education, health, welfare and legal status of children and their families" (p. 93).

The chronology of developmental psychology offered by Cairns (1998) serves as a useful framework within which to specify some of the distinctive or seminal elements of ADS. Cairns segments the emergence of developmental psychology (1882-1912), the middle period of institutionalization and expansion (1913-1946), and the modern era (1947-1976). His compliance with a convention that 20 years must elapse before qualifying as "historical" leaves much of the significant milestone material in the defining of ADS, to be mentioned below, outside the realm of his presentation, although he does conclude his account with a clarion anticipation of and call for more integrated interdisciplinary science, quite consistent with what we might term the *postmodern* or *contemporary era* (1977 to the present). Indeed, it will be from this most recent period that we draw our substantive examples of ADS, after the conclusion of this historical sketch.

Most accounts, including Cairn's (1998) "emergence" analysis, portray the dialectic at the base of ADS as pioneered by G. Stanley Hall, the first professor of psychology in America (appointed in 1883 at Johns Hopkins University), the first president of the American Psychological Association (1891), and founder of the first child development research institute at Clark University and of the journal, *Pedagogical Seminary.*

> Hall was a remarkable teacher and catalyst for the field. Some of the most significant areas for developmental study—mental testing, child study, early education, adolescence, life span psychology, evolutionary influence on development—were stimulated or anticipated by Hall. Because of shortcomings in the methods he employed and the theory he endorsed, few investigators stepped forward to claim Hall as a scientific mentor. His reach exceeded his grasp in the plan to apply the principles of the new science to society. Psychology's principles were too modest, and society's problems too large. Perhaps we should use a fresh accounting to judge Hall's contributions, one that takes into account the multiple facets of his influence on individuals, the discipline, and society. The audit would reveal that all of us who aspire to better the lot of children and adolescents can claim him as a mentor. (Cairns, 1998, p. 43)

White (1992) points to the work of Bronfenbrenner as being consistent with his own perspective. For instance, Bronfenbrenner et al. (1986) noted,

> The simple fact is that G. Stanley Hall marched away from experimental psychology toward the study of children because at least six different constituencies existed in American society, basically still our constituencies today—scientists, college administrators, child savers and social workers, mental health workers, teachers, and parents. These constituencies wanted certain kinds of knowledge about children. *Mirabile dictu,* without even being developmental psychologists and before we came into existence, they were all collecting data that look like ours. So, if you look at the social history that surrounds the birth of the Child Study Movement, you gradually come to the conclusion that perhaps we represent a professionalization of trends of knowledge gathering and knowledge analysis that existed in our society before our coming. That doesn't completely detach us from the mainstream of the history of psychology, but it certainly throws a very different light on the emergence and evolution of the field and its basic issues. (p. 1221)

Among Hall's most significant contributions, according to White (1992), were the concern with descriptions of children in their natural contexts and the priority need "to arrive at a scientific synthesis on the one side and practical recommendations on the other" (as cited in Cairns, 1998, p. 43). Contemporary ADS continues in its value in the former and aspires to overcome the too-dichotomous implications of the second; it emphasizes the reciprocal and mutual interactions of the scientific and practical that were typical in this earliest era.

Within the last quarter of a century, a key milestone in the elaboration of the field's territory occurred with the founding of the *Journal of Applied Developmental Psychology,* in 1980, an international multidisciplinary life span journal. The masthead proclaimed:

A forum for communication between researchers and practitioners working in life span human development fields, a forum for the presentation of the conceptual, methodological, policy, and related issues involved in the application of behavioral science research in developmental psychology to social action and social problem solving. (Sigel & Cocking, 1980, p. i)

In welcoming the new journal in an inaugural editorial, Zigler (1980) narrowed the definition of the journal's purview to what he called a "field within a field" (i.e., presumably, applied developmental psychology within developmental psychology) but set high and broad expectations that "these pages shall attest to the synergistic relationship between basic and applied research" (p. 1).

Almost 20 years later, Zigler (1998) issued a similar note of hope, celebration, and welcome in a significant essay called "A Place of Value for Applied and Policy Studies," this time in the pages of *Child Development*, the prestigious archival journal of the Society for Research in Child Development (SRCD). *Child Development* had been singularly devoted to . . .

Theory-driven, basic research. Now, after more than six decades of advancing science as a means to expand our understanding of human development, SRCD has formally welcomed into its major journal research that uses this knowledge on children's behalf . . . the result of a very gradual transformation within SRCD from a scientist's science toward a more public science. (Zigler, 1998, p. 532)

The continuing vicissitudes of the gaps and synergies between applied and basic research will be a theme of the historical sketch offered below (see also Garner, 1972).

In 1991, the National Task Force on Applied Developmental Science convened representatives from a broad, but not exhaustive, range of professional scientific organizations concerned with the application of the developmental psychology knowledge base to societal problems. Organizations represented included the American Psychological Association (APA), the Gerontological Society of America, the International Society for Infant Studies, the National Black Child Development Institute, the National Council on Family Relations, the Society for Research on Adolescence, and the Society for Research in Child Development. Goals included the articulation of the definition and scope of ADS along with guidelines for graduate training in this emergent interdisciplinary field. A consensus process produced a complex four-point definition of ADS, quoted here at length to document the current parameters of content, process, methods, and values:

1.1. Applied developmental science involves the programmatic synthesis of research and applications to describe, explain, intervene, and provide preventive and enhancing uses of knowledge about human development. The conceptual bases of ADS reflects the view that individual and family functioning is a combined and interactive product of biology and the physical and social environments that continuously evolve and change over time. ADS emphasizes the nature of reciprocal person-environment interactions among people, across settings, and within a multidisciplinary approach stressing individual and cultural diversity. This orientation is defined by three conjoint emphases:

Applied: Direct implications for what individuals, families, practitioners, and policymakers do.

Developmental: Systematic and successive changes within human systems that occur across the life span.

Science: Grounded in a range of research methods designed to collect reliable and objective information systematically that can be used to test the validity of theory and application.

1.2. ADS recognizes that valid applications of our knowledge of human development depend on scientifically based understanding of multilevel normative and atypical processes that continually change and emerge over the life cycle.

1.3. ADS reflects an integration of perspectives from relevant biological, social, and behavioral sciences disciplines in the service of promoting development in various populations.

1.4. The nature of work in ADS is reciprocal in that science drives application and application drives science. ADS emphasizes the bidirectional relationship between those who generate empirically based knowledge about developmental phenomena and those who pursue professional practices, services, and policies that affect the well-being of members of society. Accordingly, research and theory guide intervention strategies, and evaluations of outcomes of developmental interventions provide the basis for the reformulation of theory and for modification of future interventions. (Fisher et al., 1993, pp. 4-5)

By 1997, these parameters defining ADS were adopted as the editorial scope of a new journal, *Applied Developmental Science,* with further explication of a more inclusive range of methodologies and audiences. According to Lerner, Fisher, and Weinberg (1997), the journal publishes . . .

Research employing any of a diverse array of methodologies—multivariate longitudinal studies, demographic analyses, evaluation research, intensive measurement studies, ethnographic analyses, laboratory experiments, analyses of policy and/or policy-engagement studies, or animal comparative studies—when they have important implications for the application of developmental science across the life span. Manuscripts pertinent to the diversity of development throughout the life span—cross-national and cross-cultural studies; systematic studies of psychopathology; and studies pertinent to gender, ethnic and racial diversity—are particularly welcome. . . . (The audience includes) developmental, clinical, school, counseling, aging, educational, and community psychologists; life course, family and demographic sociologists; health professionals; family and consumer scientists; human evolution and ecological biologists; practitioners in child and youth governmental and nongovernmental organizations. (p. 1)

This amplified definition of ADS postulates a number of hallmarks of ADS key to the discussion of its history, content, and special concerns. Among these hallmarks are the following:

1. A historical context and perspective reflecting the perennial balancing of related constructs such as basic and applied research or science and practice or knowledge generation and use. This includes a sensitivity to historical and sociopolitical contexts captured in the notion of ADS as . . .

Scholarship for our times. . . . As we enter the 21st century, there is growing recognition that traditional and artificial distinctions between science and service and between knowledge generation and knowledge application need to be reconceptualized if society is to successfully address the harrowing developmental sequelae of the social, economic and geo-political legacies of the 20th century. Scholars, practitioners and policymakers are increasingly recognizing the role that developmental science can play in stemming the tide of life chance destruction caused by poverty, premature births, school failure, child abuse, crime, adolescent pregnancy, substance abuse, unemployment, welfare dependency, discrimination, ethnic conflict, and inadequate health and social resources. (Lerner et al., 1997, p. 2)

2. A broadened and deepened awareness of the ethical challenges and imperatives involved in implementing the scope of ADS. This awareness evolves from challenges in the use of scientific methods in new ways such that protection of the autonomy and well-being of participants is increasingly complex. Research participants become partners in the inquiry process and new, more complicated collaborations among diverse multidisciplinary professionals and communities become key elements of defining research questions and problems and seeking answers and solutions.

Moreover, as implied earlier in the chapter, some leaders of ADS have seen the need to further broaden the potential scope of this field, suggesting elements of a blueprint for promoting civil society and social justice, a provocative and compelling elaboration of both the substance and ethical orientation of the field (Lerner et al., 2000b). Others have focused on more traditional, academic, or incremental stocktaking for defining ADS, with attention to advancing the numerous knowledge bases and methodologies (e.g., Schwebel, Plumert, & Pick, 2000; Shonkoff, 2000; Sigel & Renninger, 1998). However, given the presence of this range of interests and activities, ADS is now considered "an established discipline" (Fisher, Murray, & Sigel, 1996), one that is operationalized by the diverse foci of work pursued under this framework but is linked by a common conceptual/theoretical perspective about human development: *developmental systems theory.* To understand the diversity of empirical, methodological, and ethical interests and activities of contemporary ADS, it is important to appreciate the developmental systems theoretical orientation that rationalizes the use of developmental science for the promotion of positive human development and the enhancement of civil society.

FROM DEVELOPMENTAL SYSTEMS THEORIES TO APPLIED DEVELOPMENTAL SCIENCE

Paul Mussen, the editor of the third edition of the *Handbook of Child Psychology*, presaged what today is abundantly clear about the contemporary stress on systems theories of human development. Mussen (1970) said, "The major contemporary empirical and theoretical emphases in the field of developmental psychology . . . seem to be on *explanations* of the psychological changes that occur, the mechanisms and processes accounting for growth and development" (p. vii). This vision alerted developmental scientists to a burgeoning interest—not in structure, function, or content per se, but in change, in the processes through which change occurs, and in the means through which structures transform and functions evolve over the course of human life.

Today, Mussen's (1970) vision has been crystallized. The cutting edge of contemporary developmental theory is represented by systems conceptions of the process of how structures function and how functions are structured over time. Thus, developmental systems theories of human development are not necessarily tied to a particular content domain, although particular empirical issues or substantive foci (e.g., motor development, successful aging, wisdom, extraordinary cognitive achievements, language acquisition, the self, psychological complexity, or concept formation) may lend themselves readily as exemplary sample cases of the processes depicted in a given theory (see Lerner, 1998a).

The power of developmental systems theories lies in their ability to not be limited or confounded by an inextricable association with a unidimensional portrayal of the developing person. In developmental systems theories, the person is neither biologized, psychologized, nor sociologized. Rather, the individual is *systemized*. A person's development is embedded within an integrated matrix of variables derived from multiple levels of organization. Development is conceptualized as deriving from the dynamic relations among the variables within this multitiered matrix.

Developmental systems theories use the polarities that engaged developmental theory in the past (e.g., nature/nurture, individual/society, biology/culture; Lerner, 1976, 1986, 2002b). They are not used to "split" depictions of developmental processes along conceptually implausible and empirically counterfactual lines (Gollin, 1981; Overton, 1998) or to force counterproductive choices between false opposites (e.g., heredity or environment, continuity or discontinuity, constancy or change; Lerner, 2002b), but rather to gain insight into the integrations that exist among the multiple levels of organization involved in human development. These theories are certainly more complex than their one-sided predecessors. They are also more nuanced, more flexible, more balanced, and less susceptible to extravagant or even absurd claims: for instance, that nature split from nurture can shape the course of human development; that there is a gene for altruism, militarism, or intelligence; or that when the social context is demonstrated to affect development, the influence can be reduced to a genetic one (e.g., Hamburger, 1957; Lorenz, 1966; Plomin, 1986, 2000; Plomin, Corley, DeFries, & Faulker, 1990; Rowe, 1994; Rushton, 1987, 1988a, 1988b, 1997, 1999).

These mechanistic and atomistic views of the past have been replaced, then, by theoretical models that stress the dynamic synthesis of multiple levels of analysis, a perspective having its roots in systems theories of biological development (Cairns, 1998; Gottlieb, 1992; Kuo, 1930, 1967, 1976; Schneirla, 1956, 1957; von Bertalanffy, 1933). In other words, *development,* understood as a property of systemic change in the multiple and integrated levels of organization comprising human life and its ecology (ranging from biology to culture and history), is an overarching conceptual frame associated with developmental systems models of human development.

Explanation and Application: A Synthesis

This stress on the dynamic relation between the individual and his or her context results in the recognition that a synthesis of perspectives from multiple disciplines is needed to understand the multilevel integrations involved in human development. In addition, to understand the basic process of human development, both descriptive and explanatory research must be conducted within the actual ecology of people's lives.

Explanatory studies, by their very nature, constitute intervention research. The role of the developmental researcher conducting explanatory research is to understand the ways in which variations in person-context relations account for the character of human developmental trajectories, life paths that are enacted in the natural laboratory of the real world. To gain an understanding of how theoretically relevant variations in person-context relations may influence developmental trajectories, the researcher may introduce policies and/or programs as experimental manipulations of the proximal and/or distal natural ecology. Evaluations of the outcomes of such interventions become a means to bring data to bear on theoretical issues pertinent to person-context relations. More specifically, these interventions have helped applied developmental scientists understand the plasticity in human development that may exist and that may be capitalized on to enhance human life (Csikszentmihalyi & Rathunde, 1998; Lerner, 1984).

The interindividual differences in intraindividual change that exist as a consequence of these naturally occurring interventions attest to the magnitude of the systematic changes in structure and function—the *plasticity*—that characterizes human life. Explanatory research is necessary, however, to understand which variables, from which levels of organization are involved in particular instances of plasticity that have been seen to exist. In addition, such research is necessary to determine which instances of plasticity may be created by science or society. In other words, explanatory research is needed to ascertain the extent of human plasticity or in turn, to test the limits of plasticity (Baltes, 1987; Baltes, Lindenberger, & Staudinger, 1998; Lerner, 1984).

From a developmental systems perspective, the conduct of such research may lead the scientist to alter the natural ecology of the person or group he or she is studying. Such research may involve either proximal and/or distal variations in the context of human development (Lerner & Ryff, 1978); but in any case, these manipulations constitute theoretically guided alterations of the roles and events a person or group experiences at, or over, a portion of the life span.

These alterations are indeed, then, interventions: They are planned attempts to alter the system of person-context relations that constitute the basic process of change; they are conducted to ascertain the specific bases of or to test the limits of particular instances of human plasticity (Baltes, 1987; Baltes & Baltes, 1980; Baltes et al., 1998). These interventions are a researcher's attempt to substitute designed person-context relations for naturally occurring ones in an attempt to understand the process of changing person-context relations that provides the basis of human development. In short,

then, basic research in human development is intervention research (Lerner et al., 1994).

Accordingly, the cutting edge of theory and research in human development lies in the application of the conceptual and methodological expertise of human developmental scientists to the natural ontogenetic laboratory of the real world. This placement of explanatory research about the basic relational process of development into the actual ecology of human development, then, involves the fusion of application with basic developmental science. To pursue the study of ontogeny from a developmental systems perspective, a research/application agenda that focuses on the relations between diverse individuals and their similarly diverse contexts is brought to the forefront (Lerner, 2002b). In addition, however, scholars involved in such research must have at least two other concerns deriving from the view that basic explanatory research in human development is, in its essence, intervention research.

Research in human development that is concerned with one or even a few instances of individual and contextual diversity cannot be assumed to be useful for understanding the life courses of all people. Similarly, policies and programs derived from such research or associated with it in the context of a researcher's tests of ideas pertinent to human plasticity cannot hope to be applicable or equally appropriate and useful in all contexts or for all individuals. Accordingly, policy development and program (intervention) design and delivery that are developmental and oriented to individual differences must be a key part of the approach to applied developmental research for which we are calling.

The variation in settings within which people live means that studying development in a standard (for example, a *controlled)* environment does not provide information pertinent to the actual (ecologically valid) developing relations between individually distinct people and their specific contexts (for example, their particular families, schools, or communities). This point underscores the need to conduct research in real-world settings (Bronfenbrenner, 1974; Zigler, 1998) and highlights the ideas that (a) policies and programs constitute natural experiments, that is, planned interventions for people and institutions, and (b) the evaluation of such activities becomes a central focus in the developmental systems research agenda we have described (Cairns, Bergman, & Kagan, 1998; Lerner, 1995; Lerner, Ostrom, & Freel, 1995; Ostrom, Lerner, & Freel, 1995).

In this view, then, policy and program endeavors do not constitute secondary work or derivative applications conducted after research evidence has been complied. Quite to the contrary, policy development and implementation and program design and delivery become integral components of the ADS approach to research; the evaluation component of such policy and intervention work provides critical feedback about the adequacy of the conceptual frame from which this research agenda should derive (Zigler, 1998; Zigler & Finn-Stevenson, 1992).

In essence, then, a developmental systems perspective leads us to recognize that if we are to have an adequate and sufficient science of human development, we must integratively study individual and contextual levels of organization in a relational and temporal manner (Bronfenbrenner, 1974; Zigler, 1998). We may also seek to serve America's citizens and families through our science and help develop successful policies and programs through our scholarly efforts that result in the promotion of positive

human development. To do this, we may make great use of the integrative, temporal, and relational model of the person and of his or her context that is embodied in developmental system theories of human development.

From Developmental Systems Theory to the Core Principles of ADS

As has been argued before us—for example, by Fisher (e.g., Fisher et al., 1993; Fisher & Lerner, 1994); Weinberg (e.g., Lerner et al., 1997, 2000a, 2000b); Sherrod (e.g., 1999a, 1999b); Eccles (Eccles, Lord, & Buchanan, 1996); Takanishi (1993); Lerner (Lerner, 1998b, 2002a, 2002b); and Wertlieb (2003)—ADS is scholarship predicated on a developmental systems theoretical perspective. Within this context, Fisher et al. (1993) summarize the five conceptual components that together characterize the core principles of ADS. Taken together, these conceptual principles make ADS a unique approach to understanding and promoting positive development.

The first conceptual component of ADS is the notion of the temporality, or historical embeddedness, of change pertinent to individuals, families, institutions, and communities. Some components of the context or of individuals remain stable over time, and other components may change historically. Because phenomena of human behavior and development vary historically, one must assess whether generalizations across time periods are legitimate. Thus, temporality has important implications for research design, service provision, and program evaluation.

Interventions are aimed at altering the developmental trajectory of within-person changes. To accomplish this aim, the second conceptual feature of ADS is that applied developmental scientists take into account interindividual differences (diversity) among, for instance, racial, ethnic, social class, and gender groups, and intraindividual changes, such as those associated with puberty.

The third conceptual feature of ADS places an emphasis on the centrality of context. There is a focus on the relations among all levels of organization within the ecology of human development. These levels involve biology, families, peer groups, schools, businesses, neighborhoods and communities, physical/ecological settings, and the socio-cultural, political, legal, moral, and economic institutions of society. Together, bidirectional relations among these levels of the developmental system necessitate systemic approaches to research, program and policy design, and program and policy implementation.

The fourth principle of ADS emphasizes descriptively normative developmental processes and primary prevention and optimization, rather than remediation. Applied developmental scientists emphasize healthy and normative developmental processes and seek to identify the strengths and assets of individuals, groups, and settings, rather than focusing on deficits, weaknesses, or problems of individuals, families, or communities. Instead of dwelling on the problems faced by people, applied developmental scientists aim to find combinations of individual and ecological assets associated with thriving among people (e.g., Benson, 1997; Benson, Leffert, Scales, & Blyth, 1998; Leffert et al., 1998; Scales, Benson, Leffert, & Blyth, 2000) and with the "5 Cs" of positive individual development: competence, confidence, connection, character, and caring/compassion (Hamilton & Hamilton, 1999; Lerner, 2002b; Little, 1993; Pittman, 1996).

The final principle of ADS is the appreciation of the bidirectional relationship between knowledge generation and knowledge application. By acknowledging bidirectionality, applied developmental scientists recognize the importance of knowledge about life and development that exists among the individuals, families, and communities being served by ADS. For applied developmental scien-tists, collaboration and colearning between researchers/universities and communities are essential features of the scholarly enterprise (Lerner, 1998a, 1998b). Such community-collaborative efforts are termed *outreach scholarship* (Lerner & Miller, 1998).

In other words, given the developmental systems perspective on which ADS is predicated, applied developmental scientists assume the following:

> There is an interactive relationship between science and application. Accordingly, the work of those who generate empirically based knowledge about development and those who provide professional services or construct policies affecting individuals and families is seen as reciprocal in that research and theory guide intervention strategies and the evaluation of interventions and policies provides the bases for reformulating theory and future research. . . . As a result, applied developmental [scientists] not only disseminate information about development to parents, professionals, and policymakers working to enhance the development of others, they also integrate the perspectives and experiences of these members of the community into the reformulation of theory and the design of research and interventions. (Fisher & Lerner, 1994, p. 7)

Given the theoretically predicated set of principles defining ADS, it is clear that not all possible realms of developmental science would lend themselves to this view of scholarship (e.g., genetic-reductionist approaches to human development would not fit within this approach; for a more thorough discussion of this point, see Lerner, 2002b). It is useful, then, to discuss the dimensions of scientific work that are brought to the forefront by an ADS perspective framed by developmental systems thinking.

FOCI OF APPLIED
DEVELOPMENTAL SCIENCE

Human developmental science has long been associated with laboratory-based scholarship devoted to uncovering "universal" aspects of development by stripping away contextual influences (Cairns et al., 1998; Hagen, 1996). However, the mission and methods of human development are being transformed into an ADS that is devoted to discovering diverse developmental patterns by examining the dynamic relations between individuals within the multiple embedded contexts of the integrated developmental systems in which they live (Fisher & Brennan, 1992; Fisher & Lerner, 1994; Fisher & Murray, 1996; Horowitz, 2000; Horowitz & O'Brien, 1989; Lerner, 1998a, 1998b, 2002a, 2002b; Lerner et al., 2000a, 2000b; Morrison, Lord, & Keating, 1984; Power, Higgins, & Kohlberg, 1989; Sigel, 1985). This theoretical revision of the target of developmental analysis, from the elements of relations to interlevel relations, has significant implications for applications of developmental science to policies and programs aimed at promoting positive human development. Arguably, the most radical feature of the theoretical, research, and applied agenda of applied developmental scientists is the idea that *research about basic relational processes of development and applications focused on enhancing person-context relations across ontogeny are one and the same endeavor.* Within this synthetic approach to basic and applied scholarship, several specific domains of scholarship are pursued by applied developmental scientists.

The National Task Force on Applied Developmental Science (Fisher et al., 1993) indicates that the activities of ADS span a continuum from knowledge generation to knowledge application (see also Wertlieb, 2003). These activities include, but are not limited to,

the following: research on the applicability of scientific theory to growth and development in natural, ecologically valid contexts; the study of developmental correlates of phenomena of social import; the construction and use of developmentally and contextually sensitive assessment instruments; the design and evaluation of developmental interventions and enhancement programs; and the dissemination of developmental knowledge to individuals, families, communities, practitioners, and policymakers through developmental education, printed and electronic materials, the mass media, expert testimony, and community collaborations.

To illustrate, Table 1.1 lists many of the topics of inquiry and action that are recurrently part of the broad scope of ADS. Recent textbooks (e.g., Fisher & Lerner, 1994); review chapters (e.g., Zigler & Finn-Stevenson, 1999); handbooks; (e.g., Lerner, 2002a, 2002b; Sigel & Renninger, 1998); special issues of journals (e.g., Hetherington, 1998); and regular sections of journals, such as the "Applied Developmental Theory" section of *Infants and Young Children,* provide ongoing articulation of ADS inquiry. Journals such as the *Journal of Applied Developmental Psychology, Applied Developmental Science,* and *Children's Services: Social Policy, Research and Practice* are among the central outlets for new work in ADS.

Applied Developmental Science and the Concept of Outreach Scholarship

Given (a) their belief in the importance for developmental analysis of systemically integrating all components within the ecology of human development and (b) their stress on integrating the expertise of the researcher with the expertise of the community through collaboration and colearning,

Table 1.1   Areas of Inquiry and Action in Applied Developmental Science

Topic	Sample Study or Review
Early child care and education	Lamb (1998); Scarr (1998); Zigler & Finn-Stevenson (1999); Ramey & Ramey (1998)
Early childhood education	Elkind (2002)
Education reform and schooling	Fishman (1999); Adelman & Taylor (2000); Renninger (1998); Strauss (1998)
Literacy	Adams, Trieman, & Pressley (1998);
Parenting and parent education	Collins, Maccoby, Steinberg, Hetherington, & Bornstein (2000); Cowan, Powell, & Cowan (1998)
Poverty	McLoyd (1998); Black & Krishnakumar (1998)
Developmental assets	Benson (1997); Scales & Leffert (1999); Weissberg & Greenberg (1998)
Successful children and families	Masten & Coatsworth (1998); Wertlieb (2001)
Marital disruption and divorce	Wertlieb (1997); Hetherington, Bridges, & Insabella (1998)
Developmental psychopathology	Richters (1997); Cicchetti & Sroufe (2000); Rutter & Sroufe (2000); Cicchetti & Toth (1998b)
Depression	Cicchetti & Toth (1998a)
Domestic violence and maltreatment	Emery & Laumann-Billings (1998)
Adolescent pregnancy	Coley & Chase-Landsdale (1998)
Aggression and violence	Loeber & Stouthamer-Loebe (1998)
Children's eyewitness reports	Bruck, Ceci, & Hembrooke (1998)
Pediatric psychology	Bearison (1998)
Mass media, television, and computers	Huston & Wright (1998); Martland & Rothbaum (1999)
Prevention science	Kaplan (2000); Coie et al. (1993)

proponents of ADS believe that researchers and the institutions within which they work are part of the developmental system that ADS tries to understand and to enhance. They emphasize that the scholar- and university-community partnerships they seek to enact are an essential means of contextualizing knowledge. By embedding scholarship about human development within the diverse ecological settings in which people develop, applied developmental scientists foster bidirectional relationships between research and practice. Within such relationships, developmental research both guides and is guided by the outcomes of community-based interventions, for example, public policies or programs aimed at enhancing human development.

The growth of such outreach scholarship (Lerner & Miller, 1998) has fostered a scholarly challenge to prior conceptions of the nature of the world (Cairns et al., 1998; Overton, W., 1998; Valsiner, 1998). The idea that all knowledge is related to its context has promoted a change in the typical ontology within current scholarship. This change has emerged as a focus on relationism and an avoidance of split conceptions of reality, such as nature versus nurture (Overton, W., 1998). This ontological change has helped advance the view that all existence is contingent on the specifics of the physical and social cultural conditions that exist at a particular moment of history (Overton, 1998; Pepper, 1942). Changes in epistemology that have been associated with this revision in ontology and contingent knowledge can be understood only if relationships are studied.

Accordingly, any instance of knowledge (e.g., the core knowledge of a given discipline) must be integrated with knowledge of (a) the context surrounding it and (b) the relation between knowledge and context. Thus, knowledge that is disembedded from the context is not basic knowledge. Rather, knowledge that is relational to its context, for example, to the community as it exists in its ecologically valid setting (Trickett, Barone, & Buchanan, 1996), *is* basic knowledge. Having an ontology of knowledge as ecologically embedded and contingent rationalizes the interest of ADS scholars in learning to integrate what they know with what is known of and by the context (Fisher, 1997). It thus underscores the importance of colearning collaborations between scholars and community members as a key part of the knowledge generation process (Higgins-D'Alessandro, Fisher, & Hamilton, 1998; Lerner & Simon, 1998a, 1998b).

In sum, significant changes that have occurred in the way social and behavioral scientists—and more specifically, human developmentalists—have begun to reconceptualize their roles and responsibilities to society is in no greater evidence than in the field of ADS (Fisher & Murray, 1996; Lerner, 2002a, 2002b; Lerner et al., 2000a, 2000b). However, the key test of the usefulness of the integrative relational ideas of applied developmental scientists lies in a demonstration of the greater advantages for understanding and application of a synthetic focus on person-context relations—as compared with an approach to developmental analysis predicated on splitting individuals from their contexts or splitting any level within the developmental system from another, for example, splitting biological from individual/psychological or social levels through genetic reductionism (e.g., as in Rowe, 1994; Rushton, 1999, 2000). In other words, can we improve our understanding of human development and enhance our ability to promote positive outcomes of changes across life by adopting the relational approach of an ADS predicated on developmental systems thinking?

THE PLAN OF THIS TEXT

We believe the answer to this question is "yes," and to support our position, in this text we present scholarship that illustrates how a focus on the person-context relation may enhance understanding of the character of human development and also of the ways in which applications linking persons and contexts in positive ways can enhance human development across the life span. The scholarship represented in this text considers the importance of understanding the match, congruence, quality of fit, or integration between attributes of individuals and characteristics of their contexts in understanding and promoting healthy, positive human development.

Key Themes of the Text

Throughout this book, a central theme in current ADS is underscored: the need to develop policies and programs that appropriately treat the *bidirectional* (or, in other terms, *reciprocal, dynamic,* or *systemic*) *relations* between diverse individuals and their diverse contexts. In addition, the chapters in this volume highlight another level of relation that is central in understanding the distinct developmental trajectories involved in diverse person-context relations. This level is the bidirectional linkage that exists between theory and application. Throughout the volume, authors explain how a developmental systems view of youth development is both a product and a producer of an integrated understanding of the theory ← → application relation involved in the promotion of positive youth development.

The developmental systems perspective also has implications for the methods and ethics of ADS. Ideas about methods and ethics are also thematic dimensions of the chapters in this volume. It is important to discuss the role of these themes in current and future work in ADS.

METHODOLOGICAL AND ETHICAL DIMENSIONS OF ADS

In addition to the developmental systems theoretical orientation framing, the substantive domain of scholarship included in this volume and also found more broadly in ADS, we must emphasize that other features of scholarship are emblematic of ADS. That is, specific views of methodology and of ethics are involved in this field of work. As we have noted earlier in this chapter, the empirical parameters of ADS are addressed only to a limited extent by traditional research methods and designs.

Acknowledgment of the conceptual complexity imposed by the relevant developmental contextual and bioecological theories engages increasingly sophisticated methodological approaches. Orchestration of a researcher's perspectives on a set of problems with a society's perspectives on the problem—be they concerns about how to provide a type of care for children or how to sustain the health and development of an ill child—requires extension and innovation by the applied developmental scientist. Some of the extension and innovation is relatively incremental.

For example, the study of children's adaptation to illness becomes the province of interdisciplinary teams of pediatricians, pediatric psychologists, nurses, and child psychiatrists. Bolder innovation advances ADS when (a) families and communities are recognized and embraced as legitimate partners in the research enterprise, (b) the audience or "consumer" of research is broadened to include service providers and policymakers, and (c) traditional institutional structures and functions associated with the "ivory tower" of the university are challenged or modified. A leading perspective in capturing these extensions and innovations is, as previously mentioned, termed outreach scholarship (Chibucos & Lerner, 1999; Lerner & Miller, 1998).

Jensen, Hoagwood, and Trickett (1999) contrast university-based research, traditionally supported by the National Institute of Health in an *efficacy model,* with *an outreach model* that reflects emergent approaches to research consistent with the parameters of ADS and basic to advancement in the numerous domains of inquiry and action listed in Table 1.1. Outreach research or outreach scholarship characterizes the "engaged university" (Kellogg Commission, 1999) more so than the traditional "ivory tower" university (e.g., McCall, Groark, Strauss & Johnson, 1995). In outreach scholarship, knowledge advances as a function of collaborations and partnerships between universities and communities such that scientists and the children, families, and communities they seek to understand and help are defining problems, methods, and solutions together. Communities include policymakers as well as the families and service providers, who both implement and consume interventions and programs. Lerner et al. (2000b) properly note that this involves a "sea change in the way scholars conduct their research" (p. 14) and then note the principles of outreach scholarship that characterize these special collaborations and methods in ADS. These principles include the following:

> (1) An enhanced focus on external validity, on the pertinence of the research to the actual ecology of human development . . . as opposed to contrived, albeit well-designed, laboratory type studies; (2) incorporating the values and needs of community collaborators within research activities; (3) full conceptualization and assessment of outcomes, that is, a commitment to understanding thoroughly both the direct and indirect effects of a research-based intervention program on youth and their context and to measuring these outcomes; (4) flexibility to fit local needs and circumstances, that is, an orientation to adjust the design or procedures . . . to the vicissitudes of the community within which the work is enacted; (5) accordingly, a willingness to make modifications to research methods in order to fit the circumstances of the local community; and (6) the embracing of long-term perspectives, that is the commitment of the university to remain in the community for a time period sufficient to see the realization of community-valued developmental goals for its youth . . . [and in addition] co-learning (between two expert systems—the community and the university); humility on the part of the university and its faculty, so that true co-learning and collaboration among equals can occur; and cultural integration, so that both the university and the community can appreciate each other's perspective. (Lerner et al., 2000b, p. 14)

As articulated in the definitional parameters of ADS that opened this chapter and as reflected in the specific examples of inquiry and action, the extensions and innovations involved in outreach scholarship provide a means to address the conceptual and methodological challenges inherent in attending to the synergy and advancement of science and practice. Along with these tools and potentials come a series of ethical imperatives reflecting responsibilities of both researchers and practitioners. These complex challenges have been a central concern to ADS from its earliest contemporary renditions, with the frameworks offered by Fisher and Tryon (1990) continuing to serve well as an agenda.

Fisher and Tryon (1990) noted that along with the synergy and integration of research and application basic to the advance of the field, the applied developmental scientist is bound by the ethics of research, by the ethics of professional service, and by a complicated admixture that emerges with the acknowledgment of their interdependence. In addition, as the notion of outreach scholarship shifts the applied developmental scientist away from narrow and traditional notions of research subjects, patients, and clients to more appropriate notions of partners, consumers, and collaborators, there emerge areas as yet uncharted by the ethical standards of extant disciplines and professions. Indeed, even the imperative— that ethical behavior in ADS reflects some consensus or amalgam of the applied ethics embraced over time by diverse disciplines or traditions now teaming up in any of the areas of inquiry and action noted earlier—invokes challenge. Distinctive, perhaps even unique, ethical issues arise when the articulation of basic bioecological and contextual theories are parlayed into methods, measures, research designs, interventions, programs, and policies. Furthermore, whether in the traditional disciplines or in emergent ADS, ethical considerations are encumbered and enriched by the mores and pressures of the historical context. Thus, the particular exigencies of our evolving multicultural and global societies manifested in concerns about diversity and cultural sensitivity and competence become deep and abiding concerns for applied developmental scientists as they develop and test their theories, design and evaluate interventions, provide health or social services, or engage policymakers around social programs and policies.

As one example of the special ethical challenges that ADS must master, consider the research on early child care and education. As noted, the sociohistorical shift involving the entry of more women into the workforce has fueled the interest and concern of both society and developmental scientists. Hoffman (1990) describes the manner in which bias in the scientific process characterized much of the early research on maternal employment. Knowledge was produced and applied with an emphasis on documenting defects or deficits in children left in nonparental day care. As the more sophisticated concepts and methods of ADS were engaged to address social concerns over nonparental care, there were more nuanced and accurate notions of direct and indirect effects of individual differences and quality variables in home-based and center-based care settings. In addition, as dire as some of the ethical challenges were in the conduct of the science aimed at generating understanding about the impact of different care arrangements, the risks involved in the communication of findings to the public and to policymakers could also be harrow-ing and daunting. Hoffman (1990) concludes her account with the following position:

> While there is a social responsibility to make findings available for social policy and individual decision, there is also a

responsibility to communicate the results accurately and to educate the public about what the data can and cannot say. The tentative nature of our findings, their susceptibility to different interpretations, and the complications of translating them into individual or policy actions must be communicated to achieve an ethical science. (p. 268)

A second example to capture some of the particular ethical challenges facing ADS pertains especially to this particular historical moment in which ADS is gaining recognition as an "established discipline" (Fisher, Murray, & Sigel, 1996, p. xvii). Training programs to produce the next generation of applied developmental scientists are only just emerging. Whereas some of the root or allied disciplines may have sophisticated quality control and credentialing procedures in place to increase the likelihood that ethical standards are met, ADS cannot borrow completely from these traditions. ADS must generate new and appropriate standards reflecting the exigencies of its special methods (e.g., outreach scholarship or university-community partnerships) and the special expectations and demands faced by new applied developmental scientists as they pursue work in many, or any, of the domains of inquiry and action listed in Table 1.1.

For instance, traditional developmental psychologists can be trained and their allegiance to the ethical standards of the APA (1992) inculcated during their graduate training. Clinical psychologists, as another example, can be educated and held accountable both through their graduate training and professional careers in APA standards and in a variety of state and national licensing and credentialing conventions. Although applied developmental scientists now emerging from traditionally regulated fields, such as clinical, school, or counseling psychology, will have a starting point in these traditional ethical guidelines, neither they nor their colleagues from diverse disciplinary and multidisciplinary training bases are yet equipped with explicit ethical principles or credentials for the "practice" of ADS. Indeed, Koocher (1990) alerted the field to this challenge a decade ago, and though the sociopolitical scene has evolved in complex ways since then, the challenge remains for ADS to attend very seriously to issues of graduate training and ethics commensurate with its appropriately broadened scope and deepened mission.

CONCLUSIONS

A focus on person-context relations underscores the key implications of developmental systems models for research and application pertinent to promoting positive human development. At any given point in ontogenetic and historical time, neither individuals' attributes nor the features of their contexts (e.g., the demands of their parents regarding a temperamental style) per se are the foremost predictors of their healthy functioning. Instead, the *relations* between the child, the parent, the school, the community, and the other levels of organization within the developmental system are most important in understanding the character of human development and of the role of the ecology of human development in a person's ontogeny.

Essentially, the developmental systems model specifies that applied developmental scholarship pertinent to understanding and enhancing the life course should focus on the relational process of human development by longitudinally integrating the study of both the actions of the individual and the actions of parents, peers, teachers, neighbors, and the broader institutional context within which the individual is embedded. Bearing in mind the centrality of this complex relational system, the synthetic research and application agenda seems clear. Applied developmental scientists must continue to educate themselves about the best means

available to promote (through integrating the developmental system) enhanced life chances among all individuals and families, but especially among those whose potential for positive contributions to civil society is most in danger of being wasted (Dryfoos, 1990, 1998; Hamburg, 1992; Lerner, 2002b; Lerner et al., 1999; Schorr, 1988, 1997).

The collaborative expertise of the research and program delivery communities can provide much of this information, especially if it is obtained in partnership with strong, empowered communities. Such coalitions could become integral components of an integrated child, family, and human development policy aimed at creating caring communities with the capacity to further the healthy development of children, adolescents, adults, and families (Jensen et al., 1999; Kennedy, 1999; Overton, B.J., & Burkhardt, 1999; Sherrod, 1999b; Spanier, 1999; Thompson, 1999). Given the enormous and historically unprecedented challenges facing the youth and families of America and the world, there is no time to lose in the development of such collaborations if there is the aspiration to raise healthy and successful children capable of leading civil society productively, responsibly, and morally across the 21st century (Benson, 1997; Damon, 1997; Lerner, 1995; Lerner et al., 2000a, 2000b).

As was originally the case, the understanding of children, their development, and their needs is pursued only in part for the intellectual bounty. It is the use of this knowledge to enhance the quality of life for children that launched the discipline of developmental psychology in the late 19th century and propels ADS in the early 21st century. The field of human development has an opportunity through the publication of its ADS research to serve our world's citizens and demonstrate that there is nothing of greater value to civil society than a science devoted to using its scholarship to improve the life chances of all people.

REFERENCES

Adams, M. J., Treiman, R., & Pressley, M. (1998). Reading, writing, and literacy. In W. Damon (Series Ed.), I. E. Sigel & K. A. Renninger (Vol. Eds.), *Handbook of child psychology: Vol. 4. Child psychology in practice* (5th ed., pp. 275-356). New York: Wiley.

Adelman, H. S., & Taylor, L. (2000). Looking at school health and school reform policy through the lens of addressing barriers to learning. *Children's services: Social policy, research, and practice, 3*(2), 117-132.

American Psychological Association. (1992). Ethical principles of psychologists and code of conduct. *American Psychologist, 47*(12), 1597-1611.

Baltes, P. B. (1987). Theoretical propositions of life-span developmental psychology: On the dynamics between growth and decline. *Developmental Psychology, 23,* 611-626.

Baltes, P. B., & Baltes, M. M. (1980). Plasticity and variability in psychological aging: Methodological and theoretical issues. In G. E. Gurski (Ed.), *Determining the effects of aging on the central nervous system* (pp. 41-66). Berlin, Germany: Schering AG (Oraniendruck).

Baltes, P. B., Lindenberger, U., & Staudinger, U. M. (1998). Life-span theory in developmental psychology. In W. Damon (Series Ed.) & R. M. Lerner (Vol. Ed.), *Handbook of child psychology: Vol. 1. Theoretical models of human development* (5th ed., pp. 1029-1144). New York: John Wiley.

Bearison, D. J. (1998). Pediatric psychology and children's medical problems. In W. Damon (Series Ed.), I. E. Sigel & K. A. Renninger (Vol. Eds.), *Handbook of child psychology: Vol. 4. Child psychology in practice* (5th ed., pp. 635-712). New York: Wiley.

Benson, P. L. (1997). *All kids are our kids: What communities must do to raise caring and responsible children and adolescents.* San Francisco: Jossey-Bass.

Benson, P. L., Leffert, N., Scales, P. C., & Blyth, D. A. (1998). Younger and older adults collaborating on retelling everyday stories. *Applied Developmental Science, 2*(3), 138-159.

Black, M. M., & Krishnakumar, A. (1998). Children in low income, urban settings: Interventions to promote mental health and well-being. *American Psychologist, 53,* 635-646.

Boring, E. G. (1950). *A history of experimental psychology* (2nd ed.). New York: Appleton-Century-Crofts.

Bronfenbrenner, U. (1974). Developmental research, public policy, and the ecology of childhood. *Child Development, 45,* 1-5.

Bronfenbrenner, U., Kessel, F., Kessen, W., & White, S. (1986). Toward a critical social history of developmental psychology. *American Psychologist, 41*(11), 1218-1230.

Bronfenbrenner, U., & Morris, P. A. (1998). The ecology of developmental process. In W. Damon (Series Ed.) & R. M. Lerner (Vol. Ed.), *Handbook of child psychology: Vol. 1. Theoretical models of human development* (5th ed., pp. 993-1028). New York: Wiley.

Bruck, M., Ceci, S. J., & Hembrooke, H. (1998). Reliability and credibility of young children's reports: From research to policy and practice. *American Psychologist, 53*(2), 136-151.

Cairns, R. B. (1998). The making of developmental psychology. In W. Damon (Series Ed.) & R. M. Lerner (Vol. Ed.), *Handbook of child psychology: Vol. 1. Theoretical models of human development* (5th ed., pp. 993-1028). New York: Wiley.

Cairns, R. B., Bergman, L. R., & Kagan, J. (Eds.). (1998). *Methods and models for studying the individual: Essays in honor of Marian Radke-Yarrow.* Thousand Oaks, CA: Sage.

Chibucos, T., & Lerner, R. M. (1999). *Serving children and families through community-university partnerships: Success stories.* Norwell, MA: Kluwer.

Cicchetti, D., & Sroufe, L. A. (2000). The past as prologue to the future: The times, they've been a-changin'. [Editorial]. *Development and Psychopathology, 12*(3), 255-264.

Cicchetti, D., & Toth, S. L. (1998a). The development of depression in children and adolescents. *American Psychologist, 53*(2), 221-243.

Cicchetti, D., & Toth, S. L. (1998b). Perspectives on research and practice in developmental psychopathology. In W. Damon (Series Ed.), I. E. Sigel & K. A. Renninger (Vol. Eds.), *Handbook of child psychology: Vol. 4. Child psychology in practice* (5th ed., pp. 479-484). New York: Wiley.

Coie, J. D., Watt, N. F., West, S. G., Hawkins, J. D., Asarnow, J. R., Markman, H. J., Ramey, S. L., Shure, M. B., & Long, B. (1993). The science of prevention: A conceptual framework and some directions for a national research program. *American Psychologist, 48*(10), 1013-1022.

Coley, R. L., & Chase-Lansdale, P. L. (1998). Adolescent pregnancy and parenthood: Recent evidence and future directions. *American Psychologist, 53*(2), 152-166.

Collins, W. A., Maccoby, E. E., Steinberg, L., Hetherington, E. M., & Bornstein, M. H. (2000). Contemporary research on parenting: The case for nature and nurture. *American Psychologist, 55*(2), 218-232.

Cowan, P. A., Powell, D., & Cowan, C. P. (1998). Parenting interventions: A family systems perspective. In W. Damon (Series Ed.), I. E. Sigel & K. A. Renninger (Vol. Eds.), *Handbook of child psychology: Vol. 4. Child psychology in practice* (5th ed., pp. 3-72). New York: Wiley.

Csikszentmihalyi, M., & Rathunde, K. (1998). The development of the person: An experiential perspective on the ontogenesis of psychological complexity. In W. Damon (Series Ed.) & R. M. Lerner (Vol. Ed.), *Handbook of child psychology: Vol. 1. Theoretical models of human development* (5th ed., 635-684). New York: Wiley.

Damon, W. (1997). *The youth charter: How communities can work together to raise standards for all our children.* New York: Free Press.

Davisdon, E. S., & Benjamin, L. T. Jr. (1987). A history of the child study movement in America. In J. A. Glover & R. R. Ronning (Eds.), *Historical foundations of educational psychology* (pp. 41-60). New York: Plenum.

Dryfoos, J. G. (1990). *Adolescents at risk: Prevalence and prevention.* New York: Oxford University Press.

Dryfoos, J. G. (1998). *Safe passage: Making it through adolescence in a risky society.* New York: Oxford University Press.

Eccles, J. S., Lord, S., & Buchanan, C. M. (1996). School transitions in early adolescence: What are we doing to your young people? In J. A. Graber,

J. Brooks-Gunn, & A. C. Petersen (Eds.), *Transitions through adolescence* (pp. 251-284). Mahwah, NJ: Lawrence Erlbaum.

Elkind, D. (2002). Early childhood education. In R. M. Lerner, F. Jacobs, & D. Wertlieb (Eds.), *Promoting positive child, adolescent, and family development*. Thousand Oaks, CA: Sage. Manuscript in preparation.

Emery, R. E., & Laumann-Billings, L. (1998). An overview of the nature, causes, and consequences of abusive family relationships: Toward differentiating maltreatment and violence. *American Psychologist, 53*(2), 121-135.

Fisher, C. B. (1997). A relational perspective on ethics-in-science decision making for research with vulnerable populations. *IRB: A Review of Human Subjects Research, 19*, 1-4.

Fisher, C. B., & Brennan, M. (1992). Application and ethics in developmental psychology. In D. L. Featherman, R. M. Lerner, & M. Perlmutter (Eds.), *Life-span development and behavior* (Vol. 11, pp. 189-219). Hillsdale, NJ: Lawrence Erlbaum.

Fisher, C. B., & Lerner, R. M. (Eds.). (1994). *Applied developmental psychology*. New York: McGraw-Hill.

Fisher, C. B., & Murray, J. P. (1996). Applied developmental science comes of age. In C. B. Fisher, J. P. Murray, & I. E. Sigel (Eds.), *Applied developmental science: Graduate training for diverse disciplines and educational settings* (pp. 1-22). Norwood, NJ: Ablex.

Fisher, C. B., Murray, J. P., Dill, J. R., Hagen, J. W., Hogan, M. J., Lerner, R. M., Rebok, G. W., Sigel, I., Sostek, A. M., Spencer, M. B., & Wilcox, B. (1993). The national conference on graduate education in the applications of developmental science across the lifespan. *Journal of Applied Developmental Psychology, 14*, 1-10.

Fisher, C. B., Murray, J. P., & Sigel, I. E. (Eds.). (1996). *Applied developmental science: Graduate training for diverse disciplines and educational settings*. Norwood, NJ: Ablex.

Fisher, C. B., & Tryon, W. W. (Eds.). (1990). *Ethics in applied developmental psychology: Emerging issues in an emerging field* (Vol. 4). Norwood, NJ: Ablex.

Fishman, D. B. (1999). *The case for pragmatic psychology*. New York: New York University Press.

Garner, W. R. (1972). The acquisition and application of knowledge: A symbiotic relation. *American Psychologist, 27*, 941-946.

Gollin, E. S. (1981). Development and plasticity. In E. S. Gollin (Ed.), *Developmental plasticity: Behavioral and biological aspects of variations in development* (pp. 231-251). New York: Academic Press.

Gottlieb, G. (1992). *Individual development and evolution: The genesis of novel behavior*. New York: Oxford University Press.

Hagen, J. W. (1996). Graduate education in the applied developmental sciences: History and background. In C. B. Fisher & J. P. Murray (Eds.), *Applied developmental science: Graduate training for diverse disciplines and educational settings, advances in applied developmental psychology*. (pp. 45-51). Norwood, NJ: Ablex.

Hamburg, D. A. (1992). *Today's children: Creating a future for a generation in crisis*. New York: Times Books.

Hamburger, V. (1957). The concept of development in biology. In D. B. Harris (Ed.), *The concept of development* (pp. 49-58). Minneapolis: University of Minnesota Press.

Hamilton, S. F., & Hamilton, M. (1999). Creating new pathways to adulthood by adapting German apprenticeship in the United States. In W. R. Heinz (Ed.), *From education to work: Cross-national perspectives* (pp. 194-213). New York: Cambridge University Press.

Hernandez, D. J. (1993). *America's children: Resources for family, government, and the economy.* New York: Russell Sage.

Hetherington, E. M. (1998). Relevant issues in developmental science: Introduction to the special issue. *American Psychologist, 53*(2), 93-94.

Hetherington, E. M., Bridges, M., & Insabella, G. M. (1998). What matters? What does not? Five perspectives on the association between marital transitions and children's adjustment. *American Psychologist, 53*(2), 167-184.

Higgins-D'Alessandro, A., Fisher, C. B., & Hamilton, M. G. (1998). Educating the applied developmental psychologist for university-community partnerships. In R. M. Lerner & L. A. K. Simon (Eds.), *University-community collaborations for the twenty-first century: Outreach scholarship for youth and families* (pp. 157-183). New York: Garland.

Hoffman, L. W. (1990). Bias and social responsibility in the study of maternal employment. In C. B. Fisher & W. W. Tyron (Eds.), *Ethics in applied developmental psychology: Emerging issues in an emerging field.* (Vol. 4, pp. 253-272). Norwood, NJ: Ablex.

Horowitz, F. D. (2000). Child development and the PITS: Simple questions, complex answers, and developmental theory. *Child Development, 71,* 1-10, 8, 58.

Horowitz, F. D., & O'Brien, M. (1989). In the interest of the nature: A reflective essay on the state of our knowledge and challenges before us. *American Psychologist, 44,* 441-445.

Huston, A. C. (Ed.). (1991). *Children in poverty: Child development and public policy.* Cambridge, UK: Cambridge University Press.

Huston, A. C., McLoyd, V. C., & Garcia Coll, C. (1994). Children and poverty: Issues in contemporary research. *Child Development, 65,* 275-282.

Huston, A. C., & Wright, J. C. (1998). Mass media and children's development. In W. Damon (Series Ed.), I. E. Sigel & K. A. Renninger (Vol. Eds.), *Handbook of child psychology: Vol. 4. Child psychology in practice* (5th ed., pp. 999-1058). New York: Wiley.

Jensen, P., Hoagwood, K., & Trickett, E. (1999). Ivory towers or earthen trenches? Community collaborations to foster "real world" research. *Applied Developmental Science, 3*(4), 206-212.

Kaplan, R. M. (2000). Two pathways to prevention. *American Psychologist, 55*(4), 382-396.

Kellogg Commission on the Future of State and Land-Grant Colleges. (1999). *Returning to our roots: The engaged institution.* Washington, DC: National Association of State Universities and Land-Grant Colleges.

Kennedy, E. M. (1999). University-community partnerships: A mutually beneficial effort to aid community development and improve academic learning opportunities. *Applied Developmental Science, 3*(4), 197-198.

Koch, S., & Leary, D. E. (Eds.). (1985). *A century of psychology as science.* New York: McGraw-Hill.

Koocher, G. P. (1990). Practicing applied developmental psychology: Playing the game you can't win. In I. E. Sigel (Ed.), *Ethics in applied developmental* psychology: Emerging issues in an emerging field (pp. 215-225). Norwood, NJ: Ablex.

Kuo, Z. Y. (1930). The genesis of the cat's response to the rat. *Journal of Comparative Psychology, 11,* 1-35.

Kuo, Z. Y. (1967). *The dynamics of behavior development.* New York: Random House.

Kuo, Z. Y. (1976). *The dynamics of behavior development: An epigenetic view.* New York: Plenum.

Lamb, M. E. (1998). Children in poverty: Development, public policy, and practice. In W. Damon (Series Ed.), I. E. Sigel & K. A. Renninger (Vol. Eds.), *Handbook of child psychology: Vol. 4. Child psychology in practice* (5th ed., pp. 73-134). New York: Wiley.

Leffert, N., Benson, P. L., Scales, P. C., Sharma, A. R., Drake, D. R., & Blyth, D. A. (1998). Developmental assets: Measurement and prediction of risk behaviors among adolescents. *Applied Developmental Science, 2*(4), 209-230.

Lerner, R. M. (1976). *Concepts and theories of human development.* Reading, MA: Addison-Wesley.

Lerner, R. M. (1984). *On the nature of human plasticity.* New York: Cambridge University Press.

Lerner, R. M. (1986). *Concepts and theories of human development* (2nd ed.). New York: Random House.

Lerner, R. M. (1995). *America's youth in crisis: Challenges and options for programs and policies.* Thousand Oaks, CA: Sage.

Lerner, R. M. (Ed.). (1998a). *Handbook of child psychology: Vol. 1. Theoretical models of human development* (5th ed.). New York: Wiley.

Lerner, R. M. (1998b). Theories of human development: Contemporary perspectives. In W. Damon (Series Ed.) & R. M. Lerner (Vol. Ed.), *Handbook of child psychology: Vol. 1. Theoretical models of human development* (5th ed., pp. 1-24). New York: John Wiley.

Lerner, R. M. (2002a). *Adolescence: Development, diversity, context, and application.* Upper Saddle River, NJ: Prentice Hall.

Lerner, R. M. (2002b). *Concepts and theories of human development* (3rd ed.). Mahwah, NJ: Lawrence Erlbaum.

Lerner, R. M., & Fisher, C. B. (1994). From applied developmental psychology to applied developmental science: Community coalitions and collaborative careers. In C. B. Fisher & R. M. Lerner (Eds.), *Applied developmental psychology* (pp. 502-522). New York: McGraw-Hill

Lerner, R. M., Fisher, C. B., & Weinberg, R. A. (1997). Applied developmental science: Scholarship for our times. *Applied Developmental Science, 1*(1), 2-3.

Lerner, R. M., Fisher, C. B., & Weinberg, R. A. (2000a). Applying developmental science in the twenty-first century: International scholarship for our times. *International Journal of Behavioral Development, 24,* 24-29.

Lerner, R. M., Fisher, C. B., & Weinberg, R. A. (2000b). Toward a science for and of the people: Promoting civil society through the application of developmental science. *Child Development, 71*(1), 11-20.

Lerner, R. M., & Galambos, N. (1998). Adolescent development: Challenges and opportunities for research, programs, and policies. In J. T. Spence (Ed.), *Annual Review of Psychology* (Vol. 49, pp. 413-446). Palo Alto, CA: Annual Reviews.

Lerner, R. M., & Miller, J. R. (1998). Developing multidisciplinary institutes to enhance the lives of individuals and families: Academic potentials and pitfalls. *Journal of Public Service and Outreach, 3*(1).

Lerner, R. M., Miller, J. R., Knott, J. H., Corey, K. E., Bynum, T. S., Hoopfer, L. C., McKinney, M. H., Abrams, L. A., Hula, R. C., & Terry, P. A. (1994). Integrating scholarship and outreach in human development research, policy, and service: A developmental contextual perspective. In D. L. Featherman, R. M. Lerner, & M. Perlmutter (Eds.), *Life-span development and behavior* (Vol. 12, pp. 249-273). Hillsdale, NJ: Lawrence Erlbaum.

Lerner, R. M., Ostrom, C. W., & Freel, M. A. (1995). Promoting positive youth and community development through outreach scholarship: Comments on Zeldin and Peterson. *Journal of Adolescent Research, 10,* 486-502.

Lerner, R. M., & Ryff, C. (1978). Implementation of the life-span view of human development: The sample case of attachment. In P. B. Baltes (Ed.), *Life-span development and behavior* (Vol. 1, pp. 1-44). New York: Academic Press.

Lerner, R. M., & Simon, L. A. K. (1998a). Directions for the American outreach university in the twenty-first century. In R. M. Lerner & L. A. K. Simon (Eds.), *University-community collaborations for the twenty-first century: Outreach scholarship for youth and families* (pp. 463-481). New York: Garland.

Lerner, R. M., & Simon, L. A. K. (1998b). The new American outreach university: Challenges and options. In R. M. Lerner & L. A. K. Simon (Eds.), *University-community collaborations for the twenty-first century: Outreach scholarship for youth and families* (pp. 3-23). New York: Garland.

Lerner, R. M., Sparks, E. S., & McCubbin, L. (1999). *Family diversity and family policy: Strengthening families for America's children.* Norwell, MA: Kluwer.

Little, R. R. (1993). *What's working for today's youth: The issues, the programs, and the learnings.* Paper presented at the ICYF Fellows Colloquium, Michigan State University, East Lansing.

Loeber, R., & Stouthamer-Loeber, M. (1998). Development of juvenile aggression and violence: Some common misconceptions and controversies. *American Psychologist, 53*(2), 242-259.

Lorenz, K. (1966). *On aggression.* New York: Harcourt, Brace & World.

Martland, N., & Rothbaum, F. (1999). Cameo feature news: University and community partnership disseminates child development information. In T. R. Chibucos & R. M. Lerner (Eds.), *Serving children and families through community-university partnerships: Success stories* (pp. 173-180). Boston: Kluwer.

Masten, A. S., & Coatsworth, J. D. (1998). The development of competence in favorable and unfavorable environments: Lessons from research on successful children. *American Psychologist, 53*(2), 205-220.

McCall, R., & Groark, C. (2000). The future of applied child development research and public policy. *Child Development, 71,* 197-204.

McCall, R. B. (1996). The concept and practice of education, research, and public service in university psychology departments. *American Psychologist, 51*(4), 379-388.

McCall, R. B., Groark, C. J., Strauss, M. S., & Johnson, C. N. (1995). The University of Pittsburgh office of child development: An experiment in promoting interdisciplinary applied human development. *Journal of Applied Developmental Psychology, 16,* 593-612.

McLoyd, V. C. (1998). Socioeconomic disadvantage and child development. *American Psychologist, 53*(2), 185-204.

Meszaros, P. S. (2003). Family and consumer sciences: A holistic approach stretching to the future. In R. M. Lerner, F. Jacobs, D. Wertlieb, & F. Jacobs (Eds.), *Handbook of applied developmental science: Vol. 4. Adding value to youth and family development: The engaged university and professional and academic outreach*. Thousand Oaks, CA: Sage.

Morrison, F. J., Lord, C., & Keating, D. P. (1984). Applied developmental psychology. In F. J. Morrison, C. Lord, & D. P. Keating (Eds.), *Applied developmental psychology* (Vol. 1, pp. 4-20). New York: Academic Press.

Mussen, P. H. (Ed.). (1970). *Carmichael's manual of child psychology* (3rd ed.). New York: Wiley.

Nickols, S. Y. (2002). Family and consumer sciences in the United States. In N. J. Smelser & P. B. Baltes (Eds.), *International encyclopedia of the social and behavioral sciences*. Oxford, UK: Elsevier.

Ostrom, C. W., Lerner, R. M., & Freel, M. A. (1995). Building the capacity of youth and families through university-community collaborations: The development-in-context evaluation (DICE) model. *Journal of Adolescent Research, 10*(4), 427-448.

Overton, B. J., & Burkhardt, J. C. (1999). Drucker could be right, but . . . : New leadership models for institutional-community partnerships. *Applied Developmental Science, 3*(4), 217-227.

Overton, W. (1998). Developmental psychology: Philosophy, concepts, and methodology. In W. Damon (Series Ed.) & R. M. Lerner (Ed.), *Handbook of child psychology: Vol. 1. Theoretical models of human development* (5th ed., pp. 107-187). New York: Wiley.

Parke, R. D., Ornstein, P. A., Reiser, J. J., & Zahn-Waxler, C. (Eds.). (1994). *A century of developmental psychology*. Washington, DC: American Psychological Association.

Pepper, S. C. (1942). *World hypotheses: A study in evidence*. Berkeley: University of California Press.

Pittman, K. (1996, Winter). Community, youth, development: Three goals in search of connection. *New Designs for Youth Development*, pp. 4-8.

Plomin, R. (1986). *Development, genetics, and psychology*. Hillsdale, NJ: Lawrence Erlbaum.

Plomin, R. (2000). Behavioural genetics in the 21st century. *International Journal of Behavioral Development, 24*, 30-34.

Plomin, R., Corley, R., DeFries, J. C., & Faulker, D. W. (1990). Individual differences in television viewing in early childhood: Nature as well as nurture. *Psychological Science, 1*, 371-377.

Power, F. C., Higgins, A., & Kohlberg, L. (1989). *Lawrence Kohlberg's approach to moral education*. New York: Columbia University Press.

Ramey, C. T., & Ramey, S. L. (1998). Early intervention and early experience. *American Psychologist, 53*(2), 109-120.

Renninger, K. A. (1998). Developmental psychology and instruction: Issues from and for practice. In W. Damon (Series Ed.), I. E. Sigel & K. A. Renninger (Vol. Eds.), *Handbook of child psychology: Vol. 4. Child psychology in practice* (5th ed., pp. 211-274). New York: Wiley.

Richters, J. E. (1997). The Hubble hypothesis and the developmentalist's dilemma. *Development and Psychopathology, 9*, 193-229.

Rowe, D. (1994). *The limits of family influence: Genes, experience, and behavior.* New York: Guilford.

Rushton, J. P. (1987). An evolutionary theory of health, longevity, and personality: Sociobiology, and r/K reproductive strategies. *Psychological Reports, 60,* 539-549.

Rushton, J. P. (1988a). Do r/K reproductive strategies apply to human differences? *Social Biology, 35,* 337-340.

Rushton, J. P. (1988b). Race differences in behavior: A review and evolutionary analysis. *Personality and Individual Differences, 9,* 1009-1024.

Rushton, J. P. (1997). More on political correctness and race differences. *Journal of Social Distress and the Homeless, 6,* 195-198.

Rushton, J. P. (1999). *Race, evolution, and behavior* (Special abridged ed.). New Brunswick, NJ: Transaction Publishing.

Rushton, J. P. (2000). *Race, evolution, and behavior* (2nd special abridged ed.). New Brunswick, NJ: Transaction Publishing.

Rutter, M., & Sroufe, L. A. (2000). Developmental psychopathology: Concepts and challenges. *Development and Psychopathology, 12*(3), 265-296.

Scales, P. C., Benson, P. L., Leffert, N., & Blyth, D. A. (2000). Contribution of developmental assets to the prediction of thriving among adolescents. *Applied Developmental Science, 4*(1), 27-46.

Scales, P. C., & Leffert, N. (1999). *Developmental assets: A synthesis of the scientific research on adolescent development.* Minneapolis, MN: Search Institute.

Scarr, S. (1998). American child care today. *American Psychologist, 53*(2), 95-108.

Schneirla, T. C. (1956). Interrelationships of the innate and the acquired in instinctive behavior. In P. P. Grassé (Ed.), *L'instinct dans le comportement des animaux et de l'homme.* Paris: Mason et Cie.

Schneirla, T. C. (1957). The concept of development in comparative psychology. In D. B. Harris (Ed.), *The concept of development: An issue in the study of human behavior* (pp. 78-108). Minneapolis: University of Minnesota Press.

Schorr, L. B. (1988). *Within our reach: Breaking the cycle of disadvantage.* New York: Doubleday.

Schorr, L. B. (1997). *Common purpose: Strengthening families and neighborhoods to rebuild America.* New York: Doubleday.

Schwebel, D. C., Plumert, J. M., & Pick, H. L. (2000). Integrating basic and applied developmental research: A new model for the twenty-first century. *Child Development, 71*(1), 222-230.

Sears, R. R. (1975). Your ancients revisited: A history of child development. In E. M. Hetherington (Ed.), *Review of child development research* (Vol. 6, pp. 1-73). Chicago: University of Chicago Press.

Sherrod, L. R. (1999a). Funding opportunities for applied developmental science. In P. Ralston, R. M. Lerner, A. K. Mullis, C. Simerly, & J. Murray (Eds.), *Social change, public policy, and community collaboration: Training human development professionals for the twenty-first century* (pp. 121-129). Norwell, MA: Kluwer.

Sherrod, L. R. (1999b). "Giving child development knowledge away": Using university-community partnerships to disseminate research on children, youth, and families. *Applied Developmental Science, 3*(4), 228-234.

Shonkoff, J. (2000). Science, policy, and practice: Three cultures in search of a shared mission. *Child Development, 71,* 181-187.

Siegel, A. W., & White, S. H. (1982). The child study movement: Early growth and development of the symbolized child. In H. W. Reese (Ed.), *Advances in child development and behavior* (Vol. 17, pp. 233-285). New York: Academic Press.

Sigel, I. E. (1985). *Parental belief systems: The psychological consequences for children.* Hillsdale, NJ: Lawrence Erlbaum.

Sigel, I. E., & Cocking, R. R. (1980). Editors' message. *Journal of Applied Developmental Psychology, 1*(1), i-iii.

Sigel, I. E., & Renninger, K. A. (Eds.). (1998). *Handbook of child psychology: Vol. 4. Child psychology in practice* (5th ed.). New York: John Wiley.

Spanier, G. B. (1999). Enhancing the quality of life: A model for the 21st century land-grant university. *Applied Developmental Science, 3*(4), 199-205.

Strauss, S. (1998). Cognitive development and science education: Toward a middle level model. In W. Damon (Series Ed.), I. E. Sigel & K. A. Renninger (Vol. Eds.), *Handbook of child psychology: Vol. 4. Child psychology in practice* (5th ed., pp. 357-400). New York: Wiley.

Takanishi, R. (1993). An agenda for the integration of research and policy during early adolescence. In R. M. Lerner (Ed.), *Early adolescence: Perspectives on research, policy, and intervention* (pp. 457-470). Hillsdale, NJ: Lawrence Erlbaum.

Thompson, L. (1999). Creating partnerships with government, communities, and universities to achieve results for children. *Applied Developmental Science, 3*(4), 213-216.

Tobach, E. (1994). Personal is political is personal is political. *Journal of Social Issues, 50,* 221-224.

Trickett, E. J., Barone, C., & Buchanan, R. M. (1996). Elaborating developmental contextualism in adolescent research and intervention: Paradigm contributions from community psychology. *Journal of Research on Adolescence, 6*(3), 245-269.

Valsiner, J. (1998). The development of the concept of development: Historical and epistemological perspectives. In W. Damon (Series Ed.) & R. M. Lerner (Vol. Ed.), *Handbook of child psychology: Vol. 1. Theoretical models of human development* (5th ed., pp. 189-232). New York: Wiley.

von Bertalanffy, L. (1933). *Modern theories of development.* London: Oxford University Press.

Weissberg, R. P., & Greenberg, M. T. (1998). School and community competence-enhancement and prevention programs. In W. Damon (Series Ed.), I. E. Sigel & K. A. Renninger (Vol. Eds.), *Handbook of child psychology: Vol. 4. Child psychology in practice* (5th ed., pp. 877-954). New York: Wiley.

Wertlieb, D. (2001). *Converging trends in family research and pediatrics: Recent findings for the AAP task force on the family.* Unpublished manuscript.

Wertlieb, D. (2003). Applied developmental science. In I. B. Weiner (Series Ed.), R. M. Lerner, M. A. Easterbrooks, & J. Mistry (Vol. Eds.), *Handbook of psychology: Vol. 6. Developmental psychology.* New York: Wiley.

Wertlieb, D. L. (1997). Children whose parents divorce: Life trajectories and turning points. In I. Gotlieb & B. Wheaton (Eds.), *Stress and adversity over the life course: Trajectories and turning points* (pp. 179-196). Cambridge, UK: Cambridge University Press.

White, S. H. (1992). G. Stanley Hall: From philosophy to developmental psychology. *Developmental Psychology, 28,* 25-34.

Zigler, E. (1980). Welcoming a new journal. *Journal of Applied Developmental Psychology, 1*(1), 1-6.

Zigler, E. (1998). A place of value for applied and policy studies. *Child Development, 69*(2), 532-542.

Zigler, E., & Finn-Stevenson, M. (1992). Applied developmental psychology. In M. H. Bornstein & M. E. Lamb (Eds.), *Developmental psychology: An advanced textbook* (3rd ed., pp. 677-729). Hillsdale, NJ: Lawrence Erlbaum.

Zigler, E. F., & Finn-Stevenson, M. (1999). Applied developmental psychology. In M. H. Bornstein & M. E. Lamb (Eds.), *Developmental psychology: An advanced textbook* (4th ed.). Mahwah, NJ: Lawrence Erlbaum.

CHAPTER 2

Neural Development and Lifelong Plasticity

CHARLES A. NELSON

The formation and growth of the human brain is surely one of the most remarkable, albeit unfinished, scientific stories of the past 25 years. Although in the United States, the 1990s were declared to be the "decade of the brain," it is clear as we enter the early 21st century that our knowledge of brain function and development is far from complete. A point I hope to emphasize throughout this chapter is that knowledge of brain development is surely critical to understanding all of child development. In particular, although it is commonly believed that brains develop on their own accord, largely under the direction of genes and hormones, I will make clear in the following pages that brains desperately need both endogenous and exogenous experiences to grow properly. This is particularly true during the postnatal period, in which, unfortunately, the least is known about brain development.

In the sections that follow, I will describe the major events that give rise to the human brain. Once this blueprint is established, I will then proceed to talk about the role of experience in influencing the brain. I will do so by drawing on the role of early as well as late experience to make the point that although brain development is largely limited to the first two decades of life, brain *reorganization* continues to occur through much of the life span.

BRAIN DEVELOPMENT: A PRÉCIS

As students of human embryology are aware, shortly after conception, rapid cell division in the zygote results in the formation of the blastocyst. By the end of the first week, the blastocyst itself has separated into two layers. The outer layer will become support structures, such as the amniotic sac, umbilical cord, and placenta, whereas the inner layer will become the embryo itself. Over the

AUTHOR'S NOTE: Reproduced with permission from *Millennial Dialogue for Healthy Child Development (MDC)*, Toronto, Canada.

course of the next week, the embryo begins to subdivide into layers, and it is from the outer, ectodermal layer that the nervous system will form. How this miraculous transformation occurs, from a thin layer of unspecified tissue into the highly complex organ known as the brain, is the subject of intense study. In the following section, the major prenatal and postnatal events that give rise to the human brain are described. The major prenatal events consist of neural induction and neurulation, cell proliferation and migration, followed by differentiation, apoptosis (cell death), and axonal outgrowth. Myelination and synaptogenesis begin prenatally (subsequent to the formation of processes, axons, and dendrites), with both processes continuing well into the second decade of life.

PRENATAL DEVELOPMENT

Neural Induction

As illustrated in Figure 2.1, *neural induction* is the process whereby the undifferentiated cells that comprise a portion of the ectodermal layer of the embryo go on to become neural tissue itself. In the human, this event occurs at 16 days gestation (O'Rahilly & Gardner, 1979). The mechanisms that permit this ectodermal transformation are still not clear. The traditional view is that a chemical agent is secreted from the mesoderm, which induces the dorsal side ("toward the rear") of the ectoderm to develop into the nervous system (Spemann & Mangold, 1924). More recent discoveries in developmental neurobiology have revealed that members of the transforming growth factor β (TGF-β) superfamily (e.g., activin) play an important role in induction, whereas several proteins (e.g., follistatin) permit neuralization by inhibiting these TGF-βs (Hemmati-Brivanlou, Kelly, & Melton, 1994).

Neurulation

Neurulation involves converting the neural plate into a neural tube (see Figure 2.1). The plate itself emerges as a thickening along the midline of the dorsal ectoderm during induction. Once the neural plate appears, it becomes elongated along the rostrocaudal (top to bottom) axis (Smith & Schoenwolf, 1997). Gradually, the neural plate is transformed into a tube, which will later go on to form the brain and spinal cord. The widest section of the neural fold represents the future forebrain, and the presumptive midbrain is identified by a bend in the neural axis called the cranial flexure (Sidman & Rakic, 1982).

Although I have greatly simplified a very complex process, it should be recognized that the very complexity of neurulation brings with it a risk of failure—that is, errors in the formation of the neural tube. So-called neural tube defects, such as anencephaly, commonly lead to termination of the fetus or profound birth defects. Other defects, such as spina bifida, are less catastrophic but still debilitating: For example, such children frequently suffer from motor problems, often with secondary medical complications such as hydrocephalus and infection.

Assuming the neural tube closes correctly, the tube itself is comprised of progenitor cells that give rise to the neurons and glia of the central nervous system. Specifically, the rostral ("toward the front") portion of the tube will form the brain, while the caudal portion becomes the spinal cord. In addition, lying adjacent to and outside the neural tube (i.e., sandwiched between the outer layer of the ectoderm and the neural tube; see Figure 2.1) lies the neural crest. The cells that make up the neural crest will eventually give rise to the peripheral (autonomic) nervous system.

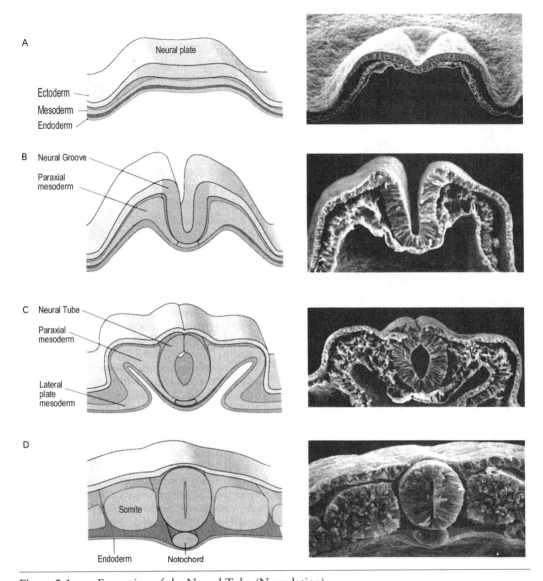

Figure 2.1   Formation of the Neural Tube (Neurulation)

SOURCE: From "The Induction and Patterning of the Nervous System," by T. M. Jessell and J. R. Sanes, 2000, in E. R. Kandel, J. H. Schwartz, and T. M. Jessell (Eds.), *Principles of Neural Science* (4th ed., p. 1020, Fig. 52-1), New York: McGraw-Hill. Reproduced by permission.

Cell Proliferation

In primates and rodents, *proliferation* includes a symmetrical and an asymmetrical stage (Rakic, 1988; Smart, 1985; Takahashi, Nowakowski, & Caviness, 1994). Chenn and McConnell (1995) have discussed how, early in the proliferation period, the mitosis of a progenitor cell produces two progenitor cells. Because one cell produces two identical cells, this first phase of proliferation has been described as *symmetrical*. Here, the cells travel back and forth between the inner and outer sides of the ventricular zone (the first

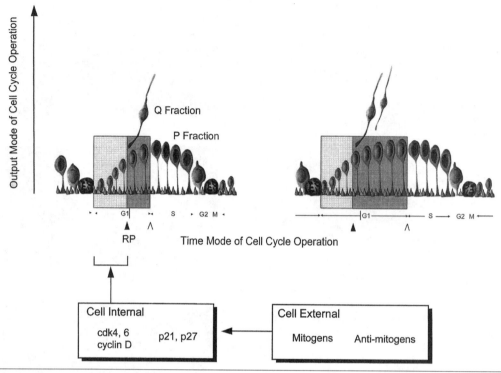

Figure 2.2   Cell Migration and Proliferation

SOURCE: From "Neocortical Neurogenesis: Regulation, Control Points, and a Strategy of Structural Variation," by T. Takahashi, R. S. Nowakowski, and V. S. Caviness Jr., 2000, in C. A. Nelson and M. Luciana (Eds.), *Handbook of Developmental Cognitive Neuroscience* (p. 9, Fig. 1.5), Cambridge: MIT Press.

layer of the nervous system, where early duplication occurs). Once duplication has occurred, the cell travels down the ventricular layer, where it divides again. The two progenitor cells then independently begin the process of mitosis again. During the proliferation period, the marginal zone is formed, which contains the processes (axons and dendrites) of cells from the underlying ventricular zone (for review, see Takahashi, Nowakowski, & Caviness, 2001; see Figure 2.2 for illustration of these two layers).

The second phase of proliferation (during which the first neurons are formed) begins at approximately 7 weeks in the human, and this process continues until mid-gestation (Rakic, 1978). Here, progenitor cells create one other progenitor cell and a postmitotic neuron, that is, a cell that no longer divides.

Because two different types of cells are created, this form of proliferation is termed *asymmetrical*. Again, cells synthesize DNA and divide as they travel back and forth between the two sides of the ventricular zone. While the newly formed progenitor cell goes on to generate other cells, the postmitotic neuron is believed to stop dividing and instead begins to migrate to its final destination (Rakic, 1988).

There are a multitude of subtle molecular interactions that must occur to permit and regulate cell proliferation. As a result, the embryo is very vulnerable to slight environmental perturbations. For instance, microencephaly (a heterogeneous group of disorders whose hallmark feature is that of a small brain) results from aberrations in neural proliferation. Microencephaly can be caused by a number of exogenous experiences, including exposure to radiation, rubella, and maternal alcoholism (for discussion, see Shonkoff & Phillips, 2000). In addition, exposure to these environmental events during the proliferation phase may lead to an end of symmetrical proliferation, which in turn can cause a reduction in the final number of neurons.

Mechanisms of Migration

Once an immature neuron is formed, it must migrate from the ventricular or subventricular zone to its final destination. In the human, migration begins at around 8 weeks gestation when the progenitor cells begin to produce postmitotic neurons (Rakic, 1978). Proliferation ends at approximately 4 to 5 months gestation, and thus, the last cells begin their migration at this time.

Migration occurs in two distinct waves. In the first wave, migratory postmitotic neurons are primarily derived from the ventricular zone, whereas in the second wave, they are primarily derived from the subventricular zone (Rakic, 1972). Cortical neurons migrate in an inside-out pattern, meaning that neurons with earlier "birthdays" migrate to lower cortical layers and the cells with later "birthdays" travel over other neurons for destinations in the outer cortex (Rakic, 1974; see Figure 2.3). Consequently, neurons generated in the ventricular zone occupy the lower layers of the brain (Layers 4, 5, and 6), whereas neurons that are derived from the subventricular zone become located in the outer regions of the brain (roughly, Layers 2 and 3). An exception to this is the molecular layer (Layer 1) of the cortex (Chong et al., 1996). Here, the cells migrate at about the same time as the innermost layer, and it is thought that the early formation of the molecular and innermost layers may provide scaffolding for the subsequent patterning of the neurons that will reside in the middle layers (Chong et al., 1996).

There are two types of migration: radial and tangential (reviewed in Hatten, 1999; Rakic, 1995). In *radial migration,* neural precursors travel along radial glia from the proliferation zones to the outer areas of the central nervous system (Rakic, 1971, 1972, 1978). As a result, glia cells provide a path for the neurons to travel from the deep layers of the proliferation zones to their final destinations. Following the migration period, many radial glia are transformed into astrocytes, another type of glial cell (Rakic, 1990).

In contrast to radial migration, *tangential migration* permits neurons to travel parallel to the surface of the developing brain and thus to enter and exit different brain regions (Rakic, 1990). Where in the developing brain does tangential migration take place? O'Rourke, Chenn, and McConnell (1997) found evidence in the fetal ferret brain for tangential migration of postmitotic cells in the ventricular and subventricular zones. Thus, at least some of the tangential dispersion is due to postmitotic cell movement that occurs even before the cell reaches the presumptive cortex. As will be discussed in the section on differentiation, whether cell migration follows a radial or tangential path will determine whether genetic or epigenetic influences are primarily responsible for determining the precise future location of the cell. That is, if cells were distributed radially, then the birth date and location of the postmitotic neuron's progenitor cell will determine where the neuron will reside. However, if tangential migration is also involved, this would indicate that cell fate may not be completely determined by birth date and progenitor location of the progenitor and that environmental cues could influence the cell's placement in the cortex.

Many neurons must migrate distances as far as thousands of micrometers (Rakic, 1972), an enormous distance given the size of a neuron. Because migrating neurons rely on a vast array of molecular signals for guiding

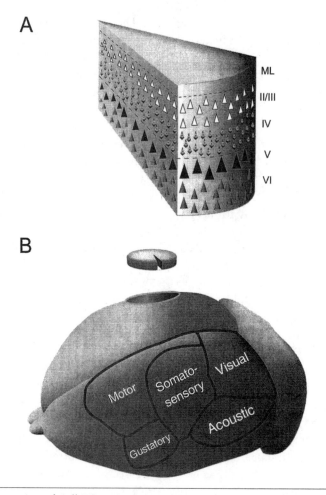

Figure 2.3   Illustration of Cell Migration

SOURCE: From "Neocortical Neurogenesis: Regulation, Control Points, and a Strategy Of Structural Variation," by T. Takahashi, R. S. Nowakowski, and V. S. Caviness Jr., 2001, in C. A. Nelson and M. Luciana (Eds.), *Handbook of Developmental Cognitive Neuroscience* (p. 4, Fig. 1.1), Cambridge: MIT Press. Reproduced with permission.

their route of migration, it is likely that deleterious perturbations during this period could lead to errors of cell migration. For example, in microgyria, an environmental insult during the migration period in human fetuses causes routing errors in traveling neurons and subsequent massive deformity of the overall brain (McBride & Kemper, 1982; Norman, 1980). Receiving even more speculation is whether schizophrenia represents an error of cell migration (see Elvevåg & Weinberger, 2001). Unfortunately, errors of cell migration are not well understood.

Anatomical Changes Due to Proliferation and Migration

As cell migration continues, the immature cortex is transformed from a single sheet composed entirely of progenitor cells to a multilayered structure with many different types of cells (see Figure 2.4). By the 6th week of gestation, the marginal zone appears superficially to the ventricular zone. Between the 6th and 8th week, the intermediate zone emerges between the ventricular and marginal zones. By and large,

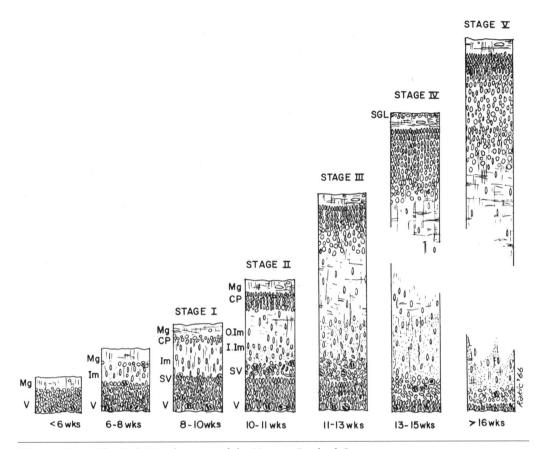

Figure 2.4   The Early Development of the Human Cerebral Cortex

SOURCE: From "Development of the Human Central Nervous System," by R. Sidman and P. Rakic, 1982, in W. Haymaker and R. D. Adams (Eds.), *Histology and Histopathology of the Nervous System* (p. 29, Figure 1-14), Springfield, IL: Charles C Thomas. Reproduced with permission.

NOTE: The key to the abbreviations are as follows: ventricular zone (V), marginal zone (Mg) intermediate zone (Im), inner intermediate zone (I. Im), outer intermediate zone (O. Im), subventricular zone (SV), cortical plate (CP). The interruptions on the two right columns indicate that the intermediate zone becomes disproportionately thick relative to the other layers.

the cells of the intermediate zone are postmitotic.

The subventricular zone (which is heavily involved in proliferation; see Rakic, 1978) emerges between the ventricular and intermediate zones, between the 8th and 10th weeks (Sidman & Rakic, 1973). As the ventricular zone becomes depleted of cells from the first wave of migration, the subventricular zone provides the majority of the neurons in the second wave of migration (Rakic, 1978). The cortical plate (which later develops into the six layers of the cerebral cortex) is also formed between the intermediate and marginal zones (Rakic, 1972). Subsequently, branching neurons from the cortical plate cause the preplate to split into the marginal zone and subplate. This subplate region is involved in determining the organization of the cerebral cortex (O'Leary, Schlaggar, & Tuttle, 1994).

In the first wave of migration, the proliferation of progenitor cells in the ventricular zone leads to the formation of vesicles, or

Three-vesicle stage

Five-vesicle stage

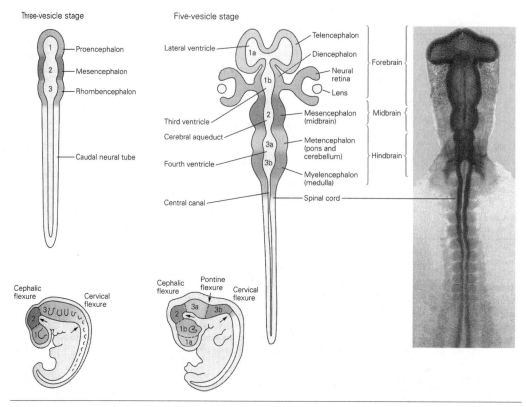

Figure 2.5 Development of the Neural Tube From Three to Five Vesicles

SOURCE: From "The Induction and Patterning of the Nervous System," by T. M. Jessell and J. R. Sanes, 2000, in E. R. Kandel, J. H. Schwartz, and T. M. Jessell (Eds.), *Principles of Neural Science* (4th ed., p. 1021, Fig. 52-2), New York: McGraw-Hill. Reproduced by permission.

bulges, in the neural tube itself. By the 20th day of human gestation, the nervous system is comprised of three primary vesicles (O'Rahilly & Müiler, 1994). The three vesicles are the proencephalon (forebrain), mesencephalon (midbrain) and rhombencephalon (hindbrain). (See Figure 2.5.) At 5 weeks, further proliferation gives rise to the five-vesicle stage. At this point, the proencephalon splits to become the telencephalon and the diencephalon. In addition, although the mesencephalon does not divide, the hindbrain is segmented into the metencephalon as well as the myelencephalon.

The second wave of migration occurs between the 11th and 16th weeks of gestation (Rakic, 1972). During this period, the telencephalon dramatically expands and differentiates to form the cerebral cortex, the basal ganglia, the corpus callosum, and other structures, including the thalamus (Martin & Jessell, 1991). By the 20th week of gestation the cortical plate has divided into three layers, and by the 7th month of gestation, all six layers (lamina) of the cortex can be observed, the same number as in the adult brain (Layer 6 is the deepest layer, whereas Layer 1 is the most superficial layer).

Axonal Outgrowth and Synaptogenesis

Once neurons migrate to their destinations, their axons must extend to establish connections with other neurons (Tessier-Lavigne & Goodman, 1996). Growth cones (which lie at the tip of moving axons) play a key role in axonal navigation. Growth cones are comprised of two basic structures: lamellipodia and filopodia (Suter & Forscher, 1998). Whereas lamellipodia are fan shaped, filopodia protrude from the lamellipodia as small spikes. These processes expand and retract to sample the molecular surroundings and thereby determine the direction of movement for the axon.

Once the axon arrives at its target destination, synaptic connections must be formed and strengthened, a process that involves neurotrophic factors. Neurotrophic factors are signaling molecules that are necessary for neural survival (Henderson, 1996). Examples include neurotrophin-4/5 (NT-4/5) and brain-derived neurotrophic factor (BDNF). However, over and above these (and other) neural growth factors (NGFs), much of synaptic modeling and remodeling depends on experience, a topic to which I shall return in subsequent sections of this chapter. Suffice to say, as axons extend and dendrites arborize, the developing nervous system becomes more densely packed, and the surface of the brain acquires convolutions (sulci and gyri) to accommodate this increased cortical mass. Thus, through these processes of axonal outgrowth and synaptogenesis, the brain increases in size, connections are formed, and the brain takes on a more mature appearance.

Differentiation

Cellular differentiation refers to the process whereby cells become more specialized over time. Exactly *when* a cell is specified to reside in a particular location is a problem of enduring interest; different locations and cortical layers tend to exhibit distinct neural characteristics (Chenn, Braisted, McConnell, & O'Leary 1997).

Two primary theories have been offered to account for when and how cells are specified to reside at particular destinations. Rakic's (1988, 1995) protomap hypothesis postulates that the proliferative ventricular zone contains a "blueprint" for the placement of all neurons within the adult cortex. The destination of the cell on the horizontal plane is determined by the location of the precursor cell in the ventricular zone, and the cell's position on the vertical plane is determined by the time of origin (Rakic, 1995). In contrast, in the protocortex hypothesis (Chenn et al., 1997; O'Leary et al., 1994), emphasis is placed on epigenetic influences and the role of events that occur once the neuron has reached its destination. In contrast to the protomap hypothesis, the protocortex hypothesis suggests that the spatial relationship between progenitors in the ventricular zone may not be maintained by the daughter cell in the cortex. Rather, cells from common genetic backgrounds have the capacity to travel to disparate locations of the brain via tangential migration (Walsh & Cepko, 1992, 1993). This form of migration may not follow a predetermined pattern, but instead, traveling cells may be responsive to various environmental cues for determining their fate. Thus, tangential migration may provide for both positive and negative influences to alter the movement and eventual differentiation of cortical neurons.

Collectively, there is evidence to support the observation that cells travel from ventricular and subventricular zones out to the cortex in a point-to-point fashion, as the protomap theory would predict. However, there is also evidence that not all cell fate is predetermined. Via tangential migration, cell movement—and thus cell morphology—might be somewhat plastic. This plasticity may allow for the amelioration of errors in migration and other developmental processes but at the same time might also permit environmental perturbations to adversely affect the developing nervous tissue during the latter parts of fetal development.

Apoptosis

It has been estimated that during development, roughly half of all brain cells die, a process referred to as *apoptosis* (Raff et al., 1993). Apoptosis is a form of programmed cell death (most likely mediated by neurotrophic factors) characterized by overall shrinkage of the cell, with the organelles and plasma membrane remaining unaffected (Kerr, Wyllie, & Currie, 1972). Other cells or macrophages then quickly absorb the dead cell (Jacobson, Weil, & Raff, 1997). This rapid response prevents leakage of the cell contents as well as inflammation. Because apoptosis is involved in the degeneration of *nearly 50%* of all neurons during development, the appropriate unfolding of this process is crucial for normal development. Indeed, perturbations in apoptosis are linked to mental retardation. For example, neurons from fetuses with Down syndrome experience high rates of apoptosis when cultured, relative to cells from control brains (Busciglio & Yankner, 1995). It is suggested that this neuronal defect may at least partly account for the mental retardation associated with Down syndrome.

Summary of Prenatal Development

The central nervous system is formed through the intricate processes of induction, neurulation, proliferation, migration, axon extension/dendritic arborization, synaptogenesis, differentiation, and apoptosis. Even the smallest perturbations during any of these periods may severely alter the developmental trajectory of the organism. On the other hand, we know that these same perturbations frequently have little effect on brain function (e.g., heterotopias—a pathological state in which cell bodies are found where normally only processes reside—is not uncommon among perfectly normally functioning individuals). Thus, a crucial area of future investigation lies in explaining the broad range of individual differences that lead to different *functional* developmental trajectories.

Having established the prenatal blueprint for the developing brain, in the next section, I briefly turn to a discussion of crucial postnatal events.

POSTNATAL DEVELOPMENT

As stated at the outset, the major two postnatal events concerns *synaptogenesis* and *myelination*, topics to which I now turn.

Formation of Axons and Dendrites

To produce a functional synapse, axons must make appropriate connections with dendrites. It is well established that axons are produced in excess numbers during perinatal life (i.e., the end of the prenatal period and the beginning of the postnatal period) and the final number may be achieved by the process of competitive elimination postnatally. For example, in the corpus callosum of the infant rhesus monkey, the number of axonal fibers is at least 3.5 times that of the adult monkey (LaMantia & Rakic, 1990). Similarly, in the visual cortex of the rhesus monkey, the peak number of axons occurs at about 5 postnatal months, and the peak of synaptogenesis occurs around the 8th postnatal month (Michel & Garey, 1984).

During the first postnatal year, growth of dendritic trees and spines can be seen in all six layers of the cortex, although these spines are still immature. In the visual cortex, for example, there is rapid development between the 2nd and 4th postnatal month, with maximum dendritic arborization occurring by approximately the 5th postnatal month, followed by regression to adult levels by the 2nd postnatal year (Michel & Garey, 1984).

Unfortunately, the formation of appropriate axonal projections may be perturbed in a number of ways, such as early head trauma, anoxia, toxins, malnutrition, or genetic anomalies. Similarly, abnormalities of dendritic development have been linked to (among other factors) inappropriate cell location, neurotoxins, and undernutrition, as well as developmental pathologies (e.g., Fragile X; see Volpe, 1995). For example, children with mental retardation have abnormalities of dendritic branching and spines (e.g., Huttenlocher, 1975, 1979; Purpura, 1975, 1982) in which dendrites may be thinner, have smaller numbers of spines, or have shorter stalks. In autopsy studies, individuals with severe mental retardation of unknown etiology present with defects in the number, length, and spatial arrangement of dendritic branching and dendritic spines.

Synaptogenesis

Synaptic Overproduction

Although there are two types of synapses, electrical (e.g., gap junctions) and chemical, I will focus most on the latter, about which more is known. In a *chemical synapse,* an electrical signal from the presynaptic cell is converted into a chemical signal that can be transferred through extracellular space to the postsynaptic cell. In synaptic transmission, an electrical signal is transferred from the soma (cell body), down the axon, and signals the release of chemical messengers into extracellular space. The chemical messengers (most commonly neurotransmitters and neuropeptides) can open or close ion channels on dendritic spines, changing the electrical current in the postsynaptic cell. This process allows for intercellular communication, with most synapses occurring between axons and dendrites (but also axon to cell, dendrite to dendrite, and axon to axon).

Both spontaneous (Molliver, Kostovic, & Van der Loos, 1973) and environmentally induced neuronal activity lead to the formation and stabilization of synapses. Early-developing synapses are labile, and most likely, this mechanism is preparing the system for environmental input. Synapses may become stabilized through one of several mechanisms. For example, they may represent coordinated activity at pre- and postsynaptic sites (Schlaggar, Fox, & O'Leary, 1993). Formation of adult patterns of connection involves the elimination of a limited number of immature labile connections, with the elaboration and addition of appropriate connections. Synapses that make functional connections receive a larger amount of coordinated activity and are stabilized, whereas those that do not may be eliminated or reabsorbed (Changeux & Danchin, 1976).

Synapse stabilization may also occur through the local release of various neurotrophic factors (such as NGFs). It has been suggested, for example, that axons whose parent cells have recently been activated are able to respond to neurotrophic factors (e.g., Katz & Shatz, 1996; Thoenen, 1995).) The N-methyl D-aspartate (NMDA) subtype of glutamate receptors may also function in a similar manner by mediating postsynaptic activation of cortical cells (e.g., Schlaggar et al., 1993).

The first synapses may occur as early as the 23rd week of gestation. For example, Molliver and colleagues (1973) identified the first synaptic junctions in the cortical plate at about this age. However, most synapses develop postnatally, particularly during the first year of postnatal life. Although the timing of synaptogenesis is varied, adult values and peak levels of synaptic density in the auditory cortex, visual cortex, and medial frontal gyrus show similar aggregate values, suggesting that peak densities and synaptic elimination occur to a similar degree throughout the cortex (Huttenlocher & Dabholkar, 1997). For example, Huttenlocher and colleagues (Huttenlocher, 1979, 1984;

Huttenlocher & Dabholkar, 1997; Hutten-locher & de Courten, 1987) have carefully documented synaptogenesis in the visual cortex and prefrontal cortex using postmortem tissue. In the visual cortex, for example, the greatest increases in synaptogenesis occur between the 2nd and 8th postnatal months, with the most rapid increases between 2 and 4 months (Huttenlocher & de Courten, 1987), though some synapses can be seen as early as the 28th week of gestation. In contrast, in the frontal cortex, synapse formation begins at 27 weeks gestation and does not reach its maximum density until after 15 postnatal months. In the middle frontal gyrus (MFG), an area believed to be involved in higher forms of cognition, synaptic density reaches its maximum number of synapses at 3.5 years (Huttenlocher & Dabholkar, 1997).

It has been proposed that the initial over-production of synapses in the cortex may be related to the functional property of the immature brain that allows recovery and adaptation after focal injury or malformation (Huttenlocher, 1984) and may represent a critical or vulnerable period. This overproduction may also be the mechanism by which the brain is made ready to receive specific input from the environment. Studies of synaptogenesis demonstrated important developmental increases in the postnatal period, and Goldman-Rakic (1987) proposed that the period of early overgrowth is important for the onset of cognitive function.

Synaptic Pruning

The elimination of synapses may be universal to all neuronal systems, and patterned connections within the brain may be based predominantly on large-scale regressive events (Changeux & Danchin, 1976; Huttenlocher & Dabholkar, 1997; Rakic, Bourgeois, Eckenhoff, Zecevic, & Goldman-Rakic, 1986; but see Purves, 1989). *Pruning,*

or loss of synapses in the absence of cell death, refers to environmentally regulated changes in the density of synapses per unit of dendritic length. Synapse elimination occurs late in childhood and in adolescence (Huttenlocher & Dabholkar, 1997). Although there are topographical differences in the time course of synapse formation and elimination, quantitative measures have found a common pattern: The number of synapses seen at peak during childhood is reduced by approximately 40% to reach the adult value (Huttenlocher, 1979; Huttenlocher & de Courten, 1987).

Presynaptic neurotransmitters play a role in the stabilization of synapses and modulation of cortical neuron activity (Kostovic, 1990). In particular, changes in the distribution of excitatory and inhibitory input may lead to pruning. For example, Diebler and colleagues (Diebler, Farkas-Bargeton, & Wehrle, 1979) propose that the amount of inhibitory neurotransmitter (GABA) at cortical synapses may drive elimination.

Second, pruning is thought to be caused by limited availability of neurotrophic factors derived from the target neuron and by trophic interactions with afferents. This may occur by way of specific neurotransmitters, NGF, NT-3, or BDNF, or thyrotrophin-releasing hormone (Patterson & Nawa, 1993). Thus, only collaterals that are electrically active can respond to synaptogenic factors, and synaptic contacts that are not incorporated into neuronal circuits may be gradually eliminated (Changeux & Danchin, 1976).

Furthermore, it is most likely that only inappropriate synapses and their branches disappear, whereas arborization in appropriate layers may increase in size and complexity.

Summary of Synaptogenesis

Overall, some synapses form as early as 4 months before term, although the majority of synapses are formed later in gestation and carry forward into the postnatal period. Indeed, it is now well documented that the developing brain massively overproduces synapses, which is followed by a reduction to adult numbers. The period of overproduction and pruning varies by area, with synapses reaching adult values in the visual cortex by the 5th to 6th postnatal year, whereas adult number of synapses in the frontal cortex are not obtained until mid- to late adolescence. As will be elaborated in a subsequent section, it is believed that the processes of overproduction and pruning are powerfully influenced by experience.

Myelination

Myelin is a fatty sheath that insulates axons and provides for more rapid impulse conduction. In the peripheral nervous system, myelin is comprised of Schwann cells, whereas in the central nervous system, it is composed of oligodendrocytes.

Myelination is thought to occur in a caudal to rostral direction. Importantly, the areas of the brain to myelinate first are the same that appear to develop function first. For example, Gibson and Brammer (1981) found that primary sensory and motor projection areas of the cortex develop in advance of the association areas; layers subserving communication with the brainstem and spinal cord (Layers 1, 4, 5, and 6) myelinate prior to layers subserving communication with the cortex (Layers 2 and 3).

The neural tracts that control body posture and orientation and the vestibular system are fully myelinated before birth. The major tracts of the visual system (superior colliculus, optic tract, and optic nerve) begin to myelinate prior to birth and are mature by the 9th postnatal month (Brody, Kinney, Kloman, & Gilles, 1987). In the first 2 postnatal years, myelination of the corticospinal tract (motor system) correlates with gains

in neuromuscular functioning (Brody et al., 1987), reaching mature levels in the brain stem by about 1 year and mature levels at the spinal cord by approximately 28 months. In contrast, myelination in frontal association areas are still developing through the adolescent period (e.g., Giedd et al., 1999; Sowell, Thompson, Holmes, Jernigan, & Toga, 1999) and by some estimates, may not reach adult levels until the third to fourth decade of life (Yakovlev & LeCours, 1967).

As is the case with other aspects of brain development, disruptions in myelination are likely to contribute to deviations in normal developmental trajectory. Thus, decreases in myelination can lead to decreased conduction velocity, increased refractory periods after action potential firing, more frequent conduction failures, temporal dispersion of impulses, and increased susceptibility to extraneous influences (Konner, 1991). Possible origins of myelin deficiencies can occur for a variety of reasons, including congenital hypothyroidism, undernutrition, and periventricular leucomalacia (a common affliction of the very premature infant; Volpe, 1995).

CONCLUSIONS

The foundational elements of the developing brain are clearly laid down long before birth. They begin with the formation of the neural tube just a few weeks after conception and conclude by the time cell migration has completed its course by about the 5th prenatal month. At this time, the formation of neural circuits begins with the earliest formation of synapses, followed shortly thereafter by the myelination of axons in various sensory systems. However, the vast majority of synaptogenesis and myelination occurs postnatally (see Figure 2.6 for a schematic overview of these major events). Both of these processes are under a combination of endogenous

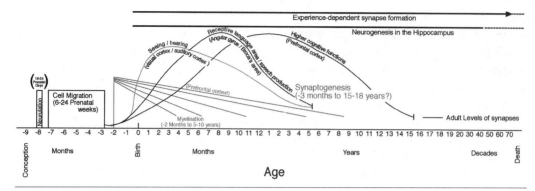

Figure 2.6   General Overview of Brain Development

SOURCE: From "Developmental Science and the Media: Early Brain Development, by R. A. Thompson and C. A. Nelson, 2001, *American Psychologist*, 56(1) pp. 5-15.

(e.g., genetic, humoral) and exogenous (e.g., experience) control. The latter occupies the next and final section of this paper.

THE DEVELOPMENT AND MODIFICATION OF NEURAL CIRCUITS: NEURAL PLASTICITY

In the preceding section, I discussed how the brain is built from conception through the adolescent period. Unfortunately, space limitations prevented me from discussing in detail the molecular mechanisms by which these events transpire. Clearly, some aspects of development are largely or entirely under genetic or humoral control and thus are impervious to exogenous or endogenous experience. Even here, however, "experience" can exert an effect. Witness the case of prenatal exposure to teratogens or nutritional deprivation (see Shonkoff & Phillips, 2000), both of which can affect cellular differentiation (e.g., microcephaly), myelination, and possibly even neurulation (cf. the epidemiological link between folic acid deficiencies and neural tube defects). However, areas in which the effects of experience have the most powerful and compelling influence on brain development pertain to the formation

of synaptic circuits. Here, the evidence is overwhelming that both positive and negative experiences can influence the wiring diagram of the brain. In this context, it is worth noting that Greenough and colleagues (e.g., Black, Jones, Nelson, & Greenough, 1998; Greenough, Black, & Wallace, 1987) have argued that the overproduction and retraction of synapses represent the prototype of a plastic system: specifically, a period of both opportunity and vulnerability. Thus, subject to the experiences the child has, synapses may be beneficially affected (e.g., the pruning of inappropriate synapses or the construction of new, beneficial synapses) or deleteriously affected (e.g., the *failure* to prune inappropriate synapses or the construction of new synapses that negatively affect the organism). In this context, it would be useful to review Greenough's model of plasticity.

Greenough (Greenough et al., 1987) has proposed that experience can exert its effects on neural circuits in one of two ways. In an *experience-expectant* system, development is based on the expectation that appropriate environments (and thus appropriate experiences) will provide the information the brain needs to select the appropriate subset of synaptic connections. Thus, for any given species, assumptions are made about what experiences can and should be reasonably expected by all members of the species. Classic examples may include the development of speech perception or some aspects of visual development (e.g., stereoscopic depth perception); less well-established examples may include the formation of attachment relationships (the assumption here being that the immaturity of our species' young calls for a caregiver). In contrast, in an *experience-dependent* system, development is unique to each person and most likely involves the active formation of new synaptic connections throughout the life span, based on each individual's concourse with the environment. Examples here include learning and memory and in the context of language, the acquisition of a vocabulary.

Inherent in both experience-expectant and experience-dependent models is the notion that "experience cuts both ways." By this, it is meant that the nature of the experience itself—coupled with the maturity of the brain at the time the experience occurs—will determine (or at least influence) whether the resulting neural change is beneficial or deleterious to the organism. In the sections that follow, I provide examples of both good and bad outcomes, as well as examples of plasticity that are restricted to the developing organism and those that are seemingly unconstrained by age. I shall begin, however, by discussing some general principles that account for how the structure of experience is incorporated into the structure of the brain.

NEUROBIOLOGICAL MECHANISMS UNDERLYING NEURAL PLASTICITY

As a rule, there are a number of mechanisms whereby experience induces changes in the brain. An *anatomical* change might reflect the ability of an existing synapse to modify its activity by forming new axons or by expanding the dendritic surface. For example, as we shall see in the section on *learning*

and memory, rearing rats in complex environments can lead to an increase in dendritic spines, which will ultimately lead to the formation of new synapses. A *neurochemical* change might be reflected in the ability of an existing synapse to modify its activity by increasing neurotransmitter synthesis and release. For example, is it now well established that NMDA, an excitotoxic amino acid used to identify a specific subset of glutamate, is known to modify pre- and postsynaptic activity and can trigger the formation of new dendritic spines (for review, see Yuste & Sur, 1999). Third, an example of a *metabolic* change might be the fluctuations in cortical and subcortical metabolic activity (e.g., glucose usage, O_2) in response to experience. Again, as we shall see in the section of *motor plasticity*, rats taught acrobatic feats tend to increase the number of capillaries in the region of the brain involved in motor movements (for review, see Black et al., 1998). Finally, in all cases, it is assumed that changes in gene expression occur with experience; for example, Rampon et al. (2000) have recently shown that adult mice that received a period of environmental enrichment (for as little as 3 hours and as much as 14 days) showed changes in a variety of genes associated with DNA/RNA synthesis, neuronal signaling, neuronal growth and structure, and apoptosis. Collectively, experience works its way into the brain through a number of molecular mechanisms.

Having established the mechanisms whereby experience exerts its effects on brain structure and function, I shall now turn to a discussion of specific behaviors and abilities and their neural correlates that are affected by experience.

Visual Development

Stereoscopic depth perception refers to the ability to discern depth cues on the basis of the different visual perspectives each eye receives. The development of this ability is made possible by the development of ocular dominance columns, which represent the connections between each eye and Layer 4 of the visual cortex. If for some reason, the two eyes are not properly aligned, thereby preventing them from converging effectively on a distant target (as would occur with strabismus), then the ocular dominance columns that support normal stereoscopic depth perception will fail to develop normally. If this condition is not corrected by the time the number of synapses begins to reach adult values (generally by the end of the preschool or early elementary school period; see Figure 2.6), the child will not develop normal stereoscopic vision. The result is not only poor stereoscopic vision but also the possibility of poor vision in general in one eye.

Until very recently, it had been thought that the development of ocular dominance columns was largely driven by postnatal visual experience. For example, David Hubel and Torsten Wiesel reported in the 1960s that in monkeys and cats, seeing out of both eyes was essential to the development of ocular dominance columns; thus, it was believed that such columns develop out of visual activity. Recently, however, there are reports that the initial development of such columns is not, in fact, activity-dependent at all (Crowley & Katz, 1999); moreover, Crowley and Katz (2000) have suggested that the formation of these columns may depend most on innate molecules that guide growing axons to their target destinations, not on visual experience per se. Although not accepted by all, these findings do raise intriguing questions about the role of experience in the development of ocular dominance columns. At the very least, they suggest that such columns develop before visual experience can exert its effect (i.e., before birth), a finding consistent with an observation by Bourgeois and colleagues that being born

prematurely or even removing the eyes of monkeys prior to birth has little effect on the overproduction of synapses in the visual cortex (Bourgeois, Reboff, & Rakic, 1989); less is known about the retraction of such synapses, however.

Turning this issue on its head, Maurer and colleagues (Maurer, Lewis, Brent, & Levin, 1999) have reported on a longitudinal study of infants born with cataracts. An elegant aspect of this work was that the investigators were able to study infants who had the cataracts removed at different ages. The basic finding was the powerful role of experience in facilitating vision, post–cataract removal; thus, for example, in infants operated on within months of birth, even just a few *minutes* of visual experience led to a rapid change in visual acuity. And as expected, the longer the infant lived with cataracts, the less experience led to favorable changes in vision. This process resembles the experience-expectant model of plasticity discussed earlier: Specifically, our species has evolved to expect certain visual experiences to occur within a certain period of time, and if the organism is deprived of such experience beyond this sensitive period, development is deleteriously affected.

Linguistic Development

A number of elements of language development are germane to our discussion of the role of experience. These include the development of speech perception, the acquisition of a second language, and the effects of congenital deafness on visual function.

Speech Perception

Let us begin with an example from the speech-perception literature to demonstrate the role of experience on brain and behavioral development. It has been known for some time that English-speaking adults who have not been exposed to languages such as Swedish, Thai, or Japanese are unable to discriminate speech contrasts from these languages. This stands in marked contrast to the ceiling level ability to discriminate speech contrasts from their own (English) language (e.g., "ba" vs. "ga"). Among others, Kuhl (e.g., Kuhl, Williams, Lacerda, Stevens, & Lindblom, 1992) has demonstrated that between 6 and 12 months of life, the infant's ability to discriminate phonemes from languages to which they are not exposed diminishes greatly (for review, see Werker & Vouloumanos, 2001). Thus, although a 6-month-old infant raised in an English-speaking home may be able to discriminate contrasts from English as well as those from Swedish or Thai, by 12 months of age, such infants become more like English-speaking adults. In other words, infants lose the ability to discriminate contrasts from nonnative languages. These data have been interpreted to suggest that the speech system remains open to experience for a certain period of time, but if experience in a particular domain (such as hearing speech contrasts in different languages) is not forthcoming, the window begins to close early in life. Again, this represents an example of an experience-expectant model.

These findings should not be construed to suggest that *all* aspects of speech perception are tied to a sensitive or critical period. For example, there is evidence that some aspects of speech perception can be altered by experience fairly late in childhood. Tallal and colleagues (e.g., Tallal et al., 1996) have speculated that some children with language problems (language-learning impairments) have difficulty in distinguishing the phonemes embedded in ongoing speech. The basis for this disability is presumably the inability of the auditory system to keep up with the speed at which these phonemes are presented, leading to difficulty in discriminating speech sounds. Tallal had previously reported that performance could be improved if the rate of change of the phonetic transitions were slowed down (e.g., Tallal & Piercy, 1973). More recently, Tallal and Merzenich (e.g., Merzenich et al., 1996; Tallal et al., 1996) reported that when children with language-learning impairments were given 4 weeks of intensive training in the temporal processing of speech, approximately 2 years in both speech discrimination and language comprehension were gained.

Collectively, although the initial acquisition of the ability to recognize speech appears in the first months of life, with a narrowing of this ability after 12 months, there is evidence that training in speech discrimination can be accomplished well beyond the infancy period.

Second-Language Acquisition/ Neural Representation of Language

What about the neural representation of language? Dehaene and colleagues (Dehaene et al., 1997) reported a number of years ago that the neural representation of a second language was identical to that of a first language *if* the individual was truly bilingual; if, however, the mastery of the second language was not as strong as the first, then the functional neuroanatomy, based on positron emission tomography imaging (PET), was different. Because nearly all the bilinguals studied in this work had acquired their second languages at an early age, the initial conclusion drawn was that a second language needed to be learned early in life to share the same neural representation as the first language. This conclusion has recently been questioned, however. These same authors (see Perani et al., 1998) wondered whether it was the *age* at which the second language was acquired that was the critical variable or, rather, the subject's *proficiency* in speaking this language. In a follow-up study, the age at which the second language had been mastered was crossed with the proficiency of speaking this language. The authors observed that it was the latter dimension that proved critical. Thus, regardless of when the second language was acquired, speaking this language with equal proficiency as the first language led to shared neural representation for both languages. Similar findings have recently been obtained with congenitally deaf individuals with mastery in sign language: The areas of the brain involved in "speaking" in sign are the same as those of hearing speakers using spoken language (see Petitto et al., 2000). Collectively, these findings call into question the critical-period hypothesis for acquiring a second language.

Note, however, that the issue of shared neural representation for multiple languages should not be confused with the issue of speaking a second language without an accent. Thus, Newport (e.g., Johnson & Newport, 1989) demonstrated that individuals who acquire a second language before the age of 10 years are far more likely to speak that language without an accent than those who acquire that language after the age of 10.

The Effects of Deafness on Visual Function

Popular lore has it that individuals who are born deaf have superior visual function relative to hearing people. Although this is largely apocryphal, it is the case that *some* visual functions differ in deaf versus hearing individuals. Thus, for example, Neville (e.g., Neville et al., 1998) has shown that attending to visual targets in the periphery is superior in congenitally deaf individuals compared with hearing individuals. Neville has interpreted these findings to suggest that the lateral geniculate nucleus (a major way station in the visual system) has been reorganized due to the lack of input to the superior geniculate nucleus (a major way station in the auditory system).

Collectively, the work on several aspects of language clearly shows the effects of experience on brain function. However, it should also be clear that there is not a critical qua critical period for doing so; rather, the extent to which experience exerts its effects varies by the particular domain being studied. This is a theme to which I shall return several times.

Learning and Memory

In the context of the effects of experience on brain and behavior, no area has received more attention than that of learning and memory. For example, it has been known for more than 20 years that rats raised in complex laboratory environments (i.e., those containing lots of toys and social contacts) outperform rats reared in isolation on certain cognitive tasks (e.g., the former make fewer errors on tasks of spatial cognition; Greenough, Madden, & Fleischmann, 1972). At the cellular level, some of the changes observed among rats raised in such environments include the following: (a) Several regions of the dorsal neocortex (e.g., visual areas) are heavier and thicker and have more synapses per neuron; (b) dendritic spines and branching patterns increase in number and length; and (c) there is increased capillary branching, thereby increasing blood and oxygen volume (for examples, see Black et al., 1998; Greenough & Black, 1992; Greenough, Juraska, & Volkmar, 1979; Greenough et al., 1972; see also Nelson, 2000). Importantly, these effects are not simply due to increased motor activity; for example, Black and colleagues have demonstrated that rats engaged in repetitive motor acts that require no learning (e.g., simply running on a treadmill) show only a subset of the changes comparable to those in rats that were engaged in learning tasks (for review, see Black et al., 1998).

The neural basis for long-term changes in the brain responsible for learning and memory has been extensively studied for many years. Hebb's postulate that strengthening of synaptic circuits occurs through repeated use of that circuit (Hebb, 1949) eventually led to the discovery of long-term potentiation (LTP) (Bliss & Lømo, 1973). LTP is the process whereby the nearly simultaneous occurrence of presynaptic activity and postsynaptic depolarization facilitates glutamate to bind to postsynaptic NMDA receptors and to expel the magnesium (Mg^{2+}), which normally block the NMDA receptor-gated ion channel. This in turn leads to a substantial influx of calcium (Ca^{2+}) ions. LTP produces changes in synaptic strength and importantly, promotes the development of new dendritic spines. Whether LTP is the mechanism responsible for *all* forms of learning and memory is unlikely, but at present, it does provide one such mechanism (or at least one model).

Unfortunately, LTP is typically studied in cell culture. What about more functional changes at the system level that are correlated with learning and memory? Erickson, Jagadeesh, and Desimone (2000) recently reported a study in which monkeys were presented with multicolored complex stimuli (some objects, some abstract designs). Some of the stimuli were novel (never seen before), and others were familiar. Single neurons were recorded from the perirhinal cortex, an area of the temporal lobe known to be strongly involved in episodic memory. The authors reported that after only 1 day of experience viewing the familiar stimuli, performance of neighboring neurons became highly correlated, whereas viewing novel stimuli revealed little correlated neuronal activity. The implication of these findings is that visual experience leads to functional changes in an area of the brain known to be involved in memory. Although this finding may on the surface not be surprising, it is among the first to provide concrete evidence of how experience influences brain function.

Collectively, it is now well established that learning and memory are correlated with changes in the brain at multiple levels, from the molecular (e.g., changes in pre- and post-synaptic functioning mediated by glutamate receptors) to the molar (e.g., changes in neuronal firing). There is no sense that there is a sensitive period for learning and memory to occur (for a tutorial on the *development* of learning and memory, see Nelson, 1995, 2000). Indeed, there is some sense that activities that engage the learning and memory system may confer some protection on lifelong learning and memory function (for discussion, see Nelson, 2000).

Motor and Somatosensory Systems

There is now extensive work to suggest that the motor and somatosensory systems are modified by experience, regardless of the age of the organism. In the 1970s, Edward Taub was an investigator at the National Institutes of Health, studying the effects of deaffrentation on monkey somatosensory cortex. Covert filming of the lab conditions by an animal rights activist posing as a lab member led to the closing down of the lab. A court battle ensued, with one side proposing the animals be euthanized, and the other suggesting they be released to a preserve in Florida. As these things go in the United States, the litigation dragged on for many years. Immediately prior to the animals being euthanized, however, Timothy Pons and Edward Taub and their colleagues studied the brains of these animals. Specifically, Pons et al. (1991) recorded neuronal responses from a region of somatosensory cortex that would normally correspond to the deafferented portion of the limb, including the fingers, palm, and adjacent areas (Area S1).

Because the limb had been deafferented 12 years earlier, the investigators were not expecting much in the way of cortical reorganization. Much to their surprise, however, it was revealed that this region of the brain now responded to stimulation in an area of the face (this region would normally border the cortical region innervated by the deafferented limb), pointing to a reorganization of somatosensory cortex of rather massive proportions (i.e., 10-14 mm).

This report was followed by others (for discussion, see Pons, 1995) and collectively demonstrated that large-scale cortical reorganization can occur following injury even in the mature primate. Reports of the adult human followed. For example, Ramachandran, Rogers-Ramachandran, and Stewart (1992) speculated that an individual who had experienced the amputation of a limb (such as the forearm) should show sensitivity on the area of the body represented by the area of the brain adjacent to the amputated limb. Adults who had experienced various forms of amputation were examined and were found to experience sensation in the limb that had in fact been amputated. Ramachandran examined one patient's sensitivity to tactile stimulation along the region of the face known to innervate the somatosensory cortex adjacent to the area previously innervated by the missing limb; the patient reported sensation in both the face and the missing limb. Using magnetoencephalography (MEG), Ramachandran was able to determine the degree to which the cortical surface had been reorganized to take over responsibility for the area previously occupied by the missing limb.

In both the monkey and human work, cortical reorganization was thought to be facilitated by stimulation of parts of the body that were adjacent to the deafferentated/ amputated limb, suggesting a form of "natural" intervention. To more directly evaluate whether the motor and/or somatosensory cortex can be reorganized on the basis of experience, Nudo, Wise, SiFuentes, and Milliken (1996) mapped the motor cortex of monkeys before and after an ischemic lesion was made. As would be expected to occur in the human suffering a stroke in the same region of the brain, the infarct led to a deficit in use of that limb—in this case, the animal's inability to retrieve food pellets. The animals then received intensive training in hand use, which resulted in a return to performance comparable to preinjury levels. Cortical mapping revealed substantial rearrangement of the area of the brain that represented the hand surrounding the lesion site.

These findings on monkeys and humans suggest that the representation of the limbs in the adult primate can be altered as a function of experience. Building on this model, Taub (2000) has recently developed a form of rehabilitation that involves restraining the patient from using the unaffected limb in order to "teach" the affected (by stroke) limb to work. Relatively brief periods of restraint (on the order of weeks) coupled with massed activity of the affected limb appear to show very beneficial effects; that is, such patients gain dramatic use of the affected limb.

In summary, there is now evidence to support the thesis that cortical reorganization is possible following injury to the peripheral nervous system in the adult human and nonhuman primate. Might similar reorganization occur in the noninjured, "healthy" individual? Also using MEG, Elbert, Pantev, Wienbruch, Rockstroh, and Taub (1995) mapped the somatosensory cortex of adults with and without experience in playing a stringed instrument (e.g., guitar, violin). The investigators reported that in the musicians, the area of the somatosensory cortex that represented the fingers of the left hand (used on the fingerboard) was larger than the area represented by the right hand (which was used to bow), and larger than the left hand area in the nonmusicians. Moreover, there was a tendency toward greater cortical representation in individuals who had begun their musical training before the age of 10 years. Collectively, this work suggests that the brain of the adult human can reorganize not just on the basis of negative experience (e.g., injury), but on positive experiences (e.g., musical training) as well.

Brain Injury

The final topic I would like to discuss concerns the effects of brain injury on brain and behavioral development.

Early in the 20th century, Kennard induced unilateral lesions in the precentral (motor) cortex of newborn monkeys (e.g., Kennard, 1942). Somewhat surprisingly, these lesions appeared to have minimal effects compared with the same lesions in adults—that is, the animals seemed to be spared from significant motor deficits on the side contralateral to the injury (i.e., hemiparesis would have been expected). This observation led to the principle that early brain damage "spares" the organism from significant behavioral sequelae, at least relative to when such damage is done later in life. However, Kennard followed up her monkeys, and it was revealed that these same early-lesioned animals tested in adulthood had learning deficits, thus refuting the concept of full neural plasticity in infants.

Countless studies with animals and humans have been conducted over the last 75 years, and the consensus is that the extent to which either recovery of function or sparing (no functions were affected to begin with) occurs depends to a great degree on (a) what specific area was damaged, (b) the age at which this damage occurred (and thus, the maturity of the structure at the time of the damage), and (c) individual differences.

Because the last of these is the least understood (although admittedly, it is also the most interesting), I will focus my comments on the first two. I will do so by drawing on three bodies of literature: work on the development of spatial cognition and language in humans who have suffered focal brain injuries, and work with rats in situations where such injury was induced at different developmental points.

Recovery From Early
Brain Injury in Humans:
The Development of Spatial Cognition

Stiles and colleagues (for review, see Stiles, 2001) have been studying the development of spatial cognition in a cohort of children who had suffered a focal lesion—that is, a lesion confined to one region of the brain. Two primary questions are being addressed in this work. First, what is the typical developmental trajectory of the ability to recognize objects on the basis of parts versus wholes; for example, when asked to draw a picture of a house, when do children attend to both the holistic features of the house (e.g., general shape and outline) as well as the individual features of the house (e.g., windows and doors)? It is well-known that the right hemisphere tends to mediate the perception of holistic information, whereas the left mediates the perception of more piecemeal, featural information. This leads to the second question: whether children who have suffered discrete brain damage to the right or left hemisphere show normal or atypical developmental trajectories of spatial cognitive ability and if *abnormal*, whether they evince more or less sparing and/or recovery of function. It is well-known that adults who suffer damage to the posterior right hemisphere show persistent problems in responding to holistic information and conversely, those suffering damage to the left hemisphere show persistent problems in responding to piecemeal information. An early hypothesis in this work was that the earlier in life such damage was incurred, the greater the recovery of function or the greater the sparing. However, contrary to expectations, it now appears that although such children do, in fact, show some recovery of function, they never recover fully; that is, even years after the injury (which typically occurs during the perinatal period), such children continue to show residual deficits.

Recovery From Early Brain Injury in Humans: Language Development

Bates and colleagues (for review, see Bates & Roe, 2001) have been studying the same population of children as has Stiles, except that they have been interested in the extent to which children with early focal lesions (a) develop normal language or (b) show early deficits followed by recovery of function. Two hypotheses might be put forth here. First, if one adopts a very nativist view of language development, then one would predict that early damage to the areas of the brain involved in language would lead to lifelong impairments in language, given that the dedicated neural hardware was corrupted. Conversely, from a more neuropsychological perspective, one might argue that children would show greater recovery of function from early insult than would adults (such as those who suffered a stroke to Broca's or Wernicke's area).

From this prospective work, Bates (Bates & Roe, 2001) has demonstrated specific correlations between lesion sites and profiles of language delay. However, these correlations look very different from lesion-symptom correlations in adults; most important, these correlations gradually disappear across the course of language development. To quote Bates and Roe (2001),

The classic pattern of brain organization for language observed in normal adults may be

the product rather than the cause of language learning, emerging out of regional biases in information processing that are relevant for language, but only indirectly related to language itself. If those regions are damaged early in life, other parts of the brain can emerge to solve the language-learning problem. (p. 281)

Collectively, the work on recovery from early neural injury in the domains of spatial cognition and language yields very different patterns, with less sparing and less recovery of function in the former and far greater in the latter. Still, in both cases, children with these injuries are less affected than adults with the same injuries. This reinforces the point made at the outset, which is that the degree to which behavior is affected by neural trauma varies as a function of the age at which the trauma occurred as well as the particular behavioral function targeted for study.

Recovery From Early Versus Late Brain Injury: Work With Rats

Although the work reviewed above provides compelling information about the remarkable plasticity of the developing human brain, such work suffers from the shortcoming that one has little control over the precise regions of the brain affected and when they are affected (e.g., in the work by Stiles and Bates, such children often suffered damage to two or more lobes of the brain, and the timing of when the damage occurred was frequently unknown). It is here, of course, that animal models are so important, because far greater control can be exerted over exactly what areas are damaged and when. Work by Kolb and colleagues (for review, see Kolb & Gibb, 2001) most elegantly exemplifies this approach.

For more than two decades, Kolb has been engaged in a systematic effort to examine not only the effects of neural damage on behavioral function but also, importantly, to elucidate the mechanisms responsible for sparing and/or recovery of function. He has reported, for example, that damaging the brain during the period of neurogenesis (embryonic days 12-20) typically leads to good functional outcome, whereas damaging the brain during the period of cell migration (the 1st postnatal week of life) is associated with very poor outcome. Damaging the brain during the period of maximum astrocyte development and synaptogenesis (the 2nd postnatal week of life) results in good functional outcome. Finally, damaging the brain after the 2nd week of life, when synaptic pruning is occurring, leads to progressively poorer outcome. Kolb and Gibb (2001) underscore the point that it is the developmental status of the brain at the time of injury that determines the outcome, not the chronological age of the subject. This is graphically illustrated in Figure 2.7.

Overall, this brief discussion of the animal literature on plasticity reinforces the need for us to carefully consider the issue of timing when considering the degree of plasticity in the adult or developing brain.

IS THERE A DIFFERENCE BETWEEN DEVELOPMENTAL AND ADULT PLASTICITY?

In the first part of this chapter, I offered a generic description of brain development, whereas in the second part, I talked about how the structure and function of the brain are powerfully influenced by experience. In the third part of the chapter, I turned my attention to the plasticity of the brain in the face of neural injury. Here, the focus was on the extent to which the timing and site of the injury relates to outcome.

Implicit through this discussion was the assumption that plasticity may differ in the juvenile versus the mature organism. For example, early damage to language centers leads

to relatively little in the way of significant, long-term impairment, whereas comparable damage later in life can lead to more severe and often sustained damage. This leads us to ask whether the mechanisms that underlie developmental plasticity truly differ from those that underlie adult plasticity. A definitive answer to this question is currently unknown, although there are some tempting cues that may point us in the right direction.

The primary question we need to ask is whether the mechanisms that lead to the initial appearance of a given behavior—for example, the ability to acquire language—are the same as those involved in acquiring a new behavior as an adult—for example, the ability to acquire a second language. Most likely, the answer is "no." Given the lack of neuroscientific evidence for innate hardware modules (which, if they existed, would lead to a lack of plasticity in the brain, which we know is not the case), the bulk of the evidence suggests that experience powerfully influences the developing brain. In the case of face recognition, for example, I have suggested that the infant is born with the neurobiological substrate that has the *potential* to become specialized for face recognition. However, it is exposure to faces that drives subsequent development and that leads to the commitment of the face areas of the brain (e.g., fusiform gyrus, superior temporal sulcus) to become specialized for face recognition (Nelson, 2001; also see Pascalis, de Haan, & Nelson, 2002). The goal of infancy, then, is to develop these neural circuits in the service of some behavior (presumably the same thing happens for other behaviors, such as language). However, in the adult, these systems are already in place and must simply be reconfigured for a different, albeit related, purpose for example, acquiring a second or third language.

Another very fundamental difference between the developing versus the developed

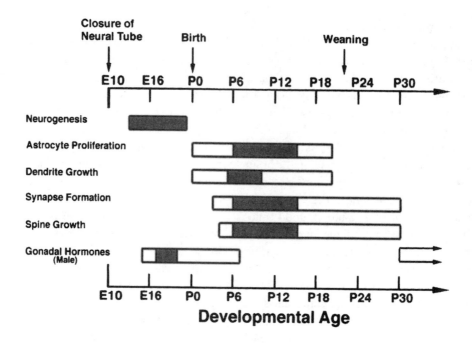

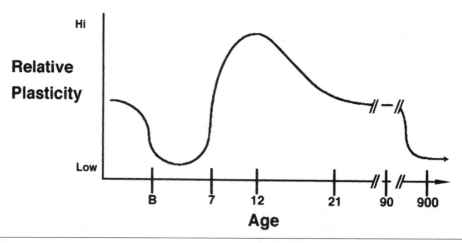

Figure 2.7   Relation Between the Timing of Neural Injury and Degree of Plasticity in the Rat Brain

SOURCE: From "Early Brain Injury, Plasticity, and Behavior," by B. Kolb and R. Gibb, 2001, in C. A. Nelson and M. Luciana (Eds.), *Handbook of Developmental Cognitive Neuroscience* (p. 180, Fig. 13.4), Cambridge: MIT Press. Reproduced with permission.

(if such a thing can ever be said) brain is that the former is still making new cells, killing others (apoptosis), myelinating axons, overproducing synapses, and so on. In the latter, of course, many of these events are now static, and experience must make due with the existing biological substrate—it cannot, for example, move cells from Layer 4 to Layer 2.

Overall, then, my main thesis is that although experience exerts a powerful effect on many aspects of brain function through much of the life span, it does so through different mechanisms at different points in time. Once we have a better understanding of the precise mechanisms whereby the brain is influenced by experience and how these mechanisms differ by (a) the age of the organism and (b) the circuits involved, we will be in a better position to explain the mechanisms that underlie not only behavioral development but behavioral modification as well. Once we have identified the key to unlocking this mystery, we will be in a far better position to understand how to intervene in the lives of children *and* adults in a meaningful way; this in turn will lead to better options for treating both psychopathological as well as neuropathological diseases and disorders. At least one can hope that this is the case.

REFERENCES

Bates, E., & Roe, K. (2001). Language development in children with unilateral brain injury. In C. A. Nelson & M. Luciana (Eds.), *Handbook of developmental cognitive neuroscience* (pp. 281-307). Cambridge: MIT Press.

Black, J. E., Jones, T. A., Nelson, C. A., & Greenough, W. T. (1998). Neuronal plasticity and the developing brain. In N. E. Alessi, J. T. Coyle, S. I. Harrison, & S. Eth. (Eds.), *Handbook of child and adolescent psychiatry: Vol 6. Basic psychiatric science and treatment* (pp. 31-53). New York: John Wiley.

Bliss, T. V. P., & Lømo, T. (1973). Long-lasting potentiation of synaptic transmission in the dentate area of the anaesthetized rabbit following stimulation of the perforant path. *Journal of Physiology, 232,* 331-356.

Brody, B. A., Kinney, H. C., Kloman, A. S., & Gilles, F. H. (1987). Sequence of central nervous system myelination in human infancy: Part I. An autopsy study of myelination. *Journal of Neuropathology & Experimental Neurology, 46(3),* 283-301.

Bourgeois, J. P., Reboff, P. J., & Rakic, P. (1989). Synaptogenesis in visual cortex of normal and preterm monkeys: Evidence from intrinsic regulation of synaptic overproduction. *Proceedings of the National Academy of Sciences, 86,* 4297-4301.

Busciglio, J., & Yankner, B. A. (1995). Apoptosis and increased generation of reactive oxygen species in Down's syndrome neurons *in vitro. Nature, 378,* 776-779.

Changeux, J. P., & Danchin, A. (1976). Selective stabilisation of developing synapses as a mechanism for the specification of neuronal networks. *Nature* 64(5588), 705-712.

Chenn, A., Braisted, J. E., McConnell, S. K., & O'Leary, D. D. M. (1997). Development of the cerebral cortex: Mechanisms controlling cell fate, laminar and areal paterning, and axonal connectivity. In W. M. Cowan, T. M. Jessell, & S. L. Zipursky (Eds.), *Molecular and cellular approaches to neural development.* New York: Oxford University Press.

Chenn, A., & McConnell, S. K. (1995). Cleavage orientation and the asymmetric inheritance of Notch1 immunoreactivity in mammalian neurogenesis. *Cell, 82,* 631-641.

Chong, B. W., Babcook, C. J., Salamat, M. S., Nemzek, W., Kroeker, D., & Ellis, W. G. (1996). A magnetic resonance template for normal neuronal migration in the fetus. *Neurosurgery, 39,* 110-116.

Crowley, J. C., & Katz, L. C. (1999). Development of ocular dominance columns in the absence of retinal input. *Nature Neuroscience, 2,* 1125-1130.

Crowley, J. C., & Katz, L. C. (2000). Early development of ocular dominance columns. *Science, 290,* 1321-1324.

Dehaene, S., Dupoux, E., Mehler, J., Cohen, L., Paulesu, E., Perani, D., van de Moortele, P. F., Lehericy, S., & Le Bihan, D. (1997). Anatomical variability in the cortical representation of first and second language. *Neuroreport, 8,* 3809-3815.

Diebler M. F., Farkas-Bargeton E., & Wehrle, R. (1979). Developmental changes of enzymes associated with energy metabolism and the synthesis of some neurotransmitters in discrete areas of human neocortex. *Journal of Neurochemistry, 32*(2), 429-435.

Elbert, T., Pantev, C., Wienbruch, C., Rockstroh, B., & Taub, E. (1995). Increased cortical representation of the fingers of the left hand in string players. *Science, 270*(5234), 305-307.

Elvevåg, B., & Weinberger, D. R. (2001). The neuropsychology of schizophrenia and its relationship to the neurodevelopmental model. In C. A. Nelson & M. Luciana (Eds.), *Handbook of developmental cognitive neuroscience* (pp. 577-595). Cambridge: MIT Press.

Erickson, C. A., Jagadeesh, B., & Desimone, R. (2000). Clustering of perirhinal neurons with similar properties following visual experience in adult monkeys. *Nature Neuroscience, 3,* 1143-1148.

Gibson, A., & Brammer, M. J. (1981). The influence of divalent cations and substrate concentration on the incorporation of myo-inositol into phospholipids of isolated bovine oligodendrocytes. *Journal of Neurochemistry, 36*(3), 868-874.

Giedd, J. N., Blumenthal, J., Jeffries, N. O., Castellanos, F. X., Liu, H., Zijdenbos, A., Paus, T., Evans, A. C., & Rapoport, J. L. (1999). Brain development during childhood and adolescence: A longitudinal MRI study. *Nature Neuroscience, 2*(10), 861-863.

Goldman-Rakic, P. S. (1987). Development of cortical circuitry and cognitive function. *Child Development, 58*(3), 601-622.

Greenough, W. T., & Black, J. E. (1992). Induction of brain structure by experience: Substrates for cognitive development. In M. R. Gunnar & C. A. Nelson (Eds.), *Developmental Behavioral Neuroscience* (Vol. 24, pp. 155-200). Hillsdale, NJ: Lawrence Erlbaum.

Greenough, W. T., Black, J. E., & Wallace, C. S. (1987). Experience and brain development. *Child Development, 58*(3), 539-559.

Greenough, W. T., Juraska, J. M., Volkmar, F. R. (1979). Maze training effects on dendritic branching in occipital cortex of adult rats. *Behavioral & Neural Biology, 26*(3), 287-297.

Greenough, W. T., Madden, T. C., & Fleischmann, T. B. (1972). Effects of isolation, dailing handling, and enriched rearing on maze learning. *Psychonomic Science, 27,* 279-280.

Hatten, M. E. (1999). Central nervous system neuronal migration. *Annual Review of Neuroscience, 22,* 511-539.

Hebb, D. O. (1949). *The organization of behavior.* New York: Wiley.

Hemmati-Brivanlou, A., Kelly, O. G., & Melton, D. A. (1994). Follistatin, an antagonist of activin, is expressed in the Spemann organizer and displays direct neuralizing activity. *Cell, 77,* 283-295.

Henderson, C. E. (1996). Role of neurotrophic factors in neuronal development. *Current Opinion in Neurobiology, 6,* 64-70.

Huttenlocher, P. R. (1975). Synaptic and dendritic development and mental defect. *UCLA Forum in Medical Sciences, 18,* 123-140.

Huttenlocher, P. R. (1979). Synaptic density in human frontal cortex: Developmental changes and effects of aging. *Brain Research, 163*(2), 195-205.

Huttenlocher, P. R. (1984). Synapse elimination and plasticity in developing human cerebral cortex. *American Journal of Mental Deficiency, 88*(5), 488-496.

Huttenlocher, P. R., & Dabholkar, A. S. (1997). Regional differences in synaptogenesis in human cerebral cortex. *Journal of Comparative Neurology, 387*(2), 167-178.

Huttenlocher P. R., & de Courten, C. (1987). The development of synapses in striate cortex of man. *Human Neurobiology, 6*(1), 1-9.

Jacobson, M. D., Weil, M., & Raff, M. C. (1997). Programmed cell death in animal development. *Cell, 88,* 347-354.

Jessell, T. M., & Sanes, J. R. (2000). The induction and patterning of the nervous system. In E. R. Kandel, J. H. Schwartz, & T. M. Jessell (Eds.), *Principles of neural science* (4th ed.). New York: McGraw-Hill.

Johnson, J. S., & Newport, E. L. (1989). Critical period effects in second language learning on the production of English consonants. *Cognitive Psychology, 21,* 60-99.

Katz, L. C., & Shatz, C. J. (1996). Synaptic activity and the construction of cortical circuits. *Science, 274,* 1133-1138.

Kennard, M. (1942). Cortical reorganization of motor function. *Archives of Neurology, 48,* 227-240.

Kerr, J. F. R., Wyllie, A. H., & Currie, A. R. (1972). Apoptosis: A basic biological phenomenon with wide-ranging implications in tissue kinetics. *British Journal of Cancer, 26,* 239-257.

Kolb, B., & Gibb, R. (2001). Early brain injury, plasticity, and behavior. In C. A. Nelson & M. Luciana (Eds.), *Handbook of developmental cognitive neuroscience* (pp. 175-190). Cambridge: MIT Press.

Konner, M. (1991). Universals of behavioral development in relation to brain myelination: In K. Gibson & A. Peterson (Eds.), *Brain maturation and cognitive development: Comparative and cross cultural perspectives* (pp. 181-223). New York: Aldine.

Kostovic, I., & Rakic, P. (1990). Developmental history of the transient subplate zone in the visual and somatosensory cortex of the macaque monkey and human brain. *The Journal of Comparative Neurology, 297,* 441-470.

Kuhl, P. K., Williams, K. A., Lacerda, F., Stevens K. N., & Lindblom, B. (1992). Linguistic experience alters phonetic perception in infants by 6 months of age. *Science, 255,* 606-608.

LaMantia, A. S., & Rakic, P. (1990). Axon overproduction and elimination in the corpus callosum of the developing rhesus monkey. *Journal of Neuroscience, 10*(7), 2156-2175.

Martin, J. H., & Jessell, T. M. (1991). Development as a guide to the regional anatomy of the brain. In E. R. Kandel, J. H. Schwartz, & T. M. Jessell (Eds.), *Principles of neural science* (3rd ed.). Norwalk, CT: Appleton & Lange.

Maurer, D., Lewis, T. L., Brent, H. P., & Levin, A. V. (1999). Rapid improvement in the acuity of infants after visual input. *Science, 286,* 108-110.

McBride, M. C., & Kemper, T. L. (1982). Pathogenesis of four-layered microgyric cortex in man. *Acta Neuropathologica, 57,* 93-98.

Merzenich, M., Wright, B., Jenkins, W., Xerri, C., Byl, N., Miller, S., & Tallal, P. (1996). Cortical plasticity underlying perceptual, motor, and cognitive skill development: Implications for neurorehabilitation. *Cold Spring Harbor Symposia on Quantitative Biology, 61,* 1-8.

Michel, A. E., & Garey, L. J. (1984). The development of dendritic spines in the human visual cortex. *Human Neurobiology, 3*(4), 223-227.

Molliver, M. E., Kostovic, I., & Van der Loos, H. (1973). The development of synapses in cerebral cortex of the human fetus. *Brain Research, 50*(2), 403-407.

Nelson, C. A. (1995). The ontogeny of human memory: A cognitive neuroscience perspective. *Developmental Psychology, 31,* 723-738.

Nelson, C. A. (2000). Neural plasticity and human development: The role of early experience in sculpting memory systems. *Developmental Science, 3,* 115-130.

Nelson, C. A. (2001). The development and neural bases of face recognition. *Infant and Child Development, 10,* 3-18.

Neville, H. J., Balvelier, D., Corina, D., Rauschecker, J., Karni A., Lalwani, A., Braun A., Clark, V., Jezzard, P., & Turner, R. (1998). Cerebral organization for language in deaf and hearing subjects: Biological constraints and effects of experience. *Proceedings of the National Academy of Sciences, 95,* 922-929.

Norman, M. G. (1980). Bilateral encephaloclastic lesions in a 26-week gestation fetus: Effect on neuroblast migration. *Canadian Journal of Neurological Sciences, 7,* 191-194.

Nudo, R. J., Wise, B. M., SiFuentes, F., & Milliken, G. W. (1996). Neural substrates for the effects of rehabilitative training on motor recovery after ischemic infarct. *Science, 272*(5269), 1791-1794.

O'Leary, D. D., Schlaggar, B. L., & Tuttle, R. (1994). Specification of neocortical areas and thalamocortical connections. *Annual Review of Neuroscience, 17,* 419-439.

O'Rahilly, R., & Gardner, E. (1979). The initial development of the human brain. *Acta Anatomica, 104,* 123-133.

O'Rahilly, R., & Müller, F. (1994). *The embryonic human brain: An atlas of developmental stages.* New York: Wiley-Liss.

O'Rourke, N. A., Chenn, A., & McConnell, S. K. (1997). Postmitotic neurons migrate tangentially in the cortical ventricular zone. *Development, 124,* 997-1005.

Pascalis, O., de Haan, M., & Nelson, C. A. (2002). Is face processing species specific during the first year of life? *Science, 296,* 1321–1323.

Patterson P. H., & Nawa, H.(1993). Neuronal differentiation factors/cytokines and synaptic plasticity. *Cell, 72*(Suppl.), 123-137.

Perani, D., Paulesu, E, Galles, N. S., Dupoux, E., Dehaene, S., Bettinardi, V., Cappa, S. F., Fazio, F., & Mehler, J. (1998). The bilingual brain. Proficiency and age of acquisition of the second language. *Brain, 121,* 1841-1852.

Petitto, L. A., Zatorre, R. J., Gauna, K., Nikeiski, E. J., Dostie, D., & Evans, A. C. (2000). Speech-like cerebral activity in profoundly deaf people processing signed languages: Implications for the neural basis of human language. *Proceedings of the National Academy of Sciences of the United States of America. 97*(25), 13961-13966.

Pons, T. (1995). Abstract: Lesion-induced cortical plasticity. In B. Julesz & I. Kovacs (Eds.), *Maturational windows and adult cortical plasticity* (pp. 175-178). Reading, MA: Addison-Wesley.

Pons, T. P., Garraghty, P. E., Ommaya, A. K., Kaas, J. H., Taub, E., & Mishkin, M. (1991). Massive cortical reorganization after sensory deafferentation in adult macaques. *Science, 252,* 1857-1860.

Purpura, D. P. (1975). Dendritic differentiation in human cerebral cortex: Normal and aberrant developmental patterns. *Advances in Neurology, (12)*91-134.

Purpura, D. P. (1982). Normal and abnormal development of cerebral cortex in man. *Neurosciences Research Program Bulletin, 20*(4), 569-577.

Purves, D. (1989). Assessing some dynamic properties of the living nervous system. *Quarterly Journal of Experimental Physiology, 74*(7)1089-1105.

Raff, M. C., Barres, B. A., Burne, J. F., Coles, H. S., Ishizaki, Y., & Jacobson, M. D. (1993). Programmed cell death and the control of cell survival: Lessons from the nervous system. *Science, 262,* 695-699.

Rakic, P. (1971). Guidance of neurons migrating to the fetal monkey neocortex. *Brain Research, 33,* 471-476.

Rakic, P. (1972). Mode of cell migration to the superficial layers of fetal monkey neocortex. *Journal of Comparative Neurology, 145,* 61-83.

Rakic, P. (1974). Neurons in rhesus monkey visual cortex: Systematic relation between time of origin and eventual disposition. *Science, 183,* 425-427.

Rakic, P. (1978). Neuronal migration and contact guidance in the primate telencephalon. *Postgraduate Medical Journal, 54*(Suppl. 1), 25-40.

Rakic, P. (1988). Specification of cerebral cortical areas. *Science, 241,* 170-176.

Rakic, P. (1990). Principles of neural cell migration. *Experientia, 46,* 882-891.

Rakic, P. (1995). Radial versus tangential migration of neuronal clones in the developing cerebral cortex. *Proceedings of the National Academy of Sciences, 92,* 11323-11327.

Rakic, P., Bourgeois, J. P., Eckenhoff, M. F., Zecevic, N., & Goldman-Rakic, P. S. (1986). Concurrent overproduction of synapses in diverse regions of the primate cerebral cortex. *Science, 232*(4747), 232-235.

Ramachandran, V. S., Rogers-Ramachandran, D., & Stewart, M. (1992). Perceptual correlates of massive cortical reorganization. *Science, 258,* 1159-1160.

Rampon, C., Jiang, C. H., Dong, H., Tang, Y. P., Lockhart, D. J., Schultz, P. G. Tsien, J. Z., & Hu, Y. (2000). Effects of environmental enrichment on gene expression in the brain. *Proceedings of the National Academy of Sciences, 97,* 12880-12884.

Schlaggar, B. L., Fox, K., & O'Leary, D. D. (1993). Postsynaptic control of plasticity in developing somatosensory cortex. *Nature, 364*(6438), 623-626.

Sidman, R. L., & Rakic, P. (1973). Neuronal migration, with special reference to developing human brain: A review. *Brain Research, 62,* 1-35.

Sidman, R., & Rakic, P. (1982). Development of the human central nervous system. In W. Haymaker & R. D. Adams (Eds.), *Histology and histopathology of the nervous system.* Springfield, IL: Charles C Thomas.

Shonkoff, J. P., & Phillips, D. A. (2000). *From neurons to neighborhoods: The science of early childhood development.* Washington, DC: National Academy of Sciences Press.

Smart, I. H. M. (1985). A localised growth zone in the wall of the developing mouse telencephalon. *Journal of Anatomy, 140,* 397-402.

Smith, J. L., & Schoenwolf, G. C. (1997). Neurulation: Coming to closure. *Trends in Neurosciences, 20,* 510-517.

Sowell, E. R., Thompson, P. M., Holmes, C. J., Jernigan, T. L., & Toga, A. W. (1999). In vivo evidence for post-adolescent brain maturation in frontal and striatal regions. *Nature Neuroscience, 2*(10), 859-861.

Spemann, H., & Mangold, H. (1924). Uber induktion von embryonalanlagen dürch implantation artfremder organisatoren. *Archiv Fuer Mikroskopische Anatomie Entwicklungsmechanik, 100,* 599-638.

Stiles, J. (2001). Spatial cognitive development. In C. A. Nelson & M. Luciana (Eds.), *Handbook of developmental cognitive neuroscience* (pp. 399-414). Cambridge: MIT Press.

Suter, D. M., & Forscher, P. (1998). An emerging link between cytoskeletal dynamics and cell adhesion molecules in growth cone guidance. *Current Opinion in Neurobiology, 8,* 106-116.

Takahashi, T., Nowakowski, R. S., & Caviness, V. S. Jr. (1994). Mode of cell proliferation in the developing mouse neocortex. *Proceedings of the National Academy of Sciences, 91,* 375-379.

Takahashi, T., Nowakowski, R. S., & Caviness, V. S. Jr. (2001). Neocortical neurogenesis: Regulation, control points, and a strategy of structural variation. In

C. A. Nelson & M. Luciana (Eds.), *Handbook of developmental cognitive neuroscience* (pp. 3-22). Cambridge: MIT Press.

Tallal, P., Miller, S. L., Bedi, G., Byma, G., Wang, X., Nagarajan, S. S., Schreiner, C., Jenkins, W. M., & Merzenich, M. M. (1976). Language comprehension in language-learning impaired children improved with acoustically modified speech. *Science, 271,* 81-84.

Tallal, P., & Piercy, M. (1973). Defects of non-verbal auditory perception in children with developmental aphasia. *Nature, 241,* 468-469.

Taub, E. (2000). Constraint-induced movement therapy and massed practice. *Stroke 31*(4), 986-988.

Tessier-Lavigne, M., & Goodman, C. S. (1996). The molecular biology of axon guidance. *Science, 274,* 1123-1133.

Thoenen, H. (1995). Neurotrophins and neuronal plasticity. *Science, 270*(5236), 593-598.

Thompson, R. A., & Nelson, C. A. (2001). Developmental science and the media: Early brain development. *American Psychologist, 56*(1), 5-15.

Volpe, J. J. (1995). *Neurology of the newborn* (3rd ed.). Philadelphia: W. B. Saunders.

Walsh, C., & Cepko, C. L. (1992). Widespread dispersion of neuronal clones across functional regions of the cerebral cortex. *Science, 255*(5043), 434-440.

Walsh, C., & Cepko, C. L. (1993). Clonal dispersion in proliferative layers of developing cerebral cortex. *Nature, 362*(6421), 632-635.

Werker, J. F., & Vouloumanos, A. (2001). Speech and language processing in infancy: A neurocognitive approach. In C. A. Nelson & M. Luciana (Eds.), *Handbook of developmental cognitive neuroscience.* Cambridge: MIT Press.

Yakovlev, P. I., & LeCours, A. R. (1967). The myelogenetic cycles of regional maternal depression. *International Journal of Family Psychiatry, 1,* 167-182.

Yuste, R., & Sur, M. (1999). Development and plasticity of the cerebral cortex: From molecules to maps. *Journal of Neurobiology, 41,* 1-6.

CHAPTER 3

The Role of Positive Psychology in Child, Adolescent, and Family Development

ANDREW J. SHATTÉ
MARTIN E. P. SELIGMAN
JANE E. GILLHAM
KAREN REIVICH

A central mission of the new movement of positive psychology is to create interventions that build human strengths in children, adolescents, and adults and to disseminate these to promote life satisfaction and fulfillment in all people. This chapter reviews the current state of protocols that putatively develop strengths such as resilience, rationality, optimism and hope, capacity for pleasure, courage, and future-mindedness. We propose that traditional psychotherapy, albeit steeped in the illness model, may have important effects on the variables of positive psychology. Primary, universal child and adolescent depression prevention programs represent a significant step toward the spirit of positive psychology, because they are focused on healthy individuals rather than the "sick." However, our review reveals that the major process in such programs is remediation of the negative, such as pessimistic explanatory style or passive or aggressive interaction styles. Few prevention programs are designed around the promotion of strengths. We briefly profile our work in the corporate sphere, our closest approximation to a positive psychology intervention, and how this work has informed our strength-building programs for children and adolescents. We spotlight the recent phenomenon of technology transfer, which facilitates dissemination to the public of intellectual property developed in universities. We suggest this as a possible means by which the work of creating positive psychology interventions may do the greatest public good.

PSYCHOLOGY'S FORGOTTEN MISSIONS

In the years before the World War II, psychologists followed three basic missions: to promote life satisfaction and fulfillment in all people, to nurture above-average talent, and to cure mental illness. But with the advent of the Veteran's Administration in 1946 and its fee-for-service structure, practitioners discovered that they could make a living by treating the sick. Followed closely by the establishment of the National Institute of Mental Health in 1947, academic psychologists gained access to research grants—provided their focus was on mental illness. The discipline of psychology underwent a sea change from which it has never recovered. In adopting an illness model with almost exclusive focus on the sick, psychology neglected its positive agenda of improving the lives of all and fostering genius (Seligman, 1998a).

POSITIVE PSYCHOLOGY

In 1998, then-president of the American Psychological Association Martin Seligman recognized that a window of opportunity lay open to restore the twin forgotten missions to prominence in psychology. Societies under conditions of threat or deficit, as was the case in the immediate postwar years, trend naturally toward a focus on the negative aspects of life. But the United States at the tail end of the 20th century was experiencing unprecedented prosperity. With the cold war all but thawed and economic indicators at all-time highs, it was time to move beyond the remedial (Seligman, 1998b). Technological innovations had enabled measurement and categorization of the negative states and investigation of their neurological underpinnings and had led to the creation of efficacious treatments. These same methodologies,

it was argued, could be brought to bear on the human strengths and civic virtues: courage, interpersonal skill, rationality and realism, insight, optimism, honesty, perseverance, capacity for pleasure, putting troubles into perspective, future-mindedness, and finding purpose, for example (Seligman, 1998b). Seligman called for the construction of a new science and practice, a discipline devoted to the neglected twin missions.

Dubbed positive psychology, this new social science aims to create an empirical corpus of knowledge of optimal human functioning. The positive psychology movement has two basic goals. The first is to increase understanding of the human strengths through the development of taxonomies and psychometrics. The second is to infuse this knowledge into effective programs and interventions designed to build participants' strengths rather than to remediate their weaknesses. Our focus in this chapter is on this second goal.

Positive psychology's shift in emphasis away from the illness model means that we are no longer only concerned with the sick. In realigning with the first of the forgotten missions, positive psychology aims to promote life satisfaction and fulfillment in all people. More relevant than ever, then, is the question of how we can take the learning of the academy and use it to transform the lives of the many. So in this chapter, we examine two fundamental questions: What is the current state of development of strength-building interventions, and how can effective programs best be made available outside the research labs in which they are developed?

BUILDING STRENGTHS

In this chapter, we will delineate three historical stages in the development of interventions designed to build human strengths:

traditional psychotherapy, prevention protocols, and positive psychology interventions. Each successive stage approaches more closely the core ideals of positive psychology. The first two stages are well under way. The final stage—the design of child, adolescent, and family interventions devoted solely to the development of the positive—is yet to be realized.

Traditional Psychotherapy

At first glance it would seem that traditional psychotherapy, steeped in the illness model, is purely a practice of remediating the negative. People seek or find themselves in therapy because they have diagnosed mental disorders or nonclinical deficits they wish to address. The therapist qua diagnostician and case conceptualizer maps the terrain of the negative—the number, frequency, and intensity of the symptoms and the social and occupational roadblocks to successful intervention. The therapeutic process then depends somewhat on the therapist's model of choice. In psychoanalytic therapies, for example, the emphasis is on resolving unconscious conflicts and releasing fixated libidinal energy. The patient is conceptualized as ill, or at least damaged, and the thrust of therapy is the restoration of normal functioning. The resolution of conflict remains as the centerpiece in more contemporary, psychodynamic therapies, with the emphasis not on libidinal conflicts but on core conflictual themes in the patient's relationships (Luborsky, Crits-Christoph, & Mellon, 1986). In the cognitive modality, the patient's pessimistic thinking and dysfunctional attitudes are the focus of therapy. But universally, the goal of therapy is to fix that which is broken.

The psychotherapy literature has been plagued by a troublesome and highly replicated finding. Although psychotherapy is robustly effective against many of the major mental disorders, there are few well-established specific effects. That is, very different treatment models typically have very similar effect sizes (e.g., Kirsch & Sapirstein, 1998). Nonspecificity has traditionally been attributed to extratheoretical variables common to all therapies, including the role of an authority figure and the attention that person provides, the establishment of rapport, payment for services, labeling the problem, and developing trust (Luborsky, 1995; Luborsky, Singer, & Luborsky, 1975; Seligman, 2002).

Another, "deeper" class of nonspecific variables has been hypothesized to enhance therapeutic outcome (Seligman, 2002), and they are recognizably in the domain of positive psychology. Competent therapists and efficacious therapies instill hope and optimism in the patient. They develop courage, interpersonal skill, insight, and rationality and realism. Specific therapeutic tools develop the capacity for pleasure, future-mindedness, and the ability to put troubles into perspective (Seligman, 2002). Efficacious therapies model honesty, nurture perseverance, and guide the patient to finding purpose. Entrenched as the discipline is in the illness model, little attention has been paid to researching these important therapy outcomes. However, it is reasonable to surmise that traditional psychotherapy does influence the variables of positive psychology, and that the development of these strengths is an important part of both therapeutic outcome and process.

Prevention Interventions and Positive Psychology

Before the launch of the positive psychology movement in the late 1990s, a small nucleus of clinical researchers were interested in prevention. In 1984, Martin Seligman attended an academic conference of psychologists and immunologists in which the future of a then-nascent field, psychoneuroim-munology or PNI, was being hotly debated. The psychologists argued that emotional stress was demonstrably linked to cancer risk. If we study how emotional states affect immune functioning and ultimately the onset of disease, they contended, we can develop psychological interventions to reverse those states and prevent the downturn in immu-nity. The immunologists argued that it was folly to hope to trace such tenuous causal pathways, implying that research money would be better spent on finding cures for the consequent disease (Seligman, Reivich, Jaycox, & Gillham, 1995). The debate was about treatment versus prevention.

In depression research, those who favor treatment have focused attention on financial cost. Many of the purported risk factors are not well validated, they argue, and many of those that are can only be measured with unreliable questionnaires and interviews. Many children who are genuinely at risk may be screened out of prevention programs, and costs will be incurred by putting children through these programs who were never truly at risk. In this view, it is better to await the onset of the depressive episode and then treat. Conversely, those who favor preven-tion focus attention on the concomitants of depression. If we wait until a child has the disorder, they suggest, that child will also be at heightened risk for nicotine, drug, and alcohol abuse (Covey, Glassman, & Stetner, 1998; Kinnier, Metha, Keim, & Okey, 1994; Riggs, Baker, Mikulich, & Young, 1995); academic decline (Kaslow, Rehm, & Siegel, 1984; Nolen-Hoeksema, Girgus, & Seligman, 1992); being suspended, expelled, or drop-ping out of school (Blechman & Culhane, 1993; Chen, Rubin, & Li, 1995; deMan & Leduc, 1995); and teen pregnancy, in the case of adolescent girls (Blechman & Culhane, 1993); as well as physical health problems (Koenig et al., 1999; Musselman,

Evans, & Nemeroff, 1998). Of course, the ultimate cost is human life, and depression is strongly linked with suicide and suicide attempts in children and adolescents (Pagliaro, 1995). Each year in the United States, approximately 13 in every 100,000 adolescents commit suicide (Lewinsohn, Rohde, & Seeley, 1996). Statistics such as these have heralded a growing commitment to prevention among clinical researchers, as well as a greater share of grant moneys earmarked for prevention work. How has the burgeoning prominence of prevention paved the way for the positive psychology movement?

Certain subsets of prevention programs represent more of a departure from the illness model than others. The discipline has drawn distinctions between primary, secondary, and tertiary prevention programs, although these lines are often blurred in practice (Gillham, Shatté, & Freres, 2000; Mrazek & Haggerty, 1994; Munoz, Mrazek, & Haggerty, 1996). Primary inter-ventions aim to prevent the onset of new cases of mental disorder in people with no history of the illness. Secondary prevention is concerned with detecting and treating new cases early in their onset. Tertiary prevention programs target existing cases with the goal of reducing the negative consequences of the disorders (Gillham et al., 2000). The Institute of Medicine's committee on prevention has further distinguished between universal, selective, and indicated prevention endeavors (Mrazek & Haggerty, 1994; Munoz et al., 1996).

Universal interventions are disseminated to entire populations regardless of their level of risk for a given disorder. Selective inter-ventions target people who currently show no signs of the disorder but who are at risk due to the life events they experience, some physical or psychological characteristic they possess, or because they fit a demographic risk factor. Indicated prevention is applied to people who already show some early symptoms or signs of the disorder. Selective and indicated interventions are often grouped as "targeted" prevention.

Primary prevention protocols are closer to the core of positive psychology than either secondary or tertiary protocols because they are provided to "healthy" people with no sign of disorder. Those programs that are both primary and universal approach most closely the rubric of positive psychology because they are applied to people who have no special vulnerability for the disorder. But distance from the illness model and "ill" populations represents only one dimension on which to evaluate degree of fit with positive psychology. The critical question is to what extent are even primary, universal prevention initiatives truly in the spirit of positive psychology? Do these programs focus on developing the strengths of their participants? Or do they aim, instead, to anticipate and preemptively shore up the weaknesses and vulnerabilities that may lead to disorder down the track?

A Brief Survey of Depression-Prevention Interventions for Children and Adolescents

Unipolar depression is perhaps the most targeted disorder for prevention research and practice to date. This is due to its documented prevalence and its associated human, social, and financial costs. It is among the most common disorders of adulthood and adolescence, with 11 million new cases emerging each year in the United States alone (Greenberg, Stiglin, Finkelstein, & Berndt, 1993). Various estimates suggest that between 10% and 25% of U.S. residents will experience an episode of clinical depression at some point in their lives (Munoz, 1987). The concomitants of depression and their effects on functioning in children, adolescents, and

adults have been well documented (see "Prevention Interventions and Positive Psychology" above). Depression brings a considerable financial cost. A conservative recalculation of the $43-billion estimate of the annual cost of unipolar and bipolar depression made by Greenberg et al. puts dysthymia's cost to business and health care at $9 billion and depression's at almost $20 billion. In fact, depression ranks fourth of all physical and mental disorders in terms of global mortality and disability (Murray & Lopez, 1997).

Rates of depression are accelerating in epidemic proportions. There was a tenfold increase in the incidence of depression across two generations in the 20th century (Robins et al., 1984). This has particularly impacted our youth, with estimates that between 15% and 20% of children and adolescents may experience clinical depression by age 18, with as many as 9% before age 14 (Harrington, Rutter, & Fombonne, 1996; Lewinsohn, Hops, Roberts, & Seeley, 1993; Garrison, Schluchter, Schoenbach, & Kaplan, 1989).

Research into psychological and environmental risk factors for depression has revealed the prevailing influence of cognitive styles and family conflict. Perhaps as a consequence, most depression prevention programs for children and adolescents have adopted a cognitive-behavioral or family systems approach. A recent, comprehensive review of these interventions concluded that the field has progressed significantly in the last decade and that several interventions were efficacious in "improv[ing] risk factors linked to depression and reduc[ing] depressive symptoms" (Gillham et al., 2000). Clearly, some of the proffered interventions are able to effectively remediate the negative. But to what extent do they seek to build strengths?

Universal and primary interventions are most likely to focus on building strengths, because they are not aimed at children and adolescents who show signs of depression or who are at identifiable risk for the disorder. Only two universal strategies for adolescent depression have been reported in the literature. The first to emerge was designed by Clarke, Hawkins, Murphy, & Sheeber (1993). In their first study, 622 predominantly white, middle-class ninth and tenth graders were recruited from the general population and randomized, by school class, to either the intervention or regular health condition. The manualized protocol consisted of three 50-minute sessions in which information was provided about depression and the students were trained in how to increase the number and quality of pleasant events, in the vein of treatments and interventions developed by Peter Lewinsohn (1974). The second study followed a similar design, was conducted with 380 students of similar demographics, and consisted of five 50-minute sessions with the same agenda. In both studies the focal outcome measures were depressive symptoms and accessing of treatment. Capacity for pleasure, an important positive psychology variable, may have been strengthened in the course of the intervention, but apparently it was not measured.

Hains and Ellman (1994) also designed a universal intervention and tested it with 21 white, high school students. The essential components of the protocol were cognitive-restructuring, relaxation, and problem solving—folded into thirteen 50-minute sessions. The cognitive restructuring was likely aimed at remediating depressogenic beliefs and relaxation to ease stress, indicating that the focus of the program was on remediating the negative. The major outcome measures reflect that: depression, anxiety, health problems, and school absences.

Not surprisingly, the targeted interventions follow a similar course. Clarke and colleagues (1995) screened and selected 150

ninth and tenth graders with particularly high levels of depressive symptoms and randomly assigned them to usual care or a 15-session protocol with focus on problem solving and challenging negative thoughts. The only outcomes were cases and symptoms of depression and schizophrenia (Clarke, Hawkins, Murphy, Sheeber, Lewinsohn, & Seeley, 1995). Petersen, Leffert, Graham, Alwin, & Ding (1997) developed a program which, on the face of it, set out to positively impact several human strengths in 486 seventh graders with elevated depression scores. Their protocol targets an increase of self-affirming thoughts, identifying goals, brainstorming, and assertiveness, along with the traditional illness model goals of reducing irrational thoughts. Interestingly, however, their outcome emphasis is again on symptoms, with a battery including self-report and interview items for depression and externalizing behaviors.

Several family and parental risk factors for depression have been identified, including marital conflict (Downey & Coyne, 1990), parental criticism (Asarnow, Goldstein, Thompson, & Guthrie, 1993), overprotectiveness (Parker, 1993), and the child's perception of receiving little parental care or support (Parker, 1993). Parental depression is strongly linked with depression in children (Beardslee, Versage, & Gladstone, 1998). While this almost certainly involves genetic factors, there is also a significant contribution due to modeling of maladaptive cognitive styles, such as pessimistic explanatory style (Cicchetti & Toth, 1998; Garber & Flynn, 1998). In addition, depressed adults are more likely to marry someone with psychopathology (Downey & Coyne, 1990), compounding the risk for their children. Conflict, economic hardship, and divorce are all more likely with at least one depressed parent (Beardslee et al., 1998; Downey &

Coyne, 1990). Depressed parents are less available for their children and may be more irritable, less caring, and less consistent in their interactions with their children (Beardslee et al., 1998; Cicchetti & Toth, 1998).

These risk factors clearly indicate the potential of family-oriented prevention measures. The review conducted by Gillham and colleagues (2000) revealed only one research group investigating this approach. William Beardslee of the Judge Baker Children's Center in Boston has developed a program for depressed parents. The focus of the program is on educating parents about the risk factors for depression as well as the promotion of resiliency, specifically teaching improved communication and the reduction of the child's self-blame for the parent's symptoms and behavior. The intervention consists of 6 to 10 sessions, including parent-only, child-only, and family sessions. In research trials, Beardslee and his colleagues (1998) did include measures of positive traits, such as self-esteem, self-reported relationship between parents and child, and global functioning, finding significant improvement in relationships and global functioning.

Our research group has also been actively involved in the depression prevention arena with the Penn Optimism Program (POP). In this chapter we spotlight the content of POP, the better to understand the relationship between depression prevention programs and the mission of positive psychology. In so doing we do not hold POP as a model but merely as an example of extant depression prevention programs.

THE PENN OPTIMISM PROGRAM (POP) FOR CHILDREN

The Penn Optimism Program (POP) was initially developed as a depression prevention program in the late 1980s. POP, a school-based intervention, targets high-risk children of 10 to 13, chosen on the basis of an already higher-than-average depressive symptom level and/or high perceived levels of family conflict or low family cohesion as measured with pencil and paper tests such as the Children's Depression Inventory (CDI) (Kovacs, 1985) and the Child's Perception Questionnaire (Emery & O'Leary, 1982; Kurdek & Sinclair, 1988). The 20-hour program has successfully prevented depressive symptoms in children and adolescents for periods of up to 2 years, without boosters (Gillham, Jaycox, Reivich, & Seligman, 1995; Jaycox, Reivich, Gillham, & Seligman, 1994). It is based on the cognitive-behavioral model and is comprised of 11 core skills.

Skill 1: ABC. The ABC model developed by Albert Ellis (1962) is the centerpiece of cognitive theory as conceptualized in POP. Ellis and Grieger (1977) based their premise on the observable data that different people behave and emote very differently in the wake of ostensibly identical events. If so, then the activating event, A, cannot be directly and proximally causal of the consequences, C (emotions and behaviors). According to Ellis, our thoughts and beliefs, B, about the event are important mediators of the effect of events on our behavior and feelings.

The kernel of the skill lies in learning that we do not have a "direct read" on reality— that our information about the world is screened through our belief systems and therefore may not be accurate, as is typically the case with the pervasive helplessness and hopelessness observed in some clinically depressed patients. POP participants learn ABC through the use of three-panel cartoons in which they are presented with the adversity and the emotional consequences and must fill in a thought bubble with a belief that fits the logic of ABC.

Skill 2: Detecting Explanatory Style. ABC represents a snapshot in time, a specific automatic thought in response to a specific activating event. However, it is well documented that our automatic thoughts are not random. We develop styles of processing information that, to some degree, predetermine our responses to stimuli. One example is explanatory style: our habitual and reflexive way of explaining the events in our lives (Abramson, Seligman, & Teasdale, 1978). Any causal attribution can be coded along three dimensions:

1. Is the negative event caused by the person or by someone else or circumstances (internal versus external)?

2. Is the cause likely to be present for a long time or is it relatively temporary (stable versus unstable)?

3. Is the cause operating in few or many life domains (global versus specific)?

Individuals have a tendency to develop explanatory styles that are either internal, stable, and global (pessimists) or external, unstable, and specific (optimists). For example, a child who attributes a math test failure to stupidity ("I'm just dumb") is making a pessimistic attribution—the failure is due to some characteristic of hers that is permanent and affects not just math performance, but most areas of functioning. Alternatively, a child who believes the math failure is because "The teacher hates me" is offering an optimistic explanation—the problem is the fault of someone else; it is only a problem for as long as he or she has this teacher and only affects the math grade.

An enormous corpus of empirical research has established a link between a pessimistic explanatory style and compromised achievement and physical and mental health (e.g., Dweck & Licht, 1980; Peterson & Seligman, 1984; Peterson, Seligman, & Vaillant, 1988;

Seligman & Schulman, 1986). POP began as a depression prevention strategy, and as such the declared goal was to guide children to an understanding of the benefits of optimism and the costs of pessimistic thinking (which leads, via ABC, to negative emotions and behaviors). This was achieved using skits that modeled optimism and pessimism and teaching participants to identify the internal, stable, and global language of pessimism ("I mess everything up," "I'm such a loser").

Skill 3: Generating Alternatives. Explanatory style provides ready-made answers to the our reflexive "Why?" questions when negative events befall us. Pessimistic explanations tend to lead to helplessness and hopelessness. Once children are equipped with an understanding of their explanatory style, they can begin the work of generating more optimistic alternatives, using the three dimensions as guidelines. If they tend to be overly internal, they are encouraged to derive plausible explanations about others or circumstances. If their explanations are overly characterological or stable, they are rewarded for generating explanations that focus on more changeable and temporary causal factors.

Skill 4: Evaluating Evidence. The goal of POP has never been blind optimism. The self-esteem movement of the 1970s encouraged children to repeat baseless mantras such as "Make loving yourself a habit" and "Everybody makes me happy" (Seligman et al., 1995). However, to the extent that these are not in accord with reality, they will merely be overwhelmed by the child's actual life experience. More importantly, they do not provide the child with the skills to do better in the world, which is the surest path to healthy self esteem. POP has always emphasized accuracy, and participants are taught to treat their initial, style-generated beliefs as well as their alternative explanations as theories to be tested with evidence. In this way, the work of generating alternatives and evaluating evidence is compared with the role of a scientist or a good detective such as Sherlock Holmes, who generates a list of suspects and then uses clues to determine the true perpetrator.

Skill 5: Putting It in Perspective. In Skill 5, attention shifts from beliefs about the past (causal explanations for past events) to beliefs about the future. Children at risk for depression are also at heightened risk for anxiety which, as ABC predicts, is often the consequence of catastrophic beliefs about the future. In this skill, children learn to identify and list their worst-case thoughts about the implications of adversity. These thoughts tend to come in chains of conditional probabilities; for example, "If my parents argue, they'll get divorced; if they get divorced, I'll never see my father again and my mother will never be happy; if that happens I'll run away from home; kids who run away from home end up in prison." The causal link between parents' arguing and prison is extremely tenuous, but the connection from link to link is more plausible. We guide children out of the chain by teaching them to estimate the probability of each link given only that the initial adversity (parents arguing) has occurred. Participants are taught to generate equally improbable best-case scenarios and then to use worst-case and best-case scenarios as anchors to arrive at most-likely outcomes.

Skill 6: Rapid Fire. The skills of POP must be useful in everyday life to effect long-lasting change. Recognizing that, the architects of the program inserted a skill that children can use to counter their pessimistic thoughts in the midst of adversity. In Rapid Fire (which combines elements of Skills 3, 4, and 5), participants are taught to quickly generate an alternative ("It's not that I'm a loser, it's just that I struck out this time at bat"), counter-evidence ("It's not true that I can't be trusted because I baby-sit my little sister all the time"), or put a catastrophic thought into perspective ("A more likely outcome is that my parents will punish me, but they'll still love me and take care of me").

Skill 7: Assertiveness and Negotiation. Using cognitive skills, children learn to challenge the negative beliefs that lead them to be overly passive or aggressive rather than assertive. They learn a four-step approach to assertiveness in which they describe the situation that is upsetting them without blame, tell the person how they feel, ask for a specific behavioral change, and let the other know how that would lead them to feel better (Bower & Bower, 1976).

Skill 8: Relaxation Techniques. In this module, children are taught controlled breathing, progressive muscle relaxation, thought stopping, and positive imagery.

Skill 9: The Graded Task. Procrastination is a common problem for children, and often negative thoughts lie at its heart. Some children believe that they are not competent to do the task. Others have perfectionistic beliefs that lead them to delay ("While the page is blank, the essay still has a chance of being perfect"). Participants learn the skill of the graded task, in which they break the task into smaller, more manageable steps and reward themselves for the successful completion of each step.

Skill 10: Decision Making. There are pros and cons to any choice. With binary choices (e.g., go to the party or stay home and study for the math exam), there are four possibilities; the pros and cons of each of the two choices (going to the party or studying for the exam). Children's cognitive styles often lead them to consider only a subset of these; for example, the fun of going to the party and the misery of staying home to study. In this skill, children are taught to carefully consider all four cells of a binary decision to achieve a more balanced and comprehensive perspective on the decision.

Skill 11: Social Problem Solving. Children at risk for depression may selectively attend to hostile cues and attribute the ambiguous behavior of others to hostile intent (Dodge, 1986; Dodge & Frame, 1982). In this module, participants learn to be skeptical toward their initial causal explanations and to generate alternatives and evaluate evidence. They learn to take the perspective of the other and to determine their own goal for the interaction. They use the four-cell, pros and cons, decision technique to choose a course of action, enact it, and modify and try again if their goal is not achieved.

Evaluating POP as a Positive Psychology Intervention

Most of the skills of the POP program are remedial in nature. This is not surprising, given that POP began as a targeted intervention for children at risk for depression. The emphasis of the program was on equipping participants with skills to help them identify their cognitive deficits—pessimistic explanatory style, tendency to catastrophize, hostile attributional bias, perfectionistic thinking—and teaching them skills that minimize the impact of those cognitive styles. Even the apparently more positive skills (such as relaxation training, assertiveness, decision making, and social problem solving) are approached from a remedial perspective; that is, redress the overactive sympathetic nervous system, curb the hostile or passive tendencies,

reduce the myopic decision-making process, and prevent rash and hasty judgments in social interactions.

The skills of POP were derived from the proven therapy techniques of the cognitive model of the treatment of depression and anxiety developed by Aaron Beck (1967, 1976; Beck, Hollon, Young, Bedrosian, & Budenz, 1985; Beck, Rush, Shaw, & Emery, 1979). The putative logic of POP was simple. Develop a depression prevention program to counter the epidemic. Select children who are at risk for depression because they show early signs or have family characteristics that are demonstrably depressogenic. Assume that the symptoms are a marker of faulty cognitions. Assume that family conflict and low family cohesion incur their effects on depression via the child's interpretation of events—the child's explanatory style and tendency to catastrophize. Finally, tackle these faulty cognitions before they lead to full-blown depression by equipping participants with the skills of cognitive therapy. POP proved to be a powerful program (Gillham et al., 1995), but its genesis was certainly illness and remediation, and the focal outcome measures were symptoms of depression, anxiety, and externalizing behaviors.

As our work progressed, we began to conceptualize the skill set, borrowed from a therapy, as much more foundational in its application. Through serendipity, in 1994, we found ourselves with a shortage of at-risk children and a surplus of available POP facilitators. We opened the groups to all children, regardless of risk, and so POP became much more of a universal intervention. As a depression prevention program and with the risk factors we employed, we had tended to select children with overly pessimistic explanatory styles. Moving them toward accuracy logically involved helping them to become more optimistic. But as a universal intervention, POP recruited children with the full spectrum of explanatory styles. Now, in group, when we discussed why a child may fail a math test, we no longer heard a unanimous "Because he's stupid" but rather subsets of children, those with optimistic explanatory style, attributing it to "The teacher hates him."

We began a complete rethinking of our work. The field of explanatory style was born out of the depression literature. There is considerable evidence that a pessimistic explanatory style is a risk factor for depression and that an optimistic explanatory style is a buffer against depression. The notion that pessimism is bad and optimism good, which is true of depression, was assumed by some psychologists to be true of almost all life domains. But what about problem solving? As we deconstructed our program we recognized that any explanatory style is limiting and either extreme is detrimental. The extreme pessimist who assumes that failure occurred due to his or her own stupidity will feel depressed and will become helpless and hopeless because intelligence and "stupidity" are stable traits. The extreme optimist who assumes that failure occurred because "The teacher hates me" will almost certainly be spared depression. But this child will probably experience anger and frustration instead and will have no more problem-solving options than a pessimistic counterpart. In essence, our explanatory style leads us automatically to a subset of causal explanations that fit that style. It leads us to systematically ignore possible causes that inhabit other regions of the three-dimensional space created by the internal, stable, and global dimensions. For this reason our explanatory styles, regardless of their composition, may cause us to channel problem-solving resources toward relatively unchangeable factors (e.g., our level of intelligence, the feelings of a teacher for a student), while systematically neglecting causes that we could alter, such as study habits. If we teach children to generate

alternative causal explanations, regardless of their explanatory style, they come to appreciate the full causal picture of their adversity and can capitalize on the full range of possible solutions. This enables participants to stay in problem-solving mode longer because they have more possible solutions to work with, and this translates into greater resilience and perseverance. As we reconceptualized POP, we realized that as a universal intervention it promoted resilience. In 1996, we officially renamed POP the Penn Resiliency Program (PRP).

This evolution has brought us even closer to the spirit of positive psychology because much of our work is with nonclinical, non-risk samples, and our skill set is aimed at general problem solving and resilience rather than depression prevention. But we still employ many of the same remedial techniques, and there are still relatively few measures of the strengths included in our assessment batteries. The program includes few explicit attempts to directly influence strengths, and our psychometric development of instruments to measure strengths has lagged behind our protocol development. We have little empirical evidence that PRP is a positive psychology intervention. But it is plausible that PRP does foster some of the variables of positive psychology.

Mapping the Impact of Remedial Skills on the Human Strengths: Anecdotal Evidence

PRP has now operated in more than 20 sites nationally and internationally, and we have collected a bank of anecdotal evidence that supports this. Here is a selection.

Courage. Joanne was only 13 years old when she joined our PRP group, but she was already struggling with many of the responsibilities of the adult world. As the oldest of four with a single mother, many of the duties of parenting fell to her. And lately her 15-year-old boyfriend had been talking about sex. A couple of weeks ago he told her it was time for them to try it, telling her that if she loved him she would want to, also. Last week he told her that everyone did it and that it would only make them closer as a couple. Just yesterday he threatened to "dump" her if she didn't. Jo was frantic. She didn't think she was ready for sex, but she didn't want to lose him and the emotional support he gave her. She was in conflict.

Joanne used ABC (Skill 1) to identify her beliefs about this situation and to track their consequences, the better to understand her anxiety and depression. She used decision making (Skill 10) to examine the costs and benefits of her choices and came to realize that she wasn't yet ready to deal with an intimate, sexual relationship. She recognized that her biggest fears were that her boyfriend would get angry with her when she told him and that he would leave. She used Putting It in Perspective (Skill 5) to decatastrophize these fears, and we helped her shape an assertive response to his demands (Skill 7).

When we last spoke with Jo at the end of the program, she had told her boyfriend that she wasn't ready. She wasn't sure if he would stay with her, but she believed that it wasn't the end of the world if he left. She thanked us for helping her gain the courage to face him and to face the decision.

Capacity for Pleasure. Linda was the treasurer of her school's student government. Student politics was a passion for her. In fact, she admitted that sometimes her enthusiasm got the better of her and she would get to class late after a meeting. A few weeks into the program, we noticed a change in Linda. Although she had been an active member of her PRP group, her leader now found it tough to keep her engaged in the program. By about the fourth session, Linda had

stopped asking questions and volunteering answers. When the leader asked Linda about her thoughts and feelings, Linda, with tears in her eyes, told her that everything was boring. She added that she'd skipped a couple of student council meetings because "they take too long, and they're all the same anyway." She said that she was going to quit as treasurer.

Linda's leader asked her to write down all the reasons she ran for the treasurer's position in the first place (Skill 1, ABC). She helped her use the graded task (Skill 9) to schedule some activities that were fun for her. As the program progressed, she helped Linda critically examine her beliefs about herself and the world, to generate alternative beliefs and evaluate their accuracy (Skills 3 and 4). By the end of the program, Linda was her old self again and still the treasurer.

Interpersonal Skill. D. J. was the kind of child who does well at everything he tries. A talented athlete and a good scholar, he was regarded highly by his teachers. He enjoyed a close relationship with his parents, who were very proud of him and his achievements at school and on the sports field. When D. J. came to group, it was a pleasure to watch him relate to the other students. He had a confident and calm demeanor that immediately put the others at ease.

So it was all the more surprising when D. J. shared that he was very upset about his relationship with his brother, 3 years D. J.'s senior. He told us, "We used to be really good friends, Tony and me, but now we just fight." D. J. felt that Tony just kept getting angry with him and that they didn't "hang out" like they used to. D. J. felt the loss of his friendship with his brother but couldn't understand it and could not work out what to do. The interpersonal skills that worked so well with his peers were failing him with sibling.

During PRP, D. J. learned to see things from his brother's perspective (Skill 11), to understand that at 14 his brother wanted more privacy and space than D. J. did at 11. He learned how to ask his brother about his thoughts and to understand how these thoughts led Tony to behave the way he did (Skill 1, ABC). He learned the critical skill of the social problem-solving component of the program (Skill 11). He learned to empathize.

Insight. Joe was the kind of rambunctious boy who is at once a joy and a frustration. At times his exuberance brought the group into PRP activity at hand, and at times it stole them away. One day Joe came to PRP looking very angry. When his PRP leader asked him what was up, he told him that he just found out that he'd failed a math test. "That math teacher hates me," he said. "He's had it in for me from the beginning."

The PRP leader pointed out to Joe that his attribution was an external belief about someone else or circumstances causing the problem. The leader encouraged Joe to come up with an internal belief about the problem, something that Joe had done to contribute to the failing grade. Joe couldn't do it. He tried and tried, but he could not come up with a single thing he had done to cause the problem. The leader told the group about explanatory style and guided Joe to an understanding that he tended to externalize (Skill 2). Joe began to realize that this same scenario played out in a lot of domains in his life: when he got angry with his football coach for pulling him out of a game, when he changed guitar teachers because "the first guy wasn't teaching me right." This provided a powerful insight into his way of navigating the world. By the end of the program, Joe was able to counter his initial instincts and generate some more internal beliefs (Skill 3). Joe told his leader, "Maybe the 15 minutes I studied on the bus wasn't enough to pass the math exam."

Future-Mindedness. A lot of things in Jim's life were uncertain, but there was one thing of which he was sure: He was going to make it into the NBA. All his spare time was spent playing basketball. He'd skip homework and even cut class to get more court time. As a result his grades were poor, and his parents were angry with him about his last report card. His game was not improving either. At 12 years of age and 5 feet 2 inches, he was much shorter than the other boys in his class. He did not have the skill that many of them had, either, so he had spent the last 2 years warming the bench.

There is nothing wrong with dreams unless pursuing them defeats other core goals or threatens safety. Jim's hopes were more about the money he would make as an NBA star than about reality or even a true drive for excellence in sports. Jim was burning bridges with his behavior, reducing his chances of making it into college and all the opportunities that affords.

PRP helped Jim to think more comprehensively about the future (Skill 5). Jim developed skills to look at both the future costs and benefits of his current behavior (Skill 10). The spark didn't leave Jim; he was just as determined to make it big in basketball. But he was also applying himself academically.

Resilience and Perseverance. Felicia lived in a world of chaos. Weekdays she spent with her mom and her brothers and sisters. But on the weekends, she and her siblings lived with an aunt or with friends of the family so her mother could work a late shift. Their inner-city apartment was small and underserviced, but it was all her mom could do to get enough work to keep their heads above water.

Felicia told her PRP leader about her living conditions during the course of the program, but this situation was not what was troubling her. She was worried about her grades. She was getting Cs and Ds in middle school when she'd been an A and B student in her old elementary school. She believed she was "just stupid" and that there was nothing she could do to improve. Her PRP leader helped her identify those beliefs and track their effects on her emotion (depression) and behavior (helplessness) (Skill 1, ABC). She learned to generate less stable and global causal alternatives, such as "I didn't study enough" and "I didn't do my homework throughout the semester," causes that are potentially changeable.

Felicia and her PRP leader set up a study agenda. Felicia put in the hours and was hopeful about her performance in the next test. To her surprise, she also failed that exam. She was devastated, but her PRP leader helped her put it in perspective (Skill 5). She led her through the iterative process of generating additional alternatives (Skills 3, 4, and 11)—Felicia often forgot to take her math text with her on the weekends, so although she was putting in the needed study hours, she was doing so without the proper materials. Felicia learned resilience and perseverance and passed her math class along the way.

Rationality and Realism. Trevor was one of those quiet and polite students who hover on the fringe of a group. He always did what his PRP group leader asked of him, but he always seemed more than a little detached. There was a profound air of sadness around Trevor. He didn't appear to really be in the world; he seemed more like a shadow than a real 11-year-old boy.

His first unsolicited remarks to the group leader told a story that started out like one we have heard a thousand times before: a father exasperated after a hard day at work, his son's homework not done, harsh words exchanged, an argument unresolved and held over until tomorrow. But Trevor's dad didn't come home the following night. He was killed in a car accident on his way home from work. For years, Trevor carried the guilt. He thought he had caused his father's death. He believed that his father had died angry with him and that he didn't love him. He felt that he was a worthless son, a worthless person. He believed that he wasn't entitled to be alive—that he deserved to be a shadow.

PRP helped Trevor dispute these beliefs (Skills 3 and 4)—to see the world more realistically and more rationally. He came to see that the accident was not his fault. He could see the mountain of evidence that showed just how much his father loved him. He felt free to reenter the world. The last time we saw Trevor was at his high school, a few years after he had graduated from PRP. He rushed over to us because he wanted to introduce us to his girlfriend. He was smiling.

Optimism and Hope. Miguel came into one of our PRP groups in Austin. He came from a loving family and was a competent student. He'd grown up in an inner city neighborhood, and he knew what it was like to be surrounded by violence. He was often afraid to walk home after school because of the drive-by shootings. Miguel knew so many of his older brother's friends who joined gangs and ended up in trouble with the law. But by and large things had been going well for him until his parents started arguing. Occasional at first, the arguments now seemed to be a nightly ritual. He couldn't stand the shouting anymore and would lock himself in his room and shut out the yelling with his headphones and music.

With each passing day, Miguel's fears grew. He believed it was inevitable that his parents would divorce. He worried that his father would move out of town and he'd never see him again. So many others in his neighborhood had lost contact with their dads, and so many of these had turned to gangs. "I'm scared I'm going to end up in a gang," he told his PRP leader. "I don't want to, but it's just what happens when your parents split up." Miguel confided that, once he was in a gang, he knew it would be just a matter of time before he got into trouble with the law. He'd be sent to juvenile hall. "The kids who come back from there get into really bad stuff. They end up spending their lives in prison. I'll never see my mother again," he said, choking back tears. "What's the point in doing anything? It's just the way it is." Miguel's tendency to catastrophize had carried him from arguments between his parents to a life spent in prison. He felt helpless and hopeless; he could see no way out of the trajectory he believed was his destiny.

Miguel's PRP leader taught Miguel to put things in perspective by evaluating worst-case, best-case, and most-likely scenarios (Skill 5). PRP developed Miguel's problem-solving skills so that he focused his resources on what he could control rather than what he could not. Miguel developed optimism and hope.

BEYOND THE ACADEMY

In 1997 the psychology department at the University of Pennsylvania was beginning a candidate search for a professorship in social psychology. At that time, Martin Seligman received an e-mail from a colleague asking if industrial psychologists should be considered in the search. He replied, "Of course—the three great realms of life are work, love, and play, and industrial psychology is the psychology of work" (Seligman, 1998c, para. 3). Later, Seligman stated that, when reflecting on the faculties of the best academic institutions in the country, he could not recall a single researcher whose primary research focus was work, love, or play.

The next day, Seligman ran into Jerome Bruner, whom he describes as having an incredible knowledge of the history of modern psychology. When asked how these major life domains had been neglected by research, Bruner replied,

It actually happened at a moment in time. About 60 years ago the chairmen of Harvard, Princeton, and Penn got together at a meeting of the Society of Experimental Psychologists and agreed that they would hire no applied psychologists! This set the hiring pattern of many of the great departments to this very day. (quoted in Seligman, 1998c, para. 6)

No applied psychologists. No role allotted for community service outside the ivory tower. This has not been the approach adopted by most of the prevention and positive psychology researchers. Their basic mission is to develop effective interventions that work in the real world. As scientists, their credo is that the best test of a theory is whether the programs derived from it are effective. Their stance has been bolstered by the emergent phenomenon of technology transfer in the country's most-respected universities.

Technology transfer is the process by which new technologies developed from research conducted at universities are formally transferred to the commercial sector. The tech transfer industry flourished after the enactment of the Bayh-Dole Act of 1980, which allowed universities, other nonprofit research organizations, and small businesses to own and patent innovations developed with federal grant money. Prior to 1980, less than 250 patents were issued annually to universities in this country, and dramatically fewer were commercialized and made available to the community. In fiscal year 1999, by comparison, 3,914 new license agreements were signed, according to the Association of University Technology Managers (AUTM) (2002).

There are now more than 300 universities and research institutions registered with AUTM and actively involved in the tech transfer process. Certainly the success of an office of technology transfer is measured, in part, by the number of deals negotiated and the amount of royalties returned to the university. But an important objective of such offices is the degree of public benefit afforded by the transaction. AUTM has developed models that estimate the potential positive impact of the product on the lives of consumers (AUTM, 2002).

In October of 1997, three of the resiliency programs developed in the Seligman lab at Penn (PRP, the APEX program for college freshmen, and a program for corporate employees) were assigned to Adaptiv Learning Systems, a technology transfer company established to facilitate the dissemination of the programs. To this end, Adaptiv has trained teachers from a consortium of school districts to implement PRP across Pennsylvania. In addition, Adaptiv has funded and spearheaded the development of Adaptiv Training for Corporations, which is proving to be the closest approximation yet to a positive psychology intervention. Adaptiv Training has been delivered in a variety of organizations including several Fortune 1000 companies, small intact research teams, and governmental and quasi-governmental organizations. A broad cross-section of employees have participated in Adaptiv Training, from frontline sales and customer service representatives through engineers, middle-level managers, and high-level executives. Adaptiv Training follows the process of the cognitive model adopted in PRP. Prework questionnaires identify participants' workplace strengths as well as their vulnerabilities, and the program focuses on the cognitions underlying each. Participants are lead to a better of understanding of the cognitive styles that provide them with strength, resilience, courage etc. in workplace areas they handle

well—such as interactions with authority or delegating work. They are led through activities that help them apply those same styles in work domains that need improving, such as the balance of work and home or procrastination. As such, Adaptiv represents a program designed to build strengths.

The program development funded by Adaptiv Learning Systems has led to a start-of-the-art instructional design for the corporate program. This knowledge has, in turn, been infused into PRP and the PRP leader certification curricula.

FUTURE DIRECTIONS OF POSITIVE PSYCHOLOGY INTERVENTIONS

In summary, there are few, if any, positive psychology interventions operating today. Traditional psychotherapy may impact such variables, but it is incidental at best. Positive psychology interventions are distinct from the illness model in two significant ways: They attempt to build strengths rather than remediate vulnerabilities, and they have the potential to benefit all people not just sick. Although state-of-the-art depression prevention programs represent an important step away from focus on the sick, all reviewed programs still focus their content on remediating vulnerability to future disorders. Perhaps programs developed for the corporate arena are the closest approximation to positive psychology interventions, because they are deployed with predominantly well-functioning people and are designed to promote productivity, performance, and work and life satisfaction.

For the mission of positive psychology to be fulfilled, ways must be discovered to disseminate its technologies beyond the academy, beyond the sick, to improve the lives of all people. The emergent process of technology transfer may prove to be a useful means of achieving this goal.

REFERENCES

Abramson, L. Y., Seligman, M. E. P., & Teasdale, J. D. (1978). Learned helplessness in humans: Critique and reformulation. *Journal of Abnormal Psychology, 87*(1), 49-74.

Asarnow, J. R., Goldstein, M. J., Thompson, M., & Guthrie, D. (1993). One-year outcomes of depressive disorders in child psychiatric in-patients: Evaluation of the prognostic power of a brief measure of expressed emotion. *Journal of Child Psychology and Psychiatry, 34,* 129-137.

Association of University Technology Managers (AUTM). (2002). *Tech Transfer: FY 2000.* Retrieved July 2, 2002, from www.autm.net/index_ie.html

Beardslee, W. R., Versage, E. M., & Gladstone, T. R. G. (1998). Children of affectively ill parents: A review of the past 10 years. *Journal of the American Academy of Child and Adolescent Psychiatry, 31,* 1134-1141.

Beck, A. T. (1967). *Depression: Causes and treatment.* Philadelphia: University of Pennsylvania Press.

Beck, A. T. (1976). *Cognitive therapy and the emotional disorders.* New York: International Universities Press.

Beck, A. T., Hollon, S. D., Young, J. E., Bedrosian, R. C., & Budenz, D. (1985). Treatment of depression with cognitive therapy and amitriptyline. *Archives of General Psychiatry, 42,* 142-148.

Beck, A. T., Rush, A. J., Shaw, B. F., & Emery, G. (1979). *Cognitive therapy of depression.* New York: Guilford Press.

Blechman, E. A., & Culhane, S. E. (1993). Aggressive, depressive, and prosocial coping with affective challenges in early adolescence. *Journal of Early Adolescence, 13*(4), 361-382.

Bower, S. A., & Bower, G. H. (1976). *Asserting yourself: A positive guide for positive change.* Reading, MA: Addison-Wesley.

Chen, X., Rubin, K. H., & Li, B. (1995). Depressed mood in Chinese children: Relations with school performance and family environment. *Journal of Consulting and Clinical Psychology, 63*(6), 938-947.

Cicchetti, D., & Toth, S. L. (1998). The development of depression in children and adolescents. *American Psychologist, 53,* 221-242.

Clarke, G. N., Hawkins, W., Murphy, M., & Sheeber, L. (1993). School-based primary prevention of depressive symptomatology in adolescents: Findings from two studies. *Journal of Adolescent Research, 8,* 183-204.

Clarke, G. N., Hawkins, W., Murphy, M., Sheeber, L. B., Lewinsohn, P. M., & Seeley, J. R. (1995). Targeted prevention of unipolar depressive disorder in an at-risk sample of high school adolescents: A randomized trial of a group cognitive intervention. *Journal of the American Academy of Child and Adolescent Psychiatry, 34,* 312-321.

Covey, L. S., Glassman, A. H., & Stetner, F. (1998). Cigarette smoking and major depression. *Journal of Addictive Diseases, 17,* 35-46.

deMan, A. F., & Leduc, C. P. (1995). Suicidal ideation in high school students: Depression and other correlates. *Journal of Clinical Psychology, 51*(2), 173-181.

Dodge, K. (1986). A social information processing model of social competence in children. In M. Perlmutter (Ed.), *Cognitive perspectives on children's social and behavioral development.* Hillsdale, NJ: Lawrence Erlbaum.

Dodge, K. A., & Frame, C. L. (1982). Social cognitive biases and deficits in aggressive boys. *Child Development, 53,* 620-635.

Downey, G., & Coyne, J. C. (1990). Children of depressed parents: An integrative review. *Psychological Bulletin, 108,* 50-76.

Dweck, C. S., & Licht, B. (1980). Learned helplessness and intellectual achievement. In J. Garber & M. Seligman (Eds.), *Human helplessness: Theory and applications*. New York: Academic Press.

Ellis, A. (1962). *Reason and emotion in psychotherapy*. New York: Lyle Stuart.

Ellis, A., & Grieger, R. (1977). *Handbook of rational-emotive therapy*. New York: Springer.

Emery, R. E., & O'Leary, K. D. (1982). Children's perceptions of marital discord and behavior problems of boys and girls. *Journal of Abnormal Child Psychology, 10*, 11-24.

Garber, J., & Flynn, C. (1998). Origins of depressive cognitive style. In D. Routh & R. J. DeRubeis (Eds.), *The science of clinical psychology: Evidence of a century's progress* (pp. 53-93). Washington, DC: American Psychological Association.

Garrison, C. Z., Schluchter, M. D., Schoenbach, V. J., & Kaplan, B. K. (1989). Epidemiology of depressive symptoms in young adolescents. *Journal of the American Academy of Child and Adolescent Psychiatry, 28*, 343-351.

Gillham, J. E., Reivich, K. J., Jaycox, L., & Seligman, M. E. P. (1995). Preventing depressive symptoms in schoolchildren: Two-year follow-up. *Psychological Science, 6*, 343-351.

Gillham, J. E., Shatté, A. J., & Freres, D. R. (2000). Preventing depression: A review of cognitive-behavioral and family interventions. *Applied & Preventive Psychology, 9*, 63-68.

Greenberg, P. E., Stiglin, L. E., Finkelstein, S. N., & Berndt, E. R. (1993). The economic burden of depression in 1990. *Journal of Clinical Psychiatry, 54*, 405-426.

Hains, A. A., & Ellman, S. W. (1994). Stress inoculation training as a preventative intervention for high school youths. *Journal of Cognitive Psychotherapy, 8*, 219-232.

Harrington, R., Rutter, M., & Fombonne, E. (1996). Developmental pathways in depression: Multiple meanings, antecedents, and endpoints. *Development and Psychopathology, 8*, 601-616.

Jaycox, L. H., Reivich, K. J., Gillham, J., & Seligman, M. E. P. (1994). Preventing depressive symptoms in school children. *Behaviour Research and Therapy, 32*, 801-816.

Kaslow, N. J., Rehm, L. P., & Siegel, A. W. (1984). Social-cognitive and cognitive correlates of depression in children. *Journal of Abnormal Child Psychology, 12*, 605-620.

Kinnier, R. T., Metha, A. T., Keim, J. S., & Okey, J. L. (1994). Depression, meaninglessness, and substance abuse in "normal" and hospitalized adolescents. *Journal of Alcohol and Drug Education, 39*(2), 101-111.

Kirsch, I., & Sapirstein, G. (1998). Listening to Prozac but hearing placebo: A meta-analysis of antidepressant medication (Article 0002a). *Prevention & Treatment, 1*. Retrieved June 9, 2002, from http//journals.apa.org/prevention/volume1

Koenig, H. G., George, L. K., Larson, D. B., McCullough, M. E., Branch, P. S., & Kuchibhatla, M. (1999). Depressive symptoms and nine-year survival of 1,001 male veterans. *American Journal of Geriatric Psychiatry, 7*, 124-131.

Kovacs, M. (1985). The Children's Depression Inventory (CDI). *Psychopharmacology Bulletin, 21*, 995-1124.

Kurdek, L. A., & Sinclair, R. J. (1988). Adjustment of young adolescents in two-parent nuclear, stepfather, and mother-custody families. *Journal of Consulting and Clinical Psychology, 56*, 91-96.

Lewinsohn, P. M. (1974). A behavioral approach to depression. In R. J. Friedman & M. M. Katz (Eds.), *The psychology of depression: Contemporary theory and research*. New York: Guilford.

Lewinsohn, P. M., Hops, H., Roberts, R., & Seeley, J. (1993). Adolescent psychopathology: I. Prevalence and incidence of depression and other DSM-III-R disorders in high school students. *Journal of Abnormal Psychology, 102,* 110-120.

Lewinsohn, P. M., Rohde, P., & Seeley, J. R. (1996). Adolescent suicidal ideation and attempts: Prevalence, risk factors, and clinical implications. *Clinical psychology: Science and Practice, 3,* 25-46.

Luborsky, L. (1995). Are common factors across different psychotherapies the main explanation for the dodo bird verdict that "Everyone has won so all shall have prizes"? *Clinical Psychology: Science and Practice, 2*(1), 106-109.

Luborsky, L., Crits-Christoph, P., Mellon, J. (1986). Advent of objective measures of the transference concept. *Journal of Consulting & Clinical Psychology, 54*(1), 39-47.

Luborsky, L., Singer, B., & Luborsky, L. (1975). Comparative studies of psychotherapies: Is it true that "Everyone has won and all must have prizes"? *Archives of General Psychiatry, 32,* 995-1007.

Mrazek, P. J., & Haggerty, R. J. (Eds.). (1994). Reducing risks for mental disorders: Frontiers for preventive intervention research. Washington, DC: National Academy Press.

Munoz, R. F. (1987). Depression prevention research: Conceptual and practical considerations. In R. F. Munoz (Ed.), *Depression prevention: Research directions.* Washington, DC: Hemisphere.

Munoz, R. F., Mrazek, P. J., & Haggerty, R. J. (1996). Institute of Medicine report on prevention of mental disorders. *American Psychologist, 51,* 1116-1122.

Murray, C. J. L., & Lopez, A. D. (1997). Global mortality, disability, and the contribution of risk factors: Global burden of disease study. *Lancet, 349,* 1436-1442.

Musselman, D. L., Evans, D. L., & Nemeroff, C. B. (1998). The relationship of depression to cardiovascular disease. *Archives of General Psychiatry, 55,* 580-592.

Nolen-Hoeksema, S., Girgus, J. S., & Seligman, M. E. P. (1992). Predictors and consequences of childhood depressive symptoms: A 5-year longitudinal study. *Journal of Abnormal Psychology, 10,* 405-422.

Pagliaro, L. A. (1995). Adolescent depression and suicide: A review and analysis of the current literature. *Canadian Journal of School Psychology, 11*(2), 191-201.

Parker, G. (1993). Parental rearing style: Examining for links with personal vulnerability factors for depression. *Social Psychiatry and Psychiatric Epidemiology, 28,* 97-100.

Petersen, A. C., Leffert, N., Graham, B., Alwin, J., & Ding, S. (1997). Promoting mental health during the transition into adolescence. In J. Schulenberg, J. L. Maggs, & A. K. Hierrelmann (Eds.), Health risks and developmental transitions during adolescence (pp. 471-497). New York: Cambridge University Press.

Peterson, C., & Seligman, M. E. P. (1984). Causal explanations as a risk factor for depression: Theory and evidence. *Psychological Review, 91,* 347-374.

Peterson, C., Seligman, M. E. P., & Vaillant, G. (1988). Pessimistic explanatory style as a risk factor for physical illness: A thirty-five-year longitudinal study. *Journal of Personality and Social Psychology, 55,* 23-27.

Riggs, P. D., Baker, S., Mikulich, S. K., & Young, S. E. (1995). Depression in substance-dependent delinquents. *Journal of the American Academy of Child and Adolescent Psychiatry, 34*(6), 764-771.

Robins, L. N., Helzer, J. E., Weissman, M. M., Orvaschel, H., Gruenberg, E., Burke, J. D., & Reiger, D. A. (1984). Lifetime prevalence of specific psychiatric disorders in three sites. *Archives of General Psychiatry, 41,* 949-958.

Seligman, M. E. P. (1998a). Building human strength: Psychology's forgotten mission. *APA Monitor, 29*(1).

Seligman, M. E. P. (1998b). Positive social science. *APA Monitor, 29*(4).

Seligman, M. E. P. (1998c). Work, love and play [President's column]. *APA Monitor Online, 29*(8). Retrieved July 3, 2002, from www.apa.org/monitor/aug98/pc.html

Seligman, M. E. P. (2002). Positive psychology, positive prevention, and positive therapy. In C. R. Snyder & S. Lopez (Eds.), *Handbook of positive psychology.* New York: Oxford University Press.

Seligman, M. E. P., Reivich, K., Jaycox, L., & Gillham, J. (1995). *The optimistic child.* New York: Houghton Mifflin.

Seligman, M. E. P., & Schulman, P. (1986). Explanatory style as a predictor of performance as a life insurance agent. *Journal of Personality and Social Psychology, 50,* 832-838.

CHAPTER 4

Child and Youth Well-Being
The Social Indicators Field

BRETT V. BROWN
KRISTIN MOORE

INTRODUCTION

Over the last decade, social indicators have become increasingly indispensable tools for policymakers, practitioners, and funders working to improve the well-being of children and youth. The social indicators field has blossomed at every level from the international arena to the local neighborhood, helping to do the following:

- Identify areas of need
- Monitor progress toward measurable social goals
- Coordinate activities across organizations
- Increase accountability for creating positive outcomes
- Assess policy and program effectiveness

The movement has been propelled forward by advances in the collection and dissemination of social indicators data, in the practical techniques and technical assistance available to promote their effective use, and in the underlying research base. The number of regularly fielded surveys collecting data on children and youth at the international, national, state, and local levels has increased dramatically since 1990 (Brown, 2001; Brown, Smith, & Harper, 2001). The number of reports on the condition of children, youth, and their families has also increased (Bradshaw & Barnes, 1999; Brown & Corbett, 2002). Moreover, practitioners have banded together in peer support networks to share information and resources on the proper use of social indicators data, and a number of national intermediary organizations have developed to provide technical assistance to such groups (Corbett, 2001; National Research Council and Institute of Medicine, 2002).

Though social indicators are first and foremost practical tools, the role of research and the researcher in advancing the field has been pivotal:

- Helping to identify the most important dimensions of well-being at each developmental stage.

- Mapping out the consequences of child and youth outcomes for long-term well-being.
- Identifying key social influences within the family, peer group, neighborhood, and community affecting the lives of children and youth throughout the development process.
- Identifying social programs and policies that are most effective in increasing the well-being of children and youth.
- Developing high-quality measures and instruments that capture the indicators accurately for the population as a whole and across key social subgroups.
- Establishing, where appropriate, defensible "cut points" from continuous measures that represent desirable or undesirable levels of well-being that are meaningful to practitioners, policymakers, and the public. This is done regularly with measures of scholastic achievement, for example, identifying cutoff levels qualifying as *basic, proficient,* and *advanced.*[1]

This chapter provides a broad overview of the child and youth indicators field. It is written with the researcher in mind, though we intend it to be useful to all interested readers. We begin with a background discussion of the properties of good child and youth indicators and systems of indictors. The body of the chapter recounts major developments over the last decade in social indicators research, data collection, dissemination, and application. We conclude with what we believe are the major opportunities in each of these areas for the coming decade and the role of the research community in making them happen.

CRITERIA FOR SOCIAL INDICATORS

Social indicators are quantitative measures of well-being that can be tracked over time and compared across social, economic, and other relevant social subgroups (Moore, 1997). Desirable properties include the following:

- *Intuitive and accessible.* Because they are predominantly tools to inform social action, social indicators must be easily understood by and meaningful to the nonscientific community, including policymakers, service providers, and citizens. So, for example, the National Education Goals Panel reported the percentage of youth who score high enough to be deemed *proficient* in math rather than reporting the average score on a scale from 0 to 800.

- *Measured on a regular basis.* Most of the uses of social indicators require that they be tracked over time. For this reason, most social indicators are taken from periodically administered cross-sectional surveys, such as the National Health Interview Survey, and regularly collected administrative data, such as birth registries.

- *Grounded in both science and social values.* When used in a policy context (which, broadly construed, is most often the case), the meaning of social indicators and the relative importance we assign to them are grounded both in science and in the values and goals of the social actors who make use of them.

- *Malleable.* Social indicators focus on aspects of well-being that are amenable to deliberate change through personal and/or social means.

- *Cost-efficient to collect.* Social indicators must be relatively economical to collect, because there is limited space on any survey instrument, and they must be collected on a regular basis. Measures based on intensive observation or long clinical diagnostic instruments are relatively expensive to collect and are for that reason impractical as social indicators. However, it is a common practice of social indicators researchers to begin with detailed indices or diagnostic batteries and create much shorter versions for administration in periodic surveys (see, for example, Moore, Halle, Vandivere, & Mariner, 2002).

- *Robust across population subgroups and over time.* Indicators should work well across gender, race/ethnicity, culture, and socioeconomic subgroups so that the experiences of children and youth in these key social cleavages can be compared. Likewise, their meaning should be consistent over time so that time trends can be followed. For example, with the development of the Internet, e-mail, and instant messaging, the meaning of "having a computer in the home" has changed dramatically in the last decade, even in the last several years.

- *Representative.* It is crucial that social indicators be based on data collection and sampling techniques that produce consistent estimates and are representative of the population of interest. Nonrigorous techniques (e.g., convenience samples, snowball samples) can provide misleading estimates and false trends. In practice, this can result in poor policy decisions that work against the interests of children and youth.

- *Based on high quality measures.* As in research, measures used for social indicators should be valid, accurately reflecting the construct they are intended to capture, and reliable, so that observed movement represents real change and not measurement volatility. When scales are used, they should have moderate-to-high internal reliability. The need for high-quality measurement sometimes conflicts with the need to be cost-efficient. In such cases, the challenge for the survey designer working in the social indicators field is to design measures that adequately capture a construct in the fewest number of questions possible.

Whole systems of child and youth indicators should have the following properties:

- *Comprehensive coverage.* Systems of indicators should provide a complete portrait covering all major life domains. A number of similar frameworks have been used to identify the key domains (Land, 2000; U.S. Department of Health and Human Services, 2001). At a minimum, a framework would include social and emotional development, physical health and safety, and intellectual/skill development. The outcomes identified for each domain would be informed by scientific theory and current research, as well as commonly held social values.

- *Developmentally sensitive.* Indicators should cover all developmental periods with measures appropriate to the central tasks and risks faced in each developmental period. These periods are generally operationalized as infancy, early childhood (age 0-5), middle childhood (age 6-11), adolescence (age 12-17), and the transition to adulthood (age 18-24). These broader age categories are sometimes subdivided in half to reflect the reality that developmental change can be quite rapid during childhood. Each stage will have indicators peculiar to itself, and often the same indicators will be operationalized differently across developmental periods.

- *Reflect social context.* Indicators of the social context that shape child and youth outcomes should be included in any complete system of child and youth indicators. These include the material and social elements of the family, peer, neighborhood, and institutional environments.

- *Geographically detailed.* The planning of activities, policies, and programs affecting children and youth happens at all geographic levels, including the nation, the state, the community, and even the neighborhood. The devolution of governmental responsibilities from the federal to the state and local levels in recent years merely underscores the need for a strong system of indicators at each of these levels.

- *Population subgroup estimates.* Data systems used to produce social indicators should be able to track separately the well-being of subgroups defined by key social cleavages such as gender (males and females), socioeconomic status (e.g., poor and nonpoor) race/ethnicity (white, black, Asian, Hispanic) and family structure (two parent, single parent).

• *Reflect well-being and well-becoming.* The meaning and relative importance of social indicators indicate both the current well-being of youth and future well-being, sometimes referred to as *well-becoming.* (Ben-Arieh et al., 2001). For example, adolescent depression is important both because of the current misery it reflects and because of what it portends for future happiness and successful transition to adulthood.

• *Positive and negative outcomes.* Because so many of our government programs have been set up to address social problems and social needs, the data systems developed to support their work tend to focus on negative behaviors, outcomes, and conditions. As a result, our systems of child and youth indicators and the research that helped to create them have focused overly on negative outcomes and risk factors. However, in the last decade, there has been a strong movement toward a *positive development* framework, particularly in youth programs and community-based programs of all sorts (Pittman, Irby, & Ferber, 2000). Karen Pittman, of the International Youth Foundation, summarizes the feelings of many program staff, parents, and youth when she says that "problem free is not fully prepared" (Pittman & Irby, 1996). This is an area in which there is much work to be done in measurement and data development.

• *Forward-looking.* To the extent possible, indicators systems should try to anticipate new social developments requiring new measures. This is important in order to provide baseline data for emerging trends. For example, children's access to, time on, and activities on the Internet are quickly

becoming an important part of their daily lives in ways that may have important implications for parenting, education, the reproduction of poverty and privilege, and for social policy in general (Novak & Hoffman, 1998; Papert & Negroponte, 1996). Unfortunately, even now, the measures and data sources for tracking these activities are meager.

A BRIEF HISTORY OF SOCIAL INDICATORS IN THE UNITED STATES

The use of social indicators as practical tools in the United States extends at least to the 1920s, with the development of a "community scorecard" by the U.S. Department of Interior's Bureau of Education. The scorecard was intended to "direct the attention of communities to important factors in their organization and maintenance and to supply a measuring stick by which they can rate themselves with reference to other communities" (Federal Council of Citizenship Training, 1924). The scorecard covered the following dimensions of well-being: mental development, health and physical development, vocational development, patriotic development (citizenship), and social and moral development.[2] A short time later, *Recent Trends in the United States* was released (President's Research Committee on Social Trends, 1933), a path-breaking national report created under the supervision of William Ogburn, chair of Herbert Hoover's Research Committee on Social Trends (Land, 2000).

The collection and use of social indicators took another leap at the national level during the 1960s and 1970s, partly in response to the expansion of federal social programs (Kingsley, 1998). By the 1970s, social indicators had become sufficiently important that the Social Science Research Council established of the Center for the Coordination of

Research on Social Indicators (CCSC). The goal of the CCSC was to establish a comprehensive system of child and family indicators and the means to track them. The CCSC understood the policy relevance of its work but was focused more on the scientific implications of such a system for increasing our understanding of social change.

By the early 1980s, however, support for child, youth, and family indicators had waned. The CCSC closed its doors. A few activities did continue during this period. A Congressional committee, the Select Committee on Children, Youth, and Families, released several comprehensive reports prepared by Child Trends on the condition of children and youth, which featured indicators data culled from across the federal data system (Select Committee on Children, Youth, and Families 1983, 1987, 1989). On the whole, however, there was little activity.

A decade later, the social indicators field began a revival and since that time has experienced strong and steady growth in all aspects of the field and at every geographic level. Reasons identified for that revival include the devolution of power from the federal to the state and local levels, and the ongoing information technology (IT) revolution (Brown & Corbett, 2002; Kingsley, 1998). Devolution created a need for more and better data at the state and local levels to support planning, goals tracking, and accountability. It also placed a greater emphasis on achieving measurable outcomes rather than carrying out particular federally designed programs. The IT revolution has made the collection, manipulation, and dissemination of all data, including social indicators data, much cheaper. It has also vastly expanded the audience of potential users as larger and larger segments of the population have direct access to powerful computers and the Internet.

INDICATORS OF CHILD, YOUTH, AND FAMILY WELL-BEING: A DECADE OF PROGRESS

The 1990s was a decade of rejuvenation and development in the child and youth indicators field. In this section of the report, we highlight key developments and activities during that period in the areas of practice, data development, dissemination, and research.[3]

Child and Youth Indicators in Practice

Social indicators of child, youth, and family well-being are being used for a number of different purposes. Most of the uses are applied, though they are used for purely scientific purposes as well. All of these uses are important to understand, because they put a somewhat different set of requirements on the indicators and the data systems used to track them.[4]

Monitoring and Needs Assessment. Indicators are commonly used to monitor well-being and assess social needs and social resources, often as a prelude to action. For example, the U.S. Centers for Disease Control and Prevention (CDC) has set up a variety of health and disease surveillance systems to identify emerging threats to the health of the nation, as well as to specific communities and population subgroups throughout the country. In addition to monitoring, which requires ongoing measurement, indicators are often used for one-time needs and assets assessments to guide program development and deployment. For example, hundreds of communities focusing on the needs of youth have fielded the Search Institute's Profiles of Student Life: Attitudes and Behaviors Survey (PSL-AB) to identify areas of need, as well as the personal and social assets that can be mobilized to meet needs and improve outcomes for youth.

Goals Tracking. Social indicators are also commonly used to track progress toward measurable goals that have been adopted by whole communities, states, or the nation. These entities commonly begin with a benchmark measurement to establish the current level of the indicator (e.g., the percentage of youth who get regular exercise) and proceed to adopt an attainable goal to be achieved over, for example, a 5- to 10-year period. These are intended to focus participating government and civic organizations on a limited set of common goals. Participating groups often will adopt measurable goals of their own that are related to the larger goal but that will reflect the fruits of their own activities (e.g., for a community-wide goal of improving the physical health of youth, a local school system may focus on increasing the percentage of public high school students who take physical education classes). A variant on this approach is based on the notion of *continuous improvement,* in which indicators are used to track progress over time, though no specific targets are set.

The federal government has launched two major goal-driven initiatives affecting children and youth, one in health, and the other in education. The Healthy People initiative, developed by the U.S. Department of Health and Human Services, is a comprehensive effort to improve the health of all Americans. Healthy People 2010 (HP2010), the latest incarnation of the initiative, identifies 467 specific, measurable objectives for the coming decade, many of which are directly relevant for children and youth. The objectives were identified in concert with 250 state agencies and several hundred national organizations, most of which have planned activities that will be pivotal in achieving the goals. Nearly all states and many communities have their own HP2010 efforts, using the national objectives

as guidelines, while setting reachable goals for their own populations. Toward this end, there has been a great deal of data development at the national, state, and local levels over the last several decades, so that objectives can be benchmarked and progress can be tracked over time.

The Education Goals 2000 initiative, launched in 1989 and adopted into law in 1994, set eight national goals, including goals to increase early school readiness; to promote competency in reading, math, science, languages, civics, economics, the arts, history, and geography; and to increase high school graduation rates. The National Education Goals Panel (NEGP), a bipartisan, multilevel government effort, encouraged the voluntary adoption of specific education standards among the states (49 states now have them in some form) and worked to increase the supply of comparable state level data to measure educational progress, in part through encouraging state participation in the National Assessment of Educational Progress. Its flagship report, the annual *National Education Goals Report,* provided state level estimates on 34 indicators related to the national goals.[5]

States have been very active participants in both of these federally coordinated initiatives, but have also been quite active on their own. The Oregon Benchmarks initiative is the oldest and most developed comprehensive state initiative seeking to base state planning across agencies, at the state and local levels, inside and outside of government, on a limited set of achievable goals that are quantifiable and tracked over time. The initiative process was launched in a series of public meetings in 1989. The initiative is currently focusing on 90 benchmarks, with specific goals for 2005 and 2010. Goal areas include the economy, education, civic engagement, social support, public safety, community development, and the environment. State agencies must address all relevant benchmark goals in their annual budget justifications. At the local level, local commissions in each county focusing on child and family benchmarks engage in comprehensive community planning to meet local goals.

Results-Based Accountability. Government and private funders are increasingly using social indicators to hold states, communities, agencies, and individual programs accountable for improving *outcomes* for children and youth. This represents a change from a period in which accountability was based on process (how well a program or policy was implemented) rather than outcome. The change to an outcomes focus is in part a result of the devolution of control over social policies and programs to lower levels of government, providing local actors with more program flexibility, while holding them accountable for the ultimate results. Which measures are used and the levels of improvement that must be met are commonly, though not always, negotiated. Failure to demonstrate improvement may result in additional technical assistance to overcome problems or, in some cases, may lead to reduced funding and loss of autonomy.

In the child and youth policy arena, this use of indicators has been most developed in public education, though private foundations and local governments are also beginning to adopt this approach for a variety of outcomes. The state of Virginia, for example, through its Standards of Learning (SOL) initiative, has a number of additional reporting and instructional requirements for poorly performing schools that fail to demonstrate improvement in student academic performance, and sanctions for schools that lose their accreditation.

Accountability can be based on reward as well as sanctions. As part of the SOL program, Virginia offers rewards to high-performing schools in the form of exemption from certain regulations and reporting requirements. At the federal level, under the Temporary Assistance for Needy Families (TANF) welfare reform, states that reduce the nonmarital birth rate the most without increasing the abortion rate have been rewarded with bonus payments in the millions of dollars each.

Reflective Practice. Communities and individual programs are using a social indicators approach to inform their own practice on an ongoing basis. Many develop formal logic models that relate particular program activities to expected outcomes for participating children, youth, and their families using an explicit theory of change (Gambone, 1998; United Way of America, 1999; Weiss, 1995).[6] In the case of a community-wide initiative, such a model would include input from multiple participating programs (public and private) as well as measurable outcomes for the community's children and youth. If program measures indicate that programs are being effectively implemented and well-being indicators move in the expected direction, then the initiative is judged to be effective. If the child and youth indicators do not move in the expected direction, then the underlying assumptions of the logic model are called into question and one or more aspects of the service approach are changed. Alternatively, if the logic model is sound, it could point to deficiencies in the *implementation* of the program. The process is similar for individual programs, though outcomes are generally limited to program participants.

At a practical level, reflective practice functions like an internal program evaluation. It lacks the methodological rigor to produce scientific knowledge but is an increasingly popular management tool for initiatives focused on child and youth well-being (National Research Council and Institute of Medicine, 2002).

Evaluation. Generally speaking, social indicators make poor tools for formal scientific evaluations of programs and policies. Such evaluations have depended primarily on experimental and quasi-experimental methods (Hollister & Hill, 1995). Traditionally, the role of indicators in evaluations has been very limited, functioning as "miners' canaries" identifying policies or programs that may be particularly promising (or dysfunctional) and deserving of formal evaluation using more rigorous techniques.

One area in which indicators have figured more prominently has been the evaluation of comprehensive community initiatives (CCIs). The intervention model of CCIs is complex, involving many programs, organizations, and services, and is intended to affect numerous outcomes at the community level. Their complexity and ubiquity makes standard evaluation techniques inapplicable, because no counterfactual comparison can be generated. Instead, evaluators have been working on an approach called *theory-driven evaluation,* which is based on the construction of complex logic models that relate changes in programs, services, and activities involved in the intervention to each other and to the final desired outcomes (e.g., improved early child development; see Connell & Kubisch, 1998). It looks similar to a path model. The evaluation is highly dependent on social indicators, including benchmark levels for each element in the model and monitoring changes in each indicator over time. This is a creative though controversial approach to evaluation, and it is still in its early stages of development.[7]

One such comprehensive community initiative is being carried out in Cleveland. The Cleveland Community-Building Initiative is focusing on four low-income neighborhoods in the city, using a comprehensive development approach that includes health, investment, education, family development, and human resource development. The evaluators, in this case, the Center for Urban Poverty and Social Change (all researchers based at Case Western Reserve University), worked with a variety of stakeholder groups, including the initiative's staff, board of trustees, and the village councils, to draw out and reconcile their respective *theories of change:* their concrete ideas on how this development would take place. Out of this came a detailed logic model to guide the projects and provide a framework for the evaluation. A series of indicators were chosen to reflect key elements of the logic model, and sources of data were identified for benchmarking and monitoring progress over time. The initiative is fortunate to have at its disposal one of the most advanced and comprehensive community Geographic Information System (GIS) databases in the country, the Cleveland Area Network for Data and Organizing (CANDO), developed by the evaluation team. Data from CANDO provide information for planning and provide feedback to stakeholders, who, in response, evaluate and modify their activities on an ongoing basis.

Other Scientific Uses. Social indicators are also used simply to inform and improve our understanding of social change. Social scientists are often inspired by the coincidence of change in several indicators (for example, decreases in youth employment rates and increases in crime) to develop hypotheses that they pursue using more rigorous methods. Macrolevel models using social indicators data, common in the field of economics, can be used to model the likely ripple effects of social change from one area to another. For example, on the basis of research (e.g., Maynard, 1997), one could develop a model to predict the effects of a 10% reduction in teen birth rates on a host of other outcomes, from high school completion to marriage rates, family income, infant health, and so on.

Limitations. Social indicators can be powerful tools for science and social policy, but they also have significant limitations and are subject to unintended and, occasionally, deliberate misuse, resulting in poor policy outcomes.[8] A major limitation is the well-documented lack of data for some important aspects of child and youth well-being, particularly at the state and community levels (Brown, 1997; Coulton & Hollister, 1998). Many aspects of well-being can only be tracked with surveys, which are relatively plentiful at the national level but not commonly available in communities. In addition, high-quality measures are simply lacking for many outcomes, including mental health, disability, and many aspects of positive youth development (Federal Interagency Forum on Child and Family Statistics, 2001; Hogan, Rogers, & Msall, 2000; Moore, Evans, Brooks-Gunn, & Roth, 2001).

The lack of adequate training by and technical assistance for practitioners and policymakers who would use social indicators leads to underuse and, on occasion, misuse of these important tools. Common problems include the use of poor-quality data, the use of inappropriate or weak measures, and the tendency to draw causal conclusions when they are not supported by the data or the methodology. In addition to lack of training, political pressures can produce a similar set of problems. This is particularly likely when indicators are used to enforce accountability or when proponents are motivated to use positive or negative trends for their political advantage.

These limitations can be addressed to some extent through basic research, data development, and the expansion of training and technical assistance. Indeed, the last decade has seen significant progress in all these areas (Child Trends, 2001). The remaining challenges are substantial, however, and their limitations should be kept firmly in mind.

Data Development

The capacity to track change over time is the hallmark of a social indicators data system. Such a system relies on two sources: repeated, cross-sectional surveys and censuses (e.g., the Current Population Surveys), and administrative data (birth and death records, disease registries, child abuse and neglect reports, school graduation records, and program data).

There has been a substantial expansion in the amount and the variety of child and youth indicators data available at all geographic levels, from the international level to the local community. The national level clearly enjoys the richest resources, though the state level has seen the greatest expansion of data collected in the last decade (Brown, 2001).

International Estimates

The United States participates in a number of periodically fielded international surveys on children and youth, as well as others that may or may not be repeated in the future. International comparisons of well-being are important because they provide a larger policy context in which to evaluate the well-being of our children. In addition, such comparisons are of practical importance in an increasingly competitive global environment.[9]

Most of these surveys are education related. They include the Trends in Mathematics and Science Study (TIMSS, fielded in 1995, 1999, and 2003), the IEA Civics Study (1997-98), the Program for International Student Assessment (PISA), and the Progress in International Reading Study (PIRLS, 2001). TIMSS collects data on youth in the fourth and eighth grades; the IEA Civics Study, on 14-year-olds; and PIRLS, on youth in the fourth grade. All collect detailed information, including skill assessments, activities known to affect attainment (e.g., study and television habits), and detailed measures of the family and school context. These surveys allow for systematic comparisons of U.S. student achievement and social environments with dozens of developed and developing countries around the world.

In addition, the United States recently entered into two health-related international surveys of youth. The Health Behavior of School-Aged Children (HBSC) is a long-standing survey of 11-, 13-, and 15-year-olds focusing on health-related behaviors and their determinants. It has been fielded approximately every 4 years and currently includes more than 27 countries. The HBSC, developed with the support of the World Health Organization-Europe, includes countries in Eastern and Western Europe, as well as Canada, the United States, and Israel. The United States participated in the 1997 to 98 survey and is participating in the 2001 to 2002 survey. Data on a wide variety of positive and negative health behaviors and statuses are collected, as well as characteristics of the family, peer, and school environments. Another health survey, the Global Youth Tobacco Survey, has been collected in 40 countries, with another 38 countries in the process of fielding the survey. This survey, first fielded in the United States in 1999, includes detailed questions on tobacco use and attitudes about use among students in the 6th through 12th grades.

National Estimates

Despite some important gaps, the United States has perhaps the richest variety and depth of regularly collected child and youth indicators data of any country in the world. During the 1990s, there were important enhancements to the data system's ability to produce national level estimates of child well-being, but perhaps the most important development was the creation of the Federal Interagency Forum on Child and Family

Statistics (the Forum). The Forum, a consortium of 20 federal statistical agencies, was formally established in 1997 by executive order of the President of the United States with the mission to "foster coordination and collaboration in the collection and reporting of Federal data on children and families" (Federal Interagency Forum on Child and Family Statistics, 2001, inside cover page). The Forum has chosen to focus much of its initial efforts on the development and dissemination of child and youth indicators, as well as improving data collection in the areas of fatherhood and family structure. Their premier product is the annual *America's Children* report, described in the section on dissemination (next). In producing that collection of essential indicators measures, the Forum has also identified important dimensions of well-being for which high-quality national estimates are not currently available. These include indicators of disability, child mental health, child abuse and neglect, parent/child interactions, time use, neighborhood quality, early child development, homelessness, and positive development. Participating agencies are working alone and in concert with other member agencies to address many of these shortcomings. Current joint activities include research and measurement development on children's disabilities, fathering, marriage and family structure, and mental health. Despite these important gaps, the existing data system provides regular estimates on hundreds of important indicators of child, youth, and family well-being.

National Health Indicators Data. The amount of data on health status and disease prevalence among children and youth is very substantial. These include data from the birth and death records of the vital statistics system (collected continuously); health status, behaviors, and service receipt from the National Health Information Survey (NHIS, annual); early child immunization data from the National Immunization Survey (annual); detailed medical data based on medical examination and interview from the National Health and Nutrition Examination Survey (NHANES, collected about every 6 years); detailed youth drug use from the National Household Survey of Drug Abuse (NHSDA, annual); and measures of drug use, sexual activity, violence, suicide ideation, physical activity, and nutrition among students in grades 9 to 12 from the Youth Risk Behavior Survey (YRBS, biennial). In addition, Monitoring the Future (MTF) has collected data on 12th-grade youth on an annual basis since 1976 and on 8th- and 10th-grade youth since 1991; it focuses on drug use but also asks questions on attitudes and values covering a wide variety of topics, as well as measures of religious, political, and volunteer activities; happiness, self-esteem, and locus of control; and risk behaviors, violence, and victimization.

National Education Indicators Data. In education, there are three primary sources of social indicators data. For assessments of academic achievement, the National Assessment of Educational Progress (NAEP) has been tracking performance with periodic assessments in math, science, reading, writing, history, civics, and the arts since 1969 (about every 2 to 6 years, depending on the topic). It also includes a number of activities known or believed to affect achievement, including hours of homework, television-watching habits, and access to a computer in the home. The NAEP focuses on youth in the 4th, 8th, and 12th grades.[10]

The National Household Education Survey (NHES) is a general-purpose education survey designed primarily to provide trend data on issues of importance to policymakers, researchers, and educators. Broad topic areas are covered in detail on a rotating

basis about every 4 years. These include parent and family involvement in education, early childhood program participation, before- and after-school programs and activities, and school readiness.

The third mainstay of education indicators is the annual October supplement to the Current Population Survey (CPS). The CPS is a monthly survey collecting data related to employment. The October supplement also collects data on a number of education-related topics, including enrollment and attainment, preschool attendance, language proficiency, disability, and computer access.

National Social and Emotional Well-Being Indicators Data. National indicators of the emotional well-being of children and youth are surprisingly limited. The YRBS asks teens if they have ever seriously contemplated or attempted to commit suicide, and the NHIS includes limited questions on behavioral and emotional problems for children and adolescents.

Indicators related to social well-being are much more numerous, though they tend to focus on negative behaviors of youth related to violence, drug use, and sexual activity. The sources for these data include the YRBS, the NHSDA, the MTF, and birth record data. Estimates of children and youth as victims of crime are limited to child abuse and neglect data gathered through the National Child Abuse and Neglect Data System (NCANDS, continuous) and to victimization of youth data on a wide variety of crimes through the National Crime Victimization Survey (NCVS, annual).

Some positive measures related to civic involvement, volunteering, and prosocial values are available from the MTF and the NHES. Repeated national estimates for any of these measures are not available for children below the age of 12.

National Social Context Indicators Data. The family is the most critical social environment affecting the development of children and youth and the best represented in the national statistical system. Detailed family structure and family economic characteristics are available annually from the March Current Population Survey (annual). This is the primary source for such indicators. The American Housing Survey provides data on children's housing quality, and the Survey of Income and Program Participation is a source for some detailed family and economic characteristics not covered by the March CPS. The social dynamics of families (e.g., parent and child time together, parenting styles, conflict resolution techniques, religious activities) are, unfortunately, not well represented in regularly fielded national surveys, though they are present in special surveys, such as the National Surveys of Families and Households, the National Longitudinal Survey of Adolescent Health (Add-Health), the Panel Study of Income Dynamics, the National Longitudinal Survey of Youth 1997 Cohort, and the Early Childhood Longitudinal Surveys.

Indicators of the community environment in national data sources are limited primarily to indicators of the school environment, which are present in several surveys sponsored by the National Center for Education Statistics, including the Common Core of Data (annual) the Schools and Staffing Survey (every 4 to 6 years), and the NHES. Sociodemographic indicators of children's neighborhoods (e.g., percent of neighbors who are poor, single-parent families, or in the labor force) have been generated from the U.S. Census, but these are available only once every 10 years.

Data on the friends and peers of children and youth are also scarce in regularly fielded national surveys. There are some questions about peer norms and beliefs in the MTF,

and the HBSC asks some questions about perceived peer support and number of close friends. National estimates for such measures prior to adolescence are nonexistent.

State and Local Estimates

The last decade has produced substantial increases in the amount and the breadth of child and youth indicators data available at the state and local levels through the federal statistical system, though they still lag far behind what is available at the national level. Indicators-driven national initiatives such as Healthy People 2000 (and now 2010), and National Education Goals 2000 were in no small part responsible for this increase, though it is also a response to the generally increased need for such data by state and local governments.[11]

In the education area, the NAEP was extended in 1990 on a voluntary basis to the state level in the areas of reading, writing, math, and science. In 2001, 41 states participated. In addition, in recent years, most states have adopted their own comprehensive systems of regular educational assessment for children and youth from the third grade and up, with results often available down to the individual school level (Archbald, 1998).

The Schools and Staffing Survey (SASS), first fielded in the late 1980s and repeated about every 4 years, provides state level estimates of student and staff characteristics, staffing patterns, programs and services offered, and graduation rates for both public and private schools. Some of these indicators are also available on an annual basis from the Common Core of Data (CCD), which is also capable of producing estimates for school districts. Data from the CCD are limited to public schools, however.

In the health area, the vital statistics system is the major source of community level data for a host of birth- and death-related indicators, including prenatal care receipt, low birthweight, smoking and drinking during pregnancy, death rates by age, and for major causes of child and youth death. For many small communities, the incidence of these events is small enough that several years of data must be combined to produce stable estimates.

A number of disease surveillance systems provide child- and youth-based estimates for states and major metropolitan areas for diseases, including HIV/AIDS, tuberculosis, and sexually transmitted diseases.

The CDC has, since 1990, designed and implemented several surveys specifically to help states and large cities track youth health risk behaviors. The YRBS (see above for details), which began in 1990, was fielded in 42 states and 16 major metropolitan areas in 1999. A handful of states have used their own financial resources to expand the survey sample so that indicators can be generated for individual school districts.

More recently, the National Youth Tobacco Survey (NYTS) has been fielded to gather detailed information on youth behaviors and attitudes related to smoking and tobacco use. The survey was fielded in 27 states in 2000, up from 3 states in 1998. A national sample is also surveyed. Fresh data are collected every year or two, depending on the state. The NYTS is administered to youth in grades 6 through 12, focusing on seven topic areas: tobacco use, tobacco-related knowledge and attitudes, the role of the media and advertising in young people's tobacco use, access to tobacco, exposure to tobacco-related school curriculum, exposure to secondary smoke, and cessation of use. Data are also collected internationally through the Global Youth Tobacco Survey.

A third survey, the Student Survey of Risk and Protective Factors, and Prevalence of Alcohol, Tobacco, and other Drug Use (SSRP), focuses on risk and protective factors influencing drug use, violence, and other

behavior problems for youth age 12 to 18. Although direct measures of youth outcomes are focused on these negative behaviors, measures related to family, peer, and school influences are more well-rounded, with many positive measures such as close and supportive parent-child relationships and perceptions of the availability of useful roles for youth in the community. Most of the indicators are based on multi-item scales, with strong psychometric properties and strong grounding in the research literature. The survey, which was developed by the Social Development Research Group at the University of Washington,[12] is being field-tested in six states and is intended for use by states, communities, and youth programs.

In addition to these efforts, the National Institute for Drug Abuse (NIDA) recently expanded the sample size of the NHSDA so that annual state level estimates of drug abuse can be generated for youth age 12 to 17 and 18 to 25. Though less detailed than the other surveys discussed above, the survey includes youth who are out of school, which the others do not.

The CDC has also been active in developing state surveys for the other end of the child age spectrum. Since 1994, the National Immunization Survey (NIS) has provided detailed estimates of immunization among 2-year-olds on an annual basis for each of the 50 states and selected major metropolitan areas. Another survey, the Pregnancy Risk Assessment Monitoring System (PRAMS), provides data that include detailed information on prenatal care receipt; maternal attitudes about the pregnancy, illness, and other health-related problems during pregnancy; infant health care receipt; sleeping position; and breast-feeding practices; The survey, which began in 1987, is now fielded on an annual basis in 22 states and in New York City.

In the area of child welfare, two national reporting systems developed during the last

10 years provide state level estimates for child abuse, neglect, adoption, and foster care. These are the National Child Abuse and Neglect Data System (NCANDS) and the Adoption and Foster Care Analysis System (AFCARS) (U.S. Department of Health and Human Services, 2000). These systems are intended to provide a core set of indicators that are common across states, though differences in state definitions and practices limit the comparability that can be achieved.

For detailed demographic and socioeconomic data on children and their families at the state and local level, the decennial census is the major data source. Its strength is its capacity to provide data for very small geographic areas, down to the city block level for some measures. Its major weakness, from the standpoint of users, is the fact that data are collected only once every 10 years. That limitation is about to be overcome, however. Beginning in 2003, the American Community Survey (ACS) will provide annually updated estimates of virtually all measures now collected in the decennial census. The survey will produce independent annual estimates for states and large communities and 5-year rolling average estimates down to the census track level. The importance of this survey for those who depend on social indicators at the state and local level can hardly be overestimated.

In addition to this, the Census Bureau recently started producing estimates of child poverty for every county in the country. Estimates have been generated for 1989, 1993, 1995, and 1997. In the future, state level estimates will be produced annually, and estimates for counties and school districts every other year.

A limited set of sociodemographic estimates of child well-being are also being produced using the CPS (see above). Federal agencies have put out a very limited number of such estimates. The Annie E. Casey Foundation has used this extensively to produce state level estimates for its annual Kids Count report. Small-state sample sizes in the CPS mean that several years of data must be combined to produce stable estimates, and even then, estimates for smaller states have a wide margin of error. Beginning in 2001, however, the sample sizes for the CPS, especially the March CPS, were substantially expanded to increase the stability of state level estimates.

DISSEMINATION

In the last decade, there has been an explosion in the dissemination of child, youth, and family well-being indicators data. The reasons for this include more available data, better technology for dissemination (i.e., the Internet), and more interested users. Publications include issue-specific and cross-cutting reports, in hard copy and on-line. Most are written for a broad audience.

Federal agencies have developed several cross-cutting compendia that include trend data on many domains of child and youth well-being. *Trends in the Well-Being of America's Children and Youth*, updated annually and disseminated by the Office of the Assistant Secretary for Planning and Evaluation of the U.S. Department of Health and Human Services, contains national estimates for more than 100 indicators of child and youth well-being. Each indicator includes a brief, research-based discussion of why the indicator is important, followed by a description of historical trends and salient population subgroup differences (e.g., by gender, race, and poverty status), plus accompanying figures and tables. The indicators initially chosen for the volume were based on recommendations from papers presented at a major national research conference on child and youth indicators held in 1994 (Hauser, Brown, & Prosser, 1997).

America's Children: Key National Indicators of Well-Being is an annual report to the President of the United States. Initially released in 1997, it is the flagship document of the Federal Interagency Forum on Child and Family Statistics. The report contains trend data for a stable set of 24 indicators of child and youth well-being across four domains of well-being (economic security, health, behavior and social environment, and education) and one or more "special features" that change each year.

Finally, *Youth Indicators*, produced by the U.S. National Center for Education Statistics approximately every 3 years, contains trend data on more than 60 indicators for youth in the areas of family, education, work, health, behaviors, and attitudes.

In addition, many area-specific and survey-specific national publications contain child and youth indicators data disseminated by federal agencies in hard copy and over the Internet. *Health, United States,* produced by the CDC, is an annual report presenting trend data on more than 140 health and health-related indicators, many of which focus on or include estimates for children and youth. The report draws on a wide variety of data sources. Another annual report, *Child Health USA,* provides trend data for more than 40 indicators of child health on an annual basis.

The U.S. Department of Education produces two major annual compendia of education statistics: the *Digest of Education Statistics* and the *Condition of Education.* Both draw on a wide variety of data sources. The National Education Goals Panel, an independent agency no longer in existence, produced the annual *National Education Goals Report.*

In addition to these compendia, most of the data sources described in the previous section have their own regular publication series. Finding these publications can be a challenge for the uninitiated. Recently, however, the Federal Interagency Forum on Child and Family Statistics has begun to list such publications by topic area on its Web site, with links to individual agency Web sites (see Appendix, end of this chapter). For a guide to federal reports containing state and local level indicators of child and youth well-being, see Brown (2001).

Kids Count, sponsored by the Annie E. Casey Foundation since 1990, is the most widely known and far-reaching effort by a nongovernmental organization to disseminate social indicators data on children and youth. The national Kids Count group produces an annual report featuring comparable indicators for each of the 50 states and the District of Columbia and produces occasional reports on specific topics, with data for both state and major metropolitan areas. In addition, Kids Count organizations within each state produce their own annual reports featuring social indicators data at the county level. Most of the state project reports are produced and used by child advocacy organizations to further the cause of children and youth, though state agencies are the main sponsors in a few states.

State governments and state agencies have also become increasingly active in the dissemination of social indicators data on child development and well-being. A number of states have multiagency projects devoted to the dissemination and active use of indicators data to inform planning and policy development at the state and community levels. The state of Vermont, for example, has developed a series called *Community Profiles,* which provides essential trend data on the well-being of children, youth, and families in each community, drawing on a variety of administrative and survey data resources. The state of Minnesota puts out a *Children's Report Card* series, which reports on 26 indicators of child and youth well-being for each county in the state. Massachusetts has developed the Massachusetts Community Health

Information Profile (MassCHIP) system, which provides access to community level data from more than 24 data sets, including many measures on children, youth, and their families.

Many states also produce and disseminate education "report cards" on a regular basis, drawing on their own assessment and school administrative data. The reports are commonly used to support education accountability initiatives and are often widely disseminated to parents as well. Similar reports focused on youth health data are also produced on a regular basis by state health or education departments.

Finally, there has been a strong movement at the state and community level to produce comprehensive indicators databases to support social planning and increase accountability. This development has only been made possible by the declining costs of collecting, storing, manipulating, and accessing data in an electronic format that have taken place in the last decade. At the state level, there has been a movement to develop data warehouses that provide one-stop access to social indicators and program data collected across many state agencies.

At the community level, it takes the form of GIS-based databases that allow communities to generate indicators down to the neighborhood level. Using these diverse data resources, it is possible to develop complex profiles of needs and resources for neighborhoods throughout the community and identify areas of need. They would also form the data backbone for any evaluation of a comprehensive community initiative (for details, see Coulton & Hollister, 1998).

Interestingly, many of the community databases are being developed by nonprofit organizations outside the government to support community development. Projects in 12 cities are sharing information and doing peer consulting through the National Neighborhood Indicators Project (NNIP), coordinated by the Urban Institute and funded by the Annie E. Casey and Rockefeller Foundations. Perhaps the most advanced of these efforts is the CANDO, headed by Claudia Coulton at the Center on Urban Poverty and Social Change. An interactive on-line database allows users to examine and map data for individual neighborhoods in the areas of economics, birth and death, housing, crime, and maltreatment, drawing on locally available administrative data sources.

Research

Theories and Frameworks

Basic research plays an important role in the social indicators field, helping to identify key constructs of well-being, the implications of that construct for long-term well-being, as well as elements of the social environment (family, peer, community) that influence development.

Most of this research has been carried out within frameworks specific to one stage of development. Early-childhood researchers commonly use a developmental/ecological framework such as that developed by Bronfenbrenner (Bronfenbrenner & Morris, 1998). Youth researchers have used a number of frameworks including deficit and risk resilience models that focus on negative behaviors and outcomes (Garmezy, 1991; Rutter, 1984) and more recently, more comprehensive developmental models that include positive outcomes and behaviors (Moore et al., in press; Moore & Glei, 1995; Seligman & Peterson, in press). Research on middle childhood (about age 6 to 11) has been sparse, though recent work has also adopted a developmental approach emphasizing outcomes that lay the foundation for adult competence (Ripke, Huston, & Eccles, 2001).

One of the contributions of the social indicators field has been to identify the need for a broader framework, one that encompasses every developmental period from infancy through the transition to adulthood and the links among those stages. Such a notion has not yet greatly penetrated basic research but is commonly used to identify holes in the existing system of social indicators measures that need attention from the research community (Federal Interagency Forum on Child and Family Statistics, 2001) and to organize comprehensive systems of data collection (Brooks-Gunn, Brown, Duncan, & Moore, 1995). Such a framework has three basic features:

- It is based on the whole child, covering all dimensions of well-being.
- It is developmental, focusing on essential developmental tasks (and risks) at each stage of development.
- It is ecological, incorporating key elements of the social environment affecting development at each stage.

Social Indicators Research. In 1994, a major national conference was held to assess the state of research on indicators of child and youth well-being and the measures and data available to track it. Papers were offered by national experts in the areas of health, education, social development, economic security, and social context (Hauser et al., 1997). Each paper identified key constructs of well-being for a particular domain and period of development (e.g., health indicators for preschool children), as well as areas in which further research was needed to carry the field forward. The results of this comprehensive review formed the scientific grounding for the U.S. Department of Health and Human Services annual report, *Trends in the Well-Being of America's Children and Youth,* containing trend data on more than 100 indicators, and *America's Children: Key*

National Indicators of Well-Being, previously mentioned.

The conference also identified major research gaps to be filled in the coming decade. These included the following:

- The need for better measures of positive outcomes for each developmental stage (Aber & Jones, 1997; Takanishi, Mortimer, & McGourthy, 1997)
- Measures of social development and health-related behaviors in early and middle childhood to match the considerable body of measures available for adolescents
- Strong measures of neighborhood quality, almost totally lacking at the time of the conference (Furstenberg & Hughes, 1997)
- Better measures for outcomes of particular social importance, including child abuse and neglect, mental health, school readiness, learning disabilities, parenting, and homelessness

In June 2001, 7 years later, a second conference was held to assess the progress that had been made, identify what remained to be accomplished and discuss new issues that had developed (for details, see Child Trends, 2001). Research advances and measurement development in the areas of school readiness, parent/child relationships, and neighborhood social context have been substantial (Eccles, Templeton, & Brown, 2001; Morenoff & Sampson, 2001; Ripke et al., 2001; Zaslow et al., 2001). Research on indicators of positive development had also started to progress, particularly in the youth development field (Roth, Borbely, & Brooks-Gunn, 2001). Work on indicators of psychological and social development in middle childhood had also advanced, as had appreciation for middle childhood as a distinct period of development. This has been made evident in the recent work of the MacArthur Research Network on Middle Childhood, whose representatives presented some of its findings at the conference (Ripke et al., 2001).

Authors have made the point, nevertheless, that positive indicators and indicators of early and middle childhood are areas in which a great deal of conceptual and measurement work remains to be done. In addition, work to explore the robustness of existing indicators across major socioeconomic and cultural subgroups is also needed. Finally, there is a clear need for researchers and practitioners in the social indicators field to work together more closely so that research can better reflect the needs of users.

Recent research to develop a single summary index of child well-being, similar in concept to the gross national product, was a central focus of discussion (Land, Lamb, & Mustillo, in press). A number of researchers have worked in recent years to develop such summary measures (Bennett, 2001; Land et al., in press; Miringoff, Miringoff, & Opdicke, 2001). The justification for the construction of such a measure is intuitively appealing, especially for journalists and those in the policy arena. With literally hundreds of indicators of child and youth well-being available, with some trends getting better while others are getting worse, there is a need for summary measures that let us know how children and youth are doing overall. Professor Kenneth Land has presented research in which he and colleagues thoroughly explore the potential for constructing such a measure as well as the limits to such an effort given currently available data.

CHALLENGES FOR THE COMING DECADE IN THE CHILD AND YOUTH INDICATORS FIELD

The child and youth indicators field has made great strides in the last decade in research, data development, data dissemination, and practical application. Indeed, the interdependent nature of these efforts requires advances in each area for the field as a whole to move forward. Below, we identify what we see as the greatest opportunities for the coming decade in each of these areas, with a particular eye to the role of researchers.

Research

A Single Theoretical Framework to Guide Child and Youth Indicators Research. The frameworks that have defined the basic research used in the social indicators field have tended to be particular to each developmental period, from the developmental framework of early-childhood research to the risk/resilience frameworks for adolescence and the transition to adulthood framework for older youth. Each area has been dominated by different disciplines (child psychologists for early childhood, health and education researchers for adolescence, sociologists and economists for the transition to adulthood), each of which has their own terminology and disciplinary biases.

We believe that the social indicators field has encouraged more cross-disciplinary approaches for research on each developmental stage, with the result that key constructs are increasingly shared. The notion of positive development, for example, once concentrated in early-childhood research, increasingly includes research on middle childhood and adolescence. The field would benefit if this convergence were done in a more deliberate manner, with the development of a single, developmentally and ecologically focused framework covering infancy through early adulthood. Such a framework would have maximum consistency of constructs across stages of development and well-delineated links from one developmental period to the next; would enrich research on children and youth in general; and would help to create a common language for the social indicators field.

A Focus on Indicators of Well-Being in Early and Middle Childhood. There is a relative wealth of indicators at infancy and youth, but for the period between those ages, the world of social indicators is sparsely populated. Over the last several years, there has been a substantial amount of research to identify key elements of early and middle child development and the contextual factors that assist or retard that development. This work needs to continue if the field is to agree on a common set of key constructs and develop effective measures that can be built into the regularly fielded surveys that support our system of social indicators. The Early Childhood Longitudinal Study is a very promising data resource for future research and measurement development in early and middle childhood. Data for the kindergarten cohort (ECLS-K) are already available, and more will become available as they are followed up through at least the 5th grade. A separate birth cohort (ELCS-B) who will be followed through entry into school will provide a rich and unique data source for development in early childhood.

More Research on Indicators of Positive Development and the Contextual Factors That Promote It. Indicators of positive outcomes are lacking in general, though particularly in the area of youth development. Federal programs have tended to focus on the incidence and the prevention of negative outcomes rather than building positive strengths, and this has skewed federally sponsored data collection and research. Measures of drug use, violence, unsafe and promiscuous sexual activity, and delinquency are common, but indicators of kindness, tolerance, character, volunteering, social capacity, emotional strength, and other positive attributes are both underdeveloped conceptually and rarely available in any form in existing survey data (Moore & Halle, 2001).

However, many practitioners at the community level who work with children and youth prefer to focus on positive development even among at-risk populations and are frustrated by the lack of positive indicators at their disposal (Murphey, 2001).

Research activities that are needed in this area include (a) analyzing existing national and local longitudinal databases that contain positive outcome measures to identify the antecedents and long-term consequences of positive development; (b) developing new measures and indices of positive youth development suitable for large-scale surveys and self-administered youth surveys; and (c) promoting methodological research, including qualitative studies, that will allow for the development of indicators that link positive child and adolescent outcomes to positive outcomes later in life.

Technical Work to Improve the Quality of New and Existing Indicators Measures. Measurement development is often not the most glamorous of research activities, but it is extremely important scientific work. Important activities for the social indicators field include the following:

• *Developing shorter indexes that can be included in large-scale surveys.* Many measures related to emotional well-being, for example, are based on a long battery of questions that are not suitable for large-scale surveys. Shorter indices based on the lengthy Child Behavior Checklist, for example, have been developed for the National Health Interview Survey and the National Longitudinal Survey of Youth 1997 Cohort (Moore et al., 2001).

• *Research to establish defensible cut points to categorize continuous measures.* Many of the measures developed to track well-being are continuous, but users often want to know at what point they should either swing into action or be satisfied with the results. Often, the answer to this question is subjective or political, but there are occasions when research can identify important nonlinearities that can be used to identify meaningful cut points. For example, cutoff points for depression based on continuous survey measures of mental health have been validated against clinical diagnoses (Devins & Orme, 1985).

- *Cross-cultural and cross-subgroup validation of existing indicators.* Many of the indicators of child and youth well-being have not been well tested on minority and low-income populations. In some cases, although constructs are valid across groups, the operationalization needs to be modified or broadened. Differences in cultural values may sometimes produce different indicators of positive development across groups (National Research Council and Institute of Medicine, 2002; Zaff, Blount, & Phillips, 1999). This need is especially urgent because many programs and policies focus on particular minority and low-income groups in which the use of existing indicators measures may be suboptimal or inappropriate.

Longitudinal Analyses to Identify the Indicators of Child and Youth Well-Being (and Contextual Factors) That Predict Most Strongly to a Successful Transition to Adulthood. The world of social policy is focused strongly on the long-term implications of child and youth development for productivity and well-being in adulthood. Yet the research that connects key markers of child and youth well-being to adult outcomes is surprisingly scant. This is particularly so at younger ages, but even critical aspects of youth well-being such as mental health and most aspects of positive development are not well understood as they relate to adult well-being. This is to some extent due to the lack of longitudinal data covering the appropriate

time span and the lack of a sufficiently broad set of measures in which longitudinal data are available. Several recent surveys, the National Longitudinal Survey of Adolescent Health (Add-Health), the National Longitudinal Survey of Youth 1997 Cohort (NLSY-97), and the National Education Longitudinal Survey 1988 (NELS88), contain many of the measures needed to substantially expand our understanding of the critical factors in adolescence leading to a healthy and successful transition to adulthood.

Focus Research on Critical Outcomes That Currently Lack Adequate Measures. Beyond the broad categories of indicators described above, a number of discrete indicators of particular importance to policy lack adequate measures. These include mental health, disability, child abuse and neglect, homelessness, and indicators of neighborhood quality. There are ongoing efforts to develop such measures in several of these areas. One effort, led by Dr. Dennis Hogan, of Brown University, and involving academic researchers and staff from major national statistical agencies is seeking to develop better measures of child and youth disability for use in future surveys (Hogan & Wells, 2001). This sort of active cooperation between researchers and the statistical agencies that design and field national surveys on children and youth can help to focus research where it is most needed and to quickly turn the fruits of that research into indicators data.

Dissemination

People can make use of indicators data only if they can find it easily and quickly understand its importance for their work and their lives. In the last several years, there has been an explosion of child and youth indicator reports, data books, fact sheets, report cards, databases, and other data-carrying vehicles, most of it available on the Internet. There are a number of practical and research-based steps that can be taken to improve effectiveness of these dissemination efforts.

Effectiveness Assessments of Child and Youth Indicators Dissemination Products. For all the publications out there, what little is known about their impact, who they reach, and how they are used is based largely on anecdote. Research to identify the most effective content, presentation, and marketing strategies for reaching key audiences (e.g., journalists, youth program staff, parents, etc.) could pay enormous dividends for the social indicators field.[13]

Access to Existing Reports Featuring Child and Youth Indicators Data. At the moment, there is no organized access to what are probably hundreds of relevant reports containing youth indicators data at the state and local levels. For the most part, they sit on individual agency Web sites, often unknown even to staff from other agencies in the same state. This produces a lot of "reinventing the wheel" by groups in other states seeking to develop similar publications and limits access to end users as well. An Internet porthole that provides organized access to these products could substantially expand their audiences and promote more efficient, rapid development of similar reports across the country.

Research to Determine Key Dimensions of Well-Being and Social Supports That Children and Youth Identify as Being Most Important to Them. We believe that children and youth are pivotal and poorly understood audiences for social indicators data about themselves and their social environment. Identifying measures that reflect and connect with the ways they think about their own lives and developing dissemination strategies that bring insights back to this audience is a

worthwhile and underdeveloped area in the indicators field.

Data Development

A number of concrete steps can be taken to improve the quality, breadth, and availability of child and youth indicators data collected in the coming decade.

Greater Coordination of Measures Between Longitudinal Surveys (In Which Research Critical to Indicators Development Usually Takes Place) and Cross-Sectional Surveys (In Which Indicators Are Tracked Over Time).[14] Longitudinal surveys cover many important dimensions of child and youth well-being, but rarely, if ever, is the construction of better social indicators measures a criterion in their design. As a result, they do not always cover issues of substantial importance to the indicators field. And when they do, the measures used in such surveys may be significantly different from those used to represent the same constructs in cross-sectional surveys. A more deliberate effort on the part of federal statistical agencies to coordinate the measures across these types of surveys could lead to what has been called a "system of continuous improvement" in our stock of child and youth indicators (Stagner & Zweig, 2001). For example, measures of early child development from the longitudinal ECLS-K could be analyzed specifically to identify key measures, which could then be added to the periodically fielded NHES survey.[15]

More Measures of Positive Child and Youth Development in Major Surveys. The development of strong measures of positive development is still in its infancy. Promising measures should be added whenever possible to major longitudinal surveys to support in-depth research that can lead to the identification of strong positive indicators. As they are identified, systematic efforts are needed to add them to the cross-sectional surveys that are the major source of indicators data.

Greater Availability of Data to Support State and Local Level Indicators Estimates. This is an area in which great progress has been made with the advent of community GIS databases and increases in the amount of survey and assessment data collected at the state and local levels. The need for such data, particularly data that can be collected only in surveys, far outstrips what is currently available in most states and communities. The YRBS offers an excellent model for the development and funding of surveys supporting indicators data collection at the state and local levels. In fact, the YRBS itself could be expanded with optional topical modules on positive development and other neglected areas.

Collection of Indicators Data on Out-Of-School Youth. The paucity of indicators data on out-of-school youth is largely a matter of economics; it is far cheaper to collect survey data on youth in school. Most of the major youth surveys, including Monitoring the Future, the Youth Risk Behavior Survey, the National Assessment of Educational Progress, the Youth Tobacco Survey, and the Profiles of Student Life: Attitudes and Behaviors Survey, are limited to youth attending school. There are ways to improve this situation, at least at the national level, by attaching special youth modules to household-based surveys. This was done in 1992, when the questions in the YRBS were fielded to youth in the NHIS. It should be done more systematically by federal data collection agencies. These youth are, after all, more likely to be at risk in many dimensions of well-being.

Practical Application

The use of social indicators to inform policy and practice is the driving force behind the growth in the child and youth indicators field. The continued development of the field will depend in no small part on the ability of the research community to provide the tools and technical assistance that practitioners need to carry out their work.

There are several notable examples of such work. Professor Clara Pratt, of Oregon State University, has been working for several years with the Oregon Office of Children and Families to overcome a significant limitation of the benchmark approach adopted throughout the state, namely, that such broad, goal-oriented indicators tend to change slowly and in response to the work of multiple influences. She and her colleagues have been working to identify *interim indicators* that are sensitive to short-term change and that can be tied to the activities of particular agencies or groups. "We are trying to help agencies figure out what their part of the elephant is" (Child Trends, 2000, p. 2; for details, see Pratt, Katzev, Henderson, & Ozretich 1997; Pratt, Katzev, Ozretich, Henderson, & McGuigan, 1998).

The Chapin Hall Center for Children, a nonprofit research organization located on the campus of the University of Chicago, has undertaken a number of practice-oriented indicators projects. For example, for the last several years, staff have been providing technical assistance to a consortium of agencies in 14 states that are working to institutionalize the use of child and youth indicators in their state planning processes. Chapin Hall researchers provide valuable expert advice on the choice, measurement, and application of social indicators and assist the states in developing a peer assistance network.

The National Neighborhood Indicators Project, located at the Urban Institute, in Washington, D.C., has been working for a number of years with community groups who are developing and employing their own indicators databases. In the process, it has developed a number of useful handbooks and guides for building community-based data systems and is using them effectively in local planning efforts.

The sort of research work just described is important to the future development of the child and youth indicators field. At present, the need far outstrips the amount of work being done, in part because the academic community does not tend to actively reward such practice-oriented research. To promote such work, we make the following recommendations:

• *Increase the involvement of top-flight social scientists in the development of practical tools for practitioners in the field.* The development of interim indicators and production of practical toolkits and guidebooks such as those described above are sorely needed, and more must be done to expand the pool of competent scientists involved in such activities. Although it can be difficult to change academic culture, it is possible to change the flow of funds to support this sort of work. If government agencies and private foundations that are interested in social indicators work increase the funding to support such research, more academics will be attracted to the field.

• *Increase new training opportunities for interested researchers.* This sort of research requires an understanding of research and measurement issues combined with a thorough grasp of the challenges of designing and executing child and youth programs and policies, a relatively rare combination. Training opportunities will be needed if we are to significantly expand the pool of researchers

working on these practice-focused activities. Supplementary funding to support such training would be usefully directed to the groups that are already the most active in this area, such as Chapin Hall, the NNIP, and Dr. Pratt's research group at the University of Oregon.

CONCLUSIONS

Indicators of child and youth well-being have become important everyday tools of social policy and practice, supporting activities ranging from planning and needs assessment to goals tracking, accountability, reflective practice, and in some circumstances, program evaluation. They are used at every level, from international planning bodies such as the World Health Organization down to local community planning boards and individual child and youth programs.

Over the last decade, the use of social indicators has expanded dramatically and with it, supporting data resources, research, and dissemination activities. This progress needs to continue in all these areas for the child and youth indicators field as a whole to move forward. In this chapter, we have attempted to highlight the recent accomplishments of the field and to identify the key challenges for the coming decade in each area.

Future progress will require a sustained and coordinated effort among researchers, policymakers, service staff, and data developers. Social scientists have important roles to play in this process. The social indicators field provides researchers with a unique opportunity to produce research that can directly affect the well-being of children, youth, and their families. To fully realize this opportunity may require some change in academic culture and its supporting system of rewards, a culture that is more appreciative of and sensitive to the research and information needs of the practice world. We believe it is well worth the effort and will produce substantial dividends for the practice community, for children's research, and ultimately, for children.

NOTES

1. See National Assessment of Educational Progress (2001) for details.
2. Information on the Community Score Card taken from *On the Plus Side: Key Indicators of Community Investment in Youth Development,* a proposal to the William T. Grant Foundation, submitted by the Center for Youth Development and Policy Research/AED, June 2000.
3. Resources described throughout the rest of the chapter are listed in the Appendix with Web site addresses, when available, for those who desire further information.
4. The following discussion is based primarily on a typology of uses for social indicators developed by Brown and Corbett (2002).
5. The NEGP was disbanded in 2001.
6. This theory of change is based on science, where it is available, as well as the beliefs and expectations of those who are participating in the initiative.
7. For a critical review of the theory-driven methodology, see Cook (2000).
8. For a detailed discussion, see Brown and Corbett (2002).
9. For a review of these and other international surveys, see Brown, Smith, and Harper (2001).
10. A separate sample is used to follow long-term trends and focuses on children and youth age 9, 13, and 17.
11. For a detailed review of federal sources of state and local level indicators of child and youth well-being, see Brown (2001).
12. This survey is being developed with federal funding from the Center for Substance Abuse Prevention within the Substance Abuse and Mental Health Services Administration (SAMHSA), U.S. Department of Health and Human Services.
13. For example, see O'Hare and Reynolds (2001).
14. This recommendation also appears in National Research Council and Institute of Medicine (2002).
15. Some work of this sort is already under way.

REFERENCES

Aber, J. L., & Jones, S. (1997). Indicators of positive development in early childhood. In R. Hauser, B. Brown, & W. Prosser (Eds.), *Indicators of children's well-being.* New York: Russell Sage.

Archbald, D. (1998). *The reviews of state content standards in English language arts and mathematics: A summary and review of their methods and findings and implications for future standards development.* Washington, DC: National Education Goals Panel.

Ben-Arieh, A., Kaufman, N., Andrews, A., Goerge, R., Lee, B., & Aber, J. L. (2001). *Measuring and monitoring children's well-being.* Dordrecht, Holland: Kluwer.

Bennett, W. (2001). *The index of leading cultural indicators 2001.* Retrieved from the World Wide Web on May 25, 2002, at Empower.org, Washington, D.C.

Bradshaw, J., & Barnes, H. (1999, September 30-October 2). *How do nations monitor the well-being of their children?* Paper presented at the conference, "Child Well-Being in Rich and Transition Countries," Luxembourg, Belgium.

Bronfenbrenner, U., & Morris, P. (1998). The ecology of developmental process. In W. Damon (Series Ed.) & R. M. Lerner (Vol. Ed.), *Handbook of child psychology: Vol. 1. Theoretical models of human development* (5th ed., pp. 993-1028). New York: Wiley.

Brooks-Gunn, J., Brown, B., Duncan, G. J., & Moore, K. A. (1995). Child development in the context of family and community resources: An agenda for national data collections. *Integrating federal statistics on children: Report of a workshop.* Washington, DC: National Academy Press.

Brown, B. V. (1997). Indicators of children's well-being: A review of current indicators based on data from the federal statistical system. In R. Hauser, B. Brown, & W. Prosser (Eds.), *Indicators of children's well-being.* New York: Russell Sage.

Brown, B. V. (2001). Tracking the well-being of children and youth at the state and local levels using the federal statistical system. *Assessing the New Federalism* (Occasional Paper No. 52). Washington, DC: Urban Institute.

Brown, B. V., & Corbett, T. (2002). Social indicators and public policy in the age of devolution. In R. Weissberg, L. Weiss, O. Reyes, & H. Walberg (Eds.), *Trends in the well-being of children and youth.* Washington, DC: Child Welfare League of America Press.

Brown, B. V., Smith, B., & Harper, M. (2001). *International surveys containing information on children and their families: An overview.* Washington, DC: Child Trends.

Child Trends. (2000). Social indicators and social programs: Researcher forges new links. *The Child Indicator Newsletter, (1)2,* 2. Washington, DC: Author.

Child Trends. (2001). Highlights from the national conference on child and youth indicators. *The Child Indicator Newsletter (3)2,* 1. Washington, DC: Author.

Connell, J., & Kubisch, A. (1998). Applying a theory of change approach to the evaluation of comprehensive community initiatives: Progress, prospects, and problems. In K. Fulbright-Anderson, A. Kubisch, & J. Connell (Eds.), *New approaches to evaluating community initiatives: Vol. 2. Theory, measurement, and analysis.* Washington, DC: Aspen Institute.

Cook, T. (2000). The false choice between theory-based evaluation and experimentation. In P. Rogers, T. Hacsi, A. Petrosino, & T. Huebner (Eds.), *Program theory in evaluation challenges and opportunities: New directions for evaluation.* San Francisco: Jossey-Bass.

Corbett, T. (2001, June 14-15). *Social indicators as a policy tool: Welfare reform as a case study.* Paper presented at conference, "Key Indicators of Child and Youth Well-Being: Completing The Picture," Bethesda, MD.

Coulton, C., & Hollister, R. (1998). Measuring comprehensive community initiative outcomes using data available for small areas. In K. Fulbright-Anderson, A. Kubisch, & J. Connell (Eds.), *New approaches to evaluating community initiatives: Vol. 2. Theory, measurement, and analysis.* Washington, DC: Aspen Institute.

Devins, G. M., & Orme, C. M. (1985). Center for epidemiological studies depression scale. In D. J. Keyser & R. C. Sweetland (Eds.), *Test critiques* (pp. 144-160). Kansas City, MO: Test Corporation of America.

Eccles, J., Templeton, J., & Brown, B. (2001, June 14-15). *A developmental framework for selecting indicators of well-being during adolescent and young adult years.* Paper presented at conference, "Key Indicators of Child and Youth Well-Being: Completing the Picture," Bethesda, MD.

Federal Council of Citizenship Training. (1924). *Community scorecard*. U.S. Department of the Interior, Bureau of Education. Washington: U.S. Government Printing Office.

Federal Interagency Forum on Child and Family Statistics. (2001). *America's children: Key national indicators of well-being 2001*. Washington, DC: U.S. Government Printing Office.

Furstenberg, F., & Hughes, M. (1997). The influence of neighborhoods on children's development: A theoretical perspective and a research agenda. In R. Hauser, B. Brown, & W. Prosser (Eds.), *Indicators of children's well-being*. New York: Russell Sage.

Gambone, M. (1998). Challenges of measurement in community change initiatives. In K. Fulbright-Anderson, A. Kubisch, & J. Connell (Eds.), *New approaches to evaluating community initiatives: Vol. 2. Theory, measurement, and analysis*. Washington, DC: Aspen Institute.

Garmezy, N. (1991). Resiliency and vulnerability to adverse developmental outcomes associated with poverty. *American Behavioral Scientist, 34,* 416-430.

Hauser, R., Brown, B. V., & Prosser, W. (Eds.). (1997). *Indicators of children's well-being*. New York: Russell Sage.

Hogan, D., Rogers, M., & Msall, M. (2000). Functional limitations and key indicators of well-being in children with disability. *Archives of Pediatric and Adolescent Medicine, 154,* 1042-1048.

Hogan, D., & Wells, T. (2001). *Developing concise measures of childhood limitations*. Unpublished manuscript.

Hollister, R., & Hill, J. (1995). Problems in the evaluation of community-wide initiatives. In J. Connell, A. Kubisch, L. Schorr, & C. Weiss (Eds.), *New approaches to evaluating comprehensive community initiatives: Concepts, methods, and contexts*. Washington, DC: Aspen Institute.

Kingsley, T. (1998). *Neighborhood indicators: Taking advantage of the new potential*. Chicago: American Planning Association. Manuscript in preparation.

Land, K. (2000). Social indicators. In E. Borgatta and R. Montgomery (Eds.), *Encyclopedia of sociology* (Rev. ed.). New York: Macmillan.

Land, K., Lamb, V., & Mustillo, S. (in press). Child and youth well-being in the United States: Some findings from a new index. *Social Indicators Research*.

Maynard, R. (1997). *Kids having kids*. Washington, DC: Urban Institute.

Miringoff, M., Miringoff, M., & Opdicke, S. (2001). *The social report: A deeper view of prosperity. Assessing the progress of American by monitoring the well-being of its people*. Bronx, NY: Fordham Institute.

Moore, K. A. (1997). Criteria for indicators of child well-being. In R. Hauser, B. Brown, & W. Prosser (Eds.), *Indicators of children's well-being*. New York: Russell Sage.

Moore, K. A., Evans, V. J., Brooks-Gunn, J., & Roth, J. (2001). What are good child outcomes? In A. Thornton (Ed.), *The well-being of children and families: Research and data needs*. Ann Arbor: University of Michigan Press.

Moore, K. A., & Glei, D. A. (1995). Taking the plunge: New measures of youth development that cross outcome domains and assess positive outcomes. *Journal of Adolescent Research, 10*(1), 15-40.

Moore, K., & Halle, T. (2001). Preventing problems vs. promoting the positive: What do we want for our children? In T. Owens & S. Hofferth (Eds.), *Children of the millennium: Where have we come from, where are we going?* (Vol. 6, pp. 141-170). New York: Elsevier.

Moore, K., Halle, T., Vandivere, S., & Mariner, C. (2002). Scaling back scales: How short is too short? *Sociological Methods & Research, 30*(4), 530-567.

Morenoff, J., & Sampson, R. (2001, June 14-15). *Constructing community indicators of child well-being.* Paper presented at conference, "Key Indicators of Child and Youth Well-Being: Completing the Picture," Bethesda, MD.

Murphey, D. (2001, June 14-15). *Creating community capacity to use indicators.* Paper presented at conference, "Key Indicators of Child and Youth Well-Being: Completing the Picture," Bethesda, MD.

National Assessment of Educational Progress. (2001). *2000 Science assessment results.* Washington, DC: National Center for Education Statistics.

National Research Council and Institute of Medicine. (2002). Community programs to promote youth development. In J. Eccles & J. A. Gootman (Eds.), *Committee on community level programs for youth* (Commission on Behavioral and Social Sciences and Education, Board on Children, Youth, and Families). Washington, DC: National Academy Press.

Novak, T., & Hoffman, D. (1998). Bridging the racial divide on the Internet. *Science, 280,* 390.

O'Hare, W., & Reynolds, M. (2001, October). *Media coverage of social indicators reports: The KIDS COUNT experience.* Paper presented at the Meetings of the Southern Demographic Association, Miami Beach, FL.

Papert, S., & Negroponte, N. (1996). *The connected family: Bridging the digital generation gap.* Marietta, GA: Longstreet.

Pittman, K., & Irby, M. (1996). *Preventing problems or promoting development: Competing priorities or inseparable goals?* Takoma Park, MD: International Youth Foundation.

Pittman, K., Irby, M., & Ferber, T. (2000). *Unfinished business: Further reflections on a decade of promoting youth development.* Takoma Park, MD: International Youth Foundation.

Pratt, C., Katzev, A., Henderson, T., & Ozretich, R. (1997). *Building results: From wellness goals to positive outcomes for Oregon's children, youth, and families.* Salem, OR: Oregon Commission on Children and Families.

Pratt, C., Katzev, A., Ozretich, R., Henderson, T., & McGuigan, W. (1998). *Building results III: Measuring outcomes for Oregon's children, youth, and families.* Salem, OR: Oregon Commission on Children and Families.

President's Research Committee on Social Trends. (1933). *Recent trends in the United States.* New York: McGraw-Hill.

Ripke, M., Huston, A., & Eccles, J. (2001, June 14-15). *The assessment of psychological, emotional, and social development indicators in middle childhood.* Paper presented at conference, "Key Indicators of Child And Youth Well-Being: Completing the Picture," Bethesda, MD.

Roth, J., Borbely, C., and Brooks-Gunn, J. (2001, June 14-15). *Developing indicators of confidence, character, and caring in adolescents.* Paper presented at conference, "Key Indicators of Child and Youth Well-Being: Completing the Picture," Bethesda, MD.

Rutter, M. (1984, March). Resilient children. *Psychology Today,* pp. 57-65.

Select Committee on Children, Youth, and Families. (1983). *U.S. children and their families: Current conditions and recent trends, 1983.* Washington, DC: U.S. Government Printing Office.

Select Committee on Children, Youth, and Families. (1987). *U.S. children and their families: Current conditions and recent trends, 1987.* Washington, DC: U.S. Government Printing Office.

Select Committee on Children, Youth, and Families. (1989). *U.S. children and their families: Current conditions and recent trends, 1989.* Washington, DC: U.S. Government Printing Office.

Seligman, M., & Peterson, C. (in press). *Positive clinical psychology*. In L. Aspinwall & U. Staudinger (Eds.), *A psychology of human strengths: Perspectives on an emerging field*. Washington, DC: American Psychological Association.

Stagner, M., & Zweig, J. (2001, June 14-15). *Indicators of youth well-being: Taking the long view*. Paper presented at conference, "Key Indicators of Child and Youth Well-Being: Completing the Picture," Bethesda, MD.

Takanishi, R., Mortimer, A., & McGourthy, T. (1997). Positive indicators of adolescent development: Redressing the negative image of American adolescents. In R. Hauser, B. Brown, & W. Prosser (Eds.), *Indicators of children's well-being*. New York: Russell Sage.

United Way of America. (1999). *Achieving and measuring community outcomes: Challenges, issues, some approaches*. Alexandria, VA: United Way of America.

U.S. Department of Health and Human Services. (2000). *Child welfare outcomes 1998: Annual report*. Washington, DC: U.S. Department of Health and Human Services. Available on the World Wide Web at http://www.acf.dhhs.gov/programs/cb.

U.S. Department of Health and Human Services. (2001). *Trends in the well-being of America's children and youth 2000*. Washington, DC: Author.

Weiss, C. H. (1995). Nothing as practical as good theory: Exploring theory-based evaluation for comprehensive community initiatives for children and families. In J. Connell, A. Kubisch, L. Schorr, & C. Weiss (Eds.), *New approaches to evaluating comprehensive community initiatives: Concepts, methods, and contexts*. Washington, DC: Aspen Institute.

Zaff, J. F., Blount, R. L., & Phillips, L. (1999, April). *Coping in adolescence: A multi-ethnic, cross-situational approach*. Poster presented at the Annual Conference of the Society for Research in Child Development, Albuquerque, NM.

Zaslow, M., Reidy, M., Moorehouse, M., Halle, T., Calkins, J., & Margie, N. (2001, June 14-15). *Progress and prospects in the development of indicators of school readiness*. Paper presented at conference, "Key Indicators of Child and Youth Well-Being: Completing the Picture," Bethesda, MD.

APPENDIX

Summary Listing of Web Sites for Child and Youth Indicators Projects and Data Sources Mentioned in the Chapter

Adoption and Foster Care Analysis System (AFCARS)
http://www.acf.dhhs.gov/programs/cb/dis/afcars/index.html

American Community Survey
http://factfinder.census.gov/home/en/acsdata.html

America's Children: Key National Indicators of Well-Being
http://childstats.gov/americaschildren

Child Health USA
http://www.mchirc.net/CH-USA.htm

Cleveland Area Network for Data and Organizing (CANDO)
http://povertycenter.cwru.edu/cando.htm

Common Core of Data
http//nces.ed.gov/ccd

Condition of Education
http://nces.ed.gov/pubsearch/pubsinfo.asp?pubid=2001072

Current Population Survey (CPS)
http://www.bls.gov/cps/home.htm

Digest of Education Statistics
http://nces.ed.gov/pubs2001/digest/

Early Childhood Longitudinal Surveys
http://nces.ed.gov/ecls/

Education Goals 2000 Initiative
http://www.ed.gov/G2K/

Federal Interagency Forum on Child and Family Statistics (the Forum)
http://childstats.gov/

Global Youth Tobacco Survey
http://www.cdc.gov/tobacco/research_data/youth/gytsfactsheets.pdf

Health Behavior of School-Aged Children (HBSC)
http://www.ruhbc.ed.ac.uk/hbsc/

Health, United States
http://www.cdc.gov/nchs/products/pubs/pubd/hus/hus.htm

Healthy People 2010
http://www.health.gov/healthypeople/

IEA Civics Study
http://nces.ed.gov/surveys/cived/

Kids Count
http://www.aecf.org/kidscount/

Massachusetts Community Health Information Profile (MassCHIP)
http://masschip.state.ma.us/

Minnesota Children's Report Card
http://www.mnplan.state.mn.us/datanetweb/chi.html

Monitoring the Future (MTF)
http://www.monitoringthefuture.org/

National Assessment of Educational Progress (NAEP)
http://nces.ed.gov/nationsreportcard/

National Child Abuse and Neglect Data System (NCANDS)
http://www.acf.dhhs.gov/programs/cb/dis/index.htm

National Crime Victimization Survey (NCVS)
http://www.ojp.usdoj.gov/bjs/cvict.htm#ncvs

National Education Goals Report
http://www.negp.gov/

National Education Longitudinal Survey 1988 (NELS88)
http://nces.ed.gov/surveys/nels88/

National Health and Nutrition Examination Survey (NHANES)
http://www.cdc.gov/nchs/nhanes.htm

National Health Interview Survey (NHIS)
http://www.cdc.gov/nchs/nhis.htm

National Household Education Survey (NHES)
http://nces.ed.gov/nhes/

National Household Survey of Drug Abuse (NHSDA)
http://www.samhsa.gov/oas/nhsda.htm

National Immunization Survey (NIS)
http://www.cdc.gov/nis/

National Longitudinal Survey of Adolescent Health (Add-Health)
http://www.cpc.unc.edu/addhealth/

National Longitudinal Survey of Youth 1997 Cohort (NLSY-97)
http://www.bls.gov/nls/

National Neighborhood Indicators Project (NNIP)
http://www.urban.org/nnip/

National Surveys of Families and Households
http://www.nichd.nih.gov/about/cpr/dbs/res_national4.htm

National Youth Tobacco Survey (NYTS)
http://www.cdc.gov/tobacco/research_data/youth/ss50.04.intro.htm

Panel Study of Income Dynamics
http://www.isr.umich.edu/src/psid/

Pregnancy Risk Assessment Monitoring System (PRAMS)
http://www.cdc.gov/nccdphp/drh/srv_prams.htm

Profiles of Student Life: Attitudes and Behaviors Survey
http/www.search-institute.org/surveys/

Program for International Student Assessment (PISA)
http://nces.ed.gov/surveys/pisa/

Progress in International Reading Study (PIRLS)
http://www.timss.org/pirls2001.html

Schools and Staffing Survey (SASS)
http://nces.ed.gov/surveys/sass/index.asp

Small Area Income and Poverty Estimates
http://www.census.gov/hhes/www/saipe.html

Trends in Mathematics and Science Study (TIMSS)
http://www.timss.org/

Trends in the Well-being of America's Children and Youth
http://aspe.hhs.gov/hsp/01trends/

Vermont "Community Profiles"
http://www.ahs.state.vt.us/publs.htm#compro

Vital Statistics
http://www.cdc.gov/nchs/nvss.htm

Youth Indicators (1996)
http://nces.ed.gov/pubs/yi/

Youth Risk Behavior Survey (YRBS)
http://www.cdc.gov/nccdphp/dash/yrbs/index.htm

CHAPTER 5

Participant Consultation

Ethical Insights Into Parental Permission and Confidentiality Procedures for Policy-Relevant Research With Youth

CELIA B. FISHER

At the dawn of the 21st century, the failure of social policies attempting to stem the tide of conditions threatening the development of our nation's youth has rekindled public anxiety about the fate of future generations. Concern about the imbalance between developmental risk and opportunity in the lives of adolescents has risen in response to the number of teenagers still living in poverty, abusing drugs and alcohol, perpetrating or being victimized by community violence, engaging in other health-compromising behaviors, failing in schools, and suffering from mental health disorders (Dryfoos, 1990; Hamburg, 1992; Hammond & Yung, 1993; Jessor, 1993; Kuther & Fisher, 1998; Lerner, 1995; Lerner & Fisher, 1994; Petersen et al., 1993; Schorr, 1988; Takanishi, 1993).

In response to these public concerns, applied developmental scientists have been called on to provide knowledge and develop empirically validated intervention strategies to stem the tide of health and social problems jeopardizing development of productive and adaptive life skills during the critical years of adolescence (Fisher & Lerner, 1994; Fisher & Murray, 1996; Haggerty, Sherrod, Garmezy, & Rutter, 1996; Lerner, 1995; Lerner & Galambos, 1998; Lerner, Sparks, & McCubbin, 2000; Schulenberg, Maggs, & Hurrelmann, 1997). The pressing need for empirically informed public policies aimed at positive youth development has challenged applied developmental scientists to modify traditional research paradigms and reevaluate their roles with

AUTHOR'S NOTE: The author's work on this chapter was supported by grants from the National Science Foundation (#SBR-9710310) and the National Institute for Child Health and Human Development (#HD39332-02). The author thanks Scyatta Wallace for her contributions to the focus group portion of this project and for her comments during questionnaire development; Aixa Rodriguez, Clarisse Miller, and Katherine Jankowski for assistance in focus group implementation and analysis; and Amy Karpf, Leyla Faw, and Ronit Roth for questionnaire data collection, entry, and analysis.

and obligations to research participants in order to contribute to policies that will best serve youth needs (Fisher & Murray, 1996; Hetherington, 1998; Higgins-D'Alessandro, Fisher, & Hamilton, 1998; Lerner, Fisher, & Weinberg, 2000a, 2000b).

As the science of youth development has moved from the experimental laboratory to the ecological niches of everyday teenage life, the need to evaluate the societal costs and benefits of socially sensitive research has evolved from an abstract ethical issue to a concrete daily concern (Fisher, 1993; Fisher & Rosendahl, 1990; Fisher & Tryon, 1990; Lerner & Tubman, 1990). For example, surveys, interviews with informants, and assignment to intervention and control groups targeting adolescent drug use, sexual behaviors, suicidal ideation, violence, and other health-compromising behaviors and mental health problems can contribute to society's understanding of and strategies for ameliorating problems of youth. At the same time, these methodologies may introduce their own form of risk by focusing teenagers' attention on emotionally charged issues, introducing them to forms of risk taking about which they may have been naïve, inflicting knowledge on them about disorders for which they or their families may not be prepared, or precipitating personal or group stigmatization following data dissemination (Fisher & Wallace, 2000). The direct application of developmental science to the health and welfare of adolescents in our society thus places the integrity and adequacy of ethical procedures at the forefront of methodological concern.

PARTICIPANT CONSULTATION AND THE ETHICS OF POLICY-RELEVANT YOUTH SCIENCE

For over two decades, the ethical conduct of research involving human participants has been based on the moral values of beneficence, respect, and justice articulated by the National Commission for the Protection of Human Subjects of Biomedical and Behavioral Research (1978). These moral values, incorporated into the Code of Federal Regulations Title 45, Part 46, Protection of Human Subjects (Public Welfare, 1991a) underscore the obligation of scientists to maximize research benefits and minimize research risks, to respect a research participant's right to decision making and privacy, and to ensure that all members of society have equal opportunity to share the burdens and benefits of research. However, federal regulations for human experimentation are written in broad general terms to ensure their applicability across diverse and shifting research activities, settings, and participant populations. Thus, ethical decision making in the complicated arena of policy-relevant adolescent research requires contextually sensitive interpretations of moral principles and federal guidelines.

Engaging in this system of interpretation, scientists concerned with the promotion of youth development have traditionally drawn on organizational policies, the advice of colleagues and institutional review boards (IRBs) and their own moral compasses to plan ethical procedures that can have immediate and long-term impact on research participants and their families (Fisher & Fyrberg, 1994). However, the values guiding these ethical practices may not be shared by research participants with the unique personal vulnerabilities and life situations of adolescents and families from socially disenfranchised, historically oppressed, and other at-risk groups. Thus, an important resource for insuring the ethical practice of policy-relevant youth research is the opinions of the teenagers and families who will be the target of investigation (Fisher, 1997, 1999). The participant consultation model engages prospective participants and their family members in dialogue regarding research ethics practices and draws on their opinions to assess research risks and benefits, the adequacy of informed consent procedures, the consequences of confidentiality and disclosure policies, and the influence of research incentives to develop ethical procedures that reflect the values and merit the trust of individuals who will be recruited for research (Fisher, 1997, 1999; Levine, 1986; Levine, Dubler, & Levine, 1991; Melton, Levine, Koocher, Rosenthal, & Thompson, 1988; Osher & Telesford, 1996; Sugarman et al., 1998; Veatch, 1987).

The need to actively engage prospective participants and their communities as partners in forging new ways of conducting research has become a cornerstone of applied developmental science and cultural psychology (Ponterotto & Casas, 1991; Higgins-D'Alessandro et al., 1998; Lerner, 1995; Lerner & Fisher, 1994; Lerner & Simon, 1998a, 1998b). The participant consultation model extends this collaborative approach to research ethics deliberations (Fisher, 1997, 1999, 2000; Fisher & Wallace, 2000). This model is also rooted in the community consultation approach to AIDS research, in which investigators meet with members of the community to discuss issues of research design and procedures to learn about their acceptability (Levine, 1986; Levine et al., 1991; Melton et al., 1988). A potential limitation of community consultation in adolescent research is that the concerns and values of the community leaders and political advocates typically invited to engage in community consultation may not always reflect those of the individuals who will actually be recruited to participate in research. Such individuals (especially if they are adolescents and families from the high-risk environments of interest to policymakers) may be less powerful, less educated, less well-off,

more disenfranchised, and more desperate for services that research may provide than their community leaders. They may therefore view ethical issues through a different, more personal lens than that of community advocates, who may not themselves be prospective research participants.

Several additional moral arguments support the importance of the views of prospective research participants and their guardians in ethics-in-science decision making. First, formulating regulations and ethical judgments solely on the basis of opinions expressed by experts in the scholarly community and IRB members risks treating participants as research material rather than as moral agents with the right to judge the ethicality of investigative procedures in which they participate (Fisher & Fyrberg, 1994; Veatch, 1987). Second, failure to consider prospective participants' points of view encourages singular reliance on scientific inference or professional logic that can lead to research procedures causing misunderstanding during the informed consent stage of research. Third, failure to draw on participant perspectives can lead to the rejection of potentially worthwhile scientific procedures that participants and their families would perceive as benign and/or worthwhile. For example, in the everyday practice of science, investigators often find that guidelines designed to protect vulnerable children from experimental psychopharmacological treatments inadvertently create institutional obstacles that limit participants' autonomy and access to research protocols that may advance scientific understanding and treatment of their disorders (Jensen, Hoagwood, & Fisher, 1996). Fourth, engaging prospective participants as partners in the design and implementation of research (a) assures adequate consideration of the ethical values of beneficence, respect, and justice and (b) increases the probability of community support and cooperation (Levine et al., 1991; Melton et al., 1988).

Participant Consultation and Colearning

A major assumption of participant consultation is that colearning enhances the moral development of scientists and participants through a better understanding of the reciprocal relationship between the participant's expectations and the researcher's obligations (Fisher, 1999, 2000; Lerner & Fisher, 1994; Lerner & Simon, 1998a, 1998b). Participant consultation views scientist and participant alike as moral agents joined in partnership to construct ethical procedures to produce knowledge carrying social value, scientific validity, justice, and care (Fisher, 1994, 1997, 1999, 2000). It assumes that both investigator and participant come to the research enterprise as experts: The investigator brings expertise about the scientific method and the extant empirical knowledge base, and the prospective participants and their family members bring expertise about the fears and hopes about and value they place on the prospective research (Fisher, 1999, 2000). Investigators can use colearning procedures to share with prospective participants their views on how and why it is important to apply the scientific method to examine questions of societal import and to debates underlying areas of current ethical concern. In turn, the prospective participants, their families, or community representatives can apply their moral perspectives to critique the scientific and social value of a proposed study and share with investigators the value orientations guiding their reactions to the planned procedures (Fisher, 1999, 2000; Fisher & Wallace, 2000).

The purpose of this chapter is to illustrate how participant consultation can enhance

ethical decision making and challenge traditional assumptions regarding the informed consent procedures for policy-relevant youth research. The next two sections describe ethical challenges of parental permission and confidentiality and disclosure policies for adolescent research. This is followed by a description of a focus group approach to participant consultation implemented by the author. The chapter then turns to specific illustrations of how teenagers and parents from diverse ethnic, racial, and economic communities viewed these ethical practices. The chapter concludes with discussion of the implications of participant views for good and rightly practiced socially relevant youth research.

An Overview of Ethical Issues in Informed Consent for Adolescent Research

Informed consent is viewed by many as the primary means of protecting research participants' autonomy and welfare (Freedman, 1975). The three overarching requirements of informed consent are that it be *informed*, *rational*, and *voluntary*.

The Informed Nature of Consent

To meet the *informed* requirement of consent, investigators must provide teenagers and their guardians with all information about the experimental procedures that might influence their willingness to participate themselves or allow their children to participate. Such information typically includes a description of the procedures, the time required to participate, the profession and institutional affiliation of the investigator(s), foreseeable risks or benefits of participation, the extent as well as limits of confidentiality, the voluntary nature of participation, and how participants can obtain information regarding the results and conclusions of the research. In the absence of input from teenagers and parents, it has traditionally been left to investigators and their IRBs to determine which aspects of the study would affect participant consent decisions.

Parental Permission

Federal regulations require the permission of the parent when minors are involved in research for several reasons. With few exceptions, minors do not have the legal capacity to consent and, depending on their age and the complexity of the research context, may lack the cognitive capacity to comprehend the nature of the research and their research rights (Fisher & Rosendahl, 1990; Keith-Spiegel, 1983; Koocher & Keith-Spiegel, 1990; Levine, 1986; Thompson, 1990). However, out of respect for children and adolescents as developing persons, federal regulations also require the affirmative agreement (assent) by the child or adolescent to participate in research. According to federal guidelines, mere failure of a minor to object should not be construed as assent (Public Welfare, 1991b, 46.402[b]). Moreover, a minor's dissent (refusal to participate) overrides parental permission except when the research offers the child or adolescent the possibility of a direct benefit that is important to his or her well-being and is available only in the context of the research (Public Welfare, 1991b, 46.408[e]).

Waiving Guardian Permission Requirements

Federal guidelines also provide for situations in which it is appropriate to waive the requirement for parental permission. For example, the "emancipated minor" legal status is conferred on persons who have not yet attained the age of legal competency as defined by state law but who are entitled to be treated as if they had such status by virtue of assuming adult responsibilities, such as self-support, marriage, or procreation. Similarly, a "mature minor" is someone who has not reached adulthood (as defined by state law) but who, according to state law, may be treated as an adult for certain purposes (e.g., consenting to treatment for venereal disease, drug abuse, or emotional disorders). In that the law grants teenagers the autonomy to make decisions concerning their medical treatment in such instances, scholars have argued that it seems both reasonable and ethical to grant them the same autonomy to decide whether or not to participate in research that examines their reasons for or reactions to seeking these treatments (Fisher, 1993; Holder, 1981; Rogers, D'Angelo, & Futterman, 1994; Scarr, 1994). However, teenagers and parents may have very different views of the reasonableness of such an approach.

Best Interests of the Child

For those adolescents who are neither emancipated nor mature minors, requiring guardian consent assumes that the teenager comes from a reasonably secure family setting in which the youth and his or her guardians share loving relationships (Gaylin & Macklin, 1982; Levine, 1986). However, the high-risk physical and social conditions that bring teenagers to the attention of applied developmental scientists and policymakers (e.g., child abuse, health compromising sexual behaviors, drug abuse) may in themselves make obtaining consent from identified guardians difficult, violate the teenager's privacy rights, or place them in jeopardy (Brooks-Gunn & Rotheram-Borus, 1994; Fisher, 1993; Fisher, Hoagwood, & Jensen, 1996). In the absence of specific consent policies regarding the "best interests of the child," applied developmental scientists are torn between excluding teenagers or waiving parental consent and the participant protection such consent is designed to afford.

The Rational Nature of Consent

The *rational* requirement of consent reflects an acknowledgment that the conditions that identify teenagers as potential participants may make it difficult for them and their guardians to understand the procedures described or to recognize the limited or non-existent benefits of participation in research that is intended to be descriptive rather than intervening (Fisher, 1993). For example, the family of an adolescent who has a pattern of school failure and no professional support may misconstrue participation in purely descriptive studies or in research that includes random assignment to nontreatment groups, as a potential source of assistance with the problem. Engaging teenagers and their parents in dialogue about the nature and value of different types of research approaches can help to ensure that assent and parental permission are rational.

Capacity to Consent

There is increasing evidence that by age 14, teenagers have the capacity to understand information presented in informed consent protocols at the same level as adults (Belter & Grisso, 1984; Grisso & Vierling, 1978; Melton, 1980; Morton & Green, 1991; Ruck, Keating, Abramovitch, & Koegl, 1998; Weithorn, 1983). However, when risk behaviors (e.g., drug use) or mental disorders (e.g., conduct disorder) are the focus of adolescent research, cognitive impairments associated with these disorders may interfere with a teenager's ability to rationally comprehend research-related information. Moreover, despite increasing opportunities to make autonomous decisions, school-age teenagers remain subject to adult authority and vulnerable to coercion and rights violations. Data on how teenagers and parents view adolescent autonomy and

vulnerability can assist investigators and IRB members with the difficult task of determining the ethical legitimacy of guardian consent waivers.

The Voluntary Nature of Consent

Investigators who study the development of vulnerable and disenfranchised youth must be particularly sensitive to potential violations of the *voluntary* aspect of assent and guardian permission (Fisher, 1993; Fisher & Rosendahl, 1990). For example, vulnerable families, contacted while seeking services at community mental health or medical facilities, may be concerned that failure to consent will result in a discontinuation of services for themselves or for their children. Under these circumstances, special care needs to be taken to clarify that the right to services is not contingent on consent, and that the teenager can withdraw even after consent has been given.

Passive Consent

Difficulties in acquiring guardian consent from at-risk youth has led in recent years to renewed debate over the use of passive guardian consent. Passive consent is the procedure by which guardians are sent forms describing the research and are asked to respond only if they do *not* wish their children to participate. Some investigators argue that such procedures are necessary in populations in which the parental permission response rate is low to ensure that these adolescents reap the benefits of scientific inquiry. An implicit assumption underlying advocacy for passive consent is that a caring and knowledgeable guardian would perceive the research as important and as desirable for his or her child and therefore would be likely to acquiesce to participation. A corollary of this argument is that parents who do not return consent forms either lack the knowledge to appreciate the importance of the research or are unconcerned about their children's welfare (Fisher, 1993).

The fallacy of this argument is that it assumes, without actually testing the assumption, that the risks and benefits of research as viewed by the investigator are morally superior to those of the parents of vulnerable adolescent participants (Fisher, 1993). The IQ debate and associated tracking movements in schools and the racial scandal surrounding the government-sanctioned Tuskegee syphilis study serve to undermine trust in social scientists as guar-dians of ethical treatment when prospective subjects are minorities (Fisher, Jackson, & Villarruel, 1997). Moreover, to call this procedure "consent" is duplicitous, because the researcher cannot know for certain that the adolescent's guardian received the information or that the guardian's failure to respond reflects agreement to have the child participate. Given the paucity of data on how teenagers and their parents view these procedures, passive consent procedures risk substituting investigator paternalism for parental permission (Fisher, 1993).

AN OVERVIEW OF ETHICAL ISSUES IN CONFIDENTIALITY AND DISCLOSURE DECISIONS FOR POLICY-RELEVANT YOUTH RESEARCH

Appropriate informed consent procedures allow prospective participants and their guardians to make decisions regarding the extent to which they wish to reveal personal information. However, once participants have agreed to share such information, investigators are obligated to ensure that confidentiality practices are consistent with the informed consent agreement.

Protecting Participant Confidentiality

In many research contexts, investigators can use routine procedures for assuring the confidentiality of data, including (a) subject codes rather than identifiers, (b) secure storage and limited access, (c) disposal of unnecessary information, (d) supervision of research personnel, and (e) anonymous data collection when possible. There may be situations in which these routine procedures for assuring confidentiality are not sufficient to protect participants from harm. For example, data collected on violent or delinquent behavior, substance abuse, or certain parenting behaviors may be subject to subpoenas stemming from criminal investigations or custody disputes. In these circumstances an investigator can apply for a Certificate of Confidentiality under 301(d) of the Public Health Service Act. The certificate provides the investigator immunity from any government or civil order to disclose identifying information contained in research records (Hoagwood, 1994; Melton, 1990). A certificate is granted for research that might be recorded in a patient's medical record or is of a sensitive nature that, if released, could result in stigmatization, discrimination, or legal action and that could damage an individual's financial standing, employability, or reputation. The certificate may not override state reporting laws on child abuse or protect the research against disclosures of child data to parents; such protection can only be assured through permission by a guardian at the time of informed consent.

Protecting the Participant's Welfare or the Welfare of Others

Research on risk and resilience in adolescence often uncovers evidence of illegal behaviors, mental health problems, and other health-compromising behaviors that may be unknown to other adults concerned with a teenage participant's welfare (Fisher, 1993; Fisher, Hoagwood, et al., 1996). Whether to keep such information confidential or disclose it to parents or professionals is a daunting ethical challenge for investigators conducting policy-relevant youth research (Brooks-Gunn & Rotheram-Borus, 1994; Fisher, 1994, 2000). Such research may also elicit sensitive information that could place participants or their family members in social or legal jeopardy if disclosed beyond the research setting. Federal and professional guidelines recognize that there may be legal or ethical obligations to disclose information to help an adolescent in jeopardy or to protect others.

Reporting Child Abuse

Following the 1976 Child Abuse Prevention and Treatment Act, all 50 states have enacted statutes mandating the reporting of suspected child abuse or neglect for mental health professionals, and at least 13 states, this obligation also extends to researchers, as members of the general citizenry. Investigators needs to review their own state laws to determine if they or members of their research team are mandatory reporters and whether they are legally required to release to authorities research records pertinent to the abuse after it is reported (see Liss, 1994).

Protecting the Participant From Self-Harm

During the course of a study some adolescents with mental disorders may reveal suicidal ideation or other self-harming behaviors. Investigators need to be knowledgeable about appropriate procedures for determining and managing suicidal intent (Pearson, Stanley, King, & Fisher, 2001a, 2001b). They must also establish criteria to be applied in determining whether other self-endangering behaviors require action (e.g., use of a toxic inhalant to get high) and whether such actions involve disclosing the information to other concerned adults or assisting the participant in obtaining appropriate treatment.

Protecting Third Parties From Harm

Investigators who study at-risk youth behavior may learn that a research participant is intending to harm a third party. Although there has yet to be case law in the area of research, investigators need to give appropriate consideration to whether their relationship with a research participant meets the "duty to protect" outlined by *Tarasoff v. Regents of the University of California* in 1976 that requires informing a third party of the prospect of being harmed if one has (a) A "special relationship" with the prospective assailant, (b) the ability to predict that violence will occur, and (c) the ability to identify the potential victim (Appelbaum & Rosenbaum, 1989).

Do Applied Developmental Scientists Have a Moral Obligation to Help Youth in Jeopardy?

Applied developmental scientists have been reluctant to disclose information derived from research on adolescent risk out of concern that inferences drawn from such measures may lack diagnostic validity and that treatment or referrals precipitated by disclosures will threaten the internal validity of longitudinal designs, lead to feelings of betrayal, or jeopardize recruitment (Fisher, 1993, 1994; Fisher, Hoagwood, et al., 1996; Scott-Jones, 1994). Moreover, disclosures to school counselors or child protection agencies regarding risk behaviors may harm participants or their families if those informed react punitively, incompetently, or entangle the family in criminal proceedings.

Confidentiality decisions may also be complicated by ethnic variation in the determinants of adolescent drug use and suicide and differences in attitudes toward research among diverse cultural communities (American Indian Law Center, 1994; Casas & Thompson, 1991; Fisher, Jackson, et al., 1997; Gibbs, 1988; Jenkins & Parron, 1995; Kilpatrick et al., 2000; Oetting & Beauvais, 1990). These issues are further clouded by emerging evidence that some teenagers may want investigators to actively assist them in obtaining help for drug or suicide problems (Fisher, Higgins-D'Alessandro, Rau, Kuther, & Belanger, 1996; O'Sullivan & Fisher, 1997). The extent to which experimentally derived information on adolescent risk behaviors should be kept confidential or disclosed thus depends in no small part on the expectations of participants and their parents (Beeman & Scott, 1991; Fisher, 1999, 2000; Johnson, Cournoyer, & Bond, 1995).

ENGAGING TEENAGERS
AND PARENTS IN FOCUS
GROUP DIALOGUE ON
RESEARCH ETHICS ISSUES

The participant consultation methodology described in this section was designed and implemented as part of the Fordham Adolescent Research Project's multiyear investigation of teenager and parent perspectives on ethical issues in adolescent risk research sponsored by the National Science Foundation (#SBR-9710310). The broad purpose of this project was to enhance the ethical and value dimensions of socially relevant adolescent research by giving parents and teenagers, especially members of ethnic minority groups, a voice in ethical procedures tied to the scientific examination of adolescent risk behaviors.

Participants

During the spring of 1998, 46 parents and 55 males and females in the 9th to 11th grades participated in one of a series of 13 small focus group discussions. Participants were drawn from urban public schools serving students at the extreme ends of academic achievement, including (a) a highly competitive and nationally recognized magnet school with approximately equal numbers of black (African American or Caribbean), East or South Asian, Hispanic/Latino, and non-Hispanic white students and (b) neighborhood schools in impoverished and crime-ridden districts with high rates of school dropouts and largely black (African American) and Hispanic/Latino student bodies. According to group member reports, parental education varied widely, including reports of no parental schooling, of some high school, of high school completion, and of college and graduate/professional school education. Parental occupations were similarly diverse. Some were unemployed or homemakers; others held semiskilled and craft positions as taxi drivers, maintenance workers, secretaries and paraprofessionals, medical assistants and court supervisors, and so on; others were in managerial, executive, and professional positions.

The Focus Group Format

Focus groups were multiethnic, but they were homogenous with respect to age (junior high school, senior high school), generation (parents, teens) and gender. Each focus group began with icebreaker conversations about where students got their news or the age and sex of the parents' children. This was followed by discussion of the types of problems participants thought were facing adolescents in their schools and communities. Substance abuse, depression, pregnancy and high risk sexual behaviors, eating disorders, crime and violence, peer pressure, school dropout, stress, family conflict, verbal abuse, lack of identity, lack of money, lack of adult role models, and racial tension were mentioned as pressing problems. Vicarious or direct experiences with research were also discussed.

The format then moved toward discussion of the following ethics-in-science issues: (a) research risks and benefits, (b) parental permission and passive consent procedures, (c) confidentiality and disclosure policies, and (d) monetary incentives. Each of these ethical topics was discussed in the context of research on diverse adolescent risk factors such as substance abuse, sexual activity, suicide and depression, violence, eating disorders, academic failure, and child abuse. Discussants were also asked to consider these ethical issues across five methodologies: *survey* research, *informant* research, *school-based intervention* studies, research involving drawing of *physical samples* (saliva, urine, blood tests), and research on the *genetic basis of adolescent risk behaviors*.

To assist discussion, participants viewed three television news clips obtained from the Vanderbilt University Television Archives describing research on adolescent risk behaviors. The first clip described the results of a study comparing the effect on adolescent sexual behavior of condom distribution policies associated with sex education programs in New York City and Chicago schools. The second reported on the American Association of University Women's study on the frequency of sexual harassment in the schools. The third news clip described the racial controversy surrounding the National Institute of Mental Health (NIMH) initiative to examine the biological basis of delinquent behaviors in urban settings.

The "Opinions in Progress" Approach to Participant Consultation

Ethical decision-making is a reflective, contextually and relationally based endeavor, with no cookie cutter answers (Hoagwood, Jensen, & Fisher, 1996). As scientists do not expect nondeliberative, categorical ethical opinions from their research colleagues, neither should they encourage such answers from prospective participants. Therefore, developmental scientists need to approach participant consultation with the expectation that in groups of teenagers and parents there will be differing views that will evolve through ongoing discussion of the various dimensions of an ethical problem (Fisher & Wallace, 2000). To promote the "opinions in progress" approach, focus group leaders shared with discussants the differing ethical arguments that investigators and bioethicists have raised about each ethical issue presented and encouraged teenagers and parents to consider, critique, and add to these arguments.

The opinions in progress approach also guided the content analysis of focus group discussions. Transcripts from each of the 13 taped sessions were analyzed individually following the grounded theory method (Glaser & Strauss, 1967; Guba & Lincoln, 1982; Krueger, 1988; Vaughn, Schumm, & Sinagub, 1996). For each transcript, strong, significant ethical themes marked by opinions, ideas, or feelings repeated across members of the group were distinguished from less significant ones. When there was a shift in opinion, raters traced the flow of the conversation to determine whether the shift was a function of new perspectives or whether themes varied with respect to discussions across different research paradigms and participant populations. Opinions expressed only once were noted but did not serve as major reference points. Responses that provided specific information, (e.g., a statement indicating why a particular view was being expressed or providing an illustrative example) were given more weight than responses that were vague or impersonal.

Ethical themes emerging in each of the focus groups along with illustrative quotes were combined into a hierarchically organized thematic grid and analyzed for frequency across the school, age, and gender groups. Overall, the same ethical themes emerged in all groups, although the emotional valence and time spent on such themes varied. The purpose of the focus group exploration was not to analyze age, gender, or cultural differences in ethics in science values, but to learn about the broad thematic dimensions underlying adolescent and parent valuing of socially sensitive youth research. (The focus group script and thematic grid are available from the author upon request.)

Participant Consultation in Context

Participant consultation is grounded in the premise that integrating the ethical perspectives of teenagers and their guardians into the fabric of research design can enhance the value of research for participating youth, for science, and for public policy, because each venture into participant consultation will reflect the unique community histories of the sample. The aim of this form of inquiry is thus not to document participant perspectives that can or should dictate specific research ethics practices designed for other distinctive communities (Fisher & Wallace, 2000) but to introduce a methodology that can be transferred to other scientific arenas for research on adolescent risk and to offer insight into participant opinions that can challenge current ways of thinking and point to new directions of ethical awareness. This chapter reports on teenagers' and parents' views of parental permission and confidentiality policies. A description of participant views

on research risks and benefits can be found in Fisher and Wallace (2000).

ADOLESCENT AND PARENT PERSPECTIVES ON INFORMED CONSENT PROCEDURES

Focus group discussion directed at participant views on informed consent procedures revolved around the value of parental permission policies, situations in which waiver of parental permission might be ethically justified, and the use of passive consent procedures. Overall, there were few differences in views expressed in parent and teenager groups. When there were differences, they involved the increased frequency with which adolescents applied the principle of autonomy to justify waiver of parental permission and the stronger emphasis that parents placed on protecting teenagers from deceptive recruitment practices. The next section contains a description of the strong ethical themes underlying opinions on why parental permission should be required, when it should be waived, the use of passive consent, and recommendations for consent practices.

The Value of Parent Permission Policies

Significant themes that emerged when adolescents and parents discussed the value of parental permission policies for research on adolescent risk included:

- They demonstrate respect for parental rights and values.
- They protect the parent's reputation in the community.
- They protect teenagers from coercive and deceptive recruitment procedures.
- They enable parents to help their children overcome power inequities that might

discourage the teenager from withdrawing from the study.

- They enable parents to detect signs of post-experimental distress, especially when investigators are either unavailable or not competent to address such reactions.

The following are examples of how teenagers and parents articulated some of these points.

Parental Rights and Values

Across groups, parents and teenagers commented that parental permission for research participation is important because it demonstrates respect for parental rights and values. As two female students noted, "They [researchers] want to know, let them ask them the parent's permission . . . not just go off with them, that . . . that's like going against the parents." "Parents raised you and they have the right to know." All groups commented that parents have a right to know where their children are and what they are doing and to have their role as parents and their religious values respected. Parents and teenagers also thought it important that researchers recognize that parents are legally responsible for their children and that "many parents want to have a voice in what their children do." As one parent summed up, "I think what we are hearing overwhelmingly from all [in the focus group] is we want to know what are kids are doing, we want to know where they are."

Unexpectedly, discussants also thought that parental permission procedures could protect the parent from harm. Groups expressed concern that without the parent's knowledge, a child's participation in research might harm the parent's reputation. For example, one male participant from a neighborhood school mentioned that "if the parent is somebody important or, like, is one of the big role models in the community and if they hear that a parent, like, he didn't know about it [his child's research participation]

but it would change him in his job if he knew his son was telling everybody what he do." Another female participant from an academically competitive school said that, without parental consent, "It's gonna seem like the parent didn't care, because she was oblivious to anything that her child was doing."

Protecting Youth From Research Risks

A second theme reflected the belief that parental permission could protect students from participating in studies that might encourage negative behavior or invade their privacy. In each group, there were mixed opinions about whether or not participating in surveys or intervention studies on adolescent risk behavior might actually increase the behavior under investigation. Recognizing that students might vary in their susceptibility to such research, one male student justified requiring parental permission because "It might be just one kid that gets influenced, but still there's one person, then there's still the possibility that parent consent should be." Threats to confidentiality were also considered a research risk that needed parental oversight. As one parent noted, "What might be idle gossip might become something that will really get that child [and family] in trouble with the police."

Parents were especially concerned about protecting their children from the potentially coercive and deceptive nature of recruitment practices. As one parent put it, "Sometimes when they ask permission, they don't tell you what is the whole picture . . . [then] after the science is going on [the scientist makes] more requests and sometimes they [the teenagers] are already in and they can't get out." Teenagers and parents also pointed out that if parents did not know about the research they could not identify or help their child if he or she became distressed about participating. This was a particularly important concern because many felt that researchers might not be competent or be around to deal with postexperimental stress. A few discussants in different groups were concerned that, in research involving physical specimens, the researcher might "be a pervert" or "get fresh." They also thought that if parents knew a child was in the experiment, they could be available to help the child withdraw from the study.

Preserving the Parent-Child Relationship

Both parents and teenagers mentioned that parental permission might enhance the parent-child relationship by encouraging discussion about research participation and protect the relationship by reaffirming the parent's role. As one parent said, parental permission "gives the child the information that the school is keeping the parent informed of everything. Not so much that the child is not responsible enough to participate without the parent knowing, but that the child is still a child . . . And while the child is going to school [he or she] is still under the parent's guidance. Because when you start giving the children . . . too much on their own . . . they will really think that they are grown . . . enough to handle everything."

Ethical Justifications for Waiving Parental Permission

Several significant value dimensions were also apparent when teenagers and parents discussed ethical justifications for the waiver of parental permission across different research methodologies and topics:

- It demonstrates respect for teenagers' competency and right to make autonomous decisions.
- It avoids invasions of privacy that occur when parents start questioning teenagers about behaviors associated with the study.
- It avoids parent-child conflict that emerges when parents misinterpret permission forms as an indication that their child has actually engaged in risk behaviors.

- It exposes students to a broader range of knowledge and opinions about risk behaviors.
- It is appropriate when research is anonymous and poses no risks to participants.
- It is appropriate when parents are the cause of the problem under investigation (e.g., child abuse) or have no contact with their children.

The next section contains descriptions of the ways in which focus group members articulated these justifications.

Adolescent Autonomy and Privacy

Both parents and teenagers talked about autonomy as a reason to waive parental permission. Characteristic comments of adolescents were: "Parents [are not] gonna be the ones answering the questions." "These are personal questions about individual kids." "You yourself has to come up with your own basis on what you believe is right." "They [investigators] should be all open to your own opinion and of your own decision."

Across generations, focus group discussants believed that under some circumstances parental permission could be waived to protect the teenager's privacy. For example, teens were particularly concerned that although the researcher might keep information confidential, once parents read the consent form, they would start asking students about the behaviors of scientific interest. As one female expressed, if parents received consent information about the study they "are gonna want to know like the answers to what [we] said and stuff." According to one male student "The reason I really don't think parental permission . . . should be advised . . . is because this is something a kid wants to keep private from his mom. A lot of teenagers want to keep that [sexual activity] private from their parents, and drug abuse, too. Although it should not be kept private from their parents, I think [you] have to give the teenager the choice to keep that private from their parents." In a related issue, some students were concerned that parents would misinterpret the permission form as an accusation of student involvement in bad behavior. They thought that this could harm the parent-child relationship by breeding a sense of distrust or getting parents upset for no reason.

Several parents and teenagers mentioned the teenager's competence to consent as a justification to allow adolescents to make their own consent decisions. Interestingly, the intuitive opinions of discussion groups members coincided with the extant literature: Most thought that adolescents 14 years of age and older had the competence to make decisions on their own behalf.

Risks and Benefits of Research Participation

Both parents and teens thought that waiver of consent could benefit teenagers if it enabled students to be "exposed to other opinions" that would be helpful to them. As one student said, "If your parents tell you one way—keep on planting this in your head and you're not exposed to anything else until later on—that could hurt, that could affect you for the rest of your life." Others were of the opinion that waivers could be justified if this increases the number of teenage participants and enhanced the scientific validity of the study by encouraging students to give more honest answers. And as one neighborhood parent commented, "My point of view of thinking is that for the sake of the scientific research, for the sake of the family values, for the sake of society, for the sake of national health for the country, we should not care to ask the parents because we should just want to extract the real opinion from the kids. They should be free to express their own opinion because there is a lot of misconceptions about the kids."

Some discussion group members thought that parental permission for surveys and

school-based interventions was not necessary if responses were anonymous. Many also thought parental permission could be waived for survey or school-based risk prevention programs that would not negatively affect the teenager's behavior. Several parent and teenage groups voiced the opinion that parental permission could be waived in situations in which the teenager had no contact with his or her parents or in which the parent was abusive.

Attitudes Toward Passive Consent Procedures

Across all groups and generations, participants were overwhelmingly negative about passive consent procedures. Two major themes emerged repeatedly:

1. Passive consent procedures are deceptive and undermine the purpose of parental consent practices.

2. Passive consent procedures are coercive and encourage teenagers to deceive their parents, because most teenagers would not want to stand out as the only student whose parent(s) refused to permit participation.

The Deceptive Nature of Passive Consent

Parents and teenagers used words such as "trickery" and "deception" to describe passive consent procedures. All were familiar with this approach, because it is frequently used in the schools for school-related activities. As one student summed it up, "[It's] completely immoral, because it takes away from the whole point of parent permission . . . and I think it's kind of, you know, sneaky." Passive consent was seen as trying to "hook kids into participating" when parents may not really want to give consent.

Parents and teenagers were convinced that passive consent procedures would most typically fail to inform parents of the study for various reasons:

1. Parents might never receive the form because the child forgot to or intentionally did not give it to them.

2. Parents might not understand the form.

3. Parents might be traveling or too busy to read the form. It was also perceived as a means of drawing in teenagers who do not have parental guidance and a way for researchers to ignore parent complaints about their child's participation in the research by allowing an investigator to say, "You were given a form, but you just didn't respond."

The Coercive and Corruptive Nature of Passive Consent

Across groups, members brought up the coercive potential of these procedures. Some thought students would not give the form to their parents because they would not want to stand out if they were the only kid whose parent signed the form. In this sense, participants (especially parents) were also concerned that passive consent procedures encourage teenagers to deceive their parents. They also were worried that it sends the wrong message to teenagers—that children rather than parents should be in control of the consent process. As one student said, "Even though I disagree with parental permission in almost every case, I think that [passive consent is] just basically pathetic. We had the same thing in junior high school . . . no kid showed that to their parents. . . . If you really want parental control, it has to be the dumbest thing to do."

Reasons Why Parental Permission Forms Are Often Not Returned

An implicit assumption underlying the ethical justification for passive consent is that a caring and knowledgeable guardian would perceive the research as important and as

desirable for his or her child. From this perspective, the reason for low response rates to "active" parental permission procedures is that parents simply do not have time to respond to the form. This rationale is frequently given for adolescent risk research in economically distressed locales where recruitment is often very difficult (Fisher, 1993; Fisher et al., 1997). Comments of parents and adolescents sharply contradicted the assumption that low parental permission form return rates reflect parental disinterest. Although discussants mentioned that parents sometimes forgot to sign the forms and that students do not give parents the forms out of disinterest, the majority of comments focused on concrete reasons for refusing consent. One set of reasons revolved around the fact that teenagers who did not want to participate in a study often did not give the form to their parent or did not bother to bring the form back to school if the parent had said "no" to participation. Another set of reasons referred to a parent's active decision not to give permission for their child to participate. These reasons included (a) fear that others would learn about a child's problems, (b) a desire to keep family matters private, (c) fear that experimental procedures would harm their child, (d) difficulty understanding the form, (e) disagreement with the nature and purpose of the study, and (f) a desire not to have their children treated like "guinea pigs" or "monkeys."

Suggested Procedures and the Value of Participant Consultation for Parental Permission Procedures

Participants raised two points when asked to provide additional information that might help investigators implement respectful parental permission procedures:

1. When implementing parental permission procedures, scientists must verify that

parents have received and understand the consent forms. Investigators should be wary of child-forged parental signatures. When evaluating ongoing school-based intervention programs, scientists should not assume that parents gave permission for their children to participate in the program.

2. Investigators need to ensure that permission policies do not lead parents or participants to assume they have waived their rights to withdraw, complain about a study, or hold an investigator liable for misconduct.

Ethical dilemmas are ubiquitous in decisions regarding parental permission for youth participation in adolescent risk research. Applied developmental scientists are faced with competing ethical obligations to respect the rights of parents to judge what is in their child's best interest, to protect teenagers' autonomy and privacy, and to develop practical consent procedures that will provide empirical knowledge essential to informed policymaking to promote positive youth development. The opinions that emerged from the participant consultation method described previously indicates that teenagers and parents share these concerns. Their comments suggest that they see decisions regarding the best approach to guardian permission policies as an ethically complex struggle between the scientist's obligations to ensure that waiver of parental permission does not take advantage of decisional vulnerabilities and power inequities of youth and that inflexible adherence to guardian permission policies does not deprive youth of participation in scientific studies that can generate knowledge on which effective risk prevention and treatment programs can be based. These responses underscore the value of the participant consultation approach and the potential for forging partnerships with teens and their

parents in designing parent permission policies in unique scientific and community contexts.

ADOLESCENT AND PARENT PERSPECTIVES ON CONFIDENTIALITY AND DISCLOSURE PROCEDURES

Scientists studying risk behaviors in adolescence often become privy to information suggesting that a participant's well-being is in jeopardy. When studying problems in adolescence, investigators must ethically justify why information regarding participant risk acquired during the course of research should or should not be disclosed to guardians or those expert in the field who can help a participant (Fisher, 1993; 1994; Fisher, Higgins-D'Alessandro, et al., 1996). Reasons both for and against confidentiality and disclosure policies for adolescent risk research were raised in all focus groups. In discussing these policies, parents and teenagers grappled with a scientist's conflicting moral obligations to participants: protecting participant autonomy and privacy, protecting participant welfare, and maintaining integrity in the scientist-participant relationship.

Ethical Justifications for Maintaining Confidentiality

Across generations and different research contexts, the major themes of protecting confidentiality during youth risk research included the following:

- Respect for the decision-making rights of adolescents and their families
- Avoidance of feelings of betrayal
- Avoidance of granting undue authority for researchers to decide which problems should or should not be reported to parents or service providers

- Prevention of giving credibility to false or inaccurate responses
- Protection against the damaging effects of bringing child protection or law enforcement agencies into the lives of participants and their families
- Encouragement for teenagers to take responsibility for their actions
- Autonomy Rights of Participants and Their Families

Discussion in parent and student focus groups reflected concern with autonomy rights in different ways. For example, many parents thought that it is inappropriate for a scientist to be the person to decide whether family or nonfamily members should be informed of a child's problems. Some parents pointed out that the type of information that is considered appropriate for children to communicate to parents is often cultural. As one parent said, "This idea of telling a parent is sometimes . . . cultural. I came from a society in which you don't just talk about everything, so no matter how close I am with my mother, my daughter . . . there are certain things that you don't talk about." Another parent exclaimed that "any relationship of honesty between them [my daughters] and me has to do with us and doesn't have to do with some third party who's also bound to tell me what they said to them." In addition, as one male student emphasized, allowing the researcher to decide to break confidentiality might be "dangerous . . . because then the person doing the survey has the power to think which is, what's confidential. I mean, what's dangerous and what's not."

Students in particular thought that it is important for teenagers to be responsible for their own welfare. For example, in situations in which the researcher learned that participants were involved in fights with other students, some teenagers thought that most students know what they are doing and that teenagers need to learn how to deal with

problems by themselves. These attitudes are illustrated in the following comments from a male and a female student: "Now if I tell you a kid wants to fight me, watch me beat his ass. I don't think you should worry that means what I'm a do. I get jumped, I'm a man, let him learn, let him get a beating if he does." "The researcher should keep it confidential, because . . . that person knows how it made them feel [and] it's up to them to build up the courage, if it was that serious to tell [someone] themselves."

Other students thought that promises of confidentiality would provide them with an opportunity to vent their feelings without worrying about the consequences. As one female explained, "Cause sometimes, I know if I am getting abused at home and I go and I tell my counselor . . . I want them to help me. I don't want her to go back and tell somebody else cause then I don't want everybody to know my business."

Trust and Betrayal

Many groups raised the importance of trust and the obligation of researchers who promise confidentiality to keep their word. One parent explained, "My concern is a word. If you tell a child it is confidential, then you are bound as far as I'm concerned. [If you do not keep your word] then where . . . will this society go?" Some students also questioned whether it is the responsibility of the researcher to help someone who "had no ethics" and was not taking personal responsibility for his or her actions. Respondents thought that breaking confidentiality could lead to feelings of betrayal that might have future repercussions. As one female student put it, if a participant finds out the researcher disclosed personal information, "They won't trust nobody and then they won't tell their problems to the person that can help them."

Validity of Risk Assessments

Group members were concerned about the accuracy of reports. Many cited instances outside the research context in which teenagers had been untruthful about a problem or threat. One female student warned that some teenagers "[lie] about the problem to get out of the house." Others thought that some problems might be minor and go away on their own. One student noted, "If it maybe like a ... small drug, they're not really addicted, but like they may have it once in a while, like maybe they [researchers] shouldn't [disclose]." Parents also cautioned against prematurely disclosing a teenager's problems without ascertaining whether other people in the community were already alerted to the problem.

There was also grave concern that a falsely accused person could be harmed by a scientist's disclosure. Participants told stories of teachers and parents falsely accused of harassment and abuse and the negative impact it had on the family and on the students who lost a good teacher. Students and parents consistently raised concerns that a scientist's report could have the damaging effect of having child protection services or law enforcement brought into a family's life. Parents in particular were hesitant about disclosure policies because they believed that the researchers might not know the appropriate person to tell or might not possess the skills or competence to handle the problem.

Ethical Justifications for Disclosing Information

Teenagers and parents in each group also grappled with situations in which it might be appropriate to disclose information to parents or other concerned adults to protect a participant, agreeing on several points:

- Investigators, as professionals and adults, have a fiduciary responsibility to protect youth from known harm.

- Disclosure policies teach teenagers about the importance of addressing their problems.
- Teenagers who reveal to an investigator that they are in jeopardy are often seeking help.

Are Adults Morally Obligated to Protect Children From Harm?

Teenagers and parents also raised concerns about the moral obligation of an adult to protect children from known harm. As one parent put it, "You're trying to protect the person when you keep something confidential, but in a case like this [e.g., a life-threatening situation], you wouldn't be protecting the person, you're causing more damage." Parents also thought that disclosure policies are helpful because adolescents "need to know that some things are just not secrets for their own well-being, for their own protection ... because it's not going to go away."

A number of student groups brought up the perspective that by not trying to help a youth who had revealed an intention of harming self or someone else, the investigator would be guilty of what one male called "criminal indifference ... this person is gonna get hurt and you have to do something about it." Others thought that if something bad happened to the student, the investigator would feel distressed and could be viewed as an accomplice. As one neighborhood male exclaimed, "'Cause you can't just let that happen, you know, 'cause that makes ... a blame on you and then it also makes you one of the persons who did it because you didn't say nothing, you kept quiet."

Participant Intent

Many discussants thought that, as one female put it, "If a child comes up to you and says this is happening, I think that means they are offering the right for you to go to a higher authority." This sentiment was expressed by another student, "So, in a way, they're telling what happens ... hoping that the researcher might tell someone else because they can't do it themselves."

To Whom Should a Researcher Disclose Information?

When asked to discuss whether it would be best to tell parents, counselors, school administrators, community physicians, or law enforcement officers if disclosure was judged to be necessary, several major themes emerged:

- Although parents can often be their child's best ally, some parents may overreact to a disclosure with punitive measures and others may not know how to help their child.
- Although school counselors are often helpful, many students and parents distrust their motives or are afraid that counselors are required by law or school policy to inform child welfare or other government agencies about a student's problems.
- Physicians and mental health professionals outside the school are often in the best position to help and influence teenagers.

Disclosing to Parents

Some students thought parents were their best allies, that school counselors would tell their parents anyway or that nothing could be accomplished until parents knew about the problem. Drawing on past experience, one male student explained, "Going to a counselor really didn't solve much until they decided to go to my parents and tell them about it." Some students were concerned that telling the parent might lead the parent to harm the child, which in turn would lead the child to run away or increase his or her risk behavior. As one male explained, "It's risky telling parents 'cause some parents they don't know how to handle like that news, they overreact. They make it worse cause if you find out your son is doing drugs or your

daughter you can overreact and scream on them. 'Cause it's going to make it worse cause if you scream on them they going to stimulate their mind [take drugs] 'cause they don't want to talk about it or worry about it."

Students were also fearful that reporting that a third party had harmed or had threatened to harm the teenager might lead a parent to overreact against the perpetrator. Other concerns were that disclosing would get the family in trouble or that the parent would not know what to do and would feel helpless.

Disclosing to School Counselors

Disclosing information to school counselors received mixed reactions. Some thought counselors were in the best position to help the researcher determine if the teen was telling the truth, and also in the best position to help the teen. Others reported instances where they had felt betrayed by a counselor because the counselor broke a confidence or because the counselor did not seem to understand the problem. According to a female student, "I went to my counselor, but she asked me first if I wanted ... somebody to be called. She asked for my permission and I told her no ... She did it anyway."

Social Services and Law Enforcement Agencies

Child protection services were viewed negatively by many parents and teenagers from the more impoverished neighborhoods. One female described her personal experience, "I had problems in my house and I went to my counselor and she called the [child] welfare. ... I felt bad because my whole family went against me." Another student explained, "If you send for BCW [child welfare] or somebody on your family ... you're not fixing the problem." Some thought law enforcement could help protect a teenager who is threatened by another. Others thought that police are part of the problem and engage in illegal behaviors themselves; one male student said, "Police smoke [dope] and everything."

Practitioners Outside the School

Parents and students thought that a mental health professional or physician outside the school setting might be the most helpful person to disclose to. Discussants believed that these practitioners would be most qualified to judge the nature of the problem, to determine if the teenager was telling the truth, and to offer help and guidance. They also thought that such professionals might be less biased than school personnel, who might be pressured to diagnosis a student with a disorder to obtain additional school funding.

RECOMMENDATIONS FOR ENSURING THE ADEQUACY OF CONFIDENTIALITY AND DISCLOSURE POLICIES AND THE VALUE OF PARTICIPANT CONSULTATION

When asked how investigators might improve their confidentiality and disclosure procedures teenagers and parents made several valuable suggestions:

• Participants and their parents should be informed about the researcher's confidentiality and disclosure policies at the beginning of a study. The most preferable policy is one in which the investigator discusses the problem with the teenager and obtains the teenager's permission to disclose information.

• Prior to initiating a study, researchers who anticipate the need to disclose information should ensure that they are (a) competent to assess levels of risk requiring assistance and (b) understand the legal ramifications of disclosures for the teenager, his or her family, and for the investigator.

• Before disclosing information, investigators should (a) determine if the participant is telling the truth, (b) distinguish between problems that need immediate attention and problems that are minor, and (c) find out if other adults in a position to help the teenager are already aware of the problem.

The Importance of Obtaining the Teenager's Permission to Disclose Information

Obtaining the permission of the participant to disclose information to an adult who can provide assistance was a common preference across focus groups. Some thought investigators should seek student permission only if the teenager revealed information that the investigator felt should be disclosed. The majority of discussants, however, believed that teenagers need to be informed about the nature of the investigator's confidentiality and disclosure policies during informed consent. One male magnet school student described this approach as a "don't ask, don't tell situation, because if you don't want me to tell anybody else about some guy slapping you in your ass, then don't tell me because then you put me in an awkward situation." Another female student explained, "It is really important that before you do the research you make it very clear that the line . . . you have to cross for . . . the researcher to be able to go and report it. Like so that the person knows how much . . . what they'll say that will make the researcher . . . report it. That way they . . . both know what the situation is and what . . . and how much information they can share."

A variation of this procedure was proposed by a female student. "First of all, before they interview the student they must need a paper saying either, if something is going on real bad I need your permission to tell . . . your parent or tell your guardian or something, or a paper saying that you can't do that. So before the student tells you, if the paper say that you can tell somebody and the student didn't sign it, you can't tell nobody, because the student didn't give you permission."

If the participant did not want information disclosed, discussants recommended that investigators offer help directly (for example, by walking home with a student home who expressed concern that another student was waiting to attack him or her. Participants thought that researchers needed to be committed to help participants if parents were not going to be told.

Precautionary Steps to
Take Before Disclosing Information

Prior to initiating a study, focus group members suggested that researchers who anticipate the need to disclose information should ensure that they are competent to assess the degree of risk requiring assistance and understand the legal ramifications of disclosures for the teenager, his or her family, and the investigator. In addition, as described previously, focus group participants also recommended that before disclosing information, investigators should (a) determine if the participant is telling the truth, (b) distinguish between problems that need immediate attention and problems that are minor, and (c) find out if other adults in a position to help the teenager are already aware of problem.

According to group members, advance planning should also include developing a plan for reporting. This student comment illustrated their suggestions, "You have to like have a set . . . idea of what you're gonna do when you get your answers." "You don't just tell the parent, 'Oh, your kid is planning on committing suicide tomorrow night,' you say 'Your child is planning on committing suicide tomorrow night, and I'm also telling

you here are people you can call, here's things you can do to stop this.'"

Shared Understandings

In the discussion groups, teenagers and parents grappled with a fundamental ethical question: *Do social scientists have a moral duty to help adolescents who reveal on a survey that they have a drug or suicide problem?* Responses indicated that adolescents and their parents believe scientists have a fiduciary obligation to help youth in jeopardy but that decisions to disclose must be tempered by investigator caution regarding the validity of risk assessment and the potential harmful consequences of disclosure. These findings are consistent with previous work on adolescent and parent expectations (Fisher, Higgins-D'Allesandro, et al., 1996; O'Sullivan & Fisher, 1997) and raise the disconcerting possibility that strict confidentiality policies for youth risk survey research may unintentionally communicate to troubled adolescents that their problem is unimportant, that no services are available, or that knowledgeable adults cannot be depended on to help adolescents in need (Fisher, 1993, 1994, 1999, 2000).

PARTICIPANT PERSPECTIVES:
SOUND EVIDENCE FOR
ETHICAL PRACTICE

The value of applied development science for providing an empirical foundation for youth development policies depends on the ability of investigators to implement ethical procedures that provide scientifically sound responses and adequate protections for participant rights and welfare. The ability to meet these dual obligations can be enhanced through careful consideration of the expectations, fears, and hopes with which teenagers and their parents approach socially sensitive youth research.

Participant consultation can produce sound evidence on which to base the selection of parent permission and confidentiality policies. However, the knowledge, training, and status that place investigators in a fiduciary relationship with participants obligate scientists to take ultimate responsibility for the rights and welfare of survey respondents (Fisher, 1999, 2000). Thus, community perspectives must inform, but cannot substitute for ethical deliberation by individual scientists (Fisher & Fyrberg, 1994). A commitment to engage participants in dialogue regarding ethical procedures will help ensure that policy relevant youth research meet standards of good scientific design and moral responsibility and reflects the values and merits the trust of teenagers and their families.

REFERENCES

American Indian Law Center. (1994). The model tribal research code: With materials for tribal regulation for research and checklist for Indian health boards. Albuquerque, NM: Author.

Appelbaum, P. S., & Rosenbaum, A. (1989). *Tarasoff* and the researcher: Does the duty to protect apply in the research setting? *American Psychologist, 44*, 885-894.

Beeman, D., & Scott, N. (1991). Therapists' attitudes toward psychotherapy informed consent with adolescents. *Professional Psychology: Research & Practice, 22*, 230-234.

Belter, R. W., & Grisso, T. (1984). Children's recognition of rights violations in counseling. *Professional Psychology and Practice, 15*, 899-910.

Brooks-Gunn, J., & Rotheram-Borus, M. J. (1994). Rights to privacy in research: Adolescents versus parents. *Ethics & Behavior, 4*, 109-121

Casas, J. M., & Thompson, C. E. (1991). Ethical principles and standards: A racial-ethnic minority research perspective. *Counseling & Values, 35*, 186-195.

Dryfoos, J. G. (1990). *Adolescents at risk: Prevalence and prevention.* New York: Oxford University Press.

Fisher, C. B. (1993). Integrating science and ethics in research with high-risk children and youth. *SRCD Social Policy Report, 7*, 1-27.

Fisher, C. B. (1994). Reporting and referring research participants: Ethical challenges for investigators studying children and youth. *Ethics & Behavior, 4*, 87-95.

Fisher, C. B. (1997). A relational perspective on ethics-in-science decision making for research with vulnerable populations. *IRB: Review of Human Subjects Research, 19*, 1-4.

Fisher, C. B. (1999). Relational ethics and research with vulnerable populations. *Reports on research involving persons with mental disorders that may affect decision-making capacity* (Vol. II, pp. 29-49). Commissioned Papers by the National Bioethics Advisory Commission, Rockville, MD.

Fisher, C. B. (2000). Relational ethics in psychological research: One feminist's journey. In M. Brabeck (Ed.), *Practicing feminist ethics in psychology* (pp. 125-142). Washington, DC: American Psychological Association.

Fisher, C. B., & Fyrberg, D. (1994). Participant partners: College students weigh the costs and benefits of deceptive research. *American Psychologist, 49*(5), 417-427.

Fisher, C. B., Higgins-D'Allesandro, A., Rau, J. M. B., Kuther, T., & Belanger, S. (1996). Reporting and referring research participants: The view from urban adolescents. *Child Development, 67*, 2086-2099.

Fisher, C. B., Hoagwood, K., & Jensen, P. (1996). Casebook on ethical issues in research with children and adolescents with mental disorders. In

K. Hoagwood, P. Jensen, & C. B. Fisher (Eds.), *Ethical issues in research with children and adolescents with mental disorders* (pp. 135-238). Hillsdale, NJ: Lawrence Erlbaum.

Fisher, C, B., Jackson, J., & Villarruel, F. (1997). The study of African American and Latin American children and youth. In W. Damon (Series Ed.) & R. M. Lerner (Vol. Ed.), *Handbook of child psychology: Vol. 1. Theoretical models of human development* (5th ed., pp. 1145-1207). New York: Wiley.

Fisher, C. B., & Lerner, R.M. (1994). Foundations of applied developmental psychology. In C. B. Fisher & R. M. Lerner (Eds.), *Applied developmental psychology* (pp. 3-20). New York: McGraw-Hill.

Fisher, C. B., & Murray, J. P. (1996). Applied developmental science comes of age. In C. B. Fisher, J. P. Murray, & I. E. Sigel (Eds.), *Graduate training in applied developmental science for diverse disciplines and educational settings* (pp. 1-22). Norwood NJ: Ablex.

Fisher, C. B., & Rosendahl, S. A. (1990). Risks and remedies of research participation. In C. B. Fisher & W. W. Tryon (Eds.), *Ethics in applied developmental psychology: Emerging issues in an emerging field* (pp. 43-59). Norwood, NJ: Ablex.

Fisher, C. B., & Tryon, W. W. (Eds.). (1990). *Ethics in applied developmental psychology: Emerging issues in an emerging field* (pp. 43-59). Norwood, NJ: Ablex.

Fisher, C. B., & Wallace, S. A. (2000). Through the community looking glass: Re-evaluating the ethical and policy implications of research on adolescent risk and psychopathology. *Ethics & Behavior, 10,* 99-118.

Freedman, B. (1975). A moral theory of informed consent. *Hastings Center Report, 5,* 32-39.

Gaylin, W., & Macklin, R. (1982). *Who speaks for the child: The problems of proxy consent.* New York: Plenum.

Glaser, B. G., & Strauss, A. L. (1967). *The discovery of grounded theory: Strategies for qualitative research.* Chicago: Aldine.

Gibbs, J. T. (1988). Conclusions and recommendations. In J. T. Gibbs, A. F. Brunswick, M. E. Conner, R. Dembo, T. E. Larson, R. J. Reed, & B. Solomon (Eds.), *Young, black, and male in America: An endangered species (pp. 317-363).* Dover, MA: Auburn.

Grisso, T., & Vierling, L. (1978). Minors consent to treatment: A developmental perspective. *Professional Psychology, 9,* 412-427.

Guba, E. G., & Lincoln, Y. S. (1982). Epistemological and methodological bases of naturalistic inquiry. *Educational communication & Technology Journal, 30,* 233-252.

Haggerty, R. J., Sherrod, L. R., Garmezy, N., & Rutter, M. (Eds.). (1996). *Stress, risk, and resilience in children and adolescents: Processes, mechanisms, and interventions.* New York: Cambridge University Press.

Hamburg, D. A. (1992). *Today's children: Creating a future for a generation in crisis.* New York: Times Books.

Hammond, W. R., & Yung, B. (1993). Psychology's role in the public health response to assaultive violence among young African American men. *American Psychologist, 48*(2), 142-154.

Hetherington, E. M. (1998). Relevant issues in developmental science: Introduction to special issue. *American Psychologist, 53,* 93-94.

Higgins-D'Alessandro, A., Fisher, C. B., & Hamilton, M. G. (1998). Educating the applied developmental psychologist for university-community partnerships. In R. M. Lerner & L. A. K. Simon (Eds.), *University-community collaborations for the twenty-first century: Outreach scholarship for youth and families* (pp. 157-183). New York: Garland.

Hoagwood, K. (1994). The Certificate of Confidentiality at NIMH: Applications and implications for service research with children. *Ethics & Behavior, 4,* 123-121.

Hoagwood, K., Jensen, P. S., & Fisher, C. B. (1996). Towards a science of scientific ethics in research on child and adolescent mental disorders. In K. Hoagwood, P. Jensen, & C. B. Fisher (Eds.), *Ethical issues in research with children and adolescents with mental disorders* (pp. 3-14). Hillsdale, NJ: LawrenceErlbaum.

Holder, A. R. (1981). Can teenagers participate in research without parental consent? *IRB: Review of Human Subjects Research, 3,* 5-7.

Jenkins, R.R., & Parron, D. (1995). Guidelines for adolescent health research: Issues of race and class. *Journal of Adolescent Health, 17,* 314-322.

Jensen, P. S., Hoagwood, K., & Fisher, C. B. (1996). Bridging scientific and ethical perspectives: Toward synthesis. In K. Hoagwood, P. Jensen, & C. B. Fisher (Eds.), *Ethical issues in research with children and adolescents with mental disorders* (pp. 287-297). Hillsdale, NJ: Lawrence Erlbaum.

Jessor, R. (1993). Successful adolescent development among youth in high-risk settings. *American Psychologist, 48,* 117-116.

Johnson, H. C., Cournoyer, D. E., & Bond, B. M. (1995). Professional ethics and parents as consumers: How well are we doing? *Families in Society, 76,* 408-420.

Keith-Spiegel, P. C. (1983). Children and consent to participate in research. In G. P. Melton, G. P. Koocher, & M. J. Saks (Eds.), *Children's competence to consent.* New York: Plenum.

Kilpatrick, D. G., Acierno, R., Saunders, B., Resnick, H. S., Best, C. L., & Schnurr, P. P. (2000). Risk factors for adolescent substance abuse and dependence: Data from a national sample. *Journal of Consulting and Clinical Psychology, 68,* 19-30.

Koocher, G. P., & Keith-Spiegel, P. C. (1990). *Children, ethics, and the law.* Lincoln: University of Nebraska Press.

Krueger, R. A. (1988). *Analyzing and reporting focus group results.* Thousand Oaks: Sage.

Kuther, T., & Fisher, C. B. (1998). A profile of victimization in suburban early adolescents. *Journal of Early Adolescence, 18,* 53-76.

Lerner, R. M. (1995). *America's youth in crisis: Challenges and options for programs and policies.* Thousand Oaks, CA: Sage.

Lerner, R. M., & Fisher, C. B. (1994). From applied developmental psychology to applied developmental science: Community coalitions and collaborative careers. In C. B. Fisher & R. M. Lerner (Eds.), *Applied Developmental Psychology* (pp. 503-522). New York: McGraw-Hill.

Lerner, R. M., Fisher, C. B., & Weinberg, R. A. (2000a). Towards a science for and of the people: Promoting civil society through the application of developmental science. *Child Development, 71,* 11-20.

Lerner, R. M., Fisher, C. B., & Weinberg, R. A. (2000b). Applying developmental science in the twenty-first century: International scholarship for our times. *International Journal of Behavioral Development, 24,* 24-29.

Lerner, R. M., & Galambos, N. (1998). Adolescent development: Challenges and opportunities for research, programs, and policies. In J. T. Spence (Ed.), *Annual review of psychology* (Vol. 49, pp. 413-446). Palo Alto, CA: Annual Reviews.

Lerner, R. M., & Simon, L. A. K. (Eds.). (1998a). *University-community collaborations for the twenty-first century: Outreach scholarship for youth and families.* New York: Garland.

Lerner, R. M., & Simon, L. A. K. (1998b). The new American outreach university: Challenges and options. In R. M. Lerner & L. A. K. Simon (Eds.), *University-community collaborations for the twenty-first century: Outreach scholarship for youth and families* (pp. 3-23). New York: Garland.

Lerner, R. M., Sparks, E. E., & McCubbin, L. (2000). Family diversity and family policy. In D. Demo, K. Allen, & M. Fine (Eds.), *Handbook of family diversity* (pp. 380-401). New York: Oxford University Press.

Lerner, R. M., & Tubman, J. G. (1990). Plasticity in development: Ethical implications for developmental interventions. In C. B. Fisher & W. W. Tryon (Eds.), *Ethics in applied developmental psychology: Emerging issues in an emerging field* (pp. 113-132). Norwood, NJ: Ablex.

Levine, R. (1986). *Ethics and regulation of clinical research* (2nd ed.). Baltimore: Urban & Schwarzenberg.

Levine, C., Dubler, N. N., & Levine, R. J. (1991). Building a new consensus: Ethical principles and policies for clinical research on HIV/AIDS. *IRB: A Review of Human Subjects Research, 13*(1-2), 1-17.

Liss, M. (1994). State and federal laws governing reporting for researchers. *Ethics & Behavior, 4,* 133-146.

Melton, G. B. (1980). Children's concepts of their rights. *Journal of Clinical Child Psychology, 9,* 186-190.

Melton, G. B. (1990). Certificates of Confidentiality under the Public Health Service Act: Strong protection but not enough. *Violence & Victims, 5,* 67-71.

Melton, G. B., Levine, R. J., Koocher, G. P., Rosenthal, R., & Thompson, W. C. (1988). Community consultation in socially sensitive research: Lessons from clinical trials of treatments for AIDS. *American Psychologist, 43,* 573-581.

Morton, K. L. & Green, V. (1991). Comprehension of terminology related to treatment and patients' rights by inpatient children and adolescents. *Journal of Clinical Child Psychology, 20,* 392-399.

National Commission for the Protection of Human Subjects of Biomedical and Behavioral Research. (1978). *The Belmont report* (DHEW Publications OS 78-0012). Washington, DC: U.S. Department of Health, Education and Welfare.

Oetting, E. R., & Beauvais, F. (1990). Adolescent drug use: Findings of national and local surveys. *Journal of Consulting and Clinical Psychology, 58,* 385-394.

Osher, T. W., & Telesford, M. (1996). Involving families to improve research. In K. Hoagwood, P. Jensen, & C. B. Fisher (Eds.), *Ethical issues in research with children and adolescents with mental disorders* (pp. 29-42). Hillsdale, NJ: Lawrence Erlbaum.

O'Sullivan, C., & Fisher, C. B. (1997). The effect of confidentiality and reporting procedures on parent-child agreement to participate in adolescent risk research. *Applied Developmental Science, 1*(4), 185-197.

Pearson, J. L., Stanley, B., King, C., & Fisher, C. B. (2001a). *Issues to consider in intervention research with persons at high risk for suicidality.* NIMH Suicide Research Consortium. Retrieved June 7, 2002, from www.nimh.nih.gov/research/suicide.htm

Pearson, J. L., Stanley, B., King, C., & Fisher, C. B. (2001b). Intervention research for persons at high risk for suicidality: Safety and ethical considerations. *Journal of Clinical Psychiatry Supplement, 62,* 17-26.

Petersen, A. C., Compas, B. E., Brooks-Gunn, J., Stemmler, M., Ey, S., & Grant, K. E. (1993). Depression in adolescence. *American Psychologist, 48,* 155-168.

Ponterotto, J. G., & Casas, J. M. (1991). *Handbook of ethnic minority counseling research.* Springfield, IL: Charles C Thomas.

Public Welfare, Department of Health and Human Services, Protection of Human Subjects, 45 C.F.R. § 46 (1991a).

Public Welfare, Department of Health and Human Services, Protection of Human Subjects, 45 C.F.R. § 46, Subpart D: Additional Protections for Children Involved as Subjects in Research (1991b).

Rogers, A. S., D'Angelo, L., & Futterman, D. (1994). Guidelines for adolescent participation in research: Current realities and possible solutions. *IRB: A Review of Human Subjects Research, 16*, 1-6.

Ruck, M. D., Keating D. P., Abramovitch, R., & Koegl, C. J. (1998). Adolescents' and children's knowledge about rights: Some evidence for how young people view rights in their own lives. *Journal of Adolescence, 21*, 275-289.

Scarr, S. (1994). Ethical problems in research on risky behaviors and risky populations. *Ethics & Behavior, 4*(2), 147-156.

Schorr, L. B. (1988). *Within our reach: Breaking the cycle of disadvantage.* New York: Doubleday.

Scott-Jones, D. (1994). Ethical issues in reporting and referring in research with low-income minority children. *Ethics & Behavior, 4*, 97-108.

Schulenberg, J., & Maggs, J. L., & Hurrelmann, K. (Eds.). (1997). *Health risks and developmental transitions during adolescence.* New York: Cambridge University Press.

Sugarman, J., Kass, N. E., Goodman, S. N., Parentesis, P., Fernandes, P., & Faden, R. (1998). What patients say about medical research. *IRB: A Review of Human Subjects Research, 10*, 1-7.

Takanishi, R. (1993). The opportunities of adolescence—Research interventions and policy: Introduction to the special issue. *American Psychologist, 48*, 85-87.

Thompson, R. A. (1990). Vulnerability in research: A developmental perspective on research risk. *Child Development, 61*, 1-16.

Vaughn, S., Schumm, J. S., & Sinagub, J. M.(1996). *Focus group interviews in education and psychology.* Thousand Oaks, CA: Sage.

Veatch, R. M. (1987). *The patient as partner.* Bloomington: Indiana University Press.

Weithorn, L. A. (1983). Children's capacities to decide about participation in research. *IRB: A Review of Human Subjects Research, 5*, 1-5.

Section II

ENHANCING INDIVIDUAL ↔ CONTEXT RELATIONS

CHAPTER 6

Families and Ethnicity

HARRIETTE P. MCADOO
ALAN MARTIN

It is every American's wish to have a "better future." Every ethnic family dreams of having a brighter future and a more positive environment in which to raise their children to preserve their distinctive ethnic heritage. As those of the dominant culture wish to preserve their heritage and positively develop their families, ethnic families wish for the same. The presumptive notion of "Come learn family development from us" or more subliminally, "Assimilate into our culture" will do nothing positive, except to further the debate on self-imposed superiority.

It is the purpose of this chapter to fully inform the readers of crucial concerns, programs, and principles that must undergird future policy innovations with respect to ethnic families. It is hoped that present programs and policies toward ethnic families will be given another look, especially in light of their changing demographics and increasingly urgent needs. Key considerations must be given to matters in the realm of education, socialization, health practices, and just

policies. Failing in these respects will simply accrue much greater future headaches for the various systems in which each individual, and hence each ethnic family, is nested.

The ethnic family forms a crucial part of this society's social system and is thus expected to positively contribute to the societal system in which it is embedded (Hildebrand, Phenice, Gray, & Hines, 2000). The general system's theoretical tenet that the "whole is greater than the sum of its parts" will lead us to the high ground of accepting and understanding the important contribution of each ethnic person, and thus each ethnic family, in the greater scheme of development. No ethnic group, culture, or individual must be viewed as unimportant or merely incidental, for such a notion will sorely detract from the healthy and positive development of the "whole." The contributions of each ethnic group must be valued, respected, considered, and used to enhance and develop the entire system: that is, American society.

DEFINING ETHNIC FAMILIES

It is believed that we all came from one "mother" in the Nile Valley, eons ago. Our families moved out from that center to all parts of the globe. We have migrated over the centuries and responded over the course of time to the geographical conditions of our diverse environments. Our families developed different cultures, different races, different ways of viewing the world, and different rituals as they faced the mysteries and uncertainties of life. We have diversified; each group, in its own place, has developed a culture appropriate to its time and environment.

As we have come together over time in this land of the United States, we have not done so equally in power and resources. Families and individuals from diverse groups came to America to escape tyranny or poverty or to seek a better way of life for their families, or were brought against their wills to work. Of the families who came to this land from European countries, some were poverty stricken and oppressed and some were wealthy (Zinn & Eitzen, 1990). Many came with an assurance of their culture, their God, and their "manifest destiny" that has continued into the present. Native Americans, who were already here, were subjugated and decimated. Enslaved Africans were brought to shore up the economy and were denied the right to be human. Asians were brought in to labor in the western part of the country and were never looked on as equals; but many Asians are now becoming part of powerful economic forces in America. Families from Spanish-speaking lands have been in North America for centuries; some were indigenous, some were immigrants, and those who arrived later gained in importance. As we look at the various families in our country today, we may well be amazed at the variety we find. Each group brought with it its members' uniqueness; each brought parts of another culture as well as other elements of ethnicity that continue to flourish today.

A family's ethnicity is critical to many aspects of life in the United States. "Ethnicity is the identification of the entire family within a cluster of individuals who may or may not be aligned in racial grouping or land of origin" (McAdoo, 1999, p. ix). Furthermore, "Family ethnicity is the sum total of people's ancestry and cultural dimensions, as families collectively identify the core of their beings" (McAdoo, 1999, p. ix). It involves the handing down of distinctive family customs, proverbs, and stories from generation to generation and similarly incorporates the celebrations, foods, religious ceremonies, and migration stories.

The term *ethnicity,* in general, is also principally used to convey cultural distinctness that is derived mainly from national origin, language, religion or a combination thereof (Wilkinson, 1999). The range of definitions from various researchers attests to the fact that a family's ethnic identity is composed of multiple complex factors. Yeh and Huang (1996) purport that one's ethnicity is strongly related to and influenced by one's social context and external factors, such as geographic location, educational setting, relationships, stereotypes, and racism.

Families primarily transmit and perpetuate language, fundamental beliefs, folkways, values, lifestyles, national pride, racial distinctions, ethnic traditions, ancestral history and connections, and social class to their offspring (Wilkinson, 1999). Most scholars who attempt to define family ethnicity are careful not to define it too narrowly, lest they create confusion. For the sake of simplicity and clarity, we shall therefore define it as a family's reference to their descent, ethnicity, ancestry, lineage, national group, and country in which the person or the person's ancestors or parents were born (Wilkinson, 1999). Ethnic families, therefore, are ethnic groups who may technically be in the minority in terms of numbers in the United States population and whose ethnic status, with the exception of Native Americans, begins in locations outside the North American continent.

In current times, ethnic families are thought of as being people within groups who are informally classified as *people of color* or one of the nondominant subgroups in the United States (McAdoo, 1999). The concept of *racial/ethnic* refers to groups who constitute socially, politically, and economically subordinated populations (Jackson, 2001; McAdoo, 1999; Wilkinson, 1999). These are groups with fewer opportunities and less political power; they are economically disadvantaged and therefore have lower family incomes than the dominant and privileged descendents from the European continent. These groups have experienced political subordination, social discrimination, and forms of exclusion.

The Ethnic Family: Increasing in Importance

Family ethnicity is becoming increasingly important in the 21st century as a result of the diverse representation within the United States population (McAdoo, 1999; U.S. Bureau of the Census, 2001). Its importance is, and will also largely be, due to the increasing awareness of individuals and families about moving beyond social class, racial groupings, regional differences, and even country of origin. America is experiencing a changing complexion. The simplistic bicategorization of the population into "black and white" is a method of the past. The 2000 census data show that 2.4% of Americans identified themselves as members of more than one race (U.S. Bureau of the Census, 2001). The rapid growth among ethnic groups in the United States necessitated an unprecedented 63 race categories on the last census forms (U.S. Bureau of the Census, 2001). That accounts for 58 more categories

than the last census. This is a definite testimony to the increasing importance of becoming eminently aware of family ethnicity within the U.S. population.

The growth rate for America's Anglo population, in contrast to that of all other ethnic groups, was much slower (U.S. Bureau of the Census, 2001). The total of all non-Hispanic whites increased by no more than 5.3%, to 198.2 million. This is a clear indication that the gap between the dominant or majority Caucasian group and all other ethnic groups is certainly decreasing. This in itself bears major program and policy implications for families in ethnic groups of color.

The Ethnic Family's Changing Demographics

The wider implications of the present and future population explosion of ethnic families of color warrants our urgent attention. Every facet of ethnic family life will be affected by the drastic demographic shifts. The United States will be a bit older and much more ethnically diverse a century from now. The Census Bureau predicts that the current population of 281 million will more than double to 571 million by the year 2100, with a median age rising above 40, and much larger proportions of ethnic people of color (Schmid, 2000).

Close to 1 million new immigrants are flowing into the United States annually. The latest 2000 population census growth figures from 1990 to 2000 showed a massive demographic change (U.S. Bureau of the Census, 2001). The figure for African Americans increased by 21.1%, to 35.4 million people, comprising nearly 13% of the total population. The figure for the Asian population increased by 74.3%, to 11.5 million people, or about 4% of the total population. The figures for American Indians, Eskimos, and Aleuts increased by 14%, to 2.4 million people, or just below 1% of the total population. More astoundingly, the figure for Hispanics (who may be of any race) increased by 57.9%, to 35.3 million, or about 13% of the total population. It is also projected that within the next 5 years, a further phenomenal growth spurt will be witnessed among Hispanics, who are to become the new majority among ethnic people of color (U.S. Bureau of the Census, 2001).

The American population is growing even more complex in that 2.4%, or 6.8 million, identified themselves in the 2000 census as members of more than one race.

Socialization in the Ethnic Family

A key aspect in developing positive child and family development for ethnic families is the importance of proper ethnic socialization within this multinested, multicultural society. One area of continuing concern is that of explaining ethnic diversity to children. Parents of children of color face the same task that all other parents must complete to help their children develop into functioning, self-sufficient adults. It is more difficult to raise children to have pride in their ethnic group's concepts when the group is perceived in a negative manner by the wider societal system (McAdoo, 1999). Clinical and empirical evidence have shown a normal distribution of feelings of self-worth in ethnically diverse children. Some feel very good about themselves and move successfully through their developmental tasks. Others are overwhelmed by limited opportunities and poor prospects for future advancement.

Families are the primary developmental and socialization agents for perpetuating nationality, racial distinctions, values, lifestyles, and social class status within their ethnicity (Wilkinson, 1999). In examining ethnic socialization, Marshall (1995) reminded us that the family is responsible for preparing children for different environments by giving them a positive sense of ethnic

identity. Ethnic groups especially need to give their children confidence in an environment that has historically made them feel inferior and less than welcome (Jackson, 2001). The socialization process within families is key to instilling within children a sense of ethnic pride, loyalty, and identification (McAdoo, 1999). It is through an ethnically distinctive socialization process that the child will be less insecure about his or her place and worth in society (Hochschild, 1995). This will provide children of ethnic families with a true sense of belonging, "family weness," and group orientation.

The following three social fields are important in this process of socialization among ethnic groups: first, the primary group, made up of the child's closest kin—most important, the mother, father, or parent surrogate(s). The child will primarily adopt their behavior, attitudes, and emotional responses as his or her own (Naylor, 1999; Reminick, 1983). An essential aspect to understanding socialization among ethnic families is the cultural self-identification of the family (Martinez, 1999). Children must be socialized to know exactly who they are and to which group they biologically, racially, and ethnically belong. McAdoo & Rukuni (1993) agree that family cultural ethnicity and its relation to the resiliency and functioning of children is a very important concept. Family ethnicity, culture, and the meanings derived from familial and extra-familial interactions are the core of individual, familial, and community identity (Martinez, 1999; McAdoo, 1999).

The second social field is the extended kin or relatives outside the primary family group who may have some influence on the developing child. Among ethnic groups, the three-generation, extended-kin group plays a most important and preserving role in ethnic tradition (Reminick, 1983). Extended family support in the child socialization process is very important in all classes of ethnic families

(McAdoo, 1999). Among certain ethnic groups (e.g., Mexican and African American), both lineal (brothers and sisters) and collateral (uncles, aunts, and cousins) relatives play key roles as part of a cohesive ethnic family unit responsible for socializing children (Chahin, Villarruel, & Viramontez, 1999; McAdoo, 1999). Fictive kin (i.e., unrelated relatives) are also considered as part of the extended family network, with rights and privileges afforded to all relatives in relation to child socialization. In many respects, it is equivalent to the African concept of "the village raising the child."

The final social field is that of some secondary groups, such as church, school, and voluntary associations, whose ideals, goals, and values are consistent with those of the ethnic family and extended family (McAdoo, 1999; Reminick, 1983). Among these microsystems, church has played a key role in the socialization process of children within ethnic families. African American men and women consider religiosity and spirituality as critical factors in the rearing and socialization of their children because it provides them with the coping mechanisms necessary to face difficult life events (McAdoo, 1999; Mattis, 1997). By far, women have been the backbone of the African American church (Billingsley, 1992). Furthermore, they serve as the primary vehicles through which religious and cultural values are informally transmitted and sustained within and across generations (Taylor, Jackson, & Chatters, 1997). In fact, the effect of maternal socialization is evidenced in part by the religious affiliation of the mother being a strong predictor of the religious affiliation of adults (Taylor et al., 1997).

THE ETHNIC FAMILY: EDUCATIONAL INEQUITIES

A very high value is placed on education in the United States, for it is purported to be the doorway to multiple opportunities for those who obtain it at the tertiary level. Sadly, though, not all opportunities are created equal when it comes to ethnic families. One would think that at the turn of the 21st century, the cheerleading nation of democracy would be viewed as the modeling architect of equal education for all individuals. It is universally known that there is such a thing as pursuing the "American dream" and that idealistic (in many cases mythical) dream begins by achieving competence in school (Hochschild, 1995). But what if such achievement is hampered by a system that does not treat all people as equal? What if such achievement has multiple highways to its pinnacle, on which some have unhindered and smooth rides and others have to struggle through the morass of obstructions (economic deprivation, political injustice, and social inequities)? For some, then, education may turn out to be the ideal American dream, but for others, an American nightmare and a continual uphill battle.

Historically, ethnic families have always been deprived, in some form or fashion, in the educational arena (Naylor, 1999). The dominance of Anglocentrism and the marginality of multilingual and multicultural education are seed forms of greater discrepancies and discriminatory practices in the education system (Macedo, 1994). Ethnic families have historically been subjugated to labor under an educational system that in the main, catered to only the majority population. A sound educational system is one that will engender the principles of democracy by showing commitment to develop the human potential of all its students (Gutmann, 1987). Education is necessary to maintain the economy's vitality and growth, but how will it thrive if only a certain sector of the population is provided with its privileges (Weiner, 2000)? Major efforts must be expended in eliminating the kind of historical constriction and discrimination ethnic families face on a regular basis. Given the social and economic problems that are the results of structural aspects of the culture, they are often poorly prepared to successfully pursue higher education. Subsequently, they will thus be poorly prepared to deal with the mainstream American workplace (Wilcox, 1999).

The "Public School" Dilemma in Education

Theoretically, the public school system of education means that class differences are leveled and everyone is educated equally to pursue the idealized American dream. Many, especially the privileged, really believe that this theory is true but fail to fully acknowledge the discriminatory practices in the current educational system. A major concern continues to be the inability of certain school districts to meet the individualized needs of students, especially students of color, students with a first language other than English, students with special needs, and economically disadvantaged students who are typically disproportionately immersed in public school settings (Gardner & Talbert-Johnson, 2000).

This situation does not suggest that children of ethnic families and others with special needs are somehow predisposed to failure in school; however, they are faced with many more challenges that can interfere with success in school (Garbarino, Dubrow, Kostelny, & Pardo, 1992). Challenges such as poverty, social marginalization, racism, classism, violence, crime, and socially toxic environments are realities, especially in public schools located in urban settings (Dalaker & Naifeh, 1998; Kozol, 1991).

The attempts to desegrate schools since the landmark court decision in *Brown v. Board of Education* (1954), with the view to establishing equity in schools, have brought about few substantive changes to remedy such inequities (Talbert-Johnson, 2000).

Almost 50 years later, many of the primary issues still have not been addressed. Few attempts have been made to structure public school curricula around social issues that address race, socioeconomic status, gender, and disability (Haynes & Comer, 1990; Talbert-Johnson, 2000). Several researchers agree that profound and significant educational reform will take place only when it includes educational equity and serves the needs and interests of its diverse student population (Tate, Ladson-Billings, & Grant, 1996). Many public schools in urban communities are increasing their ethnic intakes. They are predominantly increasing in African American, Hispanic, and Southeast Asian populations (Talbert-Johnson, 2000).

According to Oakes (1985), many more ethnic students in desegregated schools are still being disproportionately placed on lower academic tracks than are white students; they are typically higher in suspension ratings, referrals to treatment centers, and higher in placements in special classrooms for remedial work. Children from ethnic families must carry this burden because they are being measured against a curriculum that is Eurocentric in focus (Irvine, 1990; Russo & Talbert-Johnson, 1997). The crucial question is "Where is the equity?"

After almost half a century, more significant progress should have been made toward a more systemic desegregation in the public school educational arena. What is called for, then, is progress that will clearly reflect the increasing ethnic and cultural diversity of students and families in communities, such as culturally relevant pedagogies, revised curricula (more representative of all cultures), adjustment in social climate, practices, and policies (Haynes & Comer, 1990; Oakes, 1985; Talbert-Johnson, 2000).

In addition, the investment in training, certifying, and maintaining teachers from diverse ethnic groups will go a long way in solving some of the public school inequity dilemmas (Howey & Zimpher, 1991). Public schools are typically staffed with female and Caucasian teachers (Gardner & Talbert-Johnson, 2000). Futrel (1999) reveals that 25% to 30% of new educators who enter the profession leave within 5 years of entering the classroom. It is, therefore, a necessity to have educators of both genders who possess an ethnic socialization awareness (Boyer & Baptiste, 1996). In this way, they will have an understanding of how individuals process their total identities as part of the learning setting. They will also be better equipped to sympathize with an individual's ethnicity, race, gender, primary language, and economic status (Gardner & Talbert-Johnson, 2000). They will thus be better equipped to make an invaluable contribution to bridging the inequity gap in education in the public school setting.

The "Alternative Choice" Dilemma in Education

Much was said about "leaving no child behind" during the 2000 national political campaign. The stark reality is that multiple efforts have already been made to achieve this very goal, but with minimal success. Among the attempted efforts to reform the public schools are shared decision making, school-based management, privatization, vouchers, choice programs, and charter schools (Gardner & Talbert-Johnson, 2000). Similar attempts to expose families and children to educational options include magnet schools, alternative schools, tax credits for private school tuition, intradistrict choice plans, interdistrict choice plans, and alternative programs within a single school (Metcalf & Tait, 1999).

This kind of school reform approach sounds good, but how will it reshape the educational system from a mind-set of desegregation (based on economics, class, and neighborhoods) to a mind-set of genuine

integration and equality? Orfield (1996) purports that the school transformation gains for children of color have been negligible. Some of the reform approaches are offered with very little consideration for the neighborhoods in which children and families live (Gardner & Talbert-Johnson, 2000). Public schools in urban settings, for example, that are populated mainly with African American and Hispanic children and steeped in poverty, increased health risks, limited social support, and personal safety issues, need much more than just an alternative school to attend (Hanson & Carta, 1996). The family and child's entire "needs package" must be addressed.

We have already discussed the reality that ethnic families and children will dramatically increase over the next few decades. Many researchers are predicting that not much will change with respect to educational inequalities in the coming decades. The problems of pervasive racial separatism, unequal patterns of poverty, political divisiveness over the educational issue, a shift in the economic power base, and culturally sensitive curricula remain (Gardner & Talbert-Johnson, 2000; Meeks, Meeks, & Warren, 2000; Orfield, 1996). These factors significantly affect children of ethnic families more than does the mere choice of a better school.

The global description may not, however, be the cry of all ethnic families. Some are beginning to experience the benefits of moving from the public school arena to charter schools in some states. A collaborative study by researchers at Harvard, Georgetown, and Wisconsin Universities found that ethnic students (African Americans in particular) who transferred to private schools scored 6 percentile points higher than those in public schools (Wyatt, 2000). Thus, despite the background, social class, and former educational training of these students, the study attested to the key characteristic of resiliency within ethnic families. With continued improved opportunities, leveling the social and economic playing fields as well as the educational field, ethnic children and adults will gain the capacity to achieve.

POLICY INNOVATIONS TOWARD ETHNIC FAMILIES

Ethnic families are embedded in multiple systems. Each family as a microsystem is either directly or indirectly affected by the powerful influences of the larger systems (Bronfenbrenner, 1979; Jervis, 1997). Policies that negatively affect ethnic families are therefore not just mere outgrowths of private or personal attitudes, but products of institutions and inequalities in the societal system (Jackman, 1994).

For many decades, ethnic families have been subjected to policies aimed at keeping them subordinated and marginalized, while protecting the rights and privileges of the majority. Some welfare policies, for example, introduced after the deficit-modeled Moynihan (1965) report, severely affected the well-being of the majority of ethnic families. Even though his report was primarily based on the African American family, its widespread effects are still being felt today by many people of color. When policymakers operate from racialized stratification ideologies, resulting policies will mirror such ideologies. If policymakers subconsciously or consciously hold to the notion that ethnic family inequality is due to a lack in motivation, willpower, or genetic ability to learn, then policy production toward them will match such beliefs (Tuch & Hughes, 1996).

The results of the 2000 census revealed that subtle policies of discrimination and segregation still exist in many areas. At the Leadership Conference on Civil Rights in April 2001, social scientists presented detailed analyses of persistent national trends of continued segregation and isolation among ethnic people of color in most metropolitan areas (U.S. Bureau of the Census, 2001). The report stated two overall policies factors that affected various ethnic groups: (a) There has hardly been any change since 1990 in the levels of segregation, and the average Caucasian continues to live in neighborhoods that look vastly different from those of blacks, Hispanics, and Asians, and (b) a major increase is needed in fair-housing enforcement, stronger penalties for violators, and a stronger push by suburban governments and schools to expect and prepare for a wave of social change. The scientists informed the authorities that the most dangerous implications of these factors continue to exist and that subtle developments reinforced other societal inequalities. They urged the national government to reverse the trend of residential segregation along ethnic lines and to make the implementation of such policies a national priority.

Unfair policies, whether overt or covert, continue to plague and poison the national system of true democracy. A more sensitive policy that has dominated the news media headlines over the last few years is that of *racial profiling*. Racial profiling can be defined as the identification of potential criminal suspects on the basis of skin color or accent (Cureton, 2000; Goldberg, 2000; Koch, 2000; McAlpin, 2000). It has become obvious that the key targets for this unjust and inhumane practice are ethnic groups of color. Should policy implementation and justice be dependent on the social, economic, and cultural characteristics of a group's ethnicity? (Arrigo, 1999; Hagan, 1994). Is there a justifiable reason for the disproportionate numbers of ethnic people of color (versus Caucasians) being stopped, harassed, and even imprisoned? At the Leadership Conference on Civil Rights (2000), the following example was illuminated with respect to such practices toward ethnic people of color:

> On April 25, 1997, a tortilla factory in Salt Lake City owned by Rafael Gomez, an American citizen, was the subject of a police

raid in which 75 heavily armed police officers brandished rifles and pistols, struck Gomez in the face with a rifle butt, pointed a gun at his six-year old son, ordered the 80 factory employees to lie down on the floor, and dragged Gomez' secretary across a room by her hair. The raid, based on an anonymous tip, uncovered no illegal activity. (p. 8)

Numerous such incidents occur on a daily basis, but because the results do not culminate in someone's death or some tragic result, they are kept from public attention. This in itself is partial justice toward ethnic people of color and gross inequality before the law (Cureton, 2000). Covert policies of discrimination or prejudice at the local levels speak to much greater implications and responsibilities at the federal level. Stronger laws and policies with more stringent and attention-getting consequences need to be enforced at the national level, to eradicate or minimize racial profiling practices.

HEALTH NEEDS
OF ETHNIC FAMILIES

The cultural diversity of the U.S. population makes it quite difficult to merely talk about health issues in terms of the general population. This is a crucial matter, because inequities still exist between racial or ethnic groups. (Crespo, 2000). The present health estimates are unable to provide a complete and definitive health profile of all racial or ethnic groups in the country. However, there are enough data on non-Hispanic blacks and Hispanics that reveal increasing health disparities (Montgomery & Carter-Pokras, 1993; National Center for Health Statistics, 1998). Inequities in one system will have deleterious consequences on another. Ethnic families of color have historically experienced lower economic opportunities and, therefore, limited access to health insurance, prescription medication, and health care (Crespo, 2000). Discrimination in the realm of education,

which is strongly related to health behaviors, has again placed ethnic families at a crucial disadvantage. The combined disadvantages of limited education and economics have constructed the foundation for ethnic families to be mainly employed in more manual occupations, compared with the privileged majority, that require higher energy expenditure. How would they find the energy and time to devote to activities of a preventative nature when they are employed in very taxing jobs; have to work for long hours to make ends meet; work in conditions in which perhaps their health is compromised; live in neighborhoods with limited resources and recreational opportunities and facilities; and reside in residential environments that may be stressful?

In addressing racial/ethnic disparities in health care, Srinivasan and Guillermo (2000) suggest that the Asian American and Native Hawaiian/Pacific Islander groups are virtually "invisible" for serious consideration. Western practices of medicine and application of clinical therapies may seriously miss the mark with these subgroups. Srinivasan and Guillermo cite the example of Alzheimer's disease and how it is perceived among the Chinese:

The Chinese understand it as an imbalance in the chi (the source of life and energy). They thus have a different notion of Alzheimer disease and do not follow a Western or allopathic biomedical model of the disease and its progression. (p. 1)

The authors strongly suggest that a fuller understanding of alternative medical therapies appropriate to the increasing numbers of Asian and Native Hawaian/Pacific Islanders needs to be taken into account. Furthermore, these groups are daily faced with the obstacle of the lack of appropriate, cultural and linguistical services, which adds to their marginalization.

Several researchers have highlighted several major persistent racial and ethnic disparities in the realm of access to health (DeLew &

Weinick, 2000; Williams & Rucker, 2000). These researchers purport that disparities in access to care remain disproportionate, even after controlling for health insurance coverage and income. Andrews and Elixhauser (1998) report that Hispanic Americans are far less likely to receive major therapeutic procedures than are white Americans. The rate of diabetes-related amputations are 25% higher among African Americans than among whites (Sondik, Wilson-Lucas, Madans, & Smith, 2000). Ethnic people of color continue to have higher rates of morbidity and mortality than do white people, despite the advances in medical technology (Williams & Rucker, 2000). Native Americans and Hispanics continue to have higher rates than whites of diseases and deaths for multiple conditions (Bunker, Frazier, & Mosteller, 1995). These examples merely scratch the surface with respect to the multiple discrepancies that exist in health care toward ethnic families.

Several researchers maintain that the harbinger of the above inequities in health care, and access to it, is systematic discrimination (DeLew & Weinick, 2000; Sondik et al., 2000; Williams & Rucker, 2000). McAdoo (1999) posits that racism and discrimination is rooted in an ideology of inferiority that drives and directs societal resources according to ranked categories. History will attest to the fact that nondominant racial/ethnic groups have, either by law or custom, received inferior treatment in major societal institutions, and medical care is no exception (Williams & Rucker, 2000). Racial/ethnic groups and the poor have long since been at the receiving end of inferior care and are usually not considered as desirable patients by health care providers (Van Ryan & Burke, 2000). What, then, is the antidote for such a historical dilemma?

As the nation grows to be more and more diverse in its cultural makeup, health care organizations must and should strive to change the way they deliver care to meet the diverse needs of a multicultural society. One of the major suggestions by researchers on this issue is for health care organizations to provide culturally appropriate care to ethnic families. Several suggestions for the enactment of this approach are forthcoming from various researchers (Crespo, 2000; Srinivasan & Guillermo, 2000; Van Ryan & Burke, 2000):

1. Culturally appropriate social marketing

2. Facilitating the language barrier impediment

3. Translation of written materials and patient documentation

4. Sensitivity to cultural practices, mores, and values

5. Consideration of ethnically sensitive spiritual and religious factors in treatments

6. Cross-cultural consultation on health care practices

7. The training of staff in cultural competency matters

8. Culturally sensitive hospital menu

9. Recruitment of staff who match the ethnic population(s) being served

10. Desensitizing medical staff in discrimination and stereotyping of ethnic families

The above list is certainly not an exhaustive one, but will go a long way in blazing the trail to a more culturally sensitive and equitable approach to treating ethnic families.

Patients of a particular ethnic group are emotionally, psychologically, and ultimately biologically affected by the attitude of care of those who attend to them. This is especially the case if they feel that medical staff view them as a less valuable patients than those in the dominant group. It is the moral responsibility of everyone in the policy arena to ensure that the necessary policy guidelines are firmly set and implemented to reduce the inequities and disparities that currently exist in this society with respect to health care (Krieger, 1999; Williams, 1999; Williams & Rucker 2000). To be more appropriately informed, it may even be necessary for policymakers and health care providers to form a much more active collaboration with ethnically diverse communities. A discourse with those directly affected (i.e., the ethnic families in communities) will serve a much more practically informed purpose than a mere theoretically driven approach.

The true challenge for researchers is to uncover the basis for all the existing disparities in the health care system and ignore the political pressures at work. The federal government has already outlined regulations that would prohibit discrimination in government programs receiving federal funding; it is now time for industry to examine their corporate behavior with respect to this matter as well (Suro, 2000). Antiquated assumptions with respect to the needs, diagnosis, and treatment of ethnic families of color must cease to be based on the predominantly homogenous, western, white male model. Strong efforts should be made to implement the suggested culturally relevant modifications to meet the health needs of an increasingly diversified society (Suro, 2000; Van Ryan & Burke, 2000). We are not holding our breath.

CONCLUSIONS

As society becomes more and more diverse, it is important that the essential needs of burgeoning ethnic families not be overlooked. A new language should be formed that will positively convey the inclusion of every ethnic group in America and foster a true sense of belonging. Concomitantly, each ethnic group must feel and be valued for its distinctive cultural characteristics and practices and be fully allowed to participate in American economical, political, and social life (Barlow, Taylor, & Lambert, 2000).

Hochschild's (1995) suggestions of what it would take for every ethnic person to feel part of the American dream are worth noting. Her suggestion is for every individual to have the following: (a) equal opportunity, (b) the promise of success, (c) individual control over his or her own destiny, and (d) personal virtue conferred on the successful. These tenets are the cornerstones of any just society. The total embrace of each ethnic group, with all its diverse contributions, will move this society toward more closely promoting positive child, adolescent, and family development.

It is time to move beyond contemplating suggestions. Many laws currently exist with respect to improving the lot of the ethnic family but are not strictly enforced. One has to wonder about the rationale behind the nonenforcement. Could it have something to do with a political system that still, at its core, protects European values?

REFERENCES

Andrews, R. M., & Elixhauser, A. (1998). *Access to major procedures: Are Hispanics treated differently than non-Hispanic whites?* Rockville, MD: Agency for Health Care Policy and Research.

Arrigo, B. (1999). *Social justice, criminal justice: The maturation of critical theory in law, crime, and deviance.* Belmont, CA: Wadsworth.

Barlow, K. M., Taylor, D. M., & Lambert, W. E. (2000). Ethnicity in America and feeling "American." *The Journal of Psychology, 134*(6), 581-591.

Billingsley, A. (1992). *Climbing Jacob's Ladder: The enduring legacy of African American families.* New York: Simon & Schuster.

Boyer, J. B., & Baptiste, H. P. (1996). The crisis in teacher education in America: Issues of recruitment and retention of culturally different (minority) teachers. In J. Sikula, T. Buttery, & E. Guyton (Eds.), *Handbook of research on teacher education* (2nd ed., pp. 779-794). New York: Macmillan.

Bronfenbrenner, U. (1979). *The ecology of human development.* Cambridge, MA: Harvard University Press.

Brown v. Board of Educ., 347 U.S. 483 (1954).

Bunker, J. P., Frazier, H. Y., & Mosteller, F. (1995). The role of medical care in determining health: Creating an inventory of benefits. In B. C. I. Amick, S. Levine, A. R Tarlov, & D. C. Walsh (Eds.), *Society and health.* New York: Oxford University Press.

Chahin, J., Villarruel, F. A., & Viramontez, R. A. (1999). Dichos y Regranes: The transmission of cultural values and beliefs. In H. P. McAdoo (Ed.), *Family ethnicity: Strength in diversity* (pp. 153-170). Thousand Oaks, CA: Sage.

Crespo, C. J. (2000). Encouraging physical activity in minorities. *The Physician and Sports Medicine, 28*(10), 36-51.

Cureton, S. T. (2000). Justifiable arrests or discretionary justice? Predictors of racial arrest differentials. *Journal of Black Studies, 30*(5), 703-719.

Dalaker, J., & Naifeh, M. (1998). *Poverty in the United States: 1997, current population reports* (Series P60-201). Washington, DC: Government Printing Office.

DeLew, N., & Weinick, R. M. (2000). An overview: Eliminating racial, ethnic, and SES disparities in health care. *Health Care Financing Review, 21*(4), 1-7.

Futrel, M. H. (1999). Recruiting minority teachers. *Educational Leadership, 56*(8), 30-33.

Garbarino, J., Dubrow, N., Kostelny, K., & Pardo, C. (1992). *Children in danger: Coping with the consequences of community violence.* San Francisco: Jossey-Bass.

Gardner, R., & Talbert-Johnson, C. (2000). School reform and desegregation: The real deal or more of the same? *Education and Urban Society, 33*(1), 74-87.

Goldberg, J. (2000, June 20). The color of suspicion. *The New York Times,* p. 50.

Gutmann, A. (1987). *Democratic education.* Princeton, NJ: Princeton University Press.

Hagan, J. (1994). *Crime and disrepute.* London: Pine Forge.

Hanson, M. J., & Carta, J. J. (1996). Addressing the challenges of families with multiple risks. *Exceptional Children, 62*(3), 201-212.

Haynes, N. M., & Comer, J. (1990). Helping black children succeed: The significance of some social factors. In K. Lomotey (Ed.), *Going to school: The African-American experience* (pp. 103-112). New York: State University of New York Press.

Hildebrand, V., Phenice, L. A., Gray, M. M., & Hines, R. P. (2000). *Knowing and serving diverse families.* Columbus, OH: Merrill.

Hochschild, J. L. (1995). *Facing up to the American dream: Race, class, and the soul of the nation.* Princeton, NJ: Princeton University Press.

Howey, K. R., & Zimpher, N. L. (1991). *Restructuring the education of teachers.* Reston, VA: Association of Teacher Educators.

Irvine, J.(1990). *Black students and school failure.* Westport, CT: Greenwood.

Jackman, M. R. (1994). *The velvet glove: Paternalism and conflict in gender, class and race.* Berkeley: University of California Press.

Jackson, J. S. (2001). New directions in thinking about race in America: African Americans in a diversifying nation. *African American Research Perspective, 7*(1), 1-36.

Jervis, R. (1997). System effects: *Complexity in political and social life.* Princeton, NJ: Princeton University Press.

Koch, A. (2000, May 17). Can police, blacks bridge racial divide? *The Seattle Times*, p. A1.

Kozol, J. (1991). *Savage inequalities: Children in America's schools.* New York: Harper.

Krieger, N. (1999). Embodying inequality: A review of concepts, measures, and methods for studying health consequences of discrimination. *International Journal of Health Services, 29*(2), 295-352.

Leadership Conference on Civil Rights. (2000). *Justice on trial: Racial disparities in the criminal justice system.* Retrieved from the World Wide Web on September 5, 2001, at http://www.civilrights.org.

Macedo, D. (1994). English only: The tongue-tying of America. In D. Macedo (Ed.), *Taking sides: Clashing views on controversial issues in race and ethnicity* (pp. 135-145). Guilford, CT: Dushkin.

Marshall, S. (1995). Ethnic socialization of African American children: Implications for parenting, identity development, and academic achievement. *Youth and Adolescence, 24*(4), 337-357.

Martinez, E. A. (1999). Mexican American/Chicano families: Parenting as diverse as the families themselves. In H. P. McAdoo (Ed.), *Family ethnicity: Strength in diversity* (pp. 121-134). Thousand Oaks, CA: Sage.

Mattis, J. S. (1997). The spiritual well-being of African Americans: A preliminary analysis. *Journal of Prevention and Intervention in the Community, 16,* 103-120.

McAdoo, H. P. (Ed.). (1999). *Family ethnicity: Strength in diversity.* Thousand Oaks, CA: Sage.

McAdoo, H. P., & Rukuni, M. (1993). A preliminary study of family values of the women of Zimbabwe. *Journal of Black Psychology, 190,* 48-62.

McAlpin, J. P. (2000, November 28). Report: More minorities searched. *The Record,* n.p.

Meeks, L. F., Meeks, W. A., & Warren, C. A. (2000). Racial desegregation: Magnet schools, vouchers, privatization, and home schooling. *Education and Urban Society, 33*(1), 88-101.

Metcalf, K. K., & Tait, P. A. (1999). Free market policies and public education: What is the cost of choice? *Phi Delta Kappan, 81*(1), 65-75.

Montgomery, L. E., & Carter-Pokras, O. (1993). Health status by social class and/or minority status: Implications for environmental equity research. *Toxicology Industrial Health, 9*(5), 729-773.

Moynihan, D. P. (1965). *The Negro family: The case for national action.* Washington, DC: Government Printing Office.

National Center for Health Statistics. (1998). *Socioeconomic status and health chartbook in health* (DHHS Publication No. PHS 98-1232). Washington, DC: U.S. Department of Health and Human Services.

Naylor, L. L. (1999). Introduction to American cultural diversity: Unresolved questions, issues, and problems. In L. L. Naylor (Ed.), *Problems and issues of diversity in the United States* (pp. 1-18). Westport, CT: Bergin & Harvey.

Oakes, J. (1985). *Keeping track: How schools structure inequality.* New Haven, CT: Yale University Press.

Orfield, G. (1996). Turning back to segregation. In G. Orfield & S. E. Eaton (Eds.), *Dismantling desegregation: The quiet reversal of Brown v. Board of Education* (pp. 1-22). New York: New Press.

Reminick, R. A. (1983). *Theory of ethnicity: An anthropologist's perspective.* New York: University Press of America.

Russo, C. J., & Talbert-Johnson, C. (1997). The overrepresentation of African American children in special education: The resegregation of educational programming. *Education and Urban Society, 29*(2), 136-148.

Schmid, R. E. (2000, January 13). Twice as many Americans by 2100. *Augusta Chronicle,* n.p.

Sondik, E. J., Wilson-Lucas, J., Madans, J. H., & Smith, S. S. (2000). Racial/ethnicity and the 2000 census: Implications for public health. *American Journal of Public Health, 90*(11), 1709-1713.

Srinivasan, S., & Guillermo, T. (2000). Toward improved health: Disaggregating Asian American and Native Hawaiian/Pacific Islander data. *American Journal of Public Health, 90*(11), 1731-1734.

Suro, R. (2000, February). Beyond economics. *American Demographics,* pp. 48-55.

Talbert-Johnson, C. (2000). The political context of school desegregation: Equity, school improvement, and accountability. *Education and Urban Society, 33*(1), 8-16.

Tate, W. F., Ladson-Billings, G., & Grant, C. A. (1996). The *Brown* decision revisited: Mathematizing a social problem. In M. J. Shujaa (Ed.), *Beyond desegregation: The politics of quality in African American schooling* (pp. 29-50). Thousand Oaks, CA: Corwin.

Taylor, R. J., Jackson, J. S., & Chatters, L. M. (Eds.). (1997). *Family life in black America.* Thousand Oaks, CA: Sage.

Tuch, S. A., & Hughes, M. (1996). Whites' racial policy attitudes. *Social Science Quarterly, 77*(4), 723-745.

U.S. Bureau of the Census. (2001). *Census 2000: U.S. Department of Commerce, Economics, and Statistics Administration.* Washington, DC: Author.

Van Ryan, M., & Burke, J. (2000). The effect of patient race and socio-economic status on physicians' perceptions of patients. *Social Science & Medicine, 50*(6), 813-828.

Weiner, L. (2000). Democracy, pluralism, and schooling: A progressive agenda. *American Educational Studies Association, 31,* 212-224.

Wilcox, D. M. (1999). American core values and question of diversity. In Naylor, L. L. (Ed.), *Problems and issues of diversity in the United States* (pp. 19-53). Westport, CT: Bergin & Garvey.

Wilkinson, D. (1999). Reframing family ethnicity in America. In H. P. McAdoo (Ed.), *Family ethnicity: Strength in diversity* (pp. 15-60). Thousand Oaks, CA: Sage.

Williams, D. R. (1999). Race, SES, and health: The added effects of racism and discrimination. *Annals of New York Academy of Sciences, 896,* 173-188.

Williams, D. R., & Rucker, T. D. (2000). Understanding and addressing racial disparities in health care. *Health Care Financing Review, 21*(4), 75-90.

Wyatt, E. (2000, August 29). Study finds higher test scores among blacks with vouchers. *The New York Times,* p. A10.

Yeh, C. J., & Huang, K. (1996). The collective nature of ethnic identity development among Asian-American college students. *Adolescence, 31*(123), 645-661.

Zinn, M. B., & Eitzen, D. (1990). *Diversity in families.* New York: Harper & Row.

CHAPTER 7

Positive Parenting and Positive Development in Children

MARC H. BORNSTEIN

In the Universal Declaration of Human Rights, the United Nations has proclaimed that childhood is entitled to special care and assistance.

Preamble, *Convention on the Rights of the Child[1]*

POSITIVE PARENTING

States Parties agree that the education of the child shall be directed to: (a) The development of the child's personality, talents and mental and physical abilities to their fullest potential; . . . (c) The development of respect for the child's parents, his or her own cultural identity, language and values, for the national values of the country in which the child is living, the country from which he or she may originate, and for civilizations different from his or her own.

Article 29, *Convention on the Rights of the Child*

Shards of pottery found at the Oracle of Delphi attest that parents in the ancient Greek world asked the priestess *Pythia,*

"How can I ensure that my children will do something useful?" Parents are charged with myriad portentous and enduring responsibilities associated with preparing children to fare and flourish in the material, social, and economic worlds they will inherit. Numerous factors influence children's development, but parents are the "final common pathway" to childhood development and stature, adaptation, and success. Parenting is a process that formally begins during or before pregnancy but continues through the balance of the life course. Practically speaking, for most, *once a parent, always a parent.* Therefore, parents must be enlisted and empowered to parent positively and provide children with positive experiences and environments that optimize their positive development.

Yet at the start of the 21st century, parenting is in an agitated state of question, flux, and redefinition on account of strong contemporary secular and historical currents. Societywide changes in industrialization, urbanization, poverty, demographic shifts in family size, population growth, and longevity and mortality patterns, as well as the changing constellation of family structure (maternal employment[2] and female-headed households, divorced and blended families, lesbian and gay parents, teens versus 50-year-old first-time parents) exert multiple stresses on parenting, on interactions between parents and children, and consequently on parents' ability to provide for the positive development of their children.

Until now, parents, researchers, and policymakers have principally occupied themselves with children's disorders, deficits, and disabilities, even when they have had the salutatory goals in mind to develop interventions, remediations, or preventions of childhood's ills. Indeed, modern psychology is devoted to understanding and healing human functioning within a disease model; the main mode of psychological intervention has been to repair damaged habits, damaged drives, and damaged bodies. But as Seligman (1998) has written,

> Psychology is not just the study of weakness and damage, it is also the study of strength and virtue. Treatment is not just fixing what is broken, it is nurturing what is best. Human strengths—courage, optimism, interpersonal skill, work ethic, hope, honesty, and perseverance—can buffer against illness. (p. 559)

Indeed, successful prevention may spring from a science that systematically promotes positive competencies. On this account, the central tasks of positive parenting may be to foster the development of positive characteristics and values in the young. Moore and Keyes (2002), reviewing the study of well-being in children and adults, affirmed the paradigm shift that has occurred in developmental science from treating problems, to preventing problems, to promoting positive development.

This chapter reviews *positive parenting* and *positive development* in normal populations.[3] The issues addressed include positive development in children, who is responsible for positive parenting, the effects, domains, and principles of positive parenting, the antecedents of positive parenting, as well as programs that promote positive parenting and positive development in children. The chapter mainly focuses on the nature, conditions, and dimensions of positive parenting but begins with a discussion of positive child outcomes. Parenting competence is at least in part functionally defined by positive child outcomes (Teti & Candelaria, 2002). At least since the publication of Bartholomew of England's *De proprietatibus rerum* and Vincent of Beauvais's *Speculum majus,* 13th-century treatises of ancient and modern philosophies and recommendations about proper child care (Gabriel, 1962; Goodrich, 1975), parenting (broadly construed) has been recognized as a principal reason behind why individuals are who they are and why they turn out the way they do (see Collins, Maccoby, Steinberg, Hetherington, & Bornstein, 2000).

WHAT IS POSITIVE DEVELOPMENT IN CHILDREN?

> 1. States Parties recognize the right of every child to a standard of living adequate for the child's physical, mental, spiritual, moral and social development.
>
> Article 27, *Convention on the Rights of the Child*

What are the positive characteristics and values we would like to see in our children? The study of positive youth development is critically in need of development itself in terms of defining positive outcomes, enhancing the research base for positive constructs, undertaking longitudinal assessments of their growth, and policing their psychometric adequacy (Moore & Keyes, 2002). However, several social commentators and scientific investigators have made a start, and there are many individual and social indicators of positive child development in the intrapersonal and interpersonal realms. For example, Bennett (1993) enumerated a set of desired outcomes for youth that included perseverance, faith, friendship, courage, responsibility, and compassion. The Search Institute (Benson, 1993) identified a set of key "internal assets," such as commitment to learning, positive values, social competencies, and positive identity. More recently, Lerner, Fisher, and Weinberg (2000) developed the "5 Cs" of positive development: competence, confidence, connections, character, and caring. In considering positive developmental attributes, of course, we must keep in mind that they are always "in the parental eye": Some parents may want to see control of emotionality in their children, others want career success, and for still others, eye-hand coordination in batting seems to matter quite a lot.

Three global areas of positive development in children can be identified, each with a series of closely operationalized positive elements (for an elaboration of this scheme, see Bornstein, Davidson, Keyes, Moore, & the Center for Child Well-Being, 2003). Positive development encompasses physical, social and emotional, and cognitive domains. The elements that comprise any one domain are not exhaustive, but represent a core set of essentials that help to define that domain and positive development in children overall.[4]

The Physical Domain of Childhood Positive Development

Positive development in the physical domain includes minimally good nutrition, health care, physical activity, safety and security, and reproductive health.

✓ Good *nutrition* is essential to rapid growth and optimal development throughout the life course; healthy eating habits mean avoiding excesses as much as deficiencies.

✓ Maintaining *physical health* is critical to positive development, and positive development also includes enhancing *desirable physical attributes*.

✓ *Physical activity* and *sleep* are both requisite to healthy function; that is, movement and exercise as well as rest are vital to health and a hearty lifestyle.

✓ Children's *felt safety* and *security* in the home as well as at school and in the surrounding community are requisite to creating a climate conducive to positive development.

✓ In adolescence, *reproductive health* comes on-line as an issue of positive child development; this includes sexual development, safe sexual practices, and reproductive knowledge.

The Social and Emotional Domain of Childhood Positive Development

Temperament, emotional understanding and regulation, coping and resilience, trust, a self-system, character, and social competencies likewise contribute to positive development in children.

✓ Possessing a positive *temperament*, including an approach orientation and an adaptive style, is a positive trait in development.

✓ *Emotional intelligence*, that is, emotion expression, regulation, and understanding, is essential to social and emotional positive development. Empathy is the emotional response to what another person is feeling, and sympathy is the emotional reaction to another's stress; both constitute elements of social and emotional positive development.

✓ *Coping* implies the ability to interact with the environment positively, constructively, and adaptively (especially under conditions of stress, threat, or harm). Relatedly, *resilience* implies the ability to recover and regain equilibrium in the face of negative environments and experiences.

✓ *Trust* is a hallmark of secure attachment and the ability of the child to use the caregiver as a secure base from which to explore.

✓ Near to the core of social and emotional positive development is children's sense of *self,* including a positive self-concept, identity, and regard, as well as possessing self-efficacy, being able to self-regulate, and having a sense of self-determination.

✓ *Character* includes values and moral behaviors—altruism, courage, honesty, duty, and responsibility—that constitute human strengths and virtues.

✓ Good *social competencies* include understanding one's place in the social world and navigating interpersonal relations well, so as to develop quality, warm, and trusting relationships with others, notably parents, siblings, and peers.

The Cognitive Domain of Childhood Positive Development

Thinking, communicating thought, and the products of thought in everyday life are essential to individual positive development. There are many specific positive elements within the cognitive domain, including information processing and memory, curiosity and exploration, mastery motivation, intelligence, problem solving, language and literacy, educational achievement, moral reasoning, and talent.

✓ Cognitive science has identified two interrelated general mechanisms that are implicated in children's mental performance across a wide range of tasks: One is *information processing* (the execution of fundamental mental processes), and the other process is *memory* (the ongoing cognitive processing of that information).

✓ *Curiosity* can be defined as the desire to learn more, and *exploration* as the behavior that is energized and directed by curiosity.

✓ *Mastery motivation,* an achievement disposition that underlies the person's drive to learn in various situations, reflects the psychological force that leads individuals to master tasks for the intrinsic feeling of efficacy, rather than for extrinsic reward.

✓ *Thinking* involves basic processes, such as perceiving objects and events in the external environment, and high-level mental processes, such as reasoning, symbolizing, and planning. Traditional global measures of thinking include intelligence tests, but a more encompassing contemporary view of intelligence embraces understanding oneself and others, creativity, and artistic abilities.

✓ *Problem solving* is the sequence of steps that attempts to identify and create alternate solutions for both cognitive and social problems, including the ability to plan, resourcefully seek help from others, and think critically, creatively, and reflectively.

✓ *Language* and *literacy* constitute a set of critical verbal elements of positive cognitive development that are key to entering the social community and to academic and career success through schooling.

✓ *Educational achievement* is commonly measured by children's readiness to learn, the state in which the capacities and competencies of the child match the expectations and requirements of adults and school; achievement test scores; and report card grades, which directly assess children's mastery of specific skills.

✓ Cognitive ability is strongly related to several components of *morality*: moral judgment, moral emotions, and moral action.

✓ Additional elements of positive cognitive development are *creativity* and *talent,* whether intellectual, social, athletic, artistic, or other.

Some Characteristics of the Three Domains of Positive Development

These domains constitute a strengths-based approach to positive development in childhood. Certainly, the elements listed are not the only ones; the elements included here hardly exhaust all possible features of positive development. Moreover, the "surface" behaviors represented in each of these domains may change during the course of the life span; however, the "latent" strengths they represent probably remain constant, thereby creating a continuity of elements of positive development across (at least parts of) the life course. Further to that point, many elements of positive development will show stability from childhood to maturity. Thus, the foundations of positive development, as well as their antecedents in so-called flourishing adults (Rowe & Kahn, 1998), may be laid down early in life.

Elements of positive development within a domain mutually influence one another, just as elements in the physical, social and emotional, and cognitive domains interact with and support one another. Thus, for example, elements of positive development within the social and emotional domain are themselves positively associated: Children's self-regulation of their internal emotional reactions contributes to the quality of their relationships with parents and others. An example of cross-domain mutual support is the fact that good nutrition, especially during the early years of rapid brain growth, can facilitate or enhance cognitive development, just as positive cognitive development enables children to make better choices and understand more fully the consequences of their behaviors and decisions with respect to their physical health. Finally, attaining positive development in each element in a domain is important, but overall positive development in the life course presumably depends on the human being's ability to attain and sustain reasonably high levels in all domains.

WHO IS RESPONSIBLE FOR POSITIVE PARENTING?

2. States Parties shall respect the rights and duties of the parents and, when applicable, legal guardians, to provide direction to the child in the exercise of his or her right in a manner consistent with the evolving capacities of the child.

Article 14, *Convention on the Rights of the Child*

1. States Parties shall use their best efforts to ensure recognition of the principle that both parents have common responsibilities for the upbringing and development of the child. Parents or, as the case may be, legal guardians, have the primary responsibility for the upbringing and development of the child. The best interests of the child will be their basic concern.

Article 18, *Convention on the Rights of the Child*

Cultures variously distribute the tasks of child caregiving. In the minds of many, motherhood is principal in the development of children, and the roles of mothers are scripted and universal. Mothers are the traditional caregivers to young children, and cross-cultural surveys attest to the primacy of biological mothers in all forms of caregiving (Barnard & Solchany, 2002; Hart Research Associates, 1997; Holden & Buck, 2002; Leiderman, Tulkin, & Rosenfeld, 1977). Fathers are invested in caregiving as well (Parke, 2002). Men generally have fewer opportunities to acquire and practice central skills of caregiving, however. Because the paternal role is less well articulated and defined than is the maternal role, maternal support often helps to crystallize appropriate paternal behavior. In the West, moreover, mothers and fathers tend to interact with and care for their children in complementary ways; that is, they tend to divide the labors of caregiving and engage children by emphasizing different types of interactions (e.g., mothers are more nurturant and affectionate, fathers are more playful). Perhaps time budget constraints and variation in interests and abilities cause mothers and fathers to devote different amounts of time and resources to children across different domains, such as physical health, social and emotional development, and mental growth.

In the minds of others, pluralistic caregiving arrangements of children are much more common and on this account, more significant in the lives of children. In many places around the globe, siblings, grandparents, and various nonparental caregivers play salient roles that vary depending on a variety of factors about the child care provider, including age, gender, age gap, quality of attachment, personality, and so forth (Clarke-Stewart & Allhusen, 2002; Smith, P.K., & Drew, 2002; Zukow-Goldring, 2002). Often, these caregivers behave in a complementary fashion to one another as well, dividing the full labor of child caregiving by individually emphasizing different parenting responsibilities and functions. In short, many individuals (other than mother and father) play roles in positive child development. However, the implications of these diverse patterns of early "parenting" relationships for children's positive development are still unclear. It is a curious and sad fact that superb substitute parenting is often low in value and remuneration, even though the positive development of our children is at risk (Honig, 2002).

It is critical to acknowledge in this connection that as important as the biological role of "begetter" is, it is less central than the social role of "nurturer" in the full meaning of parenthood to children (Leon, in press). In short, in-the-trenches parenting matters more than blood ties to positive child development.

WHAT ARE THE EFFECTS, DOMAINS, AND PRINCIPLES OF POSITIVE PARENTING?

2. The parent(s) or others responsible for the child have the primary responsibility to secure, within their abilities and financial capabilities, the conditions of living necessary for the child's development.

Article 27, *Convention on the Rights of the Child*

Parenting children is a 24/365 job, and parenting responsibilities are clearly greatest during childhood. That is because young human offspring are totally dependent on their parents for survival and caregiving and their ability to cope alone is minimal. Reciprocally, childhood is a period normally attended to and invested in by parents the world over, and childhood is the phase of the life cycle when parenting is believed to exert its most significant and salient influences: Not only is the sheer amount of interaction between parents and children greatest then, but children may be particularly susceptible and responsive to parent-provided experiences (Bornstein, 2002a). Indeed, the opportunity of enhanced parental influence and prolonged childhood learning of positive characteristics and values is thought to be an evolutionary reason for the extended duration of human childhood (Bjorklund, Yunger, & Pellegrini, 2002; Gould, 1977).

Childhood is the time when human beings first grow and develop physically, forge their first social bonds, first learn how to express and read basic human emotions, and first make sense of and understand objects in the world (Bornstein & Lamb, 1992). Parents escort children through all of these dramatic "firsts." Not surprisingly, all of these developmental dynamics are tracked by parents, and all in turn shape parenting. Finally, influences of these developments reverberate through the balance of childhood: In the view of some social theorists, the child's first relationships with parents set the tone and style for the child's later social relationships (Cummings & Cummings, 2002), and a history of shared work and play activities with parents is positively linked to the child's smooth transition into school, just as parents' involvement with their children's school-related tasks and school partnerships relate positively to their children's school experience and performance (Epstein & Sanders, 2002). It would appear that all elements of positive physical, social and emotional, and cognitive development in childhood can be changed—and presumably, enhanced.

From an ecological stance (Bronfenbrenner & Crouter, 1983; Lerner, Rothbaum, Boulos, & Castellino, 2002), the development and growth of any element or domain of positive development depends on children themselves as well as on the many facets of the child's environment and experience. Therefore, only by taking multiple contexts into account can positive child development be fully appreciated.

Mothers, fathers, and other nonparental caregivers guide the development of their charges via many direct and indirect means. Direct effects are of two kinds: genetic and experiential. Of course, biological parents endow a significant and pervasive genetic makeup to their children, with its beneficial or other consequences. Thus, heredity can contribute to positive development. For example, twin studies of children's reactions to simulations of distress in others point to a genetic component for sympathy and prosocial activity (Zahn-Waxler, Robinson, & Emde, 1992); self-reports of sympathy and prosocial behavior appear to have a genetic basis in adulthood, too (e.g., Rushton, Fulker, Neale, & Nias, 1989).

Although genes contribute to children's positive characteristics and values, all prominent theories of human development put experience in the world as either the principal source of individual growth or as a major contributing component (Dixon & Lerner, 1999). Such experiences are of two kinds: beliefs and behaviors.

Parents hold parenting beliefs and communicate them to their offspring (Harkness & Super, 1996). Beliefs constitute a significant force over the positive development of children, whether they are perceptions about, attitudes toward, or knowledge of parenting. Seeing one's own children in a particular way has consequences for one's affect, thinking, and behavior in child-rearing situations: Parents who regard their children as "easy" are more likely to pay attention and respond to their children, and in turn, responsiveness fosters child growth (Bornstein, 1989; Putnam, Sanson, & Rothbart, 2002). Seeing childhood in a particular way functions likewise: Parents who believe that they can affect children's physical health, social and emotional growth, or cognitive development are more proactive and successful in cultivating their children's competencies (Bandura, Barbaranelli, Caprara, & Pastorelli, 1996; Coleman & Karraker, 1998; Elder, 1995; Gross, Fogg, & Tucker, 1995; King & Elder, 1998; Schneewind, 1995; Teti & Gelfand, 1991). Finally, seeing oneself in a particular way vis-à-vis children leads to certain cognitions or behaviors: Parents hold different beliefs about the meaning and significance of their own parenting behaviors as well as the behaviors and development of their children, and parents act on these beliefs about children as much as they do on their own experiences with children (Bugental & Happaney, 2002; Sigel & McGillicuddy-De Lisi, 2002).

Perhaps more salient in the phenomenology of childhood, however, are parents' behaviors: the tangible experiences parents provide their children. Parents model specific behaviors, possibly leading to the expression of those behaviors by children as the result of children's observations and practice. Parents promote positive behaviors in children as well, for example, through praise or reward of emotions, cognitions, and actions they appreciate. Parental involvement, monitoring, and communication have been associated with children's positive health, social-emotional, and academic development (Crouter & Head, 2002).

For most elements of positive development, parents exercise duty and authority over their children early in life and plan that their socialization practices will result, when child independence ultimately takes hold, in children's self-regulation of their own positive characteristics and values (Eisenberg & Valiente, 2002). Parents promote and ensure children's health and safety by attending to their preventative health care needs (such as immunizations); teaching children how to maintain healthy diets; modeling and participating with children when engaging in physical activities; and ensuring and provisioning a safe and secure environment (Melamed, 2002; Tinsley, Markey, Ericksen, Kwasman, & Oritz, 2002). Warmth and responsiveness in parent-child relationships promote the development of trust and autonomy (Cummings & Cummings, 2002). Security from infancy improves the likelihood of success in later social relationships in terms of negotiating and resolving subsequent developmental tasks (Thompson, 1999). So, to continue the above example, a variety of types of positive parenting links to the development of children's prosocial behavior or sympathy (Eisenberg & Valiente, 2002). Parents who are authoritative (in Baumrind's, 1989, sense of being supportive and demanding of appropriate behavior from their children) tend to have children who exhibit prosocial behavior, and the use of reasoning in discipline appears to be especially important to prosocial development (Krevans & Gibbs, 1996). In short, parenting that is responsive, warm, and supportive; relies on reasoning for discipline; and demands more mature behavior tends to promote positive social and emotional development in children (Dekovic & Janssens, 1992; Janssens & Dekovic, 1997).

Taken as a totality, this constellation of caregiving constitutes a varied and demanding set of parenting tasks, and the contents of parent-child interactions that correspond to the domains of children's positive development are dynamic and varied. Of course, adults differ among themselves in terms of their positive caregiving and in how successful

they may be. At the same time, individual parenting styles are reasonably consistent (Holden & Miller, 1999). Over the long-term, the precise nature and structure of positive parenting behaviors can be expected to change, as in response to their children's development. Consider two functions, surveillance and responsiveness, as examples. Positive parenting means keeping track of and tending to children and letting children know that parent and child coexist in a loving and trusting relationship (Crouter & Head, 2002), and parenting actions associated with those goals certainly vary with child age, for example, minding a toddler or giving a cell phone to a newly licensed teen driver.

Parents' nurturing, social-emotional, and didactic behaviors and styles constitute direct-experience effects of parenting. Mothers and fathers exercise indirect effects on positive child development as well. Indirect effects are more subtle and less noticeable than direct effects, but perhaps no less meaningful. Parents indirectly incline their children toward positive development in several ways: Parents influence one another, for example by marital support and communication (Grych, 2002), and parents influence their children through their influence on each other (Grych & Fincham, 2001). Parents' attitudes about themselves, their spouses, and their marriages thereby modify the quality of their interactions with their children and in turn, their children's chance for positive development.

Thus, although some contend that "parents matter less than you think" (Harris, 1998), parents manifestly exert both direct and indirect influences on their children. Consider again children's interactions with their peers. Parents directly influence their children's peer relationships when they cultivate children's social skills, organize their children's social environment, provide access to social play partners, choose playmates, and plan and monitor children's peer activities

(Ladd & Pettit, 2002). Parents indirectly affect their children's peer relationships through behaviors that encourage or hinder children's social competencies, through attachment quality, family emotional climate, support, discipline, and beliefs (Ladd & Pettit, 2002).

Principles of Positive Parenting

To fathom how parenting young children relates to children's later positive functioning, we need to distinguish individual differences and child effects in children from the roles of parent-provided experience. Experiences vital to positive child development can be contemporaneous, early occurring, or cumulative (see Bornstein & Tamis-LeMonda, 1990; Bornstein, Tamis-LeMonda, & Haynes, 1999). In a model of effective contemporary parenting, child positive characteristics and values reflect the effects of parent-provided experiences at a given time, separate from stability of individual differences to that time and the effects of prior parent-provided experience. Contemporary experience is unique and can override earlier experience. The database for this model typically consists of recovery of functioning from early severe deprivation, failure of early intervention studies to show long-term effects, and the like (Kagan, 1998; Lewis, 1997). In a model of effective early parenting, child positive characteristics and values reflect the effects of earlier parent-provided experiences, separate from stability of individual differences in the child and the effects of contemporaneous parent-provided experience. Data derived from ethology, behaviorism, and neuropsychology (e.g., sensitive periods; Bornstein, 1989) support this model. In a model of cumulative parenting, child positive characteristics and values reflect the combined effects of earlier as well as later parent-provided experiences, separate from the stability of individual differences in the child (Bornstein

et al., 1999). Cumulative effects appear to result from consistent environmental influences. To promote positive characteristics and values in young children and to fathom their antecedents in positive parenting, it is necessary to isolate and measure the stability of individual differences in the child and to differentiate among different temporal and causal models of parent-provided experience.

Specificity, Transaction, and Interdependence

Parenting that promotes positive development in children follows several additional noteworthy principles. The *specificity principle* asserts that specific experiences parents provide children at specific times exert specific effects over specific aspects of child development in specific ways. It is probably not the case that the overall level of parental stimulation, for example, directly affects the overall level of children's functioning and compensates for selective deficiencies. That is, simply providing an adequate financial base, a big house, or the like does not guarantee or even speak to a child's good nutrition, development of an empathic personality, cognitive competence, or other desirable positive attributes or capacities. This is apparently counterintuitive, because nearly 90% of parents in the United States think simplistically that the more stimulation a baby receives, the better off the baby is (Hart Research Associates, 1997). Rather, on a goodness-of-fit model, parents need to carefully match the amount and kinds of stimulation they offer to their child's level of development, interests, temperament, mood at the moment, and so forth (Lerner et al., 2002). Furthermore, to maintain appropriate influence and guidance through development, parents must effectively adjust their interactions, cognitions, emotions, affections, and strategies for exerting parental influence to the changing abilities, activities, and experiences of their children.

The *transaction principle* asserts that positive parenting will help to shape the positive characteristics and values of children through time, just as reciprocally, the characteristics and values of children help to shape their parenting. Children and their parents co-construct the child's physical, social and emotional, and intellectual development. Children influence which experiences they will be exposed to as well as how they interpret those experiences, and thereby how those experiences might affect them (Scarr & Kidd, 1983). Parents and children stimulate and provide feedback to—they mutually influence—one another. In general, parents face a continuous onrush of transitions in children's physical maturity, emotional adjustments, social opportunities and settings, and cognitive capabilities.

The *interdependence principle* asserts that to understand the responsibilities and functions of one member of a family in promoting positive development in children, the complementary responsibilities and functions of other family members also need to be acknowledged. All family members—mothers, fathers, and children, as well as other interested parties—influence each other both directly and indirectly. Furthermore, all families are embedded in, interact with, and are themselves affected by larger social systems (Lerner et al., 2002). These include both formal and informal support systems, extended families, community ties to friends and neighbors, work sites, educational and medical institutions, as well as their culture at large. To understand positive parenting and positive child development requires taking multiple factors into consideration so that individual, dyadic, family, and social level contributions to parenting and child development can be appreciated. Each piece of parenting occurs in multiple immediate and broader contexts, all

of which determine its effect and how it is perceived (Bronfenbrenner & Crouter, 1983; Darling & Steinberg, 1993).

At the intersection of these several parenting principles is *uncertainty* in what can be predicted about the positive characteristics and values of individual children, their origins, and how they will unfold . . . the question ancient Greek parents put to the Delphic oracle. There are many pathways to positive child development. Some populations we expect to fail miserably (teen parents, children born to crack-addicted mothers) just as those we think should have it made (high socioeconomic status [SES]) almost always show surprising diversity of outcomes. To detect regular relations between positive parenting and positive child development, one needs to seek and to find the right combinations of variables. The multiple pathways and dynamics of positive parenting and positive child development challenge parents and children alike (see Box 9.1). Researchers must develop new paradigms and methodologies to accommodate the chaos; similarly, this perspective renders the initiation and implementation of parenting programs and policy "nightmarish." Some will fail. Yet only by appreciating and addressing the complexity of this real-world situation can we gain access to more that is valid about positive development in children and their parents.

WHAT ARE THE ANTECEDENTS OF POSITIVE PARENTING?

The family, as the fundamental group of society and the natural environment for the growth and well-being of all its members, particularly children, should be afforded the necessary protection and assistance so that it can fully assume its responsibilities within the community.

Preamble, *Convention on the Rights of the Child*

Box 9.1   Lessons for Promoting Cognitive Competence

It is difficult to predict the developmental course of a given child, and cause-effect relations between parental actions and positive child development are notoriously complex. Nonetheless, some guidelines about possible influences of parents on children's positive development can be identified. Williams and Sternberg (2002), for example, offer 10 lessons to parents who wish to develop cognitively competent and successful children.

✓ *Lesson 1:* Recognize what can and cannot be changed in children. Watch children as they attempt to acquire new skills and meet new experiences and then encourage them to pursue skills and explore areas in which they display talents or profess interests. Expose children broadly to many skill areas.

✓ *Lesson 2:* Challenge children, rather than bore or overwhelm them. Strike a balance between tasks that are just beyond children's reach and those that children can succeed at some but not all of the time.

✓ *Lesson 3:* Teach children that the main limitation on what they can do is what they tell themselves they cannot do. Children have to be told that they have the ability to meet any challenge, and what they need to decide is how hard they are willing to work to meet a challenge.

✓ *Lesson 4:* Move children to learn what questions to ask and how to ask them and when to learn what the answers to the questions are. How we think is often more important than what to think, and how we ask questions is more important than what answers we might receive. What matters more is not what facts children know but rather their ability to use those facts.

✓ *Lesson 5:* Discover and capitalize on what excites children. To excel, children need to genuinely love what they do and to be motivated to work.

✓ *Lesson 6:* Encourage children to take sensible intellectual risks. Creativity is related to risk taking, and parents should teach children to take intellectual risks and develop a sense of when to take a risk and when not to.

✓ *Lesson 7:* Teach children to take responsibility for both their successes and their failures.

✓ *Lesson 8:* Socialize children to delay gratification and be able to wait for rewards. Children need to learn from their parents about the long term and not just the here-and-now.

✓ *Lesson 9:* Teach children empathy, the importance of understanding, respecting, and responding to the viewpoints of others.

✓ *Lesson 10:* Understand that the quality of interaction parents have with children redounds to both parent and child positively.

SOURCE: Williams & Sternberg (2002).

2. The parent(s) or others responsible for the child have the primary responsibility to secure, within their abilities and financial capacities, the conditions of living necessary for the child's development.

Article 27, *Convention on the Rights of the Child*

Each day, about three fourths of a million adults around the world experience the joys and heartaches, challenges and rewards, of becoming new parents. Which ones will parent positively? What factors will make parents the kind of parents they are? The origins of variation in parents' beliefs and behaviors are extremely complex, but certain factors seem to be of paramount importance: biological determinants, individual-differences characteristics, actual or perceived characteristics of children, and contextual influences, including social situational factors, family background, SES, and culture (Bornstein, 2002b).

Several aspects of positive parenting initially arise out of biological processes, those, for example, associated with pregnancy and parturition. Pregnancy in human beings causes the release of hormones thought to be involved in the development of positive—protective, nurturant, and responsive—feelings toward offspring (Stallings, Fleming, Corter, Worthman, & Steiner, 2001). Prenatal biological events—parental age, diet, and stress—affect postnatal parenting as well as child development. Adults already know (or think they know) something about parenting by the time they first become parents; that is, human beings appear to possess some intuitive knowledge about parenting, and some characteristics of parenting may be "wired" into our biological makeup (Papoušek & Papoušek, 2002). For example, speaking to babies is vitally important to child development, and parents speak to babies even though they know that babies cannot understand language and will not respond in kind; parents even speak to babies

in a special speech register that fosters child language development (e.g., Papoušek, Papoušek, & Bornstein, 1985).

Parenting calls on transient as well as enduring individual-differences characteristics, including personality and intelligence, traits and attitudes toward the parenting role, motivation to become involved with children, and child development and child-rearing knowledge and skills (Belsky & Barends, 2002; Bornstein, Hahn, Suizzo, & Haynes, 2001; Holden & Buck, 2002). Some personality characteristics that would favor positive parenting include empathic awareness, attuned responsiveness, and emotional availability. More educated parents project a positive authoritative style of child rearing. Perceived self-efficacy is likely to affect parenting positively because parents who feel effective vis-à-vis their children are motivated to engage in further interactions with their children, which in turn provide them with additional opportunities to understand and interact positively with their children (Teti & Candelaria, 2002).

Characteristics of children influence positive parenting and, in turn, child development (Bell, 1968; Bell & Harper, 1977). These characteristics may be obvious (age, gender, or physical appearance), or they may be subtle (temperament). Positive parenting likewise entails understanding and responding to dynamic developmental change as well as individual variation among children.

Biology, individual differences, and child characteristics constitute prominent factors that influence positive parenting. Beyond these, contextual factors motivate and help to define positive beliefs and behaviors of parents. Social situation, social class, and cultural worldview encourage specific parenting attitudes and actions. In some places, mothers and their children are isolated from other social contexts; in others, children are reared in extended families in which care is provided by many individuals (Bornstein & Lamb, 1992).

The ways in which spouses provide support and show respect for each other in parenting—how they work together as a coparenting team—influence their positive parenting (McHale, Khazan, Rotman, DeCourcey, & McConnell, 2002). In the West, frequency of contact with significant others, such as community and friendship supports, improves parents' sense of their own efficacy and competence as well as the positive quality of parent-child relationships (Cochran & Niego, 2002). For example, parents develop feelings of competence and satisfaction through contact with advice givers, role models, and persons who share their responsibilities. Mothers with social support (especially from husbands) feel less harried and overwhelmed, have fewer competing demands on their time, and as a consequence are more sensitive and responsive to their children. SES also exerts differential effects on parenting through the education of parents and provisions in the environment it may afford (Bornstein & Bradley, 2003). For example, high-SES parents compared with low-SES parents typically provide children with more opportunities for variety in daily stimulation, more appropriate play materials, and more total stimulation, especially language (Hoff, Laursen, & Tardif, 2002), and high-SES parents also tend to be more involved than low-SES parents at school (Shumow & Miller, 2001). Finally, virtually all aspects of child rearing and child development are shaped by cultural habits (Bornstein, 1991; Harkness & Super, 1996). We acquire many of our understandings of parenting and childhood simply by living in a culture: Generational, social, and media images of parenting, childhood, and family life, handed-down or co-constructed, play significant roles in helping people form their parenting beliefs and guide their parenting behaviors (Goodnow, 2002). For example, parents from different cultures differ in their opinions about which specific positives in child development spell success.

Contemporary family research teaches that parenting combines intuitive knowledge, self-constructed aspects, shared cultural constructions, and direct experiences with children (Borkowski, Ramey, & Bristol-Power, 2002; Bornstein, 2002b). No one factor is determinative and trumps all others; rather, in a comprehensive systems view of parenting and human development, many factors—biology and genetics, environment and experience—influence positive parenting and positive child development. Understanding the role of each improves explanatory power.

PROGRAMS THAT PROMOTE POSITIVE PARENTING AND POSITIVE DEVELOPMENT IN CHILDREN

1. In all actions concerning children, whether undertaken by public or private social welfare institutions, courts of law, administrative authorities or legislative bodies, the best interests of the child shall be a primary consideration.

Article 3, *Convention on the Rights of the Child*

3. States Parties shall ensure that the institutions, services and facilities responsible for the care or protection of children shall conform with the standards established by competent authorities, particularly in the areas of safety, health, in the number and suitability of their staff, as well as competent supervision.

Article 3, *Convention on the Rights of the Child*

Positive characteristics and values in the physical, social-emotional, and cognitive domains of development can all be targeted for promotion and are all responsive to effective interventions. That is, individual, interpersonal, and environmental factors can be brought to bear to promote the positive development of children. Of course, some positive characteristics and values may be more plastic than others. Reciprocally, in everyday life, positive parenting is not always in effect. Parenting is often time-consuming, effortful, complex, and sometimes ineffective. The time available for positive parenting has diminished, and economic pressures on parents have caused children to receive inadequate care and even to be placed in less-than-positive environments at ever earlier times in their lives. Today, many ills infect parenting and impede positive child development: Increasing numbers of births worldwide occur to single or teenage mothers, babies are born crack addicted, many children are not fully immunized, the very young are common victims of abuse and neglect, and many youth are reared in poverty.

Since the 1880s and the publication of the *Handbook for Friendly Visitors Among the Poor,* by the Charity Organization Society of the City of New York, the state has had manifest interest in improving parental education and social support services for parents in need (Smith, C., Perou, & Lesesne, 2002). For both positive and negative reasons mentioned earlier, contemporary parenting has witnessed an explosive growth in parenting programs. Still, these efforts have focused on the prevention of negative outcomes more than on the promotion of positive parenting and positive child development.

Children are reared in families but also in child care programs, in schools, and in community settings. From the perspective of an ecological model (Lerner et al., 2002), parents influence the "social health" of the environments their children inhabit through their citizenship and politics (Garbarino, Vorrasi, & Kostelny, 2002), and those environments contribute in critical ways to support positive characteristics and values in children. Fortunately, much is known today about the patterns and periods of early learning and the quality of environments that benefit young children's development (Bornstein et al.,

2002). Belief in the potential of the early years as a time when families can foster developmental and educational processes in children is strong. From birth through the lower primary grades, children's physical health, social and emotional development, and mental growth requirements can be better managed by many disadvantaged or taxed parents through supportive efforts from professionals. Parent programs make significant contributions to positive parenting and to positive child development. The best programs educate parents and other caregivers in ways that enhance positive parenting.

The family is the principal source of care and development of the young child. The responsibility for determining the child's best interests rests first and foremost with parents, and parental involvement remains the indispensable ingredient for sustaining the accomplishments of extrafamilial childhood education programs. Therefore, the doctrine of parental rights must remain a fundamental premise of parent education efforts (Smith, C., et al., 2002). However, substantial variation exists among parents, and some parental nurturing styles, socioemotional interactions, and cognitive exchanges appear to be less conducive to providing "optimal developmental environments" for positive development in children. Thus, for those who want it, the primary socializing function of the family can be profitably supplemented with child-rearing information and guidance. Furthermore, the ability of parents to care for and educate their children can be strengthened by support from neighbors, friends, relatives, social groups, and professionals.

Parenting programs usually involve psychological support and information about child rearing and child development, and they normally focus on children's health, social, psychological, and educational needs. Contemporary programs are highly diverse in their theoretical and conceptual frameworks, the populations they serve, the intensity of service, and the types of intervention activities they advocate, depending on needs and cultural context. Moreover, parenting programs are usually guided by several assumptions: most notably that parents are normally the most consistent and caring people in the lives of their children; when parents are provided with knowledge, skills, and supports, they can respond more positively and effectively to their children; and parents' own emotional and physical needs must be met if they are to respond positively and effectively to their children.

The general orientation of parent support programs is to help families to provide stable, nurturing, and healthy environments for children. Parents come to feel that they are not rearing their children in isolation and that there are people in programs to which they can turn for information and for a shared sense of the challenges and satisfactions surrounding child and family development. Tools commonly found in parenting programs promote positive parenting (see Box 9.2).

Positive programs for parents are guided by beliefs in the consummate role of families in rearing their own children and the importance of family participation in defining its own priorities and identifying appropriate intervention strategies. Families are best served when they are helped to enhance their own skills and traditions, rather than when decisions are made and solutions imposed on or implemented for them. Interventions that will foster positive parenting and positive development in children need to be sensitive to sociocultural diversity in families, and they do well to build on strengths within the family. Because individuals who share sociocultural similarities can still differ significantly in goals, values, and resources, endeavors to enhance positive parenting must still respond to unique characteristics of the family, such as the age of parents and children, gender of offspring, and ethnicity of the family.

Some practitioners have contended that the central responsibility for a family lies with the family and that it is outside the purview of government or other institutions to intervene. However, public and private responsibility must be viewed not as at odds, but rather as complementary. The degree to which the formal structures in a community supply families with helpful supports depends at least in part on the characteristics, desires, and current circumstances of individual families. Even small positive experiences aggregate to large, long-term gains (Abelson, 1985). Thus, increasing child care needs, resulting, for example, from changes in family structures or women's work patterns, combined with recognition of the developmental needs of the child provide powerful arguments for governments, communities, employers, and families to identify appropriate and affordable solutions to the provision of effective parenting programs. Only through complex and sensitive interventions, however, can parent and family, and context and environment be brought to bear on the route and terminus of the child's development. That pursuing such programs challenges us does not mean we should shrink from them. Our children's positive development is at stake.

POSITIVE PARENTING: A POSTSCRIPT

2. For the purpose of guaranteeing and promoting the rights set forth in the present Convention, States Parties shall render appropriate assistance to parents and legal guardians in the performance of their child-rearing responsibilities and shall ensure the development of institutions, facilities and services for the care of children.

Article 18, *Convention on the Rights of the Child*

Box 9.2   Tools for Positive Parenting

Parenting programs are guided by beliefs that emphasize the importance of addressing family needs when serving individual children, recognizing the family as a social system, and considering environmental and cultural influences when evaluating family needs and resources. Certain tools can help to address these requirements for positive parenting. They include the following:

✓   *Knowledge about child development.* Positive parenting benefits from knowledge of parenting itself and how children develop. Children's normative patterns and stages of physical, nutritional, and health needs, emotional and social requirements, and verbal and cognitive necessities at different stages should be part of the knowledge base for parenthood. Understanding the patterns and processes of development helps parents to develop more realistic expectations of child development and the requisite skills for children's achieving positive competencies.

✓   *Observing skills.* Parents need to know how to observe their children. Child watching can help one understand a child's level of development in relation to what one would like the child to learn or accomplish. Parents need information and observation skills to help them discover the match between their child's ability or readiness and ways and means to help their child achieve developmental goals.

✓   *Strategies for problem prevention and discipline.* Parents need creative insights for managing their children's behavior. Knowledge and skills regarding alternative methods of discipline and problem avoidance are basic. Knowing how to implement positive rewards can help a child more fully enjoy and appreciate the exploration and struggles required in mastering new skills and stages of growth.

✓   *Supports for emotional and social, cognitive and language development.* Parents who learn to speak and read to their children and to present their children with appealing solvable problems will enrich the actions the child carries out and the feelings the child expresses. Knowing how to take advantage of settings, routines, and activities at hand to create learning and problem-solving opportunities enhances parenting and positive development.

✓   *Personal sources of support.* Positive parenting draws on patience, flexibility, and goal orientation, and parents must command an ability to extract pleasure from their encounters with children. Parents need to understand the positive impact they can have on their children's lives through their expressed attention, pleasure, listening, and interest. These activities nourish a child's growing sense of self, just as food nourishes a child's growing body.

Parents intend much in interacting with their children: They ensure their children's physical health through the sustenance they provide, the protections they establish, and the models may afford. They foster their children's emotional regulation, development of self, and social awareness and sensitivity in meaningful relationships and experiences in and outside the family through their own behaviors and the values they display.

And they promote their children's mental development through the structures they create and the meanings they place on those structures. In fact, a parent's main job is to facilitate positive child development—a healthy and fit body, self-confidence, capacity for intimacy, achievement motivation, pleasure in play and work, friendships with peers, and early and continued intellectual success and fulfillment. A *mens sana in a corpore sano*.

The good news is that we can influence not just some, but *all* positive characteristics and values we want to see children develop. Intelligence may be inherited in part, but to be inherited does not mean to be immutable. Longitudinal studies of intelligence show that individuals change over time (Neisser et al., 1996). Even heritable traits depend on learning for their expression, and they are subject to experiential influences. Attention deficit hyperactivity disorder (ADHD) is partly biologically determined. But if parents give their children skills training, make certain their children receive appropriate medication, and hire dedicated and knowledgeable tutors, they will change the trajectory of their children's lives for the positive (Hodapp, 2002). Such positive parenting makes the difference between the ADHD children who drop out of school and those who complete college.

A full understanding of what it means to parent a child positively, however, depends on the dynamics of the family and the ecology in which that parenting takes place (Bornstein, 2002b). Within-family experiences exercise a major impact during the early years of life, and the nuclear family triad—mother, father, child—constitutes the crucible within which young children initially grow and develop. Young children also naturally form important familial relationships with siblings and grandparents, and they have significant experiences with peers and nonfamilial adults outside the family, often through enrollment in alternative-care settings. Family support, social class, and cultural variation affect patterns of parenting and exert salient influences on the ways in which young children are reared and what is expected of them as they grow. These early diverse relationships all ensure that the "parenting" children experience is rich and multifaceted. What also needs to be ensured is that all (or as much as possible) of this parenting coordinates the positive for parents and for children.

Of course, human development is too subtle, dynamic, and intricate to admit that parental caregiving alone determines the course and outcome of child development; positive development is shaped by individuals themselves and by experiences that take place after childhood and outside the scope of parents' influence. Mature characteristics possess a partly biological basis, health, temperament, and intelligence among them. Unquestionably, peer dynamics influence children. At the same time, it makes little sense to argue (as has Harris, 1998) that children are susceptible to influences from outside the family, but not from inside the family and from individuals they spend the most time with: their own parents. Thus, positive parenting does not fix the route or terminus of child development. Still, there is meaning and possibly enduring significance to positive parenting from the start.

Parenting is central to childhood, to child development, and to a society's long-term investment in children. Parents are fundamentally invested in young children: their survival, their socialization, and their education. So, we are motivated to know about the meaning and importance of parenting as much for itself as out of the desire to improve the lives of children. Parenting portends much about the later life of children *and* parents.

If we are fatalists, we accept the situation we live in. If we are not, we parent positively, and we take affirmative social and political steps to organize superb child care, to ensure children's associations with respectable peers, to erect supportive environments for children with appropriate stimulation, to guarantee children more than merely adequate schooling, and to enroll children in growth-promoting extracurricular activities. Positive parenting lies at the foundation of a science of strength and resilience: making normal people stronger and more productive, as well as actualizing human potential. Policy sometimes needs to focus on interventions that attempt to cure, but policy needs equally to guarantee experiences that are positive in their own right because they improve prevailing conditions. "Models of care" are just as important as "models of cure." Positive parenting will prevent deficit, disorder, and disability; but positive parenting will also promote human strengths, such as courage, optimism, interpersonal skill, work ethic, hope, responsibility, future mindedness, honesty, and perseverance. This in itself is a noble and desirable goal.

ACKNOWLEDGMENTS

This chapter summarizes selected aspects of my research, and portions of the text have appeared in previous scientific publications cited in the references.

NOTES

1.   The United Nations *Convention on the Rights of the Child* (United Nations General Assembly, 1990) has been signed by 191 countries; only Somalia and the United States have not signed.

2.   Women's labor force participation peaks between 25 and 44 years, which is also the period in which women normally experience a peak in child care responsibilities.

3.   The chapter presents a synopsis of theory, data, and principles about positive parenting and child development derived from the body of available Western research; much less is currently known scientifically about non-Western parents and children. It could be that positive characteristics and values in development vary in situations that are, for example, less individualistic and capitalistic in their ideology than is found in the United States and Western Europe. For children in the European American middle class, for example, the authoritative parenting style (combining high levels of warmth with moderate-to-high levels of discipline and control; Baumrind, 1989) is associated with achievement of social competence and overall adaptation when compared with other parenting styles, such as authoritarian parenting (high levels of control but little warmth or responsiveness to children's needs), which has generally been associated with poor developmental outcomes in children. In non–European American ethnic groups, other patterns may obtain. For example, adolescents from European American and Latin American homes who report having experienced authoritative parenting in growing up perform well academically, better than those coming from nonauthoritative households. However, school performance is similar for authoritatively and for nonauthoritatively reared Asian Americans and African Americans (Bornstein, 1995). Furthermore, ethnographic observations suggest that authoritarian parenting may be adaptive in some situations. European American parents in different income groups who engage in intrusive and controlling behaviors typically score high on scales of authoritarian parenting. However, work among low-income African American families suggests that a directive style of interaction is adaptive and is not harsh control. That is, an authoritarian style may constitute an appropriate adjustment in circumstances

(e.g., certain inner-city neighborhoods) in which it is a parent's job to impress on the child the necessity of following rules (Steinberg, Dornbusch, & Brown, 1992). Indeed, authoritarian parenting in some contexts may achieve the same ultimate function—successful social adaptation—that authoritative parenting serves in other contexts (Bornstein, 1995).

    4.   Order of presentation does not imply any precedence of one domain or element over another.

REFERENCES

Abelson, R. P. (1985). A variance explanation paradox: When a little is a lot. *Psychological Bulletin, 97,* 129-133.

Bandura, A., Barbaranelli, C., Caprara, G. V., & Pastorelli, C. (1996). Multifaceted impact of self-efficacy beliefs on academic functioning. *Child Development, 67,* 1206-1222.

Barnard, K. E., & Solchany, J. E. (2002). Mothering. In M. H. Bornstein (Ed.), *Handbook of parenting: Vol. 3. Status and social conditions of parenting* (2nd ed., pp. 3-25). Mahwah, NJ: Lawrence Erlbaum.

Baumrind, D. (1989). Rearing competent children. In W. Damon (Ed.), *Child development today and tomorrow* (pp. 349-378). San Francisco: Jossey-Bass.

Bell, R. Q. (1968). A reinterpretation of the direction of effects in studies of socialization. *Psychological Review, 75,* 81-95.

Bell, R. Q., & Harper, L. (1977). *Child effects on adults.* Hillsdale, NJ: Lawrence Erlbaum.

Belsky, J., & Barends, N. (2002). Personality and parenting. In M. H. Bornstein (Ed.), *Handbook of parenting: Vol. 3. Status and social ecology of parenting* (2nd ed., pp. 415-438). Mahwah, NJ: Lawrence Erlbaum.

Bennett, W. J. (Ed.). (1993). *The book of virtues: A treasury of great moral stories.* New York: Simon & Schuster.

Benson, P. L. (1993). *The troubled journey: A portrait of 6th-12th grade youth.* Minneapolis, MN: Search Institute.

Bjorklund, D. F., Yunger, J. L., & Pellegrini, A. D. (2002). The evolution of parenting and evolutionary approaches to childrearing. In M. H. Bornstein (Ed.), *Handbook of parenting: Vol. 2. Biology and ecology of parenting* (2nd ed., pp. 3-30). Mahwah, NJ: Lawrence Erlbaum.

Borkowski, J. G., Ramey, S. L., & Bristol-Power, M. (Eds.). (2002). *Parenting and the child's world: Influences on academic, intellectual, and social-emotional development.* Mahwah, NJ: Lawrence Erlbaum.

Bornstein, M. H. (1989). *Maternal responsiveness: Characteristics and consequences.* San Francisco: Jossey-Bass.

Bornstein, M. H. (1989). Sensitive periods in development: Structural characteristics and causal interpretations. *Psychological Bulletin, 105,* 179-197.

Bornstein, M. H. (Ed.). (1991). *Cultural approaches to parenting.* Hillsdale, NJ: Lawrence Erlbaum.

Bornstein, M. H. (1995). Form and function: Implications for studies of culture and human development. *Culture & Psychology, 1,* 123-137.

Bornstein, M. H. (2002a). Parenting infants. In M. H. Bornstein (Ed.), *Handbook of parenting: Vol. 1. Children and parenting* (2nd ed., pp. 3-43). Mahwah, NJ: Lawrence Erlbaum.

Bornstein, M. H. (Ed.). (2002b). *Handbook of parenting (Vols. 1-5).* Mahwah, NJ: Lawrence Erlbaum.

Bornstein, M. H., & Bradley, R. H. (Eds.). (2003). *Socioeconomic status, parenting, and child development*. Mahwah, NJ: Lawrence Erlbaum.

Bornstein, M. H., Davidson, L., Keyes, C. M., Moore, K., & the Center for Child Well-Being. (Eds.). (2003). *Well-being: Positive development across the life course*. Mahwah, NJ: Lawrence Erlbaum.

Bornstein, M. H., Hahn, C.-S., Suizzo, M. A., & Haynes, O. M. (2001). *Mothers' knowledge about child development and childrearing: National and cross-national studies*. Unpublished manuscript, National Institute of Child Health and Human Development.

Bornstein, M. H., & Lamb, M. E. (1992). *Development in infancy: An introduction* (3rd ed.). New York: McGraw-Hill.

Bornstein, M. H., & Tamis-LeMonda, C. S. (1990). Activities and interactions of mothers and their firstborn infants in the first six months of life: Covariation, stability, continuity, correspondence, and prediction. *Child Development, 61,* 1206-1217.

Bornstein, M. H., Tamis-LeMonda, C. S., & Haynes, O. M. (1999). First words in the second year: Continuity, stability, and models of concurrent and predictive correspondence in vocabulary and verbal responsiveness across age and context. *Infant Behavior and Development, 22, 65-85.*

Bronfenbrenner, U., & Crouter, A. C. (1983). The evolution of environmental models in developmental research. In P. H. Mussen (Series Ed.) & W. Kessen (Vol. Ed.), *Handbook of child psychology: Vol. 1. History, theory, and methods* (pp. 357-414). New York: Wiley.

Bugental, D. B., & Happaney, K. (2002). Parental attributions. In M. H. Bornstein (Ed.), *Handbook of parenting: Vol. 3. Status and social conditions of parenting* (2nd ed., pp. 509-535). Mahwah, NJ: Lawrence Erlbaum.

Clarke-Stewart, K. A., & Allhusen, V. D. (2002). Nonparental caregiving. In M. H. Bornstein (Ed.), *Handbook of parenting: Vol. 3. Status and social conditions of parenting* (2nd ed., pp. 215-252). Mahwah, NJ: Lawrence Erlbaum.

Cochran, M., & Niego, S. (2002). Parenting and social networks. In M. H. Bornstein (Ed.), *Handbook of parenting: Vol. 4. Applied parenting* (2nd ed., pp. 123-148). Mahwah, NJ: Lawrence Erlbaum.

Coleman, P. K., & Karraker, K. H. (1998). Self-efficacy and parenting quality: Findings and future applications. *Developmental Review, 18, 47-85.*

Collins, W. A., Maccoby, E. E., Steinberg, L., Hetherington, E. M., & Bornstein, M. H. (2000). Contemporary research on parenting: The case of nature *and* nurture. *American Psychologist, 55, 218-232.*

Crouter, A. C., & Head, M. R. (2002). Parental monitoring and knowledge of children. In M. H. Bornstein (Ed.), *Handbook of parenting: Vol. 3. Status and social conditions of parenting* (2nd ed., pp. 461-483). Mahwah, NJ: Lawrence Erlbaum.

Cummings, E. M., & Cummings, J. S. (2002). Parenting and attachment. In M. H. Bornstein (Ed.), *Handbook of parenting: Vol. 5. Practical parenting* (2nd ed., pp. 35-58). Mahwah, NJ: Lawrence Erlbaum.

Darling, N., & Steinberg, L. (1993). Parenting style as context: An integrative model. *Psychological Bulletin, 113, 487-496.*

Dekovic, M., & Jassens, J. M. A. M. (1992). Parents' child-rearing style and child's sociometric status. *Developmental Psychology, 28, 925-932.*

Dixon, R. A., & Lerner, R. M. (1999). History of systems in developmental psychology. In M. H. Bornstein & M. E. Lamb (Eds.), *Developmental psychology: An advanced textbook* (4th ed., pp. 3-45). Mahwah, NJ: Lawrence Erlbaum.

Eisenberg, N., & Valiente, C. (2002). Parenting and children's prosocial and moral development. In M. H. Bornstein (Ed.), *Handbook of parenting: Vol. 5. Practical parenting* (2nd ed., pp. 111-142). Mahwah, NJ: Lawrence Erlbaum.

Elder, G. H. (1995). Life trajectories in changing societies. In A. Bandura (Ed.), *Self-efficacy in changing societies* (pp. 46-68). New York: Cambridge University Press.

Epstein, J. L., & Sanders, M. G. (2002). Family, school, and community partnerships. In M. H. Bornstein (Ed.), *Handbook of parenting: Vol. 5. Practical parenting* (2nd ed., pp. 407-437). Mahwah, NJ: Lawrence Erlbaum.

Gabriel, A. L. (1962). *The educational ideas of Vincent of Beauvais.* Notre Dame, IL: University of Notre Dame Press.

Garbarino, J., Vorrasi, J. A., & Kostelny, K. (2002). Parenting and public policy. In M. H. Bornstein (Ed.), *Handbook of parenting: Vol. 5. Practical parenting* (2nd ed., pp. 487-507). Mahwah, NJ: Lawrence Erlbaum.

Goodnow, J. J. (2002). Parents' knowledge and expectations: Using what we know. In M. H. Bornstein (Ed.), *Handbook of parenting: Vol. 3. Status and social conditions of parenting* (2nd ed., pp. 439-460). Mahwah, NJ: Lawrence Erlbaum.

Goodrich, M. (1975). Bartholomaeus Anglicus on child-rearing. *History of Childhood Quarterly: The Journal of Psychohistory, 3,* 75-84.

Gould, S. J. (1977). *Ontogeny and phylogeny.* Cambridge, MA: Harvard University Press.

Gross, D., Fogg, L., & Tucker, S. (1995). The efficacy of parent training for promoting positive parent-toddler relationships. *Research in Nursing & Health, 18,* 489-499.

Grych, J. H. (2002). Marital relationships and parenting. In M. H. Bornstein (Ed.), *Handbook of parenting: Vol. 4. Applied parenting* (2nd ed., pp. 203-225). Mahwah, NJ: Lawrence Erlbaum.

Grych, J. H., & Fincham, F. D. (Eds.). (2001). *Interparental conflict and child development: Theory, research and application.* New York: Cambridge University Press.

Harkness, S., & Super, C. M. (Eds.). (1996). *Parents cultural belief systems: Their origins, expressions, and consequences.* New York: Guilford.

Harris, J. R. (1998). *The nurture assumption.* New York: Free Press.

Hart Research Associates. (1997). *Key findings from a nationwide survey among parents of zero-to three-year-olds.* Washington, DC: Author.

Hodapp, R. M. (2002). Parenting children with mental retardation. In M. H. Bornstein (Ed.), *Handbook of parenting: Vol. 1. Children and parenting* (2nd ed., pp. 355-381). Mahwah, NJ: Lawrence Erlbaum.

Hoff, E., Laursen, B., & Tardif, T. (2002). Socioeconomic status and parenting. In M. H. Bornstein (Ed.), *Handbook of parenting: Vol. 2. Biology and ecology of parenting* (2nd ed., pp. 231-252). Mahwah, NJ: Lawrence Erlbaum.

Holden, G. W., & Buck, M. J. (2002). Parental attitudes toward childrearing. In M. H. Bornstein (Ed.), *Handbook of parenting: Vol. 3. Status and social conditions of parenting* (2nd ed., pp. 537-562). Mahwah, NJ: Lawrence Erlbaum.

Holden, G. W., & Miller, P. C. (1999). Enduring and different: A meta-analysis of the similarity in parents' childrearing. *Psychological Bulletin, 125,* 223-254.

Honig, A. S. (2002). Choosing child care for young children. In M. H. Bornstein (Ed.), *Handbook of parenting: Vol. 5. Practical parenting* (2nd ed., pp. 375-405). Mahwah, NJ: Lawrence Erlbaum.

Janssens, J. M. A. M., & Dekovic, M. (1997). Child rearing, prosocial moral reasoning, and prosocial behavior. *International Journal of Behavioral Development, 20,* 509-527.

Kagan, J. (1998). *Three seductive ideas.* Cambridge, MA: Harvard University Press.

King, V., & Elder, G. H. (1998). Perceived self-efficacy and grandparenting. *Journals of Gerontology Series B-Psychological Sciences & Social Sciences, 53B,* S249-S257.

Krevans, J., & Gibbs, J. C. (1996). Parents' use of inductive discipline: Relations to children's empathy and prosocial behavior. *Child Development, 67,* 3263-3277.

Ladd, G. W., & Pettit, G. D. (2002). Parents and children's peer relationships. In M. H. Bornstein (Ed.), *Handbook of parenting: Vol. 5. Practical parenting* (2nd ed., pp. 269-309). Mahwah, NJ: Lawrence Erlbaum.

Leiderman, P. H., Tulkin, S. R., & Rosenfeld, A. (Eds.). (1977). *Culture and infancy: Variations in the human experience.* New York: Academic Press.

Leon, I. (in press). Adoption losses: Naturally occurring or socially constructed? *Child Development.*

Lerner, R. M., Fisher, C. B., & Weinberg, R. A. (2000). Toward a science for and of the people: Promoting civil society through the application of development science. *Child Development, 71,* 11-20.

Lerner, R. M., Rothbaum, F., Boulos, S., & Castellino, D. R. (2002). Developmental systems perspective on parenting. In M. H. Bornstein (Ed.), *Handbook of parenting: Vol. 2. Biology and ecology of parenting* (2nd ed., pp. 285-309). Mahwah, NJ: Lawrence Erlbaum.

Lewis, M. (1997). *Altering fate.* New York: Guilford.

McHale, J., Khazan, I., Rotman, T., DeCourcey, W., & McConnell, M. (2002). Co-parenting in diverse family systems. In M. H. Bornstein (Ed.), *Handbook of parenting: Vol. 3. Status and social conditions of parenting* (2nd ed., pp. 75-107). Mahwah, NJ: Lawrence Erlbaum.

Melamed, B. G. (2002). Parenting the ill child. In M. H. Bornstein (Ed.), *Handbook of parenting: Vol. 5. Practical parenting* (2nd ed., pp. 329-348). Mahwah, NJ: Lawrence Erlbaum.

Moore, K. A., & Keyes, C. L. M. (2003). The study of well-being in children and adults: A brief history. In M. H. Bornstein, L. Davidson, C. M. Keyes, K. Moore, & the Center for Child Well-Being (Eds.), *Well-being: Positive development across the life course.* Mahwah, NJ: Lawrence Erlbaum.

Neisser, U., Boodoo, G., Bouchard, T. J., Boykin, A. W., Brody, N., Ceci, S. J., & Urbina, S. (1996). Intelligence: Knowns and unknowns. *American Psychologist, 51,* 77-101.

Papoušek, H., & Papoušek, M. (2002). Intuitive parenting. In M. H. Bornstein (Ed.), *Handbook of parenting: Vol. 2. Biology and ecology of parenting* (2nd ed., pp. 183-203). Mahwah, NJ: Lawrence Erlbaum.

Papoušek, M., Papoušek, H., & Bornstein, M. H. (1985). The naturalistic vocal environment of young infants: On the significance of homogeneity and variability in parental speech. In T. M. Field & N. Fox (Eds.), *Social perception in infants* (pp. 269-297). Norwood, NJ: Ablex.

Parke, R. D. (2002). Fathers and families. In M. H. Bornstein (Ed.), *Handbook of parenting: Vol. 3. Status and social conditions of parenting* (2nd ed., pp. 27-73). Mahwah, NJ: Lawrence Erlbaum.

Putnam, S. P., Sanson, A. V., & Rothbart, M. K. (2002). Child temperament and parenting. In M. H. Bornstein (Ed.), *Handbook of parenting: Vol. 1. Children and parenting* (2nd ed., pp. 255-277). Mahwah, NJ: Lawrence Erlbaum.

Rowe, J. W., & Kahn, R. L. (1998). *Successful aging.* New York: Pantheon.

Rushton, J. P., Fulker, D. W., Neale, M. C., & Nias, D. K. (1989). Aging and the relation of aggression, altruism and assertiveness scales to the Eysenck Personality Questionnaire. *Personality & Individual Differences, 10,* 261-263.

Scarr, S., & Kidd, K. K. (1983). Developmental behavior genetics. In P. H. Mussen (Series Ed.), M. M. Haith & J. J. Campos (Vol. Eds.), *Handbook of child psychology: Vol. 2. Infancy and developmental psychobiology* (pp. 345-433). New York: Wiley.

Schneewind, K. A. (1995). Impact of family processes on control beliefs. In A. Bandura (Ed.), *Self-efficacy in changing societies* (pp. 114-148). New York: Cambridge University Press.

Seligman, M. E. P. (1998). The president's address. *American Psychologist, 54,* 559-562.

Shumow, L., & Miller, J. (2001). Parents' at home and at school involvement with young adolescents. *Journal of Early Adolescence, 21,* 68–91.

Sigel, I. E., & McGillicuddy-De Lisi, A. (2002). Parental beliefs and cognitions: The dynamic belief systems model. In M. H. Bornstein (Ed.), *Handbook of parenting: Vol. 3. Status and social conditions of parenting* (2nd ed., pp. 485-508). Mahwah, NJ: Lawrence Erlbaum.

Smith, C., Perou, R., & Lesesne, C. (2002). Parent education. In M. H. Bornstein (Ed.), *Handbook of parenting: Vol. 4. Applied parenting* (2nd ed., pp. 389-410). Mahwah, NJ: Lawrence Erlbaum.

Smith, P. K., & Drew, L. M. (2002). Grandparenthood. In M. H. Bornstein (Ed.), *Handbook of parenting: Vol. 3. Status and social conditions of parenting* (2nd ed., pp. 141-172). Mahwah, NJ: Lawrence Erlbaum.

Stallings, J., Fleming, A. S., Corter, C., Worthman, C., & Steiner, M. (2001). The effects of infant cries and odors on sympathy, cortisol, and autonomic responses in new mothers and non-postpartum women. *Parenting: Science and Practice, 1,* 71-100.

Steinberg, L., Dornbusch, S. M., & Brown, B. B. (1992). Ethnic differences in adolescent achievement: An ecological perspective. *American Psychologist, 47*(6), 723-729.

Teti, D. M., & Candelaria, M. (2002). Parenting competence. In M. H. Bornstein (Ed.), *Handbook of parenting: Vol. 4. Applied parenting* (2nd ed., pp. 149-180). Mahwah, NJ: Lawrence Erlbaum.

Teti, D. M., & Gelfand, D. M. (1991). Behavioral competence among mothers of infants in the first year: The mediational role of maternal self-efficacy. *Child Development, 62,* 918-929.

Thompson, R. A. (1999). The individual child: Temperament, emotion, self, and personality. In M. H. Bornstein & M. E. Lamb (Eds.), *Developmental psychology: An advanced textbook* (4th ed., pp. 377-409). Mahwah, NJ: Lawrence Erlbaum.

Tinsley, B. J., Markey, C. N., Ericksen, A. J., Kwasman, A., & Oritz, R. V. (2002). Health promotion for parents. In M. H. Bornstein (Ed.), *Handbook of parenting: Vol. 5. Practical parenting* (2nd ed., pp. 311-328). Mahwah, NJ: Lawrence Erlbaum.

United Nations General Assembly. (1990). *Convention on the rights of the child.* New York: United Nations Children's Fund.

Williams, W. M., & Sternberg, R. J. (2002). *How parents can maximize children's cognitive abilities. In M. H. Bornstein (Ed.), Handbook of parenting: Vol. 5. Practical parenting* (2nd ed., pp. 169-194). Mahwah, NJ: Lawrence Erlbaum.

Zahn-Waxler, C., Robinson, J. L., & Emde, R. N. (1992). The development of empathy in twins. *Developmental Psychology, 28,* 1038-1047.

Zukow-Goldring, P. (2002). Sibling caregiving. In M. H. Bornstein (Ed.), *Handbook of parenting: Vol. 3. Status and social conditions of parenting* (2nd ed., pp. 253-286). Mahwah, NJ: Lawrence Erlbaum.

CHAPTER 8

Promoting Child Adjustment by Fostering Positive Paternal Involvement

MICHAEL E. LAMB
SUSAN S. CHUANG
NATASHA CABRERA

Programs and policies designed to improve the well-being of children have generally assumed that mothers are more likely than fathers to protect, nurture, and take care of their children. When programs and policies have targeted fathers, they have emphasized economic responsibility rather than social and emotional relationships. Thus, for example, policies concerned with nonresident fathers focus on child support payments but seldom address visitation rights. This conception of contrasting maternal and paternal responsibilities and obligations has been challenged recently by both policymakers and researchers who have offered new perspectives on families and parenthood. The emergent conception of fatherhood is multidimensional and does not focus narrowly only on the father's provider role. Instead, scholars and policymakers have

noted that fathers play diverse roles in their children's lives and that many men enjoy being nurturing fathers, not just economic providers.

At the research level, evidence accumulated over the last 40 years has documented that children form significant and important attachments to their fathers in infancy, that fathers continue to be involved in their children's lives as they develop, and that positive father involvement has beneficial effects on both children and their fathers. At the same time, it has become clear that fathers face many barriers that prevent them from being the fathers they would like to be. These barriers include personal characteristics, partners' expectations and beliefs, and institutional or structural barriers.

Increased awareness that fathers can be actively and directly involved in their children's lives, that this involvement can have beneficial effects on children, and that there are social and personal barriers to their involvement has prompted efforts to promote child adjustment by fostering paternal involvement. These efforts have involved the removal of barriers that impede father involvement in the workplace and in educational settings by substituting policies that encourage and facilitate father involvement in their children's lives. In this chapter, we (a) describe the evidence that children become attached to their fathers in infancy and that these relationships continue over time, (b) show that father-child relationships have significant effects on child development, (c) identify some of the factors that affect parental involvement, and (d) describe policies and programs designed to increase positive paternal involvement in their children's lives.

THE DEVELOPMENT AND SIGNIFICANCE OF FATHER-CHILD RELATIONSHIPS

Father-Infant Relationships

Until the 1970s, most studies of infant-parent attachment focused on infant-mother dyads. Many researchers showed that secure attachments form when adults (most researchers studied mothers) respond promptly and appropriately to their infants' signals (e.g., cries, smiles). Infants treated in this manner come to perceive their parents' responses as predictable or reliable, whereas insecure attachments develop when adults do not respond predictably and infants are thus uncertain about their reliability (Ainsworth, Blehar, Waters, & Wall, 1978; DeWolff & van IJzendoorn, 1997; Lamb, Thompson, Gardner, & Charnov, 1985). Although such processes could allow infants to form attachments to adults other than mothers who respond to them appropriately and regularly, the notion that infants might also form

significant attachments to their fathers was not initially of great interest to developmentalists. In the early 1970s, however, several researchers began to examine infant-father attachments and the possible differences between infants' attachments to their mothers and fathers. The results of these studies prompted scholars to start viewing fathers as important individuals in their children's lives because it became clear that infants typically form attachments to both of their parents. For example, Schaffer and Emerson (1964) found that infants started to protest separations from both their parents at 7 to 9 months of age and that 71% of the infants they studied protested paternal separation by 18 months of age, whether or not the fathers were involved in their care. Similarly, Kotelchuck (1976) observed that 12-, 15-, 18-, and 21-month-old infants predictably protested when either parent left them alone in an unfamiliar playroom, whereas infants who were accompanied by one of the parents seldom protested when the other parent left. Although the majority of the infants protested separation from the mothers most vigorously, almost 25% protested separations from fathers most intensely, and 20% showed no preference for either parent. Infants and toddlers also protested separation from either parent similarly in nursery school settings (Field et al., 1984).

These conclusions were further supported by Lamb's (1977a, 1977b) examination of infant-parent interaction in naturalistic settings. Lengthy home observations in traditional Euro-American families revealed that 7- to 24-month-old infants showed no preference for either parent on attachment behavior measures and preferred either parent over adult visitors. Similar patterns were evident among 8- to 16-month-old infants on Israeli kibbutzim (Sagi, Lamb, Shoham, Dvir, & Lewkowicz, 1985), and observations of Swedish infants likewise revealed that infants become attached to both of their parents, regardless of variations in fathers' relative involvement in child care (Lamb, Frodi, Hwang, & Frodi, 1983). In the American studies, furthermore, infants' separation and reunion responses at home did not favor either parent, although during the second year of life, many of the infants began to show preferences for their fathers (Lamb, 1976). In short, studies in a variety of cultures and contexts have shown clearly that most infants develop attachments to their fathers and mothers at the same time.

Building on the evidence that infants become attached to their fathers, researchers later focused on the quality of infant-parent interactions, with some researchers reporting that fathers and mothers were equivalently sensitive. For example, Braungart-Rieker, Garwood, Powers, and Notaro (1998) reported that mothers and fathers were equally sensitive to their 4-month-old infants and showed similar patterns of affect and self-regulation in face-to-face and still-face paradigms. Both parents are also sufficiently sensitive to developmental changes in their children's abilities and preferences that they adjust their play and stimulation patterns (Crawley & Sherrod, 1984), although the Israeli fathers of 6-month-olds studied by Mansbach and Greenbaum (1999) believed that the infants' cognitive maturity and social autonomy developed more slowly than mothers did.

Belsky, Gilstrap, and Rovine (1984) found that although fathers were less actively "engaged" than mothers in interaction with their 1-, 2-, and 9-month-old infants, the differences decreased over time. Other researchers have found that levels of paternal responsiveness vary depending on the extent to which fathers assume responsibility for child care (Donate-Bartfield & Passman, 1985; Zelazo, Kotelchuck, Barber, & David, 1977). This may explain why low-income fathers who lived with their infants appeared more sensitive to their children than did

nonresident fathers (Brophy-Herb, Gibbons, Omar, & Schiffman, 1999). Similarly, fathers who were more affectionate, spent more time with their 3-month-old infants, and had more positive attitudes were more likely to have securely attached infants 9 months later (Cox, Owen, Henderson, & Margand, 1992).

Like the quality of infant-mother attachment, the quality of infant-father attachment affects infant social development. Main and Weston (1981) and Sagi, Lamb, and Gardner (1986) found that the security of both infant-parent attachments affected their responses to unfamiliar individuals but only the security of attachments to fathers (but not to mothers) affected the sociability of Swedish infants (Lamb, Hwang, Frodi, & Frodi, 1982).

Paternal sensitivity not only affects attachment security but also influences cognitive and motivational development directly. Yarrow et al. (1984) thus found that paternal stimulation significantly affected the development of mastery motivation in sons but not in daughters in the first year of life. Wachs, Uzgiris, and Hunt (1971) reported that higher paternal involvement was associated with better scores on the Uzgiris-Hunt scales. Magill-Evans and Harrison (1999) reported that both the fathers' and mothers' levels of sensitivity to their 3- and 12-month-olds predicted individual differences in linguistic and cognitive abilities when the children were 18 months old, and Yogman, Kindlon, and Earls (1995) found associations between levels of paternal involvement and children's IQ scores, even after controlling for socioeconomic factors. Similarly, Labrell (1990) reported that paternal scaffolding (i.e., providing indirect rather than direct help) promoted the children's independent problem-solving skills by the age of 18 months.

The quality of paternal behavior continues to affect child development beyond infancy, however. According to Verscheuren and Marcoen (1999), for example, 5-year-old children who believed that they had secure attachments with their fathers took more initiative, were more self-confident, more independent, more socially competent with peers, less anxious and withdrawn, and better adjusted to school stresses than children with insecure representations of attachments to their fathers. Moreover, children with two secure attachments were more socially competent and popular with peers, less anxious and withdrawn, better adjusted to school stress, and had higher self-esteem than children with two insecure attachment representations. Children with contrasting attachment representations to their parents, regardless of which relationships were secure, were more socially and emotionally competent and had more positive evaluations of themselves than did children with two insecure attachment representations, although their scores were lower than for children with two secure attachment representations. These findings suggest that secure attachments to one parent can compensate for insecure attachments to the other parent.

Lieberman, Doyle, and Markiewicz (1999) also reported that the security of children's attachment to their two parents predicted some positive friendship qualities (helpfulness, closeness, and security). Interestingly, even though secure attachments to both parents were associated with reduced levels of conflict with peers, fathers' availability was particularly important. Perhaps this is because children learn to regulate their emotions and to resolve conflict through interactions with their fathers (MacDonald & Parke, 1984).

When fathers are observed with their infants and toddlers, they tend to engage in more physically stimulating and unpredictable play than mothers do (Clarke-Stewart, 1978; Crawley & Sherrod, 1984; Dickson, Walker, & Fogel, 1997; Lamb, 1976, 1977a), although these play interactions decrease as children grow older

(Crawley & Sherrod, 1984). Because these types of play elicit positive responses from infants, young children often prefer interacting with their fathers when they have a choice (Clarke-Stewart, 1978; Lamb, 1977a). Not only do fathers and mothers play differently, play is an especially salient component of infant-father relationships (Lamb, 1976, 1977a). As Yarrow et al. (1984) reported, for example, more than 40% of the time the average father spent alone with his 6- to 12-month-old was spent in play.

Recent studies have suggested that the fathers' style of play affects their children's development, particularly their peer relationships (for reviews, see Parke, 1996; Parke & O'Neil, 2000). Parke and his colleagues found that fathers who exhibited high levels of both physical play and positive affect with their 3- and 4-year-old children had children who were rated by their teachers as most popular with peers. Fathers who were both highly physical and low in directiveness had the most popular sons, whereas fathers who were highly directive had less popular children (Parke, Burks, Carson, Neville, & Boyum, 1993). Moreover, more egalitarian father-child interactions, in which both fathers and children make and follow each others' suggestions, are associated with higher peer acceptance, greater social competence, and lower levels of aggression (Lindsey, Mize, & Pettit, 1997). Other researchers, too, have noted that paternal playfulness, patience, and understanding are associated with lower levels of filial aggression in children (Hart, Nelson, Robinson, Olsen, & McNeilly-Choque, 1998). Parke and Bhavnagri (1989) suggest that through interaction with their fathers, children learn how to read others' emotions and later use these skills when interacting with peers.

In short, the results of these studies underscore that fathers' influences on their children begin in infancy but continue into adulthood. There is substantial evidence that fathers are not only capable of being sensitive and responsive to their children but also that their behaviors materially affect social and personality development.

Beyond Early Childhood

Fathers' relationships with their children become more complex and multidimensional as children grow older. Even though children's social worlds expand considerably beyond parents to include peers and other adults, their relationships with their parents remain formatively important in later childhood and adolescence (Lamb, Hwang, Ketterlinus, & Fracasso, 1999), with dimensions of parental support and control being particularly important (Baumrind, 1968; Maccoby & Martin, 1983; Rollins & Thomas, 1979). Support includes affection, responsiveness, encouragement, instruction, and involvement. It promotes in children a basic sense of trust and security, enhancing children's self-conceptions of their worth and competence and fostering the acquisition of practical skills. Parental control, on the other hand, is a measure of discipline and is reflected in parents' rules, discipline, monitoring, and supervision (Baumrind, 1973).

In an extensive review focused mainly on paternal support and control, Amato (1998) concluded that, in two-parent families, the quality of father-child relationships is positively related to indices of the children's well-being. For example, Astone and McLanahan (1991) showed that fathers' monitoring of school progress was positively correlated with their adolescent children's high school grades, attendance, and attitudes toward school; and among both Anglos and Latinos, adolescents' feelings of closeness to their fathers were associated with lower levels of substance abuse (Coombs & Landsverk, 1988).

Similarly, children's reports of their fathers' and mothers' support were associated with the parents' reports of their children's social competence and self-control (Amato, 1998). For instance, Forehand, Long, Brody, and Fauber (1986) concluded that after controlling for variations in the mother-child relationships, the quality of the father-child relationships (as reported by both the children and parents) independently predicted the children's academic grades (as reported by the teachers).

Not surprisingly, negative paternal behavior can affect children as well. For example, the fathers' displays of negative emotions, such as anger, adversely affect children's acceptance by peers (Boyum & Parke, 1995; Carson & Parke, 1996). Rejected aggressive boys report that they received less affection from their fathers (but not their mothers) than do rejected but nonaggressive neglected boys (MacDonald & Parke, 1984).

Levels of Paternal Involvement

Since the early 1980s, many scholars have wondered whether variations in the levels of paternal involvement are associated with variations in their levels of impact on child development. In much of the relevant research, researchers have embraced Lamb, Pleck, Charnov, and Levine's (1987) conceptualization of father involvement. These scholars distinguished conceptually among three types of father involvement: (a) engagement, which comprises direct interaction with the child, including caretaking and play; (b) accessibility or availability to the child; and (c) the assumption of responsibility for the child by ensuring that the child is appropriately cared for and reared.

As Pleck (1997) noted in his thorough review, studies conducted in the 1980s to 1990s revealed that fathers were available to their children 35% to 40% as much as mothers were and were accessible about two thirds as much as mothers were. Time use studies indicated that father involvement had increased between the late 1970s and early 1980s and the early- to mid-1990s, perhaps suggesting that changing levels of maternal employment and growing emphasis on fathers' multifaceted roles had indeed prompted changes in the behavior of many fathers.

Paternal involvement also affects children's social, emotional, and cognitive development (Biller, 1993; Parke, 1996; Pleck, 1997). Radin (1982), for example, reported that fathers who were highly engaged and accessible to their preschoolers (performing 40% or more of within-family child care) had children who were more cognitively and linguistically competent, more empathic, less sex-role stereotyped, and had a more internal locus of control. Positive father engagement was also associated with academic achievement and social maturity at ages 6 and 7 (Gottfried, Gottfried, & Bathurst, 1988), as well as lower levels of externalizing and internalizing symptoms, and higher sociability (getting along with others, fulfilling responsibilities) among both white and African American 5- to 18-year-olds in two-parent families, even when positive maternal engagement, parental control, race, and sociodemographic background were taken into account (Mosley & Thomson, 1995). Moreover, high positive paternal engagement predicted fewer school behavior problems for boys and more self-direction for girls, as well as greater levels of cognitive, social, and personal maturity (Amato & Rivera, 1999; Furstenberg & Harris, 1993; Yogman et al., 1995), and better performance at school (Furstenberg & Harris, 1993; Nord, Brimhall & West, 1997) for both girls and boys. Greater paternal accessibility to adolescents also predicted acceptance by other children (Almeida & Galambos, 1991).

Increased paternal participation in their children's lives also appears to affect fathers' feelings about their children and perceptions of their father-child relationships (Grønseth, 1978; Hood & Golden, 1979; Radin, 1982; Russell, 1982). Russell (1982) found that the majority of fathers who were highly involved in child care reported becoming closer to, understanding of, and sensitive toward their children, as well as being more positive about their relationships. As Lamb and Easterbrooks (1981) and Kelly and Lamb (2000) argued, fathers need opportunities for interacting with their children in ways that provide practice in differentiating among, interpreting, and responding to children's signals. Interestingly, many fathers believe that the time spent with sole responsibility for their children's care and supervision was most important (Grønseth, 1978; Russell, 1982).

Nonresident Fathers

Because half of the children in the United States today spend at least part of their childhood in single-parent (usually mother-headed) families, the effects of fatherlessness have attracted the attention of both policymakers and researchers. After decades of controversy, there is now substantial agreement that children are better adjusted psychologically, perform better in school, have superior employment and income trajectories, are more socially competent with peers, and are less antisocial when they live in two-parent rather than single-parent families (see reviews by Amato, 1993, 2000; Goodman, Emery, & Haugaard, 1998; Hetherington & Stanley-Hagan, 1997; Lamb, 2002; McLanahan & Teitler, 1999). The effects of paternal absence due to paternal separation are more profound and reliable than the effects of father absence due to paternal death (Amato & Keith, 1991; Maier & Lachman, 2000). It is important to note, however, that the majority of children who grow up apart from their fathers develop quite normally, and this has led scholars to ask what accounts for the variability in outcomes and thus the weak associations between father absence or contact and child outcomes (see Lamb, 2002). Among the factors affecting child adjustment are the extent and longevity of conflict between the parents, economic circumstances, and the quality of the relationships with both of the parents.

As Amato and Gilberth (1999) showed in their recent meta-analysis, the amount of contact between nonresident fathers and children in and of itself is not very important. However, children's well-being is significantly enhanced when they have positive relationships with their nonresident fathers and these fathers regularly engage in "active parenting." Simons, Whitbeck, Beaman, and Conger (1994) thus reported that nonresident fathers who behaved authoritatively (providing emotional support to children, praising children's accomplishments, and disciplining them effectively) had adolescents who were better adjusted after the divorce. Other researchers have also found that children benefit when their nonresident fathers participate actively in routine everyday activities (Clarke-Stewart & Hayward, 1996; Hetherington, Bridges, & Insabella, 1998; Simons, 1996). Unfortunately, however, many nonresident fathers are not actively involved parents; instead, they either drift out of their children's lives or avoid discipline or limit setting, perhaps for fear that participation in such parental activities will alienate their children (Amato, 1987; Amato & Gilbreth, 1999; Furstenberg, Nord, Peterson, & Zill, 1983). Although these father-child interactions are enjoyable, they do not foster rich father-child relationships and ultimately reduce the impact that these fathers have on their children's development (Amato & Gilbreth, 1999). All of these findings thus suggest that children's well-being would be enhanced if postdivorce arrangements were designed to maximize positive and meaningful paternal involvement so as to ensure that children continue to benefit from the active participation of both parents (Kelly & Lamb, 2000; Lamb, 2002).

Factors Affecting Father-Child Relationships

Whether or not children's parents live with one another, the quality of the relationships between the parents has a powerful impact on children's adjustment. Positive coparental relationships provide children with models of emotional support, effective communication, conflict resolution, compromise, and negotiation (Cummings & O'Reilly, 1997). In addition, cooperative parents are able to provide a consistent and unified authority structure (Amato, 1998). By contrast, marital discord adversely affects children's academic successes, conduct, emotional adjustment, self-esteem, and social competence (Cummings & O'Reilly, 1997; Davies & Cummings, 1994; Emery, 1988; Grych & Fincham, 1990). When fathers are less warm toward mothers, mothers are more hostile toward fathers and discipline their children inconsistently (Conger & Elder, 1994), whereas when fathers show positive affect toward mothers, children are more likely to be popular with their peers (Boyum & Parke, 1995).

When fathers' psychological adjustment was controlled for, Cox, Owen, Lewis, and Henderson (1989) reported that fathers in close, confiding marriages had more positive attitudes toward their 3-month-old infants and toward their parental roles than did fathers in less successful marriages. The mothers were warmer and more sensitive as well (see also Levy-Shiff & Israelashvili, 1988). High marital quality was also associated with increased maternal and paternal sensitivity as well as improved child functioning, and as a result, parents who are better adapted to one another provide better parental care than parents who have poor or declining marital adaptation (Durrett,

Richards, Otaki, Pennebaker, & Nyquist, 1986; Heinicke & Guthrie, 1992; Jouriles, Pfiffner, & O'Leary, 1988; Meyer, 1988).

Interestingly, marital quality appears to influence paternal behavior more than maternal behavior (Belsky et al., 1984; Dickie & Matheson, 1984; Lamb & Elster, 1985), perhaps because paternal engagement is somewhat discretionary, whereas mothers are guided by clearer expectations that they need to be involved in their children's care. Each member of the family influences the others both directly and indirectly (Parke, Power, & Gottman, 1979). Mothers' attitudes and characteristics obviously affect levels of paternal involvement such that fathers are more involved in caregiving activities when mothers value their participation and view them as competent (Beitel & Parke, 1998; Haas, 1991; Palkovitz, 1984). Unfortunately, many mothers continue to feel ambivalent about father involvement (Coltrane, 1996; Dienhart & Daly, 1997), perhaps because they fear that fathers' involvement intrudes on their turf and may ultimately compromise their power and privilege in the home (Allen & Hawkins, 1999). This attitude may reflect maternal "gatekeeping," which at the worst of times may "inhibit a collaboration effort between men and women in families by limiting men's opportunities for learning and growing through caring for home and children" (Allen & Hawkins, 1999, p. 200).

Summary

Overall, there is substantial evidence that most children form emotionally significant relationships with their fathers in infancy and that the quality of father-child relationships plays an important role in shaping the behavior and development of infants, children, and adolescents whether or not their fathers live with them on a daily basis. The benefits associated with positive father-infant relationships are enhanced when fathers remain actively involved in their children's lives, and this has thus fostered public and private policies designed to promote father involvement, as we explain in the next section.

EFFECTS OF PUBLIC POLICIES ON FATHER INVOLVEMENT

Until recently, policymakers viewed fathers' provision of child support as the most important and regulatable form of father involvement. As a result, the goal of child support legislation is not to increase the amount of time that fathers spend with their children, but rather to insist that they live up to their economic responsibilities, whether or not this affects the amounts of time that fathers and children spend together. Such policies have been aggressively promoted and implemented in the last decade or so, especially since passage of the 1996 federal welfare reform legislation (the Personal Responsibility and Work Opportunity Reconciliation Act [PRWORA]). In contrast, policies designed to make the workplace fatherfriendly, increase health coverage of employed noncustodial parents, or increase paternal involvement in schools and child care centers have not been enforced widely, and their design and implementation vary from state to state. This has made it difficult to determine with certainty whether any of these policies had their desired effects. In this section, we focus on a handful of policies that appear to affect parental involvement and thus child well-being.

Paternity Establishment

Almost a decade before the passage of welfare reform, men were encouraged by law to take responsibility for their children. The Family Support Act of 1988, building on laws that had been in place since the 1950s, strengthened requirements that states establish the paternity of all children born out of wedlock and requires all unmarried fathers to pay child support until their children reached 18 years of age. As intended, passage of this law was associated with an increase in the proportion of children born outside of marriage whose fathers were both identified and required to pay child support (McLanahan, Seltzer, Hanson, & Thomas, 1995).

Paternity establishment policies traditionally operated under the assumption that nonmarried fathers would try to deny paternity to avoid their responsibilities, and thus coercive measures such as genetic testing and default proceedings (e.g., failure to appear at a paternity hearing is viewed in most states as acknowledgment of paternity) were deemed necessary. More recently, however, there has been an emphasis on the voluntary acknowledgment of paternity. Sonenstein, Holcomb, and Seefeldt (1994) found that states and counties that encouraged voluntary acknowledgment had a paternity establishment rate of 65%, 43% higher than in states and counties that did not encourage voluntary acknowledgement. Researchers have also shown that unmarried mothers frequently continue their relationships with fathers during pregnancy and through the first few years of their children's lives (Carlson & McLanahan, 2002; Price & Williams, 1990), suggesting that efforts to establish paternity should be made early, when fathers are more likely to be involved.

The 1996 welfare reform legislation required all states to have voluntary paternity acknowledgment programs in birthing hospitals in the hope that such programs would foster paternity establishments, child support payments, and fathers' involvement with their children. To date, however, no researchers have examined the relationships among legal paternity establishment, father involvement, and the quality of father-child relationships.

Welfare policies affect father involvement in other ways as well. In place of Aid to Families with Dependent Children (AFDC), the PRWORA created block grants that allow states to run welfare programs of their own design, within broad federal guidelines. The PRWORA had four interrelated goals: (a) to enable children to stay with their families, (b) to encourage work and marriage, (c) to prevent and reduce out-of-wedlock pregnancies, and (d) to encourage the formation and maintenance of two-parent families. The PRWORA included bonuses for "high-performing," states that met the act's overall objectives. The emphasis on marriage promotion was intended to increase proportions of children raised in two-parent families, which, as noted earlier, appears to promote better child adjustment, perhaps in part by enhancing the ability of fathers to interact with their children. Given wide variations in the design and implementation of child support laws, however, it is difficult to establish the effects of those laws. Some child support collection policies may even unintentionally discourage family formation, paternity establishment, and father involvement.

Custodial parents who apply for public assistance must take active roles in establishing paternity and pursuing child support, and the PRWORA requires states to increase the collection of child support dollars. In 1997, for example, Virginia launched the Kids First Campaign, which netted $25 million from noncustodial parents who owed back support by instituting the mandatory suspension of driving, hunting, and fishing licenses and sending letters to delinquent fathers, arresting them, and using "boots" to disable their cars. In some states, such as Wisconsin, all child support payments are forwarded to the custodial parents, whereas other states, such as Minnesota, add the funds to general revenues. In other states, welfare payments are reduced by one dollar for each dollar of child support collected. In the past, consequently, many men and women decided not to declare paternity so that all payments made by the fathers went directly to the children and their mothers, rather than to the state (Doherty, Kouneski, & Erikson, 1998). This is no longer possible. Mothers can lose their benefits if they withhold information about the fathers, although mothers can still prevent fathers from seeing their children for many reasons, including the failure to make child support payments (Nelson, Clamptet-Lundquist, & Edin, 2002). Many fathers resent sending money without having access to their children, and when they refuse to pay, mothers must report them or face steep penalties (Nelson et al., 2002). Paternal and maternal cooperation may thus be undermined just when it is most important for child well-being. Increasing hostility between parents minimizes the potential benefits for the children. As welfare reform proceeds, child support may well be an increasing source of financial support to mothers who have obtained employment, but if fathers' payments are devoted to covering back payments, fathers may be less able to support their families after mothers leave the welfare system. Unemployed fathers owe the state money for the benefits their children receive. This ongoing debt further jeopardizes father-child relationships, especially because mothers owe nothing after they get off welfare.

Although many researchers have found that income from child support is more beneficial to children than income from other sources (e.g., Knox & Bane, 1994; McLanahan et al., 1995), some have found that child support may have little or no enduring effects on child development. For example, Peters and Mullis (1997) found that child support had positive effects on cognitive test scores measured during adolescence, but not on later measures of educational attainment, earnings, and labor market experience. Knox (1996) reported

significant effects on achievement test scores, but not on measures of the home environment. Argys and Peters (1996) argued that the differential effects of child support dollars on children's outcomes might depend on the relationships between the mothers and fathers. Parents who get along are more likely to agree about how the money should be spent and to make expenditures on children in a cooperative and efficient way.

Other studies suggest that child support may influence parent-child and mother-father relationships, which in turn affect children's well-being. For example, payment of child support is an indicator of a fathers' success in the "economic provider role"; this success may then motivate nonresident fathers to become involved with their children in other beneficial ways. Similarly, mothers who are "gatekeepers" may allow fathers access to their children only if child support has been paid (Nelson et al., 2002). On the other hand, the positive relationship between child support and father involvement may simply reflect selection: Fathers who care more about their children and want to maintain involvement are also more likely to pay child support.

Finally, McLanahan et al. (1995) have suggested that child support payments may influence the degree of conflict between the two parents in diverse ways. Conflict is likely to decrease when fathers fulfill their financial obligations, but if child support leads to increases in paternal involvement, this may also increase opportunities for conflict between the parents. Argys, Peters, Brooks-Gunn, and Smith (1998) report findings that make the important distinction between cooperative and noncooperative awards. They found that the effects of child support on cognitive development are greatest when the payments are voluntary. This suggests that the increased levels of child support brought about by recent coercive practices may not be as beneficial as policymakers had hoped.

Divorce and Child Custody

For some nonresident fathers, the issue of custody is critical. Braver and O'Connell (1998) argue that divorce laws, which often presumptively identify mothers as custodial parents, keep men from remaining involved with their children. As custody laws become gender neutral, shared custody has become more common, and this has implications for child support and father involvement (Seltzer, 1998). Amato and Gilbreth (1999) argue that nonresident fathers are becoming more active in their children's upbringing and that social policies could play a key role in promoting this involvement. In the same vein, the U.S. Commission on Child and Family Welfare (1996; as cited in Levine & Pittinsky, 1997) recommended that court orders avoid terms such as *custody* and *visitation,* which imply that one parent "wins" the children, and instead promote parenting plans that emphasize the responsibilities of both parents.

Similarly, Braver and O'Connell (1998) argue that joint legal custody is beneficial for children and parents and that both visitation and support payment orders should be enforced; this is currently not the case in most states. As noted above, the ability to actively parent, which is more likely if there is meaningful midweek as well as weekend contact, is linked to many indices of superior child adjustment (Amato & Gilbreth, 1999; Lamb, 1999).

Because joint custody is gaining acceptance, there is a growing interest in identifying the conditions under which such arrangements are most likely to be successful. Many marriages that end in divorce are characterized by intense and often unresolved conflict prior to the divorce (Cherlin, 1992; Kelly, 2000). Educational programs for divorcing parents that stress the importance of cooperative parenting reduce conflict and promote child well-being (Kelly, 1994, 2000, 2002; U.S. Commission of Child and Family Welfare, 1996, as cited in Levine & Pittinsky, 1997).

Workplace-Related Policies

Even when fathers live with their children, structural barriers can hinder their ability to fulfill their parental obligations. In 1993, President Clinton thus signed the Family and Medical Leave Act (FMLA), which allowed parents to take up to 6 weeks of unpaid leave to care for new children or sick family members, provided they work in establishments with 50 or more employees and have been employed at least half-time for a full year. Before the passage of FMLA, 11 states had similar family leave policies (Klerman & Leibowitz, 1997).

Both paid and unpaid parental leave have become available in the United States only quite recently, whereas it has been available in other countries for much longer and has become increasingly popular. In Sweden, for example, Haas (1991) reports that only 3% of the eligible fathers took leave in 1974, the first year paid paternal leave was available, whereas by 1989, 44% of the eligible fathers took leave (Pleck, 1997). Even in Sweden, however, fathers take much less leave time than mothers do (53 versus 225 days, on average). In the United States, fathers typically take about 5 days of leave when their children are born (Levine & Pittinsky, 1997), and 91% of fathers now take at least some leave (Hyde, Essex, & Horton, 1993), although most fathers who take time off from work use paid vacation or sick leave rather than unpaid parental leave. Paid parental leave is fairly rare in the United States. In 1993, only 3% of medium and large establishments and 1% of small establishments offered paid parental leave (Blau, Ferber, & Winkler, 1998).

In addition to parental leave, other structural barriers in the workplace may discourage or impede active parental involvement.

In particular, men on the "daddy track" (those who take time off to care for or be with their children) get off the "career track" and hurt their careers. In recent years, however, some managers have begun to argue that "happy fathers" are more productive workers and have initiated institutional changes designed to make the workplace father-friendly. For example, many companies have begun to conduct focus groups, survey employees, provide flexible scheduling, reward performance rather than desk time, encourage fathers' participation in their children's schools, and support fathers who need to stay home to take care of sick or newborn children (Levine & Pittinsky, 1997).

Policies in Educational Settings

Children also benefit when their fathers are actively involved in their education. Parents are more likely to be involved in their children's school life when they live together (Zill & Nord, 1994), and children who live with only one parent have lower grade point averages, lower college aspirations, poorer attendance records, and higher dropout rates than students who live with both parents (McLanahan & Sandefur, 1994). Similarly, children who live with one parent spend fewer hours studying, have declining academic performances, have lower cognitive skills, and are about twice as likely to drop out of high school as children who live with both parents (Dawson, 1991; Luster & McAdoo, 1994; McLanahan & Sandefur, 1994). Involvement in schooling and active involvement in children's lives by both resident and nonresident fathers are associated with greater academic achievement and enjoyment of school by children (Nord et al., 1997). Regardless of residential status, fathers of kindergartners are just as likely as single mothers to attend PTA meetings. Single fathers and mothers are equally likely to attend PTA meetings and open houses, although fathers in two-parent

families are less likely than mothers and single fathers to attend parent-teacher conferences (West, Brimhall, Smith, & Richman, 2001). Presumably, fathers and mothers in two-parent households make different decisions regarding who will attend school activities and who will mind the children during these events.

There are, however, structural barriers that affect fathers' levels of involvement in their children's education, regardless of residential status. For example, inflexible working hours and the inability of school officials to make schools father-friendly may curb parents' involvement with school, especially for those who might have nontraditional working hours. Parents with flexible schedules are more likely to participate in their children's school activities (Cabrera & Peters, 2000). The majority of low-income men employed by small firms or in the service industry have jobs with inflexible hours and do not offer any of these benefits (Levine & Pittinsky, 1997). Few programs are designed to promote fathers' involvement in their children's schools (McBride & Rane, 1997). Although most programs focus on parents, some programs are aimed at teachers and are designed to encourage and facilitate father involvement in pre-K programs. For example, McBride, Rane, and Bae (1999) evaluated an intervention that provided support services to teachers rather than providing direct services to children and their families. Teachers were taught to plan, implement, and evaluate specific initiatives to encourage father/male involvement in the program. A major aspect of the program was teachers' attitudes toward father involvement. This intervention appeared to have positive effects on teachers and on father involvement.

New Policies and Initiatives

Policymakers in the United States now appear eager to confront the barriers to father involvement for both resident and nonresident fathers and to enhance effective services and outreach to low-income fathers. The Department of Health and Human Service policies on fathers are currently shaped by five principles: (a) All fathers can be important contributors to the well-being of their children; (b) parents are partners in raising their children, even when they do not live together; (c) fathers play diverse roles in families that and related to cultural and community norms; (d) men should receive the education and support necessary to prepare them for the responsibility of parenthood; and (e) government can encourage and promote father involvement through its programs and workforce policies.

Other federal programs and policies also promote fatherhood. In 1999, for example, the U.S. House of Representatives passed the Fathers Count Act, which would have made millions of dollars in federal grants available to fatherhood programs. The goal of this legislation was to promote marriage and successful parenting and to help fathers improve their economic status by providing job search services, job training, subsidized employment, and career-advancing education. Another recent bill, the Children First Child Support Act, also targets low-income families struggling to provide for their families. This bill would allow all child support payments to families on welfare to "pass through" to the children and would give states the option of disregarding any child support payments when assessing program eligibility. In neither case were funds appropriated to support these activities, however.

Like President Clinton, President Bush has made promoting involved, committed, "responsible fatherhood" a national priority. To further expand these efforts, the Department of Health and Human Service (DHHS) fiscal year 2002 budget request includes $131 million to support two new fatherhood initiatives: $64 million primarily to support competitive grants to faith-based and community-based organizations that work to strengthen the role that fathers play in their families' lives, and $67 million to support state grants to mentor children of prisoners (DHHS, 2001).

Another federal focus is on child health and fathering. Over 10 million children in the United States are without health care coverage, including approximately 3 million of the 21 million children who are eligible for child support enforcement services (DHHS, 2000). These children have substantially less access to health care, and the Medical Support Working Group has recommended that states maximize the enrollment of children in appropriate health insurance programs. These recommendations have not become law, however.

In addition to these national policies, the states have also attempted to increase public awareness of the importance of father involvement by convening statewide conferences and sponsoring media campaigns to promote positive father involvement. The initiatives profiled by the states fall into six categories: services for low-income, noncustodial fathers; parenting skills training; public awareness campaigns; state fatherhood commissions; comprehensive funding streams; and premature fatherhood prevention (Knitzer, Brenner, & Gadsden, 1997). Unfortunately, no efforts have yet been made to determine which approaches work best for which groups of fathers, because program evaluations rarely accompany initiatives.

PUBLIC EDUCATION AND INTERVENTION PROGRAMS

Recent changes in the conceptualization of male family roles have tremendous implications for program design and implementation. Targeted changes in parental behavior brought about by intervention programs can have positive effects on children's outcomes. Thousands of programs across the country target fathers, including unmarried and adolescent males, and provide job training and parenting (Louv, 1994). In addition, several parent-training models targeted at fathers have been developed (e.g., Levine, Murphy, & Wilson, 1993; Levine & Pitt, 1995; McBride & McBride, 1993; Palm, 1998). Organizations such as the National Center on Families and Fathers (NCOFF) (http://www.ncoff.gse. upenn.edu/fif/fif-intro.htm) and the National Association of Practitioners (http://www. npa.org) provide technical assistance, compile research information, provide forums for meetings, and organize workshops for practitioners and educators. Similarly, the National Center for Strategic Nonprofit Planning and Community Leadership (NPCL) is a nonprofit organization created for charitable and educational purposes. The NPCL offers a series of workshops to help community-based organizations and public agencies to better serve young, low-income single fathers and fragile families, and it sponsors an annual international conference on fatherhood (http://www.npcl.org).

Programs for low-income men fall into two broad categories. Some endorse "responsible fatherhood" approaches and make marriage a primary goal, whereas others presume that "marriageable" men need training and education. Public education efforts that promote sexual responsibility and responsible fatherhood have focused on teenage fathers. These programs are believed to have beneficial effects on children because they focus on training and parenting skills and encourage paternal involvement in programs such as Early Head Start (Kiselica, 1995).

Some programs have also targeted men in prisons. Incarceration can break fragile family bonds, exasperate men, and disrupt father-child relationships, but programs for incarcerated fathers are relatively new. Current federal efforts encourage incarcerated fathers to provide more reliable and regular child support for their children. These grants support a number of state and local projects that provide services to noncustodial parents who are incarcerated, unemployed, or underemployed to increase employment and reintegrate them into their communities.

In addition to programs designed to promote father involvement, a growing body of materials (including self-help books, magazines for fathers, and popular books) offer advice and suggestions about what fathers can do to become more involved in their children's lives (Levine & Pittinsky, 1997). For example, Levine and Pittinsky (1997) advise that parents focus not only on the quality of the relationships with their children but also on the relationships with "significant others" in their children's lives, including teachers, child care providers, coaches, doctors, and children's friends.

In general, little is known about the effectiveness of these programs (e.g., McBride et al., 1999) probably because few funds are available for evaluation, programs may be poorly designed and implemented, and appropriate measures have not been developed. NCOFF has published a list of quantitative and qualitative measures titled "The Fathering Indicators Framework" (FIF; NCOFF, 2001). This framework offers a set of guidelines designed to help researchers, practitioners, and policymakers conceptualize, examine, and measure change in fathering behaviors. The FIF consists of six fathering-indicator categories (e.g., father presence, caregiving, children's social competence, cooperative parenting, fathers' healthy living, and material and financial contributions) that can be measured reliably and linked to child outcomes.

CONCLUSIONS

As we have shown in this chapter, there is ample evidence that fathers typically establish emotionally salient relationships with their children and that they can make significant contributions to their children's development. Although these influences may be positive, it is also clear that fathers may fail to promote their children's well-being, either because their relationships are of poor quality or because they play little or no role in their children's lives, whether or not they live together. Recognition of these factors has fostered the development of policies, programs, and practices that promote enhancements in the quality of father-child relationships and in the extent to which fathers become or remain actively involved in their children's lives. Although the need and potential value of these programs are clear, their actual impact has not been well documented. We can only hope that this situation will improve in the next few years.

REFERENCES

Ainsworth, M. D. S., Blehar, M. C., Waters, E., & Wall, S. (1978). *Patterns of attachment.* Hillsdale, NJ: Lawrence Erlbaum.

Allen, J. M., & Hawkins, A. J. (1999). Maternal gatekeeping: Mothers' beliefs and behaviors that inhibit greater father involvement in family work. *Journal of Marriage and the Family, 61,* 199-212.

Almeida, D. M., & Galambos, N. L. (1991). Examining father involvement and the quality of father-adolescent relations. *Journal of Research on Adolescence, 1,* 155-172.

Amato, P. R. (1987). *Children in Australian families: The growth of competence.* Sydney: Prentice Hall of Australia.

Amato, P. R. (1993). *Children in Australian families: The growth of competence.* Sydney: Prentice Hall of Australia.

Amato, P. R. (1998). More than money? Men's contributions to their children's lives. In A. Booth & A. C. Crouter (Eds.), *Men in families: When do they get involved? What difference does it make?* (pp. 241-277). Mahwah, NJ: Lawrence Erlbaum.

Amato, P. R. (2000). The consequences of divorce for adults and children. *Journal of Marriage and the Family, 62,* 1269-1287.

Amato, P. R., & Gilbreth, J. G. (1999). Nonresident fathers and children's well-being: A meta-analysis. *Journal of Marriage & the Family, 61,* 557-573.

Amato, P. R., & Keith, B. (1991). Parental divorce and the well-being of children: A meta-analysis. *Psychological Bulletin, 110,* 26-46.

Amato, R. R., & Rivera, F. (1999). Paternal involvement and children's behavior. *Journal of Marriage and the Family, 61,* 375-384.

Argys, L. M., & Peters, H. E. (1996). *Can adequate child support be legislated? A theoretical model of responses to child support guidelines and enforcement efforts* [Mimeographed document]. Ithaca, NY: Cornell University, Department of Policy Analysis and Management.

Argys, L. M., Peters, H. E., Brooks-Gunn, J., & Smith, J. R. (1998). The impact of child support dollars on cognitive outcomes. *Demography, 35,* 159-173.

Astone, N. M., & McLanahan, S. S. (1991). Family structure, parental practices, and high school competition. *American Sociological Review, 56,* 309-320.

Baumrind, D. (1968). Authoritarian versus authoritative parental control. *Adolescence, 3*, 255-272.

Baumrind, D. (1973). The development of instrumental competence through social-ization. In A. D. Pick (Ed.), *Minnesota symposia on child psychology* (Vol. 7, pp. 3-46). Minneapolis: University of Minnesota Press.

Beitel, A. H., & Parke, R. D. (1998). Paternal involvement in infancy: The role of maternal and paternal attitudes. *Journal of Family Psychology, 12*, 268-288.

Belsky, J., Gilstrap, B., & Rovine, M. (1984). The Pennsylvania Infant and Family Development Project, I: Stability and change in mother-infant and father-infant interaction in a family setting at one, three, and nine months. *Child Development, 55*, 692-705.

Biller, H. B. (1993). *Fathers and families*. Westport, CT: Auburn House.

Blau, F., Ferber, M., & Winkler, A. (1998). *The economics of women, men, and work*. Upper Saddle River, NJ: Prentice Hall.

Boyum, L., & Parke, R. D. (1995). Family emotional expressiveness and children's social competence. *Journal of Marriage and Family, 57*, 593-708.

Braungart-Rieker, J., Garwood, M. M., Powers, B. P., & Notaro, P. C. (1998). Infant affect and affect regulation during the still-face paradigm with mothers and fathers: The role of infant characteristics and parental sensitivity. *Developmental Psychology, 34*, 1428-1437.

Braver, S. L., & O'Connell, D. (1998). *Divorced dads*. New York: Putnam.

Brophy-Herb, H. E., Gibbons, G., Omar, M. A., & Schiffman, R. P. (1999). Low-income fathers and their infants: Interactions during teaching episodes. *Infant Mental Health Journal, 20*, 305-321.

Cabrera, N., & Peters, H. E. (2000). Public policies and father involvement. *Marriage & Family Review, 29*, 295-314.

Carlson, M., & McLanahan, S. (2002). Fragile families, father involvement, and public policy. In C. S. Tamis-Lemonda & N. Cabrera (Eds.), *Handbook of father involvement* (pp. 461-488). Mahwah, NJ: Lawrence Erlbaum.

Carson, J., & Parke, R. D. (1996). Reciprocal negative affect in parent-child inter-actions and children's peer competency. *Child Development, 67*, 2217-2226.

Cherlin, A. J. (1992). *Marriage, divorce, remarriage*. Cambridge, MA: Harvard University Press.

Clarke-Stewart, K. A. (1978). And daddy makes three: The father's impact on mother and young child. *Child Development, 49*, 466-478.

Clarke-Stewart, K. A., & Hayward, C. (1996). Advantages of father custody and contact for the psychological well-being of school-age children. *Journal of Applied Developmental Psychology, 17*, 239-270.

Coltrane, S. (1996). *Family man*. New York: Oxford University Press.

Conger, R. D., & Elder, G. H. Jr. (1994). *Families in troubled times*. New York: de Gruyter.

Coombs, R. H., & Landsverk, J. (1988). Parenting styles and substance use during childhood and adolescence. *Journal of Marriage and Family Therapy, 50*, 473-82.

Cox, M. J., Owen, M. T., Henderson, U. K., & Margand, N. A. (1992). Prediction of infant-father and infant-mother attachment. *Developmental Psychology, 28*, 474-483.

Cox, M. J., Owen, M. T., Lewis, J. M., & Henderson, U. K. (1989). Marriage, adult adjustment, and early parenting. *Child Development, 60*, 1015-1024.

Crawley, S. B., & Sherrod, R. B. (1984). Parent-infant play during the first year of life. *Infant Behavior and Development, 7*, 65-75.

Cummings, E. M., & O'Reilly, A. W. (1997). Fathers in family context: Effects of marital quality on child adjustment. In M. E. Lamb (Ed.), *The role of the father in child development* (3rd ed., pp. 49-65). New York: Wiley.

Davies, P. T., & Cummings, E. M. (1994). Marital conflict and child adjustment: An emotional security hypothesis. *Psychological Bulletin, 116,* 387-411.

Dawson, D. (1991). Family structure and children's health and well-being: Interview survey on child health. *Journal of Marriage and the Family, 53,* 573-584.

DeWolff, M. S., & van IJzendoorn, M. H. (1997). Sensitivity and attachment: A meta-analysis on parental antecedents of infant attachment. *Child Development, 68,* 571-591.

Dickie, J., & Matheson, P. (1984, August). *Mother-father-infant: Who needs support?* Paper presented at the meeting of the American Psychological Association Convention, Toronto, Canada.

Dickson, K. L., Walker, H., & Fogel, A. (1997). The relationship between smile type and play type during parent-infant play. *Developmental Psychology, 33,* 925-933.

Dienhart, A., & Daly, K. (1997). Men and women co-creating father involvement in a nongenerative culture. In A. J. Hawkins & D. C. Dollahite (Eds.), *Generative fathering* (pp. 147-164). Thousand Oaks, CA: Sage.

Doherty, W. J., Kouneski, E. F., & Erickson, M. F. (1998). Responsible fathering: An overview and conceptual framework. *Journal of Marriage and the Family, 60,* 277-292.

Donate-Bartfield, D., & Passman, R. H. (1985). Attentiveness of mothers and fathers to their baby cries. *Infant Behavior and Development, 8,* 385-393.

Durrett, M. E., Richards, P., Otaki, M., Pennebaker, J., & Nyquist, L. (1986). Mother's involvement with infant and her perception of spousal support, Japan and America. *Journal of Marriage and the Family, 68,* 187-194.

Emery, R. (1988). *Marriage, divorce, and children's adjustment.* Newbury Park, CA: Sage.

Family and Medical Leave Act, Pub. L. No. 103-3 (1993).

Family Support Act, Pub. L. No. 100-485 (1988).

Field, T., Gewirtz, J. L., Cohen, D., Garcia, R., Greenberg, R., & Collins, K. (1984). Leave-takings and reunions of infants, toddlers, preschoolers, and their parents. *Child Development, 55,* 628-635.

Forehand, R., Long, N., Brody, G. H., & Fauber, R. (1986). Home predictors of young adolescents' school behavior and academic performance. *Child Development, 57,* 213-221.

Furstenberg, F. F. Jr., & Harris, K. M. (1993). When fathers matter/why fathers matter: The impact of paternal involvement on the offspring of adolescent mothers. In A. Lawson & D. L. Rhode (Eds.), *The politics of pregnancy: Adolescent sexuality and public policy* (pp. 189-215). New Haven, CT: Yale University Press.

Furstenberg, F. F. Jr., Nord, C. W., Peterson, J. L., & Zill, N. (1983). The life course of children of divorce. *American Sociological Review, 2,* 695-701.

Goodman, G. S., Emery, R. E., & Haugaard, J. J. (1998). Developmental psychology and law: The cases of divorce, child maltreatment, foster care, and adoption. In W. Damon (Series Ed.), I. E. Sigel & K. A. Renninger (Vol. Eds.), *Handbook of child psychology: Vol. 4. Child psychology in practice* (5th ed., pp. 775-874). New York: Wiley.

Gottfried, A. E., Gottfried, A. W., & Bathurst, K. (1988). Maternal employment, family environment, and children's development: Infancy through the school years. In A. E. Gottfried & A. W. Gottfried (Eds.), *Maternal employment and children's development: Longitudinal research* (pp. 11-58). New York: Plenum.

Grønseth, E. (1978). Work sharing: A Norwegian example. In R. Rapoport & R. N. Rapoport (Eds.), *Working couples.* St. Lucia, Australia: Queensland Press.

Grych, J. H., & Fincham, F. D. (1990). Marital conflict and children's adjustment: A cognitive-contextual framework. *Psychological Bulletin, 2,* 267-290.

Haas, L. (1991). Equal parenthood and social policy: Lessons from a study of parental leave in Sweden. In J. S. Hyde & M. J. Essex (Eds.), *Parental leave and child care: Setting a research and policy agenda* (pp. 375-405). Philadelphia: Temple University Press.

Hart, C. H., Nelson, D. A., Robinson, C. C., Olsen, S. F., & McNeilly-Choque, M. K. (1998). Overt and relational aggression in Russian nursery-school-age children: Parenting style and marital linkages. *Developmental Psychology, 34,* 687-697.

Heinicke, C. M., & Guthrie, D. (1992). Stability and change in husband-wife adaptation and development of the positive parent-child relationship. *Infant Behavior and Development, 15,* 109-127.

Hetherington, E. M., Bridges, M., & Insabella, G. M. (1998). What matters? What does not? Five perspectives on the association between marital transition and children's adjustment. *American Psychologist, 53,* 167-184.

Hetherington, E. M., & Stanley-Hagan, M. M. (1997). The effects of divorce on fathers and their children. In M. E. Lamb (Ed.), *The role of the father in child development* (3rd ed., pp. 191-211). New York: Wiley.

Hood, J., & Golden, S. (1979). Beating time/making time: The impact of work scheduling on men's family roles. *The Family Co-Ordinator, 28,* 575-582.

Hyde, J. S., Essex, M. J., & Horton, F. (1993). Fathers and parental leave: Attitudes and experiences. *Journal of Family Issues, 14,* 616-641.

Jouriles, E. N., Pfiffner, L. J., & O'Leary, S. G. (1988). Marital conflict, parenting, and toddler conduct problems. *Journal of Abnormal Psychology, 16,* 197-206.

Kelly, J. B. (1994). The determination of child custody. *The Future of Children, 4,* 121-142.

Kelly, J. B. (2000). Children's adjustment in conflicted marriage and divorce: A decade of review of research. *Journal of American Academy of Child & Adolescent Psychiatry, 29,* 963-973.

Kelly, J. B. (in press). Legal and educational interventions for families in residence and contact disputes. *Australian Journal of Family Law.*

Kelly, J. B., & Lamb, M. E. (2000). Using child development research to make appropriate custody and access decisions for young children. *Family and Conciliation Courts Review, 38,* 297-311.

Kiselica, M. S. (1995). *Multicultural counseling with teenage fathers: A practical guide.* Thousand Oaks, CA: Sage.

Klerman, J. A., & Leibowitz, A. (1997). Labor supply effects of state maternity leave legislation. In F. D. Blau & R. G. Ehrenberg (Eds.), *Gender and family issues in the workplace* (pp. 65-85). New York: Russell Sage.

Knitzer, J., Brenner, E., & Gadsden, V. (1997). *Map and track: States initiatives to encourage responsible fatherhood.* New York: National Center for Children in Poverty.

Knox, V. W. (1996). The effects of child support payments on developmental outcomes for elementary school-age children. *The Journal of Human Resources, 31,* 816-840.

Knox, V. W., & Bane, M. J. (1994). Child support and schooling. In I. Garfinkel, S. S. McLanahan, & P. K. Robbins (Eds.), *Child support and child well-being* (pp. 285-310). Washington, DC: Urban Institute.

Kotelchuck, M. (1976). The infant's relationship to the father: Experimental evidence. In M. E. Lamb (Ed.), *The role of the father in child development* (pp. 329-344). New York: Wiley.

Labrell, F. (1990). *Educational strategies and their representations in parents of toddlers.* Paper presented at the Fourth European Conference on Developmental Psychology, Sterling, England.

Lamb, M. E. (1976). Interactions between two-year-olds and their mothers and fathers. *Psychological Reports, 38,* 447-450.

Lamb, M. E. (1977a). Father-infant and mother-infant interaction in the first year of life. *Child Development, 48,* 167-181.

Lamb, M. E. (1977b). The development of parental preferences in the first two years of life. *Sex Roles, 3,* 495-497.

Lamb, M. E. (1999). Non-custodial fathers and their impact on the children of divorce. In R. A. Thompson & P. R. Amato (Eds.), *The post-divorce family: Research and policy issues* (pp. 105-125). Thousand Oaks, CA: Sage.

Lamb, M. E. (2002). Non-residential fathers and their children. In C. S. Tamis-Lemonda & N. Cabrera (Eds.), *Handbook of father involvement* (pp. 169-184). Mahwah, NJ: Lawrence Erlbaum.

Lamb, M. E., & Easterbrooks, M. A. (1981). Individual differences in parental sensitivity: Origins, components, and consequences. In M. E. Lamb & L. R. Sherrod (Eds.), *Infant social cognition: Empirical and theoretical considerations* (pp. 127-154). Hillsdale, NJ: Lawrence Erlbaum.

Lamb, M. E., & Elster, A. B. (1985). Adolescent mother-infant-father relationships. *Developmental Psychology, 21,* 768-773.

Lamb, M. E., Frodi, M., Hwang, C. P., & Frodi, A. M. (1983). Effects of paternal involvement on infant preferences for mothers and fathers. *Child Development, 54,* 450-458.

Lamb, M. E., Hwang, C. P., Frodi, A. M., & Frodi, M. (1982). Security of mother- and father-infant attachment and its relation to sociability with strangers in traditional and nontraditional Swedish families. *Infant Behavior and Development, 5,* 355-367.

Lamb, M. E., Hwang, C. P., Ketterlinus, R. D., & Fracasso, M. P. (1999). Parent-child relationships: Development in the context of the family. In M. H. Bornstein & M. E. Lamb (Eds.), *Developmental psychology: An advanced textbook* (4th ed., pp. 411-450). Mahwah, NJ: Lawrence Erlbaum.

Lamb, M. E., Pleck, J. H., Charnov, E. L., & Levine, J. A. (1987). A biosocial perspective on paternal behavior and involvement. In J. B. Lancaster, J. Atlman, & A. Rossi (Eds.), *Parenting across the life span: Biosocial dimensions* (pp. 11-42). New York: Academic Press.

Lamb, M. E., Thompson, R. A., Gardner, W., & Charnov, E. L. (1985). *Infant-mother attachment: The origins and developmental significance of individual differences in strange situation behavior.* Hillsdale, NJ: Lawrence Erlbaum.

Levine, J. A., Murphy, D., & Wilson, S. (1993). *Getting men involved: Strategies for early childhood programs.* New York: Scholastic.

Levine, J. A., & Pitt, E. W. (1995). *New expectations: Community strategies for responsible fatherhood.* New York: Families and Work Institute.

Levine, J. A., & Pittinsky, T. (1997). *Working fathers: New strategies for balancing work and family.* Reading, MA: Addison-Wesley.

Levy-Shiff, R., & Israelashvili, R. (1988). Antecedents of fathering: Some further exploration. *Developmental Psychology, 24,* 434-440.

Lieberman, M., Doyle, A. B., & Markiewicz, D. (1999). Development patterns in security of attachment to mother and father in late childhood and early adolescence: Associations with peer relations. *Child Development, 70,* 202-213.

Lindsey, E. W., Mize, J., & Pettit, G. S. (1997). Mutuality in parent-child play: Consequences for children's peer competence. *Journal of Social & Personal Relationships, 14,* 523-538.

Louv, R. (1994). *Reinventing fatherhood* (Occasional Papers Series, No. 14). New York: United Nations.

Luster, T., & McAdoo, H. (1994). Factors related to the achievement and adjustment of young African American children. *Child Development, 65,* 1080-1094.

Maccoby, E. E., & Martin, J. (1983). Socialization in the context of the family: Parent-child interaction. In E. M. Hetherington (Ed.), *Handbook of child psychology: Vol. 4. Socialization, personality and social development* (4th ed., pp. 1-104). New York: Free Press.

MacDonald, K., & Parke, R. D. (1984). Bridging the gap: Parent-child play interaction and peer interactive competence. *Child Development, 55,* 1265-1277.

Magill-Evans, J., & Harrison, M. J. (1999). Parent-child interactions and development of toddlers born preterm. *Western Journal of Nursing Research, 21,* 292-307.

Maier, E. H., & Lachman, M. E. (2000). Consequences of early parental loss and separation for health and well-being in midlife. *International Journal of Behavioral Development, 24,* 183-189.

Main, M., & Weston, D. (1981). The quality of the toddler's relationship to mother and to father: Related to conflict behavior and the readiness to establish new relationships. *Child Development, 52,* 932-940.

Mansbach, I. K., & Greenbaum, C. N. (1999). Developmental maturity expectations of Israeli fathers and mothers: Effects of education, ethnic origin, and religiosity. *International Journal of Behavioral Development, 23,* 771-797.

McBride, B. A., & McBride, R. J. (1993). Parent education and support programs for fathers: Research guiding practice. *Childhood Education, 70,* 4-9.

McBride, B. A., & Rane, T. R. (1997). Role identity, role investments, and paternal involvement: Implications for parenting programs for men. *Early Childhood Research Quarterly, 2,* 173-197.

McBride, B. A., Rane, T. R., & Bae, J. H. (1999, April). *Intervening with teachers to encourage father/male involvement in early childhood programs.* Paper presented at the meeting of the Society for Research in Child Development, Albuquerque, NM.

McLanahan, S. S., & Sandefur, G. (1994). *Growing up with a single parent: What hurts, what helps.* Cambridge, MA: Harvard University Press.

McLanahan, S. S., Seltzer, J. A., Hanson, T. L., & Thomas, E. (1995). Child support enforcement and child well-being: Greater security or greater conflicts? In I. Garfinkel, S. S. McLanahan, & P. K. Robins (Eds.), *Child support and child well-being* (pp. 239-254). Washington, DC: Urban Institute.

McLanahan, S. S., & Teitler, J. (1999). The consequences of father absence. In M. E. Lamb (Ed.), *Parenting and child development in "nontraditional" families* (pp. 83-102). Mahwah, NJ: Lawrence Erlbaum.

Meyer, H. J. (1988). Marital and mother-child relationships: Developmental history, parent personality, and child difficultness. In R. A. Hinde & J. Stevenson-Hinde (Eds.), *Relationship within families: Mutual influences* (pp. 119-139). Oxford, UK: Clarendon.

Mosley, J., & Thomson, E. (1995). Fathering behavior and child outcomes: The role of race and poverty. In W. Marsiglio (Ed.), *Fatherhood: Contemporary theory, research, and social policy* (pp.148-165). Thousand Oaks, CA: Sage.

National Center on Fathers and Families. (2001, March). *The Fathering Indicators Framework.* Retrieved from the World Wide Web on May 25, 2002, at http://www.ncoff.gse.upenn.edu/fif/fif-intro.htm.

Nelson, T., J., Clamptet-Lundquist, S., & Edin, K. (2002). Sustaining fragile fatherhood: Father involvement among low-income, non-custodial fathers in Philadelphia. In C. S. Tamis-Lemonda & N. Cabrera (Eds.), *Handbook of father involvement* (pp. 525-554). Mahwah, NJ: Lawrence Erlbaum.

Nord, C., Brimhall, D. A., & West, J. (1997). *Fathers' involvement in their children's schools*. Washington, DC: U.S. Department of Education, Office of Educational Research and Improvement.

Palkovitz, R. (1984). Parental attitudes and fathers' interactions with their 5-month-old infants. *Developmental Psychology, 35,* 1399-1413.

Palm, G. (1998). *Developing a model of reflective practice for improving fathering programs*. Philadelphia: University of Pennsylvania, National Center on Fathers and Families. Manuscript in preparation.

Parke, R. D. (1996). *Fatherhood*. Cambridge, MA: Harvard University Press.

Parke, R. D., & Bhavnagri, N. (1989). Parents as managers of children's peer relationships. In D. Belle (Ed.), *Children's social networks and social supports* (pp. 241-259). New York: Wiley.

Parke, R. D., Burks, V., Carson, J., Neville, B., & Boyum, L. (1993). Family-peer relationships: A tripartite model. In R. D. Parke & S. Kellam (Eds.), *Advances in family research, Vol. 4. Family relationships with other social systems* (pp. 115-145). Hillsdale, NJ: Lawrence Erlbaum.

Parke, R. D., & O'Neil, R. (2000). The influence of significant others on learning about relationships: From family to friends. In R. Mills & S. Duck (Eds.), *The developmental psychology of personal relationships* (pp. 15-47). London: Wiley.

Parke, R. D., Power, T. G., & Gottman, J. M. (1979). Conceptualization and quantifying influence patterns in the family triad. In M. E. Lamb, S. J. Suomi, & G. R. Stephenson (Eds.), *Social interaction analysis: Methodological issues* (pp. 231-252). Madison: University of Wisconsin Press.

Personal Responsibility and Work Opportunity Reconciliation Act, Pub. L. No. 104-193 (1996).

Peters, H. E., & Mullis, N. (1997). The role of family income and sources of income in adolescent achievement. In G. J. Duncan & J. Brooks-Gunn (Eds.), *Consequences of growing up poor* (pp. 340-382). New York: Russell Sage Foundation.

Pleck, J. H. (1997). Paternal involvement: Levels, sources, and consequences. In M. E. Lamb (Ed.), *The role of the father in child development* (3rd ed., pp. 66-103). New York: Wiley.

Price, D. A., & Williams, V. S. (1990). *Nebraska paternity project, final report*. Denver, CO: Policy Studies.

Radin, N. (1982). Primary caregiver and role sharing fathers. In M. E. Lamb (Ed.), *Nontraditional families* (pp. 173-204). Hillsdale, NJ: Lawrence Erlbaum.

Rollins, B. C., & Thomas, D. L. (1979). Parental support, power, and control techniques in the socialization of children. In W. R. Burr, R. Hill, F. I. Nye, & I. Reiss (Eds.), *Contemporary theories about the family: Vol. 1. Research-based theories* (pp. 317-364). Glencoe, IL: Free Press.

Russell, G. (1982). *The changing role of fathers*. St. Lucia, Australia: University of Queensland Press.

Sagi, A., Lamb, M. E., & Gardner, W. P. (1986). Relations between strange situation behavior and stranger sociability among infants on Israeli kibbutzim. *Infant Behavior and Development, 9,* 271-282.

Sagi, A., Lamb, M. E., Shoham, R., Dvir, R., & Lewkowicz, K. S. (1985). Parent-infant interaction in families on Israeli kibbutzim. *International Journal of Behavioral Development, 8,* 273-284.

Schaffer, H. R., & Emerson, P. E. (1964). The development of social attachments in infancy. *Monographs of the Society for Research in Child Development, 29*(Whole No. 94).

Seltzer, J. A. (1998). Father by law: Effects of joint legal custody on nonresident fathers' involvement with children. *Demography, 35,* 135-146.

Simons, R. L. (1996). *Understanding differences between divorced and intact families: Stress, interaction, and child outcome.* Thousand Oaks, CA: Sage.

Simons, R. L., Whitbeck, L. B., Beaman, J., & Conger, R. D. (1994). The impact of mothers' parenting, involvement by nonresidential fathers, and parental conflict on the adjustment of adolescent children. *Journal of Marriage and the Family, 56,* 356-374.

Sonenstein, F. L., Holcomb, P. A., & Seefeldt, K. S. (1994). Promising approaches to improving paternity establishment rates at the local level. In I. Garfinkel, S. S. McLanahan, & P. K. Robins (Eds.), *Child support and child well-being* (pp. 31 –59). Washington, DC: Urban Institute.

U.S. Department of Health and Human Services. (2000). *21 million children's health: Executive summary, 2000.* Retrieved from the World Wide Web at http://fatherhood.hhs.gov.

U.S. Department of Health and Human Services. (2001). Retrieved from the World Wide Web, May 2001, at http://fatherhood.hhs.gov.

Verscheuren, K., & Marcoen, A. (1999). Representation of self and socioemotional competence in kindergartners: Differential and combined effects of attachment to mother and to father. *Child Development, 70,* 183-201.

Wachs, T., Uzgiris, I., & Hunt, J. (1971). Cognitive development in infants of different age levels and from different environmental backgrounds. *Merrill-Palmer Quarterly, 17,* 283-317.

West, J., Brimhall, D. A., Smith, E., & Richman, N. (2001, April). *Children's experiences with school: How involved are their parents?* Paper presented at the meeting of the Society for Research in Child Development, Minneapolis, MN.

Yarrow, L. J., MacTurk, R. H., Vietze, P. M., McCarthy, M. E., Klein, R. P., & McQuiston, S. (1984). Developmental course of parental stimulation and its relationship to mastery motivation during infancy. *Developmental Psychology, 20,* 492-503.

Yogman, M. W., Kindlon, D., & Earls, F. (1995). Father involvement and cognitive/behavioral outcomes of preterm infants. *Journal of the American Academy of Child & Adolescent Psychiatry, 34,* 58-66.

Zelazo, P. R., Kotelchuck, M., Barber, L., & David, J. (1977, April). *Fathers and sons: An experimental facilitation of attachment behaviors.* Paper presented at the meeting of the Society for Research in Child Development, New Orleans, LA.

Zill, N., & Nord, C. (1994). *Running in place: How American families are faring in a changing economy and an individualistic society.* Washington, DC: Child Trends.

CHAPTER 9

Ethnotheories of Parenting

At the Interface Between
Culture and Child Development

JAYANTHI MISTRY
JANA H. CHAUDHURI
VIRGINIA DIEZ

The stage is set for a gradual, yet profound, change in the conceptualization of children's development in the field of developmental psychology. Culture and context are becoming increasingly significant constructs in the study of child development for several reasons. Forces such as economic, political, and social globalization increase the interface between the diverse communities of the world and highlight the multiple realities of humanity. Developmental psychology can no longer ignore the multiple realities of the human condition within countries of the Western world, as well as those countries that Kagitçibasi (1996) claims constitute the "majority world" (p. 3). Emphasizing the need for a global-community psychology, Marsella (1998) suggests that emerging social, cultural, political, and environmental problems around the world are placing increasing demands on the field.

> Psychology can assist in addressing and resolving these problems, especially if it is willing to reconsider some of its fundamental premises, methods, and practices that are rooted within Western cultural traditions and to expand its appreciation and use of other psychologies. (Marsella, 1998, p. 1282)

Toward these ends of broadening the vision and charge of developmental psychology, we undertake the task of integrating perspectives from within the field and beyond to represent the growing body of literature on parental ethnotheories.

Parental ethnotheories or parental belief systems serve as an excellent substantive area through which to understand the interface between cultural context and child development. As articulated succinctly by Miller and Chen (2001), studies of parenting ethnotheories provide,

> Insight into the contexts of human development, in highlighting the need to understand the impact on parenting of cultural beliefs and practices, sociopolitical and demographic forces, globalization and cohort-related historical shifts. They also raise central questions regarding the nature of socialization and of developmental change. (p. 1)

Furthermore, as contributions to the understanding of parents' cultural belief systems have emerged from various allied disciplines, including anthropology, cross-cultural psychology, cultural psychology, and developmental psychology, the area demonstrates a particularly rich potential for integrating existing perspectives and literature.

We begin by highlighting three major approaches to the study of culture and child development, drawing on the literature from developmental, cross-cultural, and cultural psychology. First, we focus on conceptualizations of culture and context within developmental psychology itself. Then, we highlight the work of cross-cultural psychologists, followed by the approaches that fit under the cultural psychology umbrella. Although all three approaches are distinct and separate in the assumptions they make about individual functioning and how it is influenced by culture, there is recent evidence of some convergence. Indeed, we draw on this convergence, as well as the complementary foci of the three subfields, to document how integrated perspectives in the study of parenting ethnotheories hold rich promise for developing culturally inclusive and comprehensive knowledge about parenting belief systems. Finally, we discuss research, program, and policy implications of research on parental ethnotheories.

MAJOR APPROACHES TO THE STUDY OF CULTURE AND DEVELOPMENT[1]

Although culture has been the focus of inquiry in several social science disciplines, in psychology, three subfields have made significant contributions to our current knowledge base on the cultural context of child development. In this section, we highlight major approaches to the study of culture and development from each subfield, focusing on the core assumptions or defining elements of each stream of knowledge. We do not intend to give an overview of each subfield; there are full-length books devoted to that task in each field (Berry et al., 1997; Damon, 1998; Miller, 1997; Shweder et al., 1998; Stigler, Shweder, & Herdt, 1990; Triandis, 1980).

Developmental Psychology: The Study of Culture as Context

The primary focus in the field of developmental psychology has been to describe and explain development and developmental processes in all domains of human physical and psychological functioning. Human development has been defined as "changes in physical, psychological, and social behavior as experienced by individuals across the lifespan from conception to death" (Gardiner, Mutter, & Kosmitzki, 1998, p. 3). As a consequence, developmental change naturally is the focus of inquiry. During the 20th century, much of the theoretical and empirical focus on the bases of developmental change centered on establishing the significance of nature versus nurture. However, contemporary developmental psychologists, going beyond prior debates between the proponents of nature versus nurture, stress that the dynamic relation between individual and context represents the basic processes of human development (Lerner, 1992, 1998, 2002; Sameroff, 1983; Thelen & Smith, 1998).

Historically, concerns about following the traditions of established science and assumptions about universality as a defining characteristic of human development have discouraged attention to the diversity and influence of varied developmental contexts. Recently however, there has been increasing focus on the contexts of psychological functioning. This attention to the contexts of development has been prompted by several intersecting trends in the past couple decades. Theoretical models and perspectives that have been developed from within the field, particularly the ecological model (Bronfenbrenner, 1979, 1986), developmental contextualism (Lerner, 1991, 1996), and the life span approaches (Baltes, Lindenberger, & Staudinger, 1998; Baltes, Reese, & Lipsitt, 1980), have been particularly influential in highlighting the significance of the contexts of individual development. In most of the ecologically based theories, context is viewed as one of the major environmental variables that facilitate or constrain individual development. Similarly, life span psychologists also emphasize social context, based on the central assumption that changes in the individual's social context across the life span interact with the individual's unique history of experiences, roles, and biology to produce an individualized developmental pathway. More recently, theorizing on the dynamic relation between individual and context has been brought to a more abstract and complex level through the concepts associated with developmental systems models of human development (Dixon & Lerner, 1999; Lerner, 2002). In such models, integrative, reciprocal, and dynamic relations and interactions between variables from multiple levels of organization constitute the core processes of developmental change (Ford &

Lerner, 1992; Gottlieb, 1997; Lerner, 1998; Thelen & Smith, 1998).

In addition to the theoretical developments noted above, there have been increasing amounts of research on the diversity of social contexts and life experiences. In summarizing current reviews of conceptual and empirical work on social, emotional, and personality development, Eisenberg (1998) identifies increasing focus on contextual and environmental inputs to development as a key theme: "Burgeoning interest in context in developmental psychology is reflected in the study of many levels of influence, including diversity in culture and subculture, race and ethnicity, sex and gender, and types of families and groups" (p. 20). Similarly, Eisenberg notes that conceptual frameworks are becoming more conditional, multifaceted, and complex and that there is increasing tendency to view development as a consequence of "social interactions that are shaped by contextual factors and characteristics of all participants in the interaction" (p. 20). Thus, investigation of the diversity of contexts of individual development has become a major research agenda in most domains of psychological functioning (Damon, 1998; Eisenberg, 1998; Masten, 1999; Wozniak & Fischer, 1993).

Applied and problem-oriented research has also contributed to the increasing relevance of context in human development. Context has been the specific focus of research aimed at understanding the particular circumstances of children growing up in poverty or adverse socioeconomic conditions (McLloyd, 1998). Similarly, research that examines children's environments to enable the design of programs to improve their welfare have specifically focused on context variables (Kagitçibasi, 1996) because it is assumed that these mediating contextual factors can be addressed by programs.

Despite the increasingly more sophisticated conceptualizations of developmental processes and contexts of children's development noted above, there appears to be a common underlying tendency to treat culture and context as synonymous in developmental psychology. Culture is operationalized as context variables and treated as independent variables. Even when investigated as a critical variable in the transactional relationship between individual and context (Sameroff, 1983) or as one of the multiple levels of organizations in dynamic developmental systems models (Lerner, 1998, 2002), it is nonetheless operationalized as separate from the individual developmental outcomes with which it interacts. This focus on culture as context may reflect the field's continued reliance on the methods of established science and the concern with establishing universal relationships between context and behavior. Interestingly, similar concerns and core assumptions about the nature of cultural influences on individual development are evident in cross-cultural approaches to human development as well. Therefore, we now turn our attention to delineating the essential features of cross-cultural psychology's approach to the study of culture.

Cross-Cultural Psychology: Focus on Cultural Variation

The defining characteristics of cross-cultural psychology as a field can be seen as rooted in the reasons for its emergence. Cross-cultural psychology emerged as a subdiscipline of psychology in reaction against the tendency in psychology to ignore cultural variations and to consider them as nuisance variables or error (Kagitçibasi & Poortinga, 2000). Thus, it has functioned as a particular methodological strategy of mainstream psychology, rather than a subfield with a specific epistemological, theoretical, or content-related emphasis (Brislin, 1983). The field is often defined by its method of comparative cross-cultural analyses aimed at exploring similarities

and differences of human psychological functioning (Berry, 1979; Brislin, 1983; Jahoda, 1992; Jahoda & Krewer, 1997).

In addition to its characteristic methodological approach, the culture-comparative approach of cross-cultural psychology is also rooted in assumptions about the universality of psychic functioning (Miller, 1997; Poortinga, 1997). Core assumptions about universality of human development and about the appropriateness of the culture-comparative method to uncover universality are reflected in the three main goals of cross-cultural psychology, often listed as the following: (a) to test or extend the generalizability of existing theories and findings in other cultural settings, (b) to document and understand variation in psychological functioning across cultures, and (c) to integrate findings in such a way as to generate a more universal psychology applicable to a wider range of cultural settings (Segall, Dasen, Berry, & Poortinga, 1999).

The centrality of assumptions of universality of psychic functioning in culture-comparative approaches is particularly well highlighted by Kagitçibasi and Poortinga (2000). They argue that assumptions of cultural relativism or universalism have important implications for methodology:

> In so far as there is non-identity of psychological processes cross-culturally, there is non-comparability of data. Insistence on the uniqueness of phenomena defies comparison and makes the use of common methods and instruments inappropriate. Thus, the entire enterprise of culture-comparative research collapses if the assumption of psychic unity of human kind is rejected. (Kagitçibasi & Poortinga, 2000, p. 131)

Although the universalist assumption serves as a core assumption for cross-cultural psychology, the assumption, at least in its current formulation, has been questioned by many within the field. Since the 1970s, "indigenous" psychologists working in developing countries have questioned Western theorists' claims that their work is objective, value-free and universal. Rather, they have countered that most theories in psychology were deeply enmeshed with Euro-American values that champion liberal, individualistic ideals (Kim, Park, & Park, 2000). Psychologists in East and Southeast Asia have been particularly vocal since the late 1970s in advocating the need to develop psychological constructs and frameworks rooted in local cultural and philosophical traditions rather than relying on imported ones (Enriques, 1977; Ho, 1988, 1998a; Sinha, D., 1986, 1997). In Confucian heritage cultures, constructs that depict the fundamental relatedness between individuals played a particularly important role in promoting the role of indigenous psychological frameworks (Choi, Kim, & Choi, 1993; Ho, 1976, 1988; Lebra, 1976).

Although the subfield of cross-cultural psychology was initially defined primarily in terms of its comparative approach, current theorists have engaged in a critical discussion of the initial approach and a rediscovery of a more socioculturally oriented tradition (Jahoda & Krewer, 1997; Poortinga, 1997; Segall et al., 1999). Though the comparative approach and the search for a culturally inclusive yet universal psychology remain hallmarks of cross-cultural psychology, recent trends indicate promising areas of convergence with other subfields of psychology that also examine the intersection of culture with human development.

Cultural Psychology: Culture and Individual Development as Mutually Constitutive

Whereas cross-cultural psychology as presented above proceeds from the perspective of searching for universals in psychological functioning, cultural psychology has often been presented from the perspective of cultural relativism. However, we contend that to portray cultural psychology as primarily representing a cultural relativist stance is inaccurate and glosses over more significant defining features of this approach to the study of culture and human development. We highlight three core features of cultural psychology.

Numerous approaches have been categorized under the cultural psychology label (Harwood, Miller, & Irizarry, 1995; Miller, 1997; Shweder et al., 1998). The most common examples include extensions of Vygotsky's (1978) sociohistorical theory (Cole, 1990, 1996; Rogoff, 1990; Wertsch, 1985, 1991) and theories that emphasize culture as the meaning systems, symbols, and practices through which people interpret experience (Bruner, 1990; Goodnow, Miller, & Kessel, 1995; Greenfield & Cocking, 1994; Markus & Kitayama, 1991; Shweder, 1991). Models that incorporate ecological constructs with those from the culture and personality school of thought (D'Andrade, 1984; LeVine, 1973; LeVine et al., 1994; Super & Harkness, 1986) and models based on "activity theory" (Eckensberger, 1990) are also included under the umbrella of cultural psychology.

Though cultural psychology does not have a unifying definition or theoretical perspective, all these approaches share a common focus on understanding culturally constituted meaning systems. The *first* core feature of these approaches is the common assumption that human beings construct meaning through the cultural symbol systems available to them in the context of social interactions. Thus, cultural psychologists view human psychological functioning as an emergent property that results from symbolically mediated experiences with the behavioral practices and historically accumulated ideas and understandings (meanings) of particular cultural communities (Shweder et al., 1998).

Along with the emphasis on the cultural meanings, the *second* unifying theme across various cultural psychology approaches is the assumption that culture and individual psychological functioning are mutually constitutive. It is assumed that culture and individual behavior cannot be understood in isolation, yet they are not reducible to each other (Cole, 1996; Miller, 1997; Rogoff, 1990). In such a view, culture and individual development are not separated into independent and dependent variables. This assumption moves the conceptualization of the relationship between individual and context beyond the bidirectionality of influence that underlies major ecological models in developmental psychology. Rather, the assumption is that human development cannot be separated from the activity in which it is observed. Particular modes of thinking, speaking, and behaving *arise from* and *remain integrally tied* to concrete forms of social practice (Cole, 1990; Vygotsky, 1978; Wertsch, 1985). "Mind, cognition, memory, and so forth are understood not as attributes or properties of the individual, but as functions that may be carried out inter-mentally or intramentally" (Wertsch & Tulviste, 1992, p. 549). Thus, instead of conceptualizing individuals as "having abilities and skills," the focus is on the "person-acting-with-mediation-means" as the appropriate unit of analysis (Wertsch, 1991, p. 119). In other words, individual *ability* and *tendency* are not separated from the contexts in which they are used. The argument is that when the focus is on human *actions*, we are immediately forced to account for the context of the actions and therefore cannot separate context from human functioning.

The *third* unifying theme in approaches to cultural psychology is the preference for interpretive methodology. Because the basic assumption is that culture and behavior are essentially inseparable, psychological functioning tends to be described and interpreted as it is experienced and understood by the members of a cultural group themselves.

Hence, the focus is on representing the meaning that particular behavior has for the behaving person. General validity is established through seeking objectified meanings within a coherence of contexts (Harwood et al., 1995; Jahoda, 1992; Jahoda & Krewer, 1997; Shweder et al., 1998). Thus, in cultural psychology, the goal is to understand the directive force of shared meaning systems and how these meanings are constructed in given contexts (D'Andrade & Strauss, 1992; Harkness & Super, 1992). Understanding context must include understanding the tacit social and interactional norms of the individuals existing within those settings, whose behaviors and expectations both shape and are shaped by the institutional structures they are a part of (Harwood et al., 1995). Although cultural psychologists recognize the multiple contexts represented in ecological models, they argue that contexts cannot be merely conceptualized as environmental influences, because these do not take into account the people's systems of making meaning in those contexts.

To summarize, we have highlighted the core assumptions of three major approaches to the study of culture and human development. Although all three approaches are distinct and will remain so, based on their different goals and assumptions, we now emphasize their complementary contributions to the study of parental belief systems by integrating the literature from all three approaches. We illustrate how it is possible to develop a culturally inclusive and comprehensive knowledge base on parental ethnotheories.

ETHNOTHEORIES OF PARENTING: AT THE INTERFACE BETWEEN CULTURE AND CHILD DEVELOPMENT

Since the early 1980s, parental beliefs and practices have increasingly engaged the attention of developmental, cultural, and cross-cultural psychologists (Bornstein, 1995; Goodnow & Collins, 1990; Sigel, 1985; Sigel, McGillicuddy-DeLisi & Goodnow, 1992; Super & Harkness, 1986). Parental beliefs have been defined as "guides to action" (McGillicuddy-DeLisi & Sigel, 1995, p. 16) and consist of specific notions about such things as the nature of children, expectations about development, the role of parents, and definitions of good parenting. Because parenting beliefs are systematically related to one another, socially constructed, and derived from larger cultural belief systems, Harkness and Super (1996) refer to them as "parental ethnotheories."

Although the study of parental beliefs occupies a small space in the vast literature on parenting (Bornstein, 1995) and family socialization (Parke & Buriel, 1998), increasing attention is being focused on parenting beliefs. Delineating contemporary perspectives on family socialization, Park and Buriel (1998) suggest that parental affect and cognitions are increasingly viewed as central to the socialization process and in understanding the nature of parent-child relationships and socialization practices within families. Furthermore, as parental beliefs are constructed within a larger sociohistorical and cultural context, their study often reveals how macrosystem level ideology and context are instantiated in microlevel interactional processes and practices of parenting.

In the following integrative review of parenting ethnotheories or parents' cultural belief systems, we draw on research from developmental, cross-cultural and cultural psychology perspectives. We begin with contributions from developmental psychology, followed by a discussion of how culture-comparative studies have enhanced our understanding of the diversity of parenting beliefs. Finally, we present examples of research driven by theoretically integrative frameworks that span disciplinary boundaries. We suggest that

interdisciplinary research holds much promise for developing culturally inclusive theories and empirical databases.

Beliefs About Parenting: Contributions From Developmental Psychology

Within the field of developmental psychology, researchers have attempted to document parents' beliefs about the nature and value of children, about the nature of development, and relatedly, about the role of parenting in development (Sigel, 1981). Early research in this area also attempted to document the linear relationships between parental beliefs and parenting behavior. However, inconsistencies in the research relating parenting attitudes to parental actions and criticisms of measurement methods (such as the use of relatively primitive self-report questionnaires) led to a temporary abandonment of this line of research (Bugental, Mantyla, & Lewis, 1989; Goodnow & Collins, 1990). The mid-1980s saw a renewed interest in parental beliefs, with an overarching goal of discovering connections that exist between parents' beliefs, their caregiving practices, and their children's development. The development of broader conceptualizations of parental beliefs, recognition of the complexity of causation, and better methodologies to study complex processes reflect great potential in developing a consistent and coherent body of knowledge addressing this goal.

One of the most important contributions from developmental psychology has been to provide the basis for general beliefs about "good" or "normal" parenting. These definitions or characterizations of parenting are typically based on research linking specific parenting behaviors to positive child development outcomes. For example, Baumrind's (1971) characterization of three types of parenting styles (authoritative, authoritarian, and permissive) has been particularly notable in defining the characteristics of good parenting in the United States, and it continues to generate research that documents parenting styles and beliefs about parental authority (Smetana, 1994). The association between authoritative parenting and positive child developmental outcomes (e.g., self-esteem, competence, adaptability, internalized control) documented by Baumrind (1971, 1991a, 1991b) has led to the positive value placed on this style of parenting in middle-class families in the United States. In contrast, authoritarian parenting is viewed negatively because of its association with negative outcomes (e.g. noncompliance, low self-esteem, low social competence) in Baumrind's work.

Similarly, definitions of appropriate parenting behavior during infancy are based on the vast body of literature on attachment. In this literature, warmth and sensitive, responsive parental care have been identified as reliable, if not robust, catalysts to secure attachment (for reviews, see Goldsmith & Alansky, 1987; Isabella, 1995; Lamb, Thompson, Garndner, Charnov, & Estes, 1984; Thompson, 1998). Likewise, research documenting patterns of parent-child language interactions that facilitate language development (Heath, 1982; Snow & Goldfield, 1982), the development of prosocial behavior and empathy (Eisenberg, 1989; Zahn-Waxler & Smith, 1992), and even early brain development have all influenced beliefs about appropriate child rearing in the United States.

Although developmental psychologists have succeeded in delineating the effects of various child-rearing beliefs and practices, much of the early work focused on European American, middle-class samples, allowing for generalizability only to a select group. Furthermore, despite attempts to incorporate contextual differences, the underlying assumptions and perspectives of this early research reflected a considerable degree of ethnocentrism. Fortunately, increasing challenges to the generalization of parenting theories developed in the United States generated a burgeoning body of research documenting the diversity of parenting beliefs and practices. We now turn to a brief presentation of this research, emphasizing the integration of research generated by cross-cultural and developmental psychology in the past 15 years.

Diversity of Parenting Beliefs and Practices: Contributions from Culture-Comparative Approaches

This selective review of cross-cultural research represents the intersection between cross-cultural and developmental psychology research (for more comprehensive reviews, see Bornstein, 1991, 1995; Goodnow & Collins, 1990; Harkness & Super, 1995; McGillicuddy-DeLisi & Sigel, 1995; Okagaki & Divecha, 1993). Several key themes regarding parental beliefs emerge, such as the nature of beliefs and expectations about children's development, the development of parenting beliefs themselves, and the links between parenting beliefs, parenting practices and child behavior.

The influence of cultural beliefs on perceptions and behavior is acknowledged in many culture-comparative studies. For example, McGillicuddy-DeLisi and Subramanium (1996) examined beliefs about intellectual development among well-educated and affluent mothers in Tanzania and the United States. Both samples were given the same questionnaire regarding knowledge acquisition. The two groups differed in the importance they placed on various learning processes such as direct instruction, experimentation, or observation. In another study, Edwards, Gandini, and Gionaninni compared the developmental timetable expectations of parents and providers in the United States and Italy, using a measure created jointly by Japanese and American researchers. Compared with other populations studied with the questionnaire, American parents had earlier developmental expectations, whereas Italian parents were midrange. In addition, the American parents had earlier expectations than their teachers, whereas Italian parents had later expectations than teachers. Yet another study compared Japanese mothers' ideas about temperament with a standardized Western measure of temperament to find that seven of nine dimensions of temperament were similarly perceived, whereas two dimensions (persistence and distractibility) were not (Shwalb, Shwalb, & Shoji, 1996). These examples typify research following the goal of cross-cultural psychology to identify and understand variation across cultures.

Diversity in parental beliefs about desirable traits in children has also been documented in the research literature. For example, Gonzalez-Ramos, Zayas, and Cohen (1998) found that respect, obedience, affection, honesty, and loyalty to family are highly valued characteristics in Puerto Rican families, whereas S.R. Sinha (1995) identified submission to authority, dependency, and passive respect for the hierarchical ordering of relationships as admirable qualities valued for Indian children. These beliefs are in contrast to the pervasive belief in the value of children's independence and autonomy that is often documented among middle-class European American parents in the United States (New & Richman, 1996; Richman et al., 1988). In fact, contrasting beliefs about independence versus interdependence, individuality versus harmony, and autonomy versus respect for authority recur in much of the research that compares the cultural beliefs and practices of European American and Asian parents (e.g., Azuma, 1994; Rothbaum, Pott, Morelli, & Constant, 2000).

Cross-cultural researchers have also recognized that factors influencing the development of parenting beliefs also contribute to variations within and across cultures. Taking a comprehensive view of research on this topic, Okagaki and Divecha (1993) delineate several factors that influence the development of parental beliefs, including child characteristics, characteristics of caregiver, marital relationships, expert advice, and larger influences from parents' work, social networks, and socioeconomic conditions. Others have attempted to expound on how both individual and cultural factors influence the development of parenting beliefs. Kojima discusses the contributions of "commonsense" psychology, ethnopsychology, and the influences of the lay person, the expert advisor, and the academic researcher on parental belief systems in his historical analysis of child rearing in Japan. Similarly, Grusec, Hastings, and Mammone examined the influence of internal working models of relationships and how these affect attributions about child behavior. They proposed a model suggesting the following:

> More general beliefs having to do with developmental timetables, methods of changing children's behavior and values are more likely to be influenced by the culture in which one lives, whereas more specific beliefs about self-efficacy and negatively biased attributions are more likely to be affected by specific experiences with one's own child. (Grusec et al., 1994, p. 16)

Current cross-cultural research on the relation between parental beliefs and practices is guided by broader conceptualizations of the complexity of these relationships than those previously represented in assumptions of linear relationships between attitudes and child-rearing practices. This focus on understanding the interconnectedness between beliefs and practices has typically focused on routine child care practices. For example, cross-cultural and subgroup variation in the settings, practices, and beliefs related to sleeping have received much attention in the literature. Differences in family sleeping arrangements between communities (within the United States or cross-nationally) have been documented to reflect the values of the larger society. Emphasis on self-reliance and the infant's capacity for self-regulation among American families has been linked to practices encouraging infants to fall asleep by themselves and separately from other family members (Harkness & Super, 1995; Morelli, Rogoff, Oppenheim, & Goldsmith, 1992; New & Richman, 1996). In contrast, emphasis on interrelatedness among families from China, Japan, Italy, and India has been linked to cosleeping practices that are more common in these parts of the world (New & Richman, 1996; Rothbaum et al., 2000; Shweder, Jensen & Goldstein, 1995; Wolf, Lozoff, Latz, & Paludetto, 1996).

Links between parenting beliefs and practices have also been observed in parent-child interactions in teaching tasks. Pomerleau, Malcuit, and Sabatier (1991) found clear group differences between three cultural groups in Montreal (Quebecois, Vietnamese, and Haitian) when settings, maternal beliefs, and mother-child interactions in a teaching task were observed. A significant relation emerged between beliefs and teaching practices that reflected cultural conceptions of child development and behavior.

Taking the relation between parenting beliefs and practices one step further, the relationship between beliefs, practices, and child behavior have also been investigated comparatively. Early research in attachment demonstrated that cultural differences exist in attachment behavior, specifically that the incidence of attachment classifications varied across cultural context (Grossmann, Grossmann, Spangler, Suess, & Unzner, 1985; Sagi et al., 1985; Takahaski, 1986). These differences were considered the result of the diverse child-rearing practices of the cultures studied (Northern Germany, the Israeli kibbutzim, Japan, and the United States). Another

example provides evidence that belief-driven parental practices result in Dutch babies actually sleeping more than American babies (Super et al., 1996). Dutch parents strongly emphasize the importance of regularly scheduled bedtimes and rest for children. Similarly, in an ethnographic study that examined infant play behavior and parental theories about development and socialization, Gaskins found that differences in the play behavior of infants in the United States and Guatemala were coherently connected with differences in parental ethnotheories.

Current research on the relation between parental beliefs and practices represents a significant advance from the earlier focus on the association between parental attitudes and behaviors. This early research, focused at the individual level of behavior, attempted to document the direct effects of stated parent beliefs on caregiving behaviors (Bugental et al., 1989). In contrast, contemporary perspectives use broader conceptualizations of parental beliefs and predict theoretically derived links between parenting beliefs and practices. Such theoretical perspectives reflect the integration of knowledge from the cross-cultural study of human development and cultural and developmental psychology and represent the promise of intersections between disciplines. In the next section, we provide examples of research that demonstrate how integration of the cultural, cross-cultural, and developmental approaches can occur.

Integrated Perspectives: Contributions From Cultural Psychology

Although research documenting diversity in parental beliefs has made a significant contribution to the literature, it is not enough for a comprehensive understanding of parenting ethnotheories. Approaches from cultural psychology have played a central role in focusing attention on the macrolevel influences of shared culture and societal institutions as they become incorporated into individual development. For example, sociocultural theory has emphasized the need to understand the role of cultural and social institutions in privileging and maintaining shared beliefs about appropriate parenting, as well as the processes whereby individuals collectively bring about change in institutions and macrolevel ideology about parenting. Though institutions and macrolevel ideology may create the conditions and contexts for social construction of parenting beliefs at the individual level, they themselves are constructed and institutionalized by collective individual actions. Thus, comprehensive perspectives on parenting ethnotheories must be able to situate parenting beliefs shared by a cultural community in the larger sociohistorical and ecological context and link these to parenting practices and child development outcomes. In addition, such perspectives must be able to explain the process of social construction whereby individuals appropriate culturally shared parenting beliefs and explain how individuals collectively bring about macro- or societal level changes.

A conceptual focus on examining culture at both the individual and societal levels can be seen in theories that systematically delineate the links between cultural-ecological context, belief systems, parenting practices, and child development outcomes. Super and Harkness's (1986) construct of the *developmental niche* is one such example. An individual's developmental niche is assumed to consist of three interrelated components that are adaptive within the larger ecological and cultural setting, mutually influence each other, and maintain each other in a state of equilibrium. These three components include the physical and social settings of children's lives, the customs and practices of child care, and the psychology of the caregiver (which includes their cultural belief systems). The assumption is that these ethnotheories or cultural belief systems are

expressed or *instantiated* in parent behaviors and activities in the settings parents organize for their children, in caregiving customs, and in the daily interactions between parents and children. Widely varying culture-specific skills, beliefs, and values are reflected in parents' caregiving practices, and children's experience is shaped by these customs of care. This can result in developmental differences observable at the level of the cultural group (Harkness & Super, 1995).

Such integrative conceptualizations enable us to go beyond merely documenting cross-cultural differences and emphasizing the cultural relativity of valued socialization goals and child care practices. It is our contention that the sociocultural and cultural psychology perspectives offer particularly useful approaches for understanding multiple cultural models of parenting, in which sociocultural context, parenting beliefs, practices, and child development outcomes are integrally linked in patterns that are culturally coherent within particular communities. LeVine et al.'s (1994) extensive research among the Gusii people of northeastern Africa and among urban, middle-class communities in northeastern United States provides an exceptional example of contrasting cultural models of early child care that exhibit cultural coherence and adaptivity within each community. We describe these models at some length to illustrate the existence of equally valid alternate conceptualizations of parenting and children's development.

LeVine et al. (1994) define cultural models of early child care as ethnographic reconstructions of the initial principles on which a community's child care practices are based. These cultural models include assumptions and beliefs about normative and desired child-rearing goals, the general strategy for attaining these goals, and the scripts for action in specific situations. LeVine et al. label the Gusii model *pediatric*, because its primary concern is with the survival, health, and physical growth of the infant, and the American model *pedagogical*, because its primary concern is with the behavioral and educational development of the infant. The adaptive and culturally coherent links between parenting goals, parenting strategies and scripts, and children's development in each model (and effectively represented in the labels) is briefly summarized from LeVine et al. (1994, pp. 248-270).

The primary goal in the pediatric model of the Gusii is to protect infants from life-threatening illnesses and environmental hazards, a goal that is particularly adaptive in the context of high mortality rates. Gusii mothers implicitly assume that infancy is a period of great danger to a child's life and requires constant protection. Therefore, they keep their infants in physical proximity as a means of providing constant protection and focus primarily on soothing distress and keeping infants satisfied and calm, assuming that these states indicate that the baby is well and safe from harm. In contrast, the goals of the American pedagogical model are to promote the infant's alertness, curiosity, interest in surroundings, exploration, and communication with others. Survival and health are background concerns, perhaps because they are more likely assured in the context of modern medicine and comparatively lower infant mortality rates. In LeVine et al.'s (1994) construction of the pedagogical model, the American mother sees herself as a teacher whose primary responsibility is to ensure the infant pupil's readiness for early education. Parenting strategies therefore focus on stimulation and proto-conversation aimed at facilitating engagement with the physical and social world.

When cultural models of child care differ, it follows that proponents of each model might be critical of the alternate model's goals and practices and consider them inappropriate and ineffective. For example, LeVine et al. (1994) acknowledge that from the perspective of the American pedagogical model, Gusii infants appear to be deprived of the stimulation and emotional support offered by American mothers and viewed as essential to facilitate social, emotional, and cognitive skills. However, from the perspective of the Gusii pediatric model, with its emphasis on physical proximity, responsive protection, and soothing, American caretaking practices appear to reflect incompetent caregiving. Practices that restrict the infant's physical contact with the mother, such as putting babies to sleep in separate beds or rooms, breast-feeding for relatively short periods of time after birth, casual responsiveness to infant crying, and lower frequencies of holding and carrying, seem harsh from the Gusii perspective.

LeVine et al.'s (1994) case study of infant care in the Gusii community goes beyond merely emphasizing the cultural relativity of child care goals and practices. Their careful and comprehensive assessment of the consequences of the Gusii pattern of care offers valuable lessons about questioning the ethnocentrism of our field's assumptions about appropriate parenting or child care practices. Even though Gusii toddlers did not experience the type of stimulation and support of cognitive and language skills common among American toddlers, the social experience of Gusii children with peer and community members after 30 months facilitated the development of capacities that were not acquired earlier.

The Gusii case teaches us that the absence during the first 2 to 3 years of specific parental practices that promote cognitive, emotional, and language skills in Western contexts does not necessarily constitute failure to provide what every child needs. Like many other peoples in Africa and elsewhere, the Gusii had socially organized ways of cultivating skill, virtue, and personal fulfillment that were not dependent on mothers after weaning and were not concluded until long after the third year of life; they involved learning through participation in established, hierarchical, structures of interaction at home and in the larger community—a kind of apprenticeship learning, once widespread in the West, which we are only beginning to understand. (LeVine et al., 1994, p. 274).

Thus, research using cultural psychology approaches has rich potential for developing theories of child development that represent multiple models and pathways for growth and development. Rogoff, Mistry, Göncü, and Mosier (1993) offer another example of culture-comparative research that illustrates contrasting patterns of behavior, each of which nonetheless reflects internal coherence between cultural context, beliefs, practices, and child behaviors. These researchers selected four cultural communities (a Mayan peasant community in Guatemala, a tribal village in India, a middle-class community in Turkey, and a middle-class community in the United States) that represented variation in the extent to which children are segregated from adult activities. Observations of caregiver-toddler interaction revealed two patterns for learning that were consistent with variations in whether children were able to observe and participate in adult activities.

In communities in which children were segregated from adult activities, adults took on the responsibility for organizing children's learning by managing their motivation, by instructing them verbally, and by treating them as peers in play and conversation. In contrast, in the communities in which children had the opportunity to observe and participate in adult activities, caregivers supported their toddlers' own efforts with responsive assistance. Toddlers appeared to take responsibility for learning by observing ongoing events and beginning to enter adult activity (Rogoff et al., 1993, p. 151). Within each community, there was a coherence of patterns linking cultural context in terms of the extent of segregation from adult activity, parental goals for children's development,

differing assumptions about who takes responsibility for learning, and patterns of caregiver-toddler interaction.

There are many reasons why we need research that documents multiple cultural models of parenting that delineate integral links between sociocultural context, parenting ethnotheories, child care practices, and child development outcomes. The theoretical implications discussed thus far have highlighted the need to develop more culturally inclusive theories of child development. However, this is by no means the only or most important reason. After all, the relevance of our field lies in our ability to use our theoretical and research knowledge base to facilitate development for all children and families. Increasing demands for relevant knowledge to guide program planning and practice also underscore the need for research documenting multiple cultural models of parenting. In the next section, we highlight a few lessons that can be derived from our discussion thus far.

IMPLICATIONS FOR RESEARCH, PROGRAM PLANNING, AND PRACTICE

The lessons we draw for research and policy to guide program planning and practice are consistent with our emphasis on integrating contrasting perspectives to the study of culture or, at the minimum, to view them as complementary. In this section, we briefly discuss lessons for researchers and program developers interested in interventions promoting positive development for children and families.

Changing Researcher Perspective

As we have discussed earlier in this chapter, there are differing perspectives on the relationship between culture and individual behavior. Convincing arguments made by cross-cultural psychologists (Poortinga, 1998) and by ecological (Bronfenbrenner, 1986) and developmental systems theorists in developmental psychology (Lerner, 1992, 1996, 2002) emphasize the need to establish lawful relations between cultural, environmental, and behavioral variables. On the other hand, rather than denying the universal aspects of psychology, cultural psychologists assume that psychological structures and processes can vary fundamentally in different cultural contexts (Miller, 1997) and that there may be multiple, diverse psychologies rather than a single psychology (Shweder et al., 1998). In our opinion, these viewpoints exemplify complementary goals that can be integrated if comparisons of behavior across cultural communities are made only after context is understood.

This integration of perspectives recognizes the importance of studying meaning along with the lawful relationships between context and behavior. By attempting to understand processes rather than just documenting group differences, research goes beyond unidimensional explanations of variations in human behavior. A culturally inclusive perspective must integrate the focus on socially constructed meaning systems with goals of establishing pan-cultural constructs or universal dimensions of behavior and meaning-making processes through culture-comparative approaches. Assuming that meaning systems are universal but varied allows us to focus on cultural meaning but leaves us open to cross-cultural comparisons and therefore, to the development of pan-cultural constructs and relationships.

Thus, conducting research from such an integrative perspective requires increasing awareness in the field about the importance of understanding meaning before making judgments and comparisons across groups. It requires "thinking out of the box" culturally to remove the blinders of our own ethnocentrism before implementing methodology and interpreting results of our culture-comparative studies. In their comparative study of attachment patterns, Harwood et al. (1995) integrated such concern with cultural meaning with an interest in establishing universal dimensions of attachment. They began by examining parents' beliefs about desirable attachment behavior, or what attachment meant for Puerto Rican mothers, before making comparisons and interpretations of traditional measures of attachment. They found that European American mothers preferred that their toddlers balance play/autonomy and relatedness and disliked it when their toddlers were clingy. Their hopes consisted of wanting their child to be self-confident, independent, happy, and able to fulfill their potential. On the other hand, Puerto Rican mothers preferred their children to be respectful and disliked highly active or avoidant behavior; they hoped for their children to be respectful, calm, courteous, and attentive. Even though the two groups differed in their ideals, the preferred group for both was the "secure" group. But this similarity is somewhat misleading. "Optimal balance for both cultures were more likely to fall in the middle range of the continuum than at either of its ends; however, the continuum itself appeared to be defined differently across the two groups" (Harwood et al., 1995, p. 143).

In drawing conclusions from their research, Harwood et al. (1995) claim that a distinction must be made between basic human mechanisms that evidence suggests are universal and the cultural constructs that human beings have built in an attempt to understand those mechanisms. Using the study of attachment as an example, they argue that there should be a common framework, but one that differentiates between two distinct levels of inquiry within that framework. For example,

Evidence suggests that it may be a human universal in later infancy for the subsystems of affiliation, wariness, exploration, and attachment to work together in coherent and recognizable patterns. It may even be that a sense of safety and emotional warmth underlie patterns of attachment behavior deemed desirable across a majority of cultures. However, these issues are separate from the cultural construct of security that we have created in U.S. psychology on the basis of these mechanisms. In particular, the concept of inner security, with its emphasis on the importance of self-sufficiency and inner resourcefulness for the autonomous, bounded individual, who is nonetheless capable of existing harmoniously and finding satisfaction in relationships with other autonomous, bounded individuals, is an ideal peculiar to the dominant U.S. culture—a culturally constructed developmental endpoint that is not shared by much of the rest of the world. (Harwood et al., 1995 p. 36)

This example, highlighting the culture-bounded nature of the construct of "attachment security," serves as a useful reminder for researchers to question the ethnocentrism of the theoretical constructs they are investigating. Scrutinizing methods used for assessment will not suffice; our theoretical constructs may also need to be questioned.

Integrating Multiple Research Methodologies

With a similar conceptual stance but targeting methodology, Garcia Coll and Magnuson (1999) call for a paradigm shift, arguing that to fully comprehend the impact of cultural processes on child development, we have to be open to the use of multiple methods of inquiry, assessment, analysis and interpretation. The main point is to ensure that understanding cultural processes is at the core, not the periphery, of conceptualizations and investigations of developmental processes. Garcia Coll and Magnuson (1999) emphasize that unpacking culture means

not treating it as a "social address" variable (Bronfenbrenner, 1986).

The question of how culture or cultural context should be operationalized lies at the center of a conceptual debate between cultural and cross-cultural psychologists and between contextualist approaches and sociocultural approaches. Should culture be conceptualized as context and as an independent influence (e.g., set of antecedent conditions) on behavior or development, or should it be conceptualized as culturally constituted meaning systems? Perhaps the more important question is this: How can we focus on understanding both the contexts and the culturally constituted meaning systems embedded in various contexts? When the focus is solely on culturally constituted meaning systems, there is the danger of relying on cultural "explanations" for variations that often tend to preclude more substantial analyses (Kagitçibasi & Poortinga, 2000). Understanding important social-structural factors such as social class standing, poverty, and low educational levels is then easily overlooked. On the other hand, focusing on context as "social address" variables (Bronfenbrenner, 1986) can reinforce past assumptions that causes of development are similar across groups but that variations between groups are caused by differential exposure to causal agents or conditions and biological predispositions.

This methodological debate between cross-cultural psychology and cultural psychology has also been linked to the emic/etic distinction (Berry, 1969). Cultural psychologists stress the uniqueness of constructs in each cultural context because meanings are derived from these contexts, whereas cross-cultural psychologists emphasize a comparative approach focusing on common constructs and common measures across cultural communities (Kagitçibasi, 1996). Behavior is *emic*, or culture specific, to the extent that it can be understood only within the cultural context in which it occurs; it is *etic,* or universal, in as much as it is common to human beings independent of their culture (Kagitçibasi, 1996; Poortinga, 1998).

The debate centers on the issue of whether a holistic, contextualized methodology or a comparative, decontextualizing methodology is to be used. Proponents of each view criticize the methodology preferred by the other. The interpretive methodologies that are particularly appropriate to study culturally unique phenomenon from an emic perspective are often not acceptable to psychologists using conventional empirical standards of methodological rigor. Similarly, culture-comparative methodologies that use etic constructs to establish lawful relationships between cultural variables and psychological phenomenon have been criticized (Greenfield, 1997) as not sensitive to cultural context.

Arguing that the search for a science of human nature must be concerned with meanings as well as lawful behavior and that no approach can fully explain or account for all behavior (Poortinga, 1998), we suggest that each approach has something unique and complementary to contribute to a comprehensive understanding of human development. Therefore, the contrasting methodological approaches to the study of culture should also be seen as complementary: "A comparative approach does not preclude a contextualist orientation" (Kagitiçibasi, 1996, p. 12). In fact, conceptualizing the context-dependency of psychological phenomenon can focus investigations to uncover causal relations in different contexts that could actually lead to better generalizability.

The research of Garcia Coll and Magnuson (1999) provides an example of integrating complementary foci of alternative methodological approaches. They ensure that culture remains at the core of processes they investigate by deriving variables conceptualized as the product of the interaction between cultural milieu and the individual.

For example, in their research among mothers from low socioeconomic backgrounds in Puerto Rico, patterns of mother-infant interaction are not viewed exclusively as the product of individual maternal characteristics. Instead, variables conceptualized as the product of the interactions between child care context and the individual are constructed in the analyses. For example, a mother's reports of a number of adults helping her with child care and her previous child care experience are constructed into a culturally meaningful variable that represents the extent to which the cultural community supports mothers, regardless of their age. The researchers found stronger associations between such variables and the qualitative aspects of the mother-infant interaction than between individual maternal characteristics (such as age or education) with discrete behaviors (such as visual contacts, verbalizations, etc.).

Furthermore, in making comparisons across cultural communities, Garcia Coll and Magnuson (1999) describe how they always chose to study each group separately to operationalize the relevant variables within each cultural group before conducting across-group comparisons. A similar strategy of developing constructs and variables within each group and examining the coherence of patterns within groups before making group comparisons was used and made explicit by Rogoff et al. (1993). They specifically reported their findings for each cultural community in separate chapters to emphasize their emic understanding of patterns of guided participation in each community before comparing these patterns to those that emerged in the other communities.

This strategy of using multiple methodological strategies is particularly relevant in program evaluation. For example, a current evaluation of a statewide program for teen parents by Easterbrooks, Jacobs, Brady, and Mistry (in preparation) includes multiple components (outcome as well as process evaluation) using multiple methodologies, including qualitative and interpretive efforts. An ethnographic component of the evaluation examines how intervention processes and approaches intersect with familial ethnotheories and cultural scripts (cultural belief systems and their behavioral expression) and thereby influence the achievement of the program's desired objectives and outcomes. This component is designed as a separate investigation of three cultural communities served by the intervention program. Across-community comparisons are made only after within-community patterns are examined and interpreted.

The implications we have highlighted for research are equally applicable in the process of program development and implementation. Although cultural issues have only recently come to the forefront in program planning and evaluation, there have been several insightful discussions that delineate challenges and implications for program development (see Bernard, 1998; Hauser-Cram, this volume, chap. 12; Slaughter, 1988; Slaughter-Defoe, 1993). In the following section, we summarize a few of these challenges.

Incorporating Cultural Relevance in Program Planning and Policy

One of the most important contributions of cultural perspectives on children's development has been to question assumptions of universality in our theories of development: universality of theoretical constructs, developmental endpoints, or developmental pathways. Although increasing attempts have been made to incorporate cultural perspectives in the theories and knowledge base of developmental psychology, the translation of these perspectives in program planning and implementation is just beginning. The problems in this translation become immediately apparent. The task of planning interventions

becomes difficult if universality of goals and best practice for facilitating goals cannot be assumed. Flexibility, rather than program standardization, becomes essential when planning programs for families in diverse sociocultural and ecological contexts. Furthermore, program planning and development has to be based on knowledge of the populations or groups being targeted.

In specifically discussing programs for ethnically diverse families, Slaughter (1988) emphasizes that an analysis of the cultural-ecological realities of racial and ethnic minority family life must precede the setting of program goals. Slaughter stresses the importance of systematic studies of research findings and literature about groups to design appropriate programs. "Too often we have not asked ourselves what we know, historically and culturally, about the families we intend to serve and what we need to know in order to design programs effectively for them" (Slaughter, 1988, pp. 467-468). Thus, delineating three essentials of program planning, Slaughter asserts that families must be respected, their perceptions about program improvement must be sought, and program content must be based on program developers' considered judgments and knowledge about a group's history and immediate social context.

Such knowledge of the communities being served is essential to ensure not only that program goals are appropriate but also that methods of delivery are appropriate. Slaughter (1988) uses the example of programs targeting teen pregnancy to emphasize that at times, the concerns of program developers might not be concerns of participants. Though program interventions may focus on the risks of teen pregnancy, the long-term consequences of teenage pregnancy might not be obvious to mothers and grandmothers who are accustomed to valuing and caring for children, irrespective of the circumstances of their birth. Similarly, Slaughter uses research documenting the importance of the extended or augmented family for African American children to emphasize that programs targeting African American families must deliver services that are family centered and do not just target mothers or a primary caregiver as the recipient of services.

Evaluations that document the implementation process suggest that standardized models of intervention are actually unrealistic. Often, program delivery varies according to the group or community being served, irrespective of the intended model. In our ongoing evaluation of a statewide program for teen parents, ethnographic studies of three communities indicate that program developers appropriate and transform programs to make them culturally relevant for their particular communities (Slive & Mistry, 2002). The program delivered in an essentially white, exurban community focuses on the individual teens, whereas the same program delivered to Spanish-speaking families in an urban community with a large Latino population targets the extended family.

Recent discussions of cultural issues in program planning and implementation have identified other concerns. Focusing on programs and policies for children with disabilities, Hauser-Cram and Howell (this volume, chap. 12) underscore the importance of cultural sensitivity in developing policies and services by presenting specific examples of cultural mismatches between service providers and program participants that impede effectiveness of service delivery. Furthermore, suggestions for ensuring the cultural relevance of programs have been suggested, such as recruiting professionals from cultural communities being served and maintaining relationships with local community groups (Hauser-Cram & Howell, this volume, chap. 12; Slaughter, 1988). Training service providers for cultural sensitivity or cultural competence has been greatly emphasized (Bernard, 1998). Training service providers

to recognize their own stereotypes and assumptions about a program and its content and to learn to listen to family stories to gain perspective on parents' values and meaning systems are particularly important aspects emphasized by Hauser-Cram and Howell.

CONCLUDING COMMENTS

In conclusion, we underscore the importance of building more comprehensive and culturally inclusive theories and empirical databases on children's development. Despite the fact that cross-cultural, cultural, and developmental psychologists approach the study of culture and human development from different perspectives, we have emphasized how it is possible to integrate literature from all three subfields to build more culturally inclusive understandings of any domain of development. In focusing on the interface between culture and human development, developmental psychology has not been at the forefront in looking outside its discipline for theoretical insights or research. However, there are promising signs of change being wrought from within the field. Theoretical frameworks and research paradigms that incorporate cultural meaning systems into the study of diverse contexts of development represent the most promising approaches to broadening our perspectives.

Such broadened perspectives and culturally inclusive knowledge of children's development are particularly relevant in our current world. Interaction and interconnections between countries due to global trade, telecommunications, and technology are bringing diverse groups of people together. Diversity within countries is also growing through factors such as increased job mobility, immigration, and urbanization. The multiplicity of human realities and the variety of conditions and circumstances under which people exist are becoming more apparent and leading to an urgent need for facilitating development among all families and communities. In this context, a culturally inclusive knowledge base about human development becomes essential if we are serious in our aims to develop appropriate policy, programs, and services for all children and families.

1. This section has been adapted from J. Mistry and T.S. Saraswathi, "The Cultural Context of Child Development," in press. To appear in. I. Weiner (Series Ed.), R.M. Lerner, A. Easterbrooks, and J. Mistry (Vol. Eds.), *Handbook of Psychology: Vol. 6. Developmental Psychology*, New York: John Wiley.

REFERENCES

Azuma, H. (1994). Two modes of cognitive socialization in Japan and the United States. In P. M. Greenfield & R. R. Cocking (Eds.), *Cross-cultural roots of minority child development* (pp. 275-284). Hillsdale, NJ: Lawrence Erlbaum.

Baltes, P. B., Lindenberger, U., Staudinger, U. M. (1998). Life-span theory in developmental psychology. In W. Damon (Series Ed.) & R. M. Lerner (Vol. Ed.), *Handbook of child psychology: Vol. 1. Theoretical models of human development* (pp. 1029-1144). New York: Wiley.

Baltes, P. B., Reese, H. W., & Lipsitt, L. P. (1980). Life-span developmental psychology. *Annual Review of Psychology, 31*, 65-110.

Baumrind, D. (1971). Current patterns of parental authority. *Developmental Psychology, 4*(1), 1-103.

Baumrind, D. (1991a). Effective parenting during the early adolescent transition. In P. A. Cowan & E. M. Hetherington (Eds.), *Family transitions: Advances in family research series* (pp. 111-163). Hillsdale, NJ: Lawrence Erlbaum.

Baumrind, D. (1991b). The influence of parenting style on adolescent competence and substance use. *Journal of Early Adolescence, 11*(1).

Bernard, J. A. (1998). Cultural competence plans: A strategy for the creation of a culturally competent system of care. In M. Hernandes & M. R. Issacs (Eds.), *Promoting cultural competence in children's mental health services* (pp. 26-52). Baltimore, MD: Brookes.

Berry, J. W. (1979). Research in multicultural societies: Implications of cross-cultural methods. *Journal of Cross-Cultural Psychology, 10*(4), 415-434.

Berry, J. W., Poortinga, Y. H., Pandey, J., Dasen, P. R., Saraswathi, T. S., Segall, M. H., & Kagitçibasi, C. (Eds.). (1997). *Handbook of cross-cultural psychology* (Vols. 1-3, 2nd ed.). Needham Heights, MA: Allyn & Bacon.

Bornstein, M. H. (Ed.). (1991). *Cultural approaches to parenting*. Hillsdale, NJ: Lawrence Erlbaum.

Bornstein, M. H. (Ed.). (1995). *Handbook of parenting: Vol. 3. Status and social conditions of parenting*. Mahwah, NJ: Lawrence Erlbaum.

Brislin, R. W. (1983). Cross-cultural research psychology. *Annual Review of Psychology, 3*, 363-400.

Bronfenbrenner, U. (1979). *The ecology of human development*. Cambridge, MA: Harvard University Press.

Bronfenbrenner, U. (1986). Ecology of the family as a context for human development. *Developmental Psychology, 22*(6), 723-742.

Bruner, J. S. (1990). Culture and human development: A new look. *Human Development, 33*(6), 344-355.

Bugental, D. B., Mantyla, S. M., & Lewis, J. (1989). Parental attributions as moderators of affective communication to children at risk for physical abuse. In D. Cicchetti & V. Carlson (Eds.), *Child maltreatment: Theory and research on the causes and consequences of child abuse and neglect.* (pp. 254-279). New York: Cambridge University Press.

Choi, S. C., Kim, U., & Choi, S. H. (1993). Indigenous analysis of collective representations: A Korean perspective. In U. Kim & J. W. Berry (Eds.), *Cross-cultural research and methodology series: Vol. 17. Indigenous psychologies: Research and experience in cultural context* (pp. 193-210). Thousand Oaks, CA: Sage.

Chugani, H. T. (1999). PET scanning studies of human brain development and plasticity. *Developmental Neuropsychology, 16*(3), 379-381.

Cole, M. (1990). Cognitive development and formal schooling. In L. Moll (Ed.), *Vygotsky & Education.* New York: Cambridge University Press.

Cole, M. (1996). *Cultural psychology: A once and future discipline.* Cambridge, MA: Belknap/Harvard University Press.

Damon, W. (Series Ed.). (1998). *Handbook of child psychology* (Vols. 1-4). New York: Wiley.

D'Andrade, R. G. (1984). Cultural meaning systems. In R. A. Shweder & R. A. LeVine (Eds.), *Culture theory: Essays on mind, self, and emotion.* (pp. 88-119). New York: Cambridge University Press.

D'Andrade, R. G., & Strauss, C. (1992). *Cultural models and human motives.* Cambridge, U.K.: Cambridge University Press.

Dixon, R. A., & Lerner, R. M. (1999). History and systems in developmental psychology. In M. Bornstein & M. Lamb (Eds.), *Developmental psychology: An advanced textbook.* (4th ed., pp. 3-45). Hillsdale, NJ: Lawrence Erlbaum.

Eckensberger, L. H. (1990). On the necessity of the culture concept in psychology: A view from cross-cultural psychology. In F. J. R. van de Vijver & G. J. M. Hutschemaekers (Eds.), *The investigation of culture: Current issues in cultural psychology* (pp. 153-183). Tilburg, Netherlands: Tilburg University Press.

Edwards, C. P., Gandini, L., & Giovaninni, D. (1996). The contrasting developmental timetables of parents and preschool teachers in two cultural communities. In S. Harkness & C. M. Super (Eds.), *Parents' cultural belief systems: Their origins, expressions, and consequences* (pp. 270-288). New York: Guilford.

Eisenberg, N. (1989). Empathy and sympathy. In W. Damon (Ed.), *Child development today and tomorrow* (pp. 137-154). San Francisco: Jossey-Bass.

Eisenberg, N. (1998). Introduction. In W. Damon (Series Ed.) & N. Eisenberg (Vol. Ed.), *Handbook of child psychology: Vol. 3. Social, emotional, and personality development* (5th ed., pp. 1-24). New York: Wiley.

Enriques, V. G. (1977). Filipino psychology in the Third World. *Philippine Journal of Psychology, 10,* 3-18.

Ford, D. L., & Lerner, R. M. (1992). *Developmental systems theory: An integrative approach.* Newbury Park, CA: Sage.

Garcia Coll, C., & Magnuson, K. (1999). Cultural influences on child development: Are we ready for a paradigm shift? In A. Masten (Ed.), *Cultural processes in child development: The Minnesota symposia on child psychology* (Vol. 29, pp. 1-24). Hillsdale, NJ: Lawrence Erlbaum.

Gardiner, H. W., Mutter, J. D., & Kosmitzki, C. (1998). *Lives across cultures: Cross-cultural human development.* Boston, MA: Allyn & Bacon.

Gaskins, S. (1996). How Mayan parental theories come into play. In S. Harkness & C. M. Super (Eds.), *Parents' cultural belief systems: Their origins, expressions, and consequences* (pp. 345-363). New York: Guilford.

Goldsmith, H. H., & Alansky, J. A. (1987). Maternal and infant temperamental predictors of attachment: A meta-analytic review. *Journal of Consulting and Clinical Psychology, 55*(6), 805-816.

Gonzalez-Ramos, G., Zayas, L. H., & Cohen, E. V. (1998). Child-rearing values of low-income, urban Puerto Rican mothers of preschool children. *Professional Psychology: Research & Practice, 29*(4), 377-382.

Goodnow, J. J., & Collins, W. A. (Eds.). (1990). *Development according to parents: The nature, sources, and consequences of parents' ideas.* Hillsdale, NJ: Lawrence Erlbaum.

Goodnow, J. J., Miller, P. J., & Kessel, F. (Eds.). (1995). *Cultural practices as contexts for development.* San Francisco: Jossey-Bass.

Gottlieb, G. (1997). *Synthesizing nature-nurture: Prenatal roots of instinctive behavior.* Mahwah, NJ: Lawrence Erlbaum.

Greenfield, P. M. (1997). Culture as process: Empirical methods for cultural psychology. In J. W. Berry, Y. H. Poortinga, J. Pandey, P. R. Dasen, T. S. Saraswathi, M. H. Segall, & C. Kagitçibasi (Series Eds.), J. W. Berry, Y. H. Poortinga, & J. Pandey (Vol. Eds.), *Handbook of cross-cultural psychology, Vol. 1: Theory and method* (2nd ed., pp. 301-346). Needham Heights, MA: Allyn & Bacon.

Greenfield, P. M., & Cocking, R. R. (1994). *Cross-cultural roots of minority child development.* Hillsdale, NJ: Lawrence Erlbaum.

Grossmann, K., Grossmann, K. E., Spangler, G., Suess, G., & Unzner, L. (1985). Maternal sensitivity and newborns' orientation responses as related to quality of attachment in Northern Germany. In I. Bretherton & E. Waters (Eds.), *Growing point of attachment theory and research* (Vol. 50, pp. 233-256). Chicago: Monographs of the Society for Research in Child Development.

Grusec, J. E., Hastings, P., & Mammone, N. (1994). Parenting cognitions and relationship schemas. In W. Damon (Series Ed.) & J. G. Smetana (Vol. Ed.), *New directions for child development: Vol. 66. Beliefs about parenting: Origins and developmental implications* (pp. 5-19). San Francisco: Jossey-Bass.

Harkness, S., & Super, C. M. (1992). Parental ethnotheories inaction. In I. E. Sigel, A. V. McGillicuddy-DeLisi, & J. J. Goodnow (Eds.), *Parental belief systems* (373-391). Hillsdale, NJ: Lawrence Erlbaum.

Harkness, S., & Super, C. M. (1995). Culture and parenting. In M. H. Bornstein (Ed.), *Handbook of parenting* (Vol. 2, pp. 211-234). Mahwah, NJ: Lawrence Erlbaum.

Harkness, S., & Super, C. M. (Eds.). (1996). *Parents' cultural belief systems: Their origins, expressions, and consequences.* New York: Guilford.

Harwood, R. L., Miller, J. G., & Irizarry, N. L. (1995). *Culture and attachment: Perceptions of the child in context.* New York: Guilford.

Heath, S. B. (1982). What no bedtime story means: Narrative skills at home and school. *Language in Society, 11,* 49-76.

Ho, D. Y. F. (1976). On the concept of face. *American Journal of Sociology, 81,* 867-884.

Ho, D. Y. F. (1988). Asian psychology: A dialogue on indigenization and beyond. In A. C. Paranjpe, D. Y. F. Ho, & R. W. Reiber (Eds.), *Asian contributions to psychology* (pp. 53-77). New York: Praeger.

Ho, D. Y. F. (1998a). Indigenous psychologies: Asian perspectives. *Journal of Cross-Cultural Psychology, 29*(1), 88-103.

Ho, D. Y. F. (1998b). Interpersonal relationships and relationship dominance: An analysis based on methodological relationalism. *Asian Journal of Social Psychology, 1*(1), 1-16.

Isabella, R. A. (1995). The origins of infant-mother attachment: Maternal behavior and infant development. In R. Vasta (Ed.), *Annals of child development: A research annual* (Vol. 10, pp. 57-81). Bristol, PA: Jessica Kingsley.

Jahoda, G. (1992). *Crossroads between culture and mind.* Cambridge, MA: Harvard University Press.

Jahoda, G., & Krewer, B. (1997). History of cross-cultural and cultural psychology. In J. W. Berry, Y. H. Poortinga, J. Pandey, P. R. Dasen, T. S. Saraswathi, M. H. Segall, & C. Kagitçibasi (Series Eds.), J. W. Berry, Y. H. Poortinga, & J. Pandey (Vol. Eds.), *Handbook of cross-cultural psychology: Vol. 1. Theory and method* (2nd ed., pp. 1-42). Needham Heights, MA: Allyn & Bacon.

Kagitçibasi, C. (1996). *Family and human development across cultures: A view from the other side.* Mahwah, NJ: Lawrence Erlbaum.

Kagitçibasi, C., & Poortinga, Y. (2000). Cross-cultural psychology: Issues and over-arching themes. *Journal of Cross-Cultural Psychology, 31*(1), 129-147.

Kim, U., Park, Y. S., & Park, D. (2000). The challenge of cross-cultural psychology: The role of the indigenous psychologies. *Journal of Cross-Cultural Psychology, 31*(1), 63-75.

Kojima, H. (1998). The construction of child-rearing theories in early modern to modern Japan. In M. C. D. P. Lyra & J. Valsiner (Eds.), *Construction of psychological processes in interpersonal communication* (Vol. 4, pp. 13-34). Stamford, CT: Ablex.

Lamb, M. E., Thompson, R .A., Garndner, W. P., Charnov, E. L. & Estes, D. (1984). Security of infantile attachment as assessed in the "strange situation": Its study and biological interpretation. *Behavioral & Brain Sciences, 7*(1), 127-171.

Lebra, T. S. (1976). *Japanese patterns of behavior.* Honolulu: University of Hawaii Press.

Lerner, R. M. (1991). Changing organism-context relation as the basic process of development: A developmental-contextual perspective. *Developmental Psychology, 27,* 27-32.

Lerner, R. M. (1992). Dialectics, developmental contextualism, and the further enhancement of theory about puberty and psychosocial development. *Journal of Early Adolescence, 12*(4).

Lerner, R. M. (1996). Relative plasticity, integration, temporality, and diversity in human development: A developmental contextual perspective about theory, process, and method. *Developmental Psychology, 32,* 781-786.

Lerner, R. M. (1998). Theories of human development: Contemporary perspectives. In W. Damon (Series Ed.) & R. M. Lerner (Vol. Ed.), *The handbook of child psychology: Vol. 1. Theoretical models of human development* (5th ed., pp.1-24). New York: Wiley.

Lerner, R. M. (2002). *Concepts and theories of human development* (3rd ed.). Mahwah, NJ: Lawrence Erlbaum.

LeVine, R. A. (1973). *Culture, behavior, and personality.* Chicago: Aldine.

LeVine, R. A., Dixon, S., LeVine, S., Richman, A., Leiderman, P. H., Keefer, C., & Brazelton, T. B. (1994). *Child care and culture: Lessons from Africa.* Cambridge, U.K.: Cambridge University Press.

Markus, H. R., & Kitayama, S. (1991). Culture and the self: Implications for cognition, emotion, and motivation. *Psychological Review, 98*(2), 224-253.

Marsella, A. J. (1998). Toward a "global-community psychology": Meeting the needs of a changing world. *American Psychologist, 53(2),* 1282-1291.

Masten, A. (Ed.). (1999). *Cultural processes in child development: Vol. 29. The Minnesota symposia on child psychology.* Hillsdale, NJ: Lawrence Erlbaum.

McLloyd, V. C. (1998). Children in poverty: Development, public policy, and practice. In W. Damon (Series Ed.), I. E. Sigel & K. A. Renninger (Vol. Eds.), *Handbook of child psychology: Vol. 4. Child psychology in practice* (pp. 135-210). New York: Wiley.

McGillicuddy-DeLisi, A. V., & Sigel, I. E. (1995). Parental beliefs. In M. H. Bornstein (Ed.), *Handbook of parenting: Vol. 3. Status and social conditions of parenting* (pp. 333-358). Mahwah, NJ: Lawrence Erlbaum.

McGillicuddy-DeLisi, A. V., & Subramanian, S. (1996). How do children develop knowledge? Beliefs of Tanzanian and American mothers. In S. Harkness & C. M. Super (Eds.), *Parents' cultural belief systems: Their origins, expressions, and consequences* (pp. 143-168). New York: Guilford.

Miller, J. G. (1997). Theoretical issues in cultural psychology. In J. W. Berry, Y. H. Poortinga, J. Pandey, P. R. Dasen, T. S. Saraswathi, M. H. Segall, & C. Kagitçibasi (Series Eds.), J. W. Berry, Y. H. Poortinga, & J. Pandey (Vol. Eds.), *Handbook of cross-cultural psychology: Vol. 1. Theory and method* (2nd ed., pp. 85-128). Needham Heights, MA: Allyn & Bacon.

Miller, J. G., & Chen, X. (2001). Culture and parenting: An overview [Special Section]. *ISSBD Newsletter, 1*(38), 1.

Morelli, G. A., Rogoff, B., Oppenheim, D., & Goldsmith, D. (1992). Cultural variation in infants' sleeping arrangements: Questions of independence. *Developmental Psychology, 28*(4), 604-613.

New, R. S., & Richman, A. L. (1996). Maternal beliefs and infant care practices in Italy and the United States. In S. Harkness & C. M. Super (Eds.), *Parents' cultural belief systems: Their origins, expressions, and consequences* (pp. 385-404). New York: Guilford.

Okagaki, L., & Divecha, D. J. (1993). Development of parenting beliefs. In T. Luster & L. Okagaki (Eds.), *Parenting: An ecological perspective* (pp. 35-67). Hillsdale, NJ: Lawrence Erlbaum.

Park, R. D., & Buriel, R. (1998). Socialization in the family: Ethnic and ecological perspectives. In W. Damon (Series Ed.) & N. Eisenberg (Vol. Ed.), *Handbook of child psychology: Vol. 3. Social, emotional, and personality development* (5th ed., pp. 463-552). New York: Wiley.

Pomerleau, A., Malcuit, G., & Sabatier, C. (1991). Child-rearing practices and parental beliefs in three cultural groups of Montreal: Quebecois, Vietnamese, Haitian. In M. H. Bornstein (Ed.), *Cultural approaches to parenting* (pp. 45-58). Hillsdale, NJ: Lawrence Erlbaum.

Poortinga, Y. H. (1997). Toward convergence. In J. W. Berry, Y. H. Poortinga, J. Pandey, P. R. Dasen, T. S. Saraswathi, M. H. Segall, & C. Kagitçibasi (Series Eds.), J. W. Berry, Y. H. Poortinga, & J. Pandey (Vol. Eds.), *Handbook of cross-cultural psychology: Vol. 1. Theory and method* (2nd ed., pp. 347-387). Needham Heights, MA: Allyn & Bacon.

Poortinga, Y. H. (1998). Cultural diversity and psychological invariance: Methodological and theoretical dilemmas of (cross-)cultural psychology. In J. G. Adair, D. Belanger & K. L. Dion (Eds.), *Advances in psychological science: Vol. 1. Social, personal, and cultural aspects* (pp. 229-245). Hove, England: Psychology Press/Lawrence Erlbaum.

Richman, A. L., LeVine, R. A., New, R. S., Howrigan, G. A., Welles-Nystrom, B., & LeVine, S. E. (1988). Maternal behavior to infants in five cultures. In W. Damon (Series Ed.), R. A. LeVine & P. M. Miller (Vol. Eds.), *New directions for child development: Vol. 40. Parental behavior in diverse societies* (pp. 81-97). San Francisco: Jossey-Bass.

Rogoff, B. (1990). *Apprenticeship in thinking.* New York: Oxford University Press.

Rogoff, B., Mistry, J., Göncü, A., & Mosier, C. (1993). *Guided participation in cultural activity by toddlers and caregivers* (Vol. 58). Chicago: University of Chicago Press.

Rothbaum, F., Pott, M., Morelli, G., & Liu-Constant, Y. (2000). Immigrant-Chinese and Euro-American parents' physical closeness with young children: Themes of family relatedness. *Journal of Family Psychology, 14*(3), 334-348.

Sagi, A., Lamb, M. E., Lewkowicz, K. S., Shoham, R., Dvir, R., & Estes, D. (1985). Security of infant-mother, -father, and -metapelet attachments among kibbutz-reared Israeli children. In I. Bretherton & E. Waters (Eds.), *Growing point of attachment theory and research* (Vol. 50, pp. 257-275). Chicago: Monographs of the Society for Research in Child Development.

Sameroff, A. J. (1983). Developmental systems: Contexts and evolution. In P. H. Mussen (Series Ed.) & W. Kessen (Vol. Ed.), *Handbook of child psychology: Vol. 1. History, theory, and methods* (pp. 237-294). New York: Wiley.

Segall, M. H., Dasen, P. R., Berry, J. W., & Poortinga, Y. H. (1999). *Human behavior in global perspective.* Needham Heights, MA: Allyn & Bacon.

Shwalb, D. W., Shwalb, B. J., & Shoji, J. (1996). Japanese mothers' ideas about temperament. In S. Harkness & C. M. Super (Eds.), *Parents' cultural belief systems: Their origins, expressions, and consequences* (pp. 169-191). New York: Guilford.

Shweder, R. A. (1991). *Thinking through cultures: Expeditions in cultural psychology.* Cambridge, MA: Harvard University Press.

Shweder, R. A., Goodnow, J., Hatano, G., LeVine, R. A., Markus, H., & Miller, P. (1998). *The cultural psychology of development: One mind, many mentalities.* In W. Damon (Series Ed.) & R. M. Lerner (Vol. Ed.), *Handbook of child psychology: Vol. 1. Theoretical models of human development* (pp. 865-938). New York: Wiley.

Shweder, R. A., Jensen, L. A., & Goldstein, W. M. (1995). Who sleeps by whom revisited: A method for extracting the moral goods implicit in practice. In J. J. Goodnow, P. J. Miller, & F. Kessel (Eds.), *Cultural practices as contexts for development* (Vol. 67, pp. 21-39). San Francisco: Jossey-Bass.

Sigel, I. E. (1981). Child development research in learning and cognition in the 1980s: Continuities and discontinuities from the 1970s. *Merrill Palmer Quarterly, 27*(4), 347-371.

Sigel, I. E. (Ed.). (1984). *Parental belief systems: The psychological consequences for children.* Hillsdale, NJ: Lawrence Erlbaum.

Sigel, I. E., McGillicuddy-DeLisi, A. V., & Goodnow, J. J. (1992). *Parental belief systems: The psychological consequences for children* (2nd ed.). Hillsdale, NJ: Lawrence Erlbaum.

Sinha, D. (1986). *Psychology in a third world country: The Indian experience.* New Delhi, India: Sage.

Sinha, D. (1997). Indigenizing psychology. In J. W. Berry, Y. H. Poortinga, J. Panday, P. R. Dasen, & T. S. Saraswathi, M. Segall, & C. Kagitçibasi (Series Eds.), J. W. Berry, Y. H. Poortinga, & J. Pandey (Vol. Eds.), *Handbook of cross-cultural psychology: Vol. 1. Theory and method* (2nd ed., pp. 129-170). Needham Heights, MA: Allyn & Bacon.

Sinha, S. R. (1995). Child-rearing practices relevant for the growth of dependency and competence in children. In J. Valsiner (Ed.), *Comparative-cultural and constructivist perspectives: Child development within culturally structured environments.* (Vol. 3, pp. 105-137). Norwood, NJ: Ablex.

Slaughter, D. (1988). Programs for racially and ethnically diverse American families: some critical issues. In H. B. Weiss & F. H. Jacobs (Eds.), *Evaluating family programs* (pp. 461-476). New York: Aldine.

Slaughter-Defoe, D. T. (1993). Home visiting with families in poverty: Introducing the concept of culture. *The Future of Children: Home Visiting, (3)*3, 172-183.

Slive, S. D., & Mistry, J. (2002). *Theories of program provider-participant relationship: Interpretation and implementation in three programs.* Working paper, Massachusetts Healthy Families Evaluation, Tufts University, Boston, MA.

Smetana, J. G. (Ed.). (1994). *New directions for child development: Vol. 66. Beliefs about parenting: Origins and developmental implications* San Francisco: Jossey-Bass.

Snow, C. E., & Goldfield, B. A. (1982). Building stories: The emergence of information structures from conversation. In D. Tannen (Ed.), *Georgetown University's roundtable on language and linguistics*. Washington, DC: Georgetown University Press.

Stigler, J. W., Shweder, R. A., & Herdt, G. (Eds.). (1990). *Cultural psychology: Essays on comparative human development*. New York: Cambridge University Press.

Super, C. M., & Harkness, S. (1986). The developmental niche: A conceptualization at the interface of child and culture. *International Journal of Behavioral Development, 9*, 545-569.

Super, C. M., Harkness, S., van Tijen, N., van der Vlugt, E., Dykstra, J., & Fintelman, M. (1996). The three R's of Dutch childrearing and the socialization of infant arousal. In S. Harkness & C. M. Super (Eds.), *Parenta' cultural belief systems: Their origins, expressions, and consequences* (pp. 447-466). New York: Guilford.

Takahaski, K. (1986). Examining the strange situation procedure with Japanese mothers and 12-month-old infants. *Developmental Psychology, 22*, 263-270.

Thelen, E., & Smith, L. B. (1998). Dynamic systems theories. In W. Damon (Series Ed.) & R. M. Lerner (Vol. Ed.), *Handbook of child psychology: Vol. 1. Theoretical models of human development* (5th ed., pp. 563-633). New York: Wiley.

Thompson, R. (1998). Early sociopersonality development. In W. Damon (Series Ed.) & N. Eisenberg (Vol. Ed.), *Handbook of child psychology: Vol. 3. Social, emotional, and personality development.* (5th ed., pp. 25-104). New York: Wiley.

Triandis, H. C. (1980). Introduction to handbook of cross-cultural psychology. In H. C. Triandis & W. W. Lambert (Eds.), *Handbook of cross-cultural psychology* (Vol. 1. pp. 1-14). Boston, MA: Allyn & Bacon.

Vygotsky, L. S. (1978). *Mind in society: The development of higher psychological processes*. Cambridge, MA: Harvard University Press.

Wertsch, J. V. (1985). *Culture, communication, and cognition: Vygotskian perspectives*. New York: Cambridge University Press.

Wertsch, J. V. (1991). *Voices of the mind*. Cambridge, MA: Harvard University Press.

Wertsch, J. V., & Tulviste, P. (1992). L. S. Vygotsky and contemporary developmental psychology. *Developmental Psychology, 28*(4), pp. 548-557.

Wolf, A. W., Lozoff, B., Latz, S., & Paludetto, R. (1996). Parental theories in the management of young children's sleep in Japan, Italy, and the United States. In S. Harkness & C. M. Super (Eds.), *Parents' cultural belief systems: Their origins, expressions, and consequences* (pp. 364-384). New York: Guilford.

Wozniak, R. H., & Fischer, K. W. (1993). *Development in context: Acting and thinking in specific environments*. Hillsdale, NJ: Lawrence Erlbaum.

Zahn-Waxler, C., & Smith, K. D. (1992). The development of prosocial behavior. In V. V. Hasselt & M. Herson (Eds.), *Handbook of social development* (pp. 229-256). New York: Plenum.

CHAPTER 10

Reforming Education: Developing 21st-Century Community Schools

MARTIN J. BLANK

WITH

BELA SHAH
SHERI JOHNSON
WILLIAM BLACKWELL
MELISSA GANLEY

The United States and its educational system have been in a particularly intensive reform mode since the issuance of the report *A Nation at Risk* in 1983. That report declared, "The educational foundations of our society are presently being eroded by a rising tide of mediocrity that threatens our very future as a Nation and a people" (National Commission on Excellence in Education, 1983, p. 1). Since that report, reform initiatives have emerged focusing on two key approaches: stimulating choice in public education and using standards-based reform. The reform strategy that has received far less attention is the community schools approach that links school, family, and community. That is the primary focus of this chapter. To put the community schools approach in context, the chapter begins with a brief overview of other education reform strategies.

EDUCATION REFORM DURING THE 1990s

The choice agenda, as it emerged during the 1990s, takes three different forms: public school choice, charter schools, and private/public school vouchers. Public school choice allows parents to send their children to any school within their own district and in some instances to schools in neighboring districts (Malone, Nathan, & Sedio, 1993). Initiated at the state level, this form of choice was codified in the Act to Leave No Child Behind (www.edworkforce.house.gov) passed in December 2001.

Charter schools use public school funds to operate schools "outside" of the school district's established rules and regulations. They are operated by many different entities, including public school systems themselves. In 2000, there were approximately 2,372 charter schools—1,376 elementary schools, 522 middle schools, and 474 high schools (Center for Education Reform, 2000). This represents less than 2.7% of American schools (National Education Association [NEA], 1999) and an even smaller percentage of students given the small size of most charter schools (Center for Education Reform, 2000). Evidence on the effectiveness of charter schools is mixed. According to a study by Manno, Finn, Bierlein, and Vanourek (1998), "The number of students doing 'excellent' or 'good' work rose 23.4% for African-Americans and 21.8% for Hispanics after enrolling in charter schools. Similar gains were made by low-income students of all races" (p. 43). The NEA (2000) praised the innovation in charter schools but noted that "researchers are finding that by commonly used measurements, charters have had mixed success in increasing student achievement, with some schools showing strong gains and others struggling or even failing" (p. 4).

Public school vouchers, sometimes called scholarships, are the most controversial form of choice. School vouchers channel education funding directly to families, bypassing school districts. Families select the schools they believe best meet the needs of their children. They may select public or private schools and may have some or all of the tuition reimbursed. "Scholarships are advocated on the grounds that parental choice and competition between public and private schools will improve education for all children. Vouchers can be funded and administered by the government, by private organizations, or by some combination of both" (School Choices, 1998, p. 1). Advocates for vouchers argue that all parents, particularly parents of children in failing schools, should have the same opportunity to choose that wealthy families have.

Opponents believe that vouchers present a threat to the historic American commitment to public education by draining resources from public education and violating the constitutional separation of church and state. Despite the rhetoric about vouchers, only the cities of Milwaukee and Cleveland and the state of Florida have instituted such programs (Center on Education Policy, 2000). A report by the RAND Corporation (2001) found no conclusive or definitive evidence that vouchers consistently improve or harm student achievement, although vouchers do seem to raise parent satisfaction.

These choice strategies have received significant attention, but it is the standards-based reform movement that was the driving force in education reform during the 1990s. In creating high standards for academic achievement, policymakers hope to level the playing field between schools and raise the academic achievement of all students. Every state except Iowa now has standards in place (Achieve, 2000). Accountability complements standards, and federal and state policies began to place more emphasis on high-stakes testing as the primary tool for accountability. Federal policy (i.e., the Act to Leave No Child Behind) now requires testing of all children in Grades 3 through 8. The comprehensive school reform movement has emerged as a way to implement standards and to help students meet standards (Hansel, 2001).

Standards and accountability have led schools to a nearly singular focus on improving the academic achievement of students. The argument is that with the right mix of school leadership, qualified teachers, professional development, effective curriculum, accountability, and assessment, schools can educate all children.

Although there is no question that schools must improve in ways that the standards movement proposes, the narrow focus on improving academic achievement ignores the roles that family and community play in children's lives. It also overlooks the implications of the extraordinary changes in the demographics of America's schoolchildren during recent years. Fully 35% of schoolchildren are now from ethnic/racial minority groups (U.S. Census Bureau, 2000), as compared with 26% in 1980 (U.S. Census Bureau, 1980). Cuban (2001) asserted that it is a myth that "schools alone can improve the life chances of poor children" (p. 7). He stated,

> Anyone who has visited an urban elementary or secondary school for at least one week (not a drive-by site visit) to sit in classes, listen to teachers and students, and observe lunchrooms, playgrounds, and offices would begin to appreciate a simple but inescapable truth: An urban school is deeply influenced by the neighborhoods from which it draws its students. (p. 8)

Thus, at the same time that the standards movement was taking hold, recognition of the multiple forces influencing the lives of children and their success in school led to a renewal of efforts to create new partnerships among schools, families, and neighborhoods to improve student learning and also to strengthen families and build healthier communities. A number of educators, along with people in the related fields of youth, family, and community development, recognized that children and youth must grow not only academically but also personally, socially, ethically, and in other ways to become contributing members of society (Council of Chief State School Officers, 1992). Foundations funded programs based on the "core

belief . . . that children develop best within loving families and the shelter of safe, supportive communities" (David and Lucille Packard Foundation, 2001, p. 2).

Educators working closely with an array of partners began to create a 21st-century community school, a school where educators and community partners from different disciplines focus on learning and development for young people while also working to strengthen their families and communities.

BACKGROUND: COMMUNITY-SCHOOL INITIATIVES DURING THE PAST DECADE

The past decade has seen exponential growth in efforts to link schools and community partners. These efforts build on a rich history of related work. Examples include John Dewey's vision of the school as center of community (Dewey, 1902), Jane Addams's work on the school as settlement house at the beginning of the 20th century (Addams, 1904), the community education movement that began during the 1930s and is still vibrant in many communities (Manley, Reed, & Burns, 1960; National Community Education Association, 2001), and the work of Communities in Schools that started during the 1970s (Communities in Schools, 2000).

Beginning during the late 1980s, schools, youth development organizations, human services agencies, community-building organizations, community organizers, parent leadership and education networks, family support groups, and others renewed efforts to create strong relationships between schools and communities. Local and state governments; United Ways; institutions of higher education; neighborhood organizations; and business, civic, religious, and social organizations also were involved. The array of initiatives grew to the point where the Charles Stewart Mott Foundation asked the Institute for Educational Leadership (IEL) to analyze the field. The resulting publication, *Learning Together,* provided an analysis of the new wave of what it called school-community initiatives (Melaville, 1998). The document "mapped" the range of activity occurring between school and community so that policymakers, administrators, and practitioners would have a clearer understanding of this burgeoning work. The analysis in *Learning Together* revealed that school-community initiatives relied on four major strategies:

Service Reform: Remove the non-academic barriers to school performance by providing access to improved health and human services to young people and families. These efforts are manifested in the creation of family support centers, health clinics, mental health services, crisis intervention programs, and other supports for students and their families, and sometimes residents, in the school.

Youth Development: Help students develop their talents and abilities to participate fully in adolescence and adult life by increasing young people's opportunities to be involved in learning, decision making, service opportunities, and supportive relationships with others. This includes after-school mentoring, community service/service-learning, recreation, leadership development, and career development programs.

Community Development: Enhance the social, economic, and physical capital of the community by focusing on economic development and job creation and emphasizing community organizing, advocacy, and leadership development among community members, parents, and students.

Education Reform: Improve educational quality and academic performance by focusing on improving the management, curriculum, instruction, and general culture within schools and classrooms. This includes engaging parents, families, and teachers more directly in school-based decision making, engaging the private sector, and a range of the activities referenced under the previous approaches. (p. 14)

Collaboration across sectors and organizations also was an overarching priority for these initiatives. Most school-community initiatives used the Service Reform and Youth Development approaches, while a few focused on Community Development and Education Reform.

Perhaps the most significant finding in *Learning Together* was the following:

While each initiative is more closely aligned with one major approach than another, most are influenced by all of them. Thus the school-community terrain is not so much characterized by disconnected or conflicting reform approaches as by blended and complementary approaches that constitute an emerging field of practice. (Melaville, 1998, p. 18)

At the practice level, a new theory of action was emerging that "brought the unique and valuable perspectives of multiple fields to bear on teaching and learning, school and education" (p. 18).

From the perspective of education reform, how were these school-community initiatives influencing teaching and learning? Not surprisingly, they followed an evolutionary path. "Beginning with parent participation, they move to affecting the school environment and eventually influence school policies and classroom instruction" (Melaville, 1998, p. 93). Preliminary data suggested positive results from most initiatives. "Evaluation findings suggest that initiatives are making a difference in the lives of individual children and families who participate" (p. 77).

Since the publication of *Learning Together,* the growth of school-community initiatives, increasingly referred to as community schools, has continued. According to the August 2001 issue of *The School Administrator,* published by the American Association of School Administrators, "The number of school-community partnerships nationally is soaring as school leaders capitalize on the potential benefits that can be gleaned from bringing schools, parents, and community agencies together to help students learn" (Pardini, 2001, p. 12).

THE CONTINUING IMPETUS FOR COMMUNITY AND SCHOOL CONNECTIONS

Several factors fuel the continued growth in school and community connections. Understanding this context helps clarify some of the challenges and opportunities that the community schools approach to education reform faces.

Demographic Changes. Educators face extraordinary changes in the students they must educate. Nearly 20% of America's school-age children now speak a language other than English at home, and 15% of those homes are outside the states of California, Florida, Illinois, New York, and Texas, where immigrants traditionally have settled (U.S. Census Bureau, 2000). The growth trend is projected to continue, with 65% of America's population growth during the next 20 years projected to come from Hispanic and Asian immigrants (U.S. Census Bureau, 2000). The reality is that educators, particularly teachers (87% of whom are Caucasian), do not feel prepared to address the needs of students and their families from diverse ethnic or cultural backgrounds or the needs of students who are learning English as a second language (MetLife Survey of the American Teacher, 2000). Schools need stronger relationships with community organizations representing these populations to involve families and to help children learn.

Parent and Neighborhood Concerns. Parents, neighborhood residents, and citizens are deeply concerned about low levels of student performance, especially among low-income children, across the country. "Over the past decade, groups organizing to improve housing and public safety began to focus on the concentration of low performing schools in their neighborhoods and to highlight the absence of accountability in these schools" (Institute for Education and Social Policy, 2001, p. 10). Community building groups—organizations with established roots in neighborhoods and a history of involvement with housing, economic development, and (sometimes) human services, such as the Logan Square Neighborhood Association in Chicago—are now more explicit about the importance of better schools to their vision of a healthy community (Jehl, Blank, & McCloud, 2001). Given the differences in organizational culture, leadership style, and problem-solving approaches, relationships between schools and these community organizations can be testy. For example, "for educators, conflict is a sign of something gone wrong, while for community builders, it is a valuable tool for change" (p. 10).

Public Engagement. Not only is the community reaching into the schools, but schools also are reaching out. Responding to concerns about public education, educators have moved to create major "public engagement" strategies as a vital component of education reform. Dialogue with the community is now commonplace, and the community is contributing to education reform and school-community connections (Annenberg Institute for School Reform, 1998). This dialogue is not always based on mutual interests, however. A recent survey by Public Agenda (2001) indicated that only 27% of superintendents saw public engagement as helping "the schools to be more responsive to the concerns of the community," while 65% saw these efforts as attempts to help "the community to be more supportive of the schools" (p. 9).

The After-School Movement. Welfare reform (e.g., the Personal Responsibility and

Opportunity Act of 1996) moved many parents whose children needed safe places after school into the workplace during the late 1990s. At the same time, there was increased recognition of the fact that most juvenile crime occurred during the after-school hours, that is, between 3 and 6 p.m. (Fox, Flynn, Newman, & Christeson, 2000). Educators also realized that some children needed extra learning opportunities. After-school programs became the major public policy response to these realities. Voters, by a two-to-one margin, prefer the schools as the place for the implementation of after-school programs (After-School Alliance, 2000).

These data led to a major expansion of after-school activities through the federal 21st Century Community Learning Centers (21st CCLC), a federal program that grew from $1 million (fiscal year 1997) to $846 million (fiscal year 2001) (U.S. Department of Education, 2001). The 21st CCLC program allowed limited funds to be used for 12 other family and community purposes. It helped to fuel the movement toward community schools by requiring that school districts "work in partnership" with community-based organizations (U.S. Department of Education, 2001). Recent changes to the Elementary and Secondary Act, of which 21st CCLC is a part, would allow community-based organizations to be direct recipients of grants funds if they have formal partnerships with schools (i.e., the Act to Leave No Child Behind).

Some states are funding similar programs (e.g., the After-School Neighborhood Partnership program in California, the Advantage Schools in New York). Many more states are using funds from the Temporary Assistance for Needy Families (TANF) program to finance after-school programs and related services for at-risk children (Children's Defense Fund, 2000; Savner & Greenberg, 2001).

Technical assistance funded by the Charles Stewart Mott Foundation (2001)

also has been a vital factor in promoting collaboration with other community agencies. In a significant partnership with the federal government, the Mott Foundation invested nearly $100 million to support the federal effort. Given its historical commitment to community education and community schools, the foundation saw this investment as not only creating more effective after-school programs but also leveraging after-school programs into more comprehensive community schools.

Challenges at the Schoolhouse Door. Violence, family crises, mental health challenges, poverty, and other child and family problems naturally find their way to the schoolhouse door. According to Joan Wynn of the Chapin Hall Center for Children, "Most students who are struggling to succeed in school don't have learning problems. They may be living in poverty, or be sick, or have parents who are unemployed or abusive" (quoted in Pardini, 2001, p. 11). Policymakers continue to put schools in a leadership position to address these issues; however, they are increasingly requiring partnerships with other organizations. For example, the federal Safe Schools/Healthy Students program, a partnership between the Departments of Education, Health and Human Services, and Justice (Safe Schools/Healthy Students, 2000), grew out of congressional concern about the tragic killings in our nation's schools. Safe Schools/Healthy Students focuses on violence prevention, mental health, and resiliency efforts in schools. School systems are required to work in partnership with law enforcement and mental health agencies. Many states have created similar programs such as Healthy Start (California), Caring Communities (Missouri), and Readiness to Learn (Washington). Other locally driven partnerships also have emerged to address these concerns (Melaville, 1998, p. 97).

Common Goals for Young People. In 1989, the Carnegie Council on Adolescent Development recommended five goals that our society should have for adolescents. Every adolescent should be an intellectually reflective person, a person en route to a life-time of meaningful work, a good citizen, a caring and ethical individual, and a healthy person (Task Force on Education of Young Adolescents, 1989). The Learning First Alliance (2001), a partnership of the nation's largest education associations, used a similar rubric in *Every Child Learning*. National and local youth development organizations have created results frameworks that focus on factors such as health, civic engagement, social skills, and employability as well as learning, thinking, and reasoning (Coalition for Community Schools, 2001). Attaining these broad goals for all youth is a task that requires schools and communities to work together.

Finally, in the authors' experience, when asked to whom schools belong, most citizens say "the community." They see the school as a center of community life, with the primary purpose of educating children but also serving as an important asset to the community in other ways. Many citizens currently believe that schools are too isolated from community. The experience of school-community initiatives during recent years, and the continuing forces that drove them, lead to a new vision for 21st-century community schools.

COMMUNITY SCHOOLS: THE EMERGING VISION AND WISDOM

A community school provides a framework within which all of the relationships between schools and many different community organizations and agencies (partners) can come together in more intentional ways to improve learning and development for all of our children while strengthening families and communities. The work of community partners is integrated with the teaching and learning work of the school, and there is an intentional focus on how their joint efforts can best reach the results that they all desire for students, their families and community. The work of community is not just an "add-on"; it is integral to the mission and life of the school. Community is helping to recreate schools as new kinds of educational and social institutions.

The Coalition for Community Schools (2000) has crafted a vision for a community school that provides a context for the design of such schools across the country. It is not a "model" of what a community school must look like; rather, it is a resource that others can use in building what will work in their own communities.

A community school, operating in a public school building, is open to students, families, and the community before, during, and after school, seven days a week, all year long. It often operates through a partnership between the school system and one anchor institution (e.g., a community-based organization, child and family service agency, community development group, institution of higher education). Families, youth, principals, teachers, neighborhood residents, and community partners help design and implement activities that promote high educational achievement and use the community as a resource for learning.

Taught by certified teachers, the school curriculum is based on high standards and expectations. The curriculum deliberately uses the history, assets, and problems of the community as a primary resource to engage students in the teaching and learning process. Service-learning is fully integrated into the curriculum. Professional development supports for teachers and other school personnel are in place, and there is a strong sense of accountability to the community.

Ideally, a full-time community school coordinator manages the supports provided by community partners and participates on the management team for the school. A before and after school learning component is rich and diverse in content, giving students opportunities to expand their horizons, build on their classroom experiences, contribute to their communities, and have fun.

A family resource center develops parent leaders; helps families with parenting education, adult education, employment, housing, and other services; and empowers parents to become better advocates for their children's education. A health clinic, offering medical, dental, and mental health services, may be located on-site. Volunteers from business, religious, and civic organizations; college faculty and students; and especially family members come into the school to share their energy and skills. Citizens, neighbors, and family members come to support, promote, and bolster what schools are working hard to accomplish—ensuring young people's academic, vocational, and interpersonal success. Community schools crackle with excitement doing, experiencing, and discovering unknown talents and strengths. Community schools open up new channels for learning and self-expression. Students come early and stay late—because they *want* to. (p. 3)

A community school also is unique because the partners working in the school facility are doing their work in various ways; it is not business as usual. The partners are working together to achieve common results; change their funding patterns; transform the practice of their staffs; and work creatively and respectfully with youth, families, and residents to create a different kind of institution—a community school that takes a comprehensive approach to strengthening children, youth, families, and communities (Coalition for Community Schools, 2000).

Just how many schools reflect this broad vision of community schools is a difficult question to answer. In 1998, *Learning Together* identified 20 different strategies being used to engage communities in more than 3,000 schools (Melaville, 1998). Two thirds (67%) of America's elementary schools now offer after-school programs (National Association of Elementary School Principals, 2001). There are more than 1,300 schools with school-based health centers (Hurwitz & Hurwitz, 2000). There are also many schools with community education programs operated by school districts. In other areas, such as family support, coordinated health and social services and use of the community as a resource for learning reveal extensive activity, but no specific numbers are available. There are community schools at the elementary, middle, and secondary school levels, and they are located in urban, suburban, and rural communities across the country. Here too, however, it is a challenge to collect specific information on the number of schools.

Why is it so difficult to count community schools? Because they do not fit into neat packages. A community school is not a separate activity easily counted by the number of programs funded. Rather, it is a synthesis of public and private programs with other community resources. Thus, an exact count is difficult to obtain. Many schools are doing pieces of a community schools vision, but far fewer integrate their resources as the community schools vision anticipates or have the kind of intentional relationship with their families and communities that is embedded in the community schools philosophy.

EFFECTIVENESS OF THE COMMUNITY SCHOOLS APPROACH

This section uses two sources of information to assess the effectiveness of community schools. The first is a synthesis of recent research on community schools initiatives by Joy Dryfoos. This research is supplemented by a review of data on the effectiveness of specific strategies that are typically included within a community schools framework.

These include education linked to community, youth development, family support, and family and community engagement strategies.

Review of Community Schools Research

Dryfoos, a recognized authority on community schools, suggested that "the weight of the evidence is substantial that community schools are beginning to be able to demonstrate their positive effects on students, families, and communities" (Dryfoos, 2000, p. 3). She reviewed 48 reports of community schools initiatives that focused on one or more outcome measures such as academic achievement, changes in student behavior, and increases in parental involvement. In 46 of the reports, some positive outcomes were reported. The quality of the reports varied enormously, from evaluations that relied on very small nonrepresentative samples to reports that were based on carefully designed management information systems and control groups. The variation in numbers reporting positive results for particular outcomes reflects the specific data that each initiative chose to collect and present. Overall, in a world where most improvements are incremental, the results are promising not only in terms of academic achievement but also with regard to conditions that are critical for student learning such as attendance, parent involvement, and the reduction of high-risk behaviors.

Achievement. Academic gains were reported by 46 of the 48 programs using any form of documentation. These were generally improvements in reading and math test scores viewed over a 2- or 3-year period.

Attendance. A total of 19 programs reported improvement in school attendance. Several programs reported lower dropout rates; one program specifically addressed pregnant and parenting teens.

Suspensions. A total of 10 programs reported reductions in suspensions, suggesting improvements in school climate.

High-Risk Behaviors. Reductions in substance abuse, teen pregnancy, or disruptive behavior in the classroom, or improvements in behavior in general, were shown in 10 of the reports.

Parent Involvement. A total of 11 programs showed increases in parent involvement. Providers reported lower rates of child abuse and neglect among participants, less out-of-home placement, better child development practices, less aggression, and generally improved social relationships. Students reported a heightened sense of adult support from both parents and teachers.

Neighborhood. Several programs (5) noted lower violence rates and safer streets in their communities. A unique finding was the reduction in student mobility reported by one program, suggesting that adding services to the school encouraged families to stay in the neighborhood.

In her "Evaluation of Community Schools: Findings to Date," Dryfoos (2000) offered two examples of comprehensive studies of community schools: the Polk Brothers Foundation initiative in Chicago and the Schools of the 21st Century initiative led by the Bush Center at Yale University.

The Polk Brothers Foundation's Full-Service School Initiative

The goal of the Polk Brothers initiative is to improve the physical and psychological well-being of children in three elementary or middle schools in order to make a positive impact on their school-related behavior and academic achievement. Support services are brought into the school that meet the needs and desires of families and strengthen the relationships between parents and school personnel. Each partnership was required to set up a governance body and hire a full-time coordinator to oversee the operations. The schools are open after school and in the evening. Each has a different set of programs, including parent involvement, recreation, tutoring, and educational enrichment.

Evidence [of the Polk Brothers success comes] from an evaluation by the Chapin Hall Center for Children at the University of Chicago:

- Reading scores improved at rates exceeding the city-wide average at all three schools. Improvement in reading has been among the toughest challenges facing Chicago public schools.
- Parents reported an increase in the number of adults in after-school programs who could be trusted to help their child with a serious problem. As parents come to see the school as a friend of the family and a safe haven, they are more likely to support the school in maintaining high expectations for learning and appropriate behavior. The climate of the school improves.
- Teachers surveyed reported an increase in the number of adults in after-school programs who know children in the school well as individuals. (Dryfoos, 2000, p. 35)

Schools of the 21st Century

[Schools of the 21st Century (21C) is a model] for school-based child care and family support services that transforms the traditional school into a year-round, multi-service center providing high-quality, accessible services from early morning to early evening. The goal is to ensure the optimal development of children. While each 21C school varies, the model includes six core components: parent outreach and education; preschool-age programs; before-/after-school and vacation programs for school-age children; health education and services; networks and training for child care providers; and information and referral services. Since its inception, more than 600 schools in 17 states have incorporated the 21C model.

Research indicates that the combination of services provided in the 21C model has strong benefits for children, parents, and schools:

- Children who participate in 21C for at least three years evidence higher scores in mathematics and reading achievement tests than children in a comparison, non-21C school.
- 21C parents reported that they experience significantly less stress, as measured by the Parental Stress Index; they spend less money on child care, and they miss fewer days of work.
- The addition of early childhood classes to the school has had a positive impact on teaching practices, with teachers in the primary grades incorporating the best aspects of early childhood classrooms.
- The expanded services provided by 21C schools have improved their standing within the larger community, as evidenced by more positive public relations, the passage of significant bond issues, and a substantial reduction in school vandalism. (Dryfoos, 2000, p. 19)

Effectiveness of Community Schools Program Components

Beyond Dryfoos's synthesis of research, there also are data on the impact of particular programs that are typically part of the community schools approach.

Connecting to Community Learning. Teaching approaches that connect students with the community, such as service learning and learning integrated with community life and issues, contribute to better results for children and youth. Service learning combines community service and learning; students learn and develop by participating in thoughtfully organized service that is conducted in and meets the needs of the community and is coordinated with their schools and the schools curriculum (Corporation for National Service, 1990). Studies show that service learning has had some impact on academic achievement, student engagement in school, sense of educational accomplishment, homework completion, maintenance of a high level of communication with parents, and sense of being able to make a difference (Billig, 2000; Center for Human Resources, 1999; Scales, 1999; Shaffer, 1993). Fully 90% of Americans strongly support service learning as a strategy for developing skills needed later in life as well as active citizenship and civic involvement (Roper Starch Worldwide, 2000). Environment as an Integrating Context (EIC) for learning developed by the State Education and Environment Roundtable (SEER) "is not primarily focused on learning about the environment. . . . It is about using a school's surroundings and community as a framework within which students can contract their own learning, guided by teachers and administrators using proven educational practices" (Lieberman & Hoody, 1998, p. 7). Examples include studying abandoned property in terms of public health, housing needs, and employment opportunities as well as building a garden in the asphalt of a school yard. A study of EIC by the SEER demonstrated positive results on standardized measures of academic achievement, reduced discipline and classroom management concerns, increased engagement and enthusiasm for learning, and greater price and ownership in accomplishments (Lieberman & Hoody, 1998).

Youth Development. A growing body of information demonstrates the value of a youth development approach. "Problem free is not fully prepared" captures the philosophy of a youth development movement that sees young people as resources for themselves and their communities and that engages young people in deciding about the supports and opportunities they want (Pittman, 1999).

After-school programs have become a focal point for youth development. Research demonstrates that children whose out-of-school time includes 20 to 35 hours of constrictive "high-yield" learning activities do better in school (Clark, 1988). High-yield activities are fun, safe, and enriched with "verbal thought" opportunities that inspire youth and give them a sense of potential accomplishment such as problem-solving activities, family/community improvement projects, social causes projects, arts, music, cultural activities, and reading. Vandell and Posner's (1999) research demonstrated that students who have access to structured after-school enrichment activities had better work habits and were better adjusted emotionally than their peers. U.S. Department of Education (1998, 2000) data indicate positive impact on student achievement and other indicators related to the conditions for learning (e.g., attendance, inappropriate behavior) through participation in after-school programs.

Mentoring programs also demonstrate positive results. Data on mentoring programs such as the Big Brothers Big Sisters program show strong improvement in antisocial behavior, academics, family relationships, and peer relationships (National Research Council and Institute of Medicine, 2002; Tierney, Grossman, & Resch, 1995). School-based mentoring programs also are proving extremely popular, and initial data suggest that they can have a positive impact as well (Schinke, Cole, & Roulin, 2000).

Finally, the National Research Council and Institute of Medicine (2002), in a report titled *Community Programs to Promote Youth Development,* confirmed the importance of youth development in reaching two key conclusions. First, "programs with more features are more likely to provide better supports for young people's positive development" (p. 8). Second, "Community programs can expand the opportunities for youth to acquire personal and social assets" (p. 8).

Family Support. Family support includes a range of services and supports for children and families, including early childhood programs; family support centers; parent involvement, health, and mental health services; and other supports that strengthen families and engage them in their children's education (Epstein, 1996). The Avance Program, for example, provided home visits and initiated many school-home links. After the first year, mothers "were providing a more educationally stimulating and emotionally encouraging environment for their children and had developed more positive attitudes toward their role as teachers of their young children" (Johnson & Walker, 1991, p. 26). The Chicago Preschool Program of the Child-Parent Centers (CPCs) offered structured prekindergarten learning experiences, including numerous parent and child visits to cultural and educational institutions in the community, a multifaceted parent involvement program, extended services into the early elementary years, and outreach activities into the home and health and nutrition services. A 15-year longitudinal study showed that CPCs contributed to a significant decrease in juvenile arrests for participating children, higher rates of school completion, significant reductions in grade retention, and reduced special education placement (Reynolds, Temple, Robertson, & Mann, 2001).

In the health area, school-based health clinics demonstrate positive effects, helping to address severe health concerns (e.g., student asthma and related problems) that lead to time lost from the classroom as well as more severe health problems (Small et al., 1995). Comprehensive school health programs that include health education, increased physical activity, nutritional services, drug and alcohol abuse prevention, and other services demonstrate that health attitudes, skills, and behavior are improved (Centers for Disease Control, 2001; Kann et al., 1995). Schools that offer intense physical activity programs see positive effects on academic achievement, including increased concentration; improved mathematics, reading, and writing test scores; and reduced disruptive behavior, even when time for physical education reduces the time for academics (Symons, 1997; U.S. Department of Health and Human Services and U.S. Department of Education, 2000).

Family and Community Engagement. Multiple studies have strongly demonstrated that active parent involvement and engagement in their children's education, not family income or socioeconomic status, is the most accurate predictor of student achievement. Experience also suggests that community partners are an important resource for engaging parents. An important way for parents to improve their children's life chances is to create a home environment that encourages learning, express high expectations for their children's achievement and future careers, and become involved in their schools and communities (Henderson & Berla, 1994). Other research suggests that the mere act of talking at home about learning and school is one of the most effective forms of parent involvement (Scales, 1999). In addition, specific activities that children and parents share, such as parents reading to their children, listening to their children read aloud on a regular basis, and open family discussions, help to improve reading achievement levels (Epstein, 1991).

Just as parents can have an impact on the school, there is some evidence that school-initiated activities can help parents to improve the home environment, which in turn has a strong influence on a child's school performance (Leler, 1983). When parents and teachers work together, both parties feel supported and have more positive views toward each other (Dauber & Epstein, 1993; Epstein, 1992; Melnick & Fiene, 1990). Several studies support Epstein's finding that teachers have higher expectations for students whose parents collaborate with them (Lareau, 1987; Snow, Barnes, Chandler, Goodman, & Hemphill, 1991; Stevenson & Baker, 1987).

In summary, research from comprehensive community schools initiatives and from specific programs typically incorporated into the community schools approach affirms the potential impact of this approach. Integrating the various services supports and opportunities that young people and their families need in a community school is, not surprisingly, a challenging endeavor.

CHALLENGES TO THE COMMUNITY SCHOOLS APPROACH TO EDUCATION REFORM

Although the case for community schools continues to grow and be bolstered by research, there remain numerous challenges to expanding the community schools approach to education reform in more schools across America. These challenges are familiar and include the following:

Differences in Philosophy and Practice. Practitioners in education, youth development, health, mental health, family support, community development, and related fields all have their distinct philosophies and practices ("mental models" in the language of Senge, 1990) of what works best to help young people succeed. Overcoming these different perspectives so that people can work together and draw on the best of each field is a slow process. Higher education institutions offer far too few interdisciplinary experiences that could help to ameliorate the problem.

Categorical Funding. Narrowly crafted funding streams, often tied to problems associated with the various disciplines referenced previously, also separate people and

organizations. They make it more difficult to integrate resources in ways that are consistent with a community schools strategy (Education and Human Services Consortium, 1991). It is differences in practice and differences in funding streams that underlie the "turf conflicts" often associated with cross-sector work.

Distraction From the Core Academic Mission. There has been concern among some educators and education researchers that linkages with community serve to distract school staff from their primary mission—teaching and learning. Principals often feel burdened by enormous administrative responsibilities (National Association of Secondary School Principals, 2001) and cannot imagine adding new responsibilities to their already overflowing plates.

The Unique Culture of Schooling. Schools are unique institutions. Principals generally have responsibility for large numbers of children and a large staff. They must interact with parents. The pressures for performance and accountability are extraordinary. These are large tasks, and administrator preparation programs have not effectively prepared principals to function in this complex environment. Instructional leadership is only now becoming a focus of programs. Moreover, principals learn little about working with family and community in their professional preparation. They are trained to manage their buildings, not to be leaders and partners in the education of children (IEL, 2000).

MOVING FORWARD

Overcoming these challenges and creating 21st-century community schools is clearly not a simple task. Here are some suggestions for making this commonsense approach a reality:

Establish an intentional, relentless strategy focused on results. A community school requires an intentional strategy among partners to support mutually agreed-on results. A results-based focus enables the schools, parents, students, and community partners to identify the services and opportunities that are most important in their particular setting. Results may be found in many domains (e.g., academic, personal, social, health, civic). With an intentional focus on results, youth development, family support, and other programs can be more strategically linked with the curriculum. If, for example, a desired result is for all children to read at their grade level by the end of the third grade, then the next question is what roles parents and families, early childhood programs, the school, after-school programs, the family support center, business, and civic groups would play in achieving that result. What does best practice tell us they should do, both individually and collectively? Thus, a conversation about results becomes a strategy session, creating a touchstone for continuous assessment and improvement of the work that people are doing together.

Build community partnerships. The community schools approach argues that communities, not just educators, are responsible for the education of our children. If community responsibility is to be a reality, then there must be a forum in the community where leaders from different sectors (e.g., K–12 education, higher education, youth development, family support, health and social services, community development, government, business, religious, philanthropy) and leaders for parents, neighborhood groups, and youth come together to talk about their children and to build and sustain a community schools strategy. These partnerships must be "significant, sustained, and systemic" (Harkavy, 2000). At the community level, they should assume responsibility for articulating a vision of community schools, defining desired results and promoting accountability, mobilizing and financing resources, educating the public and building constituency for community schools, setting broad policy, facilitating professional development, and overseeing the long-range effectiveness and financial stability of the initiative.

Organize and maintain school planning and oversight teams. School planning and oversight teams are key mechanisms for ensuring that the voices of parents and students are heard at a community school. They are the places where parents and students work with staff of the school and its community partners to plan, organize, and evaluate the community school and find ways to sustain it. These teams carry out specific tasks similar to those of community partnerships at the school level. Organizing and maintaining these teams takes a relentless commitment to the value of community participation in decision making and an understanding of the importance of these teams to building a constituency for the community school and its long-term sustainability.

Plan and coordinate school site management. Any relationship between organizations requires attention to managing that relationship. Particularly important in a school environment, where there are so many pressures on school personnel with regard to academic achievement, is how to manage the relationship between the school and its community partners. Most school-community initiatives that were reviewed in *Learning Together* chose to staff full-time coordinators (Melaville, 1998). This allowed the community school coordinator to become part of the fabric of the school; understand the school culture and the needs and assets of the school, its students, families, and staff; and become a resource to the teachers and the school principal.

Understand the role of the principal and the need for more preparation and professional development. Being a school principal is a daunting task under any circumstances. In a recent report, the IEL (2000) argued that principals must be able to exercise instructional, visionary, and community leadership to improve student learning.

Principals need to learn more about the capacity of family and community to support student learning in their preparation and professional development experience. There is little in the curriculum about the roles of family and community in their administrator preparation programs, despite the fact that standards for leadership include these factors (Council of Chief State School Officers, 1996; National Association of Elementary School Principals, 2001). Preparation and professional development programs for principals must give more attention to the principles of community development and collaborative leadership and must enhance the capacity of principals to work with families, the community, and other organizations concerned with children. Without the ability to foster such relationships, educators may inadvertently continue to take the "public" out of public schools.

Strengthen interprofessional education. Breaking down the barriers between fields and disciplines requires that people learn more about each other during their professional preparation and during in-service professional development experiences in their working lives. Progress has been made in this direction in some institutions of higher education, but far more must be done to change professional preparation so that it can more effectively help to support and sustain the community schools approach.

Focus on creating strong leaders. Leadership is recognized as key to most effective community schools strategies. "Leadership provides fuel and direction. Initiatives that last are led by people who know where they want to go and have the position, personality, and power to make others want to come along" (Melaville, 1998, p. 96). Bringing together diverse stakeholders behind a clear vision and strategy of community schools during the 21st century will require leadership from both our schools and our communities. More attention must be given to nurturing leaders who have already stepped forward and to finding and engaging other potential leaders.

CONCLUSIONS

This chapter has made the case that high-quality education alone will not prepare America's increasingly diverse student population for their roles as workers, parents, and citizens during the 21st century. Rather, education is a responsibility shared among schools, family, and community. The community schools approach, weaving together the resources that young people need to learn and succeed, is the vehicle for realizing that shared responsibility. This is not a simple approach but rather a quintessentially American strategy drawing on our natural creativity and inventiveness as well as our commitment to education and community.

Ben Canada, former school superintendent in Portland, Oregon, and a past president of the American Association for School Administrators, was active in the Schools Uniting Neighborhoods community schools initiative in Portland. He made the case for the community schools approach to education reform this way:

> For me, it's about engaging the whole community in the process of making all of us better citizens. . . . When other organizations

work closely with schools, people learn and have greater appreciation for what [schools] do. . . . They buy into what we're trying to accomplish. And I don't think any school district should deny itself the opportunity for those kinds of long-term benefits. (quoted in Pardini, 2001, p. 8)

In the long run, leadership will be the key to creating and sustaining our schools. In pursuing this approach, leaders should keep in mind the words of Gardner (1990):

In a tumultuous swiftly changing environment, in a world of multiple colliding systems, the hierarchical position of leaders within their own system is of limited value because some of the most critically important tasks require lateral leadership—cross boundary leadership—involving groups over whom they have no control. . . . Leaders unwilling to seek mutually workable arrangements with systems external to their own are not serving the long-term institutional interests of their constituents. (pp. 98-99)

REFERENCES

Achieve. (2001). *Standards and accountability: Strategies for sustaining momentum.* [Online]. Available: www.achieve.org/achieve.nsf/standardform3?openform& parentunidxxx250311191b9e438c85256aca00751c4f

Addams, J. (1904). *On education.* New Brunswick, NJ: Transaction Publishing.

After-School Alliance. (2000, July). *After-School Alert Poll Report.* [Online]. Available: www.afterschoolalliance.org

Annenberg Institute for School Reform. (1998). *Reasons for hope, voices for change.* Providence, RI: Author.

Billig, S. H. (2000). *The impacts of service learning on youth, schools, and communities: Research on K–12 school-based service learning, 1990-99.* Denver, CO: RMC Research. Available: www.learningindeed.org/research/slresearch/slrsrchsy.html

Center on Education Policy. (2000). *School vouchers: What we know and don't know . . . and how we could learn more.* [Online]. Available: www.ctredpol. org/cep.site.index.html

Center for Education Reform. (2000). *Education reform update: Charter growth on the rise.* [Online]. Available:

Center for Human Resources. (1999). *Summary report of national evaluation of Learn and Serve America: School and community-based programs.* Waltham, MA: Brandeis University, Heller School, Center for Human Resources.

Centers for Disease Control. (2001). *School health programs: An investment in our nation's future.* Atlanta, GA: Author.

Charles Stewart Mott Foundation. (2001). *21st Century Community Learning Centers: A unique public-private partnership.* [Online]. Available: www.mott.org/21.asp

Children's Defense Fund. (2000). *A fragile foundation: State child care assistance policies—Final state child care report.* Washington, DC: Author. Available: www.childrensdefense.org

Clark, R. (1988). *Critical factors in why disadvantaged children succeed or fail in school.* New York: Academy for Educational Development.

Coalition for Community Schools. (2000). *Community schools: Partnerships for Excellence.* Washington, DC: Institute for Educational Leadership.

Coalition for Community Schools. (2001). *Analysis of outcomes of youth development organizations* (taken from Boys and Girls Clubs of America, Campfire Inc., Girls Inc., Youth Development Institute of the Fund for the City of New York, and YMCA). Unpublished manuscript, Institute for Educational Leadership, Washington, DC.

Communities in Schools. (2000). *1999-2000 network report*. Alexandria, VA: Author. (previously known as Cities in Schools)

Corporation for National Service. (1990). *National and Community Service Act of 1990*. [Online]. Available: www.nationalservice.org/resources/cross/cncs_statute.pdf

Council of Chief State School Officers. (1992). *Student success through collaboration*. Washington, DC: Author. Available: www.ccsso.org/colabpol.html

Council of Chief State School Officers. (1996). *Standards for preparing school leaders*. Washington, DC: Author.

Cuban, L. (2001). *Leadership for student learning: Urban school leadership—Different in kind and degree*. Washington, DC: Institute for Educational Leadership.

Dauber, S., & Epstein, J. (1993). Parent attitudes and practices of involvement in inner-city elementary and middle schools. In N. F. Chavkin (Ed.), *Families and schools in a pluralistic society* (pp. 53-71). Albany: State University of New York Press.

David and Lucille Packard Foundation. (2001). *Build community and national commitment*. [Online]. Available: www.packard.org/index.cgi?pagexxx-childbuild

Dewey, J. (1902). The school as social center: An address delivered before the National Council of Education, Minneapolis, Minnesota, July 1902. *Elementary School Teacher, 3*, 73-86.

Dryfoos, J. (2000, September). *Evaluation of community schools: Findings to date*. Washington, DC: Coalition for Community Schools. Available: www.communityschools.org

Education and Human Services Consortium. (1991). *What it takes: Structuring interagency partnerships to connect children and families with comprehensive services*. Washington, DC: Author.

Epstein, J. L. (1991). *Effects on student achievement of teacher practices of parent involvement*. In S. Silvern (Ed.), *Advances in reading/language research,* Vol. 5: *Literacy through family, community, and school interaction*. Greenwich, CT: JAI.

Epstein, J. L. (1992). *School and family partnerships*. In M. Alkin (Ed.), *Encyclopedia of educational research* (pp. 1139-1151). New York: Macmillan.

Epstein, J. L. (1996). *Perspectives and previews on research and policy for school, family, and community partnerships*. In A. Booth & J. F. Dunn (Eds.), *Family-school links: How do they affect educational outcomes?* (pp. 209-246). Mahwah, NJ: Lawrence Erlbaum.

Fox, J. A., Flynn, E. A., Newman, S., & Christeson, W. (2000). *Fight Crime and Invest in Kids: America's after-school choice—The prime time for juvenile crime*. Washington, DC: Fight Crime and Invest in Kids.

Gardner, J. (1990). *On leadership*. New York: Free Press.

Hansel, L. (2001). *Unlocking the nine components of CSRD*. Washington, DC: National Clearinghouse for Comprehensive School Reform. Available: www.goodschools.gwu.edu/pubs/ar2000.htm

Harkavy, I. (2000, June). *Governance and the community: Higher education–school connection*. Paper delivered at the conference, "The Learning Connection: New Partnerships Between Schools and Colleges," Kansas City, MO.

Henderson, A. T., & Berla, N. (Eds.). (1994). *A new generation of evidence: The family is critical to student achievement*. Washington, DC: National Committee for Citizens in Education.

Hurwitz, N., & Hurwitz, S. (2000). Student-friendly care: The case for school-based health centers. *American School Board Journal*. [Online]. Available: www.healthinschools.org/sbhcs/papers/hurwitz.asp

Institute for Educational Leadership. (2000). *Reinventing the principalship* (Leadership for Student Learning series). Washington, DC: Author.

Institute for Education and Social Policy. (2001). *Mapping the field of organizing for school improvement.* New York: Author.

Jehl, J., Blank, M., & McCloud, B. (2001). *Education and community building: Connecting two worlds.* Washington, DC: Institute for Educational Leadership.

Johnson, D., & Walker, T. (1991). *Final report of an evaluation of the Avance Parent Education and Family Support Program* (submitted to the Carnegie Corporation). San Antonio, TX: Avance.

Kann, L., Collins, J. L., Pateman, B. C., Small, M. L., Russ, J. G., & Kolbe, L. J. (1995). The School Health Policies and Program Study (SHPPS): Rationale for a nationwide status report on school health programs. *Journal of School Health, 65,* 291-293.

Lareau, A. (1987). Social class differences in family-school relationships: The importance of cultural capital. *Sociology of Education, 60,* 73-85.

Learning First Alliance. (2001). *Every child learning.* Washington, DC: Author.

Leler, H. (1983). Parent education and involvement in relation to the schools and to parents of school-aged children. In R. Haskins & D. Adams (Eds.), *Parent education and public policy.* Norwood, NJ: Ablex.

Lieberman, G. A., & Hoody, L. L. (1998). *Closing the achievement gap: Using the environment as an integrating context for learning.* San Diego: State Education and Environment Roundtable.

Malone, M., Nathan, J., & Sedio, D. (1993). *Facts, figures, and faces: A look at Minnesota's school choice programs.* Minneapolis: University of Minnesota, Center for School Change and Other School Reform Issues. Available: www.hhh.umn.edu/centers/school-change/reform.htm

Manley, F., Reed, B., & Burns, R. (1960). *Community schools in action: The Flint Program.* Chicago: University of Chicago Press.

Manno, B., Finn, C., Jr., Bierlein, L., & Vanourek, G. (1998, Spring). Charter schools: Accomplishments and dilemmas. *Teacher's College Record.* Available: www.tcrecord.org

Melaville, A. (1998). *Learning together: The developing field of school-community initiatives.* Washington, DC: Charles Stewart Mott Foundation.

Melnick, S., & Fiene, R. (1990, April). *Assessing parents' attitudes towards school effectiveness.* Paper presented at the meeting of the American Educational Research Association, Boston.

MetLife Survey of the American Teacher. (2000). *Are we preparing students for the 21st century?* New York: Harris Interactive.

National Association of Elementary School Principals. (2001). *Principals and after-school programs: A survey of pre-K–8 principals.* Alexandria, VA: Belden, Russonello, & Stewart.

National Association of Secondary School Principals. (2001). *Priorities and barriers in high school leadership: A survey of principals.* Washington, DC: Author.

National Commission on Excellence in Education. (1983). *A nation at risk: The imperative for education reform* (report to the nation and the secretary of education). [Online]. Available: www.ed.gov/pubs/natatrisk/index.html

National Community Education Association. (2001). General information. [Online]. Available: www.ncea.com

National Education Association. (2000). *Charter schools overview.* [Online]. Available: www.nea.org/issues/charter

National Research Council and Institute of Medicine. (2002). *Community programs to promote youth development* (Committee on Community Level Programs for Youth, J. Eccles & J. A. Gootman, Eds., Board of Children, Youth, and Families, Division of Behavioral and Social Sciences and Education). Washington, DC: National Academy Press.

Pardini, P. (2001, August). School-community partnering. *The School Administrator*. [Online]. (Arlington, VA: American Association of School Administrators) Available: www.aasa.org/publications/sa/2001_08/pardini1.htm

Pittman, K. (1999, September). The power of engagement. *Youth Today*, p. 63. Available: www.forumforyouthinvestment.org/yt-powerengage.htm

Public Agenda. (2001). *Just waiting to be asked: A fresh look at attitudes on public engagement*. New York: Author. Available: www.publicagenda.org/specials/pubengage/pubengage.htm

RAND Corporation. (2001). *What do we know about vouchers and charter schools?* [Online]. Available: www.rand.org/publications/rb/rb8018

Reynolds, A. J., Temple, J. A., Robertson, D. L., & Mann, E. (2001). Long-term effects of an early childhood intervention on educational achievement and juvenile arrest: A 15-year follow-up of low-income children in public schools. *Journal of the American Medical Association, 285*, 2339-2346.

Roper Starch Worldwide. (2000). *Public opinion poll: Public attitudes toward education and service-learning* (prepared for the Academy of Educational Development and the Learning In Deed Initiative, sponsored by the W. K. Kellogg Foundation and the Ewing Marion Kauffman Foundation). [Online]. Available: www.learningindeed.org/tools/other/roper.pdf

Safe Schools/Healthy Students. (2000). General information. [Online]. Available: www.sshsac.org

Savner, S., & Greenberg, M. (2001, November). *Comments to the U.S. Department of Health and Human Services regarding the reauthorization of the Temporary Assistance for Needy Families (TANF) block grant*. Washington, DC: Center for Law and Social Policy. Available: www.clasp.org/pubs/tanf/tanf%20comments%201101.pdf

Scales, P. C. (1999, January). Does service-learning make a difference? *Source*, p. 1. (Minneapolis, MN: Search Institute)

Schinke, S. P., Cole, K. C., & Roulin, S. R. (2000). Summary of enhancing the educational achievement of at-risk youth. *Prevention Science, 1*, 51-60.

School Choices. (1998). *School vouchers: Issues and arguments*. [Online]. Available: www.schoolchoices.org/roo/vouchers.htm

Senge, P. (1990). *The fifth discipline: The art and practice of the learning organization*. New York: Doubleday Currency.

Shaffer, B. (1993). *Service-learning: An academic methodology*. Stanford, CA: Stanford University, Department of Education.

Small, M. L., Maher, L. S., Allensworth, D. D., Farquhar, B. K., Kann, L., & Pateman, B. C. (1995). School health services. *Journal of School Health, 65*, 319-325.

Snow, C. E., Barnes, W. S., Chandler, J., Goodman, I. F., & Hemphill, L. (1991). *Unfilled expectations: Home and school influences on literacy*. Cambridge, MA: Harvard University Press.

Stevenson, D. L., & Baker, D. P. (1987). The family-school relation and the child's school performance. *Child Development, 58*, 1348-1357.

Symons, C. W. (1997). Bridging student health risks and academic achievement through comprehensive school health programs. *Journal of School Health, 67*, 224.

Task Force on Education of Young Adolescents. (1989). *Turning points: Preparing America's youth for the 21st century*. Washington, DC: Carnegie Council on Adolescent Development.

Tierney, J., Grossman, J. B., & Resch, N. (1995). *Making a difference: An impact study of the Big Brothers/Big Sisters*. Philadelphia: Public/Private Ventures.

U.S. Census Bureau. (1980). General data. [Online]. Available: www.census.gov

U.S. Census Bureau. (2000). General data. [Online]. Available: www.census.gov/dmd/www/2khome.htm

U.S. Department of Education. (1998). *Safe and smart: Making the after-school hours work for kids.* Washington, DC: Author.

U.S. Department of Education. (2000). *After-school programs: Keeping children safe and smart.* Washington, DC: Author.

U.S. Department of Education. (2001). *21st Century Community Learning Centers.* [Online]. Available: www.ed.gov/21stcclc

U.S. Department of Health and Human Services and U.S. Department of Education. (2000). *Promoting better health for young people through physical activity and sports: A report to the president from the Secretary of Health and Human Services and the Secretary of Education.* [Online]. Available: www.cdc.gov/nccdphp/dash/presphysactrpt

Vandell, D., & Posner, J. (1999). After school activities and the development of low-income urban children. *Developmental Psychology, 35,* 868-879.

Section III

STRENGTHENING POLICIES AND PROGRAMS

The Role of Federal and State Governments in Child and Family Issues: An Analysis of Three Policy Areas

Jeffrey Capizzano
Matthew Stagner

Over the past decade, federal reforms to child and family policy have been driven by the prevailing belief that the substantive goals of these policies could be met better through a redistribution of policymaking authority between the federal government and the states. The Personal Responsibility and Work Opportunity Reconciliation Act of 1996 (PRWORA) (Public Law 104-193) and the Adoption and Safe Families Act of 1997 (ASFA) (Public Law 105-89) were two such reforms that significantly reconfigured the relationship between the federal and state governments. While many of the changes resulting from these reforms came in the form of devolution—a shifting of policymaking responsibility from the federal government to the states—other

changes worked to increase the level of federal oversight. The result has been a new role for states in determining the scope and direction of policies relating to children and families that is defined by a complicated array of federal policies, regulations, and incentives.

In this chapter, we develop a simple conceptual framework that identifies the parameters that define the role of the federal government and states in child and family issues. We identify key fiscal, statutory, and regulatory elements affecting the role of states, and we examine how changes in federal child and family policy have affected these elements. Specifically, we apply the framework to three areas of child and family policy—cash assistance, child care, and child welfare—in an effort to understand how PRWORA and ASFA have affected the role of state governments in these policy areas. In addition, to understand how these federal reforms have affected state policy-making behavior, we analyze policy trends in these areas. We use data and findings from two large national studies—the Urban Institute's Assessing the New Federalism Project[1] and the State Policy Documentation Project[2]—to discuss state trends in these issue areas.

CONCEPTUAL FRAMEWORK

A number of factors define how authority over a policy area is divided between the federal government and the states. For the purpose of this chapter, we focus on four factors that affect the extent to which state governments can exercise control over a policy area. These are the following:

- The *funding mechanism* used to allocate money to the states
- The *level of federal funding* for a policy area
- The *policies and regulations* governing how the money is spent
- Other *federal policies or incentives* that influence state behavior that are not specifically associated with how the money is spent

In what follows, we describe each of these elements in more detail. It is important to note, however, that while we look at these factors separately, they most often work in conjunction with one another to affect the level of state discretion in a policy area. A change in the way the federal government allocates money to states, for example, will often come with a new set of policies and regulations governing how the money is spent. Therefore, one must consider the interaction of these different elements when measuring their effect on the level of state discretion in

a policy area. Nonetheless, we find this distinction among factors useful in describing changes to the role of states in child and family policy resulting from PRWORA and ASFA.

Funding Mechanism Used to Allocate Money to the States

The means by which federal funding is allocated to states can dramatically affect state discretion in a given policy area. While the federal government uses a number of different funding mechanisms to allocate money to states (see, e.g., Break, 1980), two have been particularly important in child and family policy: the *matching grant* and the *block grant.*

Under the matching grant funding mechanism, the federal government and states share the costs of a program, with states contributing funds so as to "draw down" (i.e., gain access to) a federal match. These matching grants may be open-ended, with no theoretical limit to the amount of federal expenditure (if the state documents the need and expends its portion of the match), or they may be capped, allowing states to draw only up to a certain amount each year. Matching grants traditionally fund well-defined governmental initiatives with joint national and state interests (Break, 1980).

Block grants, on the other hand, are a fixed annual allocation of money to states that may or may not depend on a state contribution. Block grants have been used to promote national interests in more broadly defined functional areas such as "community development" and "employment and training" (Break, 1980). These grants have generally come about by combining closely related categorical grants so as to provide state governments with more freedom in how they use federal funds.

These different methods of federal funding have implications for the amount of state control over a program. For example, because matching grants are used to promote a well-defined goal, there is generally less discretion in how the funding can be used. However, when funding is intended to cover a broader functional area (as with a block grant), the federal goals are often less specific than those of a matching grant. Therefore, with a block grant, states tend to have more discretion in how to allocate money and more flexibility to determine which goals are most important to pursue.

Level of Federal Funding

The relationship between the size of a federal allocation and the amount of state discretion is straightforward. An increased level of federal funding, all else being equal, can increase the scope and/or depth of state efforts in a given policy area. As such, changes to the level of federal funding can have a profound effect on the state role. This can be especially true when changes in federal policy work to devolve to the states the authority for issues relating to children and families. From a state's perspective, devolution often means new policymaking and administrative responsibilities, which can mean an increased financial burden. Adequate federal funding, therefore, is essential in periods of devolutions if states are to play a more involved policy role.

The Policies and Regulations Governing How the Money Is Spent

Federal funding, regardless of the funding mechanism or funding level, comes with conditions on how the money can be spent (Stenberg, 1989). These conditions come in many forms—from financial reporting requirements and audits to more specific policies designed to limit the populations served or the types of services that can be provided. For example, federal funding for the Medicaid program comes with limitations

on the categories of individuals who can be covered by the program. States are required by the federal government to cover certain populations (e.g., children under 6 years of age, pregnant women below 133% of the poverty level) and are prohibited from serving others (e.g., nondisabled childless adults). The extent and types of these conditions placed on states by the federal government affect the extent of the state role in a given policy area.

Other Conditions or Incentives Placed on States

Finally, federal legislation may impose other mandates or offer incentives to influence state behavior more broadly. These constraints or incentives are not directly tied to how a particular federal funding stream operates, but they affect state behavior nonetheless. Federal legislation may mandate broad conditions for how state policy and practice operate. It also may offer incentives such as financial "bonuses" if the state invokes policies that meet national goals. For example, as we discuss later in this chapter, PRWORA mandates that states have a certain percentage of nonexempt Temporary Assistance for Needy Families (TANF) recipients in work activities each year and also provides bonuses to "high-performing" states. Neither of these federal policies *directly* affects how TANF money is spent, but the policies can significantly influence how states run their TANF programs.

THE CONCEPTUAL FRAMEWORK APPLIED: THREE AREAS OF CHILD AND FAMILY POLICY

The conceptual framework just discussed attempts to define elements of the federal-state relationship that affect the extent to which states can exercise discretion in child and family issues. In this section, we apply this conceptual framework to changes made to federal policy by PRWORA and ASFA. We investigate how these reforms have affected the state role in three major areas of child and family policy: cash assistance, child care, and child welfare. We examine how federal reforms have changed state administration of these policies (for a summary, see Table 11.1) and then discuss recent state trends in these areas.

Cash Assistance Policy

Aid to Families With Dependent Children (AFDC) was the primary cash assistance program for low-income families in the United States from 1935 to 1996. The program, established by the Social Security Act of 1935, assisted states in providing financial support to low-income families with children who were financially needy due to the death, incapacity, or absence of one or both parents.[3] The primary purpose of the program was to encourage the care of needy children in their own homes as well as to strengthen family life and promote family "self-support." To meet these goals, states provided eligible children and their caretakers with monthly cash benefits, based on the size of the family, as well as access to other social services.[4]

In 1996, the AFDC program was repealed by PRWORA and replaced with the TANF program. TANF has governed cash assistance to poor families since July 1, 1997 (earlier in some states), and was scheduled for reauthorization in 2002. Unlike AFDC, TANF offers time-limited cash assistance to low-income families that is conditioned on the parents' participation in work or a work-related activity.[5] The goals of the TANF program are different from those of the AFDC program. Specifically, the goals of TANF are (a) to aid needy families so that children can be cared for in their homes or those of relatives; (b) to end dependence of needy parents on government benefits by promoting job

preparation, work, and marriage; (c) to prevent and reduce out-of-wedlock pregnancies and establish goals for preventing and reducing their incidence; and (d) to encourage the formation of two-parent families. To meet these goals, the TANF program limits cash assistance benefits to 60 months over a recipient's lifetime, requires employable adults to work after 24 months of receiving assistance, mandates that states maintain minimum work participation rates, and rewards states for reducing out-of-wedlock birthrates.

The change from AFDC to TANF dramatically altered the statutory framework governing the relationship between the federal government and the states in the administration of cash assistance. In what follows, we describe the changes in the funding mechanism, level of funding, and policies governing state behavior.

Funding Mechanism Used to Allocate Money to States. One of the most visible reforms to the cash assistance system was the change in the mechanism by which the federal government provided states with funding. AFDC was a matching grant program in which the federal government shared with the states the cost of every dollar spent on needy families. More important, access to AFDC benefits was a federal entitlement for individuals, which meant that all eligible families were guaranteed cash assistance if they applied. As more eligible recipients joined the program, the state and federal governments shared the cost of monthly benefits. The federal contribution depended on a number of state characteristics but generally ranged from 50% to 75% of the states' cost for the program in 1996 (U.S. House of Representatives, 1998). The matching grant structure reduced states' incentive to limit welfare expenditures because every state dollar spent on cash assistance was matched with at least one federal dollar (Chernick & Reschovsky, 1996).

Table 11.1 Major Changes to Cash Assistance, Child Care, and Child Welfare Resulting From PRWORA and ASFA

	Federal Funding Mechanism	Level of Funding	Conditions Under Which the Federal Funding Must Be Spent	Other Conditions/ Incentives Imposed on States
TANF	The funding mechanism was changed from a matching grant to a block grant.	Federal funding was to remain consistent with recent state spending on AFDC, EA, and JOBS programs (about $16 billion per year). However, dropping TANF caseloads made block grant payments exceed what states would have received under the former matching grant.	The entitlement for cash assistance was ended. States were allowed to set their own income eligibility limits, and a number of specific federal eligibility restrictions and rules on how earnings affect the cash grant were eliminated. TANF funds were allowed to be spent on a broad range of social services. It was mandated that TANF recipients be in a work activity no later than 24 months after receiving benefits. TANF benefits were limited to 60 months. States were allowed to set time limits shorter than 60 months.	States must have a work participation rate of 25% in the first year (1997), rising 5% each year to 50% in 2002. The hours that a client must participate also increased during this time. High-performance bonuses were offered to states that meet a number of key indicators of success.
Child care	Four separate child care funding streams—the AFDC Child Care program, the Transitional Child Care program, At-Risk Child Care, and the Child Care and Development Block Grant—were consolidated into the Child Care and Development Fund.	Federal funding was increased dramatically, from approximately $2.1 billion in 1995 to $3.6 billion in 2000.	Child care entitlement was ended for families on welfare and families transitioning off of welfare. It was required that 70% of CCDF mandatory and matching funds be used for TANF recipients, transitional recipients, and "at-risk" recipients.	TANF work requirements create an incentive for states to fund TANF recipients over other low-income families. A state cannot reduce or terminate a TANF grant if a recipient cannot participate in a required activity due to a lack of adequate child care.

(Continued)

Table 11.1 Continued

	Federal Funding Mechanism	Level of Funding	Conditions Under Which the Federal Funding Must Be Spent	Other Conditions/ Incentives Imposed on States
			It was required that 4% of CCDF funds go to quality improvements.	Child care has recently been incorporated into the federal government's measure of "high performance."
			It limited to no more than 5% the amount of CCDF funding that can be used for administrative purposes.	
			CCDF money cannot be used for families that exceed 85% of the state's median income.	
			CCDF money cannot be used for children over 12 years of age except for special circumstances.	
Child welfare	Financing for child welfare comes through nearly 40 separate programs, including both block grants and open-ended matching grants. Some of these funding streams include Title IV-B (capped matching grant) and Title IV-E (open-ended matching grant), the Social Services Block Grant (capped block grant), and Medicaid (open-ended matching grant).	Total federal funding for child welfare services across all forms of funding was $14.4 billion in 1996. ASFA did not significantly change federal funding for child welfare.	Title IV-E funding supports out-of-home placements and adoption assistance. Federal support for preventive and in-home services was limited.	The need for states to reduce the time that children spend in foster care was reemphasized, forcing states to hold timely permanency hearings. Incentive funds for states were provided to increase adoptions out of foster care. States were allowed to quickly terminate the rights of parents to retain their children under extreme circumstances.

NOTE: PRWORA = Personal Responsibility and Work Opportunity Reconciliation Act of 1996; ASFA = Adoption and Safe Families Act of 1997; TANF = Temporary Assistance for Needy Families; AFDC = Aid to Families With Dependent Children; EA = Emergency Assistance; JOBS = Job Opportunities and Basic Skills; CCDF = Child Care and Development Fund.

Under TANF, the matching grant system was changed to a block grant that combined federal funding for the AFDC program, Job Opportunities and Basic Skills (JOBS) program, and Emergency Assistance[6] (EA). The block grant entitles states to a lump-sum payment that is based on recent spending patterns on these programs. This change ended the open-ended nature of federal funding for AFDC but provided states with more flexibility in designing their own welfare programs.

Level of Federal Funding. Federal lawmakers who created PRWORA intended to fund cash assistance through the TANF block grant at levels consistent with recent spending patterns for the AFDC, EA, and JOBS programs. The level of the federal TANF grant for each state was determined according to the highest of the following federal expenditures: (a) the average federal payment for the state for AFDC, EA, and JOBS between fiscal years (FYs) 1992 and 1994; (b) the federal payment for these programs in FY 1994; or (c) the estimated federal payment in 1995. Most states based their TANF funding on their 1994 expenditures. Annual federal TANF expenditures were then fixed at levels that were to remain constant through FY 2002. A total of 20 states, however, received authorization for modest growth in the TANF block grant (2.5% per year) through 2002 (Powers, 1999).

The block grant structure of TANF and the level of funding associated with it have turned out to be a windfall for the states. Cash assistance caseloads dropped rapidly in most states during the late 1990s as the economy expanded and welfare reform made the receipt of cash assistance less appealing. A majority of states received a TANF block grant payment that exceeded what they would have received as the matching payment under AFDC. A total of 45 states shared a funding windfall in 1997, and this has continued with rapid caseload decline (Powers,

1999). However, while the change to a block grant has initially meant a windfall in TANF funding for states, the fixed amount of the block grant will also mean fixed, rather than increased, federal funding as caseloads begin to rise, as they did in many states in 2001.

The Policies and Regulations Governing How the Money Is Spent. PRWORA fundamentally changed the conditions governing how states could spend federal funds for their welfare programs. These changes pertained to most aspects of welfare, including who is eligible for benefits, how long recipients are eligible, and the conditions for receiving a cash grant. In general, the changes made by the legislation gave states more discretion over their welfare programs. However, PRWORA also imposed a number of conditions on states regarding how welfare programs could be operated, such as limiting the length of time recipients can receive federally funded benefits.

PRWORA made a number of changes regarding who is eligible for cash assistance. First, it ended the entitlement for cash assistance. Prior to welfare reform, states were required to provide assistance to all families that met the eligibility criteria for the AFDC program established under federal and state policies. PRWORA repealed this entitlement provision, ending the federal guarantee to a cash benefit. States, therefore, have the option to set criteria for assistance within federal parameters so long as they have "objective criteria for delivery of benefits and determining eligibility."

PRWORA also dispensed with a number of specific income-related eligibility rules regarding the receipt of benefits, including eligibility restrictions on two-parent families and rules governing the manner in which earnings affect the cash grant. Under AFDC, for example, families receiving assistance were not allowed to possess more than $1,000 in countable income. While certain items were excluded from this calculation (e.g., the value of a car up to $1,500), recipients were not allowed to accumulate savings as a result of these conditions. PRWORA does not include provisions regarding asset limits, allowing states the freedom to set their own asset rules.

In addition, the earnings of AFDC recipients entering employment were subject to complex federal rules concerning how they would affect benefit levels. The federal government allowed a certain portion of earnings to be "disregarded." After the disregards were calculated, the remaining countable income resulted in a dollar reduction in the family's AFDC grant for each dollar of earned income. PRWORA allows states to set their own income eligibility limits and to make their own rules governing the treatment of earnings and other income.

PRWORA also eliminated additional eligibility restrictions placed on two-parent families. Prior to welfare reform, two-parent families were subject to a number of federal regulations, including that the principal wage earner could work no more than 100 hours per month. PRWORA eliminated the federal eligibility requirements on two-parent families, leaving the eligibility rules up to the states.

Finally, and perhaps most important for the broader field of child and family services, TANF funds can be spent on a wide range of supportive services for families not limited to cash assistance. PRWORA allows states to transfer TANF funds to other social services areas, such as the Child Care and Development Fund (CCDF) and the Social Services Block Grant as well as to use TANF funds directly on services for families that will accomplish TANF's goals.

While many provisions of PRWORA increase the discretion of states, there are also provisions that restrict state behavior. PRWORA contains a "federal work trigger" mandating that TANF recipients be in a work activity no later than 24 months after receiving benefits. In addition, while there were no time limits on benefits under the AFDC program, PRWORA precludes the use of federal funds to provide benefits for more than 60 cumulative months. States, however, are free to set their time limits to a period shorter than 60 months.

Other Conditions or Incentives Placed on States. PRWORA imposed a number of conditions on states and offered incentives that were not tied to how the TANF grant was spent. Prior to welfare reform, the federal government mandated that states have 15% of their nonexempt caseload in JOBS activities for at least 20 hours per week. Under PRWORA, a state's work participation rate was set at 25% for 1997, rising 5% each year to 50% in 2002. Similarly, the hours that TANF clients were expected to participate in work activities were also mandated to increase over that time. Failing to meet the work participation rate would result in a 5% reduction in the TANF block grant. The federal government also defines the types of activities that count toward the state's participation rate.

In an attempt to influence state behavior, PRWORA also offered a bonus to states that excel in meeting specific goals of the federal policy. One such bonus awards "high-performing" states that respond to a number of key indicators of success that are determined by the federal government with input from the states. Another bonus rewards states that reduce their rates of out-of-wedlock births while not increasing their rates of abortions. Such incentives help the federal government to continue influencing state agendas.

State Trends in Cash Assistance. The new TANF block grant, the effective increase in TANF funding, and the new conditions under which TANF funds can be spent allowed states to exercise discretion in areas of cash assistance policy not allowed under the AFDC program. While PRWORA did set strict guidelines concerning work requirements and the length of time families could stay on welfare, states now can determine the overall focus of their state welfare programs. States determine under what conditions a recipient is eligible for the TANF program, when a client should begin work (within the 24-month work trigger), time limits for cash assistance (within the 60-month federal limit), exemptions from the work requirement, and sanctions for noncompliance.

Not surprisingly, states have embraced the opportunity to reform their welfare programs with a variety of approaches, dealing with the major program components in different ways. In the following subsections, we discuss state trends in a number of major TANF program areas.

Diversion programs: Since welfare reform, states have developed what are called "formal diversion" policies to keep families in need of only short-term assistance off the welfare rolls.[7] Under these programs, states offer a one-time lump-sum payment to clients in lieu of a monthly TANF benefit. This payment is generally provided to alleviate a short-term problem that, if corrected, would help clients to remain self-sufficient or help them to achieve self-sufficiency. Families accepting these payments are generally restricted from applying for monthly TANF benefits for some period of time after the payments.

States vary enormously in their formal diversion policies. As of July 1999, nearly half of the states (22) offered formal diversion payments (Rowe, 2000). Among the states with diversion policies, most offered between 2 and 4 months of a TANF cash grant as a lump-sum payment. This payment could be in the form of cash to the recipient or could be given directly to the vendor in need of the payment (e.g., landlord, mechanic). Most states put very strict limits on how often a recipient is allowed to receive a diversion payment, but there is state variation. A number of states allow for one cash payment per year, while others allow for one cash payment per lifetime. At least one state—Nevada—allows diversion payments as often as they are needed.

Time limit policies: Because PRWORA eliminated the entitlement for welfare recipients, states may now limit the number of months that a TANF recipient is eligible for benefits. While the federal government imposed a 60-month lifetime limit, some states have made their lifetime limits shorter.[8] States also have passed periodic limits, limiting the number of consecutive months that a family can receive assistance or the total number of months that a client can receive assistance during a given period. As of July 1999, seven states (Arkansas, Connecticut, Florida, Georgia, Idaho, Indiana and Utah) had lifetime limits on assistance that were shorter than the federally mandated limit of 60 months (Rowe, 2000).[9] These shorter limits ranged from 21 months (Connecticut) to 48 months (Florida and Georgia).

In addition, at least 15 states imposed periodic time limits on benefits (Rowe, 2000), which can play a role at least as great as lifetime limits in restricting TANF eligibility. There are at least two ways in which these limits are implemented. First, states may allow recipients to receive assistance for a certain number of months followed by a period of ineligibility. For example, Delaware, while having a 5-year (60-month) *lifetime* limit, allows TANF recipients to receive assistance for only 4 years followed by 8 years of ineligibility.[10] Another way in which states may implement periodic limits is by allowing recipients to receive assistance only for a certain number of months during a given time period. Many states, for example, allow recipients to receive 24 months of assistance within a 60-month period. However, there is a lot of variation across states. South Carolina, for example, only allows 2 years of TANF benefits during a 10-year period.

Behavioral conditions for the receipt of benefits: During the years leading up to welfare reform, states had begun requesting waivers from the federal government to impose behavioral requirements as a condition of welfare benefit receipt (see, e.g., Savner & Greenberg, 1995). While the most common and well-known requirement was the work requirement, there were others that states also imposed. These included requiring that children of recipients attend school or maintain a certain grade point average, that children of recipients be immunized, and requiring that children be given health screenings. Welfare reform dispensed with the need for states to request waivers for such purposes, and currently there are a number of states that have behavioral requirements in place.

As of July 1999, 34 states required that the dependent children of TANF recipients achieve some minimum level of school performance (Rowe, 2000). These requirements could be as simple as an adequate level of school attendance or more difficult requirements such as a minimum grade point average. In addition, 26 states required that the children of recipients be immunized as a condition for receiving benefits (Rowe, 2000). Finally, 6 states required that TANF recipients either obtain health information or actually obtain regular checkups as a condition for benefits (Rowe, 2000).

Work requirements and exemptions: While the federal government requires that TANF recipients perform some type of work-related activity after 24 months of being on assistance, many states require that recipients work sooner than 24 months. However, states may exempt certain types of recipi-ents, such as those who are caring for young children or for ill or disabled family members, from participating in work-related activities.

As of July 1999, most states (32) required immediate participation in a work-related activity (Rowe, 2000). However, more than 30 states exempted recipients who were ill or incapacitated or who were caring for others who were ill or incapacitated. Most states also allowed recipients with very young children to be exempt from the work requirements. Only 6 states did *not* have a youngest child exemption in 1999 (Rowe, 2000). Most states exempted recipients with children ranging in age from 12 weeks to 36 months.

Innovative use of TANF funds: As mentioned earlier, PRWORA allows states to transfer TANF funds to other social service areas and also allows TANF funds to be spent directly on services for families. States have taken advantage of the opportunity to use these funds in innovative ways. One trend across states is to use TANF funds for families that are not traditionally served by the welfare system. For example, Denver, Colorado, uses TANF funds for a diversion program called Working Family Assistance, which provides cash assistance and supportive services such as transportation, child care, and housing to non-TANF-eligible families (Capizzano, Koralek, Botsko, & Bess, 2001).[11] In addition, Wisconsin uses TANF funds for the state's new Workforce Attachment and Advancement Program, which provides grants to local Workforce Development Boards to assist adults with incomes below 200% of the federal poverty level find and retain employment and advance into better paying jobs (Ehrle, Seefeldt, Snyder, & McMahon, 2001).[12]

States have also used TANF funds to expand services for TANF families, particularly those that are hard to serve. In Washington, TANF funds have been used to expand the number of service contractors providing services to TANF recipients. These contractors provide services such as adult basic education, employment retention services, job search, English as a second language, job skills training, preemployment training, and work experience (Thompson, Snyder, Malm, & O'Brien, 2001). In Minnesota, the state has contributed a portion of its TANF surplus to counties to address the needs and barriers of those recipients who are nearing the time limit on their TANF benefits (Tout, Martinson, Koralek, & Ehrle, 2001). The design of the services to help these clients is determined by each county.

Child Care Policy

Significant aspects of child care policy have historically fallen under the purview of state governments. For example, states have always established the income eligibility thresholds and copayment rates for child care assistance to low-income working families not associated with AFDC. States have also always determined the reimbursement rates to child care providers (i.e., the amount paid to the providers on behalf of the recipients). In addition, states have sole authority over the regulation of child care providers whereby they establish minimum standards of health and safety in child care settings. Many states have also made large investments, supplemented with local funds, to fund state prekindergarten initiatives that provide early education opportunities to young disadvantaged children.

PRWORA further expanded the role of state governments in child care policymaking. The increased focus of moving welfare recipients into work or work-related activities made child care the cornerstone of federal reform efforts, placing a significant demand on state child care subsidy systems. In response to these new demands, PRWORA changed the way in which federal funding was delivered to the states, increasing federal funds and giving states much more flexibility in how these funds could be used.

Federal Funding Mechanism Used to Allocate Money to States. The way in which the federal government allocated child care funding to the states changed significantly as a result of welfare reform. Prior to PRWORA, four separate federal child care programs assisted low-income families with child care payments. Three of the programs—AFDC Child Care, Transitional Child Care, and At-Risk Child Care—existed under Title IV-A of the Social Security Act and were associated with AFDC. The fourth child care program—the Child Care and Development Block Grant (CCDBG)—was created in 1990 to provide child care assistance to low-income working families.

Each funding stream existed to serve a specific low-income population. AFDC Child Care and Transitional Child Care were entitlement programs that guaranteed assistance to AFDC recipients who were working or in work-related activities and former AFDC recipients who had left within the past year. At-Risk Child Care was not a federal entitlement program, instead providing states a capped amount to serve the child care needs of working families "at risk" for becoming eligible for AFDC if these needs were not met. Like At-Risk Child Care, CCDBG was not a federal entitlement program, providing assistance to low-income families outside the reach of the welfare system.

This method of funding low-income child care was criticized for creating gaps in child care assistance as the low-income population moved from one category to the other (U.S. General Accounting Office, 1994). These gaps were created because programs differed in the categories of participants who could be served, the types of activities for which child care could be used, income thresholds for eligibility, and the length of time that clients could receive assistance. As low-income families moved from one population to another—AFDC recipient to transitional recipient to low-income family at risk—states found it difficult to avoid gaps in child care funding.

PRWORA consolidated the four distinct child care funding streams into the CCDF. The fund has three different components: mandatory, matching, and discretionary funds. Each state is entitled to mandatory funds, which are allocated based on a state's historical spending on child care. Mandatory allocations are based on the higher of the state's FY 1994, FY 1995, or average FY 1992-1994 federal Title IV-A child care funding (AFDC Child Care, Transitional Child Care, and At-Risk Child Care). In addition to the mandatory funds, states may also draw down matching funds if their spending exceeds their historical levels. Finally, states may also receive discretionary funds, which are subject to annual congressional appropriations. These funds are distributed to states according to a federal formula and do not require a state match.

Level of Federal Funding. Federal funding for child care increased dramatically as a result of welfare reform. In FY 1995, the year before PRWORA passed, federal spending for the four child care programs totaled approximately $2.1 billion. Entitlement

spending for AFDC Child Care and Transitional Child Care equaled approximately $893 million, while At-Risk Child Care and CCDBG were capped at $300 million and $935 million, respectively. In 2000, $2.4 billion was authorized in matching and mandatory programs, and another $1.2 billion was authorized in discretionary funding, under the CCDF. The total—$3.6 billion—marks a dramatic increase in federal funding over the $2.1 billion in 1995.

In addition to the increased federal spending, changes to federal law allow states to spend TANF funds directly on child care or to transfer up to 30% of their TANF block grant to the CCDF. This provision gave states substantial discretion over the amount they wished to spend on child care and could substantially increase their level of child care funding. This provision has become a major source of child care funding for states. In FY 2000, the amount of TANF money spent on child care was larger than the entire CCDF budget—$3.9 billion compared with $3.6 billion—giving a strong indication of the importance that states placed on child care funding (Schumacher, Greenberg, & Duffy, 2001).

The Policies and Regulations Governing How the Money Is Spent. State discretion over child care increased with the consolidation of the four child care funding streams, the significant increase in child care funding, and the opportunity to transfer funds from the TANF block grant to the CCDF. However, perhaps the single largest change to child care policy was the end of the child care entitlement for welfare recipients and families transitioning off of welfare. In other words, states no longer have to guarantee child care assistance to TANF recipients or former TANF recipients. While states always had broad discretion over which low-income working poor families could be eligible for CCDBG funding, this change now gave states similar discretion over TANF and transitional families.

Despite this discretion, a number of federal rules still place restrictions on who can be served using federal dollars and how the money can be spent. For example, federal law is specific about the portion of CCDF money that is to be spent on different populations and initiatives. According to federal law, 70% of the CCDF mandatory and matching funds must be used to meet the child care needs of TANF recipients, transitional TANF recipients, and at-risk recipients; 4% must go to quality improvements; and no more than 5% can be used for administrative purposes.

In addition to these broad guidelines on how the CCDF money should be spent, federal law also has specific guidelines governing who can be eligible for CCDF funds. While states do not have to provide assistance to all families that are eligible under federal law, states cannot use federal money to provide assistance to families that fall outside of federal guidelines. For example, states cannot use federal funding to pay for child care for children over 12 years of age or for families that exceed 85% of the state's median income. Children also must be residing with parents to receive services. States, however, can forgo these guidelines in special circumstances such as for older children with mental or physical disabilities and for families that receive child protective services.

Despite these conditions, states are free to define a number of the terms associated with these regulations. For example, while they are required to spend at least 4% of the CCDF on quality enhancements, they are free to determine what these enhancements will be. In addition, while the federal government allows states to waive eligibility for "special needs" children, it also allows them to define "special needs" or "physical and mental incapacity."

Other Conditions or Incentives Placed on the States. Changes to federal child care policy under PRWORA were made within the context of a larger welfare reform effort. As such, a number of TANF-related rules affect state child care policymaking behavior. For example, the requirement that states place a certain percentage of TANF recipients in work-related activities creates an incentive to see that welfare recipients obtain child care subsidies. In those states that lack adequate resources to fund all low-income families that apply for care, this provision may create the incentive to see that welfare recipients receive child care subsidies prior to other low-income families.

In addition, federal law created a child care protection that prohibits states from reducing a TANF recipient's grant or terminating assistance if a family cannot participate in a required activity due to a lack of child care. Because states are held to strict work participation requirements by the federal government, this provision also creates an incentive to see that TANF families are provided with the means to find adequate child care.

Finally, the federal government has also recently incorporated a child care measure into its high-performance bonus (Mezey & Greenberg, 2001). Each year, the U.S. Department of Health and Human Services (DHHS) awards $200 million to states that do an exceptional job of meeting the goals of TANF. In 2001, DHHS allocated $10 million to reward 10 states for high performance in providing child care to low-income families.

State Trends in Child Care Assistance. Changes in the level of funding and in the regulations governing how money is spent have allowed states more flexibility in administering child care subsidies to low-income families. Prior to welfare reform, states had a limited number of opportunities to define who was eligible for these subsidies. Both AFDC recipients and transitional AFDC recipients were entitled to child care. The fact that child care subsidies are no longer an entitlement for these families means that states have more discretion in determining which low-income families receive child care assistance. In the following subsections, we highlight some of the major trends in state child care policymaking since the passage of welfare reform.

State guarantee of child care: Despite the fact that PRWORA eliminated the child care entitlement for welfare and transitional welfare families, many states continue to guarantee assistance for these families. For example, 35 states reported in their child care state plans that they provide a child care guarantee for TANF families (Parizek, Falk, & Spar, 1998). In addition, 27 states continue to guarantee child care assistance for families leaving welfare (State Policy Documentation Project, 2001).

Sharing the costs of child care: Many states now ask welfare recipients to share in the costs of child care. Under pre-TANF rules, AFDC recipients were not required to pay a copay for child care. Because changes to federal child care policy do not preclude states from invoking a copay, a number of states have decided to do so. Currently, 13 states now require TANF recipients to pay a copay for child care (State Policy Documentation Project, 2001).

Using TANF money for child care: Perhaps the greatest trend in state child care policymaking is the extent to which states have used TANF money to fund child care to significantly increase their level of funding. States have both spent TANF money directly on child care and exercised the option to transfer money from the TANF block grant to the CCDF. States have used this funding for a number of purposes, including funds for transitional child care, child care licensing, regulatory services, low-income families, and other services (Schumacher et al., 2001).

Child Welfare Policy

Child welfare policy is primarily determined at the state and local levels. State and local child welfare agencies investigate child abuse or neglect and provide services to children identified through those investigations. The federal role in child welfare has never been preeminent, although it has grown during the past quarter century. Federal programs now support crucial services and provide incentives for state actions.

Much of the federal involvement in child welfare flows from a concern during the late 20th century that children were "drifting" in state child welfare systems—unnecessarily entering care or remaining in care longer than was necessary. The first major shift in federal *funding* came in 1980 with the passage of the Adoption Assistance and Child Welfare Act (Public Law 96-272). This act focused states on taking "reasonable efforts" to prevent the placement of children and provided a separate Title of the Social Security Act (Title IV-E) to support the placement costs of poor children.

State child welfare systems saw tremendous increases in child welfare caseloads throughout the 1980s and 1990s despite increasing attention to reasonable efforts to prevent placement (U.S. House of Representatives, 1998). Federal legislative changes attempted to respond to this growth in caseloads and costs. In 1993, Congress created the Family Preservation and Support

Services Program as part of the Omnibus Reconciliation Act of 1993 (Public Law 103-66) to increase funding for placement prevention services. During the mid-1990s, federal matching grant entitlements to support children in foster care and adoption assistance led to proposals to shift to a block grant structure for the major federal child welfare funding streams. Despite this proposed shift toward the states, federal child welfare programs remained intact as cash assistance and child care funding was shifted to block grants. Then, during the late 1990s, the federal government asserted an even stronger role through ASFA. This law requires states to address the disposition of children more quickly and provides incentives to increase adoptions.

The Funding Mechanism Used to Allocate Money to the States. Federal child welfare financing comes to the states through nearly 40 separate programs, including a rich mixture of capped block grant programs and open-ended matching grant programs (Geen & Tumlin, 1999). The key federal programs that determine the shape and structure of state child welfare services are Titles IV-B and IV-E of the Social Security Act. Title IV-B provides a capped block grant for a wide range of preventive and supportive child welfare services. Part 1 of Title IV-B provides a discretionary block grant for prevention services. Part 2—renamed the "Promoting Safe and Stable Families" program in 1997—provides a capped entitlement grant to states for a range of family preservation and other services.

Title IV-E provides open-ended entitlement matching funds for costs related to the placement of children in out-of-home care and for adoption assistance. It is by far the largest federal program directly supporting state child welfare services. Its use is limited to support of the costs of out-of-home

placement and adoption assistance for poor children, with federal funds matching state expenditures at the same matching rate as the Medicaid program. As state child welfare caseloads rose during the 1980s and 1990s, this funding stream pumped billions of federal dollars into state child welfare systems each year. Originally, the program tied eligibility for children to state eligibility for AFDC. Following the creation of TANF, eligibility remained tied to AFDC eligibility standards in the states in 1996. While this maintains the federal commitment to supporting poor children, it creates an administrative burden for the states who must determine eligibility based on standards different from the new TANF programs.

A number of other federal funding streams support child welfare services. Most are capped block grant programs, such as the Social Services Block Grant (SSBG). Importantly, however, many states use Medicaid—a key open-ended entitlement program—to fund certain types of child welfare services. States' use of these programs varies greatly, with some states using Medicaid to fund a large percentage of child welfare services and other states using little. The use of these funding streams has broadened the effect of federal funding well beyond programs directly supporting child welfare such as Titles IV-B and IV-E.

Level of Federal Funding. Although federal funding within Titles IV-B and IV-E was somewhat balanced during the early 1980s, skyrocketing state foster care caseloads during the 1980s and 1990s led to large annual increases in IV-E spending, while IV-B spending remained capped. By the mid-1990s, IV-E funding to match states' costs for child placement dwarfed spending on other child welfare services. This imbalance was exacerbated by several factors. First, as noted previously, caseloads grew rapidly, and with the open-ended matching structure, growth in dollars followed growth in caseloads. Second, the costs of child placement are significantly higher than the costs of preventive or supportive services.

Total spending for child welfare across all states—including all forms of funding—exceeded $14.4 billion in 1996. Most of these dollars go to out-of-home care costs. In 1996, states relied heavily on federal Medicaid, EA, and SSBG funds to pay for child welfare services. States vary greatly in their financing practices. Federal funds accounted for 44%, state funds for 44%, and local sources for 12% (Geen & Waters Boots, 1999).

The Policies and Regulations Governing How the Money Is Spent. The key restriction on federal support for child welfare in the states is the limitation of Title IV-E to the support of out-of-home placement and adoption assistance. Many child welfare analysts have lamented the relative lack of federal funds for supportive and preventive services. Some have proposed that the open-ended nature of the IV-E creates an improper incentive to place children in care or to keep them in care once they are there.

During the 1990s, federal law began to allow "waivers" from the placement restriction to allow states to experiment with Title IV-E funds (Geen & Tumlin, 1999). If states agreed to rigorous evaluation, they were allowed to expand services funded under IV-E to other types of services such as substance abuse supports and supporting guardianship of children by kin. The expectation is that each waiver will be "cost neutral" to the federal government; that is, it will lead to the same federal funding rate as would have occurred if states had followed the IV-E restrictions. With an initial rush of waivers, states sought to expand IV-E to cover services such as substance abuse treatment for parents and new guardianship arrangements

for children. However, few waivers have been sought by states during the past 3 years, perhaps because of the federal requirement that states demonstrate, through rigorous evaluation, that waiver programs cost the same as did the previous programs.

Other Conditions or Incentives Placed on States. ASFA did not significantly alter federal funding for child welfare. Title IV-E funding remains intact. The act modified some of the purposes of Part 2 of Title IV-B in changes to the allowable expenditures and in renaming the program Promoting Safe and Stable Families.

Yet ASFA has had a dramatic influence on federal and state relations in child welfare. ASFA reasserted the federal role in several ways. It reemphasized the need for states to reduce the time that children spend in foster care, forcing states to hold permanency hearings for children spending 15 of any 21 months in care. It also provided incentive funds for states to increase adoptions out of foster care, and it allowed states to quickly terminate the rights of parents to retain their children under certain extreme circumstances. States followed federal incentives quickly, increasing adoptions and modifying their laws to adjust to the new permanency time frames.

Trends in Child Welfare Policy. Although child welfare clearly remains a state and local function, federal authority in the area was reasserted in key ways during the 1990s. ASFA significantly altered some aspects of state child welfare policy. Yet state and local child welfare agencies face significant challenges as yet untouched by federal involvement as state and local staff continue to report. State systems are under increased scrutiny from the media, public commissions, elected officials, state and federal courts, and the federal administration (Malm, Bess, Leos-Urbel, & Geen, 2001).

State child welfare systems continue to face philosophical challenges, attempting to balance child safety with family preservation and reasonable efforts to maintain children at home with the need for timely placement in some cases.

Welfare reform posed numerous challenges for state child welfare systems, including the possible effects on families of work requirements and welfare sanctions as well as changes in key resource streams such as EA. EA had been a key source of prevention funding in child welfare, but it was folded into the cash assistance block grant with the creation of TANF. At the time of federal welfare reform during the mid-1990s, it was predicted that changes in cash assistance could increase the number of children who are abused or neglected, referred to Child Protective Services, or in foster care.

Thus far, there is little evidence that this has happened. State and local officials do not see federal welfare reform as a major direct influence on child welfare practice. They are far more concerned with the shifting roles and responsibilities brought on by other pressures such as increases in challenging populations (e.g., those with substance abuse or domestic violence) and the difficulty in obtaining services for these populations outside the child welfare system (Malm et al., 2001).

Child welfare staff expressed concerns about reduction in SSBG and elimination of EA following welfare reform (Geen & Waters Boots, 1999). However, more recent research shows that TANF funds have filled the gaps left by these federal sources (Bess, Andrews, Jantz, & Russell, 2002). Child welfare systems adapted slowly to TANF, but now TANF represents a major funding stream for child welfare (Bess et al., 2002). Welfare reform has not resulted in less federal money for child welfare, but if TANF demands rise because of economic recession, then states may pull TANF funding away from child welfare and back into the cash

assistance system. State child welfare budgets are vulnerable to economic downturns, even though such downturns may increase the demand for child welfare services.

CONCLUSIONS

PRWORA and ASFA significantly changed the role of state governments in the areas of cash assistance, child care, and child welfare. Many of the changes in the federal-state relationship initiated by these reforms resulted in increased state control over these policy areas. For example, PRWORA ended the individual entitlement for cash assistance and child care, dispensed with a number of specific eligibility restrictions and rules on how earnings affect cash grants, and gave states more freedom in how they spend TANF funds.

However, despite the notion that these reforms created a "devolution revolution" in these policy areas, federal controls and incentives remain. While these controls and incentives vary by policy area, federal laws continue to mandate action and constrain state policies and practices in numerous ways—even in areas where major funding streams have been block granted. In some areas of child and family policy, particularly child welfare, federal influence actually increased during the 1990s.

Nonetheless, federal reforms have afforded states an even greater opportunity to be laboratories of policy innovation in cash assistance, child care, and (to a certain extent) child welfare policymaking. Effective increases in federal funding and devolution of authority in cash assistance and child care have allowed states to develop innovative policies in these areas, and Title IV-E waiver authority in child welfare has also allowed limited experimentation. In reaction, states have passed a number of new policies and have used TANF funds in innovative ways to provide services to TANF families as well as low-income non-TANF families.

Not surprisingly, state behavior in this new federal context has been quite varied. States have used their new discretion to fund policies that, ostensibly, are positive for children and families (e.g., increasing child care funding and mandating child immunizations as a condition for parents to receive benefits) while also passing policies that could potentially be harmful (e.g., restricting the amount of time that families can receive benefits). Given the variety in state approaches to federal reform, it is important that the policy and research communities find ways in which to ensure the diffusion of effective policy ideas across states. Large national studies, such as the Assessing the New Federalism Project and the State Policy Documentation Project, as well as national conferences of state policymakers sponsored by the federal government, should continue to work to broadly disseminate those state policy ideas

that meet the goals of child care family policy.

Finally, it is important to note that much of the recent innovative state behavior has been a product not only of new flexibility in how TANF funds can be used but also of the relative abundance of TANF funds. The block grant formula created by PRWORA—combined with decreasing TANF caseloads—created increased revenues for states to spend on low-income families. Because of this windfall, states have had the opportunity to provide increased services to TANF families as well as non-TANF families and to make large transfers of TANF funds to the CCDF. Because TANF revenues are fixed, future increases in TANF caseloads will reduce the amount of federal money available for these purposes. As caseloads rise in an economic downturn, states will have to either make cuts in these services or use state funds to continue them.

NOTES

1. The Assessing the New Federalism Project used a comparative case study design to explore the implementation of a number of child and family policies in 13 states in 1997 and 1999. These states are Alabama, California, Colorado, Florida, Massachusetts, Michigan, Minnesota, Mississippi, New Jersey, New York, Texas, Washington, and Wisconsin. The specific states were chosen because they vary widely in geography, fiscal capacity, citizens' needs, and traditions of providing government services. They also contain more than 50% of the U.S. population and, thus, represent the social service systems encountered by most Americans.

2. The State Policy Documentation Project is a joint project of the Center on Budget and Policy Priorities and the Center for Law and Social Policy that tracks state policy choices on Temporary Assistance for Needy Families programs and Medicaid in the 50 states and District of Columbia.

3. During the later part of this period, the program allowed states to provide assistance to families with two unemployed parents.

4. These included, for example, services such as Medicaid and child care, which states were required to provide to AFDC recipients.

5. A portion of a state's caseload may be exempted from these requirements.

6. The JOBS and EA programs were AFDC-related programs. The JOBS program provided education and training for AFDC recipients. EA provided cash payments to families with children to assist with "emergencies," as defined by the state.

7. Some states have also passed other types of diversion policies that do not involve a cash grant to effectively divert clients from the welfare rolls. These policies involve mandating job search either before or at the same time that clients are applying for assistance. Only the diversion policies that involve a cash benefit are discussed here.

8. It is important to note that not all families are subject to time limits. "Child-only" cases, for example, are not subject to time limits.

9. Ohio has a time limit of less than 60 months (36 months). It is not counted here because after a family's benefits expire, it is possible to receive an additional 24 months of benefits under certain conditions.

10. This limit applies only to families headed by nonexempt employable adults.

11. To qualify for Working Family Assistance, a family must have a child under 18 years of age and an income of no more than 225% of the federal poverty level.

12. To qualify for the Workforce Attachment and Advancement Program, a family must have an income below 200% of the federal poverty level.

REFERENCES

Bess, R., Andrews, C., Jantz, A., & Russell, T. (2002). *The cost of protecting vulnerable children: III. What has happened since welfare reform and ASFA?* (working paper). Washington, DC: Urban Institute.

Break, G. F. (1980). *Financing government in a federal system.* Washington, DC: Brookings Institution.

Capizzano, J., Koralek, R., Botsko, C., & Bess, R. (2001). *Recent changes in Colorado welfare and work, child care, and child welfare systems* (State Update No. 9). Washington, DC: Urban Institute.

Chernick, H., & Reschovsky, A. (1996). State responses to block grants: Will the social safety net survive? *Focus, 18*(1), 25-29. (Madison, WI: Institute for Research on Poverty)

Ehrle, J., Seefeldt, K., Snyder, K., & McMahon, P. (2001). *Recent changes in Wisconsin welfare and work, child care and child welfare systems* (State Update No. 8). Washington, DC: Urban Institute.

Geen, R., & Tumlin, K. (1999). *State efforts to remake child welfare: Responses to new challenges and increased scrutiny* (Assessing the New Federalism, Occasional Paper No. 29). Washington, DC: Urban Institute.

Geen, R., & Waters Boots, S. (1999). The potential effects of welfare reform on states' financing of child welfare services. *Children and Youth Services Reviews, 21,* 865-880.

Malm, K., Bess, R., Leos-Urbel, J., & Geen, R. (2001). *Running to keep in place: The continuing evolution of our nation's child welfare system* (Assessing the New Federalism, Occasional Paper No. 54). Washington, DC: Urban Institute.

Mezey, J., & Greenberg, M. (2001). *CLASP comments on the May 10, 2001, Child Care High Performance Bonus Interim Final Rule.* Washington, DC: Center for Law and Social Policy.

Parizek, E., Falk, G., & Spar, K. (1998). *Child care: State programs under the Child Care and Development Fund* (Report 98-875). Washington, DC: Congressional Research Service.

Powers, E. (1999). *Block granting welfare: Fiscal impact on the states* (Assessing the New Federalism, Occasional Paper No. 23). Washington, DC: Urban Institute.

Rowe, G. (2000). *State TANF policies as of July 1999* (Assessing the New Federalism, Welfare Rules Databook). Washington, DC: Urban Institute.

Savner, S., & Greenberg, M. (1995). *The CLASP guide to welfare waivers: 1992-1995*. Washington, DC: Center for Law and Social Policy.

Schumacher, R., Greenberg, M., & Duffy, J. (2001). *The impact of TANF funding on state child care subsidy programs*. Washington, DC: Center for Law and Social Policy.

State Policy Documentation Project. (2001). *Findings in Brief: Child care assistance*. [Online]. Available: www.spdp.org

Stenberg, C. W. (1989). Federalism in transition: 1959-1979. In *Readings in federalism: Perspectives on a decade of change* (SR-11). Washington, DC: Advisory Committee on Intergovernmental Relations.

Thompson, T. S., Snyder, K., Malm, K., & O'Brien, C. (2001). *Recent changes in Washington welfare and work, child care, and child welfare systems* (State Update No. 6). Washington, DC: Urban Institute.

Tout, K., Martinson, K., Koralek, R., & Ehrle, J. (2001). *Recent changes in Minnesota welfare and work, child care, and child welfare systems* (State Update No. 3). Washington, DC: Urban Institute.

U.S. General Accounting Office. (1994). *Child care and welfare recipients face service gaps* (GAO/HEHS 94-87). Washington, DC: Author.

U.S. House of Representatives. (1998). *1998 Green Book: Background material and data on programs within the jurisdiction of the Committee on Ways and Means*. Washington, DC: Government Printing Office.

CHAPTER 12

Child Poverty in the United States: An Evidence-Based Conceptual Framework for Programs and Policies

Elizabeth Thompson Gershoff
J. Lawrence Aber
C. Cybele Raver

A s we enter the 21st century, the United States has just experienced a period of significant economic growth. Coupled with changes in public policy (e.g., welfare reform, tax policy changes), this growth has translated into significant reductions in the rate of poverty among children (Bennett & Lu, 2000). Nonetheless, one in six American children—more than 12 million children—still live in families whose incomes fall below the federal poverty line (U.S. Census Bureau, 2000). Indeed, 34% of all American children have spent at least 1 year in an impoverished household; this rate rises to 81% for children of single parents and to 63% for children whose parents did not complete high school (Rank & Hirschl, 1999). Numbers of

near-poor children (i.e., those in families with incomes between 100% and 200% of the poverty threshold) are growing as well, with the number of children living in near poverty rising faster than the overall poverty rate (National Center for Children in Poverty, 1996).

In this chapter, we consider poverty's effects on our nation's children. We begin by defining poverty and describing the ways in which poverty is operationalized. We then identify the serious toll that poverty takes on the well-being of many children, particularly when these children experience deep poverty, over multiple years, and early on in their development (Duncan, Brooks-Gunn, & Klebanov, 1994). As we will see, different

269

lines of social science inquiry rely on different definitions of poverty, and we briefly consider these different definitions within our review. Next, we consider developmental mechanisms through which family economic hardship may translate into negative consequences for children, so that a template for different avenues of intervention can be clearly drawn from important emerging research. We develop a framework to consider ways in which the United States has attempted to address poverty's effects on children through diverse family- and child-focused federal programs. We end by identifying several remaining obstacles to effective child poverty reduction programs.

At the outset, we acknowledge that during recent years more of the responsibility for designing poverty reduction programs within federal mandates has devolved to individual states. Because no two states are alike in how they implement federal policies (Cauthen, Knitzer, & Ripple, 2000; Meyers, Gornick, & Peck, 2001), we focus herein on federal laws and programs so as to reflect the national priorities that guide state- and community-level programs.

DETERMINING THE SCOPE OF THE PROBLEM: DEFINING AND OPERATIONALIZING POVERTY

During recent years, there has been mounting controversy on the issue of how to define and measure poverty. The United States uses what is called an "absolute" measure of poverty in that there is an imaginary poverty "line" that demarcates the poor from the nonpoor. In contrast, European and other nations use a relative measure by which families are considered poor only in relation to the median income for their country. Complements to both of these standards are subjective measures that reflect how a given family's standard of living compares with that of others in their country or region.

Research and policy discussions on poverty reflect recent discussions regarding whether to use absolute or relative measures of poverty and whether to add indexes of material deprivation or what has been termed "social exclusion." Decisions on these issues influence the design, results, and interpretation of research studies on the number of children who are identified as poor, on the effects of poverty on children, and on the effectiveness of poverty reduction policies. We briefly outline these theoretical and methodological challenges.

An Absolute Measure of Poverty: The U.S. Federal Poverty Line

The U.S. federal poverty line (FPL) is an absolute measure of a predetermined income threshold adjusted for family size and yearly cost-of-living increases. For 2001, the FPL was $17,650 for a family of four ("Annual Update," 2001). A family whose gross income (accounting for family size) falls below the poverty line is considered "poor." The U.S. federal poverty measure has been sharply criticized during recent years, particularly for (a) its failure to take into account the taxes families pay and the in-kind (non-cash) and cash-like benefits they receive (e.g., food stamps, housing subsidies) and for (b) its reliance on expenditure ratios established during the 1950s that have not been empirically confirmed and do not take into account the fact that families' housing, medical, and child care expenses have increased substantially as a proportion of their overall incomes (Aber, Bennett, Conley, & Li, 1997; Citro & Michael, 1995; Seccombe, 2000). Further problems are that regional differences in costs, particularly for housing, are not accommodated in current poverty guidelines (Aber et al., 1997; Citro & Michael, 1995;

Seccombe, 2000) and that income is generally interpreted as an individual- or family-level measure, a fact that may obscure the extent to which family income is linked to regional levels of unemployment, job loss, and economic downturns.

The policy importance of such an absolute poverty "line" is that, as will be seen, a majority of programs targeted to low-income families with children are linked to where families' incomes fall in regard to this absolute benchmark. Thus, both federal and state poverty reduction programs are disbursed according to families' incomes regardless of the cost of living for the areas in which they live. Although an annual income of 150% of the poverty line (i.e., $26,475 for a family of four) may be enough to live on in some regions of the country (e.g., small towns and rural areas in the South), it may fall far short of covering minimum expenses in others (e.g., large cities in the Northeast and West). The FPL also poses challenges to policymakers themselves: Because the poverty guidelines are based on taxable income and do not include in-kind government benefits such as food stamps and housing assistance, the guidelines hamper attempts to determine the effectiveness of policy changes on the true economic circumstances of the poor (Aber et al., 1997; Citro & Michael, 1995).

Alternative Absolute Measures of Poverty

These challenges have led a number of investigators to suggest that the FPL should be substantially amended or replaced by more theoretically and empirically meaningful measures. We now turn to a brief review of these alternative measures of poverty.

The U.S. Census's "Experimental Poverty Measure." Recently, the Census Bureau has incorporated suggested changes to the FPL (Citro & Michael, 1995) into an "experimental poverty measure" that includes the value of near-money benefits (e.g., food stamps, tax credits) as well as the costs of work-related expenses (e.g., child care) and out-of-pocket medical costs (Iceland & Short, 1999). With these adjustments, child poverty rates are somewhat higher with the experimental measure than with the official FPL, and the composition of the poor changes to include more working and two-parent families (Iceland & Short, 1999). To date, there are no official plans to adopt the experimental measure.

The Self-Sufficiency Standard. The self-sufficiency standard measures the amount of income a family would need to meet its basic needs, and thus be independent of subsidies, in a given locale (Pearce & Brooks, 2000). The self-sufficiency standard is comprised of costs for housing, child care, food, transportation, health care, miscellaneous expenses (including clothing, medicines, and household items), and taxes. The standard takes into account work expenses (including child care), the ages of children in a family, regional and local variation in costs, and the net effect of taxes and tax credits. Self-sufficiency standards have been calculated for a number of states around the nation. For example, calculation of the standard in New York State revealed that, outside of New York City, monthly self-sufficiency wage requirements for a single-parent, two-child family ranged from $30,012 (Otsego County) to $60,528 (Nassau and Suffolk counties) (Pearce & Brooks, 2000). After calculating more than 400 family budgets to represent all regions and family types in the United States, researchers at the Economic Policy Institute determined that more than two and a half times the number of families that are officially poor based on the FPL fall below estimated family budget levels (Boushey, Brocht, Gundersen, & Bernstein, 2001). This growing attention to the amount of money needed by families with children to meet their basic needs underlies the insufficiency of the current U.S. FPL and the need for poverty definitions to be tied to the income that families require to meet their basic needs in our society.

A Relative Measure of Poverty: The European Poverty Line

In contrast to the United States, European nations tend to use relative definitions of poverty, which emphasize inequality, rather than absolute definitions, which emphasize deprivation. The rationales behind the use of a relative poverty threshold are that what is considered an acceptable standard of living changes with time and that families whose resources are significantly below other members in their society will be unable to participate fully in that society (Townsend, 1992; UNICEF Innocenti Research Centre, 2000). A relative measure of poverty, typically operationalized as 50% of the median income in a society, necessarily changes as the median income in a society changes. This characteristic of a relative measure is beneficial in that it is referenced to the entire society at a given point, yet it is problematic when a recession makes an entire society worse off and some families are not considered poor even though they have very low incomes but are above half of the median income (Citro & Michael, 1995). The relative poverty measure is often used in international comparisons and yields different percentages of poverty; using a 50% of median relative measure of poverty as a standard, UNICEF recently determined that the U.S. poverty rate rises substantially (by 8% of the population) using a relative, rather than an absolute, approach. With relative poverty as the standard, the United States has one of the highest relative child

poverty rates among the world's wealthiest nations (UNICEF Innocenti Research Centre, 2000).

Subjective Measures of Poverty

In the studies reviewed thus far, researchers have considered poverty in strictly economic terms, examining the impact of low family income on child welfare. Yet these studies may underestimate the toll that material hardship may take on children by using too narrow a definition of who is considered poor according to income-based standards.

Family Financial Hardship. From a developmental perspective, income-to-needs ratios (defined as a family's income divided by the poverty threshold associated with that family's size and structure) do not provide sufficient information as to whether families perceive and are adversely affected by financial hardship such as the extent to which families are unable to purchase sufficient food, clothing, and/or shelter (Conger, Ge, Elder, Lorenz, & Simons, 1994; McLoyd, Jayaratne, Ceballo, & Borquez, 1994; Sen, 1999). Indeed, up to 65% of nonpoor families that fall between 100% and 200% of the FPL (i.e., with income-to-needs ratios of 1.0 to 2.0) experience one or more serious hardships that include food insecurity, inability to pay bills, lack of health insurance, and lack of adequate child care (Boushey et al., 2001; Children's Defense Fund, 2000). Previous studies have suggested that low income takes a negative toll on child outcomes in part through the economic pressures on family life (Elder, Eccles, Ardelt, & Lord, 1995; McLoyd et al., 1994). Under such pressures, parents make difficult "choices" about where to allocate their limited funds (Edin & Lein, 1997). Their choices will be reflected in several key indicators such as families' experiences of financial strain (Elder et al., 1995;

Gutman & Eccles, 1999; McLoyd et al., 1994), food insecurity (Carlson, Andrews, & Bickel, 1999), residential instability (Boisjoly, Duncan, & Hofferth, 1994; Leventhal & Brooks-Gunn, 2000; Pribesh & Downey, 1999), and inadequate medical care (Kenney, Ko, & Ormond, 2000; Mills, 2000; Office of Assistant Secretary for Planning and Evaluation, 1998). For example, 17% of all households with children under 18 years of age experience deprivation of basic food needs (Carlson et al., 1999; Hamilton et al., 1997), with those in poverty being 3.5 times more likely to experience food insufficiency than those with incomes above the poverty threshold (Rose, 1999). It may be these material hardships in poor families' day-to-day lives that predict increased levels of parent stress, isolation, depression, and harsh parenting, each of which, as is discussed in what follows, predicts impoverished children's deficits in behavioral and psychological functioning (Boisjoly et al., 1994; Brody et al., 1994; Chase-Landsdale, Brooks-Gunn, & Zamsky, 1994; Elder et al., 1995; Hamelin, Habicht, & Beaudry, 1999; Kleinman et al., 1998; Leventhal & Brooks-Gunn, 2000; Olson, 1999).

Social Exclusion. Researchers and policy-makers in the European Union (e.g., Burchardt, Le Grand, & Piachaud, 1999; Mikulic, Linden, Pelsers, & Schiepers, 1999; Percy-Smith, 2000), and now in the United States (e.g., Aber, Gershoff, & Brooks-Gunn, 2001), have become increasingly interested in the notion of "social exclusion" as another frame through which to understand the effects of poverty and deprivation on children. In general, families may be excluded from normative desirable experiences such as living in adequate housing, in crime-free neighborhoods, and with formal and informal social supports as well as from participation in meaningful work, educational, recreational, and civic opportunities (Burchardt et al.,

1999; Percy-Smith, 2000). For example, working parents whose incomes are poor or near poor (200% of FPL) might not be able to afford popular material goods (e.g., clothes, shoes, video games) as well as educationally enriching products and experiences (e.g., quality child care, visits to museums, computers). Children who are unable to share in these experiences may feel excluded, stigmatized, and discriminated against by their peers (Duncan & Brooks-Gunn, 1997; Klasen, 1998). Much empirical evidence indicates that U.S. children's exclusion from safe neighborhoods, adequate housing, and cognitively enriching educational systems may jeopardize their healthy development and limit their future roles as learners, workers, and citizens.

Dynamic Approaches to Measuring Poverty

Although there is an extensive literature on income dynamics (Bradbury, Jenkins, & Micklewright, 2001), it has not been well integrated with studies of developmental dynamics. Economists tend to view multiple time point measures of permanent income as more valuable than single point-in-time measures of current income, with permanent income more strongly related to child development than is current income (Blau, 1999; Brooks-Gunn & Duncan, 1997; Duncan et al., 1994). Still other researchers (Nolan & Whelan, 1996) argue that indexes of material hardship can complement measures of current income and more closely approximate permanent income (with low yearly income and high levels of material hardship approximating a measure of permanent low income). Unfortunately, all of these points of view ignore temporal fluctuations in income and potential transactional (reciprocal) paths of influence between income and hardship. The timing, variation, and directionality of income change may influence family processes over and above mean income (Brooks-Gunn & Duncan, 1997; Duncan, Yeung, Brooks-Gunn, & Smith, 1998). One needs only to conduct the mental experiment of asking which of two families with mean incomes of $10,000 per year over 5 years that one would prefer to live in: Family A with increasing incomes of $8,000, $9,000, $10,000, $11,000, and $12,000 per year or Family B with decreasing incomes of $12,000, $11,000, $10,000, $9,000, and $8,000. Although permanent income averaged across the 5-year period remains the same for both families, it is likely that Family A's outlook, as well as its income, improves over time. In contrast, Family B's economic hardship is likely to be accompanied by increasing psychological strain, worry, and emotional distress. The developmental effects of these income patterns are likely to be very different for the children in each of these families.

KNOWN EFFECTS OF POVERTY ON CHILDREN'S DEVELOPMENT

Research on the effects of growing up in poverty on children's development has consistently found negative associations between poverty and three key areas of children's lives, namely their physical, cognitive, and social-emotional development. Most of the literature on poverty and children's development uses correlational techniques. Sometimes studies control for factors that are associated with poverty (e.g., parent education, parent marital status [Mayer, 1997]), but often they do not. Even when other factors are controlled, correlational studies cannot prove causal links between poverty and child development outcomes; however, recent experimental demonstration programs that provide income supports do allow the drawing of causal conclusions. Despite these caveats, we refer to the "effects" of poverty on children's development because we believe that, taken as a whole, the extant

literature indicates that income poverty and its cofactors indeed do have significant causal influences on children's development.

Effects of Poverty on Children's Physical Development

Children who grow up in poor families are at risk for a range of detrimental physical outcomes. Being born into a poor family significantly increases the chance that a child will be of low birthweight, which in turn is associated with high risk of infant mortality (Gortmaker, 1979) and with later deficits in physical and cognitive development (Barker, 1994; Bradley et al., 1994; Brooks-Gunn, Klebanov, & Duncan, 1996). Compared with their more affluent peers, poor children are twice as likely to be in bad health, including increased rates of diarrhea, colitis, asthma, and partial or complete blindness or deafness (Brooks-Gunn & Duncan, 1997). Children in poor families are three to four times as likely as their affluent peers to suffer lead poisoning (Brooks-Gunn & Duncan, 1997; Children's Defense Fund, 1994; Klerman, 1991; Seccombe, 2000) and are much more likely to have oral health problems, including decayed primary teeth (U.S. Surgeon General, 2000), and to have an unmet need for medical care (Klerman, 1991; Vargas, Crall, & Schneider, 1998). Poor children are at risk for iron deficiency and anemia (Children's Defense Fund, 1994), both of which have been found to affect mental, motor, and social behavior throughout childhood (Klerman, 1991; Lozoff, Jimenez, & Wolf, 1991). Low family income has been found to be a significant predictor of both age-normed stunting (low height for age) and wasting (low weight for height) (Brooks-Gunn & Duncan, 1997; Klerman, 1991; Miller & Korenman, 1994). In addition, rates of injury from accidents are higher among poor children than among nonpoor children (Klerman, 1991).

Given this range of health risks, poor children unsurprisingly are twice as likely to make a visit to a hospital as are their non-poor peers (Brooks-Gunn & Duncan, 1997). The seriousness of medical problems among poor children is exacerbated by the fact that, although recent expansions in government health insurance coverage have increased the numbers of children covered by medical insurance, rates are still relatively low, with as many as 23% of poor children (families with incomes below the FPL) and 20% of near-poor children (families with incomes between 100% and 125% of the FPL) remaining uninsured (Mills, 2000).

Effects of Poverty on Children's Cognitive Development

Poor children are more likely than non-poor children to experience both developmental delays and learning disabilities (Brooks-Gunn & Duncan, 1997; Klerman, 1991), impairments that will hamper their abilities in school and beyond. Mild mental retardation is more prevalent among low-income children than among more affluent children, while both severe and profound mental retardation are fairly evenly distributed across socioeconomic status groups (Klerman, 1991). Patterns of early childhood poverty have been found to predict substantive differences in intelligence quotient (IQ) at 5 years of age (even after controlling for IQ 2 years earlier), with persistent poverty having a significantly stronger impact on IQ than does transient poverty (Brooks-Gunn et al., 1996; Duncan et al., 1994). Family income differences have been traced directly to differences in performance on standardized tests, with a one-unit improvement in the income-to-needs ratio translating into a 3.0- to 3.7-point increase in children's scores on cognitive tests (Smith, Brooks-Gunn, & Klebanov, 1997). Early poverty experiences pose particular risks for children's later academic performance (Lipman & Offord, 1997), with socioeconomic differences in math and reading test scores between the poor and nonpoor appearing as early as the first grade (Entwisle & Alexander, 1992). In turn, poor children are twice as likely as nonpoor children to repeat a grade or to drop out of school (Brooks-Gunn & Duncan, 1997; Children's Defense Fund, 1997).

Effects of Poverty on Children's Social-Emotional Development

Although children's academic success and cognitive competencies are often key policy concerns, it is equally important to consider the negative effects of poverty on children's social and emotional adjustment. The limited social capabilities of young children mean that they are highly dependent on, and shaped by, their families, and thus the course of young children's development is linked for good or for ill to their families' economic circumstances (Shonkoff & Phillips, 2000). Children from poor families are at greater risk for suffering from behavioral or emotional problems (Brooks-Gunn & Duncan, 1997). The experience of poverty, particularly that of long duration, is associated with increased likelihood that children will evidence externalizing behavior problems, such as antisocial behavior (Miech, Caspi, Moffitt, Wright, & Silva, 1999; Takeuchi, Williams, & Adair, 1991), as well as internalizing behavior problems, such as depression and poor self-image (McLeod & Shanahan, 1996; Miech et al., 1999; Takeuchi et al., 1991; Weinger, 1998). Similarly, poor children also show difficulties with aspects of social competence, including self-regulation and impulsivity (Takeuchi et al., 1991), abilities that are associated with social and emotional competence throughout childhood (Eisenberg et al., 1996; Huey & Weisz, 1997; Rothbart & Bates, 1998).

PROCESSES BY WHICH POVERTY AFFECTS CHILDREN: TARGETS FOR POLICY AND PROGRAM INTERVENTION

Policies or programs aimed at reducing child poverty or at ameliorating its negative effects are based on assumptions about the processes by which poverty and its cofactors affect children. Indeed, implicitly or explicitly, such processes constitute the potential targets for policy and program interventions. The literature to date has identified several key factors that predict family income poverty and financial hardship and that determine whether and how they in turn affect children's development. In this section, we briefly outline what is known about these processes, in part to help establish a frame within which we can discuss antipoverty policies and programs. We have summarized the processes identified in the literature in Figure 12.1.

Family-Level Characteristics as Predictors of Poverty and Associated Child Outcomes

As noted previously, a growing debate among researchers of child poverty has surrounded the assertion that causality may be incorrectly inferred between family income at one point and child outcomes at a later point when the associations between them may be better explained by a third set of unobserved variables (Duncan et al., 1998; Mayer, 1997). Factors such as parents' level of education, skills, motivation, and family structure have been suggested as possible exogenous predictors of both family income and child cognitive and social outcomes (Mayer, 2001). Other researchers have countered that such an analysis overcontrols for potential third variable threats (because many of these characteristics may be caused

by, rather than causes of, poverty). They argue that income poverty, especially extreme poverty during early childhood, does have a deleterious effect on children's development (Duncan et al., 1998). Findings from experimental demonstration projects have done much to bolster the argument that family income poverty (see Huston et al., 2001; Morris, Huston, Duncan, Crosby, & Bos, 2001; Morris & Michalopolous, 2000; Yoshikawa, 1999) and poor neighborhoods (see Ludwig, Duncan, & Pinkston, 2000) causally affect children's cognitive/academic and social/emotional development. Future work is needed to identify the individual and combined impacts of family-level characteristics and family income on children.

Mechanisms Through Which Income Poverty May Negatively Affect Children

Although economic hardship may directly limit children's access to important, educationally enriching, and emotionally rewarding goods and services, many studies have concluded that poverty exerts the bulk of its influence through parents. There are a number of mechanisms that investigators have tested as potential pathways through which income exerts an effect.

Parent Investment as a Mediator. Observed differences between poor and nonpoor children have been traced in part to differences in the quality of the home environment provided by parents for their children (Duncan et al., 1994). Specifically, lower quality home environments of poor children account for as much as half of the gap between test scores of poor versus nonpoor young children (Smith & Brooks-Gunn, 1997). The majority of studies that examine parent investment in children do so using the HOME inventory (Caldwell & Bradley, 1984), which combines

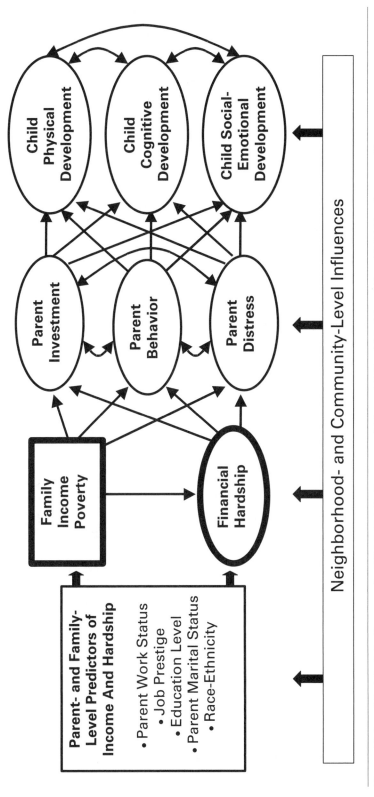

Figure 12.1 Model of the Processes by Which Family Income and Financial Hardship May Affect Child Development Outcomes

maternal reports and interviewer ratings of the quality of emotional support and cognitive stimulation that parents provide (e.g., identifying the number of child-oriented objects that families own, such as books and records/CDs, and how often they take their children to places such as museums and the library).[1] Analyses using the HOME inventory in the National Longitudinal Study of Youth have found significantly lower levels of cognitive stimulation among poor families (especially those headed by single mothers [Miller & Davis, 1997]) and that parents' investments in cognitively stimulating materials and activities strongly mediate the effects of poverty on children's intellectual development (Guo & Harris, 2000). Although the HOME cognitive stimulation subscale is now widely used as a proxy for investment, it will be important to include in future research other manifestations of parental investment, particularly in quality early childhood education.

Parent Behavior and Stress Levels as Mediators. Parents undergoing economic hardship tend to experience high levels of stress that result from active struggles to provide for their families and from increases in negative life events with which they have fewer resources to cope (Edin & Lein, 1997; McLeod & Kessler, 1990; McLoyd et al., 1994). The stress inherent in living with low incomes may precipitate both marital conflict (Conger et al., 1994) and parent depression (rates of 13%-28% [Lennon, Aber, & Blum, 1998; Shonkoff & Phillips, 2000]). Children whose parents' marriages are characterized by high conflict or whose parents have elevated levels of depressive symptoms are at greater risk for social and emotional behavior problems (Cummings & Davies, 1999; Davies & Cummings, 1994; Downey & Coyne, 1990), in large part because maritally distressed or depressed parents are more likely to withdraw from their children, to

become hostile with them, or both (Dix, Gershoff, & Miller, 2001; Jackson, Gyamfi, Brooks-Gunn, & Blake, 1998; McLoyd et al., 1994; Pinderhughes, Dodge, Bates, Pettit, & Zelli, 2000; Simons, Lorenz, Wu, & Conger, 1993; Smith & Brooks-Gunn, 1997; Tronick & Weinberg, 1997). Levels of maternal depression, generalized distress, social support, and difficulty in coping have been found in turn to partially mediate the effects of poverty on low-income children's internalizing and externalizing behavior problems (Duncan et al., 1994; Linares et al., 2001).

Because it is associated with increases in parents' psychological distress, economic hardship is argued to lead to more frequent use of corporal punishment and other negative parenting behaviors (Elder & Caspi, 1988; McLoyd, 1990; Simons et al., 1993). Indeed, associations between socioeconomic status, stress, and corporal punishment have been found in several studies (Garbarino, Kostelny, & Barry, 1997; Giles-Sims, Straus, & Sugarman, 1995; Jackson et al., 1998; McLeod & Shanahan, 1993; McLoyd et al., 1994; Pinderhughes et al., 2000; Simons, Whitbeck, Melby, & Wu, 1994). A series of meta-analyses has confirmed that parents' use of corporal punishment in particular is associated with a range of detrimental child outcomes, including increased aggression and delinquency and decreased moral internalization and mental health (Gershoff, 2002). At extreme levels, poor children are nearly eight times as likely as their nonpoor peers to experience physical maltreatment from caregivers (Brooks-Gunn & Duncan, 1997). Incidence of child maltreatment is higher among low-income families than among higher income families (Trickett, Aber, Carlson, & Cicchetti, 1991), and maltreatment among low-income families has been found to predict stronger negative child outcomes than has maltreatment among higher income families (Aber, 1994). Indeed, the form maltreatment takes may depend in part on the type of poverty experienced by the family; persistent poverty likely is associated more with neglect, whereas sudden poverty likely is associated with physical maltreatment (Aber, 1994).

Although the effects of family poverty on parenting are largely predicted to be negative, there is some evidence that parents who are able to use positive strategies, despite increased economic hardship, can buffer the effects of poverty on children. Several studies have identified protective parenting factors, including positive parent-child relations in preschool and elementary school and parents' use of age-appropriate and consistent discipline, that can mitigate the negative associations among low family income, high family financial hardship, and child outcomes (Cowen, Wyman, Work, & Parker, 1990; Masten, Morison, Pelligrini, & Tellegen, 1990; Rutter, 1990). In addition, there is some evidence that improvements in parents' activities and behaviors with their children precipitated by involvement in Head Start or Early Head Start programs are associated with later increases in children's school readiness (Parker, Boak, Griffin, Ripple, & Peay, 1999; Paulsell et al., 2000).

Neighborhoods and Communities as Moderators. Families are embedded within their neighborhoods, communities, states, and nations. The larger demographic and economic contexts in which families live are thought to affect the economic security of families and the impact of the family economy on parenting and children's development through context effects on institutional resources, social relationships, and community norms and collective efficacy (Leventhal & Brooks-Gunn, 2000). A growing body of experimental (Ludwig et al., 2000), quasi-experimental (Rosenbaum, 1991), and nonexperimental (Aber, Gephart, Brooks-Gunn, & Connell, 1997; Klebanov, Brooks-Gunn, & Duncan, 1994) research

suggests that neighborhoods do affect family human capital and income and child development net of other family factors. Although we recognize the crucial importance of taking community-level factors into account when considering the impact of programs and policies on child poverty and related child outcomes, we also recognize that neighborhood- and community-based interventions span a highly diverse area and that it is beyond the scope of this chapter to include a comprehensive review of developmental models of neighborhood influence and policy responses that capitalize on neighborhood influence.

FEDERAL PROGRAM AND POLICY INTERVENTIONS RELATED TO CHILD POVERTY

How realistic is it to expect that families' poverty status can be changed over time? Examination of family income dynamics across populations and across time underscores the ways in which family income can be powerfully affected by changes in federal policy. For example, the population of young children experienced a clear increase in their poverty rate from the 1970s to the 1990s (National Center for Children in Poverty, 1996), while the proportion of adults age 65 years or older who were poor dropped substantially during the same period (Strawn, 1992). This difference reflects in large part a decision at the federal level to marshal assistance to reduce levels of income poverty among the elderly, while comparable commitments were not made to reduce the rates of poverty experienced by children and families (Strawn, 1992).

To date, tax and transfer policies do relatively little to mitigate the incidence of child poverty in the United States; U.S. taxes and transfers reduce child poverty rates by less than 5% as compared with a 20% reduction in Sweden and an 18% reduction in the United Kingdom (UNICEF Innocenti Research Centre, 2000). Relative to past expenditures, current U.S. federal spending on programs directed toward low-income children and their families has seen a considerable increase (from 0.20% of the gross domestic product (GDP) in 1960 to 1.47% of the GDP in 1997), yet it is clear that our nation's investment in children's welfare remains a small proportion of federal programs (Clark, King, Spiro, & Steuerle, 2001), particularly in comparison with other industrialized nations (Gornick & Meyers, 2001). In addition, state decisions about how to implement, and at what levels to support, federal programs have led to wide variations in the extent to which federal programs reach and serve children in need (Meyers et al., 2001).

Within this relatively meager appropriation for poor families with children, a variety of policy and program approaches to dealing with child poverty have been implemented at the federal, state, and community levels. In what follows, we focus on the current federal policies and programs aimed at decreasing levels of poverty or ameliorating its effects on children and families. It is important to note that we recognize that other state-, neighborhood-, and school-level initiatives are also of great value in addressing child poverty and its negative consequences (Cauthen et al., 2000; Meyers et al., 2001). In this chapter, however, we restrict our discussion to family- and child-focused, federally funded interventions only such as those that help to make families less poor (e.g., the Earned Income Tax Credit [EITC]), help parents to deal with stressors associated with poverty (e.g., home visiting), and directly target the child consequences of economic hardship such as compensatory early educational programs (e.g., Head Start).

We briefly describe the substance of the major child poverty-related federal initiatives as well as any evidence of the effectiveness of these initiatives. By effectiveness, we mean (a) whether the benefit or program reaches the target population and (b) whether the benefit or program is associated with or causes improved family and/or child outcomes. Unfortunately, both types of effectiveness information are not readily available for all policies and programs to be discussed. To facilitate more integration of policy research and developmental research, we have grouped these interventions according to which process identified in Figure 12.1 is primarily targeted. We thus present six types of programs and policies targeted at the identified processes (see Figure 12.2): (a) parent-directed human capital enhancement, (b) family-directed income support, (c) family-directed in-kind support, (d) parent-directed parenting interventions, (e) two-generation interventions, and (f) child-directed interventions. (Although community-directed programs are included in Figure 12.2 for the sake of comprehensiveness, we have limited the scope of this chapter to those programs most directly targeted to family income and disadvantage.) Eligibility for a majority of these programs is linked to the FPL; funding allocations are described in terms of an October-September fiscal year (FY) or a July-June program year (PY). A brief summary of all 2001 programs targeted at low-income children and their families and listed in decreasing order by cost is provided in Appendix Table 12.A1.

Parent-Directed Human Capital Enhancement

By providing late adolescents and adults with skills that will help them to earn higher incomes, education and training programs aim to give parents access to the tools they need to lift themselves out of poverty. In numerous studies, educational attainment has been identified as one of the strongest

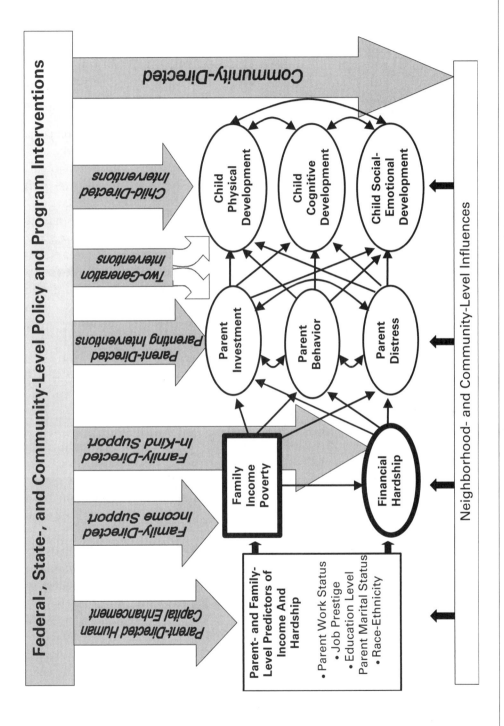

Figure 12.2   Targeted Policy and Program Interventions Related to Poverty and Its Effects on Children

281

predictors of parents' ability to lift their own and their children's social and economic status (Becker, 1993; Page & Simmons, 2000). Full-time young adult workers (25-34 years of age) without a high school diploma earned an average of $17,185 in 1996, while those young adults working full-time with a high school diploma or its equivalent earned an average of $22,567 (Pandey, Zahn, & Neeley-Barnes, 2000). Children's cognitive and social development are likely also to be positively influenced through investments in parental education. For example, investments in parents' education may affect children through the amount and quality of information and skills that parents can teach their children or through the amount and quality of material comfort and cognitive stimulation that can be purchased for children with increased family income. Parents' skills and education, viewed as human rather than material capital, have therefore been a key domain of public policy intervention.

The federal government has supported the provision of education and training services to youth and adults for more than four decades. Initially, these policies were designed in response to fears of workers' dislocation from jobs because of automation, but by the 1960s federal training and education programs were substantially reoriented toward antipoverty goals. For example, during FY 1988, 92% of the individuals served by one of the largest federal funding streams (Title IIA of the Job Training Partnership Act) were from low-income families (LaLonde, 1995). The types of training and educational programs available include remedial education, such as attainment of the General Equivalency Diploma (GED), and job training ranging from just a few weeks of minimal case management and "job club"/job search assistance to extensive year-long vocational and technical training through which individuals are guaranteed work experience in higher level clerical and technical occupations. Educational and training programs were tied to participants' welfare receipt through the passage of the Work Incentive Program (WIN) enacted in 1967 and, more recently, through the Family Support Act of 1988, which replaced WIN with the Job Opportunity and Basic Skills Program (JOBS) (LaLonde, 1995).

With the passage of the Personal Responsibility and Work Opportunity Reconciliation Act (PRWORA, discussed in more detail later) in 1996, welfare recipients' participation in federally funded training and vocational programs was substantially curtailed, with the adults facing stricter limits on funding for education and increased state and local emphasis on employment search over educational activities (Bloom & Michalopoulis, 2001). In keeping with this "work first" approach, PRWORA initiated a new federal policy (the Workforce Investment Act of 1998 [WIA]) whereby low-income individuals must complete job search efforts first, gaining access to postsecondary training only if it is determined that additional education is necessary for their employment and self-sufficiency (Golonka & Matus-Grossman, 2001). The WIA Adult Program encompasses core services (outreach and job placement), intensive services (counseling and career planning), and training services (occupational and basic skills training), each provided through One Stop Career Centers (Governmentwide Information Systems Division [GISD], 2001). All U.S. adults are eligible for core services, but states are instructed to give priority to low-income individuals; funds for the WIA Adult Program in FY 2001 were set at $950 million (Employment and Training Administration, 2001). Youth are eligible for services under WIA if their own or their families' incomes fall below the poverty line and if they themselves are deficient in basic literacy skills, school dropouts, homeless or runaways, foster children, pregnant or parents, or offenders

(GISD, 2001). Funds for the WIA Youth Activities Program in PY 2001 were estimated at $102 million (GISD, 2001).

Associate's and bachelor's degrees substantially increase low-income adults' earning power, yet only 10% of heads of household in working low-income families graduate from college, while 36% of heads of household in families at 200% above the poverty level have completed college (Golonka & Matus-Grossman, 2001). A total of $13 billion in federal funding was available in FY 2000 through a number of different financial aid packages in aiding students to attend 2- and 4-year colleges and universities (U.S. Department of Education, 2001). Of the financial aid programs targeted at low-income students, the largest is the Pell Grants Program at $8.8 billion for FY 2001, but other important programs include the Federal Work Study Program ($1 billion for FY 2001), the Federal Supplemental Educational Opportunity Grants Program ($691 million for FY 2001), the Federal Perkins Loan Program ($100 million for FY 2001), the Leveraging Educational Assistance Partnership ($55 million for FY 2001), and the Federal Family Education Loans ($29.9 million for FY 2001) (GISD, 2001). Millions of students are assisted by these programs, either separately or in conjunction, 3.8 million by Pell grants alone (GISD, 2001). Importantly, 2-year colleges are often viewed as best able to strengthen human capital among low-income families receiving public assistance because these programs have relatively open admissions policies, low tuition, and experience in serving an older and racially/ethnically diverse population (Golonka & Matus-Grossman, 2001).

In keeping with a model of investment in human capital, a number of federal policies also have been designed to encourage young, unmarried, low-income women to postpone childbearing, with the hope that this will increase the likelihood that they will attain higher levels of completed schooling and strengthen their chances of obtaining better, higher paying jobs. For example, it has been estimated that having a child as a teenager reduces a young woman's chances of obtaining a standard high school degree by 20% (although it does not decrease a young woman's chances of obtaining a GED [Maynard, 1997]). Following from the concern that welfare recipients are more likely than poor nonrecipients to have had children as unmarried teenagers, the PRWORA legislation includes funds for abstinence education and for financial incentives to states that demonstrate reductions in rates of out-of-wedlock pregnancies, the latter of which were $20 million each for Alabama, the District of Columbia, California, Massachusetts, and Michigan (U.S. Department of Health and Human Services [DHHS], 2000). PRWORA also requires that minor parents stay in school and live at home or in a supervised setting to receive public assistance through institutions such as Second Chance Homes that are aimed at providing teen parents with necessary parenting and family planning skills (Office of Assistant Secretary for Planning and Evaluation, 1997). In FY 2001, funds for the Abstinence Education Grant Program were $50 million and for Second Chance Homes were $25 million (DHHS, 2000; GISD, 2001).

Such policies are controversial because they appear to be driven solely by values and not at all by the extant research base. Indeed, any social scientific evidence to which they can be linked is itself quite controversial. Specifically, although some studies assert that teenage childbearing significantly curtails young women's future earnings, other studies suggest that the negative consequences of early childbearing have been substantially overstated and that teen mothers face a host of poverty-related stressors that serve as barriers to workforce participation (Geronimus & Korenman, 1993;

Maynard, 1997). Despite this controversy, demonstration programs such as New Chance have successfully targeted young mothers using public assistance for human capital intervention, which included motivating participants to postpone repeat childbearing and to obtain increased education and training (Quint, Bos, & Polit, 1997).

Evidence of Effectiveness. Many evaluations (including both nonexperimental and randomized experimental studies) have demonstrated human capital gains for adult women participating in federally supported education and training programs (LaLonde, 1995). Returns have included increased rates of employment among participants as well as increased numbers of hours working and increased earnings (but, given consequent cuts in eligible benefits, not overall incomes) for participants. A consensus appears to be emerging that although "work first" approaches are effective in moving more families off of public assistance and into employment in the short term, the emphasis on moving parents into unstable, low-skilled, and low-paying jobs without helping them to develop the skills needed for higher paying jobs may be shortsighted (Blank, 1995; O'Neill & O'Neill, 1997). Longer term investments in on-the-job training yield significantly higher returns via parents' earnings and via the length of time parents hold higher paying jobs (Heinrich, 1998; LaLonde, 1995). In short, it has been suggested that we "got what we paid for," with short-term, inexpensive training programs yielding returns that are effectively too small to lift families out of poverty, while greater economic and training investments in adults' skills yield substantial payoffs for both families and the state as families earn more, pay more in taxes, and are better able to support their children's development (LaLonde, 1995).

According to one recent survey, approximately 20% of college undergraduates are independent adults with incomes of less than $20,000, and among students enrolled full-time, about 30% received a Pell grant averaging just over $2,000 (U.S. Department of Education, 2001). Recent analyses of the effects of state- and federally funded financial assistance on college enrollment suggest that multiple barriers such as rising tuition costs, complex program rules, eligibility rules, and burdensome applications seriously limit low-income adults' use of financial aid and may hamper their likelihood of attending college (Kane, 1995; McPherson & Shapiro, 1991; Orfield, 1992). Clearly, federal financial aid programs such as the Pell Grants Program must be made more accessible if we hope to promote human capital gains among families who need them the most.

There is emerging evidence that some programs designed to reduce teen pregnancy, particularly those that focus on reduction of specific risky sexual behaviors, deliver consistent and strong messages and address social pressures that affect sexual behavior, can indeed delay teens' sexual behavior or increase condom and contraceptive use (Kirby, 2001). Programs that include academic support and work-related activities either instead of family life and sex education (Teen Outreach Program) or in addition to it (Children's Aid Society–Carrera Program) can delay the onset of sex, increase the use of contraception, and reduce pregnancy rates (Kirby, 2001). However, there are mixed findings on the indirect effects on marriage and childbearing from programs designed to increase income and family self-sufficiency. An analysis of the impact of increases in the EITC and changes in welfare policies on families found that, although together these changes precipitated steep increases in labor market activity among low-income single parents, there has been no accompanying increase in marriage among this population (Ellwood, 2000). Similarly, results from the New Chance welfare-to-work demonstration program, for example, found no difference between the pregnancy rates of women randomized into control and treatment groups up to 3½ years after participation in the program (Quint et al., 1997). In contrast, an evaluation of the Minnesota Family Investment Program found that two-parent families in this welfare-to-work demonstration program were 40% more likely than two-parent families receiving standard welfare to remain married after 3 years (Knox, Miller, & Gennetian, 2000).

Family-Directed Income Support

Federal expenditures designed to decrease family dependence on public aid and increase family economic self-sufficiency can be classified into five general approaches: *income supports, tax credits, federal standards for a minimum hourly wage,* the recovery of *financial support owed to children by noncustodial parents,* and efforts to *help families build assets.* Of these, the programs that have gained the most visibility during recent years have been the package of income supports and work requirements falling under the rubric of Temporary Assistance to Needy Families (TANF). In August 1996, the U.S. Congress passed the PRWORA legislation, which converted public assistance to poor families with children from a means-tested entitlement (called Aid to Families With Dependent Children [AFDC]) to a time-limited form of temporary assistance. Temporary Assistance to Needy Families has a set of clearly outlined goals, namely to (a) provide assistance to needy families; (b) end the dependence of needy parents by promoting job preparation, work, and marriage; (c) prevent and reduce out-of-wedlock pregnancies; and (d) encourage the formation and maintenance of two-parent families (Office of Family Assistance, 2001). Cash assistance is thus no longer an entitlement, as it was under AFDC, but is now time

limited and work linked. The U.S. FY 2001 block grant for TANF was $19.2 billion (GISD, 2001).

Interestingly, although public attention has focused on what has become known as "welfare reform," a greater proportion of federal resources for low-income children is delivered through tax savings offered to families. One federal tax credit program, the Earned Income Tax Credit first enacted in 1975, constitutes one of the largest federal spending programs targeted at children (Clark et al., 2001). In FY 2000, the EITC redirected $31.9 billion to 19.5 million low-income working families (GISD, 2001). In addition to the federal EITC, a growing number of states are also creating EITCs, some of which are refundable but others of which are not (Cauthen et al., 2000). The nonrefundable EITC by definition is available only to families with taxable earnings, whereas all low-income families, including those below the FPL, would be eligible for a refundable EITC. Ten states now have refundable EITCs (Cauthen et al., 2000).

A third approach to increasing family income has been to raise the minimum wage that can be paid to working parents in the United States. First enacted in 1938, the U.S. Fair Labor Standards Act sets federal standards for the minimum hourly wage to be paid to most workers, most recently setting the minimum wage at $5.15 in 1997 (U.S. Department of Labor, 2001). The current federal minimum wage is worth 25% less in real dollars than was the minimum wage in 1969 and, as a result, fails to lift even a two-person family out of poverty (U.S. Department of Labor, 2001). Based on the premise that families with at least one parent working full-time should not fall so far below the poverty line, a number of researchers, policymakers, and labor advocates have argued for a "living wage." Specifically, 11 states (Alaska, California, Connecticut, Delaware, the District of Columbia, Hawaii,

Massachusetts, Oregon, Rhode Island, Vermont, and Washington) have set their minimum wage levels above the federal level (Cauthen et al., 2000). In addition, local ordinances have been passed in approximately 19 cities to raise the minimum wage to at least $7.50 so that a family of three supported by at least one full-time worker would be raised above the poverty line (Pollin, 1998). Despite frequent arguments that raising the minimum wage would increase unemployment, there is strong research evidence that no such increase is associated with minimum wage increases (Bernstein & Schmitt, 1998).

The federal government also has taken an active role in recovering income that is owed to children by noncustodial parents. The Child Support Enforcement Program is a federal-state partnership that was established in 1975 to aid in the location of absent parents, establishment of paternity, establishment of support obligations, and enforcement of child support orders (Office of Child Support Enforcement, 2002). More than $3 billion was budgeted in FY 2001 for Child Support Enforcement (GISD, 2001). The PRWORA legislation included several strong child support items, including computerized databases of newly hired employees for tracking, streamlined paternity establishment procedures, and tough penalties such as license revocation, denial of passports, and seizure of assets from nonsupporting parents (Office of Child Support Enforcement, 2002). In addition, PRWORA allowed all states to implement full-family sanctions if custodial parents do not provide information on parents who might owe child support. Child support enforcement services are available automatically to families receiving TANF, but funds recovered are first used to reimburse state and federal programs for TANF payments to the families. Services are available for a small fee to non-TANF families.

Finally, the federal government administers a small demonstration program, called Individual Development Accounts (IDAs), to assist low-income families in saving more of what they earn. Increasingly, advocates for the poor and certain policy analysts are striving to expand policies beyond income strategies to wealth creation and asset development strategies. IDA demonstration grants are at the forefront of these efforts and were funded at $25 million for FY 2001 (GISD, 2001). Currently, among the 29 states that participate in the federal program, family savings are matched both from nonfederal and federal funds at a rate of 50¢ to $4 for every $1 saved by a participating individual. These savings cannot exceed $4,000 per household and may be used for a major capital investment such as postsecondary education, a home, or a new business. Families are eligible to participate in the federal IDA program if they are eligible for TANF or if their net worth does not exceed $10,000 excluding the value of a home and one car (Corporation for Enterprise Development, 2000; GISD, 2001). Together, income supports are thought to provide a safety net from deep poverty, whereas asset-building strategies are considered to provide a ladder up and out of poverty. Both types of strategies appear to be needed.

Evidence for Effectiveness. Welfare reform has succeeded in decreasing the number of individuals receiving cash assistance, from 14.1 million in FY 1993 to 6.3 million in FY 1999, and in increasing the percentage of adult recipients who work, from less than 7% in FY 1992 to 33% in FY 1999 (Office of Planning, Research, and Evaluation, 2000). Five years after passage of the PRWORA legislation, most evaluations of welfare reform and related demonstration programs have concluded that although many state programs have led to increases in maternal employment, they have yielded only negligible increases in parents' earnings and in family income (Duncan & Brooks-Gunn, 2000; Michalopoulos & Berlin, 2001; Morris et al., 2001). In addition, some studies have found that work participation among former welfare recipients is associated with small positive effects on young children's behavior but with small negative effects on adolescent development (Morris et al., 2001). New research suggests that these negligible effects for the total population of low-income adults may mask gains for the better-educated poor and losses for the less-educated poor (Lu, Song, & Bennett, 2001). For the group of relatively skilled, psychologically less stressed, "work-ready" parents, PRWORA appears to provide a solid set of additional supports that facilitate work participation and greater family functioning. In contrast, Paxson and Waldfogel (2001) found appreciable increases in incidence of child neglect and of out-of-home placements, suggesting that the relatively strict nature of the new welfare reform policy may be taking a serious toll on the most vulnerable families.[2]

Tax credits, in comparison, reach a much broader spectrum of both poor and near-poor families. In 1999, 19.5 million tax-payers received EITC benefits totaling $31.9 billion, with half of these payments going to families with incomes below the FPL (Hotz, Mullin, & Scholz, 2001). The EITC is credited with lifting more than 4 million families above the FPL and with increasing employment rates up to 21% for single parents with one child and up to 45% for single parents with two or more children (Hotz et al., 2001). In a recent simulation, researchers at the National Center for Children in Poverty estimated that if all 50 states adopted refundable state EITCs worth about 50% of the federal EITC, more than 1 million more children would be lifted out of poverty (Bennett & Lu, 2001).[3]

Recovery of income from noncustodial parents has demonstrated considerable success in raising larger numbers of children out of poverty. According to data published by the U.S. Census Bureau (1998), in 1997, 39% of poor parents for whom child support had been agreed or awarded did not receive any payments. Custodial parents were found to be owed $12 billion in child support payments in 1997 (U.S. Census Bureau, 1998). The Child Support Enforcement Program appears to be successful in addressing this deficit; in FY 2000, the program assisted in the collection of $17.9 billion in child support payments redirected in support of 19.4 million children (Office of Child Support Enforcement, 2001). The program is fairly efficient, garnering $3.95 in payments for every $1 spent by the program, and primarily assists families who are current or past recipients of TANF (65% of its caseload [Office of Child Support Enforcement, 2001]). The combination of child support laws and enforcement at the state and federal levels does help to increase the incomes of custodial parents, with child support comprising about one fifth of their incomes (Garfinkel, Heintze, & Huang, 2000).

Data from the first large-scale evaluation of IDAs, begun in 1997, suggest that families can be helped to save more of what they earn. Across 14 sites, working poor families attended an average of 10.5 hours of financial education and were able to save an average of $353, which then was matched to grow on average to $900 per year, amounts that constituted an increase of 1,800% in their net worth (given debts and assets at enrollment) (Schreiner et al., 2001). One drawback of the program is that its costs are quite high at $2.77 per $1 of net deposits by participants (Schriener et al., 2001). Despite the savings increases, participants used only 67% of their match eligibility; plans to bring such programs to scale will need to determine the reasons why families are unable to take full advantage of the matching funds.[4]

Family-Directed In-Kind Support

As noted in our discussions of financial hardship and social exclusion, the range of income supports developed to assist low-income families still falls short of providing families with the resources to obtain the goods and services they need for basic living. It is to this gap between goods and services needed and those that families can afford that most in-kind support programs and policies are targeted. There is a wide range of programs designed to provide additional support to low-income families with children by reducing some of the costs associated with their food, health care, child care, and housing. Through the provision of in-kind support, the federal government helps many needy children, and their parents have their basic daily needs met. Policy analysts also have pointed out that in-kind transfers allow the federal government to regulate the type of inputs provided for children by specifying the types of food that can be bought with Food Stamps, for example, or by restricting the type of housing that can be obtained with housing assistance vouchers. On the other hand, other policy analyses emphasize that in-kind programs support parents and thus help children indirectly by reducing parents' financial burden and accompanying stress.

Children's Nutrition. The Food Stamp Program provides in-kind benefits (in the form of paper coupons or electronic debit cards) with which recipients may buy eligible food in authorized retail food stores so as to improve their diets. The cost of the Food Stamp Program was $16 billion in FY 2001 (GISD, 2001). Eligibility requirements for receipt of food stamps tightened with the passage of the 1997 PRWORA legislation such that eligibility for food stamps is restricted based on family income (e.g., $1,421 per month for a family of four), amount of countable resources (e.g., $2,000 in bank accounts), allowable deductions, work status (all eligible able-bodied adults between 18 and 60 years of age must meet work requirements), and citizenship status (Food and Nutrition Service, 2000). However, states now have the option to pay the cost to provide food stamps to noncitizens made ineligible for them through welfare reform; as of December 2000, eight states had elected to do so (GISD, 2001).

The Special Supplemental Food Program for Women, Infants, and Children (WIC), a joint federal and state program authorized by Congress in 1972, provides nutrition education, food supplements, and health and social service referrals to low-income pregnant and postpartum women and their children up to 5 years of age (Food and Nutrition Service, 2001e). Women with children whose incomes are below 185% of the FPL and are certified by a health professional as at nutritional risk are eligible for WIC (Food and Nutrition Service, 2001e). In addition, 11 states supplement federal WIC funds with state funds (Cauthen et al., 2000). In FY 1999, more than 7 million people, of which 76% were children, received WIC benefits each month (Food and Nutrition Service, 2001e) at a total cost of more than $4 billion in FY 2001 (GISD, 2001).

The National School Lunch Program is sponsored by the U.S. Department of Agriculture and provides schoolchildren with one third or more of their U.S. Department of Agriculture Recommended Dietary Allowance for Key Nutrients (RDA) (Food and Nutrition Service, 2001d; Subcommittee on the Tenth Edition of the RDAs, Food and Nutrition Board, Commission on Life Sciences, National Research Council, 1989). More than $5.7 billion was budgeted for the National School Lunch Program and $1.48 billion for the School Breakfast Program in

FY 2001 (GISD, 2001). The School Breakfast Program provides one fourth or more of children's RDA (Food and Nutrition Service, 2001c). Children are eligible to receive reduced-price lunches/breakfasts if their families have annual incomes below 185% of the FPL and free lunches/breakfasts if their family incomes are below 130% of the FPL (Food and Nutrition Service, 2001c, 2001d).

Evidence for Effectiveness. Although Food Stamp Program participation per month averaged 17 million in FY 2000, with children constituting 53% of all recipients (GISD, 2001), the program has fallen short of serving the entirety of its eligible population, with 4 of 10 eligible people not receiving benefits (Castner, 2000; Schirm, 2000) and 16% of children living in poverty not receiving food stamps (U.S. General Accounting Office [GAO], 1999). Similarly, although WIC provided benefits to more than 7 million women, infants, and children in FY 2000 (GISD, 2001), it is estimated that WIC benefits fail to reach approximately 19% of eligible women, infants, and children (Food and Nutrition Service, 2001c). In FY 2000, nearly 27 million children received reduced-price or free school lunches, and more than 7 million children received reduced-price or free breakfasts (Food and Nutrition Service, 2001b, 2001c). As of FY 2000, approximately 82% of those children eligible for free lunches and 71% of those eligible for reduced-price lunches participated in the School Lunch Program (J. Tressler, Food and Nutrition Service, personal communication, August 3, 2001).

Some policy analysts have noted a sharp reduction in Food Stamp Program participation during the past 5 years, with aspects of individual states' implementation of welfare reform, such as whether they have short time limits for welfare receipt and less generous income disregards, identified as potential reasons (Jacobson, Rodriguez-Planas, Puffer, Pas, & Taylor-Kale, 2001). In addition to these potential administrative causes, it may be that families are leaving the Food Stamp Program because parents have found work and are experiencing an increase in income. However, some research suggests that this decrease in use of food stamps is not due to a decrease in material deprivation or to an improvement in family well-being; among families leaving the Food Stamp Program in Illinois, for example, more than 20% of families reported extreme poverty and moderate or severe hunger and food insecurity (Rangarajan & Gleason, 2001).

Receipt of federal nutritional assistance has repeatedly been associated with significant measurable improvements in children's nutritional and physical health. For example, receipt of food stamps is indeed associated with children's increased levels of vitamin B6, folate, and iron intake as well as with an overall increase in families' food security (Perez-Escamilla et al., 2000). WIC receipt has been associated with a range of positive outcomes for mothers and their children, including fewer premature births, lower incidence of low-birthweight babies, higher mean intakes of key nutrients, improved rates of childhood immunization, improved child cognitive abilities, and improved growth rates (Food and Nutrition Service, 1987; Heimendinger, Larid, Austin, Timmer, & Gershoff, 1984; Kowaleski-Jones & Duncan, 2001; Lee, Bilaver, & Goerge, 2001; Rose, Habicht, & Devaney, 1998). In total, every dollar spent on WIC results in $3.50 in savings, primarily due to reductions in preterm and low-birthweight infants (GAO, 1992). School food programs are effective in improving older children's diets: Low-income children who attend schools with the School Breakfast Program are significantly more likely to eat breakfasts with food energy greater than 10% of the RDA (Devaney & Stuart, 1998). Children who participate in school breakfast and/or school lunch programs obtain about half of their food energy for the day from these school-provided foods (Gleason & Suitor, 2001).

To date, developmental psychologists have not extensively considered the potential direct or indirect effects that food stamps, WIC, or subsidized school lunch/breakfast receipt might have on children's cognitive, socioemotional, or behavioral outcomes. Evaluation of WIC and school lunch programs suggests that these programs help children to do better on standardized achievement tests, to have better records of school attendance, and to need fewer special educational services (Nutrition-Cognition National Advisory Committee, 1998). Examinations of smaller scale nutrition interventions (e.g., through nutrition clinics) have found significant differences in cognitive, motor, and behavioral development among treated children as compared with control children (e.g., Hutcheson et al., 1997; Waber et al., 1981). Presumably, low-income children with greater nutritional advantage would be more likely to thrive with family, peers, and teachers than would low-income children struggling with greater food insecurity and poorer nutritional health. Greater inclusion of the potential extended effects of nutrition programs is needed in future developmentally oriented poverty research.

Children's Health Insurance Coverage: Medicaid and SCHIP. Medicaid is a federal-state health insurance program for low-income individuals and families. The Medicaid program allows states flexibility in determining eligibility requirements; as a result, income eligibility levels among a few states range as high as 350% of the FPL, yet the majority of state programs cover families with annual incomes 100% to 150% of the FPL (DHHS, 2002). In FY 2000, approximately 33.4 million individuals were enrolled in the Medicaid program (GISD, 2001); estimates that nearly half of all Medicaid

enrollees are children (DHHS, 2002) would put the number of children covered by Medicaid at 16.7 million. Total FY 2001 funds for Medicaid (for adults and children) were estimated to be $130 billion (GISD, 2001).

The State Children's Health Insurance Program (CHIP), created in 1997 under Title XXI of the Social Security Act, provides states with money to expand health care coverage to children whose families earn too much for Medicaid but too little to afford private coverage. States may cover children in families whose incomes are above the Medicaid eligibility threshold but less than 200% of the FPL or up to 50 percentage points above the state's current Medicaid income limit for children (DHHS, 2002). States implemented the program by expanding their Medicaid programs, designing new child health insurance programs, or a combination of the two. In FY 2001, $4.2 billion was budgeted for CHIP to ensure health care coverage for an estimated 2.6 million low-income children (GISD, 2001).

Evidence for Effectiveness. Estimates of health insurance coverage using the March 1998 data from the Current Population Survey have revealed that up to 28% of children whose family incomes are below 200% of the FPL do not have health insurance (Schirm & Czajka, 2000); the highest rate of noncoverage is for those children whose family incomes fell between 100% and 150% of the FPL. Even with the addition of CHIP, the number of children ineligible for health insurance is high; of the 11.5 million uninsured children in the United States, 4.2 million are eligible for Medicaid and an additional 2.4 million are eligible for CHIP, leaving 4.9 million children still ineligible for insurance (Schirm & Czajka, 2000). Unfortunately, eligibility alone does not guarantee coverage; these same analyses estimated that approximately 22% of children eligible for Medicaid remain uninsured (Schirm & Czajka, 2000).

When children do receive federal- or state-sponsored medical insurance, outcomes are typically positive. For example, the preventive care provided through Medicaid has been associated with a reduced likelihood that children will be hospitalized (Gadomski, Jenkins, & Nichols, 1998). Evaluations of the new CHIP programs are still in the beginning stages. Preliminary evidence comes from the program on which CHIP was modeled, New York State's Child Health Plus Program, which has been associated with improvements in children's use of preventive care; immunization rates; and anemia, lead level, vision, and hearing screenings (Holl et al., 2000). As with many of the other in-kind transfer programs described thus far, we do not yet have clear empirical evidence that low-income children who are healthier as a result of federal health insurance programs are also better off academically, cognitively, and/or socioemotionally than without such programs. We urge future evaluations to consider the long-term benefits that may accrue (e.g., fewer days missed of school, fewer behavior problems) across multiple domains in child well-being by such programs.

Child Care. Currently, more than 13 million children under 5 years of age spend time in a wide range of child care settings that include the homes of relatives and non-relatives, center-based care, pre-kindergarten programs, and Head Start programs (Hofferth, Shauman, Henke, & West, 1998; Innes, Denton, & West, 2001). Recent surveys suggest that 81% of kindergartners have spent some time in child care settings outside their homes during the prior year and that although the bulk of child care environments are adequate, low-income children are disproportionately likely to attend poorer quality care settings (Burchinal & Nelson, 2000; Innes et al., 2001; Peisner-Feinberg

et al., 1999). In addition, child care is extremely costly to low-income families, representing 27% of their disposable family income, with high-quality care at an affordable cost extremely hard to come by (GAO, 1994). Increasing the availability of subsidized high-quality care would substantially increase the likelihood that low-income mothers could work and thereby increase family income (GAO, 1994). In short, the twin policy challenges of child care for low-income children are to find means of increasing low-income children's access to affordable child care while at the same time improving the quality of care that low-income children receive.

With the advent of the PRWORA welfare reform legislation in 1996, a highly fragmented federal system of child care subsidies was consolidated into one federal program, the Child Care and Development Fund (CCDF). In FY 1999, the CCDF served 1.8 million children throughout the United States, 54% of whom were under 5 years of age (Child Care Bureau, 2001); with substantial funding increases over the past several years, CCDF funds for FY 2001 were budgeted at more than $4 billion (GISD, 2001). Families with children under 13 years of age and whose incomes do not exceed 85% of the state median income are eligible for CCDF funds (GISD, 2001). In addition, TANF provides states the option of transferring up to 30% of their grants to their CCDF programs such that the transferred TANF funds now account for a larger percentage of child care funding than does CCDF (Flynn, 1999). Importantly, there are no restrictions imposed on states for the type or quality of child care provided; rather, states are encouraged to respect parent preferences for family- or center-based care.

Evidence for Effectiveness. With increasing numbers of mothers moving from "welfare to work" through TANF, shortages in regulated care, particularly in low-income neighborhoods and for infants and toddlers, have been reported (Layzer & Collins, 2000), as has low program use by eligible families, with only 10% to 15% of eligible families served (Blau & Tekin, 2001). Subsidy receipt has been found to be associated with a 5 percentage point increase in employment and with an 8 percentage point increase in school attendance (Blau & Tekin, 2001). Recent research suggests that for low-income children, investments in high-quality care pay off through considerable gains in children's cognitive growth (Burchinal et al., 2000).

Housing. Poor families face the double bind of having to spend a larger proportion of their incomes on housing than do their affluent counterparts and of facing a rapidly shrinking stock of low-cost housing from which to choose. A 1997 Report to Congress by the U.S. Department of Housing and Urban Development (HUD) suggests that the number of working poor families facing "worst-case" housing needs (meaning that they spend more than half of their incomes on rent or live in seriously substandard housing) was rising rapidly during the late 1990s, with more than 2 million families with children identified as having worst-case housing problems in 1995 (HUD, 1998). Poor families also spend a greater proportion of their incomes on heating their homes; DHHS estimates that the energy burden for low-income households is 12.5% of income as compared with an average 6.3% energy burden for all households (Office of Community Services, 2000, 2001).

The federal government offers two major types of housing assistance to families whose incomes fall below 50% of the median income for the county or metropolitan area in which the family chooses to live: public housing and Section 8 housing vouchers. In both cases, families are required to pay rent of approximately 30% of their adjusted incomes. Funding for public housing is disbursed by HUD through local housing agencies that manage the housing for low-income residents at rents they can afford (HUD, 2001a, 2001b). Through the Section 8 Housing Choice Voucher Program, HUD assists very low-income families in affording safe and sanitary housing in the private market; eligibility is restricted to U.S. citizens (HUD, 2001a). More than 1.8 million housing vouchers were available in FY 2000 (GISD, 2001). In addition, the Low Income Home Energy Assistance Program (LIHEAP) assists low-income families (those with incomes at or below 150% of the FPL or 60% of state median income [GISD, 2001]) in meeting heating, cooling, weatherization, and/or energy crisis needs. Fiscal year 2001 funding for these programs was budgeted at $3 billion for public housing, $11.4 billion for Section 8 vouchers, and $2.2 billion for LIHEAP (GISD, 2001).

Evidence for Effectiveness. More than 4 million families live in HUD-assisted (via public housing or vouchers) rental units in the United States, with HUD therefore subsidizing the housing of one fourth of the 15.8 million eligible households (HUD USER, 1997). In addition, approximately 4.1 million households received some form of LIHEAP assistance in 2000 (GISD, 2001), but this assistance reached only 13% of eligible households (compared with 36% in 1981) and covered only 9% of families' energy bills (compared with 23% in 1981) (Office of Community Services, 2000). Clearly, there are many poor households that are not served by these programs, as reflected in the long waiting lists for Section 8 vouchers cited in a number of reports.

Mounting evidence suggests that housing assistance, when offered, can make a substantial difference in the lives of poor children. For example, HUD recently offered publicly housed families the opportunity to use Section

8 vouchers in low-poverty neighborhoods, with considerable counseling and support in locating and transitioning into new, more affluent neighborhoods. Efforts to fill buildings and neighborhoods with greater income mixing may have some benefits for those low-income families that are allowed to reside in the mixed-income neighborhoods, but it limits the number of low-income families served (HUD USER, 1997). Over the past several years, HUD has sponsored the Moving to Opportunity (MTO) demonstration project that randomly assigns families living in public housing to a low-poverty neighborhood housing voucher condition, a geographically unrestricted condition, or a control condition. The MTO demonstration project has found that providing the chance for families to relocate to low-poverty neighborhoods is associated with a range of positive outcomes, including a reduction in welfare receipt, increased feelings of neighborhood safety, decreased victimization, lower incidence of injuries and asthma attacks among children, and fewer child behavior problems (Del Conte & Kling, 2001; Katz, Kling, & Liebman, 2001). Regarding heating assistance, research is still needed to determine whether provision of income to cover heat alleviates the "heat or eat" dilemma that families may face, effectively freeing parents to invest an increasing portion of family income directly in their children.

Transportation. One of the barriers to employment most frequently cited among the poor is inability to pay for or to access transportation (Federal Transit Administration [FTA], 1998; Polit & O'Hara, 1989). With the passage of welfare reform and new work requirements for benefit receipt, the issue of physically getting welfare recipients to the workplace has become a prime concern. The federal government has recognized that transportation is a major challenge facing those transitioning from welfare to work.

With barriers such as distance of available jobs, the inconvenience of evening and weekend shifts, and poor service by existing transit systems, it has been estimated that fewer than half of the entry-level jobs are accessible by transit (FTA, 2000). Beginning in 1998, three federal agencies (DHHS, the Department of Labor [DOL], and the Department of Transportation [DOT]) jointly responded by establishing a systematic response to the transportation needs of welfare recipients (FTA, 2000). Funding sources from each of these agencies can be used in response to the work- and child care-related transportation needs of welfare recipients, namely the TANF block grant (DHHS), the Welfare to Work (WtW) competitive grant program (DOL), and the Job Access and Reverse Commute grant program (DOT) (FTA, 2000).

Of the $16.5 billion allocated in FY 2001 for TANF and the slightly less than $1 billion allocated in FY 2001 for WtW, funds for transportation services must be allocated according to certain guidelines, but actual amounts or percentages are left to the discretion of individual states. Federal TANF funds can be used for several transportation-related programs, including transportation allowances; reimbursements for car mileage, repair, and insurance; and subsidization of transporting children to child care (Federal Transit Administration, 2000; Office of Family Assistance, 2001). The Job Access and Reverse Commute grant program was created in 1998 to (a) develop new and expand existing transportation services for welfare recipients and low-income workers and (b) provide transportation for low-income workers from urban or rural locations to suburban employment centers (FTA, 2000, 2001). Funded at $115 million in FY 2001, the Job Access and Reverse Commute grant program funds projects such as transportation vouchers, fixed-route extensions, emergency child care transportation, guaranteed ride home programs, and additional bus lines (GISD, 2001).

Evidence of Effectiveness. The PRWORA-inspired collaboration among DHHS, DOL, and DOT is relatively new, and thus no effectiveness data are yet available. However, a group of transportation-based demonstration programs, known as JOBLINKS, was begun just before the advent of welfare reform through a collaboration between the FTA and the Community Transportation Association of America (CTAA). The goal of JOBLINKS was to test methods of helping unemployed and underemployed transportation-deficient individuals to travel to job training or employment locations (CTAA, 1999). Among the transportation solutions tested were demand-responsive van service, fixed-route reverse commute express, volunteer car pools, volunteer rural ride service, weekend fixed-route transit, and micro-business development in which welfare recipients start their own transit service (CTAA, 2001). The demonstration projects found that the provision of transportation assistance will be productive only if (a) the services could accommodate available shift time; (b) the community supported the role of publicly sponsored transportation as a means to overcoming a barrier to employment; (c) there was significant coordination among transportation providers, human services agencies, and employers; (d) the services included flexibility in designing and adjusting services in response to users' needs; and (e) transporting children to child care is included (CTAA, 1999, 2001). The extent to which these lessons will be implemented by the DHHS, DOL, and DOT programs described here awaits future evaluations.

Parent-Directed Interventions

Parent education, training, and support programs can reduce the risks associated with parenting and home environments in impoverished families by providing effective activities and strategies for parents' repertoires and/or by fostering enhancements in parents' mental states (Smith & Zaslow, 1995). There is a risk that parenting interventions targeted at low-income families unintentionally blame these families for their circumstances; to avoid this risk, such programs should balance emphases on parenting strategies and on social and economic factors in families' lives (Cowan, Powell, & Cowan, 1998).

Of the range of parenting interventions currently implemented throughout the country, few focus on a single set of parenting processes such as parent investment, parent behaviors, and parent distress. Rather, many programs attempt to provide education, training, and support in two or three of these areas. In this section, we discuss two main strategies for the delivery of parent-directed interventions: home visiting/family preservation and family support; in a later section, we briefly review interventions that combine parent- and child-directed strategies.

Home Visiting, Family Preservation, and Family Support Programs. Home visiting, family preservation, and family support programs span a broad range of theoretical orientations and types of services, from an emphasis on teaching parents about appropriate developmental milestones, effective parenting strategies, early learning activities, and available social services to mental health and public health foci oriented toward improving maternal mental health, economic self-sufficiency, and social support (Brooks-Gunn, Berlin, & Fuligni, 2000; Gomby, Culross, & Behrman, 1999). Many of these programs aim to improve families' provision of cognitive stimulation and sensitive responsive care as well as to curtail families' use of inconsistent, harsh, coercive, and emotionally volatile parenting as an indirect means of improving children's later life chances (for reviews, see Brooks-Gunn et al., 2000; Gomby et al., 1999). Home visiting programs, through which trained professionals and/or paraprofessionals give parents a range of supports and services in their home, have been implemented extensively in large demonstration projects in diverse rural and urban contexts (see Brooks-Gunn et al., 2000; Olds et al., 1998).

Funding for family preservation and family support is provided through the federal Promoting Safe and Stable Families program. Federal funds (budgeted at $295 million for FY 2001 [GISD, 2001]) are targeted to the state child welfare agencies that operate such services. *Family preservation* services are typically targeted to families that are experiencing crises or identified for serious child abuse or neglect and thus are at risk for having children removed from the home. Such services include in-home assistance in crisis intervention, managing home finances, obtaining appropriate services, and modeling of parenting techniques (Children's Bureau, 2001; Fraser, Nelson, & Rivard, 1997). *Family support* services are those that provide direct services to families so as to assist parents in meeting their responsibilities as parents (Epstein, Larner, & Halpern, 1995; Family Support America, 1996). Such services encompass respite care, early developmental screening of children, tutoring, and health education provided through both centers and home visiting programs (Children's Bureau, 2001). In addition, several states are developing *family resource centers*, which are neighborhood-based centers to offer a variety of services to parents and families, including parent education, child development screening, child care, health services, family literacy programs, and referrals to other resources (Cauthen et al., 2000).

Evidence for Effectiveness. To date, a variety of family support and family preservation methods have been used with families in need that draw from social learning, family systems, and ecological theories of child and family development (Brooks-Gunn

et al., 2000; McRoy, Christian, & Gershoff, 2000; Olds & Kitzman, 1993; Ramey & Ramey, 1992). One recent estimate suggests that communities are investing $170 million in home visiting programs targeting families from pregnancy through early childhood (Leventhal, 2001). Family support programs (e.g., Hawaii's Healthy Start Program [Duggan et al., 1999], Avance [Walker, Rodriguez, Johnson, & Cortez, 1995], Home Instruction Program for Preschool Youngsters [Baker, Piotrkowski, & Brooks-Gunn, 1999]) and family preservation programs (e.g., Homebuilders [Kinney, Madsen, Fleming, & Haapala, 1977]) have demonstrated some success in improving parenting behaviors, keeping families together, and reducing out-of-home child placements (Brooks-Gunn et al., 2000; Fraser et al., 1997; Leventhal, 2001; McRoy et al., 2000). However, when these family-focused programs are expanded "to scale" and then evaluated, results are less encouraging (see Gomby et al., 1999; Goodson, Layzer, St. Pierre, Bernstein, & Lopez, 2000; Heneghan, Horwitz, & Leventhal, 1996; Jacobs, 2001). Specifically, recent evaluations suggest wide variability in the ways in which programs are designed and implemented across different contexts (Duggan et al., 2000; Jacobs, 2001) and in which families benefit from program participation (Eckenrode et al., 2000). If successful, such preventive efforts could constitute considerable savings for families, their communities, and social service agencies, for example, with family preservation services costing $3,000 to $5,000 per family as compared with out-of-home placement services costing approximately $10,000 per year (Forsythe, 1992).

Two-Generation Interventions

In addition to providing supports to poor families, the past 40 years have also seen a rise in federal efforts to help young children directly through programs that assist parents and children at multiple levels, often called "two-generation" programs for their focus on both parents and their children (Smith & Zaslow, 1995).

Head Start and Early Intervention Programs. Foremost among these types of two-generation programs is Head Start, the chief federal early childhood program for children 3 or 4 years of age that also includes a range of health, screening, and nutrition services; indeed, 90% of Head Start enrollees are at or below the FPL (GISD, 2001). From its inception, Head Start was intended to provide direct services and supports both to low-income children and to their parents, yet the parent component has been largely neglected in Head Start programs (Zigler & Styfco, 1993). In 2000, Head Start served 857,664 children, the majority of whom were 3 or 4 years of age; the ethnic composition of the served population was 35% black, 30% white, 29% Hispanic, 3% American Indian, 2% Asian, and 1% Hawaiian/Pacific Islander (Head Start Bureau, 2001). Since its inception in 1965, Head Start has served 19.4 million low-income children (GISD, 2001). Funds for FY 2001 were budgeted at $6.2 billion (GISD, 2001). In the context of welfare reform, Head Start increasingly meets a pressing need for well-regulated and high-quality child care for low-income preschoolers (Innes et al., 2001). In addition, Head Start affords an early opportunity to identify young children in need of more intensive services through developmental screening and referral (Forness et al., 1998; Yoshikawa & Knitzer, 1997) and to provide increased services and support to more fragile families (Fantuzzo, Stevenson, Weiss, & Hampton, 1997).

Evidence for Effectiveness. Through numerous reviews and evaluations of early childhood education programs, relative consensus has emerged that high-quality, early childhood interventions such as the Abecedarian Project (Campbell & Ramey, 1994) and the High/Scope Perry Preschool (Schwienhart & Weikart, 1980) can make a nontrivial difference in children's cognitive performance (estimated at between 4 and 11 points on standardized measures of IQ [St. Pierre & Layzar, 1998]) and an even larger difference in children's early academic achievement (Karoly et al., 1998; Reynolds, 2000). Savings to taxpayers across the life of a child are also significant. It has been estimated that the Perry Preschool program enabled taxpayer savings of $13,000 per family enrolled, including reductions in welfare and criminal justice costs and increases in tax revenues (Karoly et al., 1998). One recent meta-analysis of state-funded preschools emphasized that the lack of rigorous evaluation design seriously hampers any interpretation that can be made of the few modest short-term gains regarding participating preschoolers' school readiness (effect sizes of approximately $d = .20$ [Gilliam & Zigler, 2000]). Despite these promising effects of fairly small-scale early interventions, the nationally implemented Head Start program itself has not been systematically evaluated. A national randomized trial evaluation of Head Start funded by DHHS is planned for the next few years, and the results of this study will likely provide a clearer understanding of the ways in which Head Start may make a difference for young children's emotional development and school readiness.

It is important to note that early childhood education cannot be expected to "inoculate" children from the chronic and debilitating costs of chronic exposure to poverty-related stressors during later childhood; effects of preschool-aged interventions have been found to "fade out" during the early years of children's elementary educational experiences

(Zigler & Styfco, 2001). Importantly, even with these diminished effects in children's cognitive performance, some evaluation research has convincingly demonstrated impressive benefits in children's long-term school performance such as reduced grade retention, lower rates of placement in special education classes, and higher rates of productive citizenship as young adults, with higher rates of high school graduation and employment along with lower rates of criminal behavior and reliance on public assistance (Karoly et al., 1998).

The Comprehensive Child Development Program and Early Head Start. To meet growing family needs not met by traditional child care programs, new models such as the School of the 21st Century have been developed throughout the country to meet the need for both quality and affordable early child care and after-school care as well as for parent training and mental health services (Zigler, Finn-Stevenson, & Stern, 1997). In 1988, the federal government funded a national family support demonstration, the Comprehensive Child Development Program (CCDP), that combined child-directed services (e.g., health care, developmental screenings) and parent-directed services (e.g., health care, parent education, job training, education enhancement) (Parker, Piotrkowski, Horn, & Greene, 1995; St. Pierre & Layzer, 1999). Most recent is the new Early Head Start program, which was designed to affect outcomes in four domains: child development (including health, social, and cognitive development), family development (including parenting practices, relationships between parents and children, home environment, family health, parent involvement, and economic self-sufficiency), staff development, and community development (including quality of child care and integration of family support services) (Paulsell et al., 2000). In the recent and ongoing evaluation of Early Head Start, low-income pregnant women and families with infants or toddlers were offered (through random assignment) center-based services (which included two home visits per year), home visiting services (weekly home visits), or a combination of the two (Commissioner's Office of Research and Evaluation and the Head Start Bureau, 2001).

Evidence for Effectiveness. Unfortunately, the CCDP did not yield any meaningful positive effects on participating families, with program and control families indistinguishable on key child developmental outcomes and on parent economic self-sufficiency outcomes (St. Pierre & Layzer, 1999). The program was also quite expensive at $10,849 per family per year as compared with $4,500 per family per year for Head Start (St. Pierre & Layzer, 1999).

Preliminary results suggest that Early Head Start has more positive effects, with the national evaluation of Early Head Start showing very promising effects of the program for parents and their children. Early Head Start mothers were found to be more supportive, more sensitive, less detached, more likely to engage in cognitively stimulating play with their children, and less likely to use corporal punishment than were comparison mothers (Commissioner's Office of Research and Evaluation and the Head Start Bureau, 2001). Children enrolled in Early Head Start evidenced stronger cognitive and language development than did children not enrolled in the program (Commissioner's Office of Research and Evaluation and the Head Start Bureau, 2001). It remains for future analysts to identify why some two-generation models yield positive results, while others do not.

Child-Directed Programs

Federal antipoverty efforts have also been designed to assist children directly through services provided in schools, child care, and community settings.

Title I. Enacted in 1965 as part of the War on Poverty, Title I provides federal funding to school districts with 50% or more of their students living in poverty. The need for such assistance is clear: Government research has identified an increasing achievement gap between high- and low-poverty schools, with students at high-poverty schools showing declines in achievement as compared with students at low-poverty schools showing increases in achievement (Planning and Evaluation Service, 2001a, 2001b). Title I represents the largest federal investment for both elementary and secondary education and is directed to help local school districts to assist children in greatest jeopardy of failing academically (GAO, 2000). Approximately 58% of all public schools receive Title I funds (Planning and Evaluation Service, 2001a), enabling the program to reach 12.7 million children nationally at an average cost of $472 per low-income student (GISD, 2001; Planning and Evaluation Service, 2001a). Funding was set at $8.6 billion in expenditures in FY 2001 (GISD, 2001), with disbursement of these funds (e.g., to curriculum reform, to instructional change) at the discretion of states and school districts. An increasing share of this funding is directed toward the provision of preschool services for low-income children, with more than 12% of Title I funds being spent on preschool programs serving children 3 to 5 years of age (Planning and Evaluation Service, 2001a). The reach of this program makes it one of the largest educational initiatives in its levels of federal support for low-income preschool-aged children, second only to Head Start.

Evidence for Effectiveness. Title I assistance is received by 96% of the highest poverty schools (Planning and Evaluation Service, 2001a), indicating strong penetration of the program to the eligible population. Overall, evaluations of Title I over the years have demonstrated reading and math achievement increases among children in the highest-poverty schools (Planning and Evaluation Service, 2000). However, a recently published government evaluation of school performance change found overall that children in schools receiving Title I funds did not meet national norms in achievement (Planning and Evaluation Service, 2001b). This same study did find increases when teachers rated their professional development highly and when teachers were active in outreach to the parents of low-achieving students (Planning and Evaluation Service, 2001b). It may be particularly difficult to evaluate the effectiveness of Title I dollars spent on young children's education given that Title I dollars can be combined with other federal, state, and local district funds (GAO, 2000). Despite this challenge, Title I support to low-income school districts shows continued promise for helping to increase low-income students' achievement.

After-School Programs. Recent trends of increased labor force participation of women and recognition that neighborhoods no longer provide safe and appropriate after-school environments for many children have led policymakers to focus increased attention on the funding of after-school programs (Halpern, Deich, & Cohen, 2000). Funds for after-school programs, which are those that provide organized activities for school-aged children during non-school hours, are available through more than 100 federal programs (Reder, 2000). Primary direct federal funding for after-school programs comes from four main programs. The 21st Century Community Learning Centers program provides schools with funding to expand learning opportunities and to reduce drug use and violence (De Kanter, Williams, Cohen, &

Stonehill, 2000). Congress has increased funding for this program dramatically, from $40 million in FY 1998 to $846 million in FY 2001. The Child Care and Development Fund, although primarily used to provide subsidies to low-income working families with children under 5 years of age, can be allocated by states for after-school care, and 46% of CCDF funds in FY 1999 were used to serve children age 5 years or over through after-school care (Child Care Bureau, 2001). Temporary Assistance to Needy Families provides states the option of spending their funds on after-school programs or transferring up to 30% of their grants to their CCDF programs (Flynn, 1999). The majority of the $1.6 billion spent on the Child and Adult Care Food Program in FY 1999 went to children's programs, much of which went to providing free snacks to school-aged children and youth through after-school programs in low-income areas (Food and Nutrition Service, 2001a).

Evidence for Effectiveness. Despite increasing funding, the GAO has estimated that after-school programs will meet as little as 25% of the demand in some urban areas (GAO, 1998). Indeed, as many as 8 million children 5 to 14 years of age spend time without adult supervision on a regular basis (National Institute on Out-of-School Time, 2001). The 21st Century Community Learning Centers program is relatively new, and evaluations of its effects are ongoing. Research on a range of after-school care programs has found that children in such programs spend more time in learning and academic activities (Posner & Vandell, 1999), are less likely to use drugs and to become teen parents (DHHS, 1996), and, if they attend high-quality programs, are more likely to evidence improvements in peer relations, conflict resolution skills, and conduct as compared with children not in after-school programs (Baker & Witt, 1996; Posner & Vandell, 1999).

CHALLENGES TO PROGRAM AND POLICY EFFORTS TO FURTHER REDUCE CHILD POVERTY IN THE UNITED STATES

In this chapter, we have endeavored to accomplish three goals: (a) to clarify the varying conceptual and operational definitions of poverty; (b) to summarize the extant research on the determinants and consequences of child poverty by proposing a conceptual model that is integrative of different research traditions, is testable, and makes explicit the multiple potential targets for program and policy intervention; and (c) to describe the federal program and policy initiatives to reduce child poverty and/or enhance low-income children's health and development using this conceptual framework to organize our thinking.

To our minds, there are several important implications of our descriptions. First, the processes that cause poverty and that in turn affect parents and children constitute a highly complex multilevel system that is resistant to change. Thus, it is unlikely that small fragmented program or policy changes aimed at only one part of this complex system are likely to yield dramatic results. Rather, many significant and coordinated changes are likely required to improve the economic security of low-income families and the health and development of their children. Second, although multiple changes are needed, not all program and policy changes are equally likely to lead to improved family economic security and child well-being. Some targets of change represent truly causal processes, yet some are just epiphenomenal to the causal processes. We have learned how to change some processes but not others. As well, some changes are highly consistent with broadly shared social values, while others are not. We believe that antipoverty strategies can and should be identified that are empirically demonstrated to be effective, consistent with shared American social values and within our economic means to adopt. The role of research in part is to identify those processes and strategies with the most potential leverage for promoting positive change.

Throughout the chapter, we have identified issues for which more and better research is needed. There is a very rich and compelling research agenda that should be developed and implemented to assist and guide the necessary program and policy changes. Yet although more study is critical, it is past time for our nation to act more powerfully and decisively on the knowledge base we already have. Indeed, this chapter is filled with evidence-based program and policy strategies that have demonstrated significant potential to reduce child poverty and to enhance low-income children's health and development.

What is needed to act more powerfully on the knowledge we already possess? We wish to identify here some remaining critical goals related to child poverty policies and programs:

- *Understand attitudinal barriers.* We believe that one of the most important obstacles to action is a set of American attitudes toward the poor that sap our collective political will to make changes. Great advances in understanding attitudes toward social problems have been made over the past decade. For example, in trying to explain why Americans "hate welfare," Gilens (1999) analyzed reams of polling and other opinion data and determined that the strongest influences on Americans' support for welfare programs are the extent to which they view blacks as lazy and welfare recipients as undeserving. These potential biases go against facts about poverty in the United States, namely that many welfare recipients are white (33% vs. 39% black) and do work (33%) (Office of Planning, Research, and Evaluation, 2000). In other important research, Iyengar (1990) and others have demonstrated that much media coverage of poverty and welfare issues uses "frames"

that invoke and reinforce a perception that poverty is caused by individual traits and behaviors and not by systemic or structural factors. These types of attitudinal research help to explain why policymakers emphasize personal responsibility over social responsibility in their strategies to address issues of poverty. Until we better understand attitudes toward child poverty, it will be difficult to craft effective communication strategies to develop the public will needed to promote effective programs and policies.

- *Overcome political obstacles.* In addition to attitudinal barriers, there exist significant political obstacles to acting on evidence-based program and policy strategies. Households with children are a declining percentage of all households; children do not vote, and their parents, especially low-income parents, do not vote in proportion to their percentage of the population. Therefore, low-income children and their families are underrepresented in democratic bodies at the local, state, and national levels. Although a host of voter registration and parent and citizen mobilization efforts are making important advances, the challenge remains about how to engage the vast majority of Americans in the efforts to reduce child poverty and enhance the well-being of low-income children. Interestingly, polls that we at the National Center for Children in Poverty have designed over the past several years suggest that most Americans believe that reducing child poverty should be a more important national goal. In a national survey of 1,000 registered voters during the presidential primary season of 2000, we found that 86% of Americans polled endorsed a national goal of reducing child poverty by 50% over the next 10 years and that 64% endorsed using 10% or more of the then anticipated federal budget surplus to help reduce child poverty in the United States (National Center for Children in Poverty, 2000). These findings clearly indicate a latent level of public support to reduce child poverty. Over the past few years, some countries have transformed this latent public support into government agendas; the national governments of the United Kingdom and Ireland have set clear poverty (or child poverty) reduction goals and developed concrete multisector plans and investment strategies to meet these goals.[5] Following such examples, the United States should place a very high priority on crafting a strategy that formally adopts an explicit child poverty reduction goal over a specific time period. It is hard to imagine a successful and sustained effort unless American citizens can monitor progress toward a concrete goal and hold policymakers accountable for reaching the goal.

- *Make progress on race relations and immigration policy.* A few of the most powerful demographic facts concerning child poverty are the dramatically higher rates among African American (33%) and Latino (30%) children than among white (9%) children as well as higher rates among children in immigrant families (24%) than among children in U.S.-born families (16%) (Capps, 2001; National Center for Children in Poverty, 2002). Indeed, racial minority families are more likely to be income poor, to have fewer financial assets, and to live in urban areas with concentrations of other poor families; thus, poverty, race, and neighborhood are often confounded (Duncan & Aber, 1997; Oliver & Shapiro, 1995). Poverty among immigrant families is associated with living in overcrowded housing and with difficulties in meeting food and health care needs (Capps, 2001). Adults in immigrant families are more likely to have not finished schooling beyond the eighth grade and to have difficulties in speaking English but are *not* less likely to be working (Hernandez & Charney, 1998). Although first-generation immigrant families are more likely than later-generation families to receive public assistance, likelihood of

receipt decreases substantially in subsequent generations (Hernandez & Charney, 1998). The 1996 PRWORA legislation placed severe restrictions on immigrants' eligibility for TANF, food stamps, Medicaid, and other types of assistance (although their eligibility has since been partially restored by Congress), and these restrictions have led to drastic drops in immigrant families' participation, even when they remain eligible (Fix & Passel, 1999). With one of five children living in immigrant families (Hernandez & Charney, 1998), and with "minorities" making up increasingly large proportions of the population over the next half century (Day, 1996), attending to the special needs of the minority or immigrant poor should be a priority fur future public assistance legislation.

CONCLUSIONS

The heartening conclusion from this survey is that the U.S. government has indeed recognized the need for programs and policies that help children living in poverty. Indeed, some of these initiatives are innovative and generous, and many target key developmental processes, yet many remain overly restrictive and difficult to access. During recent times of economic prosperity, the rate of child poverty in the United States has indeed declined, but whether the marketplace or policy landscape is most responsible is as yet unclear. Despite such gains, the American public and the government it represents should not be complacent so long as millions of children live in poverty. Clearly, more can and should be done to help these children.

Appendix Table 12.A1   Summary of FY 2001 Federal Programs Targeted to Low-Income Children and Their Families, in Decreasing Order by Cost

Program	FY 2001 Allocation[a]	Number Served[b]	Eligibility	Percentage of Eligible Served	Program Description	Effectiveness[c]
Medicaid	$130 billion	33.4 million low-income people (~ 50% children)	Eligibility determined by the state, dependent on income; most state programs cover families with annual incomes 100% to 150% of the FPL	78%	Determined by income; varies from full coverage to other types of medical assistance	Positive outcomes for child recipients; however, many families that are eligible do not receive Medicaid (4.2 million of the 11.5 million uninsured children in the United States)
Earned Income Tax Credit (EITC)	$31.9 billion (FY 2000)	19.5 million low-income families (FY 2000)	Family's combined income falls below a threshold (e.g., $30,850 for family with two or more children)	NA	Tax credit given for the previous year	More than 4 million families have been lifted from below the FPL; employment rates have increased up to 21% for single parents with one child and up to 45% for single parents with two or more children
Temporary Assistance to Needy Families (TANF)	$19.2 billion	6.3 million low-income individuals (FY 1999)	Families with children, as determined by the state	NA	Cash assistance with work requirement; maximum of 5 years of assistance	Mixed findings: State programs have led to increases in maternal employment but only negligible increases in parents' earnings and in family income
Food Stamp Program	$16 billion	17 million low-income adults and children per month	Determined by level of family income, amount of countable	60%	Coupons or debit cards to purchase eligible food products in	Improvements in children's nutritional and physical health and an overall increase

Program	FY 2001 Allocation[a]	Number Served[b]	Eligibility	Percentage of Eligible Served	Program Description	Effectiveness[c]
			resources, allowable deductions, work status, and citizenship status		authorized retail food stores	in families' food security
Public and Indian Housing Program; Section 8 Housing Choice Vouchers	$14.4 billion ($3 billion for public housing; $11.4 billion for Section 8 vouchers)	4 million low-income families	Families with incomes below 50% of the median income for the county or metropolitan areas in which they live; Section 8 eligibility restricted to U.S. citizens	25% of eligible receive public housing or vouchers	Public housing residence or rental assistance for decent, safe, and sanitary housing for very low-income families; families pay rent of approximately 30% of their adjusted incomes	NA
Financial Aid for Higher Education (including Pell and Perkins grants, Work Study, and Stafford)	$13.3 billion (total)	Several million (3.8 million served by Pell Grants alone)	Demonstrated financial need; U.S. citizens with a high school diploma or GED accepted or enrolled at eligible institution of higher learning	NA	Maximum award depends on program (e.g., Pell Grant maximum: $3,125 per academic year)	In general, postsecondary degrees, such as A.A. and B.A. degrees, substantially increase low-income adults' earning power
Title I	$8.6 billion	12.7 million children	Provides funding to school districts with 50% or more of their students living in poverty	NA	States and school districts choose the distribution of the funds	Reading and math achievement scores have increased in the highest-poverty schools

(Continued)

Appendix Table 12.A1 Continued

Program	FY 2001 Allocation[a]	Number Served[b]	Eligibility	Percentage of Eligible Served	Program Description	Effectiveness[c]
Head Start	$6.2 billion	857,664 low-income children	Children 3 to 4 years of age from low-income families	NA	Child care program that includes health, screening, and nutritional services	A national randomized trial evaluation is planned for the next few years; however, studies of other early childhood education programs have found the benefits to range from improvements in long-term school performance, lower rates of placement in special education classes, and higher rates of productive citizenship as young adults, with higher rates of high school graduation and employment
National School Lunch Program	$5.7 billion	27 million low-income children	Family annual income must be below 185% of the FPL for reduced-price lunches and below 130% of the FPL for free lunches	82%	School-based lunches that provide one third or more of recommended daily allowances	Improvements in children's diets and food energy levels
State Children's Health Insurance Program (CHIP)	$4.2 billion	2.3 million low-income children	Eligibility determined by the state: Either those not covered by Medicaid but	52%	Provides health care coverage for families that earn more than the Medicaid	Improvements found in children's use of preventive care; immunization rates; and anemia, lead level,

Program	FY 2001 Allocation[a]	Number Served[b]	Eligibility	Percentage of Eligible Served	Program Description	Effectiveness[c]
			below 200% of the FPL or those up to 50% above current Medcaid income limit for children		requirements but cannot afford the costs of private coverage	vision, and hearing screenings
Special Supplemental Food Program for Women, Infants, and Children (WIC)	$4 billion	7 million low-income mothers and children	Low-income pregnant and postpartum women with children up to 5 years of age; income must be below 185% of the FPL, and mother or child must be certified by a health professional as at nutritional risk	81%	Coverage includes nutritional education, food supplements, and health and social service referrals	Receipt associated with fewer premature births, lower rates of low-birthweight babies, and improved cognitive development of children; $1 spent results in $3.50 in savings, primarily in medical care
Child Care Development Fund (CCDF)	$4 billion	1.8 million low-income children (FY 1999)	Families with children under 13 years of age and whose incomes do not exceed 85% of the state median income	10%-15%	Parents allowed to choose the type and quality of child care provided	Receipt found to be associated with a 5 percentage point increase in parents' employment and an 8 percentage point increase in school attendance
Child Support Enforcement Program	$3 billion	19.4 million children	TANF recipient or for small fee if not TANF recipient	NA	Provides services designed to help custodial parents obtain income	In 1999, assisted in the collection of $16 billion in child support payments; helps to

(Continued)

Appendix Table 12.A1 Continued

Program	FY 2001 Allocation[a]	Number Served[b]	Eligibility	Percentage of Eligible Served	Program Description	Effectiveness[c]
					from noncustodial parents	increase the income of custodial parents
Low Income Home Energy Assistance Program	$2.2 billion	4.1 million low-income families	States may provide assistance to households with incomes up to the greater of 150% of the FPL or 60% of the state median income	13% (FY 1998)	Provides assistance with residential heating and cooling costs; also can be used for weatherization or energy crisis needs	Assistance in FY 1998 covered only 9% of participating families' energy bills
National School Breakfast Program	$1.48 billion	7 million low-income children	Family annual income must be below 185% of the FPL for reduced-price breakfasts and below 130% of the FPL for free breakfasts	71%	School-based breakfasts that provide one fourth or more of recommended daily allowances	Improvements in children's diets and food energy levels
Workforce Investment Act (WIA)	$1 billion ($950 million for adults; PY 2001: $102 million for youth)	NA (new program)	Adult Program: All U.S. adults, but states give preference to low-income individuals (Title IIA); Youth Program: Youth with family incomes below the FPL and those considered "at risk"	NA (new program).	Ranges from a few weeks of case management and job search assistance to a year of vocational and technical training; support for postsecondary education given only if deemed necessary for employment	In general, short-term "work first" approaches are effective in moving more families off of public assistance; long-term investments in on-the-job training significantly increase parents' earnings and length of employment

Program	FY 2001 Allocation[a]	Number Served[b]	Eligibility	Percentage of Eligible Served	Program Description	Effectiveness[c]
21st Century Community Learning Centers	$846 million	650,000 children	Rural and inner-city public elementary and secondary schools or consortia of such schools	NA	Funds to plan, implement, or expand projects that benefit the educational, health, social service, cultural, and recreational needs of the community	NA (new program)
Early Head Start	$340 million (FY 1999; Demonstration Program)	45,000 low-income families with infants or toddlers	Low-income families with infants or toddlers	NA	Center-based and home visiting services	Has been found to increase maternal support, sensitivity, and time spent in cognitively stimulating play with children; children who participated showed stronger cognitive and language development than did children not enrolled in the program
Promoting Safe and Stable Families	$295 million	NA	State child welfare agencies that operate family preservation, reunification, support, and adoption promotion services	NA	Varies by program	Some state programs have improved parenting behaviors, keeping families together and reducing out-of-home child placements

(Continued)

Appendix Table 12.A1 Continued

Program	FY 2001 Allocation[a]	Number Served[b]	Eligibility	Percentage of Eligible Served	Program Description	Effectiveness[c]
Job Access and Reverse Commute Program	$115 million	NA (new program)	Welfare recipients and low-income workers	NA (new program)	Includes transportation vouchers, fixed-route extensions, emergency child care transportation, guaranteed ride home programs, and additional bus lines	NA (new program)
Abstinence Education Grant Program	$50 million	NA (new program)	School-aged children, adolescents at risk for teen pregnancy	NA (new program)	Funds community organizations and activities based on abstinence	NA (new program)
Second Chance Homes	$25 million	NA (new program)	Unmarried teen parent TANF recipients	NA (new program)	Homes to provide teen parents with parenting and family planning skills	NA (new program)
Individual Development Accounts	$25 million (Demonstration Program)	5,000 individuals	Eligible for TANF or net worth of $10,000 or less	NA	Family savings are matched at a rate of 50 cents to $4 for every $1 saved; cannot exceed $4,000 per household	Has helped families in 29 participating states to increase their net worth by 1,800%

NOTE: FY = fiscal year; FPL = federal poverty level; NA = not available; PY = program year.
a. All funding allocations are for FY 2001 unless otherwise noted.
b. Numbers served represent those for FY 2000 unless otherwise noted.
c. See text for effectiveness references. Some effectiveness data come from related demonstrations (not necessarily the federal programs specifically) and are noted as "in general."

NOTES

1. One concern with survey instruments of family environment is that they must be able to adequately reflect competencies in parenting across diverse ethnic and racial minority communities to be considered psychometrically valid. The HOME inventory has demonstrated somewhat lower, yet adequate, levels of internal and predictive validity across African American and Hispanic populations when compared with its use within white majority populations (Bradley et al., 1989; Sugland et al., 1995).

2. Interested readers should consult the Research Forum (www.researchforum.org) for current updates on these programs.

3. See the Web sites of the Center for Budget and Policy Priorities (www.cbpp.org) and its State Fiscal Analysis Initiative (www.cbpp.org/sfai.htm) for more detailed information on the federal EITC. See also Johnson (2001) for role of state-level EITCs in helping working families.

4. See the Web site of the Corporation for Enterprise Development (www.cfed.org) for more detailed information.

5. Visit the Web sites of Ireland's Combat Poverty Agency (www.cpa.ie), the United Kingdom's Social Exclusion Unit (www.socialexclusionunit.gov.uk), and the Research Centre for Analysis of Social Exclusion (sticerd.lse.ac.uk/case).

REFERENCES

Aber, J. L. (1994). Poverty, violence, and child development: Untangling family- and community-level effects. In C. Nelson (Ed.), *Threats to optimal development: Integrating biological, psychological, and social risk factors* (Minnesota Symposium on Child Psychology, Vol. 27, pp. 229-272). Mahwah, NJ: Lawrence Erlbaum.

Aber, J. L., Bennett, N. G., Conley, D. C., & Li, J. (1997). The effects of poverty on child health and development. *Annual Review of Public Health, 18,* 463-483.

Aber, J. L., Gephart, M. A., Brooks-Gunn, J., & Connell, J. P. (1997). Development in context: Implications for studying neighborhood effects. In J. Brooks-Gunn, G. J. Duncan, & J. L. Aber (Eds.), *Neighborhood poverty,* Vol. 1: *Contexts and consequences for children* (pp. 44-61). New York: Russell Sage.

Aber, J. L., Gershoff, E. T., & Brooks-Gunn, J. (2001, May). *Social exclusion of children in the U.S.: Compiling indicators of factors from which and by which children are excluded.* Paper presented at the Social Exclusion and Children Conference, Institute for Child and Family Policy, Columbia University, New York. Available: www.childpolicyintl.org

Annual update of the HHS poverty guidelines. (2001, February 16). *Federal Register, 66*(33), 10695-10697.

Baker, A. J. L., Piotrkowski, C. S., & Brooks-Gunn, J. (1999). The Home Instruction Program for Preschool Youngsters (HIPPY). *The Future of Children, 9,* 116-133.

Baker, D., & Witt, P. A. (1996). Evaluation of the impact of two after-school recreation programs. *Journal of Park and Recreation Administration, 14,* 23-44.

Barker, D. J. (1994). Outcome of low birthweight. *Hormone Research, 42,* 223-230.

Becker, G. (1993). *Human capital: A theoretical and empirical analysis with special reference to education.* Chicago: University of Chicago Press.

Bennett, N. G., & Lu, H. (2000). *Child poverty in the states: Levels and trends from 1979 to 1998* (Childhood Poverty Research Brief No. 2). New York: National Center for Children in Poverty.

Bennett, N. G., & Lu, H. (2001). *Untapped potential: State Earned Income Credits and child poverty reduction* (Childhood Poverty Research Brief No. 3). New York: National Center for Children in Poverty.

Bernstein, J., & Schmitt, J. (1998). *Making work pay: The impact of the 1996-97 minimum wage increase.* Washington, DC: Economic Policy Institute.

Blank, R. M. (1995). Outlook for the U.S. labor market and prospects for low-wage entry jobs. In D. S. Nightingale & R. H. Haveman (Eds.), *The work alternative: Welfare reform and the realities of the job market.* Washington, DC: Urban Institute.

Blau, D. M. (1999). The effect of income on child development. *Review of Economics and Statistics, 81,* 261-276.

Blau, D., & Tekin, E. (2001). The determinants and consequences of child care subsidy receipt by low-income families. In B. Meyer & G. Duncan (Eds.), *The incentives of government programs and the well-being of families.* Evanston, IL: Joint Center for Poverty Research. Available: www.jcpr.org/book/index.html

Bloom, D., & Michalopoulos, C. (2001). *How welfare and work policies affect employment and income: A synthesis of research.* New York: Manpower Research Demonstration Corporation.

Boisjoly, J., Duncan, G. J., & Hofferth, S. (1994). Access to social capital. *Journal of Family Issues, 16,* 609-631.

Boushey, H., Brocht, C., Gundersen, B., & Bernstein, J. (2001). *Hardships in America: The real story of working families.* Washington, DC: Economic Policy Institute. Available: http: //epinet.org

Bradbury, B., Jenkins, S. P., & Micklewright, J. (2001). *The dynamics of child poverty in industrialized countries.* New York: Cambridge University Press.

Bradley, R. H., Caldwell, B. M., Rock, S. L., Barnard, K. E., Gray, C., Hammond, M. A., Mitchell, S., Siegel, L., Ramey, C. T., Gottfried, A. W., & Johnson, D. L. (1989). Home environment and cognitive development in the first 3 years of life: A collaborative study involving six sites and three ethnic groups in North America. *Developmental Psychology, 25,* 217-235.

Bradley, R. H., Whiteside, L., Mundfrom, D. M., Casey, P. H., Kelleher, K. J., & Pope, S. K. (1994). Early indications of resilience and their relation to experiences in the home environments of low birthweight, premature children living in poverty. *Child Development, 65,* 346-360.

Brody, G. H., Stoneman, Z., Flor, D., McCrary, C., Hastings, L., & Conyers, O. (1994). Financial resources, parent psychological functioning, parent co-caregiving, and early adolescent competence in rural, two-parent, African-American families. *Child Development, 65,* 590-605.

Brooks-Gunn, J., Berlin, L., & Fuligni, A. (2000). Early childhood intervention programs: What about the family? In J. Schonkoff & S. Meisels (Eds.), *Handbook of early childhood intervention* (2nd ed., pp. 549-588). New York: Cambridge University Press.

Brooks-Gunn, J., & Duncan, G. J. (1997). The effects of poverty on children and youth. *The Future of Children, 7,* 55-71.

Brooks-Gunn, J., Klebanov, P., & Duncan, G. J. (1996). Ethnic differences in children's intelligence test scores: Role of economic deprivation, home environment, and maternal characteristics. *Child Development, 67,* 396-408.

Burchardt, T., Le Grand, J., & Piachaud, D. (1999). Social exclusion in Britain 1991-1995. *Social Policy and Administration, 33,* 227-244.

Burchinal, M. R., & Nelson, L. (2000). Family selection and child care experiences: Implications for studies of child outcomes. *Early Childhood Research Quarterly, 15,* 385-411.

Burchinal, M. R., Roberts, J. E., Riggins, R., Zeisel, S. A., Neebe, E., & Bryant, D. (2000). Relating quality of center-based child care to early cognitive and language development longitudinally. *Child Development, 71,* 339-357.

Caldwell, B. M., & Bradley, R. H. (1984). *Home Observation for Measurement of the Environment.* Little Rock: University of Arkansas Press.

Campbell, F. A., & Ramey, C. T. (1994). Effects of early intervention on intellectual and academic achievement: A follow-up study of children from low-income families. *Child Development, 65,* 684-698.

Capps, R. (2001). *Hardship among children of immigrants: Findings from the 1999 National Survey of America's Families* (Assessing the New Federalism, Series B, No. B-29). Washington, DC: Urban Institute.

Carlson, S. J., Andrews, M. S., & Bickel, G. W. (1999). Measuring food insecurity and hunger in the United States: Development of a national benchmark measure and prevalence estimates. *Journal of Nutrition, 129,* 510S-516S.

Castner, L. (2000). *Trends in FSP participation rates: Focus on 1994 to 1998.* Washington, DC: Mathematica Policy Research.

Cauthen, N. K., Knitzer, J., & Ripple, C. H. (2000). *Map and track: State initiatives for young children and families* (rev. ed.). New York: National Center for Children in Poverty.

Chase-Lansdale, P. L., Brooks-Gunn, J., & Zamsky, E. S. (1994). Young African-American multigenerational families in poverty: Quality of mothering and grandmothering. *Child Development, 65,* 373-393.

Child Care Bureau. (2001). *FY 1999 CCDF data tables and charts.* Washington, DC: U.S. Department of Health and Human Services, Administration for Children and Families. Available: www.acf.dhhs.gov/programs/ccb/research/99acf800/cover.htm

Children's Bureau. (2001). *Programs: Promoting safe and stable families.* Washington, DC: U.S. Department of Health and Human Services, Administration for Children and Families. Available: www.acf.dhhs.gov/programs/cb/ programs/fpfs.htm

Children's Defense Fund. (1994). *Wasting America's future: The Children's Defense Fund report on the costs of child poverty.* Boston: Beacon.

Children's Defense Fund. (1997). *Poverty matters: The cost of child poverty in America.* Washington, DC: Author.

Children's Defense Fund. (2000). *Families struggling to make it in the workforce: A post welfare report.* Washington, DC: Author.

Citro, C. F., & Michael, R. T. (Eds.). (1995). *Measuring poverty: A new approach.* Washington, DC: National Academy Press.

Clark, R. L., King, R. B., Spiro, C., & Steuerle, C. E. (2001). *Federal expenditures on children: 1960-1997* (Occasional Paper No. 45). Washington, DC: Urban Institute.

Commissioner's Office of Research and Evaluation and the Head Start Bureau. (2001). *Building their futures: How Early Head Start programs are enhancing the lives of infants and toddlers in low-income families.* Washington, DC: U.S. Department of Health and Human Services, Administration on Children, Youth, and Families.

Community Transportation Association of America. (1999). *Assessment of the JOBLINKS II demonstration projects: Connecting people to the workplace.* Washington, DC: Author. Available: www.ctaa.org/ntrc/atj/pubs/joblinks_ii_eval

Community Transportation Association of America. (2001). *JOBLINKS: Connecting people to the workplace—Summary of the demonstration projects.* Washington, DC: Author. Available: www.ctaa.org/ntrc/atj/joblinks/job_hist#job1

Conger, R. D., Ge, X., Elder, G. H., Lorenz, F. O., & Simons, R. L. (1994). Economic stress, coercive family process, and developmental problems of adolescents. *Child Development, 65,* 541-561.

Corporation for Enterprise Development. (2000). *Individual Development Accounts: Q & A on the Assets for Independence Act (Public Law 105-285)*. Washington, DC: Author. Available: www.cfed.org

Cowan, P. A., Powell, D., & Cowan, C. P. (1998). Parenting interventions: A family systems perspective. In I. E. Sigel & K. A. Renninger (Eds.), *Handbook of child psychology*, 5th ed., Vol. 4: *Child psychology in practice* (pp. 3-72). New York: John Wiley.

Cowen, E. L., Wyman, P. A., Work, W. C., & Parker, G. R. (1990). The Rochester Child Resilience Project: Overview and summary of first year findings. *Development and Psychopathology, 2*, 193-212.

Cummings, E. M., & Davies, P. T. (1999). Depressed parents and family functioning: Interpersonal effects and children's functioning and development. In T. Joiner & J. C. Coyne (Eds.), *Advances in interpersonal approaches: The interactional nature of depression* (pp. 299-327). Washington, DC: American Psychological Association.

Davies, P. T., & Cummings, E. M. (1994). Marital conflict and child adjustment: An emotional security hypothesis. *Psychological Bulletin, 116*, 387-411.

Day, J. C. (1996). *Population projections of the United States by age, sex, race, and Hispanic origin: 1995-2050* (Current Population Reports, No. P25-1130). Washington, DC: Government Printing Office.

De Kanter, A., Williams, R., Cohen, G., & Stonehill, R. (2000). *21st Century Community Learning Centers: Providing quality afterschool learning opportunities for America's families*. Washington, DC: U.S. Department of Education.

Del Conte, A., & Kling, J. (2001, January-February). A synthesis of MTO research on self-sufficiency, safety and health, and behavior and delinquency. *Poverty Research News*, pp. 3-6. (Evanston, IL: Joint Center for Poverty Research)

Devaney, B., & Stuart, E. (1998). *Eating breakfast: Effects of the School Breakfast Program*. Alexandria, VA: U.S. Department of Agriculture, Food, and Nutrition Service, Office of Analysis, Nutrition, and Evaluation.

Dix, T., Gershoff, E. T., & Miller, P. C. (2001). *Child-orientation and depressive symptoms in mothers*. Unpublished manuscript, University of Texas at Austin.

Downey, G., & Coyne, J. C. (1990). Children of depressed parents: An integrative review. *Psychological Bulletin, 108*, 50-76.

Duggan, A. K., McFarlane, E. C., Windham, A. M., Rohde, C. A., Salkever, D. S., Fuddy, L., Rosenberg, L. A., Buchbinder, S. B., & Sia, C. C. J. (1999). Evaluation of Hawaii's Healthy Start program. *The Future of Children, 9*, 66-90.

Duncan, G., & Aber, J. L. (1997). Neighborhood models and measures. In G. Duncan, J. Brooks-Gunn, & J. L. Aber (Eds.), *Neighborhood poverty: Context and consequences for children* (pp. 44-61). New York: Russell Sage.

Duncan, G. J, Brooks-Gunn, J., Klebanov, P. K. (1994). Economic deprivation and early childhood development. *Child Development, 65*, 296-318.

Duncan, G. J., & Brooks-Gunn, J. (1997). *The consequences of growing up poor*. New York: Russell Sage.

Duncan, G. J., & Brooks-Gunn, J. (2000). Family poverty, welfare reform, and child development. *Child Development, 71*, 188-196.

Duncan, G., J., Yeung, J., Brooks-Dunn, J., & Smith, J. (1998). How much does childhood poverty affect the life chances of children? *American Sociological Review, 63*, 406-423.

Eckenrode, J., Ganzel, B., Henderson, C. R., Smith, E., Olds, D., Powers, J., Cole, R., Kitzman, H., & Sidora, K. (2000). Preventing child abuse and neglect with a program of nurse home visitation: The limiting effects of domestic violence. *Journal of the American Medical Association, 284*, 1430-1431.

Edin, K., & Lein, L. (1997). *Making ends meet: How single mothers survive welfare and low wage work*. New York: Russell Sage.

Eisenberg, N., Fabes, R. A., Guthrie, I. K., Murphy, B. C., Maszk, P., Holmgren, R., & Suh, K. (1996). The relations of regulation and emotionality to problem behavior in elementary school children. *Development and Psychopathology, 8,* 141-162.

Elder, G. H., & Caspi, A. (1988). Economic stress in lives: Developmental perspectives. *Journal of Social Issues, 44,* 25-45.

Elder, G. H., Eccles, J. S., Ardelt, M., & Lord, S. (1995). Inner-city parents under economic pressure: Perspective on the strategies of parenting. *Journal of Marriage and the Family, 57,* 771-784.

Ellwood, D. (2000). The impact of the Earned Income Tax Credit and social policy reforms on work, marriage, and living arrangements. *National Tax Journal, 53*(4), 1063-1106.

Employment and Training Administration. (2001). *Adult training programs.* Washington, DC: U.S. Department of Labor. Available: www.doleta.gov/programs/adult_program.asp

Entwisle, D. R., & Alexander, K. L. (1992). Summer setback: Race, poverty, school composition, and mathematics achievement in the first two years of school. *American Sociological Review, 57,* 72-84.

Epstein, A. S., Larner, M., & Halpern, R. (1995). *A guide to developing community-based family support programs.* Ypsilanti, MI: High/Scope Press.

Family Support America. (1996). *Making the case for family support.* Chicago: Author. Available: www.familysupportamerica.org/downloads/making%20the%20case.pdf

Fantuzzo, J. W., Stevenson, H. C., Weiss, A D., & Hampton, V. R. (1997). A partnership directed school-based intervention for child physical abuse and neglect: Beyond mandatory reporting. *School Psychology Review, 26,* 298-313.

Federal Transit Administration. (1998). *The challenge of job access: Moving toward a solution.* Washington, DC: U.S. Department of Transportation. Available: www.fhwa.dot.gov/reports/challeng.htm

Federal Transit Administration. (2000). *Use of TANF, WtW, and job access funds for transportation.* Washington, DC: U.S. Department of Transportation. Available: www.fta.dot.gov/wtw/uoft.html

Federal Transit Administration. (2001). *Job access and reverse commute grants.* Washington, DC: U.S. Department of Transportation. Available: www.fta.dot.gov/wtw/jarcgfs.htm

Fix, M., & Passel, J. S. (1999). *Trends in noncitizens' and citizens' use of public benefits following welfare reform: 1994-1997.* Washington, DC: Urban Institute.

Flynn, M. (1999). *Using TANF to finance out-of-school time and community school initiatives.* Washington, DC: Finance Project.

Food and Nutrition Service. (1987). *The national WIC evaluation: An evaluation of the Special Supplemental Food Program for Women, Infants, and Children,* Vol. 1: *Summary.* Alexandria, VA: U.S. Department of Agriculture.

Food and Nutrition Service. (2000). *Program basics: WIC at a glance.* Alexandria, VA: U.S. Department of Agriculture. Available: www.fns.usda.gov/wic/programinfo/wicataglance.htm

Food and Nutrition Service. (2001a). *Facts about the Child and Adult Care Food Program.* Alexandria, VA: U.S. Department of Agriculture. Available: www.fns.usda.gov/cnd/care/cacfp/cacfpfaqs.htm

Food and Nutrition Service. (2001b). *Food Stamp Program participation and costs.* Alexandria, VA: U.S. Department of Agriculture. Available: www.fns.usda.gov/pd/fssummar.htm

Food and Nutrition Service. (2001c). *School Breakfast Program: Fact sheet.* Alexandria, VA: U.S. Department of Agriculture. Available: www.fns.usda.gov/cnd/breakfast/aboutbfast/faqs.htm

Food and Nutrition Service. (2001d). *School Lunch Program: Fact sheet.* Alexandria, VA: U.S. Department of Agriculture. Available: www.fns.usda. gov/cnd/lunch/aboutlunch/faqs.htm

Food and Nutrition Service. (2001e). *WIC program and participation costs.* Alexandria, VA: U.S. Department of Agriculture. Available: www.fns.usda. gov/pd/wisummary.htm

Forness, S. R., Ramey, S. L., Ramey, C. T., Hsu, C., Brezausek, C. M., MacMillan, D. L., Kavale, K. A., & Zima, B. T. (1998). Head Start children finishing first grade: Preliminary data on school identification of children at risk for special education. *Behavioral Disorders, 23,* 111-123.

Forsythe, P. W. (1992). Homebuilders and family preservation. *Children and Youth Services Review, 14,* 37-47.

Fraser, M. W., Nelson, K. E., & Rivard, J. C. (1997). Effectiveness of family preservation services. *Social Work Research, 21,* 138-153.

Gadomski, A., Jenkins, P., & Nichols, M. (1998). Impact of a Medicaid primary care provider and preventive care on pediatric hospitalization. *Pediatrics, 101,* E1.

Garbarino, J., Kostelny, K., & Barry, F. (1997). Value transmission in an ecological context: The high-risk neighborhood. In J. E. Grusec & L. Kuczynski (Eds.), *Parenting and children's internalization of values: A handbook of contemporary theory* (pp. 307-332). New York: John Wiley.

Garfinkel, I., Heintze, T., & Huang, C. (2000). The effects of child support enforcement on women's incomes. *Joint Center for Poverty Research Policy Brief, 3*(5). (Evanston, IL: Joint Center for Poverty Research)

Geronimus, A., & Korenman, S. (1993). The costs of teenage childbearing: Evidence and interpretation. *Demography, 30,* 281-290.

Gershoff, E. T. (2002). Corporal punishment by parents and associated child behaviors and experiences: A meta-analytic and theoretical review. *Psychological Bulletin, 128,* 539-579.

Gilens, M. (1999). *Why Americans hate welfare.* Chicago: University of Chicago Press.

Giles-Sims, J., Straus, M. A., & Sugarman, D. B. (1995). Child, maternal, and family characteristics associated with spanking. *Family Relations, 44,* 170-176.

Gilliam, W. S., & Zigler, E. F. (2000). A critical meta-analysis of all evaluations of state-funded preschool from 1977 to 1998: Implications for policy, service delivery, and program evaluation. *Early Childhood Research Quarterly, 15,* 441-473.

Gleason, P., & Suitor, C. (2001). *Children's diets in the mid-1990s: Dietary intake and its relationship with school meal participation* (CN-01-CD1). Alexandria, VA: U.S. Department of Agriculture, Food and Nutrition Service, Office of Analysis, Nutrition, and Evaluation.

Golonka, S., & Matus-Grossman, L. (2001). *Opening doors: Expanding educational opportunities for low-income workers.* New York: Manpower Research Demonstration Corporation and National Governors Association Center for Best Practices.

Gomby, D. S., Culross, P. L., & Behrman, R. E. (1999). Home visiting: Recent program evaluations—Analysis and recommendations. *The Future of Children, 9,* 4-26.

Goodson, B. D., Layzer, J. I., St. Pierre, R. G., Bernstein, L. S., & Lopez, M. (2000). Effectiveness of a comprehensive, five-year family support program for low-income children and their families: Findings from the Comprehensive Child Development Program. *Early Childhood Research Quarterly, 15,* 5-39.

Gornick, J. C., & Meyers, M. K. (2001). Lesson-drawing in family policy: Media reports and empirical evidence about European developments. *Journal of Comparative Policy Analysis: Research and Practice, 3,* 31-57.

Gortmaker, S. L. (1979). Poverty and infant mortality in the United States. *American Sociological Review, 44,* 280-297.

Governmentwide Information Systems Division. (2001). *The catalog of federal domestic assistance.* Washington, DC: U.S. General Services Administration, Office of Acquisition Policy. Available: www.cdfa.gov

Guo, G., & Harris, K. M. (2000). The mechanisms mediating the effects of poverty on children's intellectual development. *Demography, 37,* 431-447.

Gutman, L. M., & Eccles, J. S. (1999). Financial strain, parenting behaviors, and adolescents' achievement: Testing model equivalence between African American and European American single- and two-parent families. *Child Development, 70,* 1464-1476.

Halpern, R., Deich, S., & Cohen, C. (2000). *Financing after-school programs.* Washington, DC: Finance Project.

Hamelin, A., Habicht, J., & Beaudry, M. (1999). Food insecurity: Consequences for the household and broader social implications. *Journal of Nutrition, 129,* 525S-528S.

Hamilton, W., Cook, J., Thompson, W., Buron, L., Frongillo, E., Jr., Olson, C., & Wehler, C. (1997). *Household food security in the United States in 1995: Measuring food security in the United States* (summary report). Washington, DC: U.S. Department of Agriculture.

Head Start Bureau. (2001). *2001 Head Start fact sheet.* Washington, DC: Author. Available: www2.acf.dhhs.gov/programs/hsb/about/fact2001.htm

Heimendinger, J., Larid, N., Austin, J., Timmer, P., & Gershoff, S. (1984). The effects of the WIC program on the growth of infants. *American Journal of Clinical Nutrition, 40,* 1250-1257.

Heinrich, C. J. (1998). *Aiding welfare-to-work transitions: Lessons from JTPA on the cost-effectiveness of education and training services* (Working Paper No. 3). Evanston, IL: Northwestern University, Joint Center for Poverty Research.

Heneghan, A. M., Horwitz, S. M., & Leventhal, J. M. (1996). Evaluating intensive family preservation programs: A methodological review. *Pediatrics, 97,* 535-542.

Hernandez, D. J., & Charney, E. (Eds.). (1998). *From generation to generation: The health and well-being of children in immigrant families.* Washington, DC: National Academy Press.

Hofferth, S. L., Shauman, K. A., Henke, R. R., & West, J. (1998). *Characteristics of children's early care and education programs: Data from the 1995 National Household Education Survey* (Report No. 98-128). Washington DC: U.S. Department of Education. Available: http://nces.ed.gov/pubs98/98128.pdf

Holl, J. L., Szilagyi, P. G., Rodewald, L. E., Shone, L. P., Zwanziger, J., Mukamel, D. B., Trafton, S., Dick, A. W., Barth, R., & Raubertas, R. F. (2000). Evaluation of New York State's Child Health Plus: Access, utilization, quality of health care, and health status. *Pediatrics, 105*(3, Suppl. E), 711-718.

Hotz, V. J., Mullin, C., & Scholz, J. K. (2001). The EITC and labor market participation of families on welfare. *Joint Center for Poverty Research Policy Briefs, 3*(7). (Evanston, IL: Joint Center for Poverty Research)

HUD USER. (1997, June). HUD's housing programs serve diverse groups. *Recent Research Results.* (Rockville, MD: Author) Available: www.huduser.org/periodicals/rrr/diverse.html

Huey, S. J., Jr., & Weisz, J. R. (1997). Ego control, ego resiliency, and the five-factor model as predictors of behavioral and emotional problems in clinic-referred children and adolescents. *Journal of Abnormal Psychology, 106,* 404-415.

Huston, A. C., Duncan, G. J., Granger, R., Bos, J., McLoyd, V., Mistry, R., Crosby, D., Gibson, C., Magnuson, K., Romich, J., & Ventura, A. (2001). Work-based antipoverty programs for parents can enhance the school performance and social behavior of children. *Child Development, 72,* 318-336.

Hutcheson, J. J., Black, M. M., Talley, M., Dubowtiz, H., Howard, J. B., Starr, R. H., & Thompson, B. S. (1997). Risk status and home intervention among children with failure-to-thrive: Follow-up at age 4. *Journal of Pediatric Psychology, 22,* 651-668.

Iceland, J., & Short, K. (1999, April). *Are children worse off? Evaluating child well-being using a new (and improved) measure of poverty.* Paper presented at the meeting of the Population Association of America, New York.

Innes, F. K., Denton, K. L., & West, J. (2001, April). *Child care factors and kindergarten outcomes: Findings from a national study of children.* Paper presented at the meeting of the Society for Research in Child Development, Minneapolis, MN.

Iyengar, S. (1990). Framing responsibility for political issues: The case of poverty. *Political Behavior, 12,* 19-40.

Jackson, A., Gyamfi, P, Brooks-Gunn, J., & Blake, M. (1998). Employment status, psychological well-being, social support, and physical discipline practices of single black mothers. *Journal of Marriage and the Family,60,* 894-902.

Jacobs, F. (2001). *What to make of family preservation services evaluations* (Discussion Paper No. CS-70). Chicago: University of Chicago, Chapin Hall Center for Children.

Jacobson, J., Rodriguez-Planas, M., Puffer, L., Pas, E., & Taylor-Kale, L. (2001). *The consequences of welfare reform and economic changes for the Food Stamp Program: Illustrations from microsimulation* (No. 01-003). Washington, DC: U.S. Department of Agriculture, Economic Research Service. Available: www.ers.usda.gov/publications/efanrr01003

Johnson, N. (2001). *A hand up: How state Earned Income Tax Credits help working families escape poverty in 2000: An overview.* Washington, DC: Center on Budget and Policy Priorities. Available: www.cbpp.org/12-27-01sfp.pdf

Kane, T. J. (1995). *Rising public college tuition and college entry: How well do public subsidies promote access to college?* (Working Paper No. 5164). Cambridge, MA: National Bureau of Economic Research.

Karoly, L. A., Greenwood, P. W., Everingham, S. S., Houbé, J., Kilburn, M. R., Rydell, C. P., Sanders, M., & Chiesa, J. (1998). *Investing in our children: What we know and don't know about the costs and benefits of early childhood interventions.* Santa Monica, CA: RAND.

Katz, L. F., Kling, J. R., & Liebman, J. B. (2001). Moving to Opportunity in Boston: Early results of a randomized mobility experiment. *Quarterly Journal of Economics, 116,* 607-664.

Kenney, G. M., Ko, G., & Ormond, B. A. (2000). *Gaps in prevention and treatment: Dental care for low-income children* (New Federalism: National Survey of America's Families, No. B-15). Washington, DC: Urban Institute. Available: http://newfederalism.urban.org/html/series_b/b15/b15.html

Kinney, J. M., Madsen, B., Fleming, T., & Haapala, P. (1977). Homebuilders: Keeping families together. *Journal of Consulting and Clinical Psychology, 45,* 667-673.

Kirby, D. (2001). *Emerging answers: Research findings on programs to reduce teen pregnancy* (summary). Washington, DC: National Campaign to Prevent Teen Pregnancy.

Klasen, S. (1998). *Social exclusion and children in OECD countries: Some conceptual issues.* Paris: Organization for Economic Cooperation and Development.

Klebanov, P. K., Brooks-Gunn, J., & Duncan, G. J. (1994). Does neighborhood and family poverty affect mothers' parenting, mental health, and social support? *Journal of Marriage and the Family, 56,* 441-455.

Kleinman, R. E., Murphy, J. M., Little, M., Pagano, M. E., Wehler, C. A., Regal, K., & Jellenik, M. S. (1998). Hunger in children in the United States: Potential behavioral and emotional correlates. *Pediatrics, 101,* 1-6.

Klerman, L. V. (1991). *Alive and well? Research and policy review of health programs for poor young children.* New York: National Center for Children in Poverty.

Knox, V., Miller, C., & Gennetian, L. A. (2000). *Reforming welfare and rewarding work: Final report on the Minnesota Family Investment Program.* New York: Manpower Demonstration Research Corporation.

Kowaleski-Jones, L., & Duncan, G. (2001). *The effects of WIC on children's health and development.* Madison, WI: Institute for Poverty Research.

LaLonde, R. J. (1995). The promise of public sector-sponsored training programs. *Journal of Economic Perspectives, 9,* 149-168.

Layzer, J. I., & Collins, A. (2000). *State and community subsidy: Interim report executive summary.* Cambridge, MA: National Study of Child Care for Low-Income Families, Abt Associations, and National Center for Children in Poverty.

Lee, B. J., Bilaver, L. M., & Goerge, R. (2001, March-April). Health and welfare of Illinois children: Shifting WIC and food stamp use. *Poverty Research News, 5,* 8-9. (Evanston, IL: Joint Center for Policy Research)

Lennon, M. C., Aber, J. L., & Blum, B. B. (1998). *Program, research, and policy implications of evaluations of teenage parent programs.* New York: Research Forum on Children, Families, and the New Federalism.

Leventhal, J. M. (2001). The prevention of child abuse and neglect: Successfully out of the blocks. *Child Abuse and Neglect, 25,* 431-439.

Leventhal, T., & Brooks-Gunn, J. (2000). The neighborhoods they live in: Effects of neighborhood residence on child and family outcomes. *Psychological Bulletin, 126,* 309-337.

Linares, L. O., Heeren, T., Bronfman, E., Zuckerman, B., Augustyn, M., & Tronick, E. (2001). A mediation model for the impact of exposure to community violence on early child behavior problems. *Child Development, 72,* 639-652.

Lipman, E. L., & Offord, D. R. (1997). Psychosocial morbidity among poor children in Ontario. In G. Duncan & J. Brooks-Gunn (Eds.), *Consequences of growing up poor* (pp. 239-287). New York: Russell Sage.

Lozoff, B., Jimenez, E., & Wolf, A. W. (1991). Long-term developmental outcome of infants with iron deficiency. *New England Journal of Medicine, 325,* 687-694.

Lu, H., Song, Y., & Bennett, N. G. (2001). *Estimating the impact of welfare reform on the economic well-being of children, 1987-1999* (Childhood Poverty Research Brief No. 4). New York: National Center for Children in Poverty.

Ludwig, J., Duncan, G. J., & Pinkston, J. C. (2000). *Neighborhood effects on economic self-sufficiency: Evidence from a randomized housing-mobility experiment.* Evanston, IL: Joint Center for Poverty Research.

Masten, A., Morison, P., Pelligrini, D., & Tellegen, A. (1990). Competence under stress: Risk and protective factors. In J. Rolf, A. S. Masten, D. Cicchetti, K. Nuechterlein, & S. Weintraub (Eds.), *Risk and protective factors in the development of psychopathology* (pp. 236-256). New York: Cambridge University Press.

Mayer, S. E. (1997). *What money can't buy: Family income and children's life chances.* Cambridge, MA: Harvard University Press.

Mayer, S. E. (2001). *The explanatory power of parental income on children's outcomes: Final report.* Chicago: University of Chicago, Harris School of Public Policy Studies.

Maynard, R. A. (1997). *Kids having kids: Economic costs and social consequences of teen pregnancy.* Washington, DC: Urban Institute.

McLeod, J. D., & Kessler, R. (1990). Socioeconomic status differences in vulnerability to undesirable life events. *Journal of Health and Social Behavior, 31,* 162-172.

McLeod, J. D., & Shanahan, M. J. (1993). Poverty, parenting, and children's mental health. *American Sociological Review, 58,* 351-366.

McLeod, J. D., & Shanahan, M. J. (1996). Trajectories of poverty and children's mental health. *Journal of Health and Social Behavior, 37,* 207-220.

McLoyd, V. C. (1990). The impact of economic hardship on black families and children: Psychological distress, parenting, and socio-emotional development. *Child Development, 61,* 311-346.

McLoyd, V. C., Jayaratne, T. E., Ceballo, R., & Borquez, J. (1994). Unemployment and work interruption among African American single mothers: Effects on parenting and adolescent socioemotional functioning. *Child Development, 65,* 562-589.

McPherson, M., & Shapiro, M. O. (1991). Does student aid affect college enrollment? New evidence on a persistent controversy. *American Economic Review, 81,* 309-318.

McRoy, R. G., Christian, C. L., & Gershoff, E. T. (2000). Empirical support for family preservation and kinship care. In R. G. McRoy & H. Alstein (Eds.), *Does family preservation serve a child's best interests?* (pp. 23-40). Washington, DC: Georgetown University Press.

Meyers, M. K., Gornick, J. C., & Peck, L. R. (2001). Packaging support for low-income families: Policy variation across the U.S. states. *Journal of Policy Analysis and Management, 20,* 457-483.

Michalopoulos, C., & Berlin, G. (2001). Financial work incentives for low-wage workers. In B. Meyer & G. Duncan (Eds.), *The incentives of government programs and the well-being of families.* Evanston, IL: Joint Center for Poverty Research. Available: www.jcpr.org/book/index.html

Miech, R. A., Caspi, A., Moffitt, T. E., Wright, B. R. E., & Silva, P. A. (1999). Low socioeconomic status and mental disorders: A longitudinal study of selection and causation during young adulthood. *American Journal of Sociology, 104,* 1096-1131.

Mikulic, B., Linden, G., Pelsers, J., & Schiepers, J. (1999). *Social reporting: Reconciliation of sources and dissemination of data, Task 2b—The ECHP non-monetary variables as (potential) indicators of poverty and social exclusion in the European Union.* Voorburg, Netherlands: Statistics Netherlands.

Miller, J., & Davis, D. (1997). Poverty history, marital history, and quality of children's home environments. *Journal of Marriage and the Family, 59,* 996-1007.

Miller, J. E., & Korenman, S. (1994). Poverty and children's nutritional status in the United States. *American Journal of Epidemiology, 140,* 233-243.

Mills, R. J. (2000). *Health insurance coverage: Current population reports.* Washington, DC: U.S. Census Bureau. Available: www.census.gov/hhes/hlthins/hlthin99/hlt99asc.html

Morris, P. A., Huston, A. C., Duncan, G. J., Crosby, D. A., & Bos, J. M. (2001). *How welfare and work policies affect children: A synthesis of research.* New York: Manpower Demonstration Research Corporation.

Morris, P. A., & Michalopoulos, C. (2000). *The self-sufficiency project at 36 months: Effects on children of a program that increases parental employment and income* (executive summary). New York: Manpower Demonstration Research Corporation.

National Center for Children in Poverty. (1996). *One in four: America's youngest poor.* New York: Author.

National Center for Children in Poverty. (2000, March 2). *Nearly 2 in 3 Americans endorse investing 10 percent or more of federal budget surplus to reduce child poverty* [press release]. New York: Author. Available: http://cpmcnet.columbia. edu/dept/nccp/attitpr.htm

National Center for Children in Poverty. (2002). *Low-income children in the United States: A brief demographic profile.* New York: Author. Available: http:// cpmcnet.columbia.edu/dept/nccp/ycpf.html

National Institute on Out-of-School Time. (2001). *Fact sheet on school-age children's out-of-school time.* Wellesley, MA: Wellesley College, Center for Research on Women.

Nolan, B., & Whelan, C. T. (1996). *Resources, deprivation, and poverty.* New York: Oxford University Press.

Nutrition-Cognition National Advisory Committee. (1998). *Statement on the link between nutrition and cognitive development in children.* Boston: Tufts University, School of Nutrition Science and Policy, Center on Hunger, Poverty, and Nutrition Policy. Available: http://hunger.tufts.edu/pub/statement.shtml

Office of Assistant Secretary for Planning and Evaluation. (1997). *The national strategy to prevent out-of-wedlock teen pregnancies.* Washington, DC: U.S. Department of Health and Human Services. Available: http://aspe.hhs.gov/hsp/ teenp/strategy.htm

Office of Assistant Secretary for Planning and Evaluation. (1998). *Chartbook on children's insurance status.* Washington, DC: Author. Available: http://aspe. hhs.gov/health/98chartbk/98-chtbk.htm

Office of Child Support Enforcement. (2001). *FY2000 preliminary data report.* Washington, DC: U.S. Department of Health and Human Services, Administration for Children and Families. Available: www.acf.dhhs.gov/ programs/cse/pubs/2000/datareport

Office of Child Support Enforcement. (2002). *HHS role in child support enforce-ment.* Washington, DC: U.S. Department of Health and Human Services, Administration for Children and Families. Available: www.hhs.gov/ news/press/2002pres/cse.html

Office of Community Services. (2000). *LIHEAP home energy notebook for fiscal year 1998.* Washington, DC: U.S. Department of Health and Human Services, Administration for Children and Families. Available: www.ncat.org/liheap/ notebook98/notebook-1.htm#executive

Office of Community Services. (2001). *Low Income Home Energy Assistance Program, Division of Energy Assistance/OCS/ACF: LIHEAP allotments for FY 2001.* Washington, DC: U.S. Department of Health and Human Services, Administration for Children and Families. Available: www.acf.dhhs.gov/ programs/liheap/im01-09.htm

Office of Family Assistance. (2001). *Helping families achieve self-sufficiency: A guide on funding services for children and families through the TANF program.* Washington, DC: U.S. Department of Health and Human Services, Administration for Children and Families. Available: www.acf.dhhs.gov/ programs/ofa/funds2.htm#programpurpose

Office of Planning, Research, and Evaluation. (2000). *Temporary Assistance for Needy Families (TANF) program: Third annual report to Congress.* Washington, DC: U.S. Department of Health and Human Services, Administration for Children and Families. Available: www.acf.dhhs.gov/ programs/opre/annual3.pdf

Olds, D., Henderson, C. R., Cole, R., Eckenrode, J., Kitzman, H., Luckey, D., Pettitt, L., Sidora, K., Morris, P., Powers, J. (1998). Long-term effects of nurs-ing home visitation on children's criminal and antisocial behavior: 15-year follow-up of a randomized controlled trial. *Journal of the American Medical Association, 280,* 1238-1244.

Olds, D. L., & Kitzman, H. (1993). Review of research on home visiting for pregnant women and parents of young children. *The Future of Children, 3,* 53-92.

Oliver, M., & Shapiro, T. (1995). *Black wealth/White wealth: A new perspective on racial inequality.* New York: Routledge.

Olson, C. M. (1999). Nutrition and health outcomes associated with food insecurity and hunger. *Journal of Nutrition, 129,* 521S-524S.

O'Neill, D. M., & O'Neill, J. E. (1997). *Lessons from welfare reform: An analysis of the AFDC caseload and past welfare-to-work programs.* Kalamazoo, MI: W. E. Upjohn Institute for Employment Research.

Orfield, G. (1992). Money, equity, and college access. *Harvard Educational Review, 72,* 337-372.

Page, B. I., & Simmons, J. R. (2000) *What government can do: Dealing with poverty and inequality.* Chicago: University of Chicago Press.

Pandey, S., Zahn, M., & Neeley-Barnes, S. (2000). The higher education option for poor women with children. *Journal of Sociology and Social Welfare, 27,* 109-170.

Parker, F. L., Boak, A. Y., Griffin, K. W., Ripple, C., & Peay, L. (1999). Parent-child relationship, home learning environment, and school readiness. *School Psychology Review, 28,* 413-425.

Parker, F. L., Piotrkowski, C. S., Horn, W. F., & Greene, S. M. (1995). The challenge for Head Start: Realizing its vision as a two-generation program. In S. Smith (Ed.), *Two generation programs for families in poverty: A new intervention strategy* (pp. 135-159). Norwood, NJ: Ablex.

Paulsell, D., Kisker, E. E., Love, J. M., Raikes, H., Bolles, K., Rosenberg, L., Coolahan, K., & Berlin, L. J. (2000). *Leading the way: Characteristics and early experiences of selected Early Head Start programs,* Vol. 3: *Program implementation.* Washington, DC: U.S. Department of Health and Human Services, Administration on Children, Youth, and Families, Commissioner's Office of Research and Evaluation and the Head Start Bureau.

Paxson, C., & Waldfogel, J. (2001). Welfare reform and child maltreatment. *Joint Center for Poverty Research Policy Brief, 3*(6). (Evanston, IL: Joint Center for Poverty Research)

Pearce, D., & Brooks, J. (2000). *The self-sufficiency standard for New York.* Albany: New York Association of Training and Employment Professionals.

Peisner-Feinberg, E. S., Burchinal, R. M., Culkin, M. L., Howes, C., Kagan, S. L., Yazejian, N., Byler, P., Rustici, J., & Zelazo, J. (1999). *The children of the Cost, Quality and Outcomes Study go to school: Executive summary.* Chapel Hill: University of North Caroline at Chapel Hill, Frank Porter Graham Child Development Center.

Percy-Smith, J. (2000). Introduction: The contours of social exclusion. In J. Percy-Smith (Ed.), *Policy responses to social exclusion: Towards inclusion?* (pp. 1-21). Philadelphia: Open University Press.

Perez-Escamilla, R., Ferris, A. M., Drake, L., Haldeman, L., Peranick, J, Campbell, M., Peng, Y. K., Burke, G., & Bernstein, B. (2000). Food stamps are associated with food security and dietary intake of inner-city preschoolers from Hartford, Connecticut. *Journal of Nutrition, 130,* 2711-2717.

Pinderhughes, E. E., Dodge, K. A., Bates, J. E., Pettit, G. S., & Zelli, A. (2000). Discipline responses: Influences of parents' socioeconomic status, ethnicity, beliefs about parenting, stress, and cognitive-emotional processes. *Journal of Family Psychology, 14,* 380-400.

Planning and Evaluation Service. (2000). *Promising results, continuing challenges: Final report of the national assessment of Title I.* Washington, DC: U.S. Department of Education, Office of the Deputy Secretary. Available: www.ed.gov/offices/ous/pes/exsum.htm

Planning and Evaluation Service. (2001a). *Fact sheet on Title I, Part A.* Washington, DC: U.S. Department of Education, Office of the Deputy Secretary. Available: www.ed.gov/offices/ous/pes/esed/title_i_fact_sheet.pdf

Planning and Evaluation Service. (2001b). *The longitudinal evaluation of school change and performance (LESCP) in Title I schools: Final report: Vol. 1. Executive summary.* Washington, DC: U.S. Department of Education, Office of the Deputy Secretary. Available: www.ed.gov/offices/ous/pes/esed/lescp_vol1.pdf

Polit, D. F., & O'Hara, J. J. (1989). Support services. In P. H. Cottingham & D. T. Ellwood (Eds.), *Welfare policy for the 1990s* (pp. 165-198). New York: Rockefeller Foundation.

Pollin, R. (1998). *The living wage: Building a fair economy.* New York: New Press.

Posner, J. K., & Vandell, D. L. (1999). After-school activities and the development of low-income children: A longitudinal study. *Developmental Psychology, 34,* 868-879.

Pribesh, S., & Downey, D. B. (1999). Why are residential and school moves associated with poor school performance? *Demography, 36,* 521-534.

Quint, J., Bos, J. M., & Polit, D. (1997). *New chance: Final report on a comprehensive program for young mothers in poverty and their children.* New York: Manpower Research Demonstration Corporation.

Ramey, C. T., & Ramey, S. L. (1992). Effective early intervention. *Mental Retardation, 30,* 337-345.

Rangarajan, A., & Gleason, P. M. (2001). *Food stamp leavers in Illinois: How are they doing two years later? Final report submitted to the U.S. Department of Agriculture.* Princeton, NJ: Mathematica Policy Research.

Rank, M. R., & Hirschl, T. A. (1999). The economic risk of childhood poverty in America: Estimating the probability of poverty across the formative years. *Journal of Marriage and the Family, 61,* 1058-1067.

Reder, N. (2000). *Finding funding: A guide to federal sources for out-of-school time and community school initiatives.* Washington, DC: Finance Project.

Reynolds, A. J. (2000). *Success in early intervention: The Chicago Child-Parent Centers.* Lincoln: University of Nebraska Press.

Rose, D. (1999). Economic determinants and dietary consequences of food insecurity in the United States. *Journal of Nutrition, 129,* 517S-520S.

Rose, D., Habicht, J.-P., & Devaney, B. (1998). Household participation in the Food Stamp and WIC programs increases the nutrient intakes of preschool children. *Journal of Nutrition, 128,* 548-555.

Rosenbaum, J. E. (1991). Black pioneers: Do their moves to the suburbs increase economic opportunity for mothers and children? *Housing Policy Debate, 2,* 1179-1213.

Rothbart, M. K., & Bates, J. E. (1998). Temperament. In N. Eisenberg (Ed.), *Social, emotional, and personality development* (Handbook of Child Psychology, No. 3, 5th ed., pp. 105-176). New York: John Wiley.

Rutter, M. (1990). Psychosocial resilience and protective mechanisms. In J. Rolf, A. S. Masten, D. Cicchetti, K. Nuechterlein, & S. Weintraub (Eds.), *Risk and protective factors in the development of psychopathology* (pp. 181-215). New York: Cambridge University Press.

Schirm, A. L. (2000). *Reaching those in need: Food stamp participation rates in the states.* Washington, DC: U.S. Department of Agriculture, Food and Nutrition Service. Available: www.fns.usda.gov/oane/menu/published/fsp/files/participation/reaching.pdf

Schirm, A. L., & Czajka, J. L. (2000). *State estimates of uninsured children, January 1998.* Washington, DC: U.S. Department of Health and Human Services.

Available: http://aspe.os.dhhs.gov/health/reports/state%20estimates%20of%20uninsured%20children%20(cps)/index.htm

Schreiner, M., Sherraden, M., Clancy, M., Johnson, L., Curley, J., Grinstein-Weiss, M., Zhan, M., & Beverly, S. (2001). *Savings and asset accumulation in Individual Development Accounts: Downpayments on the American Dream Policy Demonstration, a national demonstration of Individual Development Accounts.* St. Louis, MO: Center for Social Development. Available: http://gwbweb.wustl.edu/users/csd/add/addreport2001/contents.html

Schwienhart, L. J., & Weikart, D. P. (1980). *Young children grow up: The effects of the Perry Preschool Program on youths through age 15* (Monograph No. 7). Ypsilanti, MI: High/Scope Educational Research Foundation.

Seccombe, K. (2000). Families in poverty in the 1990s: Trends, causes, consequences, and lessons learned. *Journal of Marriage and the Family, 62,* 1094-1113.

Sen, A. (1999). *Development as freedom.* Garden City, NY: Anchor Books.

Shonkoff, J. P., & Phillips, D. A. (Eds.). (2000). *From neurons to neighborhoods: The science of early childhood development.* Washington, DC: National Academy Press.

Simons, R. L., Lorenz, F. O., Wu, C., & Conger, R. D. (1993). Social network and marital support as mediators and moderators of the impact of stress and depression on parental behavior. *Developmental Psychology, 29,* 368-381.

Simons, R. L., Whitbeck, L. B., Melby, J. N., & Wu, C. (1994). Economic pressure and harsh parenting. In R. D. Conger & G. H. Elder, Jr. (Eds.), *Families in troubled times: Adapting to change in rural America* (pp. 207-222). New York: Aldine de Gruyter.

Smith, J. R., & Brooks-Gunn, J. (1997). Correlates and consequences of harsh discipline for young children. *Archives of Pediatric and Adolescent Medicine, 151,* 777-786.

Smith, J. R., Brooks-Gunn, J., & Klebanov, P. K. (1997). Consequences of living in poverty for young children's cognitive and verbal ability and early school achievement. In G. J. Duncan & J. Brooks-Gunn (Eds.), *Consequences of growing up poor* (pp. 132-189). New York: Russell Sage.

Smith, S., & Zaslow, M. (1995). Rationale and policy context for two-generation interventions. In S. Smith (Ed.), *Two generation programs for families in poverty: A new intervention strategy* (pp. 1-35). Norwood, NJ: Ablex.

St. Pierre, R. G., & Layzer, J. I. (1998). *Improving the life chances of children in poverty: Assumptions and what we have learned* (Social Policy Report No. 12). Ann Arbor, MI: Society for Research in Child Development.

St. Pierre, R. G., & Layzer, J. I. (1999). Using home visits for multiple purposes: The Comprehensive Child Development Program. *The Future of Children, 9,* 134-151.

Strawn, J. (1992). *The states and the poor: Child poverty rises as the safety net shrinks* (Social Policy Report No. 6). Ann Arbor, MI: Society for Research in Child Development.

Subcommittee on the Tenth Edition of the RDAs, Food and Nutrition Board, Commission on Life Sciences, National Research Council. (1989). *Recommended dietary allowances* (10th ed.). Washington, DC: National Academy Press.

Sugland, B. W., Zaslow, M., Smith, J. R., Brooks-Gunn, J., Coates, D., Blumenthal, C., Moore, K. A., Griffin, T., & Bradley, R. (1995). The early childhood HOME inventory and HOME–Short Form in differing racial/ethnic groups. *Journal of Family Issues, 16,* 632-663.

Takeuchi, D. T., Williams, D. R., & Adair, R. K. (1991). Economic stress in the family and children's emotional and behavior problems. *Journal of Marriage and the Family, 53,* 1031-1041.

Townsend, P. (1992). *The international analysis of poverty.* Hemel Hempstead, UK: Harvester Wheatsheaf.

Trickett, P. K., Aber, J. L., Carlson, V., & Cicchetti, D. (1991). Relationship of socioeconomic status to the etiology and developmental sequelae of physical child abuse. *Developmental Psychology, 37,* 149-158.

Tronick, E. Z., & Weinberg, M. K. (1997). Depressed mothers and infants: Failure to form dyadic states of consciousness. In L. Murray & P. J. Cooper (Eds.), *Postpartum depression and child development* (pp. 54-81). New York: Guilford.

UNICEF Innocenti Research Centre. (2000). *A league table of child poverty in rich nations* (Innocenti Report Card No. 1). Florence, Italy: Author.

U.S. Census Bureau. (1998). *Child support for custodial mothers and fathers: 1997* (Current Population Reports, No. P60-212). Washington, DC: Author. Available: www.census.gov/prod/2000pubs/p60-212.pdf

U.S. Census Bureau. (2000). *Poverty in the United States, 1999* (Current Population Reports, No. P60-210). Washington, DC: Author. Available: www.census.gov/prod/2000pubs/p60-210.pdf

U.S. Department of Education. (2001). *National postsecondary student aid study: Student financial aid estimates for 1999-2000.* Washington, DC: U.S. Department of Education.

U.S. Department of Health and Human Services. (1996). *Adolescent time use, risky behavior, and outcomes: An analysis of national data.* Washington, DC: Author.

U.S. Department of Health and Human Services. (2000). *A national strategy to prevent teen pregnancy: Annual report, 1999-2000.* Washington, DC: Author. Available: http://aspe.hhs.gov/hsp/teenp/ann-rpt00

U.S. Department of Health and Human Services. (2002). *HHS fact sheet: The State Children's Health Insurance Program (SCHIP).* Washington, DC: Author. Available: www.hhs.gov/news/press/2002pres/schip.html

U.S. Department of Housing and Urban Development. (1998). *Rental housing assistance: The crisis continues—The 1997 report to Congress on worst case housing needs.* Washington, DC: Office of Policy Development and Research.

U.S. Department of Housing and Urban Development. (2001a). *Housing Choice Vouchers.* Washington, DC: Author. Available: www.hud.gov/offices/pih/programs/hcv/index.cfm

U.S. Department of Housing and Urban Development. (2001b). *HUD's public housing program.* Washington, DC: Author. Available: www.hud.gov/phprog.cfm

U.S. Department of Labor. (2001). *Minimum wage and overtime hours under the Fair Labor Standards Act.* Washington, DC: U.S. Department of Labor, Employment Standards Administration, Wage and Hour Division. Available: www.dol.gov/dol/esa/public/regs/statutes/whd/minwage1.pdf

U.S. General Accounting Office. (1992). *Early intervention: Federal investments like WIC can produce savings* (HRD-92-18). Washington, DC: Author.

U.S. General Accounting Office. (1994). *Child care: Child care subsidies increase likelihood that low-income mothers will work* (HEHS-95-20). Washington DC: Author.

U.S. General Accounting Office. (1998). *Abstracts of GAO reports and testimony, FY 97.* Washington, DC: Author.

U.S. General Accounting Office. (1999). *Food Stamp Program: Various factors have led to declining participation—Report to congressional requesters* (GAO/RCED-99-185). Washington, DC: Author.

U.S. General Accounting Office. (2000). *Title I preschool education: More children served but gauging the effect on school readiness difficult* (HEHS-00-171). Washington, DC: Author.

U.S. Surgeon General. (2000). *Oral health in America: A report of the surgeon general.* Bethesda, MD: National Institutes of Health, National Institute of Dental and Craniofacial Research.

Vargas, C., Crall, J., & Schneider, D. (1998). Sociodemographic distribution of pediatric dental carries: NHANES III, 2988-2994. *Journal of the American Dental Association, 129,* 1229-1238.

Waber, D. P., Vuori-Christiansen, L., Ortiz, N., Clement, J. R., Christiansen, N. E., Mora, J. O., Reed, R. B., & Herrera, M. G. (1981). Nutritional supplementation, maternal education, and cognitive development of infants at risk of malnutrition. *American Journal of Clinical Nutrition, 43*(Suppl. 4), 807-813.

Walker, T. B., Rodriguez, G. G., Johnson, D. L., & Cortez, C. P. (1995). Avance parent-child education program. In S. Smith (Ed.), *Two generation programs for families in poverty: A new intervention strategy* (pp. 67-90). Norwood, NJ: Ablex.

Weinger, S. (1998). Poor children "know their place": Perceptions of poverty , class, and public messages. *Journal of Sociology and Social Welfare, 25,* 100-118.

Yoshikawa, H. (1999). Welfare dynamics, support services, mothers' earnings, and child cognitive development: Implications for contemporary welfare reform. *Child Development, 70,* 779-801.

Yoshikawa, H., & Knitzer, J. (1997). *Lessons from the field: Head Start mental health strategies to meet changing needs.* New York: National Center for Children in Poverty and American Orthopsychiatric Association.

Zigler, E. F., Finn-Stevenson, M., & Stern, B. M. (1997). Supporting children and families in the schools: The school of the 21st century. *American Journal of Orthopsychiatry, 67,* 396-407.

Zigler, E. F., & Styfco, S. (1993). *Using research and theory to justify and inform Head Start expansion* (Social Policy Report No. 7). Ann Arbor, MI: Society for Research in Child Development.

Zigler, E. F., & Styfco, S. (2001). Extended childhood intervention prepares children for school and beyond. *Journal of the American Medical Association, 285,* 2378-2380.

CHAPTER 13

The Politics of Children's Issues: Challenges and Opportunities for Advancing a Children's Agenda in the Political Arena

MARYLEE ALLEN
SUSANNE MARTINEZ

Political rhetoric around the importance of America's children—the future of our nation, our greatest resource—is limitless. Yet when measured against the commitment of other industrialized nations to young people, America falls far short. Compared with 23 other industrialized countries, the United States is the only nation that fails to provide its children with a safety net that guarantees universal health coverage, paid maternal/parental leave policy, and a child allowance or grant (Children's Defense Fund, 2001c). Among these nations, America ranks 23rd in infant mortality rates, 17th in low-weight births, 11th in the proportion of children living in poverty, and 16th in efforts to lift children out of poverty. The United States has one of the widest gaps between rich children and poor children (18th in ranking) and has more children dying from gun violence than any of the other 23 nations (Children's Defense Fund, 2001c). The United States child poverty rate is roughly twice as high as the rates in Canada and Germany and is at least six times higher than the rate in France. Many experts have attributed these differences to lower spending in the United States on public benefits to help low-income families along with greater disparities in income distribution among U.S. workers (Smeeding, Rainwater, & Burless, 2000).

The poverty rate for children in America is now the highest among all age groups. In fact, children in America have traded places with the elderly. In 1969, the poverty rate for seniors exceeded 25%; today, the poverty rate for older Americans has plummeted to historic lows, falling below 10% for the first time in 1999. In contrast, a child is more likely to be poor today than was the case 30 years ago. The poverty rate for children in 2000 was 16.2%; in 1970, it was 15.1%.

A decade ago, a bipartisan National Commission on Children (1991) appointed by a Republican president and a Democratic Congress issued a report aptly titled *Beyond Rhetoric: A New American Agenda for Children and Families.* The report noted the tragic irony that the most prosperous nation on earth had failed so many of its children and that we, as a society, had lacked the vision and political will necessary to address the problems faced by millions of children. The commission, like many similar efforts that preceded it (see, e.g., Advisory Committee on Child Development, 1976; Carnegie Council on Children, 1977), outlined an ambitious set of goals to improve the health and well-being of the nation's children.

A decade later, some progress has been made, but the gap between rhetoric and reality looms as great today as it did when the National Commission on Children released its 1991 report. A new children's health insurance program enacted in 1997 has provided health insurance coverage for more than 3 million uninsured children. Yet more than 9 million children lack health insurance today—roughly 1 million more than the 8.3 million uninsured children cited in the 1991 commission report. Indeed, as millions of children have enrolled in the new Children's Health Insurance Program (CHIP), millions more have lost Medicaid health coverage as a result of 1996 welfare changes that led many to believe—mistakenly—that they were no longer eligible for Medicaid once they stopped receiving assistance or entered the workforce. One of the key recommendations in the 1991 commission report—a refundable child tax credit—was added to

the 2001 tax bill, over the objections of the Bush administration and conservative leaders in Congress (Twohey, 2001).

Other new investments in child care and child development have been achieved during the past several years. For example, in 2000, Head Start received the largest single-year increase in history—a $1 billion boost. Child care funding was increased by a similar amount following a 3-year sustained effort by child care advocates across the nation (Children's Defense Fund, 2001c). But millions of children are still left without the services necessary to help them develop into healthy productive citizens. For example, millions of children remain on waiting lists for child care assistance. Only three of five children eligible for Head Start are currently being served, and only 12% of families eligible for federal child care assistance actually receive help. Child welfare agencies are understaffed and unable to provide services and protections for the most vulnerable children. Millions of children are left in overcrowded schools and crumbling classrooms with ill-prepared teachers. Millions of children live in inadequate housing and without adequate nutrition.

Why is there such a gap in this country between the political rhetoric and reality? What are the challenges that children's advocates face in attempting to pursue gains for children in the political arena? What opportunities have helped achieve advances, and what forces work against moving forward? In this chapter, we try to address both challenges and opportunities and to provide some examples of where advocacy for children has succeeded.

THE CHALLENGES

There are many challenges that stand between what children need and effective policies and programs to address those needs. There are different perceptions about which children need what and the appropriate means for meeting those needs. Children's advocates are also often perceived as politically weak, without the resources needed to operate as a powerful political constituency. Gains for children, nevertheless, have been achieved as advocates have found ways to overcome the obstacles that hindered advancements in the politics of children's issues.

Children Do Not Vote

Although it may seem simplistic, one challenge faced by children's advocates in the political arena is the reality that children do not vote or contribute to political campaigns. The competition for time and resources is fierce, and children's advocates are often underfunded and left on the sideline by the stampede of the more politically powerful, who are able to wine and dine lawmakers, turn out voters on Election Day, and send money into campaign treasuries. Groups such as Common Cause and Public Citizen have repeatedly documented the abuses in a campaign system that benefits the wealthy and punishes both middle-income and lower-income Americans by "permitting big-money special interests to advance their agendas in Congress and at the White House—too often at the expense of working families" (Common Cause, 2001). During the 1920s, Grace Abbott, an early head of the federal Children's Bureau (1921-1934), portrayed in picturesque terms the imbalance between those moneyed interests and advocates working for children and families. In words that have inspired children's leaders for decades, but have also captured the fundamental weaknesses of children's advocacy efforts, she noted,

> Sometimes when I get home at night in Washington I feel as though I had been in a great traffic jam. The jam is moving toward the Hill where Congress sits in judgment on all the administrative agencies of the government. In that traffic jam there are all kinds of vehicles moving up toward the Capitol. . . . There are all kinds of conveyances that the Army can put into the street—tanks, gun carrier trucks. . . . There are the hayracks and binders and the ploughs and all the other things that the Department of Agriculture manages to put into the streets . . ., the handsome limousines in which the Department of Commerce rides . . ., the barouches in which the Department of State rides in such dignity. It seems so to me as I stand on the sidewalk watching it become more congested and more difficult, and then because the responsibility is mine and I must, I take a very firm hold of the handles of the baby carriage and I wheel it into the traffic. (cited in Grubb & Lazerson, 1982, p. 98)

As others have noted, the dedication of child advocates is often not enough; they are often pushed aside by more powerful interest groups in the struggle for resources and priority (Grubb & Lazerson, 1982). Indeed, in light of the limited resources available to the children's advocacy community as compared with other competing interests, the successes accomplished on behalf of children and families over the past several decades are impressive. It is not surprising, however, that the major investments of resources in children's services are in areas such as health and education where powerful allies are engaged as well.

Many believe that children's advocates must become more directly engaged in the electoral process if their voices are to be heard in the political arena. For example, one observer argued that children's issues are high on the public agenda but that to get politicians to act advocates should "consider the benefits and drawbacks of participating in [political] party and campaign activities to increase their leverage in policymaking" (Reid, 2001, p. 127). This observer contended that child advocacy groups have great experience in public education, research, and lobbying but that they need to move into the political process to get politicians to act (Reid, 2001). Others, however, have argued that children's issues must remain non-partisan and "above politics" to attract wider support. For example, one survey of children's organizations found that "there were differing comfort levels with the need to be 'political' in advancing a children's agenda. Many felt the children's community needed to be non-political and that its issues would attract a larger audience if they were packaged as 'non-political'" (The Children's Partnership, 1998, p. 15).

Ambivalence About the Role of Government in Children's Lives

Another challenge facing child advocates is a deeply rooted ambivalence about the role of government in the lives of children and their families. In America, children generally are regarded as the responsibility of their parents. The Coalition for America's Children (1999), in a recent report focusing on the challenges of pursuing a children's agenda, noted that "on nearly every issue, people point to parents as both the problem and the solution" (p. 11). In Steiner's (1976) analysis of child advocacy efforts, *The Children's Cause,* he observed that "the American social system presumes that, barring economic disaster or health crisis, a family should and will care for its children without public intervention" (p. 1). Still, as he noted, "federally supported public programs of compensatory services or cash assistance are readily accepted when the need for them results from circumstances over which either a child or a child's parents have no control" (p. 1). More recently, Imig (2001) observed, "Today, children's advocates face ambiguous, at times antagonistic political conditions.... The public is divided over policy priorities, and the role that government should play in social policy is debated on all sides" (p. 203). Imig also noted,

Child advocacy efforts ... face an uphill battle because the public itself appears conflicted about the needs of children and families. Survey after survey has shown that Americans are concerned about the problems of children.... At the same time, the public is unsure whether government should play a larger role in child policy. (pp. 199-200)

In reflecting on the American perspective, one commentator stated,

So deeply embedded is the premise that the central responsibility for children's well-being rests with parents that governmental assumption of responsibility can fail to occur even under the most dire circumstances, as in the well-publicized failures of child protective service agencies to intervene in some cases of extreme child abuse. (Heclo, 1997, p. 145)

Yet most researchers and public policy analysts believe that the American public sees a balanced role for government. Heclo (1997) argued that the public both values the family as a fundamentally private unit that should carry the prime responsibility for children and acknowledges that the welfare of children in families can be significantly strengthened or weakened depending on what the government and communities do or do not do. The key role that government can play in strengthening families has long been recognized. For example, a 1948 report, *The American Family* (National Conference on Family Life Committee, 1948), noted that when "the family is unable to supply the support and guidance that the individual [child or adult] needs, it is essential that society provide resources" (p. 373). A similar view was reflected a decade ago in the conclusions of the National Commission on Children (1991), which reaffirmed the view that "parents bear primary responsibility for meeting their children's physical, emotional, and intellectual needs and for providing moral guidance and direction," yet also concluded that "it is in society's best interests to support parents in their childrearing roles, to enable them to fulfill their obligations, and to hold them responsible for the care and support of their children" (p. xix). Accordingly, most researchers have found support for government services where parents were unable to meet the needs of their children, but resistance to having government services substitute for what are perceived to be parental responsibilities.[1]

Polling data generally have indicated widespread public support for government services to help children in low-income families. For example, a W. K. Kellogg Foundation poll in January 1999 found that 86% of those surveyed believed that child care should be available to all low-income families so that parents can work. Nearly three quarters (73%) said that the federal government should play a role in helping these families to pay for child care. In 1998, a Charles Stewart Mott Foundation survey found that 80% of those surveyed would be willing to pay higher taxes to help offer after-school programs for children. A recent poll released by the Afterschool Alliance in 2000 found that 9 of 10 voting Americans want after-school programs for children and that 8 of 10 believe that federal and state governments should set aside money for these programs.[2] Despite this widespread public support for investments in children's needs, child advocates continue to face a major challenge in translating this broad public support into political action and in underscoring the importance of government support to help parents carry out their responsibilities, not to replace parental efforts.

Concerns About Government Interference: The Family Values Debate

Children's advocates also are confronted often with conservative arguments that government services will result in government interference or control over child rearing. Although the broader public appears to be more concerned about government programs allowing parents to evade their responsibilities, the specter of government interference with family life has also had a toll on advocacy efforts. For example, opponents to U.S. ratification of the United Nations-sponsored Convention on the Rights of the Child, a document that has been approved by 191 nations, have portrayed efforts to protect the rights of children as an assault on parents (see, e.g., Sabom, 2001). One conservative organization, the Family Research Council, has adopted as its position statement in the parental rights section of its Web site the charge that "government policies routinely intrude upon the sanctity of the family unit with no compelling reason, and they denigrate the essential role of parental authority" (www.frc.org/iss/par/index.cfm). The 1975 Child and Family Services Act (H.R. 2966/S. 626) was an early victim of this kind of assault. The legislation, which would have provided basic health, education, and child care services to low-income families, was viciously attacked through an anonymous flyer that circulated throughout the country alleging that the measure would take the authority for child rearing from families and turn it over to the state (U.S. Senate, 1976).

A quarter century later, the debate over family values and similar allegations continued to surface around federal efforts to expand child care services for working families. For example, a Cato Institute (1997) paper, "The Advancing Nanny State: Why the Government Should Stay Out of Child Care," attacked the Clinton administration for hosting a White House Conference on Child Care, arguing that "child care should remain safe from government intrusion." In the same publication, the Cato Institute argued against helping low-income single mothers who need child care services to work on the grounds that "people should not bear children for whom they are unwilling or unable to provide." Child advocates thus bear the burden of clarifying that government supports for children's services do not undermine parental responsibilities but rather give hard-pressed families greater choices in caring for their children and families.

The "All Children" or "at-Risk Children" Debate

There has also been a long-standing debate among child advocates, policymakers, and the general public about whether to focus efforts on obtaining universal services ("all children") or on obtaining services needed to help vulnerable children ("at-risk children"), particularly those living in low-income families. Kamerman (1989) described this as an old debate over "universalism vs. selectivity" and fundamentally a question of whether the politics of children will support greater success for a targeted agenda rather than a broader agenda. She noted that some argue that a universal agenda attracts broader political support and ultimately results in programs that are less stigmatized and more generous. On the other hand, Steiner (1976) argued that a children's policy most feasible, and most desirable, is one targeted at poor children, children with disabilities, and/or children without permanent homes—the "unlucky children whose parents cannot provide them a start equal to that provided most children" (p. 255).

A recent case study of the establishment of a universal pre-kindergarten program for all 4-year-olds in Georgia illustrates the debate over the most effective strategies (Raden, 1999). The Georgia pre-kindergarten plan was initially focused on targeting services to the state's neediest children but was soon shifted to the provision of universal services for all children. An analysis of how and why the program focus was shifted found that

most observers believe that the decision to move toward universal provision of services ensured the future of the pre-kindergarten program in Georgia, largely because "universal programs may be more likely to generate and sustain broad political support than programs targeted towards disadvantaged children" (p. 3). On the other hand, the Georgia analysis also noted that although universal programs may erase the stigma typically attached to programs for low-income children, at the same time program elements designed for low-income populations may be unacceptable to middle- and upper-class families and may be lost in a move toward universal services. For example, when the Georgia program was initially started, it placed a great emphasis on the provision of comprehensive, family-focused social services, but as the program moved toward universal coverage, these services were criticized as overly intrusive and were cut back, igniting criticism from those who believed that the program was no longer meeting the substantial needs of low-income children and their families. Although some have taken the position that government funds should not be used to provide resources to families capable of paying for their own preschool programs, the general consensus in Georgia was that a program geared toward economically disadvantaged, politically weak populations would have remained politically vulnerable and limited (Raden, 1999).

It is clear that child advocates and policymakers will continue to debate whether efforts should be focused on targeted groups or, as with the case in Georgia, on the expansion of universal services for all children. Each approach has advantages and disadvantages, and the degree of success may vary based on time, place, and other factors. When resources are perceived to be limited, it is difficult not to argue that they should first be concentrated on those in greatest need.

Yet the public policy process may sometimes move in exactly the opposite direction. For example, for many years, child advocates have argued for a universal child tax credit or child allowance similar to that enjoyed by families in virtually all Western industrialized nations. Yet when such a credit was enacted in 1997 (Taxpayer Relief Act of 1997, Public Law 105-34, Title I, Section 101), millions of low-income children were left out. It was not until the 2001 tax bill (Economic Growth and Tax Relief Reconciliation Act of 2001, Public Law 107-16, Title II, Section 201) that the credit was made partially refundable and thus available to children whose parents' earnings were too low to have a net income tax liability. Yet some 10 million low-income children are still excluded from the credit because their parents' annual earnings are less than $10,000. The lack of refundability in the Adoption Tax Credit, which assists families who adopt children with special needs, also makes it unavailable to many foster parents and others adopting children with physical, mental, or emotional disabilities (Public Law 107-16, Title II, Section 202).

Whose Children? Issues of Class and Race

Although the majority of poor children, uninsured children, abused children, and other vulnerable children are white, the public perception remains that these children "belong to someone else." In fact, currently 62% of poor children in America are white. Fully 78% live in households where at least one person works, and more than 40% live in two-parent or father-only families. Contrary to popular belief, the majority of poor children live in rural or suburban communities, not in urban areas. Similarly, more than 40% of the uninsured children are white, about 32% are Hispanic, and 20% are black. However, the proportion of black

or Hispanic children is significantly higher in each category; specifically, 1 of 6 black children and 1 of 4 Hispanic children are uninsured, as compared with 1 of 11 white children. One third (33%) of black children live in poverty, as compared with 13.5% of white children (Children's Defense Fund, 2001c).

Most parents care deeply about the well-being of their own children. The challenge for child advocacy is to help fashion public policies aimed at providing for *all* children what every parent wants for his or her own children. Child advocates must persuade the public and policymakers that it is in everyone's best interest to ensure that *all* children receive the services they need.

In addition, too often the most vulnerable children suffer because of the perceived failures of their parents. The 1996 welfare debate was a classic example. Although the vast majority of Aid to Families with Dependent Children (AFDC) recipients were children, the welfare debate focused on the role of parents and proposed measures aimed at adult participation in the workforce. Modest efforts to provide protections for vulnerable children were rejected as the 60-year-old federal safety net was unraveled. Although the booming economy during the late 1990s prevented many of the predicted hardships from unfolding, many federal policymakers were fully prepared to take the risk that vulnerable children would be hurt in the drive to move their parents into the workforce.

Who Speaks for Children?

Another challenge for child advocacy is identifying the spokespersons. Because children have no voice, they frequently must depend on surrogates to serve as their advocates. There are only a limited number of organizations—at either the state, local, or national level—focused solely on children's advocacy. A recent Urban Institute publication examining child advocacy organizations (DeVita & Mosher-Williams, 2001) sought to identify nonprofit organizations focused on children's issues through Internal Revenue Service (IRS) records. It found that measuring the scope of child advocacy organizations was difficult because IRS reporting requirements had limited information on nonprofit advocacy activities. The authors identified some 45,000 groups registered under section 501(c)(3) of the Internal Revenue Code with a focus on children, but the vast majority of these groups provide services rather than engage in advocacy. Some 9,300 groups registered under 501(c)(4) were identified as engaged in some form of advocacy, but many of these were entities such as Kiwanis, Rotary Clubs, and Optimists, not generally regarded as advocacy organizations and certainly not solely focused on children's interests (DeVita, Mosher-Williams, & Stengel, 2001).

Often, those most knowledgeable about the gaps in services and the needs of children and their families (other than the families themselves) are professionals—the social workers, child care providers, and health care service providers or agencies that provide services for children and families. Many associations representing child-serving workers or agencies are engaged in the public policy process, but their voices are sometimes discounted as self-serving, particularly where their agencies are recipients of government grants. For example, witnesses testifying at congressional hearings are required to identify whether they have received federal funds during the current year or the 2 preceding years. Some commentators have expressed concerns about potential conflicts of interest where providers of services assume the role of child advocates. For example, Grubb and Lazerson (1982) argued that "the interests of

children cannot be fully represented as long as professionals remain the dominant groups speaking on behalf of children" (p. 100). They noted that although professionals often possess helpful expertise and experience, they also can act out of self-interest, clouding their impact as advocates for children.

Other organizations and associations with a broader focus, including faith-based entities, civil rights organizations, women's groups, and civic associations, have been engaged in child advocacy efforts at the state, local, and national levels, but they often have multiple agendas and priorities and rarely stay focused on children's agendas. Efforts to organize parents have had mixed success. Some parent groups focused on specific problems, such as access to educational services for children with disabilities and the need to advance medical research in specific child illnesses, have been highly motivated and effective. Similar groups have formed around problems such as child abuse and neglect, but financial challenges, changing leadership, and other demands have limited the strength of these voluntary associations in the political arena dominated by highly paid lobbyists and competition from many other well-financed special interest groups. More recently, broad-based coalitions such as the Million Mom March have been formed to engage mothers and others around the issue of gun violence that threatens the lives of children across America. Whether this effort will have the staying power of a similar campaign, Mothers Against Drunk Driving, is yet unknown. Still, children's advocates recognize that engaging parents, grandparents, and concerned citizens in the overall children's cause holds the most promise of building a broad-based movement to compel action in the political arena. One survey found that many children's groups have worked to develop strategies to engage parents. The respondents, however, noted that parents are the single most important group and the single most difficult group to organize (The Children's Partnership, 1998).

Other Challenges for Child Advocates

The preceding discussion highlights some of the policy obstacles that children's advocates must confront. In addition, the devolution of many policy and program decisions from the national to the state level has created a new landscape for many child advocates, where battles must be fought on new and changing terrains in different jurisdictions. State and local advocacy efforts are often underfunded. Local funders are often more comfortable with direct service efforts than with direct advocacy. Some attribute weaknesses in the child advocacy movement to problems in private foundation grant making, which tends to allocate resources on a categorical basis (e.g., by program area) rather than on a strategic basis and to fund short-term projects (e.g., 1 or 2 years) (Covington, 2001).

> Such short-term funding commitments, along with the shifting program interests of many foundations, work against child advocates' ability to think and act with a long-term view.... Child advocates are often left chasing after program dollars that may or may not fit within their own organizations' priorities and longer-range goals. (pp. 65-66)

Despite these challenges, children's advocates continue to work tirelessly at advancing the well-being of America's children and have used many different strategies to achieve this goal. As discussed in the next section, many opportunities exist for promoting a children's agenda in the political arena.

THE OPPORTUNITIES

Children's advocates have struggled over the previous decades, sometimes successfully, to overcome the challenges just described so as to pursue an agenda for children in the policy arena. They also have learned to build on and take advantage of important opportunities. In some cases, children's advocates have helped to create these opportunities with new research or by using new strategies. In other cases, they have seen opportunities arise and have used them to move their children's agendas forward. The advocacy examples discussed in this section, most of them drawn from national-level policy, demonstrate the value of using opportunities strategically on behalf of children. They also suggest what the benefits for children might be if all of these opportunities could be taken advantage of at one time in the political arena.

Hammering Home the Facts

Homework always has been a cornerstone of good child advocacy (see, e.g., Amedei, 1991; Beck, 1979). Certainly, the technological advances of the past 10 years have made it much easier to do homework—to collect and assemble data on children and to disseminate the data in ways that are advantageous to children. Over the past decades, advocates also have become more sophisticated at educating the public about the needs of children and about using data strategically to demonstrate the scope of a problem and to build support for needed reforms. Advocates believe that as citizens learn more about how children are faring and what it means for their own future and for the future of their children and the nation, the more likely it is that there will be a public will to adequately address children's needs.

Over the past decade, new sources have expanded the data easily accessible on federal, state, and local levels and have provided new opportunities for advocates to use the data as a basis for action. For example, KIDS COUNT, established in 1990 by the Annie E. Casey Foundation, produces national, state-by-state, and county-by-county data to measure the educational, social, economic, and physical well-being of children (www.aecf.org/kidscount). The first national *KIDS COUNT Data Book* was published in 1990 and continues to be published annually. The foundation also supports a national network of state-level KIDS COUNT projects, now in existence in 49 states, that record local data on children. "KIDS COUNT exists," according to the foundation, "to measure child outcomes and contribute to public accountability for those outcomes, resulting in a model for data-driven advocacy for children, their families, and their communities" (see the Annie E. Casey Foundation KIDS COUNT Web site at www.aecf.org/kidscount/index.htm). The supplementary data books from KIDS COUNT also have helped to highlight both problems and solutions in individual areas affecting children (see, e.g., Annie E. Casey Foundation, 1997, 1998). KIDS COUNT also has compiled indicators of child well-being from the 2000 U.S. census and has created an interactive database (www.aecf.org/kidscount/census).

The Annie E. Casey Foundation's combination of national, state, and local data has enabled advocates to make problems real at the community level and to track progress in addressing those problems. Such data have enabled comparisons to be made from state to state and from county to county to assess the impact of different policies and practices on outcomes for children. In Vermont, for example, progress for children is measured annually across communities and state agencies, with specific indicators under each outcome (Center for the Study of Social Policy,

2001). The state involves communities in establishing expected results. In some communities, results are printed on grocery bags and posted in laundromats. In the state, a "top 10" list of communities or areas that have shown the most progress on the most indicators is generated. Community profiles are shared with state legislators who are in positions to affect specific policies. Partnerships also are formed regionally to work toward progress on specific outcomes for children. Such efforts dramatize children's needs and instill hope for the future. They also engage citizens and the broader community in seeing the impact they can have on improving children's well-being.

The increased accessibility of federal data sources through the Internet also has made it much easier for child advocates to make timely statistics a central part of their advocacy activities. State-by-state data are available from the U.S. Bureau of the Census and from all of the other federal agencies directly responsible for programs affecting children.

Beginning in 1996, the Office of the Assistant Secretary for Planning and Evaluation in the U.S. Department of Health and Human Services (DHHS) also began publishing a series of annual reports on national trends in five key substantive areas in the lives of children and youth: population, family, and neighborhood; economic security; health conditions and health care; social development, behavioral health, and teen fertility; and education and achievement. The report, *Trends in the Well-Being of America's Children and Youth*, offers useful historical trends and population subgroup analyses on each of 74 indicators in these five areas (Office of the Assistant Secretary for Planning and Evaluation, 2000). Although the DHHS *Trends* series provides only national data, it has been useful because of the broad range of children's concerns that are addressed. It also helps to highlight major gaps in the federal statistical systems, which continue to hamper the nation's ability to monitor the well-being of its children.

Advocacy around the enactment in 1997 of the State Child Health Insurance Program (Public Law 105-33, Title IV, Subtitle J, Chapter 1, Section 4901), a landmark federal-state partnership for children's health, demonstrates the value of using data and research well. CHIP, which is discussed in greater detail later, represents one of the most significant developments for children's health in decades. The Campaign for Child Health Now, a broad-based coalition convened to advocate for passage of CHIP, was consistent in its message. There was widespread agreement that health insurance coverage is vital to children's well-being and future success and that, tragically, millions of children have no coverage whatsoever.

In the course of the campaign, certain facts were repeated over and over again. National and state data were used to build a strong case for health care for children. Some 10 million children were uninsured, and the number was growing. This fact gained national recognition. The 10 million also was a number that could be broken down state by state. Data showing that the overwhelming majority of uninsured children—90%—had parents with jobs raised the relevance of the issue for many. A strong case was made as well about the risks children incur when they go without health insurance. Research showing that children without insurance were six times as likely to go without needed medical care, were five times as likely to use the hospital emergency room as a regular source of health care, and were at greater risk of school failure was used to demonstrate the consequences of the lack of health insurance.

These facts about children's unmet health needs resonated with policymakers and the general public. They also helped to link advocates for education, social services, and other improvements for children to the call for comprehensive health coverage for all of the nation's children. For example, such data helped advocates for child care and other early childhood programs, child protection, and education recognize how improved health care could significantly enhance the impact of their own services and programs.

Building on Common Mainstream Concerns

Over the past decade, there also has been an increased effort on the part of children's advocates to rally around topics where there was evidence of common public concern. Child care and early childhood initiatives are cases in point, although education and child health also could be used as examples.

In 1990, a major initiative, the Act for Better Child Care (Public Law 101-508), moved through Congress with bipartisan support. That legislation, which established what is today the Child Care and Development Fund, still provides a significant portion of federal resources for child care. It also recognized for the first time the importance of a public role in improving the quality and supply of child care, and it included funds specifically dedicated to that purpose.

Later during that decade, however, there again was growing concern about the unmet child care needs of young children and of school-age children who were home alone after school, and there were opportunities in both areas on which to build. The public was increasingly more aware of the importance of early brain development in very young children and of the threat of violence facing children in many parts of the country.

A report by the Carnegie Task Force on Meeting the Needs of Young Children (1994), *Starting Points: Meeting the Needs of Our Youngest Children*, reinforced the critical importance of the first 3 years of life and pointed out that "the quality of young children's environment and social experience has a decisive, long-lasting impact on their well-being and ability to learn" (p. xiii). Research on the brain development of young children demonstrated that how children grow and develop depends on the interplay between nature (children's genetic endowment) and nurture (e.g., children's nutrition, surroundings, care, and stimulation) (see, e.g., Families and Work Institute, 1996a, 1996b). The "I Am Your Child" campaign, a far-reaching public education initiative begun that year, emphasized the need for better care for babies and toddlers by focusing attention on the critical brain development that takes place during the first 3 years of life.

The concern about early brain development was coupled in the public's mind with the recognition by both parents and experts that child care options for infants and toddlers are in short supply everywhere. Three of four parents of young children participating in a national poll in 1989 said that there was an insufficient supply of child care for infants in their communities (Research and Forecasts, 1989). A later study of child care needs in six cities found serious shortages of infant care (Clark & Long, 1995). A survey of child care costs by the Children's Defense Fund found that the average annual cost of child care for a 4-year-old in an urban center is more than the average annual cost of public college tuition in nearly every state and that the cost is even greater for families with younger children (Schulman & Adams, 1998), thereby putting child care out of reach for many families.

Responding to growing concerns about the nation's youngest children, Congress took steps beginning in 1994 to create better child care options for families with infants and young children. The Early Head Start program (Public Law 103-525, Title I,

Section 112) was established in 1994 to provide comprehensive child care and family support services to families with infants and toddlers from birth to 3 years of age. Activities funded under Early Head Start include quality early education in and out of the home, home visits, parent education that includes parent-child activities, comprehensive health care, nutrition, and ongoing support to parents through case management and peer support groups. Funding for Early Head Start is based on the overall amount of available Head Start funds and has increased significantly over a relatively few years. In fiscal year (FY) 2000, for example, $421.4 million was used to support nearly 600 Early Head Start child development and family support services across the country, serving about 45,000 children under 3 years of age.

The focus on early brain development and the importance of the early years also stimulated state-level action on child care and other early childhood services. One of the boldest steps was the California electorate's approval in 1998 of Proposition 10, the California Children and Families Initiative (Calif. Health & Safety Code, Section 130100). This state ballot initiative raised $650 million in 2001 alone from a tax of 50 cents per pack on cigarettes to help local communities in the state strengthen and expand early childhood services from the prenatal stage to 5 years of age. County commissions in California may use the Proposition 10 funds to provide early care and education, child health services, and parenting education and support (Miller, Melaville, & Blank, 2001).

North Carolina established the Smart Start program, which provides funding to local collaboratives to assess the gaps in early childhood development in communities and to support initiatives to fill these gaps such as increased support for child care and family support and parental education initiatives

(Children's Defense Fund, 1999). Michigan increased funding for its School Readiness Program by nearly one third in 2000 (Children's Defense Fund, 2001c). That same year, Kentucky enacted a KIDS Now! initiative that adopts a comprehensive approach to early childhood by focusing on improving maternal and child health, supporting families, and enhancing early care and education. As part of the initiative, a newly appointed Business Council, composed of business and community leaders interested in early childhood and workplaces that support families, will help to encourage the corporate community and local governments to address these issues (Children's Defense Fund, 2001c).

During this period, as there was growing concern about the needs of the youngest children, there also was increased awareness that there were millions of school-age children who needed supervision during the hours when their schools are closed and their parents are at work. These concerns were fueled, at least in part, by the public's great concern about violence and its impact on children.

In a *Newsweek*–Children's Defense Fund poll conducted in 1993, nearly three quarters of the surveyed parents and more than half of the children said that their top worry is that a family member would become a victim of violent crime (Ingrassia, 1993). A 1996 poll of police chiefs from across the country found that more than 9 of 10 of them agreed that America could sharply reduce crime by investing in programs such as early childhood, parenting education, after-school, and mentoring programs (McDevitt, 1996). Many low-income parents reported that they preferred to have their children in lessons or other organized after-school activities but that they were unable to do so because of the cost or because there are no programs available (Center for Research on Women, 1996). School-age children and teens themselves also were interested in having options

available during after-school time. There was a growing consensus about the risks, such as school failure and a range of risk-taking behaviors, that could be faced by school-age children who were left to care for themselves. A poll sponsored by the Charles Stewart Mott Foundation (1998) found striking support for after-school programs. Four of five respondents said that they would be willing to pay higher taxes to fund after-school programs in their communities. This support crossed party lines and was equally strong among parents and those who were not parents.

The significant increase in funding for the 21st Century Community Learning Centers program, which supports school-based after-school initiatives, is just one illustration at the federal level of the growing consensus about the importance of after-school programs. Funding grew from $40 million in FY 1999 to $845.6 million in FY 2001.

Although the growing concern about violence was used in a positive way to promote investments in after-school programs for children, it cannot be ignored that, at least in part, it was this very same concern about violence that helped to fuel the efforts of those who wanted to move to more punitive remedies for youth in the juvenile justice system. The success of children's advocates on that front was measured by their effectiveness in stopping efforts in Congress to pass regressive federal legislation that would have denied young people who have been adjudicated delinquent the core protections already in federal law.

Finding New Allies

Child advocates also have seized on opportunities to forge broad coalitions and important partnerships to secure gains for children over the years. Such coalitions help to provide assurances to both the public and policymakers that there is general unity around an issue and also make it much harder for political opponents to use a "divide and conquer" strategy.

Some might find a move toward broad coalitions surprising given that child advocates are sometimes criticized for their failure to come together behind a common agenda (Carson, 2001). Too often, there is only limited, if any, collaboration between advocates for specific concerns affecting children such as health care, child care, education, and child protection, and even single-issue advocates may have different and sometimes even conflicting agendas. For example, some advocates for improvements in general education are reticent to support improvements in special education out of concern that the costly needs of special education students will jeopardize their ability to make gains for all students. There have been notable instances, however, when children's advocates have worked together across special interests and also reached out to find other new powerful allies with a less obvious connection to the reforms being sought for children.

The Campaign for Child Health Now, which in 1997 advocated successfully for enactment of the landmark $48 billion bipartisan CHIP (funded in part by an increase in the tobacco tax), was coconvened by the American Cancer Society and the Children's Defense Fund. It demonstrated the value that can accrue to children when more than 250 organizations, many of which had not worked together in the past, can commit to working to achieve a common goal for children. It drew support not only from child health groups and other health organizations that have long advocated against the harmful effects of tobacco but also from a variety of education groups that recognized that children cannot learn or perform to their fullest without adequate health care. AARP, representing retired persons and others who

need a healthy next generation to support them, was an important partner. Major labor unions also were supportive. They understood how businesses would gain if their workforces had to worry less about the health care needs of their children.

There are also examples of state and local child advocacy efforts in which coalitions of groups were formed that brought in new partners. When health care coverage for children was broadly expanded for children in Massachusetts in 1996, teachers and the state's teachers unions were active and effective players in garnering support for the expansions. During the early 1990s, advocates in New York City developed an "all in the same boat" coalition to bring a wide range of advocates together to fight, in an organized way, against proposed budget cuts in children's programs. Coleman Advocates for Children and Youth in San Francisco convened an extremely broad coalition to secure enactment in 1991, and again in 2000, of a Children's Fund, a ballot initiative that mandates a percentage of San Francisco's property taxes to be set aside for children and youth.

In another example of efforts to bring together advocates for children, hundreds of thousands of adults and children gathered on June 1, 1996, at the Lincoln Memorial in Washington, D.C., to take a public stand on behalf of the nation's children. "Stand for Children," as this event was called, was organized by the Children's Defense Fund and supported by an unprecedented coalition of 3,700 national, state, and local organizations. Since then, thousands of local Stand for Children events that have brought children's advocates together, sometimes as part of formal organizations, have taken place in communities across the country on or around June 1 each year.

In 2001, the Children's Defense Fund, joined by a 16-member steering committee of national organizations, launched the

Movement to Leave No Child Behind® to build the spiritual, civic, and political will in communities across America to achieve for all children what all children need. It is a broad-based movement intent on finding new allies. It brings together disparate child advocates and service providers from a range of areas (e.g., child care, child health, child welfare, education, juvenile justice) with powerful mainstream networks (e.g., faith-based organizations, women, parents and grandparents, youth) to support, strengthen, and achieve an inspiring vision to protect the whole child and family and to rebuild community and a sense of purpose as a nation.

A key, but by no means the sole, focus of the movement is the 2001 Act to Leave No Child Behind (H.R. 1990/S. 940), which sets forth a comprehensive national policy vision that demonstrates that children do not come in pieces. The mission of the movement states,

> We *can* build a nation where families have the support they need to make it at work and at home; where every child enters school ready to learn and leaves on the path to a productive future; where babies are likely to be born healthy and sick children have the health care they need; where no child has to grow up in poverty; where all children are safe in their community and every child has a place to call home—and all Americans can proudly say "We Leave No Child Behind." (Children's Defense Fund, 2001a, p. 2)

All of these goals are part of the vision for children in the Act to Leave No Child Behind. By the end of 2001, 280 state legislators and 40 city mayors had pledged their commitment to the act. More than 900 organizations from 43 states and the District of Columbia had formally endorsed it, and momentum was building.

Finally, there also are instances in which organizations have been formed precisely to enlist new voices to advocate on behalf of children. Fight Crime: Invest in Kids is one of these. Launched in 1996, Fight Crime is led by more than 1,000 police chiefs, prosecutors, sheriffs, crime victims, and leaders of police officer organizations from communities across the country. It makes the case that a key component in any anticrime agenda must be helping children to get the right start in life. Central to the organization's plan to reduce crime and violence and to prevent school and youth violence are increased investments in programs such as Head Start, school-readiness child care, after-school youth development programs, and child abuse and neglect prevention programs. Police chiefs and others can effectively make the case that investing in kids saves lives and money (www.fightcrime.org). In addition to its work in Washington, D.C., Fight Crime had established organizations in six states as of the fall of 2001.

Generations United (GU) is another example. Initiated in 1987, GU brings children's and seniors' groups together to promote policies, strategies, and programs as well as to promote a society that values all generations. GU's members include more than 100 national, state, and local organizations representing more than 70 million Americans. GU (2001) believes that "public policy should meet the needs of all generations and that resources are more wisely used when they connect generations rather than separate them" (p. 3). GU publishes a public policy agenda for each Congress, which highlights issues that incorporate an intergenerational approach to an issue or have an impact across generations. It also has held intergenerational briefings on Capitol Hill, sponsored by the Congressional Older Americans' and Children's Caucuses.

Engaging Those Directly Affected

Although still relatively limited, there are some powerful examples of the role that those who are directly affected by policies and practices affecting children can have in the political arena. The success of such opportunities should encourage advocates for children to focus more fully on strategies that include such direct involvement when they are seeking gains for children.

Certainly, the work of the AARP is a model to be emulated. When a retired former grade school teacher contacts a member of Congress about the need for increased social security benefits, the impact is well known. Phone calls from seniors who traveled together on a bus to Canada to purchase prescription drugs not currently available in the United States or available only at a much higher cost are also powerful lobbying tools.

Young people who have "aged out" of foster care and other graduates of the child welfare system played an important role in persuading Congress to enact the federal Foster Care Independence Act of 1999 (Public Law 106-169). Leaders in the White House and in Congress who sat directly with these young people to hear about the challenges they faced in getting their basic needs met as they made the transition from foster care needed to hear little more before they were ready to support increased federal investments on behalf of others still in foster homes and group homes (Allen & Nixon, 2000). The young people worked together with other advocates for children and youth who developed, and helped to push for, the reforms.

Particularly encouraging is the role of these young people in continuing to pursue the goals of the Foster Care Independence Act once it was enacted. For example, in California, the California Youth Connection, a nonprofit advocacy and youth leadership organization for current and former foster care youth, helped to ensure that its state took advantage of the law's new option for states to extend Medicaid to young people leaving foster care (www.calyouthconn.org). In Oregon, a young man who grew up in

foster care in Washington State took the lead, together with other young people from foster care, in pushing through legislation to provide tuition assistance at Oregon colleges and universities for youth who had at least 12 months of foster care after their 16th birthdays (Grindeland, 2001). The new legislation, funded at $100,000 in the first year to at least help it to get up and running, will assist students who move directly to higher education when they leave foster care as well as students who leave foster care without a high school diploma or a general equivalency diploma (GED) but achieve them later (see National Resource Center for Youth Development, 2001).

Parents of children with disabilities also have had a powerful role in some state actions for children and also in national-level reforms. For example, the Federation of Families for Children's Mental Health, the National Alliance for the Mentally Ill, and Family Voices—all parent-led organizations—have been instrumental in helping to secure increased funding for programs and enhanced protections for children with disabilities. In each case, parents themselves have mobilized to speak to policymakers about both the positive and negative impacts of reforms being considered. The Family Opportunity Act of 2001 (S. 321/H.R. 600) would directly help parents whose incomes make them ineligible for Medicaid but who are still too poor to be able to afford the treatments that their children with disabilities need. It would help to address the needs of parents of children with serious emotional disturbances who have no insurance or are underinsured and too often are told that the only option they have for getting their children the treatment they need is the draconian choice of having to place them in the custody of the state. In part due to advocacy by parents of children with disabilities, the act, at the end of 2001, had 74 cosponsors in the

Senate and 206 cosponsors in the House of Representatives.

Young people, both current and former consumers of mental health services, are also becoming actively engaged in mental health system reform in some states, with support from groups such as the Federation of Families for Children's Mental Health and other parent advocacy organizations (Research and Training Center on Family Support and Children's Mental Health, 2000).

The Children's Defense Fund, through the Student Leadership Network for Children (SLNC) of the Black Community Crusade for Children, also is seeking to engage new leaders for children. The SLNC is a national network of servant-leaders, ages 18 to 30 years, committed to improving the lives of children. Its mission is to mobilize a new generation of leaders eager to serve, empower, and advocate for positive social change through advocacy. The SLNC trains young high school and college students, as well as older youth, through Advanced Service and Advocacy Workshops in which they are engaged in public policy awareness.

Many SLNC servant-leaders also are trained to become teachers, counselors, and program staff at Freedom School sites nationwide. Modeled after the Freedom Schools of the civil rights movement, the Freedom Schools of today, which numbered 61 in 2001, provide safe havens, academic and cultural enrichment opportunities, and social change vehicles for children ages 5 to 18 years in comprehensive summer and sometimes after-school programs during the school year. SLNC members organize and empower parents of participating children to foster change in their communities. Young people are helped to see the link between effective programs and public policy as well as the importance of community development, political advocacy, and coalition building. Members of the SLNC receive

information on national and state legislation that will affect children in their communities as well as announcements of community-based service initiatives and training for youth activists and organizers (for additional information, see www.childrensdefense.org/bccc.htm).

Identifying Champions

Many of the important gains for children over the past 20 years, at least at the national level, had identified champions for their causes and often had strong bipartisan support. Such support is key to rallying congressional support as well as mobilizing broad grassroots support for an initiative. The creation in 1993 of the House Select Committee on Children, Youth, and Families helped to highlight and bring to national attention the special needs of the nation's most needy children. There also have been other special select bodies that, over time, have focused important attention on issues such as adoption, child nutrition, and children's needs more generally.

Familiarity with the substance of an initiative and consistency of support often characterize these champions. Some members of Congress have taken leadership roles because of their prior work as prosecutors, physicians, social workers, state legislators, or board members of human service agencies where they had exposure to children's concerns. There are other personal connections as well, for example, when members of Congress are foster parents, are adoptive parents, or have lost children to specific diseases or lost family members to violence. They can speak with real authority on behalf of the gains being sought. For example, improvements over recent years on behalf of children who have been abused and neglected, are in foster care, or are waiting for adoptive families have resulted, at least in part, because of leadership from members of Congress with professional and personal connections to such children.

Bipartisan support for encouraging work has helped to expand the federal Earned Income Tax Credit (EITC) (26 U.S.C., Section 32) over time to reach more low-income working families and to protect it from efforts to limit its benefit to low-income families. The EITC is a vital work support for families with children because it is available if the families' incomes are too low to owe federal income taxes. At the same time, however, the EITC has helped to reduce child poverty. In 1999, the federal EITC lifted 2.6 million children out of poverty and had a greater impact than did all other means-tested programs combined. More than 16 million children live in these families—one of every four children under 17 years of age. Most recently, there was a bipartisan effort to further expand the credit to include families with three or more children—families that are disproportionately poor.

The major expansion of child care for low-income working families in 1988, the Act for Better Child Care, had leadership from the bipartisan team of Senators Christopher Dodd and Orrin Hatch. This helped to move it forward despite opposition from the Reagan administration. Such support helped in Congress and in mobilizing the field on behalf of these important gains for children.

Although there were many in Congress and in the Clinton administration who worked hard to find new ways for states to improve children's health, it was the tireless leadership of Senators Orrin Hatch and Edward Kennedy and of Representatives Nancy Johnson and Robert Matsui that was key to securing final passage of the CHIP legislation in 1997. This bipartisan support was helpful later in some states as state policymakers had to determine how best to translate

the new federal law into state action and decide who would be reached under the program and how.

In a more recent example, in 2001, the leadership of moderate Republican members of Congress (e.g., Senator Olympia Snowe, Representative Connie Morella), with the backing of a strong coalition of advocates, forced a reluctant Bush administration and conservative congressional leadership to accept provisions making the child tax credit refundable as part of the Economic Growth and Tax Relief Reconciliation Act of 2001 (Public Law 107-16).

Recognizing the Value of Incremental Gains

As noted earlier, change can sometimes take a long time. Therefore, it is important to recognize that incremental changes may be an effective approach that will, over time, lead to large-scale reforms. A recent analysis of child advocacy in public policy done by the Urban Institute details, for example, a series of successful incremental reforms pursued by child health advocates. The gains were achieved between 1984 and 1990 and together restructured health care coverage for children under the federal Medicaid program (Rosenbaum & Sonosky, 2001). These incremental approaches became necessary when broader health reform initiatives failed and federal investment opportunities were limited. Yet they paved the way so that when the CHIP legislation was passed in 1997, a strengthened Medicaid program was in place to serve the additional Medicaid-eligible children identified as part of CHIP outreach in many states.

Advocates for family and medical leave also have used an incremental or a staged approach to continue to move forward toward paid parental leave for families, including families with child care responsibilities or experiencing the birth or adoption of children. The enactment of the Family and Medical Leave Act of 1993 (Public Law 103-3) was a major achievement. And that act actually built on important legislation, passed a decade earlier, that prohibited employers from discriminating against or discharging pregnant workers. The Family and Medical Leave Act guaranteed that people working for employers with more than 50 employees can take up to 12 weeks of unpaid leave a year to care for their families or themselves in certain circumstances (www.nationalpartnership.org). Since the passage of the act, the National Partnership for Women and Families, the leader in the struggle for its passage, has concentrated attention on getting it implemented in states and working with states to increase family leave benefits beyond those in the act.

The Campaign for Family Leave Benefits, launched by the National Partnership for Women and Children in June 1999, has developed a menu of policy models for family leave for state and local policy leaders and also has worked to document public support for family leave benefits. About 19 states have family leave laws that are at least somewhat more generous than the Family and Medical Leave Act (see Campaign for Family Leave Benefits section at www.nationalpartnership.org). There has been particular emphasis on getting states to consider at least partial wage replacement for those who take leave. Activities such as these can then help to garner grassroots support for federal funding of paid parental leave in the future. There already have been proposals introduced in Congress that would go beyond the 1993 act. Among other things, they would expand the federal act to apply to employers with 25 or more employees rather than 50 as in the original bill. There are also proposals pending to establish demonstration projects that would offer paid leave on the birth or adoption of children so that parents could spend more time with their new infants or newly adopted children (see, e.g., Title II of the Act to Leave No Child Behind).

Putting It All Together

The ultimate challenge for those advocating for improvements for children is to take advantage of all the opportunities described earlier while overcoming the challenges that too often create barriers to political gains for children. Many of the examples cited previously are drawn from national activities at the congressional level. There are many more, both from the national level and in individual states. For a final example of a "win" for children that pulled together and built on many of the opportunities and overcame significant challenges, we turn to the local level.

The budget success of children's advocates in San Francisco is a wonderful example of politics working for children and how persistence can pay off in the end. Passage of the Children's Amendment (originally Proposition J) by San Francisco voters and its renewal in 2000 defied many of the challenges already discussed and built on numerous opportunities (San Francisco Charter, Article XVI, Miscellaneous Provision, Section 16.108). Proposition J was created and sponsored by Coleman Advocates for Children and Youth (and its tireless leader, Margaret Brodkin), which began working for children in San Francisco in 1975.[3]

Proposition J was an amendment to the San Francisco city charter that made children a permanent priority. The decision to go to voters to amend the city charter was the culmination of 4 years of intense budget advocacy for the children of San Francisco. It began in 1987 with the development of a comprehensive children's agenda by 85 children's organizations from throughout the city. Although the board of supervisors and the mayor ultimately adopted it, the agenda was not sufficient without increased resources to accompany it. So, advocacy continued for a San Francisco Children's Budget. Sophisticated analyses were prepared each year that not only looked at the needs of children but also analyzed current expenditures, made specific proposals, and laid out the cost benefits of such investments. Specific recommendations for possible revenue-generating solutions also were made. Yet when in the third year nothing new for children was added to the budget, there was a clear recognition that more must be done to gain services for children over the long run. Brodkin and Coleman Advocates for Children and Youth's (1994) analysis of children's expenditures over a 5-year period revealed that there had actually been a decrease in the percentage of the budget going to children.

Much had been learned during that 4-year budget struggle. Homework was essential. Basic facts about children were gathered and analyzed to assess their impact. The public learned more about children's needs. Multiple strategies were used to get the message across. The agenda was specific and linked to compelling public concerns. It was crafted carefully to accommodate multiple interests. Yet there was also recognition that, without political clout, meaningful change could not be seen for children.

A decision was made by advocates for children in the city to place an initiative on the ballot that would provide a public forum for making children a permanent priority in San Francisco. Proposition J amended the city charter to mandate that 2.5% of the city's property taxes be "set aside" to expand children's services each year, thereby eliminating annual budget battles. Brodkin described it as a "fiscal Bill of Rights for Children." The "Campaign for the Children's Amendment," from the initial drive for signatures for the petition to Election Day, was run as an attack on politics as usual and stressed

the need for children to have their fair share. It focused on solutions, energized the cause of children, and created significant political momentum. Children's agencies were strong endorsers, but there were many atypical allies as well—unions, religious organizations, city workers, and groups with strong political ties for their own causes. Some 100 children gathered to pull the petitions to City Hall in red wagons and get the amendment on the ballot. About half of the politicians in City Hall endorsed it; the mayor decided not to oppose it.

The Campaign for the Children's Amendment included direct mail, extensive outreach, involvement of youth themselves, and striking presentations to the media—all intended to educate the public. The focus was on the positive, on how investments for children could be used, and on making it clear that there were political points to be gained in supporting children. There was attention to building grassroots support. Results were promised; approximately 80,000 children would be served by 180 programs each year. Proposition J won with 54.5% of the votes in the November 1991 election.

Continuing action was essential, and the Kids Action Network, a citizens' action arm established to monitor Proposition J and take action on other children's issues, was a central part of the ongoing advocacy for what came to be called the Children's Fund. Implementation problems were enormous. There was a continuing focus on broadening the voices for children in the city and on raising the visibility of parents and young people. Youth Making Change and Parent Advocates for Youth both are actively engaged in the city, pushing for significant expansions in both youth development and early childhood activities. During a 9-year period, from 1991 to 2000, the Children's Amendment yielded more than $140 million in funding for services for children and youth.

In 2000, the Children's Amendment's 10-year time frame came to an end, but in the

November 2000 election it was renewed for another 15 years by 74% of San Francisco's voters. The child advocates, again led by Brodkin and Coleman Advocates for Children and Youth, made a compelling case that "the Children's Fund was vital to the well-being of the city's children" (National Association of Child Advocates, 2001). Voters overwhelmingly approved funding for the Children's Fund (this time Proposition D) for 15 more years; in addition, they increased the amount of children's "set aside" by about 20% (by increasing it from 2.5% to 3% of the city's property tax assessed valuation) and required new activities to improve oversight and planning for children in San Francisco.

The win for children in San Francisco truly represents how advocates can come together to promote significant and lasting change for children. Children were made a political issue.

CONCLUSIONS

Advocates for children face many challenges and barriers as they pursue gains for children in the political arena, but steady progress continues to build. Advocates have repeatedly found ways to overcome the obstacles to make important changes to better meet the needs of our nation's children and to seize on opportunities as they arise. Continuing these efforts and finding ways to transform rhetoric into meaningful action for children in the political arena is of critical importance now and will continue to be in the future.

APPENDIX 24.A

Current Contacts for National Organizations Referred to in This Chapter

AARP
601 E Street, NW
Washington, DC 20049
(800) 424-3410
www.aarp.com

Afterschool Alliance
P.O. Box 65166
Washington, DC 20035-5166
(202) 296-9378
www.afterschoolalliance.org

American Cancer Society
1599 Clifton Road
Atlanta, GA 30329
(404) 320-3333
www.cancer.org

Annie E. Casey Foundation
701 St. Paul Street
Baltimore, MD 21202
(410) 547-6600
(410) 547-6624 (fax)
www.aecf.org

U.S. Bureau of the Census
Washington, DC 20233
www.census.gov

Campaign for Family Leave Benefits
c/o National Partnership for Women and Families
1875 Connecticut Avenue, NW, Suite 650
Washington, DC 20002
(202) 986-2600
(202) 986-2539 (fax)
www.nationalpartnership.org

Cato Institute
1000 Massachusetts Avenue, NW
Washington, DC 20001-5403
(202) 842-0200
(202) 842-3490 (fax)
www.catoinstitute.com

Charles Stewart Mott Foundation
1200 Mott Foundation Building
Flint, MI 48502-1851
(810) 238-5651
www.mott.org

Children's Defense Fund
25 E Street, NW
Washington, DC 20001
(202) 628-8787
(202) 662-3510 (fax)
www.childrensdefense.org

Common Cause
1250 Connecticut Avenue, NW, Suite 600
Washington, DC 20036
(202) 833-1200
(202) 659-3716 (fax)
www.commoncause.org

Family Research Council
801 G Street, NW
Washington, DC 20001
(202) 393-2100
(202) 393-2134 (fax)
www.frc.org

Family Voices
3411 Candelaria NE, Suite M
Albuquerque, NM 87107
(505) 872-4774
(505) 872-4780 (fax)
www.familyvoices.org

Federation of Families for Children's Mental Health
1101 King Street, Suite 420
Alexandria, VA 22314
(703) 684-7710
(703) 836-1040 (fax)
www.ffcmh.org

Fight Crime: Invest in Kids
2000 P Street, NW, Suite 240
Washington, DC 20036
(202) 776-0027
(202) 776-0110 (fax)
www.fightcrime.org

Generations United
122 C Street, NW, Suite 820
Washington, DC 20001
(202) 638-1263
(202) 638-7555 (fax)
www.gu.org

KIDS COUNT
c/o Annie E. Casey Foundation
701 St. Paul Street
Baltimore, MD 21202
(410) 547-6600
(410) 547-6624 (fax)
www.aecf.org/kidscount

Million Mom March
1225 Eye Street, NW, Suite 1100
Washington, DC 20005
(888) 989-MOMS (6667)
(202) 371-9615 (fax)
www.millionmommarch.org

Mothers Against Drunk Driving
P.O. Box 541688
Dallas, TX 75354-1688
(800) GET-MADD (438-6233)
www.madd.org

National Alliance for the Mentally Ill
Colonial Place Three
2107 Wilson Boulevard, Suite 300
Arlington, VA 22201
(703) 524-7600
www.nami.org

National Association of Child Advocates
1522 K Street, NW, Suite 600
Washington, DC 20005-1202
(202) 289-0777
(202) 289-0776 (fax)
www.childadvocacy.org

National Partnership for Women and Families
1875 Connecticut Avenue, NW, Suite 650
Washington, DC 20009
(202) 986-2600
(202) 986-2539 (fax)
www.nationalpartnership.org

National Resource Center for Youth Development
University of Oklahoma
4502 East 41st Street
Building 4 West
Tulsa, OK 74135-2512
(918) 660-3700
(918) 660-3737 (fax)
www.nrcys.ou.edu

Office of Planning and Evaluation
c/o U.S. Department of Health and Human Services
200 Independence Avenue, SW, Suite 415F
Washington, DC 20201
(202) 690-7858
(202) 690-7383 (fax)
www.aspe.hhs.gov/aspenet/

Public Citizen
1600 20th Street, NW
Washington, DC 20009
(202) 588-1000
www.citizen.org

Stand for Children
1420 Columbia Road, NW, 3rd Floor
Washington, DC 20009
(202) 234-0095
(202) 234-0217 (fax)
www.stand.org

Student Leadership Network for Children
c/o Children's Defense Fund
25 E Street, NW
Washington, DC 20001
(202) 628-8787
(202) 662-3510 (fax)
www.childrensdefense.org/slnc.htm

Urban Institute
2100 M Street, NW
Washington, DC 20037
(202) 833-7200
(202) 331-9747 (fax)
www.urban.org

W. K. Kellogg Foundation
One Michigan Avenue East
Battle Creek, MI 49017-4058
(616) 968-1611
(616) 968-0413 (fax)
www.wkkf.org

NOTES

1. It is interesting to contrast the shift in perspectives over time toward family responsibilities for elderly members. It was not until the middle part of the 20th century, beginning with passage of the Social Security Act in 1935, that government responsibility for providing care for elderly Americans became ingrained in American social policy.

2. For a summary of a number of national polls indicating public support for child care investments, see Children's Defense Fund (2001b).

3. A full description of the campaign, from which we have drawn much in this section, can be found in Brodkin and Coleman Advocates for Children and Youth (1994). See also the Coleman Advocates for Children and Youth Web site (www.colemanadvocates.org) for more specifics on the Children's Amendment.

REFERENCES

Advisory Committee on Child Development. (1976). *Toward a national policy for children and families.* Washington, DC: National Academy of Sciences.

Allen, M., & Nixon, R. (2000). The Foster Care Independence Act and John H. Chafee Foster Care Independence Program: New catalysts for reform for young people aging out of foster care. *Clearinghouse Review: Journal of Poverty Law and Policy, 34*(3-4), 197-216.

Amedei, N. (1991). *So you want to make a difference: A key to advocacy.* Washington, DC: OMB Watch.

Annie E. Casey Foundation. (1997). *Success in school: Education ideas that count* [Online]. Available: www.aecf.org/kidscount/index.htm

Annie E. Casey Foundation. (1998). *Child care you can count on: Model programs and policies* [Online]. Available: www.aecf.org/kidscount/index.htm

Beck, R. (1979). *It's time to stand up for your children: A parent's guide to child advocacy.* Washington, DC: Children's Defense Fund.

Brodkin, M., & Coleman Advocates for Children and Youth. (1994). *From sand boxes to ballot boxes: San Francisco's landmark campaign to fund children's services.* San Francisco: Coleman Advocates for Children and Youth.

Carnegie Council on Children. (1977). *All our children.* New York: Harcourt Brace Jovanovich.

Carnegie Task Force on Meeting the Needs of Young Children. (1994). *Starting points: Meeting the needs of our youngest children.* New York: Carnegie Corporation of New York.

Carson, E. D. (2001). Introduction: How are the children? In C. J. DeVita & R. Mosher-Williams (Eds.), *Who speaks for America's children? The role of child advocates in public policy* (pp. xi-xviii). Washington, DC: Urban Institute.

Cato Institute. (1997). *The advancing nanny state: Why the government should stay out of child care.* Washington, DC: Author. Available: www.cato.org/pubs/pas/pa-285

Center for Research on Women. (1996). *"I wish the kids didn't watch so much TV": Out of school time in three low income communities.* Wellesley, MA: Wellesley College, Center for Research on Women.

Center for the Study of Social Policy. (2001). *Using data to ensure accountability: Building capacity for local decisionmaking* (Vol. 6 in a series of learning guides). Washington, DC: Author.

Charles Stewart Mott Foundation. (1998, September 24). *Polls find overwhelming support for after-school enrichment programs to keep kids safe and smart* [press release]. Flint, MI: Author. (Poll conducted by Lake Snell Perry and Associates and the Tarrance Group)

Children's Defense Fund. (1999). *The state of America's children yearbook 1999.* Washington, DC: Author.

Children's Defense Fund. (2001a). *Background materials on key sections of the Act to Leave No Child Behind.* Washington, DC: Author.

Children's Defense Fund. (2001b). *Polls indicate widespread support for increased investments in child care* [Online]. Available: www.childrensdefense.org/cc_polls.htm

Children's Defense Fund. (2001c). *The state of America's children yearbook 2001.* Washington, DC: Author.

The Children's Partnership. (1998). *Exploring constituency-building strategies for children's issues: What's working?* Santa Monica, CA: Author.

Clark, R., & Long, S. (1995). *Child care prices: A profile of six communities—Final report*. Washington, DC: Urban Institute.

Coalition for America's Children. (1999). *Effective language for communicating children's issues*. Washington, DC: Benton Foundation.

Common Cause. (2001). *Why you should care about campaign finance reform* (Common Cause series about the impact of big money in politics) [Online]. Available: www.commoncause.org

Covington, S. (2001). In the midst of plenty: Foundation funding of child advocacy organizations in the 1990's. In C. J. DeVita & R. Mosher-Williams (Eds.), *Who speaks for America's children? The role of child advocates in public policy* (pp. 39-80). Washington, DC: Urban Institute.

DeVita, C. J., & Mosher-Williams, R. (Eds.). (2001). *Who speaks for America's children? The role of child advocates in public policy*. Washington, DC: Urban Institute.

DeVita, C. J., Mosher-Williams, R., & Stengel, N. A. J. (2001). Nonprofit organizations engaged in child advocacy. In C. J. DeVita & R. Mosher-Williams (Eds.), *Who speaks for America's children? The role of child advocates in public policy* (pp. 3-37). Washington, DC: Urban Institute.

Families and Work Institute. (1996a). *Brain development for young children: New frontiers for research, policy, and practice*. New York: Author. (Materials prepared in conjunction with a conference organized by the Families and Work Institute)

Families and Work Institute. (1996b). *Rethinking the brain: New insights into early development*. New York: Author. (Materials prepared in conjunction with a conference organized by the Families and Work Institute)

Generations United. (2001). *Public policy agenda for the 107th Congress*. Washington, DC: Author.

Grindeland, S. (2001, July 5). Former foster child beats odds, inspires legislation. *Seattle Times*, p. B1.

Grubb, W. N., & Lazerson, M. (1982). *Broken promises: How Americans fail their children*. New York: Basic Books.

Heclo, H. H. (1997). Values underpinning poverty programs for children. *The Future of Children, 7*(2), 141-148.

Imig, D. (2001). Mobilizing parents and communities for children. In C. J. DeVita & R. Mosher-Williams (Eds.), *Who speaks for America's children? The role of child advocates in public policy* (pp. 191-207). Washington, DC: Urban Institute.

Ingrassia, M. (1993, November 22). Growing up fast and frightened. *Newsweek*, p. 52.

Kamerman, S. B. (1989). Toward a child policy decade. *Child Welfare, 68*, 371-390.

McDevitt, J. (1996). *Fight Crime: Invest in Kids*. Boston: Northeastern University, Center for Criminal Justice Policy Research.

Miller, L., Melaville, A., & Blank, H. (2001). *Bringing it together: State-driven community early childhood initiatives*. Washington, DC: Children's Defense Fund.

National Association of Child Advocates. (2001). *San Francisco's Coleman Advocates secures funding for children's program* (Child Advocates Making a Difference series). Washington, DC: Author.

National Commission on Children. (1991). *Beyond rhetoric: A new American agenda for children and families*. Washington, DC: Government Printing Office.

National Conference on Family Life Committee. (1948). *The American family: A factual background* (report of the interagency committee on background materials). Westport, CT: National Conference on Family Life.

National Resource Center for Youth Development. (2001). *Tuition waivers for foster care youth*. Tulsa: University of Oklahoma. Available: www.nrcys.ou.edu/tuitionwaivers/oregon.htm

Office of the Assistant Secretary for Planning and Evaluation. (2000). *Trends in the well-being of America's children and youth, 2000.* Washington, DC: Government Printing Office.

Raden, A. (1999). *Universal pre-kindergarten in Georgia: A case study of Georgia's lottery-funded pre-K program* (working paper). New York: Foundation for Child Development.

Reid, E. (2001). Building a policy voice for children through the nonprofit sector. In C. J. DeVita & R. Mosher-Williams (Eds.), *Who speaks for America's children? The role of child advocates in public policy* (pp. 105-133). Washington, DC: Urban Institute.

Research and Forecasts. (1989). *Kinder-care report: Perspectives on child care in America.* Montgomery, AL: Author.

Research and Training Center on Family Support and Children's Mental Health. (2000). Roles for youth in systems of care. *Focal Point: A National Bulletin on Family Support and Children's Mental Health, 14*(2).

Rosenbaum, S., & Sonosky, C. A. (2001). Medicaid reforms and SCHIP: Health care coverage and the changing policy environment. In C. J. DeVita & R. Mosher-Williams (Eds.), *Who speaks for America's children? The role of child advocates in public policy* (pp. 81-104). Washington, DC: Urban Institute.

Sabom, D. (2001, April 16). Should the Senate ratify the Convention on the Rights of the Child? No: It will subvert U.S. sovereignty, undermine parents, and sabotage religious teachings. *Washington Times* (Insight, symposium section), p. 41.

Schulman, K., & Adams, G. (1998). *Issue brief: The high cost of child care puts quality care out of reach for many families.* Washington, DC: Children's Defense Fund.

Smeeding, T. M., Rainwater, L., & Burless, G. (2000). *United States poverty in a cross-national context* (Luxembourg Income Study Working Paper No. 244). Syracuse, NY: Syracuse University. Available: http://lisweb.ceps.lu/publications.htm

Steiner, G. T. (1976). *The children's cause.* Washington, DC: Brookings Institution.

Twohey, M. (2001, July 7). A moderate hangs tough. *National Journal,* p. 2159.

U.S. Senate. (1976). *Background materials concerning the Child and Family Services Act, 1975, S. 626.* Washington, DC: U.S. Senate, Subcommittee on Children and Youth of the Committee on Labor and Public Welfare.

CHAPTER 14

Juvenile Justice and Positive Youth Development

ROBERT G. SCHWARTZ

The American system of juvenile justice has existed for more than 100 years because of two beliefs that have remained relatively constant: (a) that youth are not as culpable for their conduct as are adults and (b) that youth are more capable of change and need room to grow (Zimring, 1998).

Although those two beliefs have been its bedrock, their application in the juvenile justice system goes through cyclical changes (Bernard, 1992). Sometimes the system is perceived as too harsh and sometimes as too lenient. During the past century, it has often been shaped by new ideas of the day or by theories that infused the culture at large—doctrines of rehabilitation, of due process, or (most recently) of accountability. Now, early in the 21st century, positive youth development (PYD) has found a receptive audience in the fields of youth employment, community-based services, and early adolescent initiatives. But how will it be received in the insular world of juvenile justice?

Consider Gabriel, a 14-year-old boy who lives in a drug-infested neighborhood in Steve Lopez's first novel, *Third and Indiana*. The fictional Gabriel is a brilliant artist with a photographic memory. His father has abandoned the family. To raise money, Gabriel begins serving as a lookout for a gang of drug dealers. Unlike his school, the gang recognizes Gabriel's strength:

> Gabriel, who'd always had a good memory, was an especially good lookout because he never forgot a face or a vehicle. If plain-clothes cops jumped out of a car at the next intersection and threw a drug crew against a wall . . ., Gabriel would wander in close enough to study the faces of the officers. . . . Sometimes he drew sketches for the crew supervisor. He drew sketches of the unmarked cars, too, detailing a small dent, a missing hubcap. . . . That's why he was being promoted. Gabriel was looked upon in his drug gang as something of a rising star. (Lopez, 1994)

A boy like Gabriel is a challenge to the juvenile justice system. He represents everything that the newest version of juvenile justice is designed to punish: a drug-dealing gang member who later, for protection, carries a gun. In today's climate, he will be a candidate for transfer to the criminal court, where he will face a mandatory sentence for using a gun. At a minimum, he would be removed from his mother's home and placed in a residential treatment facility. Whether anyone recognizes his talent will be a matter of luck, not design.

The two questions that are the focus of this chapter apply to every "Gabriel" who comes in contact with the law. First, is there a place for PYD in juvenile justice, a system that exists to respond to negative behavior and that is not uniformly adept at discovering talent? Second, if so, is there any chance that PYD will become central to the juvenile justice culture—as opposed to a characteristic of an exemplary program here or there— so that every Gabriel will be its beneficiary?

I conclude that the tenets of PYD are more applicable in work with children who are at risk for entering the juvenile justice system than with those who are inside the formal system. Diversion programs for all children are more promising than a formal juvenile justice system that is organized, staffed, funded, and regulated by law in ways that, for the most part, work in opposition to PYD. The formal system is not hopeless, however. There are a few chinks in the system's seemingly sheer wall, and it is there that PYD advocates must apply piton and hammer if they are to have any chance of scaling the barrier that juvenile justice represents to the field.

This chapter begins with a discussion of some assumptions about what is required for PYD to succeed in the formal juvenile justice system. It then gives an overview of the juvenile justice system, suggesting possible opportunities for the injection of some aspect of PYD into the system; discusses constraints

that are inherent in the formal system; and concludes with suggestions for changes that will be necessary if PYD is to have a chance to take root and grow.

ASSUMPTIONS

Positive youth development refers to attitudes about youth, to what youth do and achieve during and at the end of their route to adulthood, and to the informal and formal systems of support that help youth to reach adulthood successfully. It includes a common vision of success at the end of adolescence, when youth develop academic or vocational "competence, personal contentment, interpersonal skills, social involvement, and staying out of trouble" (Furstenberg, 1999). This definition suggests why the formal juvenile justice system is not a fertile area for PYD. Although there are some areas of opportunity, most of those will cluster around primary or secondary prevention; that is, they will focus on all youth or on youth who have been identified as being at risk for entering the juvenile or criminal justice system. In the early 21st century, the formal system—the system that is supposed to prevent youth from reoffending after arrest—does not routinely think about children developmentally, rarely recognizes adolescents' strengths, does not routinely believe in adolescents' ability to succeed, and only spottily offers the kind of supports necessary for success. In juvenile justice, obstacles outnumber opportunities.

Discussions of PYD assume that most parents prefer to view their children through that lens. So, for PYD to operate in the juvenile justice system—and as a gatekeeper to it—there must be someone who operates as an *ordinary devoted parent* on behalf of the child. According to Furstenberg (1999), such a person would have the instincts to know the child's needs and strengths; know how to protect the child from harm; suppress the child's weaknesses; and organize the child's world to permit a transition to employment, partnership, and citizenship. Although the notion of the ordinary devoted parent was conceived in the child welfare (foster care) context (Goldstein, Freud, Solnit, & Goldstein, 1986), it is equally relevant to juvenile justice and its effort to absorb PYD into its culture.

When the juvenile justice system replaces parents by asserting the doctrine of *parens patriae* (i.e., the state is the ultimate parent of all of its children), it is assumed that the system is able to serve as an ordinary devoted parent. But in fact, it is rarely able to do so. Therefore, to the extent that PYD is what ordinary devoted parents ensure for their children, the juvenile justice system will inevitably fall short.

Despite many obstacles, the juvenile justice system may yet offer opportunities for the introduction of PYD. Decent systems attend to adolescents' education and health care needs. They build on adolescents' strengths, in particular by emphasizing skills that adolescents need to cope in the world. The best juvenile probation departments help youth when they leave institutions and assist them in the difficult transition to adulthood.

THE JUVENILE JUSTICE SYSTEM

During much of the 20th century, public rhetoric about how to respond to juvenile crime incorrectly posited antipodean positions on which policy choices should be based—child or adult, punishment or rehabilitation, judicial discretion or rigorous guidelines.[1] The reality has always been more ambiguous. Even though it is heuristically useful to divide the century's juvenile court experience into opposing epochs—the benign paternalism of the first part of the century

versus the "get tough" policies of recent decades—the lines between these orientations are less clear.

We can nevertheless divide the juvenile justice "system" between court and corrections; one is the judicial side that determines whether juveniles are delinquent and enters orders of detention and disposition, whereas the other is that part of the system that detains, rehabilitates, treats, supervises, or punishes young offenders. This section addresses both.

The Origins of the American Juvenile Justice System

Economic recessions during the early 19th century and the first wave of Irish immigrants pushed children out of work in America's new factory system during the Industrial Revolution. Concerns about poor children on the streets led to the creation of institutional care for children. In New York City, the Society for Prevention of Pauperism in 1824 became the Society for the Reformation of Juvenile Delinquents, and in 1825 it opened the nation's first House of Refuge. Boston followed a year later, and Philadelphia followed in 1828. These Houses of Refuge were designed to maintain class status and prevent unrest (Krisberg & Austin, 1993; Platt, 1977).

The concept of parens patriae provided the legal underpinning for the Houses of Refuge many years before it provided a legal framework for the juvenile court. In *Ex Parte Crouse,* the Pennsylvania Supreme Court in 1838 affirmed the state's accepting Mary Ann Crouse from her mother and putting her into Philadelphia's House of Refuge. In now-famous language, the court declared,

> The object of the charity is reformation, by training its inmates to industry; by imbuing their minds with principles of morality and religion; by furnishing them with means to

earn a living; and, above all, by separating them from the corrupting influence of improper associates. To this end, may not the natural parents, when unequal to the task of education, or unworthy of it, be superseded by the *parens patriae*, or common guardian of the community?... The infant has been snatched from a course which must have ended in confirmed depravity; and not only is the restraint of her person lawful, but it would have been an act of extreme cruelty to release her from it.

For the first time, parens patriae—a 15th-century concept for orphans—was applied to a poor child whose parents were still alive. By 1890, nearly every state had some version of a reform school (Bernard, 1992).

In 1899, Jane Addams and her Hull House colleagues in Chicago established what is generally accepted as the nation's first juvenile court. Juvenile court judges, during the early part of the 20th century, "were authorized to investigate the character and social background of both 'pre-delinquent' and 'delinquent' children. They examined personal motivation as well as criminal intent, seeking to identify the moral reputation of problematic children" (Platt, 1977, p. 141; see also Tanenhaus, 2001).

Judge Julian Mack, Chicago's second juvenile court judge, described the idealized juvenile court in the following way:

> The problem for determination by the judge is not has this boy or girl committed a specific wrong but what is he, how has he become what he is, and what had best be done in his interest and in the interest of the state to save him from a downward career. It is apparent at once that the ordinary legal evidence in a criminal court is not the sort of evidence to be heard in such a proceeding. (Mack, 1909)

The Impact of the Gault Decision

At its most idealistic, the juvenile court of the first half of the 20th century tried to act as an ordinary devoted parent would on behalf of a child. Because the system's operation was less than ideal, in 1967 the "rehabilitative" world of juvenile justice was altered forever. It was then that the U.S. Supreme Court injected due process into the system (*In re Gault*).

Gault involved a 15-year-old boy who was arrested for making calls to his next-door neighbor that the Supreme Court described as "of the irritatingly offensive, adolescent, sex variety." Gerald Gault was brought before a juvenile court judge, but he did not have notice of the charges against him, nor did he have a lawyer. The neighbor never appeared in court, but testimony was given by the arresting officer, who described what the neighbor had told him.

For an offense for which an adult could have received a fine of not more than $50 or more than 2 months in jail, the juvenile court committed Gault to the Arizona State Industrial School for up to 6 years. There was little developmental rationale behind the Arizona juvenile court's decision to send Gault to a training school for 6 years. In what sense was Gault to be rehabilitated? Indeed, the training school looked remarkably like the early Quaker penitentiaries that sought to reform prisoners by using thick-walled cells, isolation, and a Bible (Meranze, 1996).

Gault challenged his adjudication of delinquency, and the U.S. Supreme Court held that the Fourteenth Amendment's due process clause applied to children. The court ruled that in the context of adjudications of delinquency, children were "persons" within the meaning of the Fourteenth Amendment, and that no state could deprive them of liberty without due process of law. This meant that, at trial, juveniles had a right to notice of the charges, to counsel, to confront witnesses against them, and to decline to incriminate themselves.

The *Gault* decision ended benign neglect of the juvenile justice system and introduced a period during which juveniles were increasingly thought to be entitled to constitutional procedural protections similar to those of adults.[2] During the mid-1990s, and motivated by other concerns, a different sort of "adultification" occurred, one that ironically moved the juvenile court away from its rehabilitative ideal and toward a retributive model that had much in common with the philosophy of the adult criminal court. The increase in violent juvenile crime between the mid-1980s and 1993 led nearly every state to change its juvenile laws. States devised a variety of approaches to (a) removing more juveniles from juvenile court jurisdiction and placing them in criminal court, (b) increasing the severity of juvenile court dispositions, and (c) reducing the confidentiality of juvenile proceedings and records (Torbet et al., 1996).

Through the 20th century, the juvenile justice system sought to save children, nurture them, rehabilitate them, cure them, isolate them, and punish them. New punitive legislative policies have recently led some scholars to seek a middle ground between the "old" rehabilitative model of the idealized juvenile court and the "new" model of retributive justice. The latest synthesis of these various philosophies, which includes teaching youth "competencies," emerged during the late 1980s when Dennis Maloney called for a "balanced approach" to juvenile probation. The balanced approach would address public safety, accountability, and youth competency development (Maloney, Romig, & Armstrong, 1988).

Maloney's work became part of the "restorative justice" movement of the 1990s, during which criminologists Gordon Bazemore, Mark Umbreit, and others called for a juvenile justice system in which attention would be paid to making the victims whole, involving communities in fashioning

dispositions, and teaching juveniles skills (i.e., competency development) necessary to make the transition to responsible adulthood (Bazemore & Umbreit, 1994). (The balanced approach is discussed in detail later.)

Moving Through the Contemporary Juvenile Justice "System"

It is useful to imagine the juvenile justice system as a pipeline through which water flows. Along the pipeline are diversion valves—the points of decision at which children either are diverted from the pipeline or continue through its various gates and locks. These are the points of arrest, detention, adjudication, disposition, and disposition review. One of the signal characteristics of the juvenile justice system is that its diversion options extend across the pipeline's continuum; at every point of the system, it may send some children home, some to other systems, and others to noninstitutional care. Another characteristic that distinguishes the juvenile justice system from the adult system is the theoretical importance the juvenile system places on a swift flow through the pipeline. Although juvenile courts still operate more quickly than criminal courts,

> delays in the juvenile justice system should be viewed from the perspective of an adolescent offender. Professional standards suggest that even the longest case should be processed within 90 days. Yet, a 90-day process means that a 14-year-old offender will wait the equivalent of a summer vacation for services or sanctions. In many of the nation's juvenile courts, young offenders wait even longer. (Butts, 1997)

States vary greatly in the architecture of their juvenile justice systems. They may set different ages for a child's entry into the system (as young as 7 or as old as 10 years of age) or exit from it (as young as 16 or as old as 25 years of age). Every state has a different mix of decision makers and services at each stage of the pipeline; each divides power over juveniles in different ways. It is rare that a coherent philosophy governs the component parts (Ayers, 1997; Guarino-Ghezzi & Loughran, 1997).

Critical Decision Points Along the Pipeline

Despite jurisdictional differences in policies and practices, the points of decision are essentially similar—diversion, referral, intake, detention, adjudication, transfer, disposition, and release. At each stage are numerous opportunities for refashioning agency behaviors to reflect PYD principles.

Diversion. As in basketball, where not every contact is a foul, on the street, not every deed that provokes a police whistle is a crime. Indeed, adolescence, particularly for boys, is a time of experimentation, risk taking, and relative recklessness that would lead to the arrest of many if the law were applied strictly. Without invoking the law, parents, teachers, and communities have historically taught adolescents how to behave. So, simply refusing to refer a youth to the juvenile justice system is one form of diversion. And indeed, for many youth, diversion is a low-risk enterprise. Marvin Wolfgang's landmark longitudinal studies in Philadelphia showed that half of the children who committed delinquent acts were never heard from again (Wolfgang, Figlio, & Sellin, 1972).

Diversion is less common today than it was in the past, as parents and schools develop "zero tolerance" for misdeeds committed by other people's children. For example, schools across the country today are routinely expelling children and referring them to the juvenile justice system for offenses that just a few years ago would have been handled in-house. Such expulsions are inconsistent with PYD.

If parents have the resources, knowledge, and contacts, they have a chance of keeping their child from being expelled or labeled "delinquent." A few years ago, I was called by a white middle-class couple who had a 16-year-old son with serious emotional problems. He fought with other kids, smoked dope, and extorted small amounts of money from younger children. The parents, however, were concerned and active. Thus, during the boy's troubled high school years, the school district kept him in school and provided special education assessment and services. When the boy's conduct got out of hand, the parents arranged for private psychiatric care. His conduct clearly violated the criminal code, and many children—especially today—who behave as he did would end up in the juvenile justice system. This boy, with the help of ordinary devoted parents, did not.

Referral. Formal entrance into the pipeline begins with a referral to the juvenile justice system or a police arrest. Depending on the state, however, a child may be too young or too old to be "accepted." Children who are too young are most often diverted or sent to the branch of the juvenile court that has jurisdiction over neglected and abused children. Children who are too old are tried as adults.

Intake. An intake decision is made if the child enters the juvenile justice system after being arrested or referred by a private petitioner (e.g., a school, a next-door neighbor). Should the case proceed or be diverted? If the latter, should it be an informal diversion, without further involvement by the juvenile court, or should the child be sent to a formal program such as a community panel or teen court? Some cases are diverted to other systems such as the mental health system. Some cases are dropped entirely as intake officers decide that the particular combination of youth and offense does not warrant involvement in the juvenile justice system.

Detention. If the intake officer (usually a juvenile probation officer) decides that the case should proceed to a hearing, the officer faces a set of decisions—whether the child should be sent home (with or without supervision) or should be detained, and if the child is detained, should it be in a maximum-security detention center or in a detention alternative. Pretrial detention has two valid purposes: reducing the risk of flight and reducing the risk of reoffending prior to trial (Institute of Judicial Administration–American Bar Association, 1996).

Secure detention should be a last resort (Institute of Judicial Administration–American Bar Association, 1996). And because it generally occurs pretrial, no youth can be compelled to receive treatment while in detention. That would be imposing a disposition (sentence) before the trial. However, youth can *voluntarily* accept services, and the best juvenile detention centers make a range of services available. However, Lubow (1997) cautions against creating a better detention system that will lead probation officers and judges to increase its use. Any improvement of services inside detention centers must also be tied to screening and risk assessment instruments that ensure that only high-risk youth enter secure detention at all.

Transfer. State law may exclude some youth from the juvenile justice system because of their age; for example, in New York, a 16-year-old will be tried as an adult for any offense. Every state also excludes some offenses from juvenile court jurisdiction if a child is of a certain age (e.g., a state can decide that 15-year-olds who are charged with armed robbery will have their cases begin in adult criminal court). In the spring of 2001, Florida tried as adults two youths who were 12 and 13 years of age at the times of their crimes. Lionel Tate, 12, was sentenced to life without the possibility of parole for killing a 6-year-old girl with whom he was "wrestling," and Nathaniel Brazill, 13, received a 28-year term for killing his eighth-grade teacher. In Pennsylvania in 1999, then 11-year-old Miriam White was charged with murder, as an adult, after stabbing a neighbor.

Recently, there have been recommendations to make even the adult system developmentally appropriate for adolescents (American Bar Association, 2001).[3] Yet few jurisdictions have implemented the recommendations. Children moved to adult criminal court often lose their right to vote. They are often denied education when they are incarcerated, unable to return to school if they are released, and end up with inadequate physical and behavioral health care. In short, they receive little in the adult system that supports them as they continue to grow and develop (Sereny, 1999).

Adjudication. If the child continues to be detained, an adjudicatory hearing (comparable to the trial in criminal court) will usually be held within 10 to 30 days. Although this is the general rule, in some states juveniles charged with high-profile crimes, such as murder, will have a longer time to wait until their trials. Most states do not have speedy trial requirements for conducting adjudicatory hearings if the juvenile is released before trial (Butts, 1997).

Disposition. If the juvenile admits to the offense, or if the juvenile court finds with proof beyond a reasonable doubt that the child committed the offense, then the court will proceed to disposition (comparable to the sentencing decision in adult court).

Juvenile dispositions historically have aimed to provide "treatment, rehabilitation, or supervision" in a way that best serves the needs of the juvenile. Such interventions have been thought to offer the best opportunity for public protection. Some legislatures have recently included incapacitation for public safety as a valid rationale for disposition. Others have required the juvenile court to balance public safety, accountability, and some version of treatment (sometimes called competency development). Under any of the models, the juvenile court will have a range of discretion. In some states, such as Wisconsin and Pennsylvania, the juvenile court retains power over the child and has wide latitude, from ordering that the child return home under supervision—probation—to placing the child in a maximum-security institution known as a training school, reform school, or youth development center. Other states, such as California and Massachusetts, use a "youth authority" model; in theses states, the court will either order probation or, if placement is warranted, transfer custody of the child to the youth authority, which will then determine the level of care.

Release. Most juvenile court dispositions are for indeterminate periods of time. In states where the juvenile court controls all aspects of the juvenile's treatment, the court will usually "review" the juvenile's case every 6 to 9 months. States with youth authorities follow administrative procedures for reviewing the need for continued confinement. In nearly every instance, the review of placement focuses on whether the child is behaving or showing an improved attitude. Reviewing authorities rarely compare the child's progress with a treatment plan.

Many juveniles in placement, particularly those with mental health needs and those who have been placed in inappropriate placements, end up being returned to juvenile court for new dispositions because they have "failed to adjust" to the treatment program. Most often, those juveniles are placed in detention pending a new placement plan. When juveniles are released from institutions, they are placed on "aftercare probation," analogous to parole. A juvenile who is on probation or aftercare probation status can have that status revoked, or "violated," for new offenses or for violating the terms of probation such as associating with gang members, missing school, and ignoring curfew.

OBSTACLES AND CHALLENGES TO CHANGING THE SYSTEM

There are numerous obstacles to the juvenile justice system behaving so as to promote PYD. Although superb programs and visionary leaders exist, they are not the norm, and they operate in bureaucratic settings that make it difficult for them to succeed or be replicated (Schorr, 1997). These constraints on PYD are exacerbated by the vexing problem of race discrimination. During the early 1990s, the Juvenile Justice and Delinquency Prevention Act (42 U.S.C., Section 5633) required states to assess whether their juvenile justice systems disproportionately confined members of minority groups. Only one state, Vermont, found no problem. In other states, minority youth were less likely than white youth to be diverted from the juvenile justice system, and they were more likely to be detained or placed in training schools. The general public and juvenile justice decision makers tend to ascribe negative characteristics more often to minority youth—in particular those who misbehave—than to white youth. Thus, for children of color, the following hurdles loom even higher.[4]

A Confused Mission. The formal juvenile justice system's goals and operational components are often incompatible. For example, the system is meant to control, punish, treat, supervise, incapacitate, and train youth who are entrusted to its care. These mandates can work at cross-purposes to each other and often fail to promote healthy development.

Although ordinary devoted parents fill a range of roles with their children, systems have a more difficult time with these tasks. Feld (1993) aptly describes these polar competing purposes—social control, on the one hand, and social welfare, on the other. He notes,

> Juvenile courts' subordination of individual welfare to custody and control stems from its fundamentally penal focus. Delinquency jurisdiction is not based on characteristics of children for which they are not responsible and for whom intervention could mean an improvement in their lives—their lack of decent education, their lack of adequate housing, their unmet medical needs, or their family or social circumstances. . . . Rather, delinquency jurisdiction is based on criminal law violations. . . . As long as juvenile courts emphasize criminal characteristics of children least likely to elicit sympathy and ignore social conditions most likely to engender a desire to nurture and help, they reinforce punitive rather than rehabilitative impulses. Operating in a societal context that does not provide adequately for children in general, intervention in the lives of those who commit crimes inevitably serves purposes of penal social control, regardless of the court's ability to deliver social welfare.

Jaded Staff. Many of those who work in juvenile justice, in particular those in public systems where the job can become a sinecure, have lost their enthusiasm for their work and for the children they supervise. In many ways, these juvenile justice professionals are similar to what we hear about teachers; some still have passion and talent, some have always been unqualified, and some once had quality and passion but those flames have dimmed over time. Like teachers, who must believe that every child can learn if the teachers are to succeed, juvenile justice professionals must believe that every youth can become a productive adult.

Inadequate Measures of Success. Despite its competing goals, the juvenile justice system tends to use one negative measure of success: recidivism. And even that measure is not uniformly applied across jurisdictions. Some places will measure rearrest within a particular time frame. Others will measure frequency or severity of new offenses. There is no common understanding of what this negative standard is measuring.

Public juvenile justice programs—training schools, detention centers, and youth authority programs—simply do not measure positive outcomes. Private (usually nonprofit) agencies with which public agencies have contracts rarely have payment tied to performance measures (unless they are negative measures such as keeping the number of escapes below a certain percentage).

There is an exception. During the early 1990s, Philadelphia Deputy Commissioner Jesse E. Williams, Jr., then in charge of the Department of Human Services' (DHS's) Juvenile Justice Services, wanted to see whether he was getting value from the four dozen private agencies with which the city had contracts. Williams arranged with the Crime and Justice Research Institute (CJRI) at Temple University to develop ways of measuring whether children were better off leaving the programs than they were when they entered the programs. CJRI created a data collection and evaluation system called the Program Development and Evaluation System (ProDES), which began collecting data in 1994. ProDES measures client and program trends, looking at changes in adolescents' life skills, self-esteem, behavior, and other assets that were of interest to DHS. ProDES uses a pre- and postprogram assessment, a follow-up assessment, and reviews of official records to see what programs were doing. This is a rare example of an evaluation system that measures positive outcomes. ProDES provides the Philadelphia system with regular reports on trends, and it gives individual programs—as well as DHS—reports on how those programs are faring.[5]

Overreliance on the Medical Model. The juvenile justice system operates on an illness- or deficit-oriented model, as opposed to one based on assets, strengths, and wellness. It is bent on curing and saving children (Platt, 1977). Once "what is wrong" with a youth is fixed, he or she can reenter the mainstream of society.

For example, one sees this medical orientation in the system's approach to assessing risk. It is easier to use an assessment that will identify a specific problem and attach a descriptive label to that problem than it is to describe the ways in which a child is healthy.[6] Risk assessment often is reduced to negative labeling. Negative labeling pervades many child-serving fields, but in juvenile justice—a system that is invoked only *after* a child gets into trouble—it is virtually the universal language. At best, risk assessment tools have only a modest chance of sending a child to the kind of program that claims to be able to address the diagnosed problem. But many juvenile justice systems do not even use their assessment instruments that well. In too many systems, the "empty bed" remains the most frequently used diagnostic indicator. (In 2001, the MacArthur Foundation Research Network on Adolescent Development and Juvenile Justice began collecting data for a longitudinal study, "Pathways to Desistance," that may help jurisdictions to do a better job of matching programs with offenders.)

Punishment, Retribution, and Incapacitation. Increasingly, legislators are infusing juvenile justice statutes with the language of the adult system. In contrast to the juvenile justice system's historic goal of "rehabilitation," the adult criminal justice system has focused on deterrence (both of the individual and of society in general), retribution, and incapacitation (Packer, 1968).

Some reformers proposed that a punishment model should *replace* the traditional rehabilitation model; they viewed children as being no different from adults (Treanor & Volenik, 1987). Others *added* punishment to the existing juvenile justice framework. They argued that the juvenile justice system was merely a substitute parent; because parents are motivated by love when they punish their children, punishment is, in the end, no different from rehabilitation. Such sophistry had surface appeal because the major premise was true; when a parent punishes his or her child, love is indeed a motivator. The sanction is swift, directly related in time and proportion to the offense, expected by the child, and part of a context that includes love and nurturing. In those circumstances, punishment is indeed an important part of raising a child. Unfortunately, that is not the way punishment is used by the juvenile justice system.

To promote the goals of punishment, both conservatives and liberals have proposed that juvenile justice systems be required to use "graduated sanctions." As envisioned by Representative Bill McCollum, the author of the 105th Congress's H.R. 3 (which was passed by the House in 1997 but which died in the Senate), there would be a justice system response for *every* alleged delinquent act, and the response would be a sanction that would increase in severity for every subsequent offense. In anticipation of H.R. 3's passage, Congress, at the end of 1997, appropriated $250 million for the Juvenile Accountability Incentive Block Grant (JAIBG) (Public Law 105-119).

The authorized spending purposes of JAIBG reflect this posture. To qualify for JAIBG funds, states must certify that they have adopted or are considering (a) increased transfer of juveniles to criminal court, (b) a system of graduated sanctions, (c) a system of juvenile delinquency records for serious offenders that would treat their records similarly to adult records, and (d) court-ordered parental involvement and sanctions against parents for failing to supervise their children. JAIBG funds may be used only for the following purposes:

- Construction of juvenile detention or correctional facilities, including training of personnel
- Accountability-based sanctions programs
- Hiring of judges, probation officers, and defenders and funding of pretrial services
- Hiring of prosecutors
- Funding of prosecutor-led drug, gang, and violence programs
- Provision of technology, equipment, and training programs for prosecutors
- Probation programs
- Gun courts
- Drug courts
- Information-sharing systems
- Accountability-based programs for law enforcement referrals or those that are designed to protect students and school personnel from drug, gang, and youth violence
- Controlled substance testing (including interventions) for juveniles in the juvenile justice system. (Albert, 1998)

JAIBG's appropriation was far more than Congress had ever appropriated for juvenile justice prevention programs.

Language. One reason why punishment and graduated sanctions have taken root in the juvenile justice system is that the system's language has changed to reflect public attitudes about children. Most state juvenile codes, until recent years, dealt with a range of children's issues, including child abuse, neglect, status offenses, and delinquency. Everyone who was the subject of those codes was described as a "child." During the 1990s, many states changed their terminology, opting, as the Virginia legislature did, to refer to children as "juveniles" instead. "Juvenile" is a less benign term and appears to lead more easily to punishment or transfer to the adult system.

Bennett, DiIulio, and Walters (1996) introduced the term "superpredator" at that time, with profound impact. Indeed, rhetoric about superpredators fueled many of the changes in state law that occurred during the mid-1990s; when McCollum first introduced the bill that became H.R. 3, it was called the "Violent Youth Predator Act of 1996."

Reliance on Quarantine. Too often, the juvenile justice system evokes the medical model by segregating youth—both to encourage a cure and to prevent the spread of the disease. Altschuler (1984) describes how this reliance on quarantine made it difficult to implement his alternative approach to aftercare:

> The community reintegration process [which I propose] is based on a set of assumptions which fly in the face of the practice of many decades where child care institutions of various sorts were separated from mainstream socialization influences and the local community. It was their intention first to insulate the child from these influences and then to strengthen or inculcate values conducive to law abidance and other legitimate roles. The assumptions were that (1) the youths would leave the programs appropriately immunized to survive the outside world, and (2) adjustment and progress within the programs offered some reasonably sound basis for thinking successful community reintegration would follow.

Poor Institutional Conditions. Although there are many exemplary facilities for delinquent youth, those programs do not predominate. On any day, tens of thousands of American youth are held in state training schools and detention centers—institutions maintained in deplorable conditions. For example, consider this description of a Louisiana facility:

> Here in the middle of the impoverished Mississippi Delta is a juvenile prison so rife with brutality, cronyism, and neglect that

many legal experts say it is the worst in the nation. The prison, the Tallulah Correctional Center for Youth, opened just four years ago where a sawmill and cotton fields once stood. Behind rows of razor wire, it houses 620 boys and young men, age 11 to 20, in stifling corrugated-iron barracks jammed with bunks.

From the run-down homes and bars on the road that runs by it, Tallulah appears unexceptional, one new cookie-cutter prison among scores built in the United States this decade. But inside, inmates of the privately run prison regularly appear at the infirmary with black eyes, broken noses or jaws, or perforated eardrums from beatings by the poorly paid, poorly trained guards or from fights with other boys. Meals are so meager that many boys lose weight. Clothing is so scarce that boys fight over shirts and shoes. Almost all the teachers are uncertified, instruction amounts to as little as an hour a day, and until recently there were no books. Up to a fourth of the inmates are mentally ill or retarded, but a psychiatrist visits only one day a week. There is no therapy. Emotionally disturbed boys who cannot follow guards' orders are locked in isolation cells for weeks at a time or have their sentences arbitrarily extended. (Butterfield, 1998)

Thirty years ago, Jerry Miller, who gained renown for closing Massachusetts's large delinquency training schools during the early 1970s, warned about the dangers of juvenile justice institutions (Miller, 1991). It is much easier to be a guard than to function like an ordinary devoted parent. Most institutional staff believe that they have succeeded if they get through a day without incident.

The average institution across the country is mired in inadequate, or barely adequate, practice. Although the Tallulah facility just described is an extreme example, relatively poor conditions are commonplace. During the early 1990s, an Office of Juvenile Justice and Delinquency Prevention (OJJDP)-commissioned study by Abt Associates found that more than half of the country's training schools and detention centers fell below

nationally accepted standards (Parent et al., 1994).

Congress made a bad situation worse in 1996 when it passed the Prisoner Litigation Reform Act (PLRA; 42 U.S.C., Section 1997e). The new law was ostensibly enacted to reduce frivolous litigation by jailhouse lawyers, but it did much more. PLRA made it extremely difficult for adults and juveniles to bring suits about conditions of confinement. At a time when more children spend more time in overcrowded facilities, PLRA prevents juveniles, who are least able to obtain help, from complaining in federal court about institutional conditions.

Complicated Professional Roles. To the extent that there is a single professional at the top of the pyramid of service providers and custodians of youth in the juvenile justice system, it is the juvenile probation officer. In theory, probation officers are both monitors and helpers; both are necessary to promote PYD. As monitors, they note infractions, have authority to take youth into custody for those infractions, report to the juvenile court on adolescents' progress or lack thereof, and make recommendations for sanctions. As helpers, juvenile probation officers counsel youth and connect them with appropriate social and educational services and employment opportunities. Although these roles are often experienced as incompatible, the best juvenile probation officers do indeed serve as case managers and helpers in other ways while at the same time maintaining their monitoring authority. The problem is that it is difficult to design state-of-the-art interventions based on PYD when they must rely on the skills of the *best* juvenile probation officer. To be successful, these reforms must be acceptable to, and possible to implement by, the *average* probation officer.

Several barriers are obvious. First, it is simply much easier for probation officers to be monitors rather than guides. This is true both for historical reasons (monitor is the more traditional role) and because large probation officer caseloads make doing anything other than "the usual" difficult. Second, juvenile probation officers consider the client to be the youth (or perhaps the juvenile court itself); they rarely consider the family to be the client. Too often, they automatically consider the parents to be part of the problem. They do not know how to learn what parents know about their children—to become partners with parents. And indeed, given their preferential monitoring role, many parents are reluctant to treat probation officers as trusted confidants committed to helping their children develop into competent, complete adults.

A third related barrier is that many probation officers also are ill at ease working with strength-based community organizations. The probation system generally does not encourage officers to learn about—to visit, observe, and build relationships with— community-based agencies. And again, large caseloads conspire to make such activities difficult. Supervisors expect line staff to be working with individual youth, not working out in the community.

Finally, there is a developing trend to arm juvenile probation officers. For example, more than a dozen Pennsylvania counties permit juvenile probation officers to carry guns; several *require* them to be armed.

The Inclusion of Children With Disabilities. Recent studies suggest that a significant percentage of delinquent youth have mental health problems (Grisso & Barnum, 1998; Teplin, Abram, & McClelland, 1998), yet few coordinated and comprehensive services exist. There are examples of successful programs for these children; Multisystemic Therapy in South Carolina, the Willie M. program in North Carolina, and Alternative Rehabilitative Communities in Pennsylvania come to mind. Until recently, however, no state system routinely screened and diagnosed children with mental health problems or boasted staff trained to address their problems.[7]

Parents of delinquent youth are not themselves expected to serve as ordinary devoted parents. To the extent that states have turned their attention to the role of parents at all, it is to hold them accountable. Some states have given jurisdiction over parents to juvenile courts that hear delinquency cases, and increasingly juvenile courts have had authority to hold parents responsible for the delinquent conduct of their children. This situation is often frustrating to parents and is often counterproductive.

Some years ago, I was at a conference of parents of children with mental health problems. One angry parent rose and said,

> Until my child was arrested, I was the "majority shareholder" in his life. I held 51% of the stock, which meant that I had the final say, whether we were with school officials preparing an Individualized Education Program or with mental health providers developing an Individualized Treatment Plan. Then my son was arrested, and I became not only a minority shareholder, I was seen as part of the problem. Juvenile probation treated me as though I knew nothing about my son. Probation felt that I had no solutions to offer, that my son would be better off without me. And worse—they didn't come close to recognizing his problems or working energetically to help him overcome them.

OPPORTUNITIES TO AFFECT SYSTEMS CHANGE

The juvenile justice system exists to protect the public. Thus, there will always be pressure on it to remove children from the community, transfer them to the adult criminal justice system, or control and monitor adolescents' behavior. So, what opportunities are there for a PYD orientation to enter the juvenile justice system? In the beginning, it likely will be an *add-on* to current practice rather than a replacement for it. The system will not willingly yield on the goals of control and negative labeling. For PYD to take root and endure, however, it must be part of an overall system transformation. Changing a system must be viewed as a multiyear effort. It requires change in values at all levels of service delivery and decision making. It also requires new training and the addition of staff with new skills, even as old ways of doing business are phased out.

There are examples of system conversions of the type we seek—those based on new values. These are clearest in the transformation of mental health and mental retardation systems, which were once institution based, resting on negative stereotypes of the mentally ill and mentally retarded, much like today's juvenile justice system (Rothman & Rothman, 1984). There are also some examples of successful transformations of juvenile justice systems (Miller, 1991). If those examples are to be replicated, however, systems must be willing and able to pay for such a multiyear strategic transition (Conservation Company and Juvenile Law Center, 1994).

Bazemore and Terry (1997) note the difficulty of injecting PYD into the modern juvenile justice system. They are right in cautioning reforms to "start small," suggesting that "the complexity of juvenile justice requires that reform efforts be carefully planned and deliberate and that they include input from the staff as well as all other stakeholders in the system and the community."

The Communities That Care (CTC) initiative is one example. Although risk assessments in general are an obstacle to promoting PYD *after* adolescents have been referred to the juvenile justice system, there is promise in the primary and secondary prevention context. Pursuant to Title V of the Juvenile

Justice and Delinquency Prevention Act, since the early 1990s, OJJDP has sponsored the CTC initiative. Developed by David Hawkins and Richard Catalano, the CTC grant program to states calls for self-assessments by individuals, families, schools, and communities as part of an effort to reduce "risk factors" in each that lead to antisocial behavior. This risk-focused approach targets adolescent behaviors such as drug abuse, delinquency, violence, school dropout, and teen pregnancy (Hawkins & Catalano, 1992).

The CTC initiative has potential, especially to the extent that PYD requires suppression of risk factors. It is certainly true that risks work together exponentially and that elimination of *any* risks will be helpful to children and families (Schorr, 1988). Indeed, early studies show that CTC can be effective in organizing adults and youth around the common task of building strong neighborhoods (U.S. General Accounting Office, 1996).

What is less well known than CTC's emphasis on risk factors is its asset-based social development strategy, which is supposed to promote healthy behaviors. Unfortunately, this strategy is not nearly as well developed conceptually as is CTC's emphasis on risk factors, and there is little evidence that CTC communities are focusing as much on healthy behaviors as they are on the easier-to-identify CTC checklist of risk factors.

Education and Health Care. One cluster of opportunities can be seized no matter how incoherent juvenile justice policy, practice, philosophy, and goals are. At a minimum, juvenile justice can address basic needs of *any* youth in *any* system, specifically education and health care (with the latter including physical and behavioral health).

There is significant literature—much directed to juvenile justice—on correctional health care and correctional education (Center on Crime, Communities, and Culture, 1997).

Unfortunately, those responsible for serving delinquent youth often fail to meet even minimum standards. Juvenile Law Center staff see institutions that do not provide delinquent youth with basic or special education for the same number of hours provided to children in public schools. We see children who do not receive routine health screens and treatment. There is no excuse for these shortcomings. *Education and health care are basic rights, and they ought to be viewed as prerequisites for any deliberate shift to a PYD orientation.*

Delivery of health care to delinquent youth—in particular those in private residential treatment programs eligible for funding through the federal Medicaid program—will be affected by states converting Medicaid fee-for-service programs to managed care. The cautionary note, for those who see health care as a bedrock of PYD, is that health care has been unevenly provided to delinquent youth under fee-for-service arrangements, and it may well get even worse if managed care programs are not managed carefully.

Education is also unevenly delivered. At least 40% of institutionalized children have special education needs (Gemignani, 1994). If these needs had been identified before entering the institution, the adolescents' Individualized Education Programs—developed in concert with parents and teachers who know the youth well—rarely "follow them" to the institutional school. Parents are not encouraged to participate in the education of their children, and the geographic distance from home to institution is usually too great, even if they were invited to be helpful. Around the country are also examples of delinquent youth who have difficulty in returning to school after discharge from delinquency programs.

However, examples of how to address these challenges also exist. During the early 1990s, with support from OJJDP, Pennsylvania's detention centers developed a model of detention service delivery. The Juvenile Detention

Centers Association of Pennsylvania (JDCAP) standards go beyond a typical state regulatory framework (i.e., one that sets minimum health and safety standards) by establishing optimal standards for screening, assessment, education, health care, recreation, and other activities that can occur when youth are locked up, even for short periods of time (JDCAP, 1993). The JDCAP standards are an example of how proponents of PYD might approach the hundreds of thousands of juveniles who are detained each year. Juvenile detention is an opportunity for staff to learn about adolescents' strengths and to make recommendations to court and probation about disposition and the focus of the next intervention.

Aftercare. Aftercare here refers to services to youth who are leaving placements to which they were committed after adjudication and disposition.

Beginning in the late 1980s, the federal government invested in promoting aftercare probation services. OJJDP promoted a model of intensive aftercare program (IAP) developed by Altschuler and Armstrong (1992). IAP relies on the probation officer (i.e., the aftercare worker) as case manager and on five operating principles: preparing youth for progressively increased responsibility and freedom in the community, facilitating youth-community interaction and involvement, working with offenders and community support systems, developing new resources to support youth in the community, and monitoring (Altschuler & Armstrong, 1992).

For some reason—most likely routine system inertia—the Altschuler-Armstrong model of aftercare did not gain sufficient purchase to dominate the field. It should have. At its best, IAP is a model of reintegration that is consistent with PYD. The reason why IAP is such a valuable wedge for PYD is that it forces the system to imagine adolescents' future *at the time that the juvenile court or state youth authority fashions its first order of disposition.* It is impossible to plan for a youth's disposition, for example, unless one knows where the youth is going. To which school will he or she return? Where will the youth live? With which adults will he or she need to be connected? How will the order of disposition make the answers to those questions possible?

Aftercare that begins with those questions will follow a youth along a developmental pathway—through institutional care, planning with institutional staff for the future, involving family and other concerned adults, and preparing the child for school or work. Aftercare is an aggressive course of reintegrative services and supervision that should build on a youth's strengths in a ceaseless reimagining and re-creation of the youth's future.

Aftercare should be available to all children who are placed outside their homes. In a sense, aftercare should operate as an ordinary devoted parent would for a child who is in a mental health facility, special education program, or boarding school. The ordinary devoted parent, of course, has a caseload of one or several and knows how to connect the child with friends, relatives, and community institutions. Indeed, aftercare is crucial to connecting a child coming out of an institution to community-based organizations that will provide the youth's next bit of scaffolded support. Combined with independent living and the balanced approach (described next), aftercare should be a promising investment for PYD proponents.

Independent Living: Title IV-E(IL). For years, the federal government has contributed to states' expenditures on foster care, including such care for delinquent youth. The Adoption Assistance and Child Welfare Act of 1980 was designed to end foster care drift and promote permanent homes for children in the child welfare system. Because many dependent children moved in and out of the delinquency system, and because many states were quickly alert to the possibilities of refinancing their delinquency systems, federal foster care maintenance payments were soon being used for delinquent children.

The federal government pays a proportionate share of foster care (related to a state's poverty rate) pursuant to Title IV-E of the Social Security Act. Many states have been claiming Title IV-E reimbursement for delinquent youth. The case planning requirements of Title IV-E offer an opportunity to infuse PYD into the plans and services provided for Title IV-E-eligible youth. This is particularly true of those who are age 16 years or over, for whom the Title IV-E independent living requirements are applicable.

At the end of 1999, Congress enacted the Foster Care Independence Act, which expanded the Title IV-E independent living program by giving states additional dollars and options as they plan for, and support, youth who are making the transition from foster care to adulthood.

The "Balanced Approach." There is probably no better wedge for PYD than that provided by the "competency development" component of the late 1990s notion of "restorative justice." Restorative justice is an effort by juvenile justice proponents to preserve the system from attack by finding a philosophical middle ground between retributive justice, which gained favor as states sought to "get tough" on juvenile crime, and rehabilitation, which was seen as being "too soft" on crime. By the 1990s, "rehabilitation" was used as pejoratively by critics of the juvenile justice system as "liberal" was used in the political context.

A form of restorative justice had been introduced earlier—during the 1980s—by Maloney's probation staff in Bend, Oregon.

Maloney called his intervention the "balanced approach" (Maloney et al., 1988). Although he originally applied it to the purposes and uses of juvenile probation, the balanced approach soon became an organizing principle for the entire juvenile justice system. It proposes that at every stage of the juvenile justice pipeline, three principles should operate: accountability, public safety, and *competency development*. The system must hold the individual youth *accountable* (satisfying the needs of the victim and the community). *Public safety* is the reason why the system exists (here recognizing the potential for rehabilitation, incapacitation, and deterrence). *Competency* development—the link to PYD—ensures that every intervention provides more than "make-work" or incapacitation. For example, restitution or community service that requires participation in Habitats for Humanity, in which a juvenile learns a skill and increases empathy, makes more sense than having the juvenile rake leaves along a freeway.

Many state legislatures have been attracted to the balanced approach. Beginning in the mid-1990s, several states (e.g., Idaho, Illinois, Maryland, Montana, Pennsylvania, Wisconsin) changed the purposes and languages of their juvenile codes to incorporate balanced approach principles. Although some states have made tentative steps in this direction in their codes,[8] few have included sufficient content in legislation to change the culture of the state system.

Illinois, whose new code went into effect in January 1999, is an exception. Illinois's new purpose clause explicitly adopts the balanced approach. After invoking public protection and accountability, it declares as a goal equipping "juvenile offenders with competencies to live responsibly and productively." Competency is then defined as "the development of educational, vocational, social, emotional, and basic life skills which enable a minor to mature into a productive member of society" (705 Ill. C.S., Section 405/5-105).

Gordon Bazemore and Mark Umbreit have written extensively about the potential for restorative justice affecting every aspect of the juvenile justice system. At best, restorative justice is not an addition to the system but rather a reformation of it.

> Restorative justice is a way of thinking, a way of behaving, and a way of measuring. Until we change the way we think about why probation exists, we can't change our behavior. We can't measure the changes until our behavior changes. (Umbreit & Carey, 1995)

Bazemore and Terry (1997) also recognize the need for a paradigm shift if restorative justice is to become central to the juvenile justice system. They caution,

> For a new paradigm to emerge, however, professionals must not only reject the old paradigm but also understand the new and embrace its implications for a distinct change in practice. In the absence of a shared understanding of core principles, and of their implications for systemic and organizational change, the competency development model can be quickly equated with one or more treatment programs or intervention techniques transformed to fit bureaucratic agendas.

This warning is important. The danger is that juvenile justice residential programs will simply repackage existing treatment programs, calling them "competency development." Anecdotal evidence suggests that this has already occurred.

The early writings of Bazemore and Umbreit were vague where competency development was concerned. During the past few years, however, Bazemore has given increased attention to competency development. His recent article with W. Clinton

Table 14.1   Intermediate Outcomes of Intervention: Individual Treatment and Competency Development

Individual Treatment	Competency Development
Avoid negative influence of designated people, places, and activities	New positive relationships and positive behavior in conventional roles; avoiding placement of youth in stigmatizing treatments
Follow rules of supervision (e.g., curfew, school attendance)	Competent conventional behavior
Attend and participate in treatment activities (e.g., counseling)	Active demonstration of competency through completion of productive activity (service and/or work with community benefit)
Complete all required treatment and terminate supervision	Significant increase in measurable competencies (e.g., academic, social, occupational)
Make improvements in attitude and self-concept, family interaction, and psychological integration	Improvements in self-image and public image (community acceptance) and increased bonding and community integration

SOURCE: Bazemore and Terry (1997).

Terry in the journal *Child Welfare* (Bazemore & Terry, 1997) discusses how the competency development leg of the balanced approach triangle can be integrated into the juvenile justice system. The Bazemore-Terry approach is illustrated by a table from their article that shows how competency development differs from the erstwhile medical model, which is founded on individual treatment (see Table 14.1 here). This table illustrates how competency development represents an approach that can be applied at any stage of the juvenile justice pipeline. In addition, as the table also displays, a well-designed competency development program can be measured, and assessments of success can go well beyond traditional measures of recidivism.

Changing the Measure of Success. With tracking and evaluation tools such as ProDES (described earlier), juvenile justice systems have the capacity to measure aspects

of PYD orientation. Programs will be able to learn whether they are succeeding in promoting discrete aspects of PYD, and juvenile justice administrators will be in a position to reward success.

For example, at the end of 1998, ProDES looked at system trends for the 4 years during which the system tracked youth who entered the Philadelphia juvenile justice system. With solid data, the evaluators could make the following statement:

> When ProDES was being developed, programs were almost unanimous in stating that improved self-esteem, more pro-social values, and improved school and family bonding were intermediate goals of theirs (in the sense that positive change on these was expected to have a longer-term impact on delinquent behavior). *There is no evidence yet that any of these goals are being met.* Some juveniles do improve on one or more of these dimensions while in the programs; others, however, do not change or even get worse. The balance among these three outcomes has fluctuated but not

changed significantly during the more than four years of study. If these remain important goals, programs need to try alternative modes of intervention in the hope that they will have a more marked positive impact. (Jones & Harris, 1998)

It is crucial that jurisdictions develop the capacity to generate data that would enable evaluators to track adolescents' progress over time and measure aspects along dimensions consistent with the principles of PYD. For many communities, changing what is measured will inevitably change practice. For example, Tom Grisso found that when states began using the Massachusetts Youth Screening Instrument, they had to begin to offer mental health services to respond to their findings (Grisso & Barnum, 1998). Administrators found that they could not very well use mental health screens and then ignore youth whose symptoms placed them at high risk. In addition, the aggregate data collected from the screens turned out to give a clear picture of the kinds of services that were needed.

The Role of Defense Counsel. The defense counsel role holds great potential for promoting PYD. Yet youth in the juvenile justice system have often been ill served by their lawyers. Although there are excellent examples of quality legal representation across the country, for the most part, the juvenile defense bar has been beset by large caseloads and low expectations (Puritz, Burrell, Schwartz, Soler, & Warboys, 1995).

PYD will not become part of the juvenile justice culture unless there is an internal advocate for it in every case. For that to occur, defense counsel must do more than simply "show up" for adjudicatory hearings. They must get to know their clients and the adults who care about them. They must be active participants in planning their clients' dispositions and push probation staff to think

constructively. If their clients are committed to institutions, defense counsel must work with institutional and aftercare probation staff to ensure transitional plans that are developmentally sound and strengths based. Investment in training and in augmenting defense counsel's offices with social workers, for example, would create within the juvenile justice system an internal advocacy component for individual cases at every stage of the juvenile justice pipeline.

In 1999, OJJDP provided start-up funding for the National Juvenile Defender Center, the first national office designed to provide training, resources, and technical assistance exclusively to the juvenile defense bar. OJJDP saw this project as a natural evolution of the Due Process Advocacy Project it had supported since 1993. That project, led by the Juvenile Justice Center of the American Bar Association with support from the Youth Law Center and the Juvenile Law Center, produced the first national assessment of the quality and availability of counsel for delinquent youth (Puritz et al., 1995). At the end of 2001, the National Juvenile Defender Center had nine regional offices and was in the process of conducting assessments in each state of the quality of indigent juvenile defense.

CONCLUSIONS

Each of the opportunities described in the prior section has promise. If approached strategically, even the obstacles might be weeded sufficiently to allow PYD to grow. However, proponents of this approach should not be overoptimistic, nor should they overpromise quick results for children and families. The history of juvenile justice (Bernard, 1992) makes clear that most reforms are short-lived. A normal cycle would be that the system changes for a while, truly absorbs some PYD kernels, and then swings back to an approach that promotes more punitive measures.

For their part, advocates must address adolescents' negative behaviors, acknowledging that incapacitation—even transfer to adult court—is appropriate for some children. Risk management must be a central element of any PYD-oriented program promoted by the juvenile justice system, for without it, the inevitable failures will be turned into celebrated cases that precipitate a backlash. At the same time, advocates are fully justified in challenging the proponents of incapacitation and transfer to justify those parts of the system. Prisons have yet to be evaluated with the scrutiny that no doubt awaits the move toward PYD within the juvenile justice system.

Embracing the principles of PYD remains our best hope for creating a future that welcomes the majority of our children. If they are to have real life chances, we will have to rewind and edit much of the film of juvenile justice's recent past. If we are to have the benefit of the talent that youth such as Gabriel can offer society, we must toss talk of "sanctions" to the cutting room floor. The field will have to return to a rhetoric of childhood, editing out X-rated language such as "superpredator" and eliminating glib slogans such as "adult time for adult crime." If a youth is already an adult in the public mind, there is nowhere to develop *to*. If PYD means anything, it is that our children who pass through adolescence are not yet adults (Grisso & Schwartz, 2000), and all of the slogans in the world will not make them so.

NOTES

1. Much of the material in this section is adapted from Steinberg and Schwartz (2000).

2. During the years after *Gault,* the Supreme Court stopped short of making juveniles' rights identical to those of adults. Although juveniles could avoid double jeopardy (*Breed v. Jones*) and could be adjudicated delinquent only by proof beyond a reasonable doubt (*In re Winship*), the court held that they were not entitled to jury trials (*McKeiver v. Pennsylvania*) or to have strict Fourth Amendment procedures apply in schools (*T.L.O. v. New Jersey*). In addition, because children are always in some form of custody, the Supreme Court approved pretrial preventive detention for the children's own good (*Schall v. Martin*). Juveniles also have no constitutional right to bail or a speedy trial.

3. Drawing on the American Bar Association report, in 2001 Senators Leahy, Hatch, and Kennedy cosponsored S. 1174, the Children's Confinement Conditions Improvement Act of 2001, which made as its first congressional finding the fact that "recent studies have established that youth are developmentally different from adults, and these developmental differences need to be taken into account at all stages and in all aspects of the adult criminal justice system."

4. During the late 1990s, the Youth Law Center brought together a coalition of organizations, Building Blocks for Youth, to attack disproportionate minority representation. The coalition's many reports have documented the pervasiveness of the problem (www.buildingblocksforyouth.org).

5. ProDES reports are available at www.prodespromis.cjri.com.

6. For example, the Search Institute's checklist of assets is generally not used in juvenile justice systems (www.search-institute.org).

7. Since early 2000, with the support of the MacArthur Foundation, Thomas Grisso has been introducing many states to the Massachusetts Youth Screening Instrument (MAYSI), a self-report inventory instrument developed to identify potential mental health needs of youth at entry or transitional placement points in the juvenile justice system. The manual and materials for the MAYSI-2 may be obtained from Grisso at the University of Massachusetts Medical School (thomas.grisso@umassmed.edu).

8. Maine, for example, speaks of providing a juvenile in state care with "the necessary treatment, care, guidance, and discipline to assist him in becoming a responsible and productive member of society" (15 M.R.S.A., Section 3002). Florida's system is "to provide children committed to the Department of Juvenile Justice with training in life skills, including career education" (West's F.S.A., Section 39.001). New Jersey calls for a "comprehensive program" that "should provide a range of services and sanctions for juveniles sufficient to protect the public through prevention; early intervention; and a range of meaningful sanctions that ensure accountability, provide training, education, treatment, and, when necessary, confinement followed by community supervision that is adequate to protect the public and promote successful reintegration into the community" (N.J. Stat., Section 52:17B-169).

REFERENCES

Albert, R. L. (1998). *Juvenile Accountability Incentive Block Grants Program.* Washington, DC: Office of Juvenile Justice and Delinquency Prevention.

Altschuler, D. M. (1984). Community reintegration in juvenile offender programming. In R. A. Mathias, P. DeMuro, & R. S. Allinson (Eds.), *Violent juvenile offenders: An anthology.* San Francisco: National Council on Crime and Delinquency.

Altschuler, D. M., & Armstrong, T. (1992). *Intensive aftercare for high-risk juvenile parolees: A community-care model.* Washington, DC: Office of Juvenile Justice and Delinquency Prevention.

American Bar Association. (2001). *Youth in the criminal justice system: Guidelines for policymakers and practitioners.* Washington, DC: Author.

Ayers, W. (1997). *A kind and just parent: The children of juvenile court.* Boston: Beacon.

Bazemore, G., & Terry, W. C. (1997). Developing delinquent youths: A reintegrative model for rehabilitation and a new role for the juvenile justice system. *Child Welfare, 76,* 665.

Bazemore, G., & Umbreit, M. S. (1994). *Balanced and restorative justice.* Washington, DC: Office of Juvenile Justice and Delinquency Prevention.

Bennett, W. J., DiIulio, J. J., Jr., & Walters, J. P. (1996). *Body count: Moral poverty and how to win America's war against crime and drugs.* New York: Simon & Schuster.

Bernard, T. J. (1992). *The cycle of juvenile justice.* New York: Oxford University Press.

Butterfield, F. (1998, July 15). Hard time: A special report—Profits at a juvenile prison come with a chilling cost. *New York Times.*

Butts, J. (1997). *Delays in juvenile court processing of delinquency cases.* Washington, DC: Office of Juvenile Justice and Delinquency Prevention.

Center on Crime, Communities, and Culture. (1997). *Education as crime prevention: Providing education to prisoners.* New York: Open Society Institute.

Conservation Company and Juvenile Law Center. (1994). *Building bridges: Strategic planning and alternative financing for system reform*. Philadelphia: Author.

Feld, B. (1993). Juvenile (in)justice and the criminal court alternative. *Crime & Delinquency, 39,* 403.

Furstenberg, F. F. (1999). *Managing to make it: Urban families and adolescent success*. Chicago: University of Chicago Press.

Gemignani, R. J. (1994). *Juvenile correctional education: A time for change*. Washington, DC: Office of Juvenile Justice and Delinquency Prevention.

Goldstein, J., Freud, A., Solnit, A. J., & Goldstein, S. (1986). *In the best interests of the child*. New York: Free Press.

Grisso, T., & Barnum, R. (1998). *Massachusetts Youth Screening Instrument: Preliminary manual and technical report*. Worcester: University of Massachusetts Medical School, Department of Psychiatry.

Grisso, T., & Schwartz, R. G. (Eds.). (1999). *Youth on trial: A developmental perspective on juvenile justice*. Chicago: University of Chicago Press.

Guarino-Ghezzi, S., & Loughran, E. J. (1997). *Balancing juvenile justice*. New Brunswick, NJ: Transaction Publishers.

Hawkins, J. D., & Catalano, R. F. (1992). *Communities That Care*. San Francisco: Jossey-Bass.

Institute of Judicial Administration–American Bar Association. (1996). *Juvenile justice standards annotated: A balanced approach* (R. E. Shepherd, Jr., Ed.). Chicago: American Bar Association.

Jones, P. R., & Harris, P. W. (1998). *System trends 1994-1998*. Philadelphia: Crime and Justice Research Institute.

Juvenile Detention Centers Association of Pennsylvania. (1993). *Juvenile detention program standards*. Harrisburg: Pennsylvania Commission on Crime and Delinquency.

Krisberg, B., & Austin, J. (1993). *Reinventing juvenile justice*. Newbury Park, CA: Sage.

Lopez, S. (1994). *Third and Indiana*. New York: Penguin.

Lubow, B. (1997). *The juvenile detention alternatives initiative: A progress report*. Baltimore, MD: Annie E. Casey Foundation.

Mack, J. (1909). The juvenile court. *Harvard Law Review, 23,* 104-122.

Maloney, D., Romig, D., & Armstrong, T. (1988). Juvenile probation: The balanced approach. *Juvenile and Family Court Journal, 39,* 1-63.

Meranze, M. (1996). *Laboratories of virtue: Punishment, revolution, and authority in Philadelphia, 1760-1835*. Chapel Hill: University of North Carolina Press.

Miller, J. G. (1991). *Last one over the wall: The Massachusetts experiment in closing reform schools*. Columbus: Ohio State University Press.

Packer, H. L. (1968). *The limits of the criminal sanction*. Stanford, CA: Stanford University Press.

Parent, D. G., Lieter, V., Kennedy, S., Livens, L., Wentworth, D., & Wilcox, S. (1994). *Conditions of confinement: Juvenile detention and corrections facilities*. Washington, DC: Office of Juvenile Justice and Delinquency Prevention.

Platt, A. M. (1977). *The child savers: The invention of delinquency* (2nd ed.). Chicago: University of Chicago Press.

Puritz, P., Burrell, S., Schwartz, R., Soler, M., & Warboys, L. (1995). *A call for justice: An assessment of access to counsel and quality of representation in delinquency proceedings*. Chicago: American Bar Association.

Rothman, D. J., & Rothman, S. M. (1984). *The Willowbrook wars: A decade of struggle for social justice*. New York: Harper & Row.

Schorr, L. B. (1988). *Within our reach: Breaking the cycle of disadvantage*. Garden City, NY: Doubleday.

Schorr, L. B. (1997). *Common purpose: Strengthening families and neighborhoods to rebuild America.* New York: Doubleday.

Sereny, G. (1999). *Cries unheard: Why children kill—The story of Mary Bell.* New York: Metropolitan Press/Henry Holt.

Steinberg, L., & Schwartz, R. G. (2000). *Developmental psychology goes to court.* In T. Grisso & R. G. Schwartz (Eds.), *Youth on trial: A developmental perspective on juvenile justice.* Chicago: University of Chicago Press.

Tanenhaus, D. S. (2001, February). *The evolution of juvenile courts in the early twentieth century: Beyond the myth of immaculate construction.* Paper presented to MacArthur Foundation Research Network on Adolescent Development and Juvenile Justice, San Diego.

Teplin, L., Abram, K., & McClelland, G. (1998, March). *Psychiatric and substance abuse disorders among juveniles in detention: An empirical assessment.* Paper presented at the meeting of the American Psychology–Law Society, Redondo Beach, CA.

Torbet, P., Gable, R., Hurst, H., IV, Montgomery, I., Szymanski, L., & Thomas, D. (1996). *State responses to serious and violent juvenile crime.* Washington, DC: Office of Juvenile Justice and Delinquency Prevention.

Treanor, W. W., & Volenik, A. E. (1987). *The new right's agenda for the states: A legislator's briefing book.* Washington, DC: American Youth Work Center.

Umbreit, M. S., & Carey, M. (1995). Restorative justice: Implications for organizational change. *Federal Probation, 59,* 47-54.

U.S. General Accounting Office. (1996). *Juvenile justice: Status of delinquency prevention program and description of local projects* (GAO/GGD-96-147). Washington, DC: Author.

Wolfgang, M. E., Figlio, R. M., & Sellin, T. (1972). *Delinquency in a birth cohort.* Chicago: University of Chicago Press.

Zimring, F. E. (1998). *American youth violence.* New York: Oxford University Press.

CHAPTER 15

The Development of Young Children
With Disabilities and Their Families
Implications for Policies and Programs

PENNY HAUSER-CRAM

ANGELA HOWELL

Most prospective parents hope and expect to have children who exhibit typical patterns of development, yet about 12% of children in the United States have difficulty performing one or more everyday activities, including learning, communication, mobility, and self-care, such as feeding, dressing, and bathing (America's Children, 1999). These include children with biologically based developmental disabilities, such as Down syndrome or other distinct syndromes, autism or other communication disorders, and mental retardation or other forms of developmental delay. In this chapter, we examine the empirical evidence about young children with developmental disabilities and their families

from the perspective of current policies and with a view toward service provision. We begin with a discussion of service-related policies for children with developmental disabilities and their families. Next, we review the theoretical and empirical literature on the relation between family functioning and the development of children with disabilities. Third, we consider the importance of cultural perspectives in terms of parental goals, the meanings parents ascribe to a disability, family relationships, and patterns of communication. In the final section, we discuss implications for service provision. We are limiting this review to children with biologically based cognitive disabilities; others (e.g., Farran, 2000; Halpern, 2000) provide

AUTHORS' NOTE: Preparation of this chapter was partially supported by Grant No. R40 MC 00177 from the Maternal and Child Health Bureau (Title V, Social Security Act), Health Resources and Services Administration, U.S. Department of Health and Human Services, and by a grant from the Argyelan Family Educational Research Fund.

extensive discussion about the service needs of children with developmental delays due to poverty and related adverse circumstances.

The term *developmental disabilities* is rarely defined but generally refers to individuals who are exhibiting unusual or delayed patterns of cognitive development. Children with mental retardation comprise a large proportion of those with developmental disabilities. Definitions of mental retardation were once based exclusively on cognitive performance but now include limitations in at least two adaptive skill areas (e.g., communication, self-care, social skills, daily living, and other similar domains) along with substantial deficits or delays in cognitive performance (American Association on Mental Retardation, 1992). Some maintain that categories such as developmental delay and mental retardation are socially constructed (Blatt, 1985), because the delineation between typical and atypical patterns of development is arbitrary and is based on ideals of age-appropriate behaviors and skills constructed by the dominant cultural group. Nevertheless, the current need for definitions is driven by requirements to determine which children are eligible for legally mandated services.

SERVICE-RELATED POLICIES FOR YOUNG CHILDREN WITH DISABILITIES

Throughout the 20th century, many policy changes related to children with disabilities occurred in the United States. At the beginning of the century, children with disabilities were often housed in crowded institutions in which they received custodial care, little or no education, and were isolated from the rest of society (Meisels & Shonkoff, 2000). Isolation and forced sterilization were common practices based on beliefs about the link between mental retardation and criminal behavior (Kamin, 1974). More benevolent attitudes

toward those with disabilities emerged at the end of World War II, when citizens encountered and knew many disabled veterans. Further stimulated by the Civil Rights movement of the 1950s and 1960s, along with optimism about the malleability of intelligence generated by psychologists such as D.O. Hebb (1949), J. McVicker Hunt (1961), and Benjamin Bloom (1964), a change in public opinion occurred about the potential benefits of public services for the positive development of children with disabilities. In the 1970s, deinstitutionalization became an important movement, and families increasingly reared children with disabilities at home rather than placing them in institutions (Lakin, Bruininks, & Larson, 1992). As a result, service needs for young children changed from being institution based to being family focused.

Educational initiatives also reflected a change in public policies for children with disabilities. Beginning in 1975 with the Education of All Handicapped Children Act, legislation focused on the education of children of traditional school age with disabilities in the "least restrictive environment." Other important legislation followed, including the Education for All Handicapped Children Act Amendments of 1986, which mandated "free and appropriate" education for 3- and 4-year-olds with disabilities and encouraged (but did not mandate) states to provide early intervention services for children with disabilities from birth. This marked the first time that public educational services applied to children of preschool age. The act was reauthorized in 1990, renamed the Individuals with Disabilities Education Act (IDEA). Legislation passed in 1997 reauthorized IDEA and included a component, Part C, which is an optional program for infants and toddlers. Although Part C is voluntary, all states and territories are currently participating and have developed statewide systems of early intervention services for infants and toddlers with developmental delays or diagnosed disabilities and their families.

One important aspect of Part C is the requirement that early intervention programs develop an individualized family service plan (IFSP) for each family enrolled. This plan differs from the individualized education plan (IEP), which is developed for preschool and older children served by public schools through its focus on the family, rather than only on the child. For example, an IFSP may contain information about how a family's strengths could be used to enhance a child's language development. The family is considered central to the optimal development of young children, and the requirement to develop an IFSP stems from an ecological and contextual perspective of child development.

THE RELATION BETWEEN THE FAMILY SYSTEM AND CHILDREN'S DEVELOPMENT: THEORETICAL PERSPECTIVES AND EMPIRICAL EVIDENCE

The family is the primary context in which most young children learn and are nurtured (Bronfenbrenner, 1986). Relationships within families are complex and multidirectional; children affect the well-being of their siblings, parents, and other caregivers, and those individuals also influence children's development (Minuchin, 1988). Furthermore, these relationships are dynamic because constantly changing needs and influences affect the family over time (Lerner, 1991). The quality of these relationships is central to children's development (National Research Council and Institute of Medicine, 2000). In this section, we review theoretical and empirical work on the relation between the development of children with disabilities and the family system in which they are nurtured.

The family relationship most investigated in studies of children with developmental

disabilities is the one between the primary caregiver, usually the mother, and the child. In contrast, little evidence exists about the father-child relationship, even though fathers are often highly involved caregivers (Lamb & Billings, 1997). Drawing from the large body of research on relationships between mothers and their typically developing children, studies of the mother-child dyad in families in which the child has a disability have been guided by a transactional model (Sameroff & Chandler, 1975). This theoretical framework describes a dynamic interactive process through which reciprocal interaction of the mother-infant dyad continues to exhibit more complex behaviors over time and across contexts (Sameroff & Fiese, 2000). The mother-child relationship is important in its own right, as well as being predictive of social and cognitive development of children born full term or with low birthweight (Landry, Smith, Miller-Loncar, & Swank, 1997) and of children with developmental disabilities (Hauser-Cram, Warfield, Shonkoff, & Krauss, 2001).

Mothers, of course, have a larger range and repertoire of responses than do their infants. Through the early social signals of infants, mothers begin to understand their children's temperaments and usually become proficient at responding to their children's needs. The contingency of a mother's response to her child regulates the child's future behaviors as the child begins to recognize the relation between his or her actions and the responses of others (Goldberg, 1977). A mother's sensitivity and contingent responsiveness to her child's social signals are essential for the infant's development of security and attachment, which in turn supports the child's exploration of the environment and development of autonomy (Bell & Ainsworth, 1972). In contrast, mothers who exhibit high levels of control or intrusion into children's play diminish children's motivation to explore objects and the environment and reduce children's opportunities to develop self-efficacy (Heckhausen, 1993).

Thus, the quality of the mother-child transaction is central to children's optimal development (Guralnick, 2001). Referring to the rhythmic interactive pattern between mother and child as a "dance between partners," Barnard (1997) emphasized the importance of contingent responding of both partners. When one partner consistently leads, the mutuality of the relationship is diminished and the tempo is disrupted. Several researchers have reported that such disruption often occurs in dyads in which the child has a disability (Kelly & Barnard, 2000).

Investigators have reported that mothers of children with disabilities tend to adopt directive and controlling styles of interaction with their children (McCollum & Hemmeter, 1997). For example, Eheart (1982) reported that even during free play, mothers of preschool children with Down syndrome tended to instruct their children about the appropriate use of toys more often than did mothers of typically developing preschoolers.

Many researchers have focused on maternal interactive patterns with children with Down syndrome, and they suggest that children's developmental delays may make their signals difficult for parents to read. For example, Berger (1990) found that children with Down syndrome were beginning to develop eye contact at the chronological age typically developing children are using referential eye contact to engage their caregivers. Harris (1992) reported that the delayed use of referential eye contact by infants with Down syndrome elicited less verbal interactions from mothers, which in turn contributed to fewer verbal learning opportunities for the child. Others have reported that children with Down syndrome demonstrate fewer appropriate social signals (Beeghly, Perry, & Cicchetti, 1989) and have less predictable responses to caregivers (Landry & Chapieski, 1990).

The interactive relationships of children with autism and their caregivers also have been studied fairly extensively. Young children with autism often display minimal interest in people, rarely make eye contact or respond to caregivers' attempts to engage them in play (Hoppes & Harris, 1990). These behaviors may reduce the opportunities of infants with autism to engage their caregivers in "joint attention" necessary for language development. The diminished responsiveness of children with autism has been reported by parents to violate their expectations and reduce their perceptions of attachment to their children (Hoppes & Harris, 1990).

Some researchers maintain that the high levels of directiveness observed in mothers of children with developmental disabilities reflect an adaptive response by mothers to their children's competence (Marfo, 1990). For example, Crawley and Spiker (1983) found that parents were more directive of children who showed less interest in play and initiated fewer interactions. Tannock (1988) found that maternal directives assisted children with Down syndrome in participating more fully in the interaction. Thus, caregivers tend to provide more directives to children who are less responsive in attempts to engage them more fully in the ongoing activity.

Other investigators suggest that maternal directiveness may indicate diminished sensitivity of mothers to the abilities of their children with developmental disabilities. Mahoney, Fors, and Wood (1990) reported that during observations of free play, mothers of children with Down syndrome directed their children's attention away from objects they were playing with and toward potentially overly challenging tasks. In contrast, mothers of typically developing children (of similar mental age) were more focused on supporting the activities that engaged their children at the moment. These findings indicate that mothers of children with developmental disabilities may gear their behavior toward instruction but also may have difficulty judging the appropriate degree of scaffolding required by the children.

Marfo (1990) argues that directiveness is only one dimension of a complex system of interactive behaviors. Caregiver responsiveness and support are other critical dimensions less often investigated. In a study of maternal interactive behaviors with children with Down syndrome, chronologically matched peers, and mental-age-matched peers, Roach, Barratt, Miller, and Leavitt (1998) found that mothers of children with Down syndrome demonstrated both more directiveness and more supportiveness. Directives tended to occur within a supportive context in which mothers facilitated children's play by moving or steadying objects, for example, and by providing vocal praise. They further reported that maternal supports were associated with more object play and vocalization. Thus, the combination of directives and supports may be central to the development of beneficial interactive patterns between caregivers and young children with developmental disabilities.

The caregiver-child dyadic relationship occurs within the larger system of the family. Children affect their mothers and other members of the family system, including fathers and siblings. Historically, research on the effects of a child with disabilities on the family has been based on an assumption that such children disrupt and distort family life (Gallimore, Bernheimer, & Weisner, 1999). Many researchers have focused on documenting deleterious outcomes of various family members, a trend that can diminish the ability of service providers and families to recognize family strengths and develop productive partnerships (Turnbull, Turbiville, & Turnbull, 2000).

Four theoretical perspectives have guided investigations of families in which children have developmental disabilities: stage theory models, stress and coping models, family systems models, and social-ecological models. During the 1960s and 1970s, a *stage theory model* (i.e., a predictable sequence of patterns) was used to explain the patterns of adjustment that parents pass through when coping with the birth or diagnosis of a child with disabilities (Blacher, 1984). This model was influenced by reports of clinically observed stages of grieving after the death of a close family member. An assumption was made that parents of children with disabilities also experience similar grief for their longed-for typical children (e.g., Solnit & Stark, 1961). Generally, three stages were delineated. In the first stage, parents experience disbelief and often "shop" for physicians and treatments. The second stage is characterized by guilt, anger, and disappointment. In the third stage, parents reorient themselves toward adjustment and acceptance and often become advocates for their children and others with disabilities. The empirical evidence for these stages is weak (Blacher, 1984), and scholarship has turned toward understanding parental adaptation and accommodation rather than documenting parental reactions according to characteristics of purported stages.

The *ABCX model of family adaptation* (Hill, 1949) has stimulated much research over the last two decades. According to this model, the adaptation of the family to an event such as the birth of a child with a disability is postulated to be explained by several factors, including the meaning ascribed to the child's disability and the internal and external resources of the family. An expanded version of this model, the *double ABCX model,* includes a developmental component stipulating that families change over time in terms of their stressors, resources, and the meaning ascribed to the children (McCubbin & Patterson, 1982).

Several researchers have compared stress in parents of children with disabilities to that reported by other parents. Studies have been fairly consistent in finding normative levels of stress reported during the infancy period (Shonkoff, Hauser-Cram, Krauss, & Upshur, 1992), followed by increasing stress levels during early childhood (Innocenti, Huh, & Boyce, 1992), and high stress levels during middle childhood (Warfield, Krauss, Hauser-Cram, Upshur, & Shonkoff, 1999). Middle childhood appears to be a particularly vulnerable time for parents of children with disabilities; stress levels are higher than at any other childhood phase (Orr, Cameron, Dobson, & Day, 1993). Middle childhood may be a particularly vulnerable period for parents because they expect children's behaviors to be better regulated than in earlier years.

Research indicates that parent stress levels are related to children's self-regulatory behaviors and temperament rather than to the tasks of parenting per se (Innocenti et al., 1992; Warfield et al., 1999). The internal (i.e., psychological) and external (i.e., social support) resources of parents also relate to the increase in stress experienced by parents during the middle-childhood period. Mothers with more satisfying social support networks and fathers with higher levels of problem-focused coping strategies experience comparatively fewer increases in stress related to their children with disabilities from early to middle childhood than do other parents (Hauser-Cram et al., 2001).

Although fathers' perspectives are often neglected in research on children with disabilities (Lamb & Billings, 1997), a few researchers have investigated whether parenting stress differs for fathers and mothers. Some have found that maternal and paternal stress levels are similar in families with children with disabilities (e.g., Dyson, 1997; Roach, Orsmond, & Barratt, 1999). In contrast, Scott, Atkinson, Minton, and Bowman (1997) reported that mothers evinced more psychological stress than fathers. Krauss (1993) found that during the early years, fathers reported more stress related to their

children's temperaments and self-regulatory behaviors, whereas mothers reported more stress related to the parenting role (i.e., their own emotional resources and adjustments to providing children's caregiving needs). Increases in stress levels of both mothers and fathers, however, appear to be more consistently related to children's behavior problems than to the type of disability or extent of cognitive delay (Hauser-Cram et al., 2001).

Parenting stress is only one aspect of parent well-being, however. *Family systems theory* posits a broad conceptual model of family processes that relate to the well-being of both parents and children. From this perspective, the family is considered to be an open, interactive system that operates according to a generalized set of principles (Walsh, 1980). Changes in one family member affect changes among other members, producing multiple iterative responses. Thus, rather than focusing on unidirectional effects of a particular child on the family, those operating from the family systems perspective consider simultaneous, multiple, and iterative effects of family members on each other (Minuchin, 1988).

Although many researchers emphasize the value of a family systems perspective, few investigators have rigorously employed this model in empirical studies of families in which a child has a disability. The work of Mink and Nihira (1986) is unique because they have developed a series of family typologies based on the psychosocial environment of the home. They found that children with mild mental retardation had more positive self-esteem and social adjustment when they lived in more cohesive families. Their development of typologies serves as a useful model for researchers who want to move away from unidimensional questions about whether having a child with a disability affects a family to broader questions about the "fit" between the functioning of the child and the family.

From the vantage point of developmental systems theory, the family system itself operates within multilayered interacting systems (Bronfenbrenner, 1986; Lerner, 1991). Multiple systems are involved when families make accommodations to sustain the daily routines for any child (Weisner, 1993). In making arrangements for children's daily lives, parents make decisions that involve many *social-ecological systems,* including, for example, their employment, children's schooling, and community services. Gallimore and colleagues (Gallimore, Coots, Weisner, Garnier, & Guthrie, 1996) investigated the functional adjustments that families make to sustain their daily routines when raising children with disabilities. For example, parents may need to make adaptations in the home for a child with a motor impairment or may adapt their employment schedules to meet a child's medical needs. Gallimore and colleagues found that although parents made a wide range of accommodations during early childhood, they needed to make an even greater number of accommodations during the middle-childhood period. The manner in which families organize their daily activities and the meaning they attribute to their patterns of organization are essential to achieve a fuller understanding of family functioning (Gallimore et al., 1999).

In all four theoretical perspectives discussed above, the focus of research has been on the child with a disability, the mother, and to a lesser extent, the father. Siblings, however, are also an integral part of the family. Similar to early studies of parents of children with disabilities, investigations of siblings have often focused on potential pathology. Typically developing siblings were considered to be at risk for maladjustment as a consequence of the chronic stress, social stigma, and responsibilities associated with the care of brothers or sisters with disabilities (e.g., Farber, 1959). Most recent reviews of empirical research on sibling

relations, however, indicate equivocal support for the hypothesis that siblings of children with disabilities assume greater caregiving or are at greater risk for psychopathology (Damiani, 1999; Stoneman, 1998). In fact, some researchers report that typically developing siblings demonstrate more prosocial behaviors, greater maturity, patience, and a deeper understanding of individual differences than do their peers (Dyson, 1989). Some adolescent and adult siblings have indicated that the experience of living with a brother or sister with mental retardation helped them to develop greater empathy and appreciation of family relationships (Eisenberg, Baker, & Blacher, 1998).

The adjustment of siblings is related to multiple factors, including the severity of the brother's or sister's disability, the temperament of each sibling, as well as behavioral, psychological, and health problems related to the sibling's disability (Stoneman, 1998). In particular, siblings appear to have more difficult adjustments when their brothers or sisters with disabilities exhibit behavior problems (Brody, Stoneman, & Burke, 1987). Children with certain disabilities, such as Fragile X syndrome or autism, are more likely to display maladaptive behaviors and thus make the sibling relationship potentially problematic. When a child exhibits difficult behaviors, parents often expend more resources caring for that child, which results in differential treatment of siblings (Corter, Pepler, Stanhope, & Abramovitch, 1992). Perceived discrepancies in the attention parents give to their children can lead to more conflictual interaction between siblings and less prosocial behavior of typically developing siblings (Brody et al., 1987). Siblings of children with developmental disabilities, however, may adjust to such discrepancies as they come to understand the legitimacy of their siblings' needs and attribute differential attention, rather than parental favoritism, to those needs (McHale & Pawletko, 1992).

Older sisters of children with developmental disabilities often have greater child care responsibilities than other children. When examined longitudinally, these greater responsibilities have been associated with increased sibling conflict and reduced time socializing with friends outside the home (Stoneman, 1998). When the abilities of younger, typically developing siblings surpass those of older siblings with developmental delays, younger siblings often experience role reversal. These younger siblings often assume more teaching and helping roles than is found in other families (Brody, Stoneman, Davis, & Crapps, 1991).

The functioning of the larger family system appears to be especially important for the positive adjustment of typically developing siblings. Lynch, Fay, Funk, and Nagel (1993) found that conflict between parents and disorganized family functioning were associated with poor sibling outcomes. In contrast, parents who perceive their children with disabilities and the functioning of their families more positively tend to have typically developing children with more positive feelings about their families and better psychological adjustment (Weinger, 1999). Thus, sibling relationships may be sensitive to behavior problems and to caregiving responsibilities, but the ways in which the family functions and copes with those behaviors and responsibilities relate to positive outcomes of all family members.

A CULTURAL PERSPECTIVE ON FAMILIES OF CHILDREN WITH DISABILITIES

Most of the research studies on families of children with disabilities (described in the prior section) are based on families of Euro-American descent. Given the changing demographic makeup of this country, in which ethnic, cultural, and linguistic variation has

increased substantially (U.S. Bureau of the Census, 2001), a broader understanding of families of children with disabilities is needed.

Individuals usually have been the primary unit of analysis in developmental psychology. Child development research has often relegated the pervasive influence of culture to a marginal entity or conceptualized it as an aspect of context that mediates developmental outcomes (Garcia Coll & Magnuson, 2000). A contrasting and growing view, however, is that culture is an organizing principle of development (Valsiner, 1989). From that perspective, culture is defined as a multifaceted construct that serves to organize multiple dynamic systems of meaning for individuals, such as values, beliefs, and expectations. These systems of meanings are transmitted through social groups but constantly evolve as individuals construct meaning from their experiences in the environment (Super & Harkness, 1997; Valsiner & Litvinovic, 1996). Individuals often belong to more than one social group, and thus, culture involves levels of shared discourse and practices related to one's religious affiliation, socioeconomic status, and occupation (Harwood, Miller, & Irizarry, 1995). Although many aspects of culturally related dynamics are integral to parenting a child with a disability, in this section, we highlight four areas that have implications for service provision: (a) parents' goals for their children, (b) the meaning ascribed to a child's disability, (c) family relationships, and (d) patterns of communication.

Parents' Goals for Their Children

LeVine and his colleagues suggest that parental goals consist of culturally shared assumptions about skills and values necessary for children to become well-functioning adults (LeVine et al., 1994). Such assumptions are often unconscious or transparent to their users. Historically, there has been an implicit assumption within the field of developmental psychology that the values and practices of educated white middle-class North Americans constitute the optimal environment for children's development (Patterson & Blum, 1993). This view is reflected by interventions that seek to enlighten parents from minority groups about the behaviors and practices reflected in white middle-class values (Garcia Coll & Magnuson, 2000). Child-rearing practices and parental values that differ from mainstream Euro-American culture have been considered deficient, rather than alternative, pathways to normal development (Patterson & Blum, 1993). For example, cosleeping between parents and infants is common in countries throughout the world, reflecting values of close physical proximity that foster strong emotional bonds between mother and child (Morelli, Rogoff, Oppenheim, & Goldsmith, 1992). Among some Euro-Americans, however, this practice breaches cultural taboos of appropriate physical intimacy and is thought to stifle the development of independence in children, which is a highly valued trait in this culture (Morelli et al., 1992).

The assumption that Western practices and values are optimal for children's development is reflected in many standardized tests that use developmental milestones of Euro-American children as standards for normative behavior (Garcia Coll, Meyer, & Brillon, 1995). Some have argued that the conceptualization of "normative behavior" is a social construction created by members of a dominant culture who transmit the necessary knowledge to members of that culture, providing them with the resources to succeed in society. If this implicit knowledge is not transmitted to members of minority groups, it diminishes their power and resources (Delpit, 1995). Children with disabilities from minority or immigrant groups face double jeopardy because their disabilities as well as

their cultural behaviors may not meet narrow mainstream standards of development.

The cultural values of parents and professionals are likely to influence the goals that each perceives to be most crucial for a child and the needs they identify. For example, parents from cultures that value harmony among all members of a family, and especially between different generations, may seek to instill an understanding of respect and social hierarchy in their children. The goals of these parents may reflect a desire for their children to learn behaviors that demonstrate respect and deference to elders. These goals may differ from those of Euro-Americans who foster the development of independent decision making and self-assertion among children (Zuniga, 1998). Similarly, professionals from Euro-American backgrounds may expect parents and children to exhibit behaviors associated with their own values, such as maintaining direct eye contact and asserting one's opinion during conversations. These behaviors, however, may directly oppose the values held by the family. Likewise, parents who value cooperation more than competition between individuals may focus their parenting goals on the development of interpersonal skills in their children more than on the timely achievement of other cognitive milestones (Zuniga, 1998).

The transmission of parenting and socialization practices are guided in part by cultural values and in part by parents' active construction of the demands of the social context (LeVine et al., 1994). Parents must choose strategies that solve the needs of the immediate situation. Their decisions, however, also reflect future goals they have for their children with disabilities in relation to the well-being of the family system. These goals can range from securing the basic safety of their children to ensuring that their children develop the skills necessary to flourish in their future and in accordance with cultural values (LeVine et al., 1994).

Parents of children with disabilities often face uncertain futures for their children, and some seek to foster behaviors that increase the likelihood of their children being accepted and cared for by others in the future. For example, Arcia, Reyes-Blanes, and Vazquez-Montilla (2000) found that Puerto Rican and Mexican mothers of young children with Down syndrome, cerebral palsy, and spina bifida emphasized the value of respectful, compliant behavior and wanted their children to develop a sense of right and wrong, be respectful and responsible, and be close to the family. These highly valued characteristics reflect behaviors that would be adaptive and support their acceptance by others in the classroom and in related settings.

The personal experience of having a child with a disability also may influence the values and goals of parents. For example, in one study, Quirk and colleagues (Quirk, Sexton, Ciottone, Minami, & Wapner, 1984) found that Puerto Rican mothers of children with disabilities valued health and creativity more than did Puerto Rican mothers of nondisabled children; however, they reported few other differences within ethnic groups. Other studies have not found the role of disability to affect cultural values (e.g., Arcia et al., 2000). More often, studies have shown that cultural values influence the meaning parents ascribe to their children's disabilities, which can in turn influence the internal and external resources available to them for the care of their children (Blacher, Lopez, Shapiro, & Fusco, 1997).

The Meaning Parents Ascribe to a Child's Disability

Cultural values influence the meaning that parents ascribe to a child's disability and their role as parents of a child with special needs. Individuals differ in the extent to which they attribute the etiology of disability to fatalistic determination, spiritual intervention, biological chance, or personal responsibility.

Cultural beliefs and expectations about children's illnesses or disabilities influence parents' perceptions of their ability to influence the course of their children's development. Mardiros (1989) found that parents of children with disabilities who believed that their children's disabilities were the result of fatalistic or supernatural forces perceived themselves to have less control over their children's outcomes. Alternatively, parents who viewed their children's disabilities as punishment for their own personal actions were more likely to assume greater roles in helping their children develop positively (Mardiros, 1989).

Sometimes, cultural beliefs about etiology and treatment of a disability are distinctly different from those held by personnel in the mainstream service system. Fadiman (1997) describes the misunderstandings and clashes that occurred between a Hmong family whose child had epilepsy and the medical system they encountered in the United States. The parents viewed the cause of their child's disorder, which they described as a "loss of soul," as the result of a fright from the abrupt sound of a door slamming shut. Furthermore, they considered their daughter's condition to be a possible indication that she might become a shaman, a person of great respect in her community, because of her trancelike state and potential ability to see things others cannot see. They viewed healing as a holistic and spiritual matter not restricted to the taking of medication, especially preventative medications that have potentially deleterious side effects. In contrast, the Western physicians considered the parents' unwillingness to treat their child with medications that might stabilize or prevent seizures as a lack of compliance and eventually, a sign of neglect. Even when interpreters were available to assist communication between the family and Western medical personnel, the distinct belief system of each culture and the lack of knowledge of each other's belief system prevented a collaborative relationship.

The construction of meaning is dynamic, evolving through transactional interactions between individuals across multiple systems (Bronfenbrenner, 1986). For example, a parent's conception of disability may be influenced by interactions with members of their ethnic group, their religious identity, as well as their exposure to mainstream beliefs about disability. Skinner and colleagues (Skinner, Bailey, Correa, & Rodriguez, 1999) found that Catholic Latino mothers of children with disabilities differed in the extent to which they incorporated religious beliefs into the meaning they ascribed to disability and its relation to their role as parent. Some mothers incorporated the religious image of a "good mother" into their descriptions of themselves, one who sacrifices herself for the sake of caring for her children. These mothers rejected religious conceptions of disabilities as representing punishment for their sins. Many retained positive images of themselves as morally virtuous and viewed their children as symbols of God's belief in their strength and capability to care for their children's special needs. Other mothers believed that disability was the consequence of personal transgressions. They also, however, described their personal meaning of disability as providing positive transformations in their identities as advocates and more compassionate persons. In general, religious and cultural beliefs were reported by mothers to increase their internal strength and support their parenting practices.

Family Relationships

Consistent with current models of family adaptation (e.g., McCubbin & Patterson, 1982), cultural values can influence the internal (e.g., psychological well-being) and external resources (social support) available for a family. For example, interdependence among

individuals is exhibited in the value of *familism* in Latino culture, which represents loyalty and solidarity among nuclear and extended family members who rely on each other for support (Zuniga, 1998). Some practices associated with familism can serve as sources of strength for families of children with disabilities. For example, extended family members are reported to provide emotional support, which has been found to reduce stress among Mexican American mothers of children with developmental disabilities (Shapiro & Tittle, 1990). Alternatively, lack of solidarity among Latino families with children with mental retardation has been associated with higher rates of depression among mothers (Blacher et al., 1997). Similarly, South Asian mothers of children with developmental delays reported that a lack of extended family members contributed to their feelings of loneliness and dissatisfaction with social support (Raghavan, Weisner, & Patel, 1999).

Cultures that have broad definitions of family may include extended family members, such as grandparents, or non-kin, such as unofficially adopted children or godparents. Joe and Malach (1998) found that the extended family often plays a central role in obtaining and organizing services for children with disabilities among Native American cultures. Collectivist values of interdependence between family members may help to strengthen family relationships through various pathways, such as honoring of family obligations and self-sacrifice of family members for the sake of the family unit. The practices associated with these values can, however, exact a cost from parents in terms of time and effort. Turnbull, Blue-Banning, and Pereira (2000) found that extended family social networks provided the main source of friendship for many children with disabilities. Yet mothers reported that the time required to foster these family relationships reduced opportunities avail-able to help their children develop social networks outside the family. The manner in which familism and related values influence caregiving practices is important for professionals to understand; it remains a core value for many families in the United States despite different levels of acculturation (Zuniga, 1998).

The role of cultural factors in a family system is dynamic and likely to change across the family life span. Valsiner and Litvinovic (1996) emphasized that humans are "innovating carriers of the collective culture" (p. 61) as they actively reconstruct and reinterpret expectations on the basis of new experiences and unique characteristics of each situation. For example, Magana (1999) found that self-sacrifice among mothers for the sake of their children *(marianismo)* is strongly valued among some Catholic Latino families. Although this value contributes to positive maternal caregiving practices among mothers of young children with disabilities, it has also been associated with poorer health among Puerto Rican mothers of adults with mental retardation (Magana, 1999). Cultural values of familism and marianismo may contribute to positive functioning and cohesion among families with young children but may also be less adaptive as mothers age and members of the nuclear family assume their own family responsibilities.

Patterns of Communication

From a socioecological perspective, culture is embodied in a social context that pervades all aspects of an individual's life, guiding the ways people interpret and act in varied situations and influencing patterns of behavior and communication (Super & Harkness, 1997). In some cultures, communication patterns require that an individual's position in a social hierarchy (e.g., elder vs. younger person) be acknowledged (Hecht, Andersen, & Ribeau, 1989), or misunderstandings can result. For example, Fadiman (1997)

described how a physician's decision to communicate to younger rather than elder members of a family violated the social expectations in Hmong culture even though the younger members had greater facility with English. Furthermore, nonverbal aspects of communication, such as body stance, facial expressions, eye contact, and gestures often have different interpretations in different cultural groups (Hecht et al., 1989). If service providers are unaware of their own styles of communication and how they differ from the ones valued by the families whom they serve, miscommunication can result.

Cultural values influence parents' engagement in collaboration with professionals in planning and implementing services for their children. Individuals' cultural meanings are influenced by processes occurring between and within individuals in dynamic and constantly unique environments (Valsiner & Litvinovic, 1996). Garcia Coll and Magnuson (2000) suggest that cultural differences can become "risk factors" when they are misunderstood and confounded by socioeconomic status. For example, Harry (1992) found that passivity demonstrated by some African American and Puerto Rican parents of children with disabilities reflected their feelings of powerlessness over their children's programs. Parents who were unhappy with their children's programs demonstrated their disagreement by refusing to attend meetings or sign forms, rather than engaging in active confrontation with teachers. Many mothers reported that the collaborative process only minimally involved their informed consent and that they did not feel empowered to question the authority of the group of professionals, whom together, mothers viewed as wielding much greater power than an individual mother could independently.

Lack of understanding about cultural patterns of communication can impede collaboration efforts. In a 3-year longitudinal study, Harry, Allen, and McLaughlin (1995) interviewed African American mothers of preschool children with various disabilities and found that reliance on written communication, the use of unexplained jargon, and differences in the goals of parents and professionals deterred true collaboration. When mothers' conceptualizations of their childrens' programs differed from the ones provided by school personnel, mothers became disillusioned and less willing to engage in collaboration. For example, some mothers believed that the goal of preschool special education was to give children a chance to catch up with their peers. Mothers were upset when they realized that their preschoolers were increasingly stigmatized by the experience of being labeled as mentally retarded and placed in self-contained classrooms with older children who had more serious behavioral problems. A focus on labeling children's deficits rather than promoting their strengths and the failure of professionals to respect cultural differences in parenting, such as the involvement of extended family, were reported as deterrents to communication.

IMPLICATIONS FOR SERVICE PROVISION

Services provided to young children with disabilities are best conceptualized as systems designed to support families in ways that promote children's development (Guralnick, 2001). Such services often concern basic care issues such as sleeping, feeding, and health, which reflect the cultural beliefs, values, and practices of a family. Parent-child interactions occur within a family system that functions according to certain daily routines developed to accommodate the needs of many family members, including the child with disabilities. Despite strong evidence of the importance of growth-promoting parent-child (especially mother-child) interaction,

focusing on those interaction patterns without paying attention to parents' goals, values, and beliefs is misguided. Similarly unfounded are attempts to assist parents in diminishing their levels of stress without understanding (a) the relation of parent well-being to internal and external resources and (b) family values related to those resources. Intervention in the form of support to families involves an understanding of the complex developmental system.

In the case of young children with developmental disabilities, collaboration between parents and service providers often occurs at a time when parents are focusing on their children's daily needs. Differences in communication styles between professionals and parents can create fertile ground for tension and misunderstandings to develop. Cultural collisions may be most likely during periods in which parents must make crucial decisions that evoke anxiety and strong emotions (Hanson, 1998). One factor that underlies these patterns of communication is the difference in the value placed on time between Euro-Americans and members of other cultural groups. An orientation to the future and a preoccupation with managing time and achieving multiple tasks within a given period are predominant in the values of Euro-Americans, but this may clash with families who place greater value on fostering interpersonal understanding and trust between parents and professionals through conversation and casual exchange (Zuniga, 1998). Although professionals often have multiple responsibilities that must be fulfilled within limited time, the burden of adjusting one's style must not be placed solely on the parent (Harry, 1992). Rather, cultural understanding requires professionals to adapt their agendas to match the styles and tempos of families.

Another example of potential mismatch between service providers and families relates to male and female roles and power structures within families. Equality between sexes is often valued among Euro-Americans, which influences their expectations that a family structure will be democratic. Euro-Americans who work with culturally diverse families may anticipate shared decision making between spouses but may find that some families, such as those from some Middle Eastern cultures, value differential status between the sexes (Sharifzadeh, 1998). Social hierarchies play important roles in some families and guide interactions among members in ways that Euro-American service providers may misunderstand or overlook.

Cultural understanding involves facilitating meaningful communication and relationships related to the delivery of services in ways that are respectful of the cultural heritage of the family (Roberts, 1989). Although such understanding involves more than sensitivity to the families, little scientific evidence is available about the way this can be accomplished (National Research Council and Institute of Medicine, 2000). Agreement centers on the need for service providers to recognize their own cultural values, assumptions, and beliefs and to understand how those concepts influence their interactions with members of other cultural groups. In this regard, Hanson (1998) suggests that mentoring relationships with members of different cultures can assist professionals in reflecting on their own cultural perspectives.

Training in cultural understanding that involves making generalizations about specific cultural groups can result in the development of stereotypes, however. This is especially detrimental to the understanding of muticulturalism as the structures of families in the United States become progressively more diverse, more often representing bicultural marriages and blended cultural values and practices. The factors that influence individuals are dynamic and vary both within and between cultural groups, such as degree of acculturation,

socioeconomic status, occupation, and religious identity (Harwood et al., 1995). Skinner and colleagues (Skinner et al., 1999) suggest that one way to minimize the construction of stereotypes is to learn to listen to family stories as a way of gaining a perspective on parents' values and meaning systems. Researchers are increasingly acknowledging the power of personal narratives as important markers of family relationships (Fiese et al., 1999), and service providers who attempt to understand the meaning-making process in families may be more able to engage in true collaboration.

What are some ways early intervention services could more fully incorporate cultural perspective? First, involving community members in planning the range of services offered by early intervention programs and recruiting professionals and paraprofessionals from targeted cultural groups are critical steps. Positive relationships between early intervention programs, local community groups, and respected community leaders need to be created. The need for productive relationships between early intervention personnel and medical and school personnel is fundamental to most early intervention programs. The need to develop strong relationships with other community groups and leaders, however, is equally important, especially in diverse communities.

Second, service providers would benefit from experiences that make their own assumptions, for example, about how children develop and optimal child-rearing styles, *apparent* rather than *transparent*. Although no experience substitutes for that of actually living in a culture quite distinct from one's own, service providers might benefit from learning techniques that allow them to gain knowledge and perspective from personal narratives. Such techniques involve the ability to listen not only to the words of the stories but also to the meaning behind the words (Skinner et al., 1999). Personal stories indicate how parents make meaning of their children's development, but they also suggest ways in which parents cope and the strengths they bring to parenting experience.

Third, based on a medical anthropological perspective, Kleinman, Eisenberg, and Good (1978) suggest that physicians develop questions to elicit a patient's explanatory model of a particular illness. The physician then makes explicit his or her model of healing and negotiates a shared model with the patient. A similar approach could be taken by individuals providing services to families of children with disabilities. Early intervention service providers could develop questions aimed at understanding how parents perceive their children's delayed development, experiences parents consider beneficial to their children's development, and the way parents see their family supporting their children's potential trajectory. Because parents' theories of development are important frameworks within which early intervention services work, understanding those theories is a central part of the collaboration between families and service providers.

Finally, service providers might benefit from a collection of examples in which potential collisions between families and service providers were averted. For example, Fadiman (1997) describes several examples in which medical personnel worked within families' belief systems to assist the individual who was ill, sometimes necessitating changes in the processes by which the physicians usually worked. A collection of positive examples in which early intervention personnel have also revised their standard practices in ways that support family beliefs and benefit children would be advantageous to the field.

In conclusion, research clearly points to the importance of the family system in promoting the positive development of children with developmental disabilities, their siblings, and their mothers and fathers. The cultural beliefs, values, and practices of the family are an integral part of that system. Recognition and knowledge of the multiple and changing facets of the family system are essential for the promotion of positive development among all children, including those with developmental disabilities.

REFERENCES

American Association on Mental Retardation. (1992). *Mental retardation: Definition, classification, and systems of supports* (9th ed.). Washington, DC: Author.

America's Children 1999. *Key indicators of well-being.* Retrieved on November 18, 1999, from the World Wide Web at http://www.childstats.gov/ac1999/toc.asp/.

Arcia, E., Reyes-Blanes, M. E., & Vazquez-Montilla, E. (2000). Constructions and reconstructions: Latino parents' values for children. *Journal of Child and Family Studies, 9,* 333-350.

Barnard, K. E. (1997). Influencing parent-child interactions for children at risk. In M. J. Guralnick (Ed.), *The effectiveness of early intervention* (pp. 249-268). Baltimore, MD: Brookes.

Beeghly, M., Perry, B. M., & Cicchetti, D. (1989). Structural and affective dimensions of play development in young children with Down syndrome. *International Journal of Behavioral Development, 12,* 257-277.

Bell, S. M., & Ainsworth, M. D. S. (1972). Infant crying and maternal responsiveness. *Child Development, 43,* 1171-1190.

Berger, J. (1990). Interactions between parents and their infants with Down syndrome. In D. Cicchetti & M. Beeghly (Eds.), *Children with Down syndrome: A developmental perspective* (pp. 101-146). New York: Cambridge University Press.

Blacher, J. (1984). Sequential stages of parental adjustment to the birth of a child with handicaps: Fact or artifact? *Mental Retardation, 22,* 55-68.

Blacher, J., Lopez, S., Shapiro, J., & Fusco, J. (1997). Contributions to depression in Latina mothers with and without children with retardation: Implications for caregiving. *Family Relationships, 46,* 325-334.

Blatt, B. (1985). The implications of the language of mental retardation for LD. *Journal of Learning Disabilities, 18,* 625-626.

Bloom, B. (1964). *Stability and change in human characteristics.* New York: Wiley.

Brody, G. H., Stoneman, Z., & Burke, M. (1987). Child temperaments, maternal differential behavior, and sibling relations. *Developmental Psychology, 23,* 354-362.

Brody, G. H., Stoneman, Z., Davis, C. H., & Crapps, J. M. (1991). Observations of the role relations and behavior between older children with mental retardation and their younger siblings. *American Journal on Mental Retardation, 95,* 527-536.

Bronfenbrenner, U. (1986). Ecology of the family as a context for human development: Research perspectives. *Developmental Psychology, 22,* 723-742.

Corter, C., Pepler, D., Stanhope, L., & Abramovitch, R. (1992). Home observations of mothers and sibling dyads comprised of Down's syndrome and nonhandicapped children. *Canadian Journal of Behavioural Science, 24,* 1-13.

Crawley, S. B., & Spiker, D. (1983). Mother-child interactions involving two-year olds with Down's syndrome: A look at individual differences. *Child Development, 54,* 1312-1323.

Damiani, V. B. (1999). Responsibility and adjustment in siblings of children with disabilities: Update and review. *Families in Society, 80,* 34-40.

Delpit, L. D. (1995). *Other people's children: Cultural conflict in the classroom.* New York: New Press.

Dyson, L. L. (1989). Adjustment of siblings of handicapped children: A comparison. *Journal of Pediatric Psychology, 14,* 215-229.

Dyson, L. L. (1997). Fathers and mothers of school-age children with developmental disabilities: Parental stress, family functioning, and social support. *American Journal on Mental Retardation, 102,* 267-279.

Education of All Handicapped Children Act, Pub. L. No. 94-142 (1975).

Education for All Handicapped Children Act Amendments of 1986, Pub. L. No. 99-457 (1986).

Eheart, B. K. (1982). Mother-child interactions with non-retarded and mentally retarded preschoolers. *American Journal of Mental Deficiency, 87,* 20-25.

Eisenberg, L., Baker, B. L., & Blacher, J. (1998). Siblings of children with mental retardation living at home or in residential placement. *Journal of Child Psychology and Psychiatry and Allied Disciplines, 39,* 355-363.

Fadiman, A. (1997). *The spirit catches you and you fall down: A Hmong child, her American doctors, and the collision of two cultures.* New York: Farrar, Strauss, & Giroux.

Farber, B. (1959). The effects of the severely retarded child on the family system. *Monographs of the Society for Research in Child Development, 24*(2, Serial No. 71).

Farran, D. C. (2000). Another decade of intervention for children who are low income or disabled: What do we know? In J. P. Shonkoff & S. J. Meisels (Eds.), *Handbook of early childhood intervention* (2nd ed., pp. 510-548). New York: Cambridge University Press.

Fiese, B. H., Sameroff, A. J., Grotevant, H. D., Wamboldt, F. S., Dickstein, S., & Fravel, D. L. (1999). The stories that families tell: Narrative coherence, narrative interaction, and relationship beliefs. *Monographs of the Society for Research in Child Development, 64*(2, Serial No. 257).

Gallimore, R., Bernheimer, L. P., & Weisner, T. S. (1999). Family life is more than managing crisis: Broadening the agenda of research on families adapting to childhood disability. In R. Gallimore, L. P. Bernheimer, D. L. MacMillan, D. L. Speece, & S. Vaughn (Eds.), *Developmental perspectives on children with high-incidence disabilities* (pp. 55-80). Mahwah, NJ: Lawrence Erlbaum.

Gallimore, R., Coots, J., Weisner, T., Garnier, H., & Guthrie, D. (1996). Family responses to children with early developmental delays, II: Accommodation intensity and activity in early and middle childhood. *American Journal on Mental Retardation, 101*, 215-232.

Garcia Coll, C. T., & Magnuson, K. (2000). Cultural differences as sources of developmental vulnerabilities and resources. In J. P. Shonkoff & S. J. Meisels (Eds.), *Handbook of early childhood intervention* (2nd ed., pp. 94-114). New York: Cambridge University Press.

Garcia Coll, C. T., Meyer, E. C., & Brillon, L. (1995). Ethnic and minority parenting. In M. H. Bornstein (Ed.), *Handbook of parenting: Vol. 2. Biology and ecology of parenting* (pp. 189-209). Mahwah, NJ: Lawrence Erlbaum.

Goldberg, S. (1977). Social competence in infancy: A model of parent-infant interaction. *Merrill-Palmer Quarterly, 29*, 163-177.

Guralnick, M. J. (2001). A developmental systems model for early intervention. *Infants and Young Children, 14*(2), 1-18.

Halpern, R. (2000). Early intervention for low-income children and families. In J. P. Shonkoff & S. J. Meisels (Eds.), *Handbook of early childhood intervention* (2nd ed., pp. 361-386). New York: Cambridge University Press.

Hanson, M. J. (1998). Ethnic, cultural and language diversity in intervention settings. In E. W. Lynch & M. J. Hanson (Eds.), *Developing cross-cultural competence: A guide for working with young children and their families.* (2nd ed., pp. 3-22). Baltimore, MD: Brookes.

Harris, M. (1992). *Language experience and early language development: From input to uptake.* Hillsdale, NJ: Lawrence Erlbaum.

Harry, B. (1992). An ethnographic study of cross-cultural communication with Puerto Rican-American families in the special education system. *American Educational Research Journal, 29*, 471-494.

Harry, B., Allen, N., & McLaughlin, M. (1995). Communication versus compliance: African-American parents' involvement in special education *Exceptional Children, 61*, 364-376.

Harwood, R. L., Miller, J. G., & Irizarry, N. L. (1995). *Culture and attachment: Perceptions of the child in context.* New York: Guilford.

Hauser-Cram, P., Warfield, M. E., Shonkoff, J. P., & Krauss, M. W. (with Sayer, A., & Upshur, C. C.). (2001). Children with disabilities: A longitudinal study of child development and parent well-being. *Monographs of the Society for Research in Child Development, 66*(3, Serial No. 266).

Hebb, D. O. (1949). *The organization of behavior: A neuropsychological theory.* New York: John Wiley.

Hecht, M. L., Andersen, P. A., & Ribeau, S. A. (1989). The cultural dimensions of nonverbal communication. In M. K. Asante & W. B. Gudykunst (Eds.), *Handbook of international and intercultural communication* (pp. 163-185). Beverly Hills, CA: Sage.

Heckhausen, J. (1993). The development of mastery and its perception within caretaker-child dyads. In D. J. Messer (Ed.), *Mastery motivation in early childhood: Development, measurement and social processes* (pp. 55-79). London: Routledge.

Hill, R. (1949). *Families under stress*. New York: Harper & Row.

Hoppes, K., & Harris, S. L. (1990). Perceptions of child attachment and maternal gratification in mothers of children with autism and Down syndrome. *Journal of Clinical Child Psychology, 19*, 365-370.

Hunt, J. M. (1961). *Intelligence and experience*. New York: Ronald.

Individuals With Disabilities Education Act, Pub. L. No. 101-476 §20 U.S.C. 1400 (1997).

Innocenti, M. S., Huh, K., & Boyce, G. (1992). Families of children with disabilities: Normative data and other considerations on parenting stress. *Topics in Early Childhood Special Education, 12*, 403-427.

Joe, J. R., & Malach, R. S. (1998). Families with Native American roots. In E. W. Lynch & M. J. Hanson (Eds.), *Developing cross-cultural competence: A guide for working with children and their families*. (2nd ed., pp.127-164). Baltimore, MD: Brookes.

Kamin, L. (1974). *The science and politics of IQ*. Potomac, MD: Lawrence Erlbaum.

Kelly, J. F., & Barnard, K. E. (2000). Assessment of parent-child interaction: Implications for early intervention. In J. Shonkoff & S. Meisels (Eds.), *Handbook of early childhood intervention* (2nd ed., pp. 258-289). New York: Cambridge University Press.

Kleinman, A., Eisenberg, L., & Good, B. (1978). Culture, illness, and care: Clinical lessons from anthropologic and cross-cultural research. *Annals of Internal Medicine, 88*, 251-258.

Krauss, M. W. (1993). Child-related and parenting stress: Similarities and differences between mothers and fathers of children with disabilities. *American Journal on Mental Retardation, 97*, 393-404.

Lakin, K. C., Bruininks, R. H., & Larson, S. A. (1992). The changing face of residential services. In L. Rowitz (Ed.), *Mental retardation in the year 2000* (pp. 197-247). New York/Berlin: Springer-Verlag.

Lamb, M. E., & Billings, L. A. (1997). Fathers of children with special needs. In M. E. Lamb (Ed.), *The role of the father in child development* (pp. 179-190). New York: Wiley.

Landry, S. H., & Chapieski, M. L. (1990). Joint attention of six-month-old Down syndrome and preterm infants, I: Attention to toys and mother. *American Journal on Mental Retardation, 91*, 488-498.

Landry, S. H., Smith, K. E., Miller-Loncar, C. L., & Swank, P. R. (1997). Predicting cognitive-language and social growth curves from early maternal behaviors in children at varying degrees of biological risk. *Developmental Psychology, 33*, 1040-1053.

Lerner, R. M. (1991). Changing organism-context relations as the basic process of development: A developmental contextual perspective. *Developmental Psychology, 27*, 27-32.

LeVine, R. L., Dixon, S., LeVine, S., Richman, A., Leiderman, P. H., Keefer, C. H., & Brazelton, B. T. (1994). *Child care and culture: Lessons from Africa*. Boston: Cambridge University Press.

Lynch, D. J., Fay, L., Funk, J., & Nagel, R. (1993). Siblings of children with mental retardation: Family characteristics and adjustment. *Journal of Child and Family Studies, 2*, 87-96.

Magana, S. M. (1999). Puerto Rican families caring for an adult with mental retardation: Role of familism. *American Journal on Mental Retardation, 104*, 466-482.

Mahoney, G., Fors, S., & Wood, S. (1990). Maternal directive behavior revisited. *American Journal on Mental Retardation, 94*, 398-406.

Mardiros, M. (1989). Conception of childhood disability among Mexican American parents. *Medical Anthropology, 12,* 55-68.

Marfo, K. (1990). Maternal directiveness in interactions with mentally handicapped children: An analytical commentary. *Journal of Child Psychology and Psychiatry, 31,* 531-549.

McCollum, J. A., & Hemmeter, M. L. (1997). Parent-child interaction intervention when children have disabilities. In M. J. Guralnick (Ed.), *The effectiveness of early intervention* (pp. 549-576). Baltimore, MD: Brookes.

McCubbin, H. I., & Patterson, J. M. (1982). Family adaptation to crises. In H. I. McCubbin & J. M. Patterson (Eds.), *Family stress, coping, and social support* (pp. 26-47). Springfield, IL: Charles C Thomas.

McHale, S. M., & Pawletko, T. M. (1992). Differential treatment of siblings in two family contexts. *Child Development, 63,* 68-81.

Meisels, S. J., & Shonkoff, J. P. (2000). Early childhood intervention: A continuing evolution. In J. P. Shonkoff & S. J. Meisels (Eds.), *Handbook of early childhood intervention* (2nd ed., pp. 3-34). New York: Cambridge University Press.

Mink, I. T., & Nihira, K. (1986). Family life-styles and child behaviors: A study of direction of effects. *Developmental Psychology, 22,* 610-616.

Minuchin, P. P. (1988). Relationships within the family: A systems perspective on development. In R. A. Hinde & J. Stevenson-Hinde (Eds.), *Relationships within families: Mutual influences* (pp. 7-26). New York: Oxford University Press.

Morelli, G. A., Rogoff, B., Oppenheim, D., & Goldsmith, D. (1992). Cultural variation in infants' sleeping arrangements: Questions of independence. *Developmental Psychology, 28,* 604-613.

National Research Council and Institute of Medicine. (2000). *From neurons to neighborhoods: The science of early childhood development.* Washington, DC: National Academy Press.

Orr, R. R., Cameron, S. J., Dobson, L. A., & Day, D. M. (1993). Age-related changes in stress experienced by families with a child who has developmental delays. *Mental Retardation, 31,* 171-176.

Patterson, M., & Blum, R. W. (1993). A conference on culture and chronic illness in childhood: Conference summary. *Pediatrics, 91*(Suppl. 5), 1025-1030.

Quirk, M., Sexton, M., Ciottone, R., Minami, H., & Wapner, S. (1984). Values held by mothers for handicapped and nonhandicapped preschoolers. *Merrill Palmer Quarterly, 30,* 403-418.

Raghavan, C., Weisner, T. S., & Patel, D. (1999). The adaptive project of parenting: South Asian families with children with developmental delays. *Education and Training in Mental Retardation and Developmental Disabilities, 34,* 281-292.

Roach, M. A., Barratt, M., Miller, J. F., & Leavitt, L. A. (1998). The structure of mother-child play: Young children with Down syndrome and typically developing children. *Developmental Psychology, 34,* 77-87.

Roach, M. A., Orsmond, G. I., & Barratt, M. (1999). Mothers and fathers of children with Down syndrome: Parental stress and involvement in child care. *American Journal on Mental Retardation, 104,* 422-436.

Roberts, R. (1989). *Developing culturally competent programs for children with special needs.* Washington, DC: Georgetown University Development Center.

Sameroff, A. J., & Chandler, M. J. (1975). Reproductive risk and the continuum of caretaking casuality. In F. D. Horowitz, M. Hetherington, S. Scarr-Salapatek, & G. Siegel (Eds.), *Review of child development research* (Vol. 4., pp. 187-244). Chicago: University of Chicago Press.

Sameroff, A. J., & Fiese, B. H. (2000). Transactional regulation: The developmental ecology of early intervention. In J. P. Shonkoff & S. J. Meisels (Eds.),

Handbook of early childhood intervention (2nd ed., pp. 135-159). New York: Cambridge University Press.

Scott, B. S., Atkinson, L., Minton, H., & Bowman, T. (1997). Psychological distress of parents of infants with Down syndrome. *American Journal on Mental Retardation, 102,* 161-171.

Shapiro, J., & Tittle, K. (1990). Maternal adaptation to child disability in a Hispanic population. *Family Relations, 39,* 179-185.

Sharifzadeh, V. (1998). Families with Middle Eastern roots. In E. W. Lynch & M. J. Hanson (Eds.), *Developing cross-cultural competence: A guide for working with children and their families.* (2nd ed., pp. 441-482). Baltimore, MD: Brookes.

Shonkoff, J. P., Hauser-Cram, P., Krauss, M. W., & Upshur, C. C. (1992). Development of infants with disabilities and their families. *Monographs of the Society for Research in Child Development, 57*(6, Serial No. 230).

Skinner, D., Bailey, D. B., Correa, V., & Rodriguez, P. (1999). Narrating self and disability: Latino mothers' construction of identities vis-à-vis their child with special needs. *Exceptional Children, 65,* 481-495.

Solnit, A. J., & Stark, M. H. (1961). Mourning and the birth of a defective child. *Psychoanalytic Study of the Child, 16,* 523-537.

Stoneman, Z. (1998). Research on siblings of children with mental retardation: Contributions of developmental theory and etiology. In J. A. Burack, R. M. Hodapp, & E. Zigler (Eds.), *Handbook of mental retardation and development* (pp. 669-692). New York: Cambridge University Press.

Super, C. M., & Harkness, S. (1997). The cultural structuring of child development. In J. W. Berry, Y. P. Poortinga, J. Pandey, P. R. Dasen, T. S. Saraswathi, M. H. Segall, & C. Kagitçibasi (Series Ed.), J. W. Berry, P. R. Dasen, & T. S. Saraswathi (Vol. Eds.). *Handbook of cross-cultural psychology: Vol. 2. Basic processes and human development.* Boston, MA: Allyn & Bacon.

Tannock, R. (1988). Control and reciprocity in mothers' interactions with Down syndrome and normal children. In K. Marfo (Ed.), *Parent-child interaction and developmental disabilities: Theory, research, and intervention* (pp. 162-180). New York: Praeger.

Turnbull, A. P., Blue-Banning, M., & Pereira, L. (2000). Successful friendships of Hispanic children and youth with disabilities: An exploratory study. *Mental Retardation, 38,* 138-153.

Turnbull, A. P., Turbiville, V., & Turnbull, H. R. (2000). Evolution of family-professional partnerships: Collective empowerment as the model for the early twenty-first century. In J. P. Shonkoff & S. J. Meisels (Eds.), *Handbook of early childhood intervention* (2nd ed., pp. 630-650). New York: Cambridge University Press.

U.S. Bureau of the Census. (2001). *Population by race and Hispanic or Latino origin for the United States: 1990 and 2000.* Washington, DC: U.S. Department of Commerce, Economics and Statistics Administration.

Valsiner, J. (1989). From group comparisons to group knowledge: Lessons from cross-cultural psychology. In J. P. Forgas & J. M. Innes (Eds.), *Recent advances in social psychology: An international perspective* (pp. 501-510). Amsterdam: North-Holland.

Valsiner, J., & Litvinovic, G. (1996). Processes of generalization in parental reasoning. In S. Harkness & C. M. Super (Eds.), *Parent's cultural belief systems: Their origins, expressions, and consequences* (pp. 56-82). New York: Guilford.

Walsh, F. (Ed.). (1980). *Normal family processes.* New York: Guilford.

Warfield, M. E., Krauss, M. W., Hauser-Cram, P., Upshur, C. C., & Shonkoff, J. P. (1999). Adaptation during early childhood among mothers of children with disabilities. *Journal of Developmental and Behavioral Pediatrics, 20,* 9-16.

Weinger, S. (1999). Views of the child with mental retardation: Relationship to family functioning. *Family Therapy, 26,* 63-79.

Weisner, T. S. (1993). Siblings in cultural place: Ethnographic and ecocultural perspectives on siblings of developmentally delayed children. In Z. Stoneman & P. Berman (Eds.), *Siblings of individuals with mental retardation, physical disabilities, and chronic illness* (pp. 51-83). Baltimore, MD: Brookes.

Zuniga, M. E. (1998). Families with Latino roots. In E. W. Lynch & M. J. Hanson (Eds.), *Developing cross-cultural competence: A guide for working with children and their families.* (2nd ed., pp. 209-250). Baltimore, MD: Brookes.

Section IV

ENHANCING
SERVICE SYSTEMS

CHAPTER 16

Early Intervention and Family Support Programs

JOHN ECKENRODE

CHARLES IZZO

MARY CAMPA-MULLER

We now have several decades of experience in fielding and evaluating interventions designed to improve the life chances of children born into disadvantaged families. In this chapter, we review this body of work, focusing on several exemplary programs. Our review is limited to those programs serving families with preschool children without disabilities, although programs serving families of children at risk for developmental disabilities (e.g., low birth weight) are included. These programs begin during pregnancy, infancy, or early childhood and may involve a variety of intervention approaches. Information on the criteria used to select programs is discussed in the first section.

BACKGROUND

Several developments have led to the current interest among scientists and policymakers in programs for disadvantaged young families in the United States. First, the precarious state of American families has been a continuing cause for concern due to problems such as teen parenting, child abuse and neglect, a lack of community services, substance abuse, and a culture of violence (Bronfenbrenner, McClelland, Wethington, Moen, & Ceci, 1996; Garbarino, 1995; National Research Council and Institute of Medicine, 2000). Increasingly, developmental research has documented the destructive effects of poverty on children and adolescents (Huston, McLoyd, & Coll, 1994; Brooks-Gunn & Duncan, 1997).

Second, recent research on early brain development and the critical influence of environmental factors during the first 3 years of life has placed renewed attention on enhancing parenting and the home environment prior to school entry so as to diminish biological vulnerabilities and shape healthy development.

Third, since the mid-1960s "war on poverty," large-scale government programs gained wide political support for providing disadvantaged children with an enriched learning environment and other supports to compensate, in part, for the destructive effects of poverty by improving their chances of success in school (Reynolds, 2000). Other federal legislation has directed increased attention to very young children, such as the 1997 reauthorization of the Individuals with Disabilities Education Act, which mandated services to infants and toddlers with disabilities (Erikson & Kurz-Riemer, 1999; Ramey & Ramey, 1998).

Fourth, a number of grassroots "movements" have led to an increased awareness of the need to support and empower vulnerable families by building on their strengths. (Dunst & Trivette, 1994; Kagan, Powell, Weissbourd, & Zigler, 1987). As a consequence, thousands of local programs designed to support families, such as family resource centers, were established, and national organizations, such as the Family Resource Coalition, grew to support such efforts.

Finally, the growth of the "prevention science" field (Coie et al., 1993) has led to an increased understanding of the array of risk and protective factors that influence child development and the efficacy of intervention approaches that address those factors. One of the principles of prevention is that risk factors for dysfunction should be addressed before they become stabilized and before the first signs of disorder. As a result, our growing knowledge about the early signs of dysfunction and the effects of early experiences on later functioning have helped to guide the design and evaluation of early interventions.

THEORETICAL UNDERPINNINGS OF EARLY INTERVENTION AND FAMILY SUPPORT PROGRAMS

All early education and family support programs embody, either implicitly or explicitly,

a set of assumptions about the origins of human behavior; risk factors that lead to dysfunction; individual, family, or community factors that might modify these risks; and change processes that are instituted by the program. For example, Olds and his colleagues have discussed the role of human ecology, self-efficacy, and attachment theories in designing the Nurse Home Visitation Program (NHVP) (Olds, Kitzman, Cole, & Robinson, 1997).

Most programs embrace some form of human ecology theory (Bronfenbrenner, 1979, 1986), with its emphasis on the importance of multiple contexts for development (e.g., family, schools, neighborhoods, the larger culture) and the proximal processes that sustain positive development over time. The importance of both context and process is reflected in more recent conceptual frameworks for early intervention programs such as Ramey and Ramey's (1998) model of "biosocial developmental contextualism." Embedded in these broad theoretical frameworks are a number of common conceptual or theoretical propositions, including the following:

- Problematic outcomes result from multiple interrelated risk factors.
- Any given risk factor, such as poverty, may be associated with a number of problematic cognitive, social, and emotional outcomes.
- Protective factors affect problematic development either by reducing risk factors or by building competence. These can include individual characteristics (e.g., social skills) and aspects of the child's environment (e.g., a stable home).
- Development is assumed to be a joint function of biologically and environmentally determined strengths and vulnerabilities.
- Each developmental period shows the emergence of new developmental competencies and the presence of new environmental risks as children begin to interact with new contexts.
- Many later problems result from a series of interrelated and persistent early experiences

and developmental problems that form a compromised developmental trajectory. The implication is that interventions early in life can have a self-sustaining quality in the presence of a moderately supportive environment.

These theoretical propositions have contributed to an increased emphasis on starting interventions as early as possible, even in pregnancy as the impact of prenatal health behaviors (e.g., smoking, diet) on the development of the fetus becomes better known. There is also increased attention to the importance of defining intervening causal mechanisms that link risk factors to more distal child outcomes. For example, a successful early intervention designed to improve academic success requires a developmental theory that links early experiences and developmental processes to intended outcomes. These intervening processes (e.g., the parent-child relationship) become targets of the intervention.

PROGRAM CHARACTERISTICS

Most programs that fall under headings such as "family support and education" (Weiss & Jacobs, 1988) and "early childhood intervention" (Reynolds, 2000) share several characteristics in common, including the following:

- A primary focus on economically disadvantaged families, although middle-income families are sometimes served
- A goal to foster healthy child development and in some cases to support the life course development of the parents
- The provision of a range of support, including information, emotional support, and tangible aid
- A focus on building competence as well as reducing risk
- A base of operation within the most relevant ecological settings for families and children such as homes and schools
- Linkage of families to other community-based services

Some of the distinctions between programs are also worth noting because these differences may be linked to program effectiveness (Gomby, Larner, Stevenson, Lewit, & Behrman, 1995; Erikson & Kurz-Riemer, 1999). The dimensions discussed next are not completely independent of one another (e.g., programs that include a focus on health begin earlier and often involve home visitation).

Focus. It is useful to distinguish among child-focused, family-focused, and "two-generation" programs (Gomby et al., 1995). Child-focused programs typically emphasize cognitive development so as to enhance school readiness, although they can include developmental screenings and links to health services. Services may take place in a center or school and try to involve parents to reinforce the learning goals set for the child. Family-focused or family support programs serve families with children under 3 years of age and work with parents to improve the home environment and enhance the parents' caregiving skills. Two-generation programs focus jointly on the development of the child (e.g., through interventions with the child and parent support) and parental life course development (e.g., education, economic self-sufficiency, family planning).

Comprehensiveness. This term refers to the range of intervention outcomes (e.g., social, emotional, and cognitive development), target population (i.e., children, parents, or both), and types of delivery systems employed (e.g., home visits, center-based programs, links to other community-based services). There has been an evolution in early intervention programs in approach and scope. Although at one time they were focused almost exclusively on cognitive gains, current programs are more broad based and focus on reducing multiple stresses and risk factors that influence several outcomes for parents and children (e.g., health, cognitive development, social development).

Delivery System. The primary distinction here is between home-based and center-based programs. Some programs use home visits as the only mode of intervention (e.g., NHVP), others rely primarily on center- or school-based services (e.g., Chicago Child-Parent Centers [CPCs; see program descriptions later for references]), and some combine both approaches (e.g., Infant Health and Development Program [IHDP]). The literature is not yet clear on what combination of home- and center-based services is optimal for improving children's long-term social and cognitive development (Ramey & Ramey, 1998; Weiss, 1993; Yoshikawa, 1995).

Age. Although all early intervention programs begin prior to school entry, there is considerable variation in the starting ages of the children. This reflects the primary emphasis of the program (e.g., improving infant health outcomes, enhancing school readiness), the chosen delivery system (e.g., home based, center based), and cultural issues. Some family support and education programs, such as the NHVP, began during pregnancy. Several programs, such as the IHDP and Healthy Families America (HFA), recruited families soon after the births of the children. Others, such as CPCs and the High/Scope Perry Preschool Program, enrolled families when the children were 3 or 4 years of age. The optimal age to begin early intervention is an important policy question. The answer may be driven in part by the outcomes targeted by the program and the underlying theory of change (Cummings, Davies, & Campbell, 2000). Programs aimed at preventing child maltreatment generally begin prenatally or during infancy, whereas programs targeting the prevention of aggression and antisocial behaviors may begin during the preschool years. As noted, recent evidence suggests that intervening in risk processes at a very young age may be the most efficacious preventive approach. However, there are practical and political constraints in mounting and sustaining prevention programs well before target problems emerge developmentally (e.g., starting a pregnancy prevention program with toddlers).

Duration. Programs vary considerably in the duration of the services provided. Although there is intuitive appeal to the dictum that the longer the program, the more effective the intervention, few well-controlled studies have tested the minimum amount of time or intensity of intervention needed to achieve positive effects for children and families. Most model programs try to retain families for at least 2 years. But after a certain point, longer might not be better; little is known about the period of time when diminishing returns occur given the investment in resources and the well-known problem of retaining families in such programs. A few well-evaluated programs, such as the NHVP and CPCs, have systematically varied the duration of services, and some other studies have attempted to examine the strength of program effects as a function of the duration of program participation (e.g., IHDP).

Model or Community-Based Program. Most of what is known about the effectiveness of early interventions comes from university-led model demonstration programs rather than large-scale community-based projects such as Head Start (Reynolds, 2000). From a policy perspective, model programs are important because they show what can be accomplished given a well-funded, well-designed, and well-evaluated program. There are many challenges in taking the results of model programs and designing federal or state programs for larger and more diverse groups of families. Some initially small demonstration programs, such as the NHVP, have begun widespread dissemination efforts that are designed to establish the programs in new communities while maintaining integrity to the original program models. Other programs, such as HFA and Parents as Teachers (PAT), have instituted wide-scale dissemination efforts in parallel to evaluative efforts aimed at testing program effectiveness. The challenge here is how to use evaluative data to improve programs that are already widely disseminated.

EVALUATING THE EFFECTIVENESS OF EARLY INTERVENTION AND FAMILY SUPPORT PROGRAMS

Studies vary considerably in the level of evidence they have used to demonstrate the effectiveness of early intervention programs. For this review, we primarily selected programs that were evaluated in experimental designs with random assignment to intervention and control groups because these allow one to interpret more clearly whether program benefits can be attributed to the intervention. Even among randomized trials, however, several methodological issues can limit the interpretation of the results. Attrition rates are often higher in the comparison group and may also vary by demographic group. Consequently, in the final sample, intervention and comparison groups may differ both in size and in composition. Some programs, such as the IHDP, dealt with this issue by assigning a greater proportion of participants to the comparison group so as to compensate for the higher attrition rate expected in that group. In addition, most studies in this review have empirically tested the extent to which differential attrition existed (e.g., between intervention and comparison groups, between demographic groups) so that the influence of attrition on overall findings can be judged.

In many "real world" settings, however, true experimental designs are not feasible,

either because it is difficult to justify withholding services from eligible families or because in some settings (e.g., schools, neighborhoods) it is too difficult to avoid "contaminating" the control group. For these and other reasons, many early intervention programs (e.g., CPCs) use quasi-experimental designs in which there is no random assignment of families. The primary concern with these studies is that the factors that influence families' participation and retention in the program (e.g., parental resourcefulness, commitment to promoting child's cognitive development) may also predispose them to achieve better outcomes. Therefore, it is difficult to distinguish the effect of the program from the effect of these predisposing factors. To address this issue, studies such as the CPC program (Reynolds, 2000) devoted significant effort to investigating the comparability between intervention and control groups.

Another issue that makes it difficult to interpret the literature on early intervention is the wide variation across studies in sample size. Small sample size may lead one to overlook important effects because there is not enough statistical power for group differences to reach statistical significance. To compensate for this, many studies report differences that are significant at the 10% level rather than at the 5% level so that potentially important findings are not missed. Very small sample size, however, also leads one to question whether a study's findings (significant or not) can be generalized to the larger population of potential program participants. One must also consider whether statistically significant findings are large enough to be clinically significant. For example, the IHDP reported nearly a 4-point intelligence quotient (IQ) difference between treatment and control groups, but with a sample size of nearly 1,000 families, these effects are significant at the 5% level. One article critiquing the interpretation of IHDP findings judged this effect to be so small as to be clinically meaningless (Baumeister & Bacharach, 1996).

Evidence for program effectiveness can be bolstered by demonstrating that similar program effects can be replicated across different settings. Such replicability shows that observed program effects are not simply due to unique characteristics of a given sample, region, or period in time but instead are a function of a substantive program model. We have tried to include as many replicated studies as possible in this review, although few exist because replication is rare in the early intervention and family support literature. Some programs, such as the IHDP, involved targeting the same population in multiple sites simultaneously. Others, such as the NHVP and PAT, were implemented sequentially, with each trial targeting a slightly different population.

There is also substantial variability in the length of the follow-up period and in the extent to which assessments are made across a broad range of life areas. The promise of early childhood intervention is that the initial cognitive and social benefits that programs produce will place children on a positive life trajectory involving academic success, prosperity in both work and family spheres, and good citizenship. Evaluations need to reflect the ecological focus of these programs so as to document their benefits most effectively. Some evaluations in this review, such as CPCs and the Abecedarian Project, conducted follow-up assessments up to 20 years following the interventions and assessed a range of maternal life course and parenting variables as well as child outcomes. Others, such as PAT and the Home Instruction Program for Preschool Youngsters (HIPPY), extend their assessments for only 1 or 2 years beyond the programs and report few if any results for parenting or maternal life course variables, despite the potential for the programs to influence these domains. Thus, for many studies, it is difficult to know whether they could have had more stable and wider ranging benefits if their evaluations were sensitive enough to detect them.

Programs differ greatly in the extent to which their results apply to the general population or to only specific subgroups. Programs such as the NHVP and PAT reported some outcomes for only higher risk subgroups (e.g., low income), whereas the IHDP reported some effects only for lower risk subgroups (e.g., heavier birth-weight infants). These kinds of differences make it hard to make general statements about the effectiveness of early childhood intervention programs, but they do provide valuable insight for targeting interventions to specific subgroups.

Finally, it is important to note that although the rigorous studies reviewed in what follows constitute an important source of data on the effectiveness of early intervention, they represent only a small fraction of the existing knowledge base on this topic. Literally hundreds of evaluations of varying size and methodological quality have been conducted (Layzer, Goodson, Bernstein, & Price, 2001), most using quasi-experimental designs. The state of our scientific knowledge about early intervention and family support programs cannot be appreciated fully without proper attention to that massive literature as well.

PROGRAM DESCRIPTIONS

Each program is briefly reviewed in the summaries that follow. Key characteristics of each program are summarized in Table 16.1, and a detailed summary of research findings is presented in Table 16.2.

Abecedarian Project

The Abecedarian Project began in 1972 as a randomized efficacy trial of an early education intervention. Families were chosen to

(Text continues on page 420)

Table 16.1   Descriptions of Selected Early Intervention and Family Support Programs

Dimension Program	Number of Participants	Age at Start of Program	Target Recipient	Focus of Services	Type of Evaluation	Duration	Population Demographics	Delivery of Service	Sources of Data
Abecedarian Project	$N = 111$	Newborn	Entire family	Family functioning and child outcomes (mainly cognitive)	Randomized	3 years	Low SES and low education	Home visits; social work; early childhood education	Child reports
CCDP	$N = 3,961$	Children 1 year of age or under	Primary caregiver	Maternal self-sufficiency; parent education; early childhood education information	Randomized	5 years	Low income	Home visits; case management	Maternal and child reports; observations
CPCs	$Ns = 887$ to 1,539	Children entering preschool	Entire family	Children's cognitive/ educational development; parent-child interactions; parent involvement in children's education; parents' education and skill development	Quasi-experiment	Up to 6 years	Economically disadvantaged families that were not involved in Head Start	Center/ School based; parent resource teacher	Maternal, child, and teacher reports; record-level data

(Continued)

407

Table 16.1 Continued

Dimension Program	Number of Participants	Age at Start of Program	Target Recipient	Focus of Services	Type of Evaluation	Duration	Population Demographics	Delivery of Service	Sources of Data
HFA	Virginia: N = 619; Hawaii: N = 324	Newborns	Entire family	Healthy child development; parent-child interactions; maternal life course; linkage to community services	Randomized	3 to 5 years	All parents of newborns at risk for child abuse and neglect	Home visits	Maternal, child, and teacher reports; observations; record-level data
HIPPY	N = 182	Children in preschool and soon to be in kindergarten	Entire family	Parenting skills and activities for children; child educational development	Randomized	2 years	Families with little formal education	Home visits; center-based family and staff meetings	Maternal, child, and teacher reports
Houston Parent-Child Development Center	N = 170	Children 1 year of age	Entire family	Parent-child interactions; children's cognitive development; parents' family management skills and life course development	Randomized	2 years	Low-income Mexican American families with one child	Center based; home visits; family picnics	Maternal, child, and teacher reports

Dimension Program	Number of Participants	Age at Start of Program	Target Recipient	Focus of Services	Type of Evaluation	Duration	Population Demographics	Delivery of Service	Sources of Data
IHDP	$N = 985$	Newborns	Entire family	Children's cognitive development; parenting skills; maternal life course	Randomized	3 years	Premature, low-birthweight children	Home visits; child care; parent support meetings	Maternal and child reports; observations
New Chance Demonstration	$N = 2,322$	Young children	Mothers	Maternal life course development; parent-child interactions; child development	Randomized	3 years	Teenage mothers (ages 16-22 years) without high school education on AFDC	Classes; job training; child care; case management	Maternal, child, and teacher reports; observations; record-level data
NHVP	Elmira: $N = 354$; Memphis: $N = 1,139$	Prenatal	Mothers	Maternal life course; child development; parent-child interactions	Randomized	2 years	Three criteria: under 19 years of age, unmarried, or low SES having first child	Home visits	Maternal, child, and teacher reports; observations; record-level data
PAT	$N = 667$	Prenatal or newborns	Entire family	Parenting skills; child development; children's education; parent-child interactions	Randomized	3 years	Families with children age 6 months or under	Home visits; group meetings	Maternal, child, and teacher reports; observations; record-level data

(Continued)

Table 16.1 Continued

Dimension Program	Number of Participants	Age at Start of Program	Target Recipient	Focus of Services	Type of Evaluation	Duration	Population Demographics	Delivery of Service	Sources of Data
High/Scope Perry Preschool Program	N = 123	3 or 4 years	Entire family	Children's cognitive development; parent involvement in children's education	Randomized	1 to 2 years	Low-income African American families	Center based; home visits	Child reports
Syracuse University FDRP	N = 216	Prenatal	Entire family	Family environment; child development; family support	Time lag recruitment	5 years	Low-income, low-education families	Home visits; child care; parent groups	Maternal, child, and teacher reports; record-level data

NOTE: SES = socioeconomic status; CCDP = Comprehensive Child Development Program; CPCs = Child-Parent Centers; HFA = Healthy Families America; HIPPY = Home Instruction Program for Preschool Youngsters; IHDP = Infant Health and Development Program; AFDC = Aid to Families with Dependent Children; NHVP = Nurse Home Visitation Program; PAT = Parents as Teachers; FDRP = Family Development Research Program.

Table 16.2 Effects of Selected Early Intervention Programs on Maternal, Parenting, and Child Outcomes

			Maternal Outcomes	
Program	Fertility	Educational Attainment	Economic Self-Sufficiency	Physical/Mental Health
Abecedarian Project		Total education 54 months: E > C	In semiskilled or skilled employment 54 months: E > C	Locus of control 3 months: E = C
CCDP			Vocational training/work 2 years: E > C Mother employment/AFDC use 5 years: E = C Total income 5 years: E > C+	Effects for mothers of subsequent children: Alcohol use during pregnancy 5 years: E = C
CPCs				
HFA				San Diego: Depression 2 years: E < C
HIPPY				
Houston Parent-Child Development Cente	Occurrence of additional births 3 years: E = C	Effects for Hispanics Months of education 3 years: E > C		
IHDP			Months employed 3 years: E > C Early entry into workforce 3 years: E > C Effects for more educated mothers: Months on welfare 3 years: E > C	Emotional distress Post: E < C

(Continued)

Table 16.2 Continued

Program	Fertility	Educational Attainment	Economic Self-Sufficiency	Physical/Mental Health
New Chance Demonstration	Pregnancy and births 18 and 42 months: E = C Had unprotected sex 42 months: E = C *Effects for sexually active participants:* Contraceptive use 18 months: E < C	Received GED End of 18 and 42 months: E > C Received high school diploma End of 18 and 42 months: E > C Received college credit End of 18 months: E > C End of 42 months: E > C+	Ever employed Months 1 to 42: E = C Average total earnings and months on AFDC E = C Ever received AFDC Months 1 to 42: E > C Combined work with AFDC Months 1 to 42: E > C	Hospitalized at least once Months 0 to 42: E > C Average depression 18 months: E = C 42 months: E > C+ High stress levels 42 months: E > C Drug/alcohol use 18 and 42 months: E = C
Elmira NHVP	Number of subsequent pregnancies/births 4 years: E < C *Effects for poor/unmarried mothers:* Number of subsequent pregnancies/births 15 years: E < C	Educational achievement 2, 4, and 15 years: E = C *Effect for mothers who had not graduated at registration:* Graduated or enrolled in school 6 months: E > C 10 months: E = C	*Effects for poor/unmarried mothers:* Number of months employed 4 years: E > C Number of months receiving public assistance 15 years: E < C	*Effects for white mothers only:* Prenatal smoking End of pregnancy: E < C *Effects for poor/unmarried mothers:* Substance abuse 15 years: E < C
Memphis NHVP	Number of subsequent pregnancies 2 years: E < C *Mothers with fewer psychological resources:* Fewer live births 2 years: E = C	Years of education 2 years: E = C	Number of months receiving public assistance 2 years: E < C+ 5 years: E < C Number of months employed 2 years: E = C	Perceived mastery 2 years: E = C
PAT				
High/Scope Perry Preschool Program				
FDRP				

Parenting Outcomes

Program	Parent-Child Interactions	Home Environment	Child Abuse and Neglect	Parenting Skills
Abecedarian Project	Dyadic involvement 20 months: E = C *Cohorts I and II only:* Mutual activity initiated by mother E > C Mother's authoritarianism 6 and 18 months: E = C	Home environment 6, 18, and 42 months: E = C		Mother's democratic attitudes 6 and 18 months: E = C
CCDP	Parent-child interactions 3 years: E = C Mother fosters emotional development 3 years: E = C	Home environment 4 years: E = C Preventive medical care E = C	Child death E = C	Inappropriate expectations and lack of empathy for child 5 years: E = C
CPCs	Parent involvement Grade 5: E_1 = C; E_2 = C			
HFA	*Virginia:* Teaching 2 years: E = C Improved interaction 1 to 24 months: E > C *Hawaii:* Maternal involvement 6 months: E > C^+ Child's responsiveness to mother 1 year: E > C	*Virginia:* HOME composite 2 years: E > C	*Virginia:* Verified cases of child abuse/neglect 2 years: E = C *Hawaii:* Verified cases of child abuse/neglect 1 year: E < C^+ Emergency room visits 1 year: E = C *San Diego:* Physical aggression 2 years: E < C 3 years: E = C	*Hawaii:* Knowledge about parenting 1 year: E > C
HIPPY				

(Continued)

Table 16.2 Continued

Program	Parent-Child Interactions	Home Environment	Child Abuse and Neglect	Parenting Skills
Houston Parent-Child Development Center	Affection 2 years: E = C 3 years: E > C Encourages verbalization 2 years: E < C 3 years: E > C	HOME composite 2 years: E = C 3 years: E > C		
IHDP		HOME composite 1 year: E = C 3 years (post): E > C		
New Chance	Emotional support 18 months: E > C+ 42 months: E = C Harsh discipline 18, 42 months: E = C Dislike of parental role 18 months: E < C+ 42 months: E = C Aggravation with child 18 months: E = C 42 months: E < C	Physical environment 18 months: E = C Cognitive stimulation 18 months: E = C Child health coverage 42 months: E = C		Total parenting stress 18 months: E = C 42 months: E > C
Elmira NHVP	Warmth and control 4 years: E = C *Effects for poor, unmarried teenage mothers:* Conflict with/scolding babies 6 months: E < C+ Punishment/restriction 10 and 22 months: E < C 4 years: E > C Involvement with child 4 years: E > C	*Effects for poor, unmarried teenage mothers:* Appropriate play materials provided 10 and 22 months: E > C	Emergency room visits/injuries 2 years: E < C *Effects for families of poor unmarried teenagers:* Verified cases of child abuse/neglect 2 years: E < C 4 years: E = C Emergency room visits/injuries 4 years: E < C *Effects for families of poor unmarried teenagers:*	Parental coping 4 years: E > C

Program	Parent-Child Interactions	Home Environment	Child Abuse and Neglect	Parenting Skills
Memphis NHVP	Attempt breast-feeding 2 years: E > C	Homes conducive to child development 2 years: E > C	Verified cases of child abuse/neglect 4 years: E = C 15 years: E < C Health encounters for injuries/ingestions 2 years: E < C	Healthy beliefs about child rearing 2 years: E > C Maternal teaching behavior 2 years: E = C
PAT	Parent-child interaction 1 and 2 years: E = C *Effects for very low-income families:* Parent reads/sings to child 2 years: E > C	Home environment 1 and 2 years: E = C *Effects for moderate-income families:* Acceptance of child's behavior E > C	Child maltreatment precursor 2 years: E = C	Parental sense of competence 2 years: E = C Parental knowledge of child development/safety 1 and 2 years: E = C
Perry	Attend parent-teacher conferences when invited E < C			*Effects for parents of girls:* Wants child to attend college E > C Positive parenting attitudes 1 year preschool: E > C
FDRP		Home stimulation 36 months: E > C		Low expectations for youth 10-year follow-up: E < C

(Continued)

Table 16.2 Continued

Child Outcomes

Program	Cognitive Development	Social/Emotional Development	Education	Health

Abecedarian Project	IQ
	  4, 5, 12, and 21 years: E > C
	  15 years: E = C⁺
	Memory
	  42 months: E > C
	Motor skills
	  42 months: E = C
	Verbal ability
	  42 months: E > C
	Reading ability
	  15 years: E > C
	Math ability
	  15 and 21 years: E > C
		Goal-directed behavior
		  6 and 12 months: E = C
		  18 months: E > C
		Social competence
		  6 and 12 months: E > C
		Criminal or property charges
		  16 to 21 years: E = C
		Employed
		  21 years: E = C
		Skilled employment
		  21 years: E > C
			Special education
			  15 years: E < C
			Grade retention
			  12 and 15 years: E < C
			Use of special services
			  15 years: E = C
			4-year college or university
			  21 years: E > C
			Effects for females:
			Years of education
			  21 years: E > C
				Medical coverage
				  21 years: E = C
				Binge drinking
				  21 years: E = C
				Marijuana use
				  21 years: E < C
				Teenage pregnancy (before 19 years of age)
				  21 years: E < C
				Effects for those who had children:
				Age at first birth
				  21 years: E < C
				Number of children
				  21 years: E = C

CCDP	IQ
	  5 years: E = C
	Overall cognitive ability
	  5 years: E > C⁺
		Behavior problems
		  2 to 5 years: E = C
		Social behavior
		  3 years: E = C		

CPCs
(E₁ = participation in preschool only;
E₂ = participation in preschool through Grade 3)
		Classroom adjustment
		  Grades 3, 4, and 5: E₁ = C;
		  E₂ > C
		Delinquent acts at school
		  Ages 13 and 14 years: E₁ = C
		  Ages 14 and 15 years: E₁ = C
		Any arrests
		  Ages 14 and 15 years: E₁ = C
		  Age 18 years: E₁ < C
			Reading and math achievement
			  Grades 3, 4, and 5: E₁ = C;
			  E₂ > C
			Grade retention
			  Grades 3, 4, and 5: E₁ =
			  C; E₂ < C
			  Ages 14 and 15 years: E₁ < C
			Special education
			  Grades 3, 4, and 5: E₁ and
			  E₂ = C
			  Ages 14 and 15 years: E₁ < C
			High school completion
			  Age 20 years: E₁ > C	

HFA	*Virginia:* Developmental age score 1 and 2 years: E = C			*Virginia:* Pre-term delivery End of pregnancy: E = C

Program	Cognitive Development	Social/Emotional Development	Education	Health
	Hawaii: Cognitive development score 1 year: E = C *San Diego:* IQ 2 years: E > C 3 years: E = C			Birth complications End of pregnancy: E < C *Hawaii:* Immunization 1 year: E = C
HIPPY	*Cohort I* Cognitive skills Program end: E > C Reading ability Program end: E = C 1 year later: E > C Math ability Program end, 1 year later: E = C *Cohort II* Cognitive skills Program end: E = C Reading and math ability Program end, 1 year later: E = C		*Cohort I* Classroom adaptation Program end, 1 year later: E > C *Cohort II* Classroom adaptation Program end, 1 year later: E = C	
Houston Parent-Child Development Center	IQ 1 year: E = C 2 and 3 years: E > C 4 to 6 years Composite scales: E = C Information and geometric design: E > C 6 to 9 years Composite scales: E = C Block design: E > C Verbal communication 2 years: E > C 3 years: E = C	Hostility 8 to 11 years: E < C Considerateness 8 to 11 years: E > C *Effects for boys:* Destructive 4 to 7 years: E < C Overactive 4 to 7 years: E < C	Academic achievement 8 to 11 years: E > C Grades 8 to 11 years: E = C Grade retention/learning problems 8 to 11 years: E = C Special education 8 to 11 years: E = C Bilingual classes 8 to 11 years: E < C	

(Continued)

417

Table 16.2 Continued

Program	Cognitive Development	Social/Emotional Development	Education	Health
IHDP	Overall IQ 3 years: E > C Language/vocabulary 2 and 3 years: E > C Visuomotor skills 2 and 3 years: E > C *Effects for heavier children:* Overall IQ 5 and 8 years: E > C	Behavior problems 2 and 3 years: E < C 5 years: E = C	*Effects for heavier children:* Math achievement 8 years: E > C	*Effects for children of white mothers who smoked at intake:* Pre-term delivery End of pregnancy: E < C Number of health problems 3 years: E > C
New Chance	Academic performance/ability (teacher rating) E = C Academic performance/ability (maternal rating) E < C⁺	Antisocial behavior 42 months: E = C Behavioral problems and depression 42 months: E > C		Child hospitalized at least once 0 to 42 months: E = C Medical treatment for injuries/ingestions 0 to 18 months: E = C 19 to 42 months: E > C⁺
Memphis NHVP	Mental development 2 years: E = C *Children whose mothers had greater psychological resources:* Communicative/responsive to mother 2 years: E > C	Behavior problems 2 years: E = C		Birthweight E = C
Elmira NHVP	*Effect for children of poor/unmarried teenage mothers:* Developmental quotient 1 and 2 years: E > C⁺ *Effect for children of moderate/heavy-smoking mothers:* IQ 15 years: E > C	Arrests and convictions 15 years: E < C Internalizing and externalizing behavior and substance abuse 15 years: E = C *Effects for children of poor/unmarried mothers:* Alcohol use 15 years: E < C Cigarette and drug use 15 years: E = C Number of sex partners 15 years: E < C Running away 15 years: E < C	Number of absences 15 years: E < C Years retained 15 years: E = C Grade point average 15 years: E = C Number of suspensions 15 years: E = C	Receipt of well-child care 2 years: E = C Immunization status 2 years: E = C

Program	Cognitive Development	Social/Emotional Development	Education	Health
PAT	Cognitive development 2 years: E = C	Social, self-help, and communication development 2 years: E = C		Went to emergency room last year 2 years: E = C Physical development 2 years: E = C
High/Scope Perry Preschool Program	IQ Preschool (first year) to Grade 1: E > C Grades 2 to 4: E = C Vocabulary skills 4 and 5 years: E > C 6 to 9 years: E = C General literacy ability 19 years: E > C 27 years: E = C Reading ability Grades 1 and 2: E = C Grades 3 and 4: E > C Math ability Grade 1: E > C Grades 2 to 4: E = C	Positive socioemotional state Kindergarten and Grades 1 and 3: E > C Grade 2: E > C Positive social development Kindergarten and Grade 1: E = C Grade 2: E > C Grade 3: E > C+ School/personal misconduct 6 to 9 years: E < C+ Currently employed 19 years: E > C 27 years: E = C Lifetime arrests 19 and 27 years: E < C	School success Grades 1 and 2: E = C Grades 3 and 4: E > C High school grade point average E > C Academic motivation/potential 6 to 9 years: E = C Grade retention Grade 12: E = C Effects for females: High school graduation/highest grade completed 27 years: E > C	Hospitalized 27 years: E > C Alcohol use 27 years: E = C Always/usually wear seatbelt 27 years: E > C Effects for females: Births 19 and 27 years: E = C Pregnancies 19 years: E < C+ 27 years: E = C Abortions 27 years: E < C+
Syracuse University FDRP	IQ 6 months: E > C 12 months: E = C	Initiative, active problem response 36 months: E > C Kindergarten and Grade 1: E = C 10-year follow-up: E > C Threatens aggressive acts 36 months: E > C Kindergarten: E = C Grade 1: E < C On probation 10-year follow-up: E < C Effects for girls: Positive attitudes/impulse control 10-year follow-up: E > C	Placed in special education 80/81 and 84/85: E = C Plans to be in school in 5 years 10-year follow-up: E > C Effects for girls: Grade point average in failing range Grades 7 and 8: E < C Absent 20 days or more 81/82 and 82/83: E = C 83/84 and 84/85: E < C	

NOTE: E = experimental group; C = control group; CCDP = Comprehensive Child Development Program; CPCs = Child-Parent Centers; HFA = Healthy Families America; HIPPY = Home Instruction Program for Preschool Youngsters; IHDP = Infant Health and Development Program; NHVP = Nurse Home Visitation Program; PAT = Parents as Teachers; FDRP = Family Development Research Program; AFDC = Aid to Families With Dependent Children; GED = general equivalency diploma; IQ = intelligence quotient.

participate in the study based on a 13-factor risk index (Ramey & Campbell, 1991). A high-quality preschool program designed to enhance school readiness began when the children were 6 weeks old and continued year-round until 5 years of age. Following preschool, all children were randomly reassigned to the K–2 educational support program or to standard K–2 classes, thus creating four groups (control, preschool only, K–2 only, and preschool/K–2). The K–2 program was designed to involve parents in the children's learning process by supplying professional educators to provide educational training for parents in the home.

Positive results of the program were found through 21 years of age on many child cognitive and socioemotional outcomes (Barnett, 1995; Campbell, Pungello, Miller-Johnson, Burchinal, & Ramey, 2001; Campbell & Ramey, 1994, 1995; Campbell, Ramey, Pungello, Sparling, & Miller-Johnson, 2002; Clarke & Campbell, 1998; Ramey, 1980; Ramey & Campbell, 1981; Ramey et al., 2000; Ramey, Dorval, & Baker-Ward, 1983; Ramey & Haskins, 1981; Ramey, Yeates, & Short, 1984). Although this program did not continue after the initial trial, many of its key aspects were incorporated into Project Care and the IHDP (Ramey & Ramey, 1998).

Chicago Child-Parent Centers Program

The CPC program began in 1967 to provide early educational and family support services to low-income children and their parents. Funded by Title I of the Elementary and Secondary Education Act, it is the second oldest federally funded early intervention program in the nation (second only to Head Start). Two major features of the program include free child care centers that provide enhanced educational activities and intensive parental participation in activities at the centers (required in preschool and kindergarten and strongly encouraged in Grades 1-3). Children attend the centers during the preschool years and receive an enhanced academic curriculum emphasizing language arts in Grades 1 to 3. The program increases the adult-to-child ratio by providing teacher aides, parent volunteers, and smaller class sizes to allow for more individualized, intensive educational services. A full-time parent resource teacher, based at the center or school, arranges opportunities for parents to volunteer at school, receive education and training, and participate in their children's education. A full-time school-community representative conducts home visits to assess family needs and helps parents to access available community services. Finally, all instructional staff receive in-service training relevant to the program goals.

A quasi-experimental evaluation indicated program effects on school performance up to 20 years of age (Reynolds, 1994, 1995, 2000; Reynolds, Chang, & Temple, 1998). The CPCs currently operate in 24 sites throughout Chicago, all administered centrally through the Chicago Public School System.

Comprehensive Child Development Program

The Comprehensive Child Development Program (CCDP) began in 1989 as a two-generation demonstration project of the Administration on Children, Youth, and Families. Designed to build off locally available services, the CCDP provided case management services though home visits scheduled either weekly or biweekly, depending on need. As part of a legislative mandate, the program sought to target low-income families with children under 1 year of age. Case managers with previous early child experience linked families with existing community services and provided direct service where gaps existed. The main benefit of the program was outreach; all services available to CCDP families were available to families in the control group that sought them out (St. Pierre, Layzer, Goodson, & Bernstein, 1997).

The impact evaluation of the CCDP focused on 22 Cohort I CCDP projects that had run throughout the United States for 5 years, ending in 1993 (Goodson, Layzer, St. Pierre, Bernstein, & Lopez, 2000; St. Pierre et al., 1997). Overall, few positive effects were found for the program. In response to the null findings and the backlash that ensued in the government and media, Gilliam, Ripple, Zigler, and Leiter (2000) criticized both the implementation and evaluation of the CCDP. Researchers from Abt Associates defended the project and reiterated that the main benefit of the program was case management services and that this was both implemented and evaluated as specified (Goodson et al., 2000). Despite controversy and weak findings, in 1995 34 CCDP programs were reauthorized under the Head Start Act and the program was consolidated into the new Head Start initiative (Alliance for Redesigning Government, n.d.).

Healthy Families America

HFA is a nationwide initiative that employs paraprofessionals to deliver preventive home visiting services to new parents who are at risk for child abuse and neglect. HFA was launched in 1992 as an attempt to replicate the home visitation model used in the Hawaii Healthy Start Program and to increase families' access to preventive services. Although HFA's goals have broadened to include reforming child welfare and health care systems, the bulk of HFA activity has been devoted to developing and implementing home visiting programs.

Services vary by site but typically involve a systematic needs assessment of all new parents at or before childbirth, followed by home visits that first occur weekly and then on a diminishing schedule as specific goals are met. Home visits continue for 3 to 5 years, depending on need, and focus on enhancing parent-child interaction, children's social and cognitive development, parents' social support, and use of community services. Home visitors receive intensive didactic training and ongoing supervision to help maintain standards of best practice.

Evaluation results were inconsistent across the two randomized trials that exist but included modest short-term benefits on mother-infant interaction, child maltreatment, and cognitive functioning (Daro & Harding, 1999). More extensive results have been reported in the wide range of nonexperimental studies that were conducted (Daro & Harding, 1999). HFA is the most widely disseminated home visitation program in the nation, currently being delivered at more than 300 sites in more than 40 states.

High/Scope Perry Preschool Program

The High/Scope Perry Preschool Program was conducted from 1962 to 1967 to demonstrate that high-quality preschool can help to counteract the cycle that links family poverty to children's school failure and continuing poverty into adulthood.

The classroom (High/Scope) curriculum was developed based on Piaget's theories of cognitive development. As it is currently practiced, the curriculum involves activities that facilitate "active learning." Although there are no preassigned lessons for teachers to use, children follow a consistent daily routine in a setting with a low teacher-child ratio where they plan and carry out their own learning activities, and the teachers help them to extend those activities into developmentally appropriate learning experiences. Teachers conduct home visits that focus on helping mothers become involved in educating their children and implementing the curriculum with other children in the household.

Long-lasting program benefits have been reported on a wide range of cognitive, educational, behavioral, and health outcomes (Barnett, 1985; Parks, 2000; Schweinhart, Barnes, Weikart, Barnett, & Epstein, 1993; Schweinhart, Berruta-Clement, Barnett, Epstein, & Weikart, 1985; Weikart, Bond, & McNeil, 1978; Weikart & Schweinhart, 1991, 1992, 1997). The High/Scope Educational Research Foundation has widely disseminated the High/Scope educational curriculum, although there has been no replication or dissemination of the overall program as described here.

Home Instructional Program for Preschool Youngsters

HIPPY began in Israel in 1969 and now serves more than 15,000 American children in more than 120 program sites, each of which is funded and administered by local organizations. The 2-year program is designed to assist parents with little formal education in preparing their 4- and 5-year-old children for school. HIPPY trains mothers to teach their children using a 30-week learning program for the final year of preschool and the first year of kindergarten. The training location alternates weekly between home visits from paraprofessionals and center-based meetings with the program coordinator and staff. Paraprofessionals are taken from the community and trained weekly by the program coordinator. The training is structured to become increasingly difficult so that both mothers and children gain a sense of mastery and accomplishment as they move through the program (Baker, Piotrkowski, & Brooks-Gunn, 1998; Olds, Hill, Robinson, Song, & Little, 2000).

HIPPY was evaluated in a randomized trial involving two cohorts (Baker et al., 1998). Program effects were found on children's cognitive and academic functioning in the first cohort, but those findings were not replicated in the second cohort. Both cohorts were equivalent on rate of attrition and program exposure.

Houston Parent-Child Development Center

The Houston Parent-Child Development Center (HPCDC) was designed to foster the development of cognitive and social skills among disadvantaged Mexican American children. Initiated in 1970, it was one of the original parent-child development centers supported by Head Start to develop state-of-the-art early intervention programs.

From 1 to 2 years of age, families received biweekly home visits from a paraprofessional during which mothers learned about early child development, home health and safety, and how to engage in educational play with their children and also were given English language lessons. Home visitors trained mothers to enhance their children's development but did not interact directly with children. Some home visits occurred on weekends to involve fathers and siblings in the activities. From 2 to 3 years of age, mothers and their study children attended the center 4 days per week. Mothers participated in instructional activities and group discussions related to life skills and child rearing, while their children participated in educational day care.

Results of a randomized trial showed program effects on parenting behavior and on children's social, cognitive, and academic functioning (Andrews et al., 1982; Johnson, 1990; Johnson & Breckenridge, 1982; Johnson & Walker, 1987; Walker & Johnson, 1988). The program was repeated in San Antonio, Texas; however, an effort to evaluate it was terminated due to funding problems. We know of no additional replication or dissemination efforts.

Infant Health and Development Program

The IHDP is an intervention designed to prevent health and developmental problems among low-birth-weight, preterm infants. It is the first attempt to test the efficacy of an intensive preschool program for this population in a large-scale, multisite randomized trial. The intervention combines activities that have been found to be effective for disadvantaged, normal-birth-weight infants (adapted for low-birth-weight infants) with family support services.

Services to families began immediately following infants' discharge from the hospital, starting with weekly home visits until infants were 12 months old (gestational age) and moved to visits twice per month until children were 36 months old (gestational age). In addition to providing social support and information about children's health and development, home visitors helped parents to learn a set of cognitively stimulating activities and games designed to facilitate their development. From 12 to 36 months of age, children attended a child development center in which staff engaged children in developmentally appropriate educational activities and games similar to those in the home curriculum. In addition, parent support groups were available during the second and third years where parents could share their child-rearing concerns and get information on topics of interest.

Investigators reported program effects on home environment and on numerous aspects of maternal and child functioning (Baumeister & Bacharach, 1996; Bradley et al., 1994; Brooks-Gunn, Klebanov, Liaw, & Spiker, 1992; Brooks-Gunn, Liaw, & Klebanov, 1992; Brooks-Gunn, McCormick, Shapiro, Benasich, & Black, 1994; IHDP, 1990; McCarton et al., 1997). We know of no further replication or dissemination efforts.

Nurse Home Visitation Program

The NHVP delivers home visiting services designed to improve children's developmental outcomes by promoting healthy prenatal habits, effective child care practices, and positive life course development among mothers. The program began as a randomized trial in Elmira, New York, in 1977.

Registered nurses conducted home visits once every other week during pregnancy, once a week for the first 6 weeks postpartum, and then on a diminishing schedule until the children were 2 years of age. Although nurses adapted the content of their home visits to the individual needs of each family, they focused on promoting three aspects of maternal functioning: (a) health-related behaviors during pregnancy and the early years of the child's life, (b) the care parents provided to their children, and (c) maternal life course development (family planning, educational achievement, and work goals). The most notable results were long-term program effects on child maltreatment and repeated childbearing, although investigators also reported benefits on a range of other areas related to parenting, maternal life course, and child functioning (Olds et al., 1997, 1998; Olds, Henderson, Chamberlin, & Tatelbaum, 1986; Olds, Henderson, Tatelbaum, & Chamberlin, 1988). Some of these results were replicated in a second randomized trial conducted in Memphis, Tennessee, that served mostly urban African American families (Kitzman et al., 1997). Currently, the NHVP is being implemented in 72 sites across 23 states.

New Chance Demonstration

Designed to improve human capital and life course outcomes, the New Chance Demonstration was a randomized evaluation targeted at young women who had given birth during their teen years, had dropped out of high school, and were receiving welfare. The demonstration began in late 1989 and ran for 3 years in 16 communities in 10 states. Participation was voluntary and was structured to fit into existing services. The first phase of the program provided vocational and parenting skills training in a school-like atmosphere and provided free child care. The second phase was designed to involve participants in further vocational training in an actual work environment, although few made it to this phase. The program also provided case management for personal issues and work assistance (Quint, Bos, & Polit, 1997).

Despite the comprehensive services offered to New Chance mothers, the program had very little positive effect on their lives and in some instances exerted negative effects (Quint et al., 1997; Zaslow & Eldred, 1998).

Parents as Teachers

PAT is a universal access intervention that is founded on the notion that babies are born learners and that effective parenting practices can lead to enhanced cognitive development. Begun in 1981 as the New Parents as Teachers program, in its current form the PAT program operates in 48 states and 6 foreign countries, running more than 2,600 local programs. Beginning as early as prenatally, certified parent educators conduct regularly scheduled home visits providing information on child development and parenting behaviors using an age-specific curriculum. In addition, parents are offered monthly group meetings to encourage community building. All parent educators have backgrounds in teaching or early child development and receive special training to deliver the PAT curriculum. The program is designed to meet the diverse needs of many families, and curricula can be targeted to

serve specific populations, including teen parents and Native American parents (Olds et al., 2000; Wagner, Spiker, Hernandez, Song, & Gerlach-Downie, 2001; Winter & McDonald, 1997).

Three randomized trials have been conducted on the PAT program. One involving Latino parents and another involving teen parents showed mixed effects (for a summary, see Wagner & Clayton, 1999). In a more recent three-site study (Wagner et al., 2001), only one site found program effects, both on parenting and child development outcomes. The authors speculated that this site may have experienced greater benefits because it was located in an organization that offered a variety of services to families, with PAT being only a part of them, suggesting that PAT is most effective if it is part of a broader social support network.

Syracuse University Family Development Research Program

The Syracuse University Family Development Research Program (FDRP) was a comprehensive family intervention delivered during the mid-1970s. Although the program placed primary emphasis on working with parents and families, high-quality university-based preschool was also an important component. With a stated goal of helping very deprived families to increase their chances for positive development, the intervention began early in the final trimester of pregnancy and continued for 5 years. Home visitors, or child development trainers, were paraprofessionals who were trained, along with all program staff, in annual 2-week training sessions (Honig & Lally, 1982).

The evaluation of the FDRP was a quasi-experimental time lag design with matched controls. The control group was established at 36 months and was matched with the experimental group on several factors. Results from the early years are generally positive, showing effects for all children, albeit a little weaker by the first grade (Honig, Lally, & Mathieson, 1982). The follow-up showed sustained effects for program girls (Lally, Mangione, & Honig, 1988).

SUMMARY OF PROGRAM EFFECTS

What have we learned from the evaluation of early intervention and family support programs? First, let us consider an earlier influential review by Bronfenbrenner (1975) of the preschool- and family-based intervention literature as it existed more than 25 years ago. After reviewing several randomized studies of both preschool programs in group settings and family interventions in the home, Bronfenbrenner drew several conclusions. These studies focused on children's cognitive gains as the primary outcome. Center-based preschool programs typically showed short-term gains in IQ that declined after the end of the program, especially for the most economically disadvantaged children. Some preliminary evidence suggested that this decline could be offset by continuing the intervention into the early grades and including a strong parent involvement component. Home-based interventions that focused on the parent(s) as well as the child showed more positive and longer-lasting effects. The earlier the program began, the greater the cognitive gains for the child. Parent-child interventions begun during the early years appeared to reinforce the magnitude and endurance of cognitive gains that could be achieved when children were enrolled in center-based preschool programs. Finally, the parent-focused programs showed evidence that both mothers and children benefited in terms of an increased sense of competence.

Many of the programs we have reviewed drew lessons from this earlier generation of intervention studies by including a focus on improving the mother's life course development, enhancing parent-child interactions, and working directly with children. An expanded range of maternal and child outcomes has also supplanted the exclusive concern with IQ and academic gains, although these remain important measures of success. There is also better evidence on long-term effects as cohorts of families and children enrolled in some of the early studies (e.g., Perry Preschool, NHVP) have taken part in follow-up studies. We summarize results of the programs we have reviewed next.

Maternal Life Course Development

The assumption underlying many programs is that sustained and cumulative positive effects on children will occur if mothers' own life chances are improved (Benasich, Brooks-Gunn, & Clewell, 1992; Olds et al., 2000). Several programs have reported positive effects on maternal life course, even though this was not always one of the explicit goals. Important maternal life course outcomes include fertility, educational attainment, economic self-sufficiency, and health. Unfortunately, some programs that actively involve parents (e.g., PAT) have not measured maternal outcomes, limiting our knowledge base for these outcomes.

Despite the importance of the number and spacing of additional children for the mother's life course development, few studies have included fertility as an outcome. Of the 12 studies reviewed here, only 4 measured fertility outcomes, and of these, only the NHVP showed positive effects on pregnancies, births, and spacing of children, with evidence across both the Elmira and Memphis studies among higher risk mothers. Of the 27 early intervention programs reviewed by

Benasich et al. (1992), only 5 measured fertility outcomes. Each of these 5 programs, such as the Yale Child Welfare Study (Seitz, Rosenbaum, & Apfel, 1985), showed significantly lower birthrates in the intervention group. This review, however, included some studies with weaker evaluation designs (e.g., small number of families, nonrandom assignment to groups).

The effects on mother's educational achievement are mixed as well. The New Chance and Abecedarian interventions showed positive effects on outcomes such as high school completion and college attendance. The IHDP showed no effects at 5 years, and the NHVP showed some early effects at 4 years but none at 15 years, suggesting that the control group "caught up" with treatment group mothers. More detailed analyses of the effects of the timing of educational achievement relative to other maternal outcomes, such as fertility and employment, have not yet been reported.

Results for employment and welfare use are also mixed and tend to vary for subgroups of families. The NHVP reduced mothers' welfare use, the CCDP had no effect, and New Chance and the IHDP reported more welfare use. The latter result may reflect the short-term effects of linking mothers to needed services given that some of these same programs showed positive effects for number of months employed (IHDP) and number of mothers who combined work with Aid to Families With Dependent Children use (New Chance). It is interesting to note that although no long-term results for the mothers are reported for the Perry Preschool Program, when the children were 27 years old, they had spent less time on welfare and had earned more. The drastic reduction in welfare caseloads during recent years makes it difficult to test the impact of such programs on the transition from welfare to work.

Effects of these programs on maternal physical or mental health are inconclusive. The IHDP and HFA reported less emotional distress among mothers, while New Chance reported more depression. The Elmira NHVP reported some positive effects on substance use at 15 years, while New Chance reported no effects. Many other studies simply did not measure these outcomes.

Overall, the results suggest that it is difficult to influence maternal life course outcomes and that positive effects may take several years to emerge. The Elmira NHVP reported the most consistent effects for mothers' life course outcomes, although they are limited to the poor and unmarried subgroup of participants. Furthermore, some large programs, such as the CCDP, failed to measure many life course variables, even though they included efforts to support parents' personal development.

Parenting

Many programs seek to influence the parent-child relationship and the quality of the home environment. The range of outcome measures have included self-reports from parents, direct observations of parenting behaviors, assessment of the home environment, and official reports of child abuse and neglect. Several programs report positive effects for parenting attitudes and parent-child interaction measures (IHDP, Houston [HPCDC], CPCs, NHVP, Abecedarian), although most do not report positive effects across a broad range of outcomes. Other literature reviews have concluded that early intervention and family support programs have positive effects on parenting. Yoshikawa (1995) reviewed 28 programs that measured parenting outcomes, 19 of which reported generally positive effects. Benasich et al. (1992) reported that 10 of 11 programs found improved mother-infant interactions and that 7 of 10 reported positive changes in maternal knowledge or attitudes. Fewer programs have influenced the home environment as measured by the HOME scales (see also Karoly et al., 1998).

The current popularity of early home visiting programs is based to a considerable degree on their promise as a child abuse and neglect prevention strategy. Yet very few early education and family support programs have measured this outcome, and only one (Elmira NHVP) has shown positive effects on rates of substantiated child maltreatment reports within the context of a strong research design (randomized trial) and long-term follow-up data. Other programs, such as HFA, have reported changes in parental attitudes about child maltreatment (Daro & Harding, 1999), although the relation of attitudinal change to actual reductions in maltreatment is not known (Olds et al., 2000). Because child abuse and neglect is underreported in some communities, finding intervention effects through official child protective services reports is difficult and other indicators of actual maltreatment may need to be measured. For example, the Memphis NHVP found significant effects of nurse home visitation in reductions of hospital visits for injuries and ingestions consistent with a pattern of maltreatment (Kitzman et al., 1997).

In sum, model early intervention and family support programs have shown some promise in affecting parenting attitudes and behaviors, although the impact on the home environment and reductions in child abuse and neglect are more mixed and not yet fully evaluated.

Child Outcomes

Although cognitive outcomes remain important, measures of social adjustment are frequently added to more recent evaluations, particularly those examining long-term effects (e.g., Perry Preschool, NHVP, CPCs). Other reviews (e.g., Barnett, 1995) suggest that well-designed early intervention programs for disadvantaged children can have immediate and meaningful effects on cognitive ability. The strength and duration of those effects vary according to key program characteristics, as reviewed earlier. Larger and longer-lasting gains occurred when programs began early (e.g., Abecedarian, IHDP), were more intensive and comprehensive (e.g., Perry Preschool), and involved direct educational experiences for the children in addition to home visits that sought to enhance learning goals (Ramey & Ramey, 1998). Long-term follow-up studies of model and some large-scale programs showed that IQ gains can be maintained into the school-age years. Even when such gains are not maintained, there is evidence for continued effectiveness as reflected in measures of school success such as grade retention, special education placement, and high school graduation (Barnett, 1995; Karoly et al., 1998).

With respect to children's social and emotional development, the impact of programs has been measured in a variety of ways at different ages. Positive effects during the preschool years have been reported for some programs (e.g., Perry Preschool, IHDP, Abecedarian, Houston [HPCDC]). The emergence of behavioral problems and criminal activity among older children has been the focus of a smaller number of model programs (e.g., Perry Preschool, NHVP, Syracuse [FDRP]) and one large-scale program (CPCs) that followed families long enough to measure these outcomes. Although few programs report long-term effects, the results are somewhat encouraging in that the Perry Preschool Program, CPCs, the FDRP, and the NHVP (for the high-risk subgroup) all reported reductions in delinquency and criminal activity among children in the intervention groups. Yoshikawa (1995), after reviewing 42 early intervention and family support programs, concluded that the most consistent long-term effects on delinquency outcomes are found for programs that combine early education services with family support (see also Zigler, Taussig, & Black, 1992). However, because one exclusively home-based family support program (Elmira NHVP) and a primarily school-based (CPCs) approach both reported long-term effects on delinquency and criminal behaviors, this suggests that more than one type of program may be effective in preventing these social problems. The positive effects of these infancy and preschool programs also provide an interesting comparison to recent prevention trials designed to reduce conduct disorders and aggression such as FAST Track (Conduct Problems Prevention Research Group, 1992) and the Early Alliance Prevention Trial (Dumas, Prinz, Smith, & Laughlin, 1999), each of which begins in the first grade. It is too early to know whether these comprehensive, theory-based efforts will be as effective as the early interventions described previously in producing long-term effects on delinquency and criminal behavior.

A few programs have followed children long enough to measure economic activity. At 21 years of age, Abecedarian children report more skilled employment, and at 27 years of age, Perry Preschool children reported less welfare use and higher earnings. The Elmira NHVP recently collected 19-year data, which will allow a preliminary assessment of whether the gains in maternal economic self-sufficiency observed for the mothers will yield similar benefits for the participants' children as they reach adulthood.

COMMON ELEMENTS OF SUCCESSFUL PROGRAMS

What conclusions can be made about the aspects of program design and implementation

that are linked to program success? Some preliminary conclusions can be derived from the early intervention and family support literature (e.g., Barnett, 1995; Karoly et al., 1998; National Research Council and Institute of Medicine, 2000; Olds et al., 2000; Ramey & Ramey, 1998; Yoshikawa, 1995).

Timing and Duration. Programs that begin earlier and last longer are generally more effective. This conclusion is based on a few randomized studies that varied program length (e.g., NHVP) and others that attempted to link program impact as a function of amount of participation (e.g., IHDP). But relatively few studies have systematically varied timing or duration, so it is too early to identify a clear threshold age beyond which targeted interventions could not be successful. Not only are earlier and longer interventions more costly, but it is difficult to maintain family participation for lengthy periods. Although Karoly et al. (1998) demonstrated that program costs are recovered over time, there is still much to learn about when and for how long interventions should take place for maximum effectiveness.

Intensity and Comprehensiveness. Effective programs are more intense, broad, and comprehensive. These dimensions may be measured by the number of contacts (e.g., home visits) or hours spent with children and families, but they also reflect the range or breadth of services provided. Longer term effects are generally associated with programs that have multiple contacts over at least 2 or 3 years and that help parents with their own life course development in addition to focusing on the cognitive, socioemotional, and physical development of the children.

Program Quality. Not surprisingly, higher quality programs are more effective. Quality programs have a strong theoretical base, a well-defined curriculum, well-trained and supervised staff, adequate funding, a small teacher-to-child ratio (1 to 0.75 in infant/ toddler programs and 1 to 6 in preschool programs), a small home visitor-to-family ratio (1 to 10 or fewer), and strong formative and summative evaluation components. Overall program quality, however, is ultimately derived from the interpersonal relationships that staff develop with parents and children, where assistance, support, and instruction are balanced with respect for parental autonomy, authority, and cultural heritage.

Differential Effects in Subgroups. It is quite common for programs to benefit some children or families more than others. For example, long-term effects of the NHVP were generally restricted to the lower income and unmarried mothers and their children. Similarly, the IHDP reported IQ effects for the higher birth-weight children. The Syracuse (FDRP), Houston (HPCDC), and Perry Preschool programs all reported that program effects varied by gender. Programs also appear to have increased benefits to more disadvantaged families, although it is likely that there is a lower limit to this effect. For example, among poor families in the IHDP, having more risk factors in the family was associated with decreased program effectiveness (Liaw & Brooks-Gunn, 1994). Evidence of individual differences in program effects provides the rationale for more targeted versus universalistic approaches to these programs. It also suggests that even targeted programs need to be somewhat flexible in meeting the needs of specific children and families, especially as programs are disseminated in diverse community settings.

THE FUTURE OF EARLY INTERVENTION AND FAMILY SUPPORT PROGRAMS

The National Research Council and Institute of Medicine's (2000) report, *From Neurons to Neighborhoods*, summarized the state of the early intervention field in this way:

> The general question of whether early childhood programs can make a difference has been asked and answered in the affirmative innumerable times. This generic query is no longer worthy of further investigation. The central research priority for the early childhood field is to address more important sets of questions about how different types of interventions influence specific outcomes for children and families who face differential opportunities and vulnerabilities. To this end, program evaluators must assess the distinctive needs that must be met, the soundness of the intervention strategy, its acceptability to the intended recipients, the quality of its implementation, and the extent to which less intensive, broader-based programs can be developed that are both beneficial and cost-effective. (p. 379)

Improving program models that have shown some promise in affecting parent and child functioning should occur within a "culture of experimentation" (p. 380) in which the reasons for negligible, clinically insignificant, and uneven program effects (across measures, children, time, etc.) are systematically explored. For example, the initial optimism surrounding home visiting programs for young parents has given way to guarded assessments of program effectiveness even as widespread dissemination of untested models has continued (Gomby, Culross, & Behrman, 1999; Olds et al., 2000). Larger and more consistent results will occur only when programs are based on sound epidemiological research, employ behavior change strategies that are theoretically and empirically grounded, target families whose needs are most relevant to the programs, and engage in a research development process in which program elements are pilot tested before full implementation. It is also important to fully document the programs' content and methods so that replication can occur and to develop the organizational infrastructure needed to adequately support the programs in the community (Olds et al., 2000).

Public policy issues surrounding early intervention and family support programs are often cast in terms of the economic benefits derived from government-funded programs designed to aid vulnerable children and families as measured by increased productivity and decreased social problems (Karoly et al., 1998). Although cost-benefit analyses have not been numerous, there is mounting evidence that comprehensive programs targeted to families most in need can result in considerable savings over several years. For example, the Perry Preschool Program's $12,148 investment in children (in 1996 dollars) has been estimated to yield nearly $50,000 in reduced expenditures (e.g., fewer services, fewer losses to crime victims) and greater income as young adults (Karoly et al., 1998). Likewise, the $6000 investment in Elmira NHVP families will yield an estimated $30,766 in economic benefits among the higher risk families (Karoly et al., 1998).

It is not clear whether such savings could be realized with programs that began in the current welfare reform environment. The nature of the social safety net on which such programs depend for funding and through which some of the effects of the earlier programs may have depended (e.g., by linking families to needed social services) has changed. But a consideration of recent experimental evaluations of welfare reform suggests that interventions that narrowly concentrate on family economic issues (e.g., work incentives, wage supplements, income disregards) will not realize the range of benefits for families and children found with the most comprehensive and best implemented early intervention and family support programs. The Milwaukee New Hope project (Bos et al., 1999; Huston et al., 2001), the Minnesota Family Independence Program (Gennetian & Miller, 2000), and the Canadian Self-Sufficiency Program (Morris & Michalopoulos, 2000) all involved a combination of incentives to return to work, income supplements, and child care. Although some positive effects for educational achievement and classroom behavior have been reported in these programs for school-age children, younger children have been largely unaffected (National Research Council and Institute of Medicine, 2000). In addition, these programs have shown few effects on parenting behavior, maternal depressive symptoms, or changes in the home environment, which may be key to sustaining long-term cognitive, social, and emotional effects for children.

According to Ramey and Ramey (1998), "The primary issues for early intervention now are ones of the political will to aid vulnerable children, the appropriate scale of resources needed to provide potentially effective interventions, and commitment to conducting rigorous research to move the field of early intervention forward" (p. 119). We can and should work to make early intervention and family support programs better and more widely disseminated. But in the end, we must recognize that the interventions we have described are modest in scope given the enormity of the continuing problems of poverty and inequality in our society; thus, our expectations must match these realities. True reform and social change will come only when the first step of a sequential series of interventions represents an "ecological intervention" (Bronfenbrenner, 1975) to provide families with adequate housing, health care, nutrition, and employment.

REFERENCES

Alliance for Redesigning Government. (n.d.). *Comprehensive Child Development Program*. [Online]. Available: www.alliance.napawash.org/alliance/picases.nsf/504ca249c786e20f85256284006da7ab/cb06dc021d0dd70385256531005aa375?opendocument

Andrews, S. R., Blumenthal, J. B., Johnson, D. L., Kahn, A. J., Fergeson, C. J., Lasater, T. M., Malone, P. E., & Wallace, D. B. (1982). The skills of mothering: A study of Parent Child Development Centers. *Monographs of the Society for Research in Child Development, 47*(6, Serial No. 198).

Baker, A. J., Piotrkowski, C. S., & Brooks-Gunn, J. (1998). The effects of the Home Instruction Program for Preschool Youngsters (HIPPY) on children's school performance at the end of the program and one year later. *Early Childhood Research Quarterly, 13,* 571-588.

Barnett, W. S. (1985). Benefit-cost analysis of the Perry Preschool Program and its policy implications. *Educational Evaluation and Policy Analysis, 7,* 333-342.

Barnett, W. S. (1995). Long-term effects of early childhood programs on cognitive and school outcomes. *The Future of Children, 5*(3), 25-50.

Baumeister, A. A., & Bacharach, V. R. (1996). A critical analysis of the Infant Health and Development Program. *Intelligence, 23,* 79-104.

Benasich, A. A., Brooks-Gunn, J., & Clewell, B. C. (1992). How do mothers benefit from early intervention programs? *Journal of Applied Developmental Psychology, 13,* 311-362.

Bos, H., Huston, A. C., Granger, R., Duncan, G. J., Brock, T., & McLoyd, V. C. (1999). *New Hope for people with low incomes: Two-year results of a program to reduce poverty and reform welfare.* New York: Manpower Demonstration and Research Corporation.

Bradley, R. H., Whiteside, L., Mundfrom, D. J., Casey, P. H., Caldwell, B. M., & Barrett, K. (1994). Impact of the Infant Health and Development Program (IHDP), on the home environments of infants born prematurely and with low birth weight. *Journal of Educational Psychology, 86,* 531-541.

Bronfenbrenner, U. (1975). Is early intervention effective? In M. Guttentag & E. L. Struening (Eds.), *Handbook of evaluation research* (Vol. 2, pp. 519-603). Beverly Hills, CA: Sage.

Bronfenbrenner, U. (1979). *The ecology of human development: Experiments by nature and design.* Cambridge, MA: Harvard University Press.

Bronfenbrenner, U. (1986). Ecology of the family as a context for human development: Research perspectives. *Developmental Psychology, 22,* 723-742.

Bronfenbrenner, U., McClelland, P., Wethington, E., Moen, P., & Ceci, S. (1996). *The state of Americans.* New York: Free Press.

Brooks-Gunn, J., & Duncan, G. J. (1997). The effects of poverty on children and youth. *The Future of Children, 7*(2), 55-71.

Brooks-Gunn, J., Klebanov, P. K., Liaw, F., & Spiker, D. (1992). Enhancing the development of low-birthweight premature infants: Changes in cognition and behavior over the first three years. *Child Development, 64,* 736-753.

Brooks-Gunn, J., Liaw, F., & Klebanov, P. K. (1992). Effects of early intervention on cognitive function of low-birth-weight preterm infants. *Journal of Pediatrics, 120*(3), 350-359.

Brooks-Gunn, J., McCormick, M. C., Shapiro, S., Benasich, A. A., & Black, G. W. (1994). The effects of early education intervention on maternal employment, public assistance, and health insurance: The Infant Health and Development Program. *American Journal of Public Health, 84,* 924-931.

Campbell, F. A., Pungello, E. P., Miller-Johnson, S., Burchinal, M., & Ramey, C. T. (2001). The development of cognitive and academic abilities: Growth curves from an early childhood educational experiment. *Developmental Psychology, 37,* 231-242.

Campbell, F. A., & Ramey, C. T. (1994). Effects of early intervention on intellectual academic achievement: A follow-up study of children from low-income families. *Child Development, 65,* 684-698.

Campbell, F. A., & Ramey, C. T. (1995). Cognitive and school outcomes for high-risk African American students in middle adolescence: Positive effects of early intervention. *American Educational Research Journal, 32,* 743-772.

Campbell, F. A., Ramey, C. T., Pungello, E. P., Sparling, J., & Miller-Johnson, S. (2002). Early childhood education: Young adult outcomes from the Abecedarian Project. *Applied Developmental Science, 6,* 42-57.

Clarke, S. H., & Campbell, F. A. (1998). Can intervention early prevent crime later? The Abecedarian Project compared with other programs. *Early Childhood Research Quarterly, 13,* 319-343.

Coie, J. D., Watt, F., West, S. G., Hawkins, J. D., Asarnow, J. R., Markman, H. J., Ramey, S. L., Shure, M. B., & Long, B. (1993). The science of prevention: A conceptual framework and some directions for a national research program. *American Psychologist, 48,* 1013-1022.

Conduct Problems Prevention Research Group. (1992). A developmental and clinical model for the prevention of conduct disorder: The FAST Track Program. *Development and Psychopathology, 4,* 509-527.

Cummings, E. M., Davies, P. T., & Campbell, S. B. (2000). *Developmental psychopathology and family process.* New York: Guilford.

Daro, D. A., & Harding, K. A. (1999). Healthy Families America: Using research to enhance practice. *The Future of Children, 9*(1), 152-176.

Dumas, J., Prinz, R. J., Smith, E. M., & Laughlin, J. (1999). The EARLY ALLIANCE prevention trial: An integrated set of interventions to promote competence and reduce risk for conduct disorder, substance abuse, and school failure. *Clinical Child and Family Psychology Review, 2,* 37-53.

Dunst, C. J., & Trivette, C. M. (1994). Aims and principles of family support programs. In C. J. Dunst & C. M. Trivette (Eds.), *Supporting and strengthening families: Vol. 1. Methods, strategies, and practices* (pp. 30-48). Cambridge, MA: Brookline Books.

Erikson, M. F., & Kurz-Riemer, K. (1999). *Infants, toddlers, and families: A framework for support and intervention.* New York: Guilford.

Garbarino, J. (1995). *Raising children in a socially toxic environment.* San Francisco: Jossey-Bass.

Gennetian, L. A., & Miller, C. (2000). *Reforming welfare and rewarding work: Final report on the Minnesota Family Investment Program.* New York: Manpower Demonstration and Research Corporation.

Gilliam, W. S., Ripple, C. H., Zigler, E. F., & Leiter, V. (2000). Evaluating child and family demonstration initiatives: Lessons from the Comprehensive Child Development Program. *Early Childhood Research Quarterly, 15,* 41-59.

Gomby, D. S., Culross, P. L., & Behrman, R. E. (1999). Home visiting: Recent program evaluations—Analysis and recommendations. *The Future of Children, 9*(1), 4-26.

Gomby, D. S., Larner, M. B., Stevenson, C. S., Lewit, E. M., & Behrman, R. E. (1995). Long-term outcomes of early intervention programs: Analysis and recommendations. *The Future of Children, 5*(3), 6-24.

Goodson, B. D., Layzer, J. I., St. Pierre, R. G., Bernstein, L. S., & Lopez, M. (2000). Effectiveness of a comprehensive, five-year family support program for low-income children and their families: Findings from the Comprehensive Child Development Program. *Early Childhood Research Quarterly, 15*(1), 5-39.

Honig, A. S., & Lally, J. R. (1982). The Family Development Research Program: Retrospective review. *Early Child Development and Care, 10,* 41-62.

Honig, A. S., Lally, J. R., & Mathieson, D. H. (1982). Personal-social adjustment of school children after five years in a family enrichment program. *Child Care Quarterly, 11*(2), 138-146.

Huston, A., Duncan, G., Granger, R., Bos, H., McLoyd, V., Mistry, R., Crosby, D., Gibson, C., Magnusson, K., Romich, J., & Ventura, A. (2001). Work-based anti-poverty programs for parents can enhance the school performance and social behavior of children. *Child Development, 72,* 318-337.

Huston, A. C., McLoyd, V. C., & Coll, C. G. (1994). Children and poverty: Issues in contemporary research. *Child Development, 65,* 275-282.

Infant Health and Development Program. (1990). Enhancing the outcomes of low-birth-weight, premature infants: A multisite, randomized trial. *Journal of the American Medical Association, 263,* 3035-3042.

Johnson, D. L. (1990). The Houston Parent-Child Development Center Project: Disseminating a viable program for enhancing at-risk families. *Prevention in Human Services, 7*(1), 89-108.

Johnson, D. L., & Breckenridge, J. N. (1982). The Houston Parent-Child Development Center and the primary prevention of behavior problems in young children. *American Journal of Community Psychology, 10*(3), 305-316.

Johnson, D. L., & Walker, T. (1987). A follow-up evaluation of the Houston Parent-Child Development Center: School performance. *Journal of Early Intervention, 15*(3), 226-236.

Kagan, S. L., Powell, D. R., Weissbourd, B., & Zigler, E. F. (Eds.). (1987). *America's family support programs.* New Haven, CT: Yale University Press.

Karoly, L. A., Greenwood, P. W., Everingham, S. S., Hoube, J., Kilburn, M. R., Rydell, C. P., Sanders, M., & Chiesa, J. (1998). *Investing in our children: What we know and don't know about the costs and benefits of early childhood interventions.* Santa Monica, CA: RAND.

Kitzman, H., Olds, D. L., Henderson, C. R., Hanks, C., Cole, R., Tatelbaum, R., McConnochie, K. H., Sidora, K., Luckey, D. W., Shaver, D., Engelhardt, K., James, D., & Barnard, K. (1997). Effect of prenatal and infancy home visitation by nurses on pregnancy outcomes, childhood injuries, and repeated childbearing: A randomized controlled trial. *Journal of the American Medical Association, 278,* 644-652.

Lally, R. J., Mangione, P. L., & Honig, A. S. (1988). The Syracuse University Family Development Research Program: Long-range impact on an early intervention with low-income children and their families. In D. R. Powell (Ed.), *Parent education as early childhood intervention: Emerging directions in theory, research, and practice* (Vol. 3, pp. 79-104). Norwood, NJ: Ablex.

Layzer, J. I., Goodson, B. D., Bernstein, L., & Price, C. (2001). *National evaluation of family support programs: Final report: Vol. A. The meta-analysis.* Cambridge, MA: Abt Associates.

Liaw, F., & Brooks-Gunn, J. (1994). Cumulative familial risks and low-birthweight children's cognitive and behavioral development. *Journal of Clinical Child Psychology, 23,* 360-372.

McCarton, C. M., Brooks-Gunn, J., Wallace, I. F., Bauer, C. R., Bennett, F. C., Bernbaum, J. C., Broyles, R. S., Casey, P. H., McCormick, M. C., Scott, D. T., Tyson, J., Tonascia, J., & Meinert, C. L. (1997). Results at age 8 years of early intervention for low-birth-weight premature infants. *Journal of the American Medical Association, 277,* 126-132.

Morris, P., & Michalopoulos, C. (2000). *The Self-Sufficiency Project at 36 months: Effects on children of a program that increased employment and income.* Ottawa: Social Research and Demonstration Corporation.

National Research Council and Institute of Medicine. (2000). *From neurons to neighborhoods* (Committee on Integrating the Science of Early Childhood Development, J. P. Shonkoff & D. Phillips, Eds., Board on Children, Youth, and Families, Commission on Behavioral and Social Sciences and Education). Washington, DC: National Academy Press.

Olds, D. L., Eckenrode, J., Henderson, C. R., Jr., Kitzman, H., Powers, J., Cole, R., Sidora, K., Morris, P., Pettitt, L., & Luckey, D. (1997). Long-term effects of home visitation on maternal life course and child abuse and neglect: 15-year follow-up of a randomized trial. *Journal of the American Medical Association, 278,* 637-643.

Olds, D. L., Henderson, C. R., Jr., Chamberlin, R., & Tatelbaum, R. (1986). Preventing child abuse and neglect: A randomized trial of nurse home visitation. *Pediatrics, 78,* 65-78.

Olds, D., Henderson, C. R., Jr., Cole, R., Eckenrode, J., Kitzman, H., Luckey, D., Pettitt, L., Sidora, K., Morris, P., & Powers, J. (1998). Long-term effects of nurse home visitation on children's criminal and antisocial behavior: 15-year follow-up of a randomized trial. *Journal of the American Medical Association, 280,* 1238-1244.

Olds, D. L., Henderson, C. R., Jr., Tatelbaum, R., & Chamberlin, R. (1988). Improving the life-course development of socially disadvantaged mothers: A randomized trial of nurse home visitation. *American Journal of Public Health, 78,* 1436-1445.

Olds, D., Hill, P., Robinson, J., Song, N., & Little, C. (2000). Update on home visiting for pregnant women and parents of young children. *Current Problems in Pediatrics, 30,* 105-148.

Olds, D., Kitzman, H., Cole, R., & Robinson, J. (1997). Theoretical foundations of a program of home visitation for pregnant women and parents of young children. *Journal of Community Psychology, 25,* 9-25.

Parks, G. (2000). *The High/Scope Perry Preschool Project (October, 1997).* Washington, DC: U.S. Department of Justice, Office of Juvenile Justice and Delinquency Prevention.

Quint, J. C., Bos, J. M., & Polit, D. F. (1997). *New Chance: Final report on a comprehensive program for young mothers in poverty and their children.* New York: Manpower Demonstration Research Corporation.

Ramey, C. T. (1980). Social consequences of ecological intervention that began in infancy. In S. Harel (Ed.), *The at-risk infant.* Amsterdam: Excerpta Medica.

Ramey, C. T., & Campbell, F. A. (1981). Educational intervention for children at risk for mild retardation: A longitudinal analysis. In P. Mittler (Ed.), *Frontiers of knowledge in mental retardation: Social, educational, and behavioral aspects.* Baltimore: University Park Press.

Ramey, C. T., & Campbell, F. A. (1991). Poverty, early childhood education, and academic competence: The Abecedarian experiment. In A. C. Huston (Ed.), *Children in poverty: Child development and public policy* (pp. 190-221). Cambridge, UK: Cambridge University Press.

Ramey, C. T., Campbell, F. A., Burchinal, M., Skinner, M. L., Gardner, D. M., & Ramey, S. L. (2000). Persistent effects of early childhood education on high-risk children and their mothers. *Applied Developmental Science, 4*(1), 2-14.

Ramey, C. T., Dorval, B., & Baker-Ward, L. (1983). Group day care and socially disadvantaged families: Effects on the child and the family. *Advances in Early Education and Day Care, 3,* 69-106.

Ramey, C. T., & Haskins, R. (1981). The causes and treatment of school failure: Insights form the Carolina Abecedarian Project. In M. J. Begab, H. Garber, & H. C. Haywood (Eds.), *Psychosocial influences in retarded performance* (Vol. 2). Baltimore: University Park Press.

Ramey, C. T., & Ramey, S. L. (1998). Prevention of intellectual disabilities: Early interventions to improve cognitive development. *Preventive Medicine, 27,* 224-231.

Ramey, C. T., Yeates, K. O., & Short, E. J. (1984). The plasticity of intellectual development: Insights from preventive intervention. *Child Development, 55,* 1913-1925.

Reynolds, A. J. (1994). Effects of a preschool plus follow-on intervention for children at risk. *Developmental Psychology, 30,* 787-804.

Reynolds, A. J. (1995). One year of preschool intervention or two: Does it matter? *Early Childhood Research Quarterly, 10,* 1-31.

Reynolds, A. J. (2000). *Success in early intervention: The Chicago Child-Parent Centers.* Lincoln: University of Nebraska Press.

Reynolds, A. J., Chang, H., & Temple, J. (1998). Early childhood intervention and juvenile delinquency: An exploratory analysis of the Chicago Child-Parent Centers. *Evaluation Review, 22,* 341-372.

Schweinhart, L. J., Barnes, H. V., Weikart, D. P., Barnett, W. S., & Epstein, A. S. (1993). *Significant benefits: The High/Scope Perry Preschool Study through age 27* (Monographs of the High/Scope Educational Research Foundation, No. 10). Ypsilanti, MI: High/Scope Press.

Schweinhart, L. J., Berruta-Clement, J. R., Barnett, W. S., Epstein, A. S., & Weikart, D. P. (1985). Effects of the Perry Preschool Program on youths through age 19: A summary. *Topics in Early Childhood Special Education, 5*(2), 26-35.

Seitz, V., Rosenbaum, L. K., & Apfel, N. H. (1985). Effects of family support intervention: A ten-year follow-up. *Child Development, 56,* 376-391.

St. Pierre, R., Layzer, J., Goodson, B., & Bernstein, L. (1997). *National impact evaluation of the Comprehensive Child Development Program.* Cambridge, UK: Abt Associates.

Wagner, M. M., & Clayton, S. L. (1999). The Parents as Teachers program: Results from two demonstrations. *The Future of Children, 9*(1), 91-115.

Wagner, M. M., Spiker, D., Hernandez, F., Sung, J., & Gerlach-Downie, S. (2001). *Multi-site Parents as Teachers evaluation: Experiences and outcomes for children and families.* Menlo Park, CA: SRI International.

Walker, T., & Johnson, D. L. (1988). A follow-up evaluation of the Houston Parent-Child Development Center Project: Intelligence test results. *Journal of Genetic Psychology, 149,* 377-381.

Weikart, D. P., Bond, J. T., & McNeil, J. T. (1978). *The Ypsilanti Perry Preschool Project: Preschool years and longitudinal results through fourth grade* (Monographs of the High/Scope Educational Research Foundation, No. 3). Ypsilanti, MI: High/Scope Press.

Weikart, D. P., & Schweinhart, L. J. (1991). Disadvantaged children and curriculum effects. *New Directions for Child Development, 53,* 57-64.

Weikart, D. P., & Schweinhart, L. J. (1992). High/Scope Preschool Program outcomes. In J. T. McCord & R. E. Trembly (Eds.), *Preventing antisocial behavior: Interventions from birth through adolescence* (pp. 67-86). New York: Guilford.

Weikart, D. P., & Schweinhart, L. J. (1997). High/Scope Perry Preschool Program. In G. W. Albee & T. P. Gullotta (Eds.), *Primary prevention works* (pp. 146-166). Thousand Oaks, CA: Sage.

Weiss, H. B. (1993). Home visits: Necessary but not sufficient. *The Future of Children, 3*(3), 113-128.

Weiss, H. B., & Jacobs, F. H. (Eds.). (1988). *Evaluating family programs.* New York: Aldine de Gruyter.

Winter, M. M., & McDonald, D. S. (1997). Parents as Teachers: Investing in good beginnings for children. In G. W. Albee & T. P. Gullotta (Eds.), *Primary prevention works* (pp. 119-145). Thousand Oaks, CA: Sage.

Yoshikawa, H. (1995). Long-term outcomes of early childhood programs on social outcomes and delinquency. *The Future of Children, 5*(3), 51-75.

Zaslow, M., & Eldred, C. (1998). *Parenting behavior in a sample of young mothers in poverty.* New York: Manpower Demonstration Research Corporation.

Zigler, E., Taussig, C., & Black, K. (1992). Early childhood intervention: A promising preventative for juvenile delinquency. *American Psychologist, 47,* 997-1006.

CHAPTER 17

Back to Basics: Building an Early Care and Education System

Sharon L. Kagan
Michelle J. Neuman

As states expand both their interest and investments in young children, they expect, first and foremost, to have youngsters who are ready for school, youngsters who meet standards, and youngsters who are adept at preliteracy and prenumeracy skills. Make no mistake, the "basics" have returned in full force to early care and education. So prevalent is this sentiment that White House conferences, vast media attention, countless new initiatives, and fresh legislation are promoting standards, outcomes, skills, and assessments for young children. Awash with good intentions, this orientation has also, however unintentionally, obfuscated another set of less well known, but equally important, basics. Poorly understood, this second set of basics refers to what it takes to make early care and education programs function so that they can, indeed, provide the quality services necessary to achieve the basics so common in today's parlance.

Just what constitutes this second set of basics, and why are they so important? This chapter suggests that these "hidden basics" are the *infrastructure* and the *system* of early care and education. At the core of every critical policy question faced by policymakers and advocates, these basics beg for attention as America asks the following questions. How should quality services be "incentivized"? How can we break down the heretofore segregated approach to services? Who should take the lead in administering and/or regulating such efforts? How do we know that such efforts are working, and for what populations do services work best? What will such efforts cost?

Not glamorous, catchy, or well-understood words, *infrastructure* and *system* are often neglected in important discussions of early childhood policy. They are regarded as vague and are deemed remote from the daily realities that face parents and children. Little could be further from the truth. Parents care about quality early care and education for their children. And infrastructure is the sine qua non of that quality; it is the essential ingredient that enables expansion and excellence. Systems are also important to parents and policymakers. Systems make the pieces function; they are what enable tax dollars to yield returns and what congeal highly disparate, idiosyncratic, and episodic efforts. Systems eliminate redundancies and maximize efficiencies.

This chapter is about the all-important and hidden basics—the *infrastructure* and the *system*. By *infrastructure,* we mean the supports that are essential to making programs and other direct services to children and families effective. Such supports (or elements of the infrastructure), although differing somewhat according to various authors (as we delineate later), are generally accepted as including (a) professional development and training, (b) regulation, (c) quality assurance mechanisms, (d) information dissemination, (e) finance, (f) governance, and (g) accountability. *System,* as we use it, is a broader term that encompasses both the infrastructure and the direct services that children and families receive (typically, the programs and services). Using these definitions, this chapter considers the nature of systems, revealing that to date there is no single or uniform definition of an early care and education system or of its infrastructure. The chapter considers why this is the case and discusses the liability of continuing to mount programs in the absence of such definitions. It offers a more elaborated working definition of an early care and education system and of its infrastructure. The chapter asserts unequivocally that unless the system and the infrastructure are addressed and supported, there is little opportunity for achieving early care and education and the desired outcomes for children now being touted. Finally, it concludes with concrete operational suggestions for consideration as new agendas for children are being considered.

WHY A *SYSTEM* AND WHY AN *INFRASTRUCTURE?*

During recent years, investments in early care and education have increased dramatically at both the federal and state levels. Using constant 1999 dollars, federal expenditures on early care and education increased from about $8 billion to $12 billion between 1992 and 1999 (Barnett & Masse, in press). If we examine the trajectory of state investments, we see that total spending for child development and family support efforts has increased by nearly 90% since 1998 (Cauthen, Knitzer, & Ripple, 2000). In 2000, state investments alone totaled more than $3.7 billion, a dramatic increase over a mere 2-year period. In fact, 33 states reported overall funding increases of 10% or more. Although these increases were found across the early childhood age group, there are still fewer resources accorded to infants and toddlers. Between 1998 and 2000, state funding for children ages 3 to 6 years increased by 24% (from $1.7 billion to $2.1 billion), and funding for children under 3 more than doubled (from $108 to $226 million) (Cauthen et al., 2000).

These trends are mirrored—and in some cases magnified—internationally. Although European countries have had long traditions of investing in programs for young children, some nations with much shorter histories have increased their financial commitments to early care and education dramatically over the past 5 years. In Portugal, for example, the national budget for preschool education has more than doubled since 1996. Significant increases have been documented in the Netherlands and the United Kingdom as well. Most countries now spend between 0.4% and 0.6% of their gross domestic product

(GDP) on early childhood education for children between the ages of 3 and 6 years (the United States spends about 0.36%). Some countries spend significantly more when infant-toddler services and other family benefits are included in the calculations (Organization for Economic Cooperation and Development [OECD], 2001). Indeed, countries such as Belgium, Denmark, France, and Sweden routinely spend more than 1% of their GDP on early care and education. Moreover, nearly all other industrialized countries invest in important family supports, including child allowances and paid parental leave policies (Meyers & Gornick, 2000; OECD, 2001; Rostgaard & Fridberg, 1998).

Despite this rapid and significant infusion of funds, concerns about the quality of services and their ability to yield and sustain the outcomes desired by policymakers remain prevalent (Kagan & Cohen, 1997). When the Cost, Quality, and Child Outcomes Study was released in 1995 (Cost, Quality, and Child Outcomes Study Team, 1995), even those closest to the field were surprised by its findings related to the pervasiveness of low- and mediocre-quality care. Then, and still today, we correctly ask the following questions. How can quality be so low when so many centers and programs are being accredited? When so many quality initiatives are being funded? When investments are increasing so? When parents are paying the most they can pay, often more for child care than for college tuition?

There are two answers to these challenging questions. First, and most important, the resources to establish quality are insufficient to meet the true costs of American child care (Cost, Quality, and Child Outcomes Study Team, 1995). This is the case despite requirements that a certain percentage of the Child Care Development Fund and Head Start funds be allocated for quality improvement measures and despite notable complementary

efforts by states to bolster services. Unlike other nations with whom we are routinely compared, America's public investment in early care and education remains distressingly low (Meyers & Gornick, 2000; OECD, 2001). As noted earlier, although the United States ranks among the richest nations, it spends a much smaller share of its wealth on young children and families than do most other industrialized countries. In these countries, parental fees typically cover 25% to 30% of the costs of child care, with government picking up the rest of the tab. In contrast, parents in the United States carry the burden of roughly 60% of the costs of early care and education (OECD, 2001), and this makes investing in quality more difficult to finance. So, the first critical issue revolves around *how much* is being expended on young children.

Although inadequate resources is the most important issue, it is not the only issue. We need to understand that *how* resources are spent is also critically important. Historically, our public investments in early care and education have been directed to providing direct services to children and families and to increasing the supply of services. A secondary objective has been to increase affordability via subsidies to fee-paying parents. Some, but far less, attention has been paid to the quality of those services. And even less attention has been paid to nurturing the activities and supports that nourish quality.

For example, even though study after study has found that states with more stringent regulations tend to have higher quality centers (Cost, Quality, and Child Outcomes Study Team, 1995; Howes, Smith, & Galinsky, 1995) and family child care homes (Galinsky, Howes, Kontos, & Shinn, 1994), states have strengthened some regulations but not others. Many states have improved staff-child ratios for infants and preschool children but not for 2-year olds. States have added substantial numbers of hours of ongoing staff training, but preservice qualifications have not improved greatly (Morgan, in press). Although we have learned that wage enhancements are directly related to increased quality in programs (Bell, Burton, Shukla, & Whitebook, 1997), increases in wages have remained the purview of special (and worthwhile) projects rather than a prevailing characteristic of all early care and education efforts. Similarly, although research has found that programs accredited by the National Association for the Education of Young Children (NAEYC) pay higher wages to staff, report lower teacher turnover, and have retained twice as many staff members over the past decade as compared with non-accredited programs (Whitebook, Howes, & Phillips, 1998), few states provide incentives for settings to undergo this quality improvement process. Just 16 states pay a higher per-child rate to accredited programs (Morgan, in press), and only 5 states require state prekindergarten programs to be accredited (Mitchell, Ripple, & Chanana, 1998). Finally, although we understand that quality curriculum and quality pedagogy are essential to quality early care and education, only very recently have we linked these ingredients to robust calls for credentialed personnel (Bowman, Donovan, & Burns, 2001; Kagan & Cohen, 1997).

The disconnect among research, policy, and practice clearly looms large in early care and education. It is particularly problematic in early care and education now, however, because we have an opportunity to redirect a portion of the significant investments that are being made. Indeed, rather than focusing all new dollars on direct services and demand-driven subsidies to improve affordability, quality enhancement would stand a far better chance if some portion of the investments were devoted to supporting the infrastructure and building a durable coordinated system

of early care and education (European Commission Childcare Network, 1996; Kagan & Cohen, 1997; Gallagher & Clifford, 2000; OECD, 2001). To that end, Kagan and Cohen (1997) recommended that 10% of early care and education funds be invested directly in the infrastructure. This earmarking would still allow states the flexibility to determine how to allocate the money so as to meet local needs. In other countries, such as Germany and Austria, the high quality of early care and education programs has been attributed to a strong infrastructure (Tietze, Cryer, Bairrao, Palacios, & Wetzel, 1996). Not surprisingly, the European Commission Childcare Network (1996) recommended that countries allocate at least 6% of early childhood funds to develop the infrastructure. In America, however, a major part of the challenge is that we are unclear as to what we mean by a system and what we mean by infrastructure.

HOW HAVE *SYSTEM* AND *INFRASTRUCTURE* BEEN DEFINED IN THE PAST?

Webster's New World Dictionary defines a system as "a set or arrangement of things so related or connected as to form a unity or organic whole (e.g., a solar system, school system, system of highways)" (Merriam-Webster, 1970, p. 1445). Note that the nomenclature "school system" is so commonplace that *Webster's* uses it as an exemplar. This popularity of "school system" stands in stark contrast to the notion of an "early care and education system" not only in *Webster's* nomenclature but also in reality. To think of schools as functioning within the context of a system is normative; to think of early care and education as functioning within the context of a system is not, even during an era when so many parallels are drawn between compulsory (K–12) education and early childhood education.

Although it is not common to consider a system of early care and education, during the past decade such conceptualizations and nomenclature have begun to appear. For example, in 1991, Jule Sugarman discussed the characteristics of an early childhood system. He noted that although early childhood programs were gaining increased attention at the federal level, "what is missing is a sense of what system(s) would best accomplish our national objective" (Sugarman, 1991, p. xi). He suggested that the characteristics of an early childhood system had elements "with respect to" the child's program, service availability, protecting children, health and mental health, families and social services, staff, environment, funding, providers, nutrition, and other matters. For each of these items, Sugarman spelled out a set of indicators.

Taking a different approach, the Essential Functions and Change Strategies Task Force (1993) of the Quality 2000 initiative began to deal with the definition of the infrastructure. Using the *Webster's* definition of an infrastructure as the "substructure or underlying foundation" (Merriam-Webster, 1970, p. 723), it suggested that the early care and education infrastructure was composed of five essential functions: (a) collaborative planning and cross-system linkages, (b) consumer and public engagement, (c) quality assurance, (d) professional and workforce development, and (e) financing. In addition to creating subthemes for each of the five functions or pieces of the infrastructure, this group noted that each function was a specialized or essential component of the whole; "a function implies performance and action essential to the operation of the system" (Essential Functions and Change Strategies Task Force, 1993, p. 11). A function or an element of the infrastructure is a part of, but not a replacement for, a system.

Emanating from this work, *Not by Chance* (Kagan & Cohen, 1997) identified eight components of an early care and education system for consideration by those interested in designing a long-term vision for such a system: (a) quality programs; (b) child-based, results-driven system; (c) parent and family engagement; (d) individual licensing; (e) professional preparation; (f) program licensing; (g) funding and financing; and (h) governance, planning, and accountability (see Box 15.1).

Although the list of components is important, more crucial is the definition of the infrastructure and the system proffered by *Not by Chance* (Kagan & Cohen, 1997). The report suggested that a system consisted of these eight components and that all eight components had to be present for a system of early care and education to exist. Stated as a somewhat unconventional formula "$8 - 1 = 0$," *Not by Chance* suggested that if even one component of the system were taken away, the system could not function as a system; the net result would be zero or a nonsystem. Equally important, *Not by Chance* suggested another formula: The system (or all eight components) was composed of programs (Component 1) + the infrastructure (Components 2-8). Definitionally, then, it is programs plus the infrastructure that equals or composes the system.

More recently, other scholars and practitioners have highlighted the need for increased attention to the infrastructure and to systems theory. Gallagher and Clifford (2000) argued that the lack of a comprehensive infrastructure or support system for the delivery of early care and education services undermines efforts to protect and enhance the well-being of young children. They identified and discussed eight necessary components for creating a comprehensive infrastructure for an early care and education system: (a) personnel preparation, (b) technical

Box 15.1 The Eight Components of an Early Care and Education System

1. *Quality Programs.* At the core of any system must be a set of direct services to children and families that are of high quality and that are easily accessible.

   - *Create learning environments and opportunities:* Foster the effective use of materials, curriculum, and pedagogy, including multi-age and flexible grouping of children, effective staff deployment, attentiveness to cultural and linguistic variation, and appropriate balance between academic and play activities. Establish effective systems of assessment that are ongoing and that are used to improve instruction.
   - *Advance children's healthy development:* Foster concerted attention to children's physical and mental health by either providing or accessing appropriate screenings, immunizations, and services.
   - *Foster accreditation:* Provide incentives to encourage early care and education services to participate in accreditation and in other quality enhancement efforts.
   - *Create and maintain links with community resources:* Foster ongoing links with schools, resource and referral agencies, and other community services. This component stresses support for these agencies.
   - *Create and maintain links with family child care:* Support family child care and family child care networks.

2. *Child-Based, Results-Driven System (accountability)*

   - *Define appropriate results:* This includes the establishment of a state- and/or community-wide system of results across all domains of development, with appropriate benchmarks. Parents and professionals must be included in the development of such results.
   - *Establish mechanisms to collect results appropriately:* This includes the development of data collection strategies that take the ages and abilities of young children into consideration.
   - *Ensure that results are used appropriately:* This includes the establishment of appropriate safeguards so that data collected will not be used to label, track, or stigmatize young children and that data will be useful to policymakers as they plan increased services for young children and their families.

3. *Parent, Family, Community, and Public Engagement*

   - *Support parents as consumers:* Ensure that parents have options as they use early care and education services.
   - *Increase workplace commitments to families and business and community involvement in early care and education:* Ensure that incentives are provided for American businesses to be family friendly in their policies and practices and to be involved in advancing legislative and community supports for early care and education.

- *Increase community awareness of early care and education:* Provide for the development of ongoing opportunities for the public to gain information regarding the status of young children and their families.

4. *Individual Credentialing*

    - *Credential all who work with young children:* Create an appropriate set of credentials so that all who work with young children have the ability to gain transferable credentials. This suggests that the licensing of facilities should be distinct from the credentialing of individuals.
    - *Create the credentialing system and compensate teachers accordingly:* Ensure that credentials that are developed are instantiated in state regulations and are accompanied by appropriate salaries and benefits.
    - *Create administrator/director/master teacher and leadership credentials:* Recognize that an array of opportunities for adults exist in early care and education, and create credentials for them.

5. *Improve the Content of, and Resources for, Professional Development*

    - *Examine the content of all preparation programs:* Ensure that all certification and teacher preparation programs are up-to-date and focused on producing developmentally appropriate outcomes.
    - *Create the content and incentives:* Ensure that administrator/director/master teacher content is appropriate for the diverse roles and responsibilities.
    - *Create opportunities for advocacy and leadership:* Foster the development of leadership in all sectors of the early care and education system.

6. *Program Licensing*

    - *Eliminate exemptions:* Ensure that all programs serving young children are subject to state regulation.
    - *Streamline, coordinate, and adequately fund facility licensing:* Ensure that licensing is efficient and that it is funded at levels sufficient to ensure its completion.
    - *Promote national guidelines:* Create and/or support the promulgation of a set of national licensing standards that can be used as guidelines for states.

7. *Funding and Financing*

    - *Identify the costs of a quality system:* Ensure that all fiscal projections include the cost of funding the infrastructure and the full cost of care.
    - *Raise staff compensation:* Staff compensation in early care and education should be commensurate with that of public schools given equal education and experience of staff.
    - *Identify revenue sources:* Discern short- and long-term revenue sources that can fund the early care and education system.

- *Develop a long-term financing plan:* Engage civic leaders, stakeholders, and academics in the development of a comprehensive 15-year financing plan that considers the costs of creating an early care and education system, with adequate funding to support the infrastructure. Create a time line for its implementation.

8. *Governance, Planning, and Program Accountability*

- *Establish governance mechanisms at the state level:* Such mechanisms should durably provide for the oversight of the early care and education field. Such mechanisms might be boards, cabinets, or other structures, but they must be durable and take responsibility for planning, assessment, distribution of resources, and agenda setting.
- *Establish governance mechanisms at the local level:* Create mechanisms at the local level that will coordinate the delivery of services, ensure the effective use of funds, provide for the infrastructure, and coordinate efforts with the state governance mechanism.

SOURCE: Kagan and Cohen (1997).

assistance, (c) applied research and program evaluation, (d) communication, (e) demonstration, (f) data systems, (g) comprehensive planning, and (h) coordination of support elements. They discussed the various types of barriers—institutional, psychological, sociological, economic, political, and geographic—that one may face when implementing new policies to support an infrastructure.

Systems theory is prevalent also in international discussions for improving early care and education policies and programs. The 1992 European Council Recommendation on Child Care, which has been adopted by all member states, proposed specific objectives for the development of services for young children: affordability, access to services in all areas, access to services for children with special needs, combining safe and secure care with a pedagogical approach, close and responsive relations between services and parents and local communities, diversity and flexibility of services, increased choice for parents, and coherence between different services. "Taken together, these objectives form the basis for the definition of a good quality service system; fully achieved, they would ensure equal access to good quality services" (European Commission Childcare Network, 1996, p. 5). The European Commission Childcare Network (1996) proposed criteria or targets for assessing progress toward achieving the recommendation's specific objectives and establishing the conditions that would enable their achievement.

Building on this work and its own policy analysis, the OECD Thematic Review of Early Childhood Education and Care Policy proposed eight key elements of successful policy to promote equitable access to quality services (OECD, 2001): (a) a systemic and integrated approach to policy development and implementation; (b) a strong and equal partnership with the education system; (c) a universal approach to access, with particular attention to children in need of special support; (d) substantial public investment in services and the infrastructure; (e) a participatory approach to quality improvement and assurance; (f) appropriate training and working conditions for staff in all forms of provision; (g) a systematic attention to monitoring and data collection; and (h) a stable framework and long-term agenda for research and evaluation. Cross-national analyses suggest that each of these key elements needs to be addressed for the goal of quality accessible services to be achieved.

As analytic as these definitions are, their utility emerges only when they are coalesced into action and practice. In reality, however, there is little commonality in the systems of early care and education that are emerging. Each state, each leader, and each policymaker seems to be etching a unique definition. Like the veritable and venerable Rorschach Test, early care and education systems seem to derive individual meaning in, and from, the eye of the beholder.

On the one hand, such differences in interpretation are welcome. They provide the maximum amount of flexibility to states as they craft their early care and education policies. This approach does not limit ingenuity or invention, with the result that exciting efforts are being mounted to augment and enrich direct services to children. In addition, such variation leaves us with an unintended natural experiment whereby states can glean workable strategies and ideas from others. Often a pioneer state will create an effort that supports one component of the system, and when it is reviewed by other states, it is modified and improved, sometimes causing the pioneer state to alter its effort. Examples of this may be observed in the increasing authority being given to governance bodies as they proliferate across the states (Cauthen et al., 2000). As such, there is not only a cumulative building of efforts but also an approach that promotes their continuous improvement. Finally, an advantage of the "nonsystematization" of the system is that the different efforts could be subjected to qualitative and comparative evaluation.

On the other hand, the lack of a common understanding of what is meant by a system of early care and education leaves policymakers and practitioners in somewhat of a quandary. Lacking clear direction, policy initiatives often focus on one element of the system one year and on another element the next. Furthermore, without a widely accepted definition of a system, there is no organized way to ascertain whether all elements of a system are being addressed. Another risk is that as initiatives develop haphazardly in parts of the country—with some very active states and others much less so—inequities in system building emerge across states.

A scholar from another country might peer at the United States and discern that the same kind of unsystematic chaotic development of early childhood *programs* is now characterizing the development of early childhood *systems*. Indeed, the international OECD review team that reviewed U.S. early care and education in 1999 noted the following:

> We witnessed an abundance of collaborative initiatives and innovative practices, particularly at the local level, a remarkable array of energising forces intent on improving the overall situation of young children and their families. . . . In order to increase the chances of sustaining and nourishing regional partnerships (which are all based on voluntary participation), an agreed infrastructure with clear policy goals and implementation plans is necessary. What is needed is an *overall vision* of quality education and care in the early years, a coordinated policy framework to draw together these varied approaches and use them to the best advantage of young children and their families. (OECD, 2000, p. 52)

THE CURRENT STATUS OF SYSTEMS DEVELOPMENT

State efforts to build a system are so prevalent today that the most recent *Map and Track* edition (Cauthen et al., 2000), a report that profiles and analyzes state policies and initiatives for young children and families, has a special category titled "Early Childhood Systems Development." The report found that state efforts to build early childhood systems and maximize the impact of program investments are increasing but remain uneven across the country. The authors found that 30 states report some level of early childhood systems-building efforts. Although not all of these efforts focus exclusively on young children, this nonetheless represents a substantial increase over the 16 states that reported such systems-level initiatives in 1998. On the other hand, only 11 states dedicate state funds for systems development efforts, and some of these funds support programs and services. The authors summed up the situation as follows:

> Recognizing that developing individual programs is not sufficient to address the multiple needs of young children and families, state policymakers are increasingly attending to early childhood system development—developing the infrastructure, resources, and leadership necessary to create a coordinated system of services and supports to address the many needs of young children and their families. (p. 8)

But how coordinated and how comprehensive are these services really? On the positive side, many states, in addition to funding direct programs and services, are funding components of the infrastructure. We use the term *direct services* + to describe efforts that typically provide for direct services to children and families plus one or two other components of the infrastructure. In some cases, these noteworthy *direct services* + efforts include funding new supports for staff to achieve better training and compensation. For example, Rhode Island's RIteCare Health Insurance provides health insurance for child care center staff whose programs serve state-subsidized children (Mitchell,

Stoney, & Dichter, 2001). North Carolina's TEACH and WAGES models, now being replicated in many other states, provide educational scholarships and the potential for increased wages for people working in early care and education settings (Mitchell et al., 2001). In other states, *direct services* + means that funds are provided to subsidize facilities expansion. For example, Connecticut has appropriated money to lower the debt owed by providers on revenue bonds for new facilities. Early education providers who build new facilities are responsible for paying back, over a 30-year period, only 20% of the debt incurred (Mitchell et al., 2001).

In still other states, *direct services* + means establishing mechanisms that facilitate coordination and policy development. For example, Hawaii has established its Good Beginnings Alliance, a statewide public-private partnership that works to plan and coordinate services for young children. Indiana has its Building Bright Beginnings effort, a governor's initiative that has both an advisory team and a center that work to coordinate and assess services and to disseminate information to policymakers. South Carolina's First Steps to School Readiness has established public-private partnership boards in every county to assess local needs and develop strategic planning. The Governor's Early Childhood Initiative in Kentucky, funded with tobacco settlement funds, has created an Early Childhood Development Authority to oversee and administer funding, Community Councils to assess local needs, and a Business Council to promote involvement in early childhood issues (Cauthen et al., 2000).

These efforts, and many like them, clearly indicate that the idea of supporting the infrastructure is becoming more normative. Yet this progress has not been easy given both the nation's penchant to legislate incrementally and its predilection to invest in direct services. As a result, these efforts warrant accolades, as do the ardent pioneers who conceived, advocated for, and implemented them.

Internationally as well, there are countries that have demonstrated a strong commitment to developing services plus one component of the infrastructure. For example, England has set up Early Years and Childcare Development Partnerships with representatives from the public, private, and voluntary sectors; local education, health, and social services; employers, trainers, advisers, and parents in each local authority. The partnerships are a governance tool for expanding and improving early care and education services in partnership with public, for-profit, and nonprofit providers. Although the funding is decentralized to the local and services level, national standards and regulations remain. Part of the grant is earmarked for developing the local infrastructure and services, which support quality assurance (Bertram & Pascal, 1999).

Several countries have focused on strengthening the training and working conditions of staff. Finland, Italy, and Portugal recently upgraded the required training and education of lead early childhood staff to the university level (OECD, 2001). Belgium, Italy, Norway, and Portugal have improved in-service training; noncontact time is set aside in employee contracts for ongoing professional development as an essential part of forging staff relationships and of undertaking an ongoing critical evaluation of the curriculum being offered to children. In Italy, early childhood staff have a right to 6 hours of paid professional development time each week. During this time, they may undertake, for example, the process of pedagogical documentation, which is a very useful tool to deepen understanding among staff and children and to encourage reflective practice (European Commission Childcare Network, 1996).

Another example of *direct services +* is found in Australia, which is unique in having a national, government-supported accreditation system for its early care and education centers that is tied directly to the provision of funding. The Quality Improvement and Accreditation System (QIAS) is based on the NAEYC voluntary accreditation program. Like the NAEYC accreditation, the QIAS focuses primarily on assessing and improving the determining, or process, components of quality through an externally validated, center-based evaluation method. Because centers are required to take part in the QIAS process for parents to be eligible for the Child Care Benefit (the main fee subsidy in Australia), more than 98% of both private for-profit and nonprofit centers participate (Press & Hayes, 2000).

Other countries have focused their *direct services +* on improving parent and family engagement in early care and education. In the Netherlands and Portugal, for example, parent associations are among the privileged partners (along with, e.g., trade unions) in the consultation process leading to the formulation of national educational policies, including those concerning care and education. In several countries (e.g., Denmark, Finland, the Netherlands, Norway, Sweden), genuine decision making, access to information, and some powers of supervision are given to parents via parent councils and representation on governing boards (OECD, 2001).

Yet there is a problem. Only a handful of efforts are truly addressing the entire system. Although addressing one, two, or even three components of the infrastructure is better than addressing none and is extremely important, it will not render the kind of quality improvement needed over the long haul. For example, despite considerable diverse investments in training and professional development, which is often thought to be at the very heart of early care and education, gains in quality are modest. Where more robust gains appear, it is often because a combination of improvements exists. North Carolina is an excellent example. That state, through a variety of efforts such as Smart Start, Teacher Education and Compensation Helps (TEACH), and regulatory changes, has demonstrated improvements in child outcomes (Smart Start Evaluation Team, 2000). Specifically, Smart Start is a comprehensive effort that promotes county partnerships that plan and make decisions regarding early childhood education in their counties. The TEACH project aims to promote professional development and compensation of early care and education staff. Regulatory improvements have strengthened the content of and support for regulations in early care and education settings. Together, these efforts and others in North Carolina combine to form a reform approach that is producing results. Combining lessons from practice in North Carolina and from theoretical work on systems development, we can now see that it is imperative not to fund only *direct services +*. We must press ourselves to *consider the system in its entirety.*

How can this be in done in a nation characterized by episodic and flirtatious investments in children? In a nation where legislative and bureaucratic structures foster categorical programmatic separations? In a nation that is reluctant to value early care and education as a national imperative? Although not definitive or the sole answer, one response is to do what business and other disciplines and fields have done routinely—to acknowledge the importance of long-term strategic planning and to develop incremental operational strategies aligned with the long-term plan. Stated differently, considering the system in its entirety means having a dream *and* developing sequentially and systematically the process to achieve it. This approach suggests that creating a detailed vision or plan for the early care and education system is the requisite first step, to be followed by the development of implementation plans that

can be aligned with legislative initiatives over a period of years.

Is this possible? Indeed, *can* this be done? As states have considered expanding their services to young children, some have begun to shift from a program approach to considering the development of a system. Delaware, in its Early Success effort, developed a long-range blueprint that advanced the existence of a system (Early Success Steering Committee, 2000). Building incrementally, Delaware is moving toward the enactment of a comprehensive system of services. Likewise, Massachusetts has developed a similar comprehensive plan (Massachusetts Department of Education, 2001), as have North Carolina and California (Mitchell et al., 2001). Most recently, New York State education legislation that addresses universal pre-kindergarten has suggested that six critical dimensions need to be considered: universal access, diversity, collaboration, developmentally appropriate practice, teacher preparation, and financing. "The existing system not only contributes to shaping the development of hundreds of thousands of preschoolers in New York State, it also operates as a vital support system for the families to which those preschoolers belong" (Lekies & Cochran, 2001, p. 59). In sum, these states have a mandate to transcend programmatic thinking and move to systemic long-term planning that defines and envisions a system of early care and education.

Another example of comprehensive system building in American early care and education is the U.S. military. More than 200,000 young children are served every day (Campbell, Appelbaum, Martinson, & Martin, 2000). Over the past 10 years, the armed forces have developed a system of child care options with its own regulatory process, training and improved wages, and accreditation program. The large-scale program is adequately funded, addresses quality, has reasonable personnel policies, and is open to all children and families for a sliding scale fee (Morgan, in press). The military uses a systemic approach that links centers, family child care homes, before- and after-school programs, and resource and referral services to assist parents in finding care through a single point of entry. Basic standards have been established and are rigorously enforced in all settings. Moreover, 95% of all military child care centers also meet the higher NAEYC accreditation standards. In military child development centers, staff receive systematic ongoing training (24 hours every year) and increased compensation that is linked to their training. Following training and wage improvements, the system has experienced a dramatic reduction in staff turnover—from more than 300% annually at some bases to less than 30%—and staff morale and professionalism have improved (Campbell et al., 2000).

Taking a look outside the United States, a few nations have recognized that all components of the system need to be addressed so as to achieve quality, accessible services, and a solid infrastructure to support them (OECD, 2001). We discuss two examples here. First, Sweden has developed a coherent early care and education and school-age child care system for children from birth to 12 years of age. All children with working or studying parents have a *legal right* to a place in early care and education from 1 year of age (after the paid parental leave period). A free part-time session will soon be available for *all* 4-, 5-, and 6-year-olds. Since 1996, the Ministry of Education and Science has held national responsibility for policy development for early care and education and compulsory schooling, although in practice local authorities have the freedom to adapt policies to meet local needs and circumstances. National curriculum guidelines for preschool, compulsory school, and upper secondary school are linked conceptually by a coherent view of knowledge, development, and learning. A new preservice education program for lead staff who work with young children will ensure that early childhood, school-age child care, and primary school teachers share a common core of knowledge and understanding. Similar pay and working conditions already exist across the sector (Gunnarsson, Martin Korpi, & Nordenstam, 1999).

France is another country that has taken a systemic approach. In contrast to Sweden, however, there are in fact two highly developed systems in France: a system of infant-toddler centers, family child care, and drop-in centers for children from birth to 3 years of age that are available on a sliding scale fee and a system of universal free preschools for children from 2½ to 6 years of age. Each system has a distinct and coherent national regulatory framework, funding policy, professional development structure, and methods for evaluation and accountability. Although voluntary, more than 98% of 3-, 4-, and 5-year-olds attend the preschools (*écoles maternelles*), which are administratively part of the primary school system. A national curriculum organized around 3-year "cycles" encourages pedagogical continuity as children move from one class to another (French-American Foundation, 1999). Although in the past there have been few links between the infant-toddler and preschool systems, new approaches are being developed, particularly at the local level, to bridge the divide (Baudelot & Rayna, 2000). In sum, these two international examples confirm the need for efforts in all areas for the system to really work in ways that promote child and family well-being.

ACHIEVING THE VISION

There is no question that we are a long way from implementing all components of an early care and education system. Yet if we look back just a few years, the idea of a system and the idea of developing an infrastructure were not even in the lexicon. Today, armed with better research and greater public support than ever before, we sit on the cusp of making decisions that will affect the future of American early care and education and the life chances of millions of youngsters during the years to come.

Rather than asking *whether* this vision can be achieved, we must turn our energies and discourse to discerning *how* to do it. This shift is simple to state but not simple to do. The journey begins by engaging states in the process of thinking strategically about how to promote more positive outcomes for young children given that a wide gap in state-level vision and leadership exists between states that are doing little for young children and those that have mounted comprehensive early childhood systems-building initiatives. This gap reflects not only different levels of fiscal investments but also different degrees of understanding about how investing in young children relates to larger state economic and educational goals (Cauthen et al., 2000).

With this context in mind, the first step would be to coalesce knowledgeable and caring people to develop a state plan. The state plan must address all components of the system. It must delineate strategies for each. Then, the state must be self-critical and undertake an honest assessment of where it sits in each component. By identifying programs and projects that exist either at the state or local level and slotting them into one of the components, it will quickly be apparent where voids exist and, therefore, where work is necessary.

Once the tasks are identified, a time line over a period of years should be established. The point is not to achieve all elements at once but rather to have a strategic vision and time line of what and when each area will be addressed. Developing a strategy for achieving an early care and education system requires sustained long-term planning, so

perhaps it would be prudent to start with a series of 5-year plans (Gallagher & Clifford, 2000). Establishing benchmarks for accomplishment will facilitate the tracking of progress.

This work could augment current efforts in the field to build public and political will and to develop strategic planning. For example, the National Governors Association's Center for Best Practices has launched an initiative to support seven states (Georgia, Illinois, Maryland, New Hampshire, Ohio, Washington, and Wisconsin) in their efforts to build public and political will for improving access to affordable, quality early care and education. Each state team is working on establishing a vision of early childhood care and education with specific objectives and is developing a strategic plan for building public and political support for this vision. The National Governors Association has provided technical assistance and guidance to the state teams to help them achieve their goals (www.nga.org).

Engaging legislators and business leaders in the process helps tremendously. Once the power elite have a clear understanding of what is needed, why it is needed, and how it will help them, obtaining funds is less difficult. The media can be an important partner in this effort, particularly to help explain to both the public and decision makers what an infrastructure is and why it is needed to support a system of quality services (Gallagher & Clifford, 2000). For example, I Am Your Child is a national campaign that has worked with mass media, community mobilization, public education, and policy outreach to promote public awareness about, and stronger societal investments in, early childhood development. The public engagement campaign seeks to unite and expand the work being done on the national, state, and local levels to provide comprehensive, integrated early childhood development programs that include health care, quality child care, parent education, and intervention programs for families at risk (www.iamyourchild.org).

Finally, lessons from abroad highlight the importance of developing a shared vision for children across the early childhood years with coherent policy frameworks, regulations, funding, and staff training and working conditions for all early care and education programs (OECD, 2001). This approach not only is viewed as more efficient, because it resists the fragmentation and overlap of resources and services, but also is supported because it is more equitable for children and families. In addition, international experiences suggest that developing and operating a system does not have to be part of a special initiative with a catchy title or slogan. Indeed, although such efforts may

be necessary initially to garner public support, examples from other countries suggest that early care and education can become part of a set of inviolable rights for all citizens, just like public schooling.

It has been noted that to have dreams come true, we must first dream. The challenge at hand is not to squander the opportunity by thinking too narrowly or by thinking in the short term. We need to settle for nothing less than a comprehensive plan and strategy that will create a system of early care and education founded on a clear and coherent vision for children and families. In so doing, we will reaffirm that achieving the basics being called for by the popular press and policymakers will never be achieved unless the basic infrastructure and system for early care and education are well in place.

REFERENCES

Barnett, W. S., & Masse, L. (in press). Funding issues for early care and education in the United States. In D. Cryer (Ed.), *U.S.A. background report for the OECD Thematic Review.* Chapel Hill, NC: National Center for Early Development and Learning.

Baudelot, O., & Rayna, S. (Eds.). (2000). *Coordonnateurs et coordination de la petite enfance dans les communes* (Actes du colloque du Creasas). Paris: INRP.

Bell, D., Burton, A., Shukla, R., & Whitebook, M. (1997). *Making work pay in the child care industry: Promising practices for improving compensation.* Washington, DC: National Center for the Early Childhood Work Force.

Bertram, A. D., & Pascal, C. (1999). *Early childhood education and care policy in the United Kingdom* (background report prepared for the OECD Thematic Review of Early Childhood Education and Care Policy). Worcester, UK: University College Worcester, Center for Research in Early Childhood.

Bowman, B., Donovan, M. S., & Burns, M. S. (2001). *Eager to learn: Educating our preschoolers.* Washington, DC: National Research Council, National Academy of Sciences.

Campbell, N. D., Appelbaum, J. C., Martinson, K., & Martin, E. (2000). *Be all that you can be: Lessons from the military for improving our nation's child care system.* Washington, DC: National Women's Law Center.

Cauthen, N., Knitzer, J., & Ripple, C. (2000). *Map and track: State initiatives for young children and families.* New York: National Center for Children in Poverty.

Cost, Quality, and Child Outcomes Study Team. (1995). *Cost, quality, and child outcomes in child care centers* (technical report). Denver, CO: University of Denver, Center for Research in Economic and Social Policy.

Early Success Steering Committee. (2000, January). *Early Success: Creating an early care and education system for Delaware's children*. Wilmington, DE: Author.

Essential Functions and Change Strategies Task Force. (1993). *Quality 2000: The essential functions of the early care and education system: Rationale and definition*. New Haven, CT: Yale University, Bush Center.

European Commission Childcare Network. (1996). *Quality targets in services for young children*. Brussels, Belgium: Author.

French-American Foundation. (1999). *Ready to learn: The French system of early education and care offers lessons for the United States*. New York: Author.

Galinsky, E., Howes, C., Kontos, S., & Shinn, M. (1994). *The study of children in family child care and relative care*. New York: Families and Work Institute.

Gallagher, J., & Clifford, R. (2000, Spring). The missing support infrastructure in early childhood. *Early Childhood Research and Practice, 2*(1), 1-24.

Gunnarsson, L., Martin Korpi, B., & Nordenstam, U. (1999). *Early childhood education and care policy in Sweden* (background report prepared for the OECD Thematic Review of Early Childhood Education and Care Policy). Stockholm, Sweden: Ministry of Education and Science.

Howes, C., Smith, E., & Galinsky, E. (1995). *The Florida Child Care Quality Improvement Study*. New York: Families and Work Institute.

Kagan, S. L., & Cohen, N. (1997). *Not by chance: Creating an early care and education system for America's children*. New Haven, CT: Yale University, Bush Center.

Lekies, K., & Cochran, M. (2001). *Collaborating for kids: New York State universal pre-kindergarten, 1999-2000*. Ithaca, NY: Cornell University Press.

Massachusetts Department of Education. (2001). *Securing our future: Planning what we want for our youngest children*. Malden, MA: Author.

Merriam-Webster. (1970). *Webster's new world dictionary* (2nd ed.). Springfield, MA: Author.

Meyers, M., & Gornick, J. (2000). Cross-national variation in service organization and financing. In S. B. Kamerman (Ed.), *Early childhood education and care: International perspectives* (pp. 141-176). New York: Columbia Institute for Child and Family Policy.

Mitchell, A., Ripple, C., & Chanana, N. (1998). *Pre-kindergarten programs funded by the states: Essential elements for policymakers*. New York: Families and Work Institute.

Mitchell, A., Stoney, L., & Dichter, H. (2001). *Financing child care in the United States*. Kansas City, MO: Ewing Marion Kauffman Foundation.

Morgan, G. (in press). Regulatory policy in the United States. In D. Cryer (Ed.), *U.S.A. background report for the OECD Thematic Review*. Chapel Hill, NC: National Center for Early Development and Learning.

Organization for Economic Cooperation and Development. (2000). *OECD country note: Early childhood education and care policy in the United States of America*. Paris: Author.

Organization for Economic Cooperation and Development. (2001). *Starting strong: Early childhood education and care*. Paris: Author.

Press, F., & Hayes, A. (2000). *Early childhood education and care policy in Australia* (background report prepared for the OECD Thematic Review of Early Childhood Education and Care Policy). Sydney, Australia: Macquarie University, Division of Early Childhood and Education, Institute of Early Childhood.

Rostgaard, T., & Fridberg, T. (1998). *Caring for children and older people: A comparison of European policies and practices*. Copenhagen: Danish National Institute of Social Research.

Smart Start Evaluation Team. (2000). *Smart Start services and successes* (annual report, 1999-2000). Chapel Hill: University of North Carolina, Frank Porter Graham Child Development Center.

Sugarman, J. (1991). *Building early childhood systems.* Washington, DC: Child Welfare League of America.

Tietze, W., Cryer, D., Bairrao, J., Palacios, J., & Wetzel, G. (1996). Comparisons of observed process quality in early care and education programs in five countries. *Early Childhood Research Quarterly, 11,* 447-475.

Whitebook, M., Howes, C., & Phillips, D. (1998). *Worthy work, unlivable wages: The National Child Care Staffing Study, 1988-1997.* Washington, DC: Center for the Child Care Workforce.

CHAPTER 18

Child Welfare: Controversies and Possibilities

Jacquelyn McCroskey

The public child welfare system provides social services to troubled families whose children have been abused or neglected. Nationwide, an estimated 826,000 children were maltreated in 1999; of these, nearly three fifths were neglected, while one fifth were physically abused and about 11% were sexually abused. The scope of the child welfare service system, however, is both broader and deeper than might be assumed based on these numbers alone. It is broader because there were nearly 3.0 million referrals and 1.8 million investigations leading to these substantiated cases in 1999 (U.S. Department of Health and Human Services, 2001a). It is deeper because of long-term stays (some children remain in the system for years) and repeat cases (maltreated children are two to three times more likely to be reported again) (Inklas & Halfon, 1997; U.S. Department of Health and Human Services, 2001b).

Although the child welfare system touches the lives of millions of children annually, most people know very little about how it works or why it works the way it does. To the people who do know something about it, controversy seems to be a constant feature of the system. This chapter examines the roots of some major controversies. It describes the functions and components of the child welfare service system, its history, the current federal policy framework, different perspectives on how it works, and key issues for child and adolescent development. It concludes with the challenges and possibilities that will need to be negotiated so as to enhance the lives and development of maltreated children.

FUNCTIONS AND COMPONENTS OF THE CHILD WELFARE SYSTEM

The four key functions of the child welfare services system are child protection, foster care, family-centered services, and adoption. *Child protection* focuses on investigation, assessment, and treatment of children when abuse or neglect is suspected or substantiated. *Foster care* focuses on out-of-home placement to ensure the safety of children; placement may be with relatives or in non-relative foster homes, group homes, or residential treatment facilities. *Family-centered services* focus on strengthening intact families and reunifying families when children return home from foster care placement; services include family support, family preservation, and other interventions oriented to the entire family. *Adoption services* focus on finding, strengthening, and maintaining new families for children who cannot return to their birth families. In most communities, these functions are carried out by a number of public and private agencies with intertwined responsibilities and relationships.

To begin, there is the public child welfare agency, which may serve the entire state, a county, or a large city (many of the larger states have county-run social services that sometimes allow for large cities to become separate jurisdictions). It may be a stand-alone department of children's services or children and family services, it may be part of a larger department that administers income support programs and other social services, or it may be part of an umbrella department of health and human services. The responsibilities of the public child welfare agency include responding to child abuse and neglect referrals, assessing child and family needs, making immediate determination of whether to remove children from their homes, working with the court to determine long-term needs, overseeing foster care placements, and caring for children *in loco parentis* until they can return home or find a new home. In each jurisdiction, the public child welfare agency relies on a number of other public entities and many community-based partners to help accomplish these tasks. The specifics of which workers from which agencies are

responsible for which tasks on which cases, however, vary enormously across jurisdictions and may also vary within jurisdictions over time.

Other public agencies that play important roles in child welfare include the following:

- Juvenile courts that have legal jurisdiction over dependency (what happens to children and families in the child welfare system) and delinquency (when children known to child welfare are also accused of status offenses such as truancy and incorrigible behaviors that would not be crimes for an adult) or criminal behaviors
- District attorney, public defender, and prosecutor offices that represent children in court and that prosecute or defend parents on allegations of abuse
- Police departments that identify children needing help and assist social workers in making dangerous or difficult home calls
- Health, mental health, and disability departments that care for foster children
- School districts that provide regular or special education for foster children
- Public social services departments that provide welfare, food stamps, Medicaid (publicly financed health insurance), and other resources to families with children known to the system
- Probation departments that may get involved when dependent children are accused of crimes

These public agencies also work in partnership with many local not-for-profit agencies, community-based organizations, and faith-based or civic groups. Although the potential number of institutional players involved in the child welfare system is very large, the individuals with professional responsibilities in any one case may be familiar enough with the system and with each other to work together effectively as a team. In smaller communities, where people know each other and have a relatively small number of children to care for, the complexity of the system does not necessarily impede effective work with families and children. In large urban areas, however, the size and complexity of the institutions, the number of children involved, and the fact that child welfare can be the "last chance" for families with very deep and serious problems complicate matters immensely.

Sources of Controversy

To make matters even more confusing, most professionals (led in some instances by social workers but including representatives of all of the agencies and disciplines described previously) are so enmeshed in controversy that it is hard to know where to look for guidance to make this complicated system work. One of the primary sources of controversy is that definitions of child abuse and neglect can be unclear and open to interpretation. Although some proportion of the cases that come to the attention of the child welfare system are clearly abusive or clearly not abusive (i.e., they would be rated the same way by anyone trained to assess), a substantial proportion are cases involving neglect that fall somewhere in the middle. Because definitions are subjective, it is not surprising that individual judgments may depend on factors such as personal experiences, cultural background, and disciplinary training (Giovannoni, 1989).

Depending on one's point of view, the priorities of the child welfare system can also look quite different. Although the Adoption and Safe Families Act of 1997 (Public Law 105-89) (www.nicwa.org/policy/asfa.htm) clarified the federal government's intention to focus on three goals—safety, permanence, and well-being—there is still considerable uncertainty about how these goals should or will be operationalized as desired outcomes for child welfare services. States and localities are still working through the process of developing measurable indicators of goal

achievement and performance measures to track progress toward those goals.

From a *child protection* perspective, the primary goal is to ensure *safety*, usually by removing children from unsafe homes. Once taken away from their parents, foster care has a secondary goal of ensuring *permanence* or residential stability. This includes helping to find permanent homes for children in care as quickly as possible as well as helping them to stay in the same foster homes (rather than moving from home to home) whenever possible. From a broader *child welfare* perspective, once the state takes children from their families, it stands in place of the families and is responsible for the children's *well-being* and healthy development, including their mental and physical health and their education. Advocates of family-centered services suggest that the goal of promoting child well-being would be even better served in many cases by strengthening families and preventing out-of-home care in the first place.

Many observers believe that the entire system needs to be restructured. Ideas about what should be done range across the political spectrum from liberal to conservative—from believers in family-friendly humanism to those with hard-line views on law enforcement and criminal prosecution. Some authors suggest that the system should recognize that poverty is at the heart of much of what is now mislabeled as "abuse" and that services cannot combat the effects of poverty (Lindsey, 1994; Lindsey & Doh, 1996; Pelton, 1989). Others emphasize recriminalizing child abuse to ensure that abusers are punished (Orr, 1999). Still other ideas include the following:

- Narrowing the scope of the child welfare system by restricting the definition of child abuse to include only the most extreme cases (Orr, 1999; Pelton, 1997)
- Separating investigative and foster care functions from "softer" family-centered

support and service functions (Orr, 1999; Pelton, 1992, 1997)

- Changing state laws to allow for "differential response" or allowing child welfare agencies to "provide services to some cases without a formal determination of abuse and neglect" (Schene, 2001, p. 2)
- Repealing mandatory reporting laws (Orr, 1999)

Every suggestion for improvement seems to spark yet another round of argument and controversy.

HISTORY OF CHILD WELFARE SERVICES

A brief review of the history of child welfare helps to explain why today's child welfare system works the way it does and why it is so hard to figure out which way to go from here. The roots of child welfare over the past century set the stage for very different views of what the system is about and how it should function.

The English Elizabethan Poor Laws of 1601 provided the basis for government intervention in family life, holding that communities should care for the poor and vulnerable in their midst. *Parens patriae* or "ruler as parent" justified government intervention in family life by asserting that government (or the local township) should step in for parents who could or would not care appropriately for their children (Berg & Kelly, 2000).

During the 19th century, the focus in the United States was primarily on orphans and the children of very poor immigrant families who could be "saved" from their "unworthy" parents. This impulse reached its height when the New York Children's Aid Society, founded by the Reverend Charles Loring Brace, developed the "orphan trains." The society found homeless, vagabond, immigrant (largely Irish Catholic) children and

put them on trains headed toward "better" homes on the farms and in the small towns of the Protestant Midwest (Holt, 1992).

Three Roots of Child Welfare Services

From the late 1880s through the early part of the 20th century, there emerged three new approaches to providing help for children and their families; two provided social services, largely aimed at the immigrant families pouring into urban areas, and one focused on policing parents. Halpern (1999) describes the similar purposes of the two social service approaches—the community-based approach of the settlement movement and the social casework practice of the Charity Organization Societies (COS):

> One, embodied in the settlement movement, was community-focused. . . . The other, found in the emerging discipline of social casework, focused on individual and family adjustment. Both approaches seemed to proponents more powerful and constructive than charity and moral exhortation. Their mission—to strengthen the domestic practices of poor immigrant families and generally help them adjust to American society; to identify and address community and social conditions that undermined family well-being; to organize and build a sense of mutual support within poor neighborhoods; to reconcile cultural and class conflict; to address the consequences of, and when possible reign in, the worst excesses of industrial capitalism—was both ambitious and diffuse. It also set the stage for internal disagreement over purpose, emphases, and methods that would plague the service provision community throughout the century. (p. 3)

Both COS and the settlement houses had roots in the English charities and correction movement. The first American branch of the COS was established in Buffalo, New York, in 1877, and by the turn of the century there were branches in most of the large cities on the East Coast. The COS philosophy, based on "scientific charity," encouraged "friendly visitors" to complete a "social investigation" in the family home. Help was based on the advice and counsel of these "friends" rather than on financial contributions or relief. This approach established the foundations of social casework.

> COS principles were simple: To create an "independent" poor with "backbone," no material aid was to be given to them except in emergencies, and then only on a temporary basis; volunteers, usually women, were to counsel the poor as "friendly visitors"; and philanthropy was to be placed on a businesslike footing. The COS would investigate, collate data, and proffer advice, although its coercive, moralistic tone was not lost on the poor. (Walkowitz, 1999, p. 33)

The early work of Mary Richmond and other COS leaders pioneered what were to become essential social work skills—client engagement, assessment, intervention, and evaluation (Richmond, 1917). Although the skills remain essential today, their meanings changed dramatically with the advent of psychoanalytic theories. By midcentury, most social workers, including child welfare workers, relied on psychoanalytic rather than social explanations of need, and these essential social casework skills had taken on very different meanings:

> Over the next fifty years, the scientific investigation evolved into the clinical interview; the faithful friend turned into, first, the social caseworker and, later, the psychotherapist; and the personal influence came to be exercised through a therapeutic relationship. (Specht & Courtney, 1994, p. 75)

Hull House, the best-known American settlement house, was established by Jane Addams and her colleagues in Chicago in 1889—at roughly the same time that Richmond was developing casework methods of social investigation and diagnosis. The settlement movement focused attention on

social and economic conditions, creating havens in poor urban areas where immigrant families could find kindergartens, English classes, health care, youth clubs, and social activities.

In contrast to the preventive and therapeutic emphases of settlement houses and social casework, the third institution that was key to child welfare, the Societies for Prevention of Cruelty to Children (SPCC), emphasized policing and retribution for "bad" parenting. Many SPCC workers saw themselves as law enforcement agents, and some even had police powers (Folks, 1902). In 1902, Homer Folks described the influence of "the Cruelty":

> The influence of "cruelty" societies as a whole has been in favor of the care of children in institutions rather than by placing them in families. So far as [is] known, none of the societies have undertaken the continued care of children rescued by them, but all have turned them over to the care of institutions or societies incorporated for the care of children. . . . Usually they have not cooperated to any extent with placing-out societies, perhaps because of being continually engaged in breaking up families of bad character, but have rather become the feeders of institutions, both reformatory and charitable.
>   Without detracting from the great credit due to such societies for the rescue of children from cruel parents or immoral surroundings, it must be said that their influence in the upbuilding of very large institutions, and their very general failure to urge the benefits of adoption for young children, have been unfortunate. Probably their greatest beneficence has been, not to the children who have come under their care, but to the vastly larger number whose parents have restrained angry tempers and vicious impulses through fear of "the Cruelty." (pp. 176-177)

Race, Class, and Culture

Class, race, and cultural differences between the families in need and those who wanted to help them added another layer of complexity to the developing practice of child welfare. Victorian era charity and corrections movements were based largely on notions of *noblesse oblige*—the duty of the better off to provide role models for their less fortunate neighbors. Most COS and settlement house workers were upper class women who wanted to help the less fortunate while also finding work for themselves in a society that radically limited possibilities for women. Thus, the attitudes of professional helpers were largely formed by upper class white women who, as they became professionals, took their responsibility to uphold society's moral standards very seriously. Many functioned as guardians of those standards, trying to persuade immigrant families from all over the world to behave more like they did.

In *Twenty Years at Hull House,* Addams (1910) tells a story about a teacher's attempts to impart temperance principles to an Italian mother whose 5-year-old daughter came to kindergarten having breakfasted on wine-soaked bread:

> The mother, with the gentle courtesy of a South Italian, listened politely to her graphic portrayal of the untimely end awaiting so immature a wine bibber; but long before the lecture was finished quite unconscious of the incongruity, she hospitably set forth her best wines, and when her baffled guest refused one after the other, she disappeared, only to quickly return with a small dark glass of whisky, saying reassuringly, "See, I have brought you the true American drink." The recital ended in serio-comic despair with the rueful statement that "the impression I probably made upon her darkened mind was that it is the American custom to breakfast children on bread soaked in whisky instead of a light Italian wine." (p. 84)

Social workers, counselors, and other child welfare practitioners still struggle with how to reach parents and children across such deep differences in understanding and experience. How do we develop cultural competence—the ability to work competently across cultures—when talking honestly about race and class can feel like walking in a minefield (Fong, 2001)? When these "helpers" have the power to take away your children, the stakes are very high indeed. The consequences of our collective inability to deal with race, class, and cultural differences is reflected in the disproportionate number of children of color who get caught up in the child welfare system.

> Any thorough assessment of recent trends in child welfare populations (e.g., abused and neglected children, children in family foster care, children awaiting adoption) must take note of the disproportionately large number of children of color. For example, a recent analysis of prevalence rates in five states with large out-of-home care populations (California, Illinois, Michigan, New York, and Texas) found that the proportion of African American children ranged from three times as high to over ten times as high as the proportion of Caucasian children in care. (Courtney et al., 1996, p. 100)

The Inheritance of Child Welfare

Many of the tensions in child welfare through the past century can be traced back to its triple roots in the social reform tradition of the settlement houses, the individual treatment tradition of the COS, and the law enforcement tradition of "the Cruelty." Some of today's most controversial topics have their roots in the past century, including the following:

- "Saving" children from "bad" families versus building community-based social and economic supports for families
- Placing children who have been "rescued" into protective institutions versus searching for permanent adoptive families
- Focusing on fear, sanctions, and punishment versus focusing on education, information, support, and help for poor parents

- Enforcing middle-class standards of child rearing versus making active efforts to communicate across cultural and class divides

Focus on Families

During the early part of the 20th century, Progressive era advocates worked to broaden the government's role in the lives of families, including establishment of child labor laws, juvenile courts, mothers' pensions, and economic supports for families.

> This commitment represented a major shift in American poor law philosophy regarding the custody of children, probably the most significant change since the Elizabethan Poor Laws of 1601 mandated the apprenticeship of poor, idle, or vagrant children. Propelling this ideological shift was the emerging belief that poverty did not necessarily reflect moral weakness; social conditions could force otherwise worthy people into a state of poverty. A good part of the child-saving debate during the Progressive era focused on when and how to support parents so that they would not be forced to give up their children. (Mason, 2000, p. 553)

Although small-scale experimentation with family-centered social work programs had been under way for decades, the possibilities of these services as an alternative to foster care became more apparent during the 1970s and 1980s. Studies of the increasing number of children removed from family homes only to "drift" in foster care called attention to the importance of permanency and the effects of dislocation on children's development. Many questioned the ability of large institutions to care for vulnerable children, and exposés about the treatment of inmates in hospitals, prisons, and corrections facilities only underscored such doubts. Community-based care looked like a sensible alternative to institutionalization, especially when deinstitutionalization also offered the promise of cost savings.

Prevention and early intervention services that could help families before problems escalated to the point of abuse—or at least before children needed to be placed in foster care—were clearly needed, but where would the money come from? During the early 1980s, one program was brought forward with a good deal of fanfare: the Homebuilders program, a crisis-oriented, short-term, home-based, intensive treatment program designed to prevent out-of-home placement (Kinney, Madsen, Fleming, & Haapala, 1977). In brief, the model suggested that funding for preventive services could be found by investing some of the resources for "back end" child welfare placement in prevention at the "front end."

This solution appealed to legislators and policymakers, to philanthropic funders, and to many child welfare practitioners in public and private nonprofit agencies. Federal legislation enabled experimentation with a broad range of family support and family preservation models. Subsequent research on the effectiveness of these services, however, has only added more fuel to the flames of controversy in the field (Lindsey & Doh, 1996; McCroskey & Meezan, 1998; Pecora, Fraser, Nelson, McCroskey, & Meezan, 1995; Schuerman, Rzepnicki, & Little, 1994).

THE FEDERAL POLICY FRAMEWORK FOR CHILD WELFARE

Although there is not an overarching family policy framework in the United States, there have been a number of key pieces of legislation that provide guidance for child welfare services (see Table 18.1). The first major step was encouragement of mandatory reporting of child abuse by professionals, especially doctors and other health care professionals who were in a position to recognize the symptoms of the "battered child syndrome."

Table 18.1   Summary of Key Federal Legislation on Child Welfare

1974	Child Abuse Prevention and Treatment Act
• A framework for state responses to child abuse and neglect, including mandatory reporting	
1975	Title XX Amendments to the Social Security Act
• Federal funding available to states for social services, including child welfare	
1978	Indian Child Welfare Act
• Recognition of authority of tribes over placement and adoption of American Indian children	
1980	Adoption Assistance and Child Welfare Act
• Defines major elements of child welfare service system, including emphasis on permanency and "best practices"	
1993	Family Preservation and Support Act
• First federal funding made available to states for family preservation and support	
1997	Adoption and Safe Families Act
• Reaffirmation of family-centered approaches; identification of safety, permanence, and well-being as desired results of child welfare services	
1999	Foster Care Independence Act
• Supports for foster youth up to 21 years of age	

The Child Abuse Prevention and Treatment Act of 1974 (Public Law 93-247) set out a framework for child welfare that included encouraging states "to pass mandatory reporting laws" and requiring "public social service agencies to keep track of perpetrators by establishing a state registry" (Berg & Kelly, 2000, p. 26).

The states were concerned about how they could respond to these reports without dedicated funding to provide services for identified families. In 1975, the Title XX amendments to the Social Security Act authorized federal payments to the states for

provision of a broad array of social services, including child welfare services. In 1981, the Omnibus Reconciliation Act (Public Law 97-35) converted these payments into a social service "block grant" that gave states more discretion over expenditures.

In 1978, the Indian Child Welfare Act (Public Law 95-608) provided recognition of the unique status of American Indian tribes. It acknowledged special threats to the cultural identity of American Indian children removed from their families or their reservations by the child welfare system. Essentially, the act granted tribes more authority over the placement and adoption of American Indian children.

The Adoption Assistance and Child Welfare Act (Public Law 96-272), in many ways the keystone of the child welfare service system, was enacted in 1980. Many of its provisions, however, have never been fully realized, at least in part because it was developed under the Democratic Carter administration and implemented under the Republican Reagan administration. The act responded to increasing concern about "foster care drift" by emphasizing permanency and laying out a set of "best practices."

> Through the funding regulations, the act discourages state use of custodial foster care. Instead, funding prompts preplacement preventive services for families in crisis and permanency planning for children unable to remain with their own families. A new adoptions subsidy program is created as well. Finally, the act requires the maintenance or institution of a number of "best practice" requirements by state child welfare programs. (Pecora, Whittaker, & Maluccio, 1992, pp. 21-22)

These best practices included an inventory of children in care, establishment of statewide management information systems, detailed case plans, and assurance that "reasonable efforts" had been made to provide services to parents so that children could be safely returned to their own homes.

During the 1990s, federal legislation authorized funding for family-centered services and for services for youth emancipating from the foster care system. In 1993, the Family Preservation and Support Act (Public Law 103-66) earmarked federal funds for family support and family preservation services. In 1997, the Adoption and Safe Families Act (Public Law 105-89) reaffirmed the national commitment to timely, goal-directed, family-centered approaches but signaled change in congressional intent by changing the name of the program to "Promoting Safe and Stable Families." The name change signified an emphasis on desired results—safety and stability—rather than support for specific kinds of programs. Provisions included shorter time frames for permanency hearings, adoption incentive payments, and modification of the "reasonable efforts" provisions of the 1980 act.

The Foster Care Independence Act of 1999 (Public Law 106-166) is the most recent key piece of federal legislation guiding the child welfare system. The act established the John H. Chafee Foster Care Independence Program, which provides financial, housing, counseling, employment, education, health insurance, and "other appropriate services and supports" to foster youth up to 21 years of age.

DIFFERENT PERSPECTIVES

Like the elephant, which appears in different guises to the blind men trying to discover its essence from its parts, the child welfare system is many things to many people. All-too-frequent stories of kids who have been rescued from abusive families only to drift through endless placement changes—without love, support, or a sense of their place in the world—are among the most heartbreaking:

> I am sixteen years old. I have been in the state's custody since I was ten years old. . . . I was placed into a foster home shortly after I went into the state's custody. I stayed in this home for almost a year and eight months. I was then moved to [an] orphanage, then to another foster home, then to a group home, then to the orphanage again, and then to another group home. At my last group home, I was there for almost two years. . . . I knew I would never get to go home, so I gave up and decided to run away. After three months on the street going from friend to friend, I decided to contact the only person that I knew would help me.
> This person used to be a foster parent of mine. Her name is Jackie C. It took me two

days to find her 'cause she had moved. When I entered her house, she had pictures of me everywhere. It was then, after not seeing her for four years, that I realized how much she loved me. . . . DHR [Department of Human Resources] was supposed to make Jackie a foster parent for me again, but they have not called us yet. It has been over four months now. DHR don't care about me. It was bad enough that my mom let men sexually abuse me. Now the state neglects me. (Bazelon Center for Mental Health Law, 1998, p. 19)

When a child has the misfortune to be raised by the state, the possibility of drifting into criminal behavior also seems to be greater. Humes (1996) describes how it happened to "George":

While under the Juvenile Court's guidance and protection—as a victim, not a victimizer—a bright, law-abiding A student with a penchant for writing poetry was destroyed. For ten years, he was shunted from one temporary home to another. He was separated from his older brother and younger sister. He was entrusted to neglectful, drug-addicted guardians. He was allowed to roam the streets, to experiment with drugs, to drop out of school—all the while in the care and custody of the state. With each move, his pitifully meager possessions were packed into a disposable green Hefty trash bag, the foster child's luggage, which George was bright enough to see as a metaphor for his entire life. He considered himself a prisoner.

"I always wondered what it was I had done wrong," George says, "but no one would ever tell me. I just figured they thought I would turn out like my mother, and they were just getting a head start."

And when the inevitable finally came to pass, when this increasingly angry, rootless kid took solace in the streets and got involved in crime, the system geared up with all its power and programs to do what it always does in such cases.

It is preparing to abandon him. (pp. 107-108)

Although most foster parents derive great satisfaction from caring for abused and

neglected children, many believe that the system does not support them either. Hubner and Wolfson (1996) quote one long-term foster parent in California's Santa Clara County and describe the frustrations of many parents who volunteer to care for children:

"I know that many just give nominal care, but to say that most foster parents are in it for the money? That's not what I've seen. . . .

"In my own case, I've had to fight tooth and nail to get what I need for the kids—for instance, going to the Rotary Club to beg for money for plane tickets to Washington so one of the babies could be treated with a new protocol. Social services did give us money for memorial services to bury the children, though. They did do that much." (p. 20)

Based on their interviews with foster parents, Hubner and Wolfson note,

Money . . . is not even the primary frustration. While foster children have gotten more demanding, so have the legal and bureaucratic pressures placed on those who care for them. Foster parents face any number of legal liabilities. For instance, babies born addicted to drugs have a high mortality rate, and their foster parents risk being sued for inadequate care. Foster parents have also been included in lawsuits by parents charging that child welfare departments improperly removed children from their homes. (p. 21)

In the view of most advocates, the child welfare system has been "broken" for some time, and despite many well-meaning efforts, it remains desperately "in need of fixing":

The myriad of class action lawsuits and service integration and system reform initiatives in the past ten years attest to the "broken" state of child welfare. Lawsuits in both child welfare and juvenile corrections assert a range of problems throughout the system, focusing considerable attention on the quality of care and the length of stay for children placed in out-of-home care.

Remarkably, while most of these lawsuits have resulted in significantly increased resources for child welfare, most of the affected systems are still plagued with problems, in some instances, problems that have plaintiffs' attorneys threatening contempt actions. (Feild, 1996, p. 4)

Would-be reformers also face bureaucratic nightmares galore (Williams, 1995). Hagedorn (1995), part of a leadership team that tried unsuccessfully to reform the child welfare system in Milwaukee County, describes some of the frustrations of trying to shake up a resistant and entrenched child welfare bureaucracy:

I'm on my way to a meeting and another hectic day. The basic problem that we're having here is that we're overwhelmed with the complexity of the tasks ahead of us, how much we've bitten off, and our inability to get the structure, the bureaucracy itself, to react, to do these tasks for us. We end up doing everything ourselves, which is exhausting us. I like the bureaucracy's strategy better than ours—to sit back and watch us collapse. (pp. 156-157)

From the kids themselves to those trying to help them, everyone has strong feelings about what is wrong with the child welfare system. Stories of child abuse, system abuse, and the failures of even the best intentions abound, generating very deep emotions and more than a little cynicism. The next section describes recent advances in developmental theory that may help frustrated advocates to focus their efforts with the greatest hope of improving long-term outcomes for children.

KEY ISSUES FOR CHILD AND ADOLESCENT DEVELOPMENT

The recent "explosion of research" in the neurobiological, behavioral, and social sciences on early childhood development has increased knowledge about the interactions among different domains of physical, psychological, and behavioral development in young children. The research clearly reinforces the importance of nurturing relationships with parents and other adults who stimulate development by helping children to explore and interact with the world around them (National Research Council & Institute of Medicine, 2000). What happens when children do not have such nurturing relationships or when those relationships are sporadic or disrupted by episodes of maltreatment (Cicchetti & Carlson, 1989; Trickett & Schellenbach, 1998)?

For the most part, findings affirm the experiences of frontline child welfare practitioners: Although children may suffer long-term consequences as a result of abuse and neglect, they are also extraordinarily resilient, adaptable, and responsive to improved circumstances. Even children who have "missed" some developmental opportunities due to inattentive, disorganized, or disrupted parenting can, with loving attention and care, make up for lost time. The possibilities for children who do not get a second chance at loving attention and care, however, are much bleaker.

Two sets of findings are especially troubling from the perspective of child welfare. These are research on (a) the physiological effects of sustained stress and (b) the effects of prenatal exposure to alcohol and drugs. In terms of the effects of sustained stress on the developing brain, one of the research findings

concerns the detrimental effects of early and sustained stressful experiences, particularly those that derive from aberrant or disrupted caregiving environments. Evidence from research on animals suggests that such experiences overactivate neural pathways that regulate fear-stress responses in the immature brain, perhaps placing them on a "high alert" setting that may alter patterns of behavioral responding in adult animals with different rearing histories. (National Research Council & Institute of Medicine, 2000, p. 217)

Many of the children in the child welfare system have clearly experienced sustained stress, which may have led to such fear-stress patterns. More knowledge about the neurological effects of "high alert" status during early development may help to show whether and how such patterns can be modified or eliminated and help to guide intervention.

Over the past 30 years, many researchers have documented the negative effects of prenatal exposure to alcohol.

> These effects range from problems with attention and memory, to poor motor coordination, to difficulty with problem solving and abstract thinking. Infants and toddlers may be delayed in reaching important milestones, may have difficulty tuning out excess sensory stimulation, and often are hyperactive. (National Research Council & Institute of Medicine, 2000, p. 201)

Despite efforts to warn prospective parents, prenatal exposure to alcohol and other illegal drugs remains a serious problem affecting a significant proportion of babies. For example, a 1992 study of births in California estimated that 11% of all new mothers tested positive for alcohol and/or drug use (Vega, Kolodny, Hwang, & Noble, 1993).

Many of these children come to the attention of the child welfare system (Hawley, Halle, Drasin, & Thomas, 1995; Lewis, Giovannoni, & Leake, 1997), but most public child welfare agencies do not systematically track the number of cases in which drugs and/or alcohol are a primary factor in family disruption (Young, Gardner, & Dennis, 1998). Informed observers suggest that as much as 80% to 90% of the child welfare caseload could be made up of families that have problems with alcohol and/or other drugs. No one knows how many of these kids were exposed in utero, what substances they might have been exposed to, at what points during the pregnancy they might have been exposed, or whether familial use

of alcohol and/or other drugs continued through the early years of their development.

Research on the behavioral and psychological effects of different kinds of maltreatment, and the implications of maltreatment for different stages of child development, is still in its formative stages. Although studies have shown that maternal depression and physical and sexual abuse or neglect (alone or in combination) can have negative effects on children, the impact appears to vary depending on the duration and intensity of the experiences, individual susceptibility, and compensating factors in the children's environment. It is clear, however, that when maltreatment interferes with successful attachment or bonding with parents or other adult caregivers, children suffer.

> Like a row of dominoes, failure to develop an adaptive strategy sets off a chain reaction that leads to unpredictable outcomes. The absence of an organized attachment strategy makes the young child's behavior more difficult to manage, which in turn causes the caregiver to react with even more withdrawal or abuse. A damaging, interactive pattern may develop that, over time, places the child's development in further jeopardy. Difficulties in early attachment and affect regulation, a distorted view of oneself and others, and peer problems and school adjustment are some of the major developmental consequences identified among this population. Chronic problems and clinical disorders are also more common among abused children and adolescents, particularly academic problems, behavioral and emotional disorders, and criminal and antisocial behavior. Fortunately, this process is neither inevitable nor irreversible. (Wolfe, 1999, p. 55)

The effects of physical abuse have perhaps been best documented, although there is still need for more research on the effects of violence of all kinds on the developmental pathways of children and adolescents. Children who have been physically abused typically exhibit elevated levels of aggression and are more likely to attribute hostile intent to others.

> On average, children who have experienced physical abuse show less empathy for others, have difficulty recognizing others' emotions, and are more likely to be insecurely attached to their parents. Deficits have been noted in IQ [intelligence quotient] scores, language ability, and school performance, even when the effects of social class are controlled. (National Research Council & Institute of Medicine, 2000, p. 255)

There have been few studies on the effects of sexual abuse, but results suggest that sexually abused children may experience both biological and psychological effects. Possible effects include dysregulated hormones, acting out and externalizing behavior during childhood, behavior problems during adolescence and adulthood, and possible limitations on educational and occupational attainment (Trickett & Putnam, 1998).

Even children who have not been maltreated themselves may suffer as a result of exposure to domestic violence in the home or to violent incidents in the community.

> Recent research has brought some clarity to the distinction between children who are witnesses to abuse and those who are directly victimized. It has generally been found that children who observe interparental violence exhibit a level of adjustment that is somewhat "in between"; that is, their adjustment tends to be better than that of children who are physically abused or who are physically abused *and* witness interparental abuse, but it is worse than that of children in comparison or control groups. (Margolin, 1998, p. 76)

The effect of community violence on child witnesses has received little study, but there is some evidence that being close to even one episode of considerable violence can bring about symptoms "commonly accepted as indicating PTSD [posttraumatic stress disorder]" (Horn & Trickett, 1998, p. 128). Perhaps

because the impact of direct victimization has been assumed to be much more serious, the potential impact of witnessing community violence has received little attention in child welfare circles. Children who have known violence in multiple forms may face higher or at least different kinds of risk, and those closest to these children need to know what they are trying to cope with if they are to be of help. Unfortunately, some practitioners might not even ask maltreated children whether they have also been exposed to domestic or community violence. One study found that therapists in residential treatment settings serving emotionally disturbed youth did not have "substantive knowledge of their young clients' exposure to such violence" (Guterman & Cameron, 1999, p. 382).

Maternal depression also affects child development, with children of depressed mothers demonstrating more social, emotional, and behavioral problems, often leading to increased difficulties in self-control with peers and in school (National Research Council & Institute of Medicine, 2000). There appears to be a high incidence of maternal depression among families involved with child welfare where depression may have prevented (or limited) development of successful nurturing relationships for some time before families were known to the system. Experienced practitioners have long maintained that it is harder to work with, engage, or motivate depressed mothers (often referred on allegations of child neglect) than to work with nondepressed mothers accused of physical abuse (especially when the abuse stems from out-of-control "disciplinary" measures).

Because children need stimulation and exchanges with nurturing adults, neglect can have negative effects on development throughout childhood and adolescence. For example, one study linked neglect during the early years to decreases in school performance during the transition from elementary school to junior high school (Kendall-Tackett & Eckenrode, 1996). Neglect has also been associated with insecurity and poor attachment.

> Studies of neglected children, such as those reared in orphanages or removed from their homes because of severe neglect, have shown that some, but certainly not all, of these children do not seem to organize their behavior in meaningful ways around one or a few adults. They do not fit typical patterns of insecurity, but rather display inconsistent and disorganized responses to their caregivers. (National Research Council & Institute of Medicine, 2000, p. 231)

How Do Child Welfare Services Affect Child and Adolescent Development?

All of the children in the child welfare system have had negative experiences that threaten their chances for optimal development. They need a second chance to overcome these experiences, to make up for missed developmental opportunities, and to pave the way for successful future experiences. It is hoped that child welfare services can help them to find that second chance quickly, either through intervention with their biological families or by finding new families willing and able to care for them. Unfortunately, many remain in the system; the lucky ones stay in stable placements with relatives or foster families, while the unlucky ones drift in foster care, moving from placement to placement while their childhood slips away.

A limited research base on the experiences of youth who emancipate or "age out" of foster care reinforces the observations of practitioners and advocates that it is very difficult for foster youth to make it on their own at 18 or even 21 years of age. For example, Blome (1997) shows that foster youth were less likely to graduate from high school or to complete a general equivalency diploma (GED) than were a matched group of youth living with at least one parent.

Concern about the number of kids who move from foster care into delinquency, and who turn to crime later during adulthood, is increasing, but we still know very little about how big a group this is or what factors are most relevant to the evolution from victim to victimizer.

> No one knows exactly how many adjudicated children and youth have been involved with the child welfare system, but numerous studies demonstrate intricate interconnections.
>
> The Rochester Youth Development Study found that subjects who had experienced officially substantiated maltreatment before age 12 were at least 25% more likely than nonmaltreated subjects to display a variety of problem behaviors during adolescence, including serious violent delinquency, substance abuse, teen pregnancy, low academic achievement, and mental health problems. Cathy Spatz Widom in 1996 found that being maltreated increased a child's chances of having a juvenile record by a factor of almost two over children who were not substantiated as abused or neglected. (Wingfield, 2001, p. 9)

Widom (1991) also suggests that there may be a small group of abused and neglected children whose behavior problems make them especially difficult to manage and that these children are especially likely to have multiple placements and to experience the uncertainty, rejection, and anger that accompanies frequent moves:

> The presence of these children may account for the high rates of delinquency, adult criminality, and violent criminal behavior often associated with children in foster care. Whether frequent moves reflect an early predisposition to antisocial behavior or are in part a response to it, children with numerous placements are in need of special services. (Widom, 1991, p. 208)

A promising approach explored by Zingraff, Leiter, Johnsen, and Meyers (1994) suggests that good school performance may be associated with reduced risk of delinquency, especially for physically abused children:

> The type of abuse and neglect makes an important difference for risk of delinquency. Neglected children ... are most clearly at increased risk of delinquency, facing a probability of delinquency with only one substantiated maltreatment report of 10.4%. Physically abused children are also at a significantly elevated risk of delinquency; their probability with one report is 9.3%. The probabilities rise with a larger number of substantiated reports. Sexually abused children are not at a significantly higher risk of delinquent involvement than [is] the general school population. (p. 80)

Children entering the child welfare system face a number of developmental risks as a consequence of the maltreatment they have experienced. Unfortunately, the system itself may increase these risks for some of these children by lack of attention to the effects of the grief, trauma, and losses they have suffered or by its inability to find them stable homes. Without attention, stability, and permanence, many children who come into the child welfare system—thrown on the not-so-tender mercies of an overburdened bureaucratic system—will have a very hard time rallying.

ENHANCING THE POSSIBILITIES FOR HEALTHY DEVELOPMENT

The proverbial wise man could wander far and wide before finding anyone who believes that our nation's public child welfare system is on the right track. Rather, we seem to have created a dense forest of cross-purposes and confusion. After more than a century of controversy, there is no clear-cut pathway out of that forest, and there is little agreement on where to search for the trailhead. Some observers suggest that parts of the system should be cut away, encouraging focus on only the most severe cases of child abuse

(Orr, 1999). Others suggest that law enforcement should handle investigative functions, separating those from family-centered services that should be handled by the public child welfare system (Pelton, 1992, 1997). Others suggest that we need "differential" or "multiple-track" responses that allow child welfare agencies to serve families without substantiated reports of abuse or neglect (Schene, 2001).

Still others suggest that child welfare should be linked more closely with income support and that the process of reforming the nation's welfare system offers both opportunities and challenges for changing child welfare (Berns & Drake, 2000; Duncan & Chase-Lansdale, 2001). Others focus on the cost-benefit potential of "managing care" in child welfare in ways similar to "managed care" practices in the health care system (Kahn & Kamerman, 1999; Wulczyn, 1998).

The Executive Session on Child Protection, convened by the John F. Kennedy School of Government at Harvard University, recommended building community partnerships. It suggested that such partnerships could take some of the pressure off the "front end" of the system (e.g., supporting families, preventing child abuse, identifying and supporting relative and nonrelative foster families and other family-centered services) (Farrow, with the Executive Session on Child Protection, 1997; Waldfogel, 1998). Others suggest that the "patch" system that has been used to good effect in England is also relevant in America. Basically, this idea focuses on small geographic communities or patches where interdisciplinary teams representing an integrated service delivery system focus as much on prevention as they do on problem-based intervention (Adams & Krauth, 1995; Smale, 1995). This suggests the need to assign child welfare caseloads according to geographic community boundaries rather than according to types of cases or specialties of workers.

Taking an ecological perspective, we know that child development occurs through transactions between children and members of their families and communities. When child welfare is defined in organizational or systems terms (e.g., funding streams, reporting responsibilities, organizational relationships), it is easy to miss this point. Healthy child development requires more than even the best-functioning service delivery system can ever provide. It requires that families, communities, and service systems acknowledge their mutual interests in promoting healthy development and accept *shared* responsibility for *joint* goals that will help to improve the well-being of the most vulnerable children and families.

Although there is no simple recipe for improving the child welfare system, shifting the focus from stability and permanency to child well-being could help the field disentangle itself from its traditional controversies and concerns, moving toward a more proactive focus. Focus on child well-being would encourage public child welfare agencies and their partners to become more familiar with developmental theory and research, to pay more attention to the developmental needs of the children in their care, and to enhance the capacity of poor communities to support families. Getting from here to there will require work on at least three fronts simultaneously:

- Actively encouraging a broad range of community partnerships
- Integrating and aligning the functions of the many public and private organizations already involved in the child welfare system
- Significantly upgrading the research base on child development and child welfare

Encouraging Community Partnerships

Rather than one agency—the public child protective services agency—bearing the sole responsibility for protecting children, a broader array of parents, public and private agencies, organizations, and individuals should join together to carry out this fundamental public responsibility. The heart of this improved system is a community partnership for child protection. A community partnership is a way of extending "who's responsible" for child safety as well as a way of providing more rapid, intensive, and effective responses when a child is in danger of being abused or neglected. (Farrow, with the Executive Session on Child Protection, 1997, pp. vii-viii)

To be effective, such partnerships should go much further than just expanding the number of community-based agencies under contract with public agencies to provide family-centered services. True partnerships require fundamental changes in relationships between public agencies and the communities they serve. For example, in Los Angeles County, the Children's Planning Council brings together key leaders representing county agencies; schools; cities; private sector service providers; universities; and the various philanthropic, business, ethnic, and geographic communities of Los Angeles. To ensure that elected officials are active participants in shared planning, the chairmanship of the council rotates annually among the five elected members of the County Board of Supervisors.

Created in 1992, the Children's Planning Council has adopted an ongoing, incremental, data-driven approach to planning and has developed agreement on a countywide vision for children, principles for change, short- and long-term outcomes, directions, and specific action steps.

The Children's Planning Council believes that the best way to ensure that children become healthy, productive adults is to build strong communities—ones that provide the opportunities, facilities, programs, and positive environments to meet children's developmental needs. Communities can offer these essentials only if residents are full participants in their design and governance and only if the political systems of which they are a part encourage and support this self-determination. (Los Angeles County Children's Planning Council, 1998, p. ii)

Los Angeles County's public child welfare agency (the Department of Children and Family Services) and its other public agency partners in the child welfare system are members of the Children's Planning Council. The focus, however, is not on incremental changes in relationships between public agencies and their community-based partners but rather on fundamental changes in how decisions that affect children and families are made, including the following:

- Ensuring that voices from diverse communities are heard in decision-making processes
- Encouraging large bureaucratic systems to become more responsive to the multiple needs of children and families
- Linking resource allocation and expenditures to results achieved
- Supporting the efforts of community and regional groups to identify local priorities for improving the well-being of children in their communities

Integrate and Align the Functioning of the Many Agencies Involved

At the same time that they build community partnerships with nonprofit and community-based organizations and civic groups, public agencies need to better integrate the services they currently offer by improving access, decreasing fragmentation, and increasing effectiveness and efficiency. The challenges of integrating the services offered across a large number of public and private agency partners are legion (Austin, 1997), but the benefits can be substantial. For example, staff can help families to find the services they need before crises escalate

into child abuse or neglect. They can build relationships with schools to ensure that children are not moved from a familiar school setting just because they had to go to foster care or were moved from one foster care setting to another. They can ensure continuity with health care providers so that children continue to see the same providers or that medical records at least follow children from one provider to another.

Perhaps most important, shared planning for service integration can allow multiple authorities (e.g., courts, child protection, probation, police) to work out their differences about what really is "in the best interests" of children and families in interagency planning sessions that include community representatives. Talking through differences in values, assumptions, and procedures not only is good practice but also can lessen the chance that agencies will fight out their differences in contested cases where vulnerable children and families stand to lose the most.

Coordination of multiagency services through multidisciplinary teams has proven to be effective in a number of child welfare functions. Interdisciplinary teams can provide assessment and case planning (National Association of Public Child Welfare Administrators, 1999; Social Care Group, 2000), help to resolve family problems and service delivery conflicts (Winton & Mara, 2001), and help to reduce out-of-home placement and improve outcomes for children in placement (Glisson, 1994). Increased use of multidisciplinary teams clearly implies that both professional preparation and in-service training programs need to be enhanced.

In England, recognition of the interdisciplinary nature of service provision has gone well beyond the social services.

From birth, all children will become involved with a variety of different agencies in the community, particularly in relation to their health, day care, and educational development. A range of professionals . . . will have a role in assessing their general well-being and development. Children who are vulnerable are, therefore, likely to be identified by these professionals, who will have an important responsibility in deciding whether to refer them to social services for further assessment and help. The knowledge they already have about a family is an essential component of any assessment. Interagency work starts as soon as there are concerns about a child's welfare, not just when there is an enquiry about significant harm. An important underlying principle of the approach to assessment . . . , therefore, is that it is based on an inter-agency model in which it is not just the social services departments which are the assessors and providers of service. (Social Care Group, 2000, p. 14)

Focusing on supports and interventions that are known to be effective, or for which there is some evidence of promise, is also very important. Available research about what works in child welfare practice has increased during recent years, although it is still quite limited in many areas (Kluger, Alexander, & Curtis, 2000). For example, in terms of family-centered services, the most recent round of research on the placement prevention impact of family preservation services is discouraging (U.S. Department of Health and Human Services, 2001b). But other findings suggest that family-centered approaches may improve family functioning, especially when used as part of a plan to reunify families (Fraser, Nelson, & Rivard, 1997). Findings from research on early home visiting programs have been encouraging in terms of the possibilities of targeted prevention programs (Guterman, 2001; Olds et al., 1997). Findings on the impact of family-centered multisystemic therapies for adolescents, especially those involved in delinquent behaviors, have also been encouraging (Schoenwald, Borduin, & Henggeler, 1998).

Improve the Research Base

Although there have been some research studies evaluating the effects of specific intervention programs, the research base for the child welfare system is profoundly limited. Not only are there problems in the state and county information systems that are supposed to track the children and families served in each jurisdiction, but efforts to aggregate data from these systems to represent national conditions and trends over time have also been problematic. Little funding has been available at national or state levels to carry out significant research on the most essential questions confronting child welfare. Researchers have struggled to find relatively small pots of money to support small studies about limited questions. Even when investigators have tried to incorporate methodological rigor into their studies, requirements from the agencies under study or conditions in the field have seriously limited the credibility of their results.

Epstein's (1999) blistering critique of child welfare lets no one off the hook about the lamentable state of research on child welfare:

The problems with research do not simply reflect the faults of the researchers; they clearly express society's lack of concern for the safety, health, and socialization of dependent children. It is astonishing that no comprehensive information system has ever existed to describe the public child welfare system. . . .

A neglectful public has refused to approve the necessary funds for more credible research methods to investigate child welfare services. Moreover, the foster care system would be unlikely to tolerate objective scrutiny; few researchers or practitioners within the system are in positions to apply these designs dispassionately. Without rational evidence for any production function except surveillance, child welfare services serve in ceremonial roles as symbols of popular values. . . .

Notwithstanding perhaps a century of research efforts—indeed, child welfare may be the oldest subspecialty of American social welfare scholarship—there is still little if any accurate information, either descriptive or evaluative, about child welfare services. The system appears to be avoiding scrutiny, and this in itself is cause to question the quality and social role of current provisions for maltreated children. (pp. xvi-xvii)

The highest priorities of the field related to data and research should be the following:

- To ensure that all involved agencies have accurate timely data on basic conditions and trends to guide their planning
- To institute results-based accountability methods and reasonable performance measures (Friedman, 1997) for every child welfare service program, including basic services such as foster care, group homes, and residential treatment
- To ensure that every child welfare practitioner is familiar with the emerging body of research on brain development, the effects of maltreatment on child and adolescent development, and the implications of this research for treatment and intervention

There is an enormous amount of work to do in planning a research agenda for the next decades. Plans should be developed to address pressing large-scale systems questions (e.g., about which structures and interagency strategies are most effective in improving results for children) as well as smaller scale questions (e.g., about which kinds of interventions work for which families and children). Additional research is clearly needed on the knowledge, skills, and training needed by effective child welfare practitioners and on the impact of race, class, and culture on service delivery. In fact, the list of important questions for which we do not currently have adequate answers is appalling and would not be tolerated if our country were serious about promoting child, adolescent, and family development.

PROMOTING POSITIVE CHILD, ADOLESCENT, AND FAMILY DEVELOPMENT: WHERE COULD WE GO FROM HERE?

The child welfare field has struggled to maintain a delicate balance on some very difficult questions. How can child welfare support families *and* "rescue" kids who are in trouble? How can it remove children from abusive situations *and* ensure that there are better alternatives for them? How can it be culturally competent and support poor families? How can it resolve class and race-related factors that land too many kids of color in dependency and delinquency systems? How can it enhance the social capital that binds people in their communities *and* make sure that communities support and welcome families of all kinds?

But child welfare alone cannot do any of these things. It simply is not possible to resolve these troubling questions through incremental "fixes" to the current child welfare system. Rather, as a group of advocates in Los Angeles recently stated, change must be "dramatic and pervasive":

Disparities between what is desirable and current practice are not due to a lack of money. Enormous sums are being spent, though often in ways that prevent blending of funds to maximize results and streamline delivery. Frequent discussions of the crisis in the system for children and families indicates that the problem is not a lack of awareness or concern. Rather, the primary stumbling block appears to be the assumption that the current system can be fixed, despite the failure of innumerable attempts at reform. The breadth of this crisis defies incremental change. To have a chance for success, change must be dramatic and pervasive. (Aguilar et al., 2000, p. 7)

Whether and how we decide to respond to the controversies and possibilities that permeate child welfare remains to be seen. Millions of children and families await our responses.

REFERENCES

Adams, P. A., & Krauth, K. (1995). Working with families and communities: The patch approach. In P. Adams & K. E. Nelson (Eds.), *Reinventing human services: Community- and family-centered practice* (pp. 87-108). Hawthorne, NY: Aldine de Gruyter.

Addams, J. (1910). *Twenty years at Hull House with autobiographical notes.* New York: New American Library.

Aguilar, Y. F., Armstrong, B., Biondi, C. O., Buck, M., Curry, P., Lewis, L., McCroskey, J., Olenick, M., Perry, J., Riordan, N. D., Wainwright, M., & Weinstein, V. (2000). *From child welfare to child well-being.* Pasadena, CA: Casey Family Program. (75 S. Grand Avenue, Pasadena, CA 91105)

Austin, M. J. (Ed.). (1997). *Human services integration.* New York: Haworth.

Bazelon Center for Mental Health Law. (1998). *Making child welfare work: How the R. C. lawsuit forged new partnerships to protect children and sustain families.* Washington DC: Author.

Berg, I. K., & Kelly, S. (2000). *Building solutions in child protective services.* New York: Norton.

Berns, D., & Drake, B. (2000). Combining child welfare and welfare reform at a local level. *Journal for the Community Approach, 1*(3), 12-18.

Blome, W. W. (1997). What happens to foster kids: Educational experiences of a random sample of foster care youth and a matched group of non-foster care youth. *Child and Adolescent Social Work, 14*(1), 41-53.

Cicchetti, D., & Carlson, V. (1989). *Child maltreatment: Theory and research on the causes and consequences of child abuse and neglect.* Cambridge, UK: Cambridge University Press.

Courtney, M. E., Barth, R. P., Berrick, J. D., Brooks, D., Needell, B., & Park, L. (1996). Race and child welfare services: Past research and future directions. *Child Welfare, 75*(2), 99-137.

Duncan, G. J., & Chase-Lansdale, P. L. (2001, February). *Welfare reform and child well-being.* Paper prepared for the Blank/Haskins Conference, "The New World of Welfare Reform," Washington, DC.

Epstein, W. M. (1999). *Children who could have been: The legacy of child welfare in wealthy America.* Madison: University of Wisconsin Press.

Farrow, F., with the Executive Session on Child Protection. (1997). *Child protection: Building community partnerships—Getting from here to there.* Cambridge, MA: Harvard University, John F. Kennedy School of Government.

Feild, T. (1996). Managed care and child welfare: Will it work? *Public Welfare, 54*(3), 4-10.

Folks, H. (1902). *The care of destitute neglected and delinquent children* (Classics Series). Washington, DC: National Association of Social Workers.

Fong, R. (2001). Cultural competency in providing family-centered services. In E. Walton, P. Sandau-Beckler, & M. Mannes (Eds.), *Balancing family-centered services and child well-being: Exploring issues in policy, practice, theory, and research* (pp. 55-68). New York: Columbia University Press.

Fraser, M. W., Nelson, K. E., & Rivard, J. C. (1997). Effectiveness of family preservation services. *Social Work Research, 21*(3), 138-153.

Friedman, M. (1997). *A guide to developing and using performance measures in results-based budgeting.* Washington, DC: Finance Project. (See also www.raguide.org and www.fiscalpolicystudies.com)

Giovannoni, J. (1989). Definitional issues in child maltreatment. In D. Cicchetti & V. Carlson (Eds.), *Child maltreatment: Theory and research on the causes and consequences of child abuse and neglect* (pp. 3-37). Cambridge, UK: Cambridge University Press.

Glisson, C. (1994). The effect of services coordination teams on outcomes for children in state custody. *Administration in Social Work, 18*(4), 1-23.

Guterman, N. B. (2001). *Stopping child maltreatment before it starts: Emerging horizons in early home visitation services.* Thousand Oaks, CA: Sage.

Guterman, N. B., & Cameron, M. (1999). Young clients' exposure to community violence: How much do their therapists know? *American Journal of Orthopsychiatry, 69,* 382-391.

Hagedorn, J. M. (1995). *Forsaking our children: Bureaucracy and reform in the child welfare system.* Chicago: Lake View Press.

Halpern, R. (1999). *Fragile families, fragile solutions: A history of supportive services for families in poverty.* New York: Columbia University Press.

Hawley, T. L., Halle, T. G., Drasin, R. E., & Thomas, N. G. (1995). Children of addicted mothers: Effects of the "crack epidemic" on the caregiving environment and the development of preschoolers. *American Journal of Orthopsychiatry, 65,* 364-379.

Holt, M. I. (1992). *The orphan trains: Placing out in America.* Lincoln: University of Nebraska Press.

Horn, J. L., & Trickett, P. K. (1998). Community violence and child development. In P. K. Trickett & C. J. Schellenbach (Eds.), *Violence against children in the family and the community* (pp. 103-138). Washington, DC: American Psychological Association.

Hubner, J., & Wolfson, J. (1996). *Somebody else's children: The courts, the kids, and the struggle to save America's troubled families.* New York: Three Rivers Press.

Humes, E. (1996). *No matter how loud I shout: A year in the life of juvenile court.* New York: Simon & Schuster.

Inklas, M., & Halfon, N. (1997). Recidivism in child protective services. *Children and Youth Services Review, 19*(3), 139-161.

Kahn, A. J., & Kamerman, S. B. (1999). *Contracting for child and family services: A mission-sensitive guide.* New York: Columbia University, School of Social Work.

Kendall-Tackett, K. A., & Eckenrode, J. (1996). The effects of neglect on academic achievement and disciplinary problems: A developmental perspective. *Child Abuse and Neglect, 20*(3), 161-169.

Kinney, J. M., Madsen, B., Fleming, T., & Haapala, D. A. (1977). Homebuilders: Keeping families together. *Journal of Consulting and Clinical Psychology, 45,* 667-673.

Kluger, M. P., Alexander, G., & Curtis, P. A. (Eds.). (2000). *What works in child welfare.* Washington, DC: Child Welfare League of America.

Lewis, M. A., Giovannoni, J. M., & Leake, B. (1997). Two-year placement outcomes of children moved at birth from drug-using and non-drug-using mothers in Los Angeles. *Social Work Research, 21*(2), 81-90.

Lindsey, D. (1994). *The welfare of children.* Oxford, UK: Oxford University Press.

Lindsey, D., & Doh, J. (1996). *Family preservation and support services and California's families, Section A.* Background briefing report prepared for California Family Impact Seminar, Sacramento.

Los Angeles County Children's Planning Council. (1998). *Laying the groundwork for change: Los Angeles County's first action plan for its children, youth, and families* (executive summary). Los Angeles: Author.

Margolin, G. (1998). Effects of domestic violence on children. In P. K. Trickett & C. J. Schellenbach (Eds.), *Violence against children in the family and the community* (pp. 57-102). Washington, DC: American Psychological Association.

Mason, M. A. (2000). The state as superparent. In P. A. Fass & M. A. Mason (Eds.), *Childhood in America* (pp. 549-554). New York: New York University Press.

McCroskey, J., & Meezan, W. (1998). Family-centered services: Approaches and effectiveness. *The Future of Children, 8*(1), 54-70.

National Association of Public Child Welfare Administrators. (1999). *Guidelines for a model system of protective services for abused and neglected children and their families* (rev. ed.). Washington, DC: American Public Human Services Association.

National Research Council & Institute of Medicine. (2000). *From neurons to neighborhoods: The science of early childhood development* (J. P. Shonkoff & D. A. Phillips, Eds., Committee on Integrating the Science of Early Childhood Development, Board on Children, Youth, and Families, Commission on Behavioral and Social Sciences and Education). Washington, DC: National Academy Press.

Olds, D. L., Eckenrode, J., Henderson, C. R., Kitzman, H., Powers, J., Cole, R., Sidora, K., Morris, P., Pettitt, L. M., & Luckey, D. (1997). Long-term effects of home visitation on maternal life course and child abuse and neglect: Fifteen-year follow-up of a randomized trial. *Journal of the American Medical Association, 278,* 637-643.

Orr, S. (1999). *Child protection at the crossroads: Child abuse, child protection, and recommendations for reform* (Policy Study No. 262). Los Angeles: Reason Public Policy Institute. Available: www.rppi.org/socialservices/ps262

Pecora, P. J., Fraser, M. W., Nelson, K. E., McCroskey, J., & Meezan, W. (1995). *Evaluating family-based services.* Hawthorne, NY: Aldine de Gruyter.

Pecora, P. J., Whittaker, J. K., & Maluccio, A. N. (1992.) *The child welfare challenge: Policy, practice, and research.* Hawthorne, NY: Aldine de Gruyter.

Pelton, L. H. (1989). *For reasons of poverty: A critical analysis of the public child welfare system in the United States.* New York: Praeger.

Pelton, L. H. (1992). A functional approach to reorganizing family and child welfare interventions. *Children and Youth Services Review, 14,* 289-303.

Pelton, L. H. (1997). Child welfare policy and practice: The myth of family preservation. *American Journal of Orthopsychiatry, 67,* 545-553.

Richmond, M. (1917). *Social diagnosis.* New York: Russell Sage.

Schene, P. (2001, Spring). Meeting each family's needs: Using differential responses in reports of child abuse and neglect. *Best Practice, Next Practice,* pp. 1-6. (Washington, DC: National Child Welfare Resource Center for Family-Centered Practice)

Schoenwald, S. K., Borduin, C. M., & Henggeler, S. W. (1998). Multisystemic therapy: Changing the natural and service ecologies of adolescents and families. In M. Epstein, K. Kutash, & A. Duchnowski (Eds.), *Outcomes for children and youth with behavioral and emotional disorders and their families: Programs and evaluations best practices* (pp. 485-511). Austin, TX: Pro-Ed.

Schuerman, J., Rzepnicki, T., & Little, J. (1994). *Putting families first: An experiment in family preservation.* Hawthorne, NY: Aldine de Gruyter.

Smale, G. G. (1995). Integrating community and individual practice: A new paradigm for practice. In P. Adams & K. E. Nelson (Eds.), *Reinventing human services: Community- and family-centered practice* (pp. 59-85). Hawthorne, NY: Aldine de Gruyter.

Social Care Group. (2000). *Framework for the assessment of children in need and their families* (joint project of Department of Health, Department for Education and Employment, and Home Office in England). London: Her Majesty's Stationery Office. Available: www.the-stationery-office.co.uk/doh/facn/facn.htm

Specht, H., & Courtney, M. E. (1994). *Unfaithful angels: How social work abandoned its mission.* New York: Free Press.

Trickett, P. K., & Putnam, F. W. (1998). Developmental consequences of sexual abuse. In P. K. Trickett & C. J. Schellenbach (Eds.), *Violence against children in the family and the community* (pp. 39-56). Washington, DC: American Psychological Association.

Trickett, P. K., & Schellenbach, C. J. (1998). *Violence against children in the family and the community*. Washington, DC: American Psychological Association.

U.S. Department of Health and Human Services. (2001a). *Child maltreatment 1999*. Washington, DC: Government Printing Office.

U.S. Department of Health and Human Services. (2001b). *Evaluation of family preservation and reunification services* (executive summary to the interim report). Washington, DC: Author.

Vega, W. A., Kolodny, B., Hwang, J., & Noble, A. (1993). Prevalence and magnitude of perinatal substance abuse exposures in California. *New England Journal of Medicine, 329*, 850-854.

Waldfogel, J. (1998). Rethinking the paradigm for child protection. *The Future of Children, 8*(1), 104-119.

Walkowitz, D. J. (1999). *Working with class: Social workers and the politics of middle-class identity*. Chapel Hill: University of North Carolina Press.

Widom, C. S. (1991). The role of placement experiences in mediating the criminal consequences of early childhood victimization. *American Journal of Orthopsychiatry, 61*, 195-209.

Williams, S. D. (1995). Integrating the family service system from the inside out: A view from the bureaucratic trenches. *Journal of Family and Economic Issues, 16*, 413-424.

Wingfield, K. (2001). Breaking the link between child maltreatment and juvenile delinquency. *Children's Voices, 10*(2), 8-12.

Winton, M. A., & Mara, B. A. (2001). *Child abuse and neglect: Multidisciplinary approaches*. Boston: Allyn & Bacon.

Wolfe, D. A. (1999). *Child abuse: Implications for child development and psychopathology* (2nd ed.). Thousand Oaks, CA: Sage.

Wulczyn, F. H. (1998). *Federal fiscal reform in child welfare services*. Discussion paper, Chapin Hall Center for Children, University of Chicago.

Young, N. K., Gardner, S. L., & Denis, K. (1998). *Responding to alcohol and other drug problems in child welfare: Weaving together practice and policy*. Washington, DC: Child Welfare League of America.

Zingraff, M. T., Leiter, J., Johnsen, M. C., & Meyers, K. A. (1994). The mediating effect of good school performance on the maltreatment-delinquency relationship. *Journal of Research in Crime and Delinquency, 31*, 62-91.

CHAPTER 19

Housing: The Foundation of Family Life

RACHEL G. BRATT

I n 1949, the U.S. Congress first articulated the nation's housing goal: "a decent home and suitable living environment for every American family." Since then, this goal has been reaffirmed many times, but more than half a century later, it is still far from realized.[1] This is true, despite the regular bipartisan and seemingly heartfelt pronouncements about the importance of "family" in American life and the compelling logic of decent housing being an integral component of family policy. As the context for all family activities—including procreation and the socialization and nurturing of children—a safe, stable, affordable, and secure dwelling would seem to be a prerequisite for a family's ability to function, let alone thrive. Succinctly underscoring this point, the National Housing Task Force (1988) noted,

> A decent place for a family to live becomes a platform for dignity and self-respect and a base for hope and improvement. A decent home allows people to take advantage of opportunities in education, health, and employment—the means to get ahead in our society. A decent home is the important beginning point for growth into the mainstream of American life. (p. 3)

The intimate connections between family well-being and housing were articulated as far back as the 1920s, when "the welfare system recognized that adequate housing was one of the most important needs for mothers and their children" (Newman & Schnare, 1992, p. 8). Nevertheless, the housing delivery and welfare bureaucracies expanded and, for the most part, operated independently of one another. During the 1990s, there was renewed interest in trying to rationalize and better coordinate the two systems (Council of State Community Development Agencies and the American Public Welfare Association, 1991).

Although housing is indisputably central in people's lives, in general, it has continued to be viewed as separate from other components of family and social policy such as promoting economic security and creating opportunities for its residents. Yet there are several notable exceptions. Shlay (1995) has argued that housing policy should be closely linked to family life, community economic development, and social mobility, and others have underscored the relationships between welfare and housing policy (Newman & Schnare, 1993; Sard, 1998). Furthermore, as discussed later in this chapter, housing in nonpoverty areas is increasingly being viewed as a vehicle to expand employment and educational opportunities for low-income households. Finally, the growing "self-sufficiency"[2] agenda, which has used public housing as a major locus of activity, continues to expand the earlier narrow view of housing, which generally conceptualized the provision of housing as an end in itself (see Bratt & Keyes, 1998; Rohe & Kleit, 1997, 1999; Shlay, 1993).

This chapter begins with an overview of housing problems in the United States, with a particular focus on "affordability."[3] The second section explores the implications for families that spend too much for housing. This is followed by two sections exploring how physical quality and, indeed, the presence or lack of housing in one's life (e.g., homelessness) affect children and families. The chapter then goes on to present a discussion of how the location of housing affects access to educational opportunities and employment as well as social networks. This is followed by an examination of some of the connections between a family's housing and the extent to which it does or does not provide opportunities to promote a positive sense of self (see Figure 19.1). The chapter then raises two key questions relevant to the issue of whether we should promote a wider scale housing agenda: "How does project-based subsidized housing affect families and children?" and "Is the provision of subsidized housing a disincentive to productivity and employment?" The chapter concludes

with a proposal that would involve a significantly increased commitment to housing. Thus, the overriding argument being presented here is that housing is the foundation of family life and well-being and that the provision of housing is an essential component of a progressive social agenda.[4]

This chapter is largely based on a review of existing studies.[5] Three points about methodology warrant highlighting. First, research that attempts to ascribe causality to particular housing conditions struggles with the question of how to disentangle the host of variables that may be responsible for observed outcomes. Clearly, it is never possible to isolate the specific housing condition or to fully control for the characteristics of the occupants. Second, the studies reviewed here represent a range of methodological approaches, and depending on one's disciplinary perspective, some would be viewed as more rigorous than others. Third, the impacts of housing per se are difficult to disentangle from the income levels of the residents. Very low income people are challenged in a number of ways, and although each of the factors discussed in what follows has a disproportionately large impact on poor people, no effort has been made to explicitly focus on poor versus nonpoor residents. Similarly, this study does not focus on how race is likely an important mediating factor between housing and resident outcomes.

OVERVIEW OF HOUSING PROBLEMS IN THE UNITED STATES

Housing problems are particularly acute for millions of renter households. In numerous locales across the United States, it is common to hear about escalating rents and house prices and the large numbers of households whose incomes cannot cover the costs of decent quality housing at prices they can

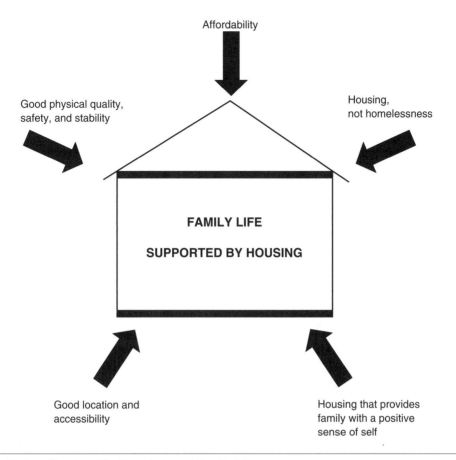

Figure 19.1   Housing: The Foundation of Family Life

afford. In no jurisdiction in the United States is the minimum wage sufficient for workers to afford apartments at what the U.S. Department of Housing and Urban Development (HUD) designates as the "fair market rent" for homes in their community (National Low Income Housing Coalition, 2001). Furthermore, HUD regularly reports on those households with "worst-case housing needs." Included in this category are some 4.9 million very low income unassisted renter households that live in severely substandard housing or pay more than one half of their incomes for rent (HUD, 2000b).[6] And the most extreme form of housing problem is homelessness—the complete absence of stable shelter—with estimates ranging from 600,000 to 750,000 individuals (National Coalition for the Homeless, 1999; HUD, 2000b).

The National Low Income Housing Coalition estimates that some 16.6 million homeowner households and some 16.7 million renter households are facing either moderate or severe housing problems.[7] Of these 33.3 million households, about 19.5 million earned less than 50% of the median income, and another 6.5 million earned less than 80% of the median income (Joint Center for Housing Studies, 1998, p. 68; National Low Income Housing Coalition/LIHIS, 2000, pp. 2-3 and Figures 7 and 9). Using a different method of calculating housing problems, Stone (in press; see also the next section of this chapter) demonstrated that a similar number of households are facing serious housing problems (more than 30 million) but that large households, renter households, and households headed by a person of color or a woman fare the worst. Thus, families with children are among those that are facing the most serious housing problems.

Housing for low-income people in the United States has been subsidized by the federal government in three major ways: through public housing, which was created in 1937 and which involves local housing authorities building, owning, and managing low-rent units; through other types of "project-based" subsidies, the earliest of which was created in 1959 and which involve private nonprofit or for-profit sponsors of housing building, owning, and managing units affordable to low-income households; and through rental vouchers and certificates, implemented on a wide scale in 1974 and generally known as the Section 8 program, which enable eligible low-income households to rent privately owned units. Overall, there are about 4.6 million households receiving rental housing assistance (1.3 million in public housing; 1.9 million in other project-based, privately owned buildings; and 1.4 million that receive rental vouchers) (Joint Center for Housing Studies, 2001, p. 24).

Based on data collected between 1996 and 1998, HUD estimated that, nationally, the average wait for a public housing unit is 11 months and the average wait for a Section 8 rental assistance voucher is 28 months. For the largest public housing authorities (those with more than 30,000 units), the wait for a public housing unit is 33 months and the wait for a Section 8 certificate is 42 months. Moreover, HUD cautioned that all of its estimates may be too low because many housing authorities have closed their waiting lists due to their overwhelming size (HUD, 1999a, pp. 7-10).

Moreover, there is not much hope of improvement. Current federal policies and priorities fall way short of meeting the demand for low-rent housing. As of 1995, an additional 4.4 million units affordable to low-income households were needed. Stated another way, there were nearly two low-income renters for every low-cost unit, and about two of three renters with incomes below the poverty level did not receive any housing subsidy (Daskal, 1998, pp. 2, 35). At the very least, the 4.9 million households that have "worst-case housing needs" would be eligible for HUD assistance.

The reasons for these problems are multi-faceted. There has been a loss of private low-cost units, estimated at 370,000 between 1991 and 1997 (HUD, 2000a, p. 22), as well as a loss of HUD-assisted units, estimated at 65,000 between 1995 and 1998 (Joint Center for Housing Studies, 1999, p. 27); rents have risen faster than the rate of general inflation and incomes (HUD, 1999b, p. 3; see also Joint Center for Housing Studies, 1999, p. 25, Table A-9); and there have been decreases in the rate of new additions to the inventory of assisted housing as well as decreases in federal funding for HUD. Since 1977, new federal budget authority for housing declined from $64.5 billion to $26.7 billion in fiscal 2001 (in constant dollars) (Dolbeare, 2000, p. 2).

Debates on how the provision of housing affordable to low-income households can be improved have included the types of housing subsidies that should be provided (e.g., project based vs. tenant based) and, if project based, whether the developments should be owned by public housing authorities, by for-profit entities, or by nonprofit entities; the extent to which regulatory controls thwart the production of housing; whether the housing resources available should be targeted to the very poor or to households with a wider income range; and the extent to which tax incentives versus direct subsidies are the preferred approach. Undergirding all these controversies is a general acceptance that housing is not an entitlement and that resources are scarce. A small group of scholars, religious leaders, and housing advocates acknowledge that resources are insufficient, but they take the argument several steps further by proposing the adoption of a new policy guaranteeing a right to housing (Hartman, 1998; Institute for Policy Studies Working Group on Housing, 1989; Law, 2000; Roisman, 1990; Smizik & Stone, 1988; U.S. Catholic Conference, 1975). The final section of this chapter returns to this issue and outlines a new housing initiative premised on the availability of decent housing for all.

In the following five sections, the impacts of the housing problems just described on children and families are explored.

IMPACTS OF A LACK OF "AFFORDABLE HOUSING"

During the 1970s and 1980s, there was increasing criticism of public housing and the other project-based housing subsidy programs. In response, rental certificates and vouchers became the preferred federal housing strategy, in part due to their ability to disaggregate the poor and to reduce some of the stigma associated with the most problem-laden housing "projects." But because rental certificates are not provided to everyone in need, and because in many market areas there is an insufficient supply of units that are affordable to certificate holders, housing is still not affordable to millions of households, as discussed earlier.

To the extent that people pay far more than they can afford, other necessities of life are compromised. This point needs little elaboration. Family well-being can be in jeopardy if too much of a family's budget is committed to the fixed costs of housing, thereby not leaving enough money to cover food, medical care, transportation, clothing, and recreational opportunities.

The issue of "what a household can afford" has been the subject of debate. Although the federal standard is that a household should not pay more than 30% of income for rent (raised from 25% in 1981), we know that for many households this percentage is too high. Stone's (1993) concept of "shelter poverty" is based on a "market basket" assessment of what families can truly afford for rent after taking into account an estimate of the amount of income needed to cover basic expenditures. The outcome of this analysis is that, for many households, 30% of income is way too much; some can afford absolutely nothing for housing.

In one study, researchers assessed the impacts on children whose families were living in assisted housing as opposed to those whose families were on waiting lists for housing assistance. Subsidized housing was found to yield positive outcomes, with the former group significantly less likely to have lower physical growth indicators than the latter group. The authors concluded that "receiving housing assistance may diminish the risk of undernutrition among children from low-income families, perhaps by freeing cash resources to provide a more adequate diet" (Meyers et al., 1993, p. 1083; see also Currie, 1995).

Another line of research related to housing affordability has investigated the possible link between high housing costs and health impacts. For example, in one study carried out in Great Britain, researchers explored the impacts of households being in mortgage arrears on the health of those homeowners as well as their use of primary health care services. While acknowledging that the nature of the associations are complex, the authors noted that "mortgage indebtedness is associated with changes in the subjective well-being of men and women and that it increases the likelihood that men in particular will visit their GPs [general practitioners]" (Nettleton & Burrows, 1998, p. 743). Further research has similarly revealed that "respondents who reported greater difficulty in meeting their housing and shelter related costs were more likely to report poorer health status" (Dunn & Hayes, 2000, p. 575) and high levels of stress (Nettleton & Burrows, 2000).

The limited work on impacts of unaffordability, combined with the inherent logic of the argument, underscores that the cost of housing is directly linked to family well-being.

IMPORTANCE OF PHYSICAL QUALITY, SAFETY, AND STABILITY OF HOUSING

It is something of an understatement to say that physically inadequate housing can be problematic and threaten family well-being. At worst, the lack of any shelter can result in death, and housing with major deficiencies can create life-threatening conditions such as an increased likelihood of fire. But even at lesser levels of severity, if housing is overcrowded, dilapidated, or otherwise inadequate, it is difficult, if not impossible, for family life to function smoothly.

There has been considerable interest in trying to measure the impacts of poor-quality housing on adult health. In a recent review of the literature, researchers noted that "a lack of decent housing and homelessness among a significant number of Americans remains a significant public health concern. In addition, a number of specific health hazards can be found even in housing that is in good condition and provides all basic amenities" (Matte &

Jacobs, 2000, p. 7). Marsh, Gordon, Heslop, and Pantazis (2000) conducted a major longitudinal study that followed some 17,000 residents of Great Britain between 1958 and 1991. They concluded that "housing deprivation has a substantial impact upon the risk of severe ill health" (p. 424; see also Whitehead, 1998). Finally, in a relatively rare controlled study, also carried out in Great Britain, it was revealed that residents living in high-quality public housing in West London were far less likely to become sick than were those living in low-quality public housing in East London (cited in Hynes, Brugge, Watts, & Lally, 2000, pp. 35-36).

Poor-quality housing is also certain to have detrimental effects on children. One study that explored the effect on children's health showed that overcrowding leads to higher rates of respiratory illness and stomach infections and even a higher probability of death (Currie & Yelowitz, 2000). Research has also shown that poorly maintained housing is closely linked to childhood injuries and that damp moldy interiors are associated with elevated incidences of respiratory disease and asthma (Sandel, Sharfstein, & Shaw, 1999, pp. 25-26). One of the specific correlates of poor-quality housing, lead paint poisoning, has been called "the most common and devastating environmental disease of young children" (U.S. General Accounting Office, 1993, p. 2), and the Centers for Disease Control and Prevention has "estimated that about 1 million U.S. children between one and five years [old] have elevated blood lead levels. . . . An estimated 14 million U.S. children in the at-risk age of 0 [to] 6 years old still live in housing built before 1960 with the highest concentration of lead paint" (cited in Sandel et al., 1999, p. 36). Hazards due to lead paint are most serious among poor non-white households, whose members have far higher incidences of lead poisoning than do their higher income white counterparts (Leonard, Dolbeare, & Zigas, 1993, p. 8; National Low Income Housing Coalition/LIHIS, 2000).

Closely tied to the physical safety of the dwelling is the stability and security provided by one's housing arrangement. Not only does housing need to shelter its occupants from external threats as well as possibly dangerous physical conditions, it also must be reliably present in a family's life. As one team of researchers put it,

> Developmental theory holds that the early security of the home and family bonds give a young person the strength to grow and the courage to explore the outer world. Perhaps when early stability and safety are violated, a person is more vulnerable to cognitive disorganization, to further victimization, and to problems in achieving a stable inner and outer life. (Ridgway, Simpson, Wittman, & Wheeler, 1994, p. 412)

However, stability and security are often elusive for low-income families, particularly if their already precarious financial situation worsens or if the housing market renders their unit unaffordable.

The importance of families securing stable housing has also been underscored in a number of recent research studies. Exploring various factors influencing high school completion rates, one study found that disrupting the physical location of a young child (age 7 years or under) or an adolescent (age 12-15 years) "has a strong negative and significant effect on achievement" (Haveman, Wolfe, & Spaulding, 1991, p. 144; see also U.S. General Accounting Office, 1994). In another study, researchers concluded that "instability impacts the emotional, behavioral, and cognitive development of children with homelessness exacerbating that impact" (Schmitz, Wagner, & Menke, 1995, p. 315). Recent research conducted by Harkness and Newman (2001) also underscored the significant contribution of residential stability as a

key factor contributing to the positive effects of homeownership on children's outcomes.

Beyond Shelter, a small Los Angeles nonprofit organization whose mission and operation are based on a "housing first" philosophy, embraces the importance of stable and secure housing for family well-being. Executive Director Tanya Tull explained her innovative approach:

> Instead of households remaining in emergency shelters or transitional housing for extended periods, homeless families are immediately relocated into permanent, affordable rental housing in residential neighborhoods and then provided with home-based case management services. . . . By situating homeless families within the larger community, the program fosters dignity and human connections. . . . [Moreover, "service-enriched housing"] provides a mechanism for meeting the long-term needs of families caught in chronic poverty and allows for resident involvement in issues that affect their lives and the environment in which they live. (cited in Bratt & Keyes, 1997, p. 36)

However, some have countered that "life stabilization . . . is necessary before poor women who head households can take advantage of affordable, permanent housing" (Sprague, 1991, p. 28). According to this view, housing in itself can neither end domestic violence and substance abuse nor help children who have led traumatic lives. Nevertheless, it is quite likely that a stable secure living arrangement, in conjunction with supportive services, can be as effective as the types of transitional programs that include these kinds of extensive services. But whether one is first housed in an emergency or transitional dwelling and then housed in a permanent home, or whether one goes straight to long-term housing, is likely less important than decent, stable living conditions being made available to all families, especially those in distress.

IMPACTS OF HOMELESSNESS ON CHILDREN AND FAMILIES

Homelessness can have profound and serious impacts on families and children. Newman (1999) noted that "most observers take it as self-evident that being homeless increases the difficulty of pursuing education or job training or getting and keeping a job" (pp. 3-4). Whether self-evident or not, psychiatrist Matthew Dumont provided this succinct statement on the impacts of homelessness on emotional well-being:

> Of all life's grating events, of all the stressors which drive people crazy, the loss of one's home ranks at the top. . . . Homeless children are subjected to the interruption of their school, the loss of their friends, malnutrition, and infection. The loss of a child's home is nothing less than an invitation to chronic illness. (cited in Smizik & Stone, 1988, pp. 229-230)

Kozol's (1988) poignant account of homeless families in New York City shelters underscores the extent to which grossly inadequate housing conditions contribute to family dysfunction: A lack of privacy creates stress for all members, the inability to have guests or to receive phone calls constricts normal social access as well as the ability to communicate with potential employers, children are unable to do homework, and adults live in constant fear that their children will be endangered by the harsh social and physical environments.

Wright, Rubin, and Devine (1988) stated that homeless people are more likely to report poor health than are other low-income respondents. Homelessness, in short, is an important cause of acute and chronic medical problems (pp. 147-148, 154). And another group of researchers summarized the following impacts of homelessness:

> Homelessness is a condition that erodes a family's sense of security, privacy, stability, control, and emotional and physical health. Homeless families are more susceptible to

violence and experience an undermining of parental authority caused by a disruption of schedule during shelter living. (Schmitz et al., 1995, p. 303)

A large body of research has focused on the impacts of homelessness on children. Summarizing several studies from the late 1980s, Blau (1992) noted that homeless children had overall poorer health, including poorer nutrition, delayed immunization, and higher levels of lead in their blood. One study concluded that the time children spent in the shelter contributed to developmental problems and that children living in shelters also missed far more days of school than did housed children (Sandel et al., 1999, p. 39).

Other studies have focused on the psychological impacts of homelessness, particularly among children. Blau (1992) noted, "Anxious, depressed, and deficient in self-control, homeless children scored lower than other students on both the reading and achievement tests. As a consequence, teachers held them back more than twice as frequently" (p. 161). In addition,

> A greater number of homeless children than housed children exhibited low self-concept and a higher level of behavioral problems. . . . Homeless families presented with poorer interpersonal relationships, less personal growth attributes, less perceived support, and less social embeddedness than housed families. (Downer, 1998, p. 6256)

Still another team of researchers found that half of all children in shelters show signs of anxiety and depression and demonstrate significantly more behavioral disturbances, such as tantrums and aggressive behavior, than do poor housed children (cited in Sandel et al., 1999, p. 39; see also Schmitz et al., 1995). Bassuk, Brooks, Buckner, and Weinreb (1999) also found a series of negative impacts of homelessness on children over 6 years of age, including a higher frequency of stressful events in their lives, a greater likelihood of sexual abuse, and a greater need for clinical referral.

Compelling evidence about the importance of homeless families attaining housing comes from a longitudinal study of poor and homeless families in New York City. Researchers found that the odds of stability were 20.6 times greater for those families who received subsidized housing than for those who did not (Shinn et al., 1998).

The problem of locating causality in research on the impacts of homelessness is particularly pronounced. There is always the possibility, for example, that some of the negative conditions observed caused or contributed to homelessness rather than the other way around. Elaborating on this point, a massive report on a 1998 homelessness symposium noted the following:

> The assessment of mental health status among homeless adolescents poses a number of problems. It is difficult to determine whether a homeless youth's emotional disturbance at a given point in time is more causally associated with an underlying emotional or mental disorder; the exigencies of homelessness; chronic stresses such as family violence or parental substance abuse; the youth's own use of alcohol or other drugs; or combinations of these. (cited in Fosburg & Dennis, 1999, pp. 3-10)

Despite the difficulty of assigning causality, it is probably reasonable to conclude that, at the very least, long-term residence in shelters can exacerbate an already problematic situation. Logic, combined with the empirical review presented earlier, points to the important and multiple connections between the presence of housing in a family's life and its well-being.

LOCATION AND ACCESSIBILITY OF HOUSING

The racial segregation and economic segregation of our neighborhoods appear to be important factors in family well-being. According to Turner (1998),

> Empirical studies generally conclude that conditions in the neighborhoods where people live influence a wide range of individual outcomes, including educational attainment, criminal involvement, teen sexual activity, and employment. High poverty rates, the absence of affluent or well-educated neighbors, high unemployment, high rates of welfare recipients, and the absence of two-parent families have all been found to affect important outcomes for children and families. (p. 375)

The literature on the impacts of dispersing low-income households to low-poverty areas underscores that housing subsidies should, in addition to providing decent affordable shelter, promote wider educational and employment opportunities. Results from both the Gautreaux Demonstration and the federal Moving to Opportunity (MTO) program point to the benefits enjoyed by low-income households that move from high- to low-poverty census tracts with the assistance of Section 8 certificates. The Gautreaux program, which was the outcome of a 1976 U.S. Supreme Court consent decree in which public housing residents in Chicago charged the public housing authority with discriminatory practices, provides housing certificates to public housing residents and those on waiting lists for public housing for use in mostly white Chicago suburbs or in the city of Chicago (see Rosenbaum, 1995). This program was followed in 1992 by the MTO program, which was aimed at "assist[ing] very low-income families with children who reside in public housing to move out of areas of high concentrations of persons living in poverty areas to areas with low concentrations of such persons" (Public Law 105-550, 42 U.S.C. 3672, Section 146).

Specifically concerning the Gautreaux program, researchers have found that a move to the suburbs improved adolescents' and younger children's education and employment prospects (Rosenbaum, 1995, pp. 263-264). Although gains were neither immediate nor easy (e.g., significant additional housing and counseling services were required), "the early experiences of low-income blacks do not prevent them from benefitting from suburban moves" (p. 266). And early reports from the MTO program indicate that participants feel safer in their new neighborhoods (Goering et al., 1999, pp. 44-45).

In one of the MTO sites, Baltimore, researchers found that "the offer to relocate families in public housing from high- to low-poverty neighborhoods improves academic achievement among elementary-school children." Although "the results appear to be more mixed for teens," the authors concluded that housing vouchers that restrict moves to low-poverty areas "can be used to produce substantial benefits to low-income families at relatively modest cost to the government" (Ludwig, Ladd, & Duncan, 2000, p. 27).

Where low-income housing is located, and where poor people live, would also seem to have a great deal to do with the ease or difficulty that potential workers have in locating employment. Since at least the late 1960s, with the publication of the Report by the National Advisory Commission on Civil Disorders (1968; i.e., the Kerner Commission), the physical separation between jobs and where workers live has been widely acknowledged (for more information on the "spatial mismatch hypothesis," see Ihlanfeldt & Sjoquist, 1998; Kain, 1992).

Both the Gautreaux program and MTO, by relocating households to low-poverty areas, attempt to provide better physical access to jobs as well as to reduce social isolation from employment networks. In the Gautreaux program, whether it was the change in physical proximity or the change in the social environment, those who moved to the suburbs were more likely to find employment than were their counterparts who remained in the city (Rosenbaum, 1995, p. 239).

Although moves to the suburbs may assist some households in their job search efforts, these programs cannot, at current funding levels, accommodate the number of people who might be eligible. But whether families live in urban neighborhoods or suburban ones, it is clear that the accessibility and attributes of one's neighborhood matter. A neighborhood without access to good educational and employment opportunities works against family stability and security.

POSITIVE SENSE OF SELF AND OPPORTUNITIES FOR EMPOWERMENT

Housing, as the physical space that is most intimately associated with one's identity, has a great deal to do with how one feels about oneself. And how adults perceive themselves clearly has enormous implications and impacts for children. More directly, how children perceive their environments translates into the formation of their own self-esteem. On a conceptual level,

> shaping the environment, exploring values, and making selections among options build a sense of personal efficacy and competence.... To a large degree, having and making choices is synonymous with personal power. Empowerment is often found in the details of the mundane world. It comes from controlling access to personal space, from being able to alter one's environment and select one's daily routine, and from having personal space that reflects and upholds one's identity and interests. (Ridgway et al., 1994, p. 413)

Some of the most widely cited research on this subject has been done by Cooper Marcus (1995), who stated, "Throughout our lives, whether we are conscious of it or not, our home and its contents are very potent statements about who we are. In particular, they represent symbols of our ego-selves" (p. 12).

Kearns, Hiscock, Ellaway, and Macintyre (2000), a team of Scottish researchers, concluded that "most people derived psychosocial benefits from the home" (p. 406).

According to psychologist Abraham Maslow's hierarchy of human needs, the basic "lowest" need that housing provides is shelter or protection. "Higher" level needs provided by housing include safety or security, a sense of belonging, self-esteem, and self-fulfillment. "Lower needs" must be met before "higher needs" (discussed in Meeks, 1980, pp. 46-49). But clearly, both are critical for optimal well-being.

A landmark study prepared in 1966 for the U.S. Department of Health, Education, and Welfare (predecessor to the U.S. Department of Health and Human Services) investigated what was known about the relationship between housing and the feelings and behavior of individuals and families. It concluded, "The evidence makes it clear that housing affects perception of one's self, contributes to or relieves stress, and affects health" (Schorr, 1966, p. 3).

Echoing these findings, a 1977 survey of middle-income people reported that the house "seemed to be a powerful symbol of order, continuity, physical safety, and a sense of place or physical belonging . . . where one could truly be oneself, in control, 'more of an individual,' capable of loving, and fully human" (Rakoff, 1977, p. 94).

Empirical evidence on the psychological importance of housing comes from studies that demonstrate that better quality housing is related to lower levels of psychological distress (Evans, Chan, Wells, & Saltzman, 2000, pp. 529-530). A survey of residents of Vancouver, British Columbia, revealed that residents who were proud of their dwellings, and who felt that their homes were a good reflection of who they were and provided a good place to live, were more likely to report better health status. In addition, "greater overall satisfaction with one's neighborhood as a whole, and greater satisfaction with personal safety in one's neighborhood, were significantly related with better mental health" (Dunn & Hayes, 2000, p. 576).

Housing also can offer opportunities for households to experience a greater sense of self-worth.[8] Reports from various community-based housing initiatives and self-help programs provide evidence that, due to the intimate role that housing plays in people's lives, it can be a critical vehicle for promoting one's sense of self. Also, to the extent that residents are able to take an active role in the development or management of their housing, they are provided with a concrete opportunity to achieve positive and productive outcomes. This, in turn, can have beneficial effects on the human need to feel potent and to fully realize one's capabilities (Bratt, 1990; Leavitt & Loukaitou-Sideris, 1995; Peterman, 1996; White & Saegert, 1997). Friedman (1992) provided a theoretical perspective on how control over one's housing situation can lead to psychological empowerment; by increasing "personal potency," there can be "recursive, positive effects on a household's continuing struggle to increase its effective social and political power" (p. 33).

It is beyond the scope of this chapter to discuss how, exactly, parents who either do or do not have a positive sense of themselves will affect their children. However, there is strong evidence on the connections between housing and psychological well-being among adults, and it would appear logical that this, in turn, would have significant impacts on children.

Finally, if it is correct that the way in which a family relates to its housing has the opportunity to translate into a sense of mastery over one's personal environment and there is no evidence to the contrary, then it would appear that this connection holds great promise for improved housing promoting far-reaching personal and social benefits. But should housing policy explicitly create opportunities for individuals to promote a positive sense of themselves? Should housing initiatives be structured so that it enables people to develop to their full potential? These questions are addressed in the final section of the chapter.

TWO LINGERING QUESTIONS

As noted at the outset of this chapter, in addition to the preceding series of explorations into the impacts of housing on family well-being, there are at least two questions that have received attention among policymakers and social scientists and that are relevant to building an argument for more public support for housing assistance. (A third key question—How does subsidized housing affect surrounding neighborhoods?—is not discussed here. Despite the conventional wisdom that low-income housing reduces property values and has other negative effects, most studies show either a neutral or a reverse effect; often, it actually improves values and neighborhood conditions (Freeman & Botein, 2002; Goetz, Lam, & Heitlinger, 1996; Lee, Culhane, & Wachter, 1999; Newman & Schnare, 1997).

How Does Project-Based Subsidized Housing Affect Families and Children?

When the public housing program was created in 1937, there were expectations that the behavior of the new residents would improve and that crime would be reduced. Embracing "physical determinism," an early poster promoting public housing heralded, "Eliminate Crime in the Slums Through Housing" (Roessner, 2000, p. 11). Despite the high hopes, current conventional wisdom

speaks to the negative images of "the projects." Stereotypes notwithstanding, although many subsidized developments have faced enormous problems, studies consistently demonstrate that these widely held perceptions are often not based on the lived experiences of the residents.

A number of surveys of public housing residents during the 1970s eloquently concluded that residents were far happier with their housing than the typical media portrayals indicated.

> The point that emerges most strongly from an examination of the tenants in the public housing program ... is that conventional public housing, for all its inadequacies and faults, served a real and important human need that would not otherwise have been served. Had the alternative been significantly superior, the occupants would have voted with their feet and done so willingly and openly, recording their dissatisfaction for all to see. (Meehan, 1975, p. 135)

And another team of researchers noted,

> Even as the image of public housing steadily deteriorates and its few remaining supporters speak in softer tones, tenants keep clamoring to get in. Is it not ironical that people should want to move into this housing of last resort? And that people in public housing don't want to leave? ... We have, in short, a paradox: Nobody likes public housing except the people who live there and those who want to get in. (Rabushka & Weissert, 1977, p. xvi)

A third study from that era collected data from residents at 10 public housing developments across the country. More than twice as many residents indicated they were satisfied as indicated they were dissatisfied with where they lived (Francescato, Weideman, Anderson, & Chenoweth, 1979). More recently, Bratt (1989) concluded that "public housing has not failed," and Atlas and Dreier (1993) observed that "the best kept secret about public housing is that most of it actually provides decent affordable housing to many people" (p. 22).

Over the past decade, research has continued to corroborate earlier studies revealing positive impacts on residents living in assisted housing. One such effort noted that "there is little evidence that projects actually harm children" (Currie & Yelowitz, 2000, p. 101); moreover, researchers found that "project families are less likely to suffer from overcrowding" and that "projects actually have positive effects on both housing quality and children's academic achievement. . . . Projects as a group have been wrongly vilified" (p. 121). Positive health impacts for low-income children living in assisted housing were also found; these children were significantly less likely to suffer from iron anemia (Meyers et al., 1993, cited in Currie, 1995).

In another study in which more than 200 public residents were interviewed, residents indicated that "public housing is much more affordable, offers better housing and services than comparable private market housing, has saved many families from homelessness and dissolution, and has given residents a critical sense of community" (quoted in Center for Community Change, 1999, p. 1). And in a third study in which 267 residents of five public housing developments in Boston were surveyed, at least half of the respondents indicated that they were pleased to be living in public housing and expressed a desire to continue living there (Vale, 1997).

In a further research project conducted during the period from 1968 to 1982 by Newman and Harkness (2001), public housing was found to enhance children's long-term outcomes and to reduce welfare dependence. The authors suggested that "these positive effects could arise because public housing improves physical conditions, reduces residential mobility, or enables families to spend more of their income on items

that benefit children's development" (p. 21). However, another study by this same team provided no conclusive evidence—either positive or negative—of any strong impacts of assisted housing on educational attainment (Newman & Harkness, 2000, pp. 41, 57). Other researchers have found no significant differences in alcohol consumption between youth living in public housing and those living in conventional housing (Williams, Scheier, Botvin, Baker, & Miller, 1997, p. 84). And another team of researchers investigated the extent to which the stereotypical high-rise public housing project[9] accounted for differences in high-risk behaviors among 9- to 15-year-olds. While acknowledging that prior studies yielded opposite results (some had found negative effects of high-rise buildings, whereas others found no effects), their research revealed that, at least in the study city, "variations in location and structure are not associated with marked differences in risk behaviors" (Li et al., 1997, p. 263).

In another line of inquiry, studies have underscored the benefits of large numbers of low-income families living in close proximity to one another. Although there is much research on the negative impacts of large numbers of poor families living in poverty-affected areas and there have been efforts to reduce concentrations of low-income households, as discussed earlier, there have also been many recent efforts to bring services to public housing and other subsidized housing developments specifically because that is where large numbers of low-income families live. A recent report noted, "The concentration of so many low-income children within public housing offers the possibility of designing service programs that help these children and their parents break through the cycle of poverty that grips many low-income American neighborhoods" (Center for Community Change, 1999, p. 2). (Some of the most innovative social programs directly connected to public or other forms of subsidized housing are discussed in Bratt & Keyes, 1997; Center for Community Change, 1999; and Lassen, 1995.)

In addition, the federal Family Self-Sufficiency Program and the various programs leading up to this initiative all provide evidence of the efficacy of using subsidized housing as the vehicle for a wide range of family support and employment programs. Created in 1990, the Family Self-Sufficiency Program promotes the development of local strategies to coordinate federal housing assistance with public and private resources so as to enable low-income public housing and Section 8 families to work toward economic independence and self-sufficiency. A HUD report underscored the agency's commitment to the self-sufficiency agenda and the notion that the provision of housing, alone, is not enough:

> Low- and moderate-income families should have greater power to make decisions about their lives, and government should support their quest for self-sufficiency. Public and assisted housing rules that have locked families into substandard housing have impeded their ability to move to self-sufficiency. . . . [Thus, one of HUD's key goals is to] make affordable housing serve as a starting point for families working toward stability and self-sufficiency by emphasizing work, education, and security. (HUD, 1995, pp. 1, 4)

A relatively new federal policy initiative is also viewing housing in connection with other non-"bricks and mortar" improvements. With the creation in 1993 of the HOPE VI program, which provides funds to public housing authorities to undertake major physical redesign and improvements, public housing developments are increasingly being seen as the locus for a broad range of community and social improvements, including child care and educational facilities, as well as social services and economic development programs.

Taken as a whole, the evidence presents a compelling story of the benefits for families

and children who are lucky enough to live in assisted housing. Although public housing and other project-based housing developments have admittedly experienced many problems, particularly in the area of poor management, the overall assessment, based on available research, leads to a far more positive appraisal than that offered by conventional wisdom.

Is the Provision of Subsidized Housing a Disincentive to Productivity and Employment?

One of the key arguments against providing subsidized housing is that the incentive to reduce dependence on the housing assistance may be negligible and that the incentive to work may be severely compromised or may disappear altogether. However, the available evidence leads to the opposite conclusion. A study based on 1,145 public housing households calculated the likelihood that a household would move out of public housing for each year between 1966 and 1992. Freeman (1998) concluded that public housing is not "habit forming for most residents" (p. 348). Emphatically rejecting the view that public housing and welfare are like "narcotics for the poor," he went on to state that receipt of public assistance, whether in the form of welfare or public housing, does not "become a trap from which it is increasingly difficult to exit as time wears on" (p. 350).

In another study, little evidence was found that

> public housing residency further reduces labor force activity. While it is true that most public housing residents do not work, their counterparts in the private real estate market are no more likely to be involved in the labor force. The perception that public housing is contributing to high levels of unemployment and joblessness appears to be an illusion. (Reingold, 1997, p. 484)

Newman (1999) examined a series of studies pertaining to the question of whether housing is an incentive or a disincentive to achieving a high level of economic security. She noted that there may be some modest positive effects among residents in assisted housing, such as greater labor force participation and/or educational attainment, and that findings indicating that "welfare recipients who also receive housing assistance have lower employment rates than those who do not receive assistance" may be due to "administrative decisions, such as preference rules for housing programs that gave priority to the most disadvantaged—not the result of the disincentive effect of housing assistance, per se" (pp. 8, 10).

In addition, a study of California residents living in Section 8 housing provided support for the view that the provision of housing does not negatively affect motivation to work. According to the author, "a well-designed housing program can help welfare recipients form a greater attachment to the labor market" (Ong, 1998, p. 791).

Sard and Lubell (2000) cited a study of welfare reform in Minnesota that found that

> most of the gains in employment and earnings attributable to the state's welfare reform initiative were concentrated among residents of public or subsidized housing. In other words, welfare reform was found to have a larger effect on employment and earnings among families receiving housing subsidies than among other families in the study. (p. 3)

They further noted that "preliminary findings from studies in Atlanta, Georgia, and Columbus, Ohio, indicate the same may be true of different initiatives undertaken in those cities" (p. 3).

Despite these findings, there is still a strong view that if housing is guaranteed, then the motivation to seek employment and to work toward economic security will be undermined. However, as noted previously, I have not found any empirical evidence that the provision of housing negatively affects

the motivation levels of workers or would-be workers. Furthermore, given the evidence to the contrary—that housing is a critical element for family well-being and that it is an essential springboard from which other career and income-enhancing initiatives can be launched—this chapter embraces the view that the provision of housing would serve as a positive force in the lives of the vast number of recipients. The logic of this position is far more compelling, believable, and consistent with psychological views on the importance of work to personal self-actualization than with the unsubstantiated view that the provision of housing encourages complacency and laziness.

HOUSING AS THE BASIS OF A NEW SOCIAL CONTRACT

Based on dozens of research studies, it is clear that the connections between housing and family well-being are profound and far-reaching. In addition, based on available research, there is no reason for the two lingering questions (discussed in the preceding section) to serve as impediments to a larger commitment to housing. Thus, in view of these arguments, as well as the level of housing need presented at the outset of this chapter, my recommendation is that we institute a far more widespread series of housing subsidy programs and initiatives based on a new social contract between government and individuals. The essence of this new contract would involve government provision or direct support of decent affordable housing in exchange for individuals meeting their core responsibilities—working toward family well-being and optimal productivity.

What does "optimal productivity" mean, and how could it possibly be assessed? This proposal may also be challenged as having a Communist ring: "From each according to his ability, to each according to his need."

However, it also has a distinctly American ring. It echoes President John F. Kennedy's oft-quoted words from his inaugural address in January 1961: "Ask not what your country can do for you, ask what you can do for your country." In both statements, there is a sense of give and take, needs and benefits, individual and community.

The "communitarian" philosophy embraces this key relationship. According to Etzioni (1995), who has been central to this movement,

> At the heart of the communitarian understanding of social justice is the idea of reciprocity: Each member of the community owes something to all the rest, and the community owes something to each of its members. Justice requires responsible individuals in a responsive community. (p. 19)

The foundation of the new social contract proposed here would be twofold. First, it would involve the government's commitment to make housing (and, hopefully in the future, other key necessities of life such as food and health care) available to all those in need. Second, it would require a commitment by citizens to enhance their productivity. There is some precedence for explicitly articulating the expectation that recipients of government assistance also provide something in return. The Personal Responsibility and Work Opportunity Reconciliation Act of 1996 incorporated the social contract idea. However, this welfare reform legislation created an arbitrary "one-size-fits-all" set of government expectations.

Most welfare recipients can now rely on public assistance for 2 consecutive years and a total of 5 years over a lifetime. Able-bodied recipients with school-age children are expected to work or perform community service for at least 20 hours per week within 60 days of receiving benefits. If a household does not comply with this requirement, then benefits will be progressively cut, with the cash grant disappearing entirely after 91 days.

The law also prevents most parents (except those under 20 years of age) from counting education or training programs as part of the work requirement. This last provision is perhaps the most troublesome, and it runs counter to the kind of social contract being proposed here. In addition, the government's expectations for what individuals will contribute are insufficient and incomplete. Government should not be content with an individual simply finding a job—any job.

Another precedent for requiring an exchange of benefits for work is found in the Quality Housing and Work Responsibility Act of 1998. Among its many provisions, each adult resident of public housing must perform community service or participate in an economic self-sufficiency program for at least 8 hours per month.

However, the current proposal would include more widely available housing assistance, and it would be both more flexible and more targeted to specific family needs and assets. Central to this proposal would be the provision of case workers to work with each individual and her or his family to develop a course of action that would enable that person to maximize productivity and optimize contributions to society. Through this relationship, an assessment of what individuals are able to provide would be carried out. It would also ensure that specific family needs are met.

The plan involves the creation of a comprehensive family support system, and all families receiving housing subsidies would be required to participate. I am arguing here that participation in such an initiative should be viewed as part of the *responsibilities* expected of the housing recipient. The rationale is that if family support can help individuals to develop their own capacities, then society at large will benefit.

It is further proposed that *all* households that receive government-sponsored or -supported housing participate in the family support program, including those that take homeowner deductions.[10] Incorporating such families into the program would achieve at least four goals. First, it would provide real support to all families, regardless of income, thereby acknowledging that family supports are necessary more broadly, not just for the poor.[11] Second, such a far-reaching program would be nonstigmatizing for the poorer participants. Third, it would make explicit how many people do, in fact, receive some form of housing subsidy in the form of homeowner deductions. Fourth, for those homeowners who do not want to participate in the family support system, homeowner deductions would be forfeited, thereby whittling away at a regressive subsidy that disproportionately benefits the wealthy (Dolbeare, 2000).

This proposal is premised on the notion that development of human capital should be at the heart of what government expects of its citizens. This is very different from the work and community service requirements contained in recent legislation noted previously, both of which have a punitive ring. With reference to Maslow's hierarchy of human needs, the first set of responsibilities that everyone must accept is the responsibility for one's self and her or his family's physical needs and safety. At the most basic level, housing would be provided and recipients would be expected to demonstrate responsibility for moving toward greater productivity and participation in social and economic life. If people were guaranteed decent places to live, with the worry of deprivation and humiliation removed, much human potential could be unleashed.

At one level, some individuals may need to work on literacy or substance abuse issues. Others may need to develop and hone parenting skills. And as family life is stabilized, education and job training programs would be provided. A revitalized social services and public works program could be part of this initiative as well. As bridges and other parts of our infrastructure continue to age, workers would be enlisted to assist in such projects. In addition, more one-on-one assistance is needed in a variety of sectors—from schools, to hospitals, to the kind of casework proposed here. These jobs may be permanent or transitory as individuals gain skills and expertise. The key point is that the stability that housing provides would enable individuals to fulfill their responsibilities to their families and to work toward realizing their potential as productive members of society.

The program outlined here would require three major kinds of funding. The first would go toward the direct support of a new production and rehabilitation program as well as a greatly expanded Section 8 voucher program. Although it is beyond the scope of this chapter to delve into the specific types of housing that would be created, my preference would be for an expanded commitment to various forms of social housing—housing owned by the public and nonprofit sectors—as well as to increasing homeownership opportunities. At the very least, for housing to promote feelings of self-worth and empowerment, it is likely that a new housing program would embrace ownership forms and management arrangements that would enable residents to maximize control over their living environments.

The second funding stream would go toward the family support initiative just outlined. Enough well-trained and competent case workers would need to be hired to ensure that caseloads are low and that each participant receives the needed attention. One of the secondary goals of the program might also be to help develop caseworker expertise among those who, themselves, have actively participated (or still are actively participating) in the family support program.

Finally, funding would be needed to support the public works and community service jobs that would be created. These kinds of jobs not only would enable workers to develop skills and expertise but also would provide needed services to the larger community.

Calculating the final price tag would not be simple, and the costs would not be low. But it is hoped that the benefits are apparent in view of the evidence presented throughout this chapter.

For those who still believe that, despite the evidence to the contrary, we would be inviting a lazy and complacent society, I suggest that we embark on a new social experiment. These tests would allow us to explore different ways of providing for basic human needs. Key to these experiments would be opportunities to evaluate how a right to housing could be balanced with individual responsibilities. And maybe—just maybe—we will tire of waiting for the results of the experiments and just decide to *do it*—to launch comprehensive social welfare guarantees, including decent affordable housing, for all.

We, as a society, do seem to have the resources to achieve this goal, particularly during an era of tax cuts. What would it take to overcome the pessimism expressed by DeParle (1996), who stated, "The federal government has essentially conceded defeat in its decades-long drive to make housing affordable to low-income Americans. Housing has simply evaporated as a political issue" (p. 52). Could arguments such as those presented throughout this chapter encourage greater recognition of the role of housing by politicians and, ultimately, result in greater resources for housing?[12]

The major argument presented here is that decent affordable housing is central to family well-being and that it must be treated as such. To fully embrace this view, I have proposed that we adopt a new type of housing program that would entail a new social contract between government and individuals. It would mean that, for the first time, individuals and families would have a guarantee of a stable environment in which to carry out the tasks of daily living—child rearing, pursuing and maintaining jobs, and participating in education/training programs. At the same time, families would be supported in those tasks, and the full potential and capabilities of each member would be realized. This would result in a true government *for* the people. It would promote a *civil society* (which has become the buzz-phrase of the new millennium). And it would result in healthier, safer, and more productive families and communities.

NOTES

1. A recent piece of housing legislation, the Quality Housing and Work Responsibility Act of 1998, amended this statement. It is arguable whether the new language constitutes a major or a modest retreat from the original national housing goal, which was to be realized "as soon as feasible." The 1998 act states: "that our Nation should promote the goal of providing decent and affordable housing for all citizens through the efforts and encouragement of federal, state, and local governments, and by the independent and collective actions of private citizens, organizations, and the private sector."

2. Although "self-sufficiency" is frequently used, there are a number of drawbacks to this term. According to Bratt and Keyes (1997), a major problem is that the term implies that people "will, at some point, no longer need any outside supports and, instead, will be totally able to care for themselves. In contrast, it can be argued that no one in our society is truly self-sufficient. Virtually all citizens receive some form of 'special assistance'" (p. 9).

3. "Affordability" is in quotations as a way of highlighting the inappropriateness of the term, although it is widely used. Indeed, all housing is affordable to someone. "Affordable housing" has come to mean housing affordable to very low-income families. That is, families earning 50% or less of the area median income paying no more than 30% of income for rent.

4. The subsequent sections of this chapter are generally expanded versions of material presented in Bratt (2002). The final section will also appear, in a somewhat different form, in Bratt (in press).

5. The literature pertaining to this issue is vast and draws from a variety of disciplines—economics, planning, social welfare, public health, medicine, sociology, public policy, housing policy, child development, and psychology. As a result, it is not possible to cite all of the relevant studies. The focus here is U.S.-based studies that have been carried out over the past 10 to 15 years, although in several cases international and earlier works are also included.

6   According to HUD, "very low-income" households are those earning less than 50 percent of area median income; "low-income" households earn less than 80 percent of area median income (HUD 1999a).

7. A moderate housing problem consists of a cost burden between 30% and 50% of income, overcrowding, and/or occupancy of moderately inadequate units; a severe housing problem consists of a cost burden above 50% of income and/or occupancy of severely inadequate units (National Low Income Housing Coalition, 2000, pp. 2-3).

8. Hayden (1984) and other architects and scholars writing from a feminist perspective have pointed out that the type of housing and its design can have the reverse effect. The typical home can be a source of frustration, isolation, and endless work for women whose homes become barriers, rather than aids, to self-actualization.

9. Although public housing is often equated with high-rise housing, this stereotype is in fact not accurate. Based on a survey of more than 200 public housing authorities, it was estimated that approximately 28% of public housing developments are in structures with four or more stories. The remainder of the stock are in developments with two- or three-story buildings (38%), one-story buildings (23%), and detached single-family structures (11%) (National Association of Housing and Redevelopment Officials, 1990, p. 19).

10. Homeowner deductions allow homeowners who itemize their income taxes to deduct both the interest portion of their mortgage payments and the amount of their property taxes from gross income. This results in substantially reduced tax liabilities for this group. In the aggregate, some $82 billion is lost to the U.S. Treasury due to these deductions (Dolbeare, 2000).

11. The suggestion that a comprehensive set of family supports be offered broadly has been made by a number of social policy analysts. See, for example, Albelda and Tilly (1997, chap. 9), Skocpol (2000, chap. 5), and Schorr (1997). Also, there is ample precedence for universal family support programs in many Western European countries.

12. This chapter was written before the September 11, 2001, terrorist attacks and the ensuing "War on Terrorism." Given this new reality, with significant resources being spent on defense, security, and military initiatives, it is uncertain when we will return to a full and robust domestic agenda. When we do, I hope that these ideas will help to chart that course.

REFERENCES

Albelda, R., & Tilly, C. (1997). *Glass ceilings and bottomless pits: Women's work, women's poverty*. Boston: South End Press.

Atlas, J., & Dreier, P. (1993). From "projects" to communities: Redeeming public housing. *Journal of Housing, 50*(1), 21-33.

Bassuk, E., Brooks, M. G., Buckner, J. C., & Weinreb, L. F. (1999). Homelessness and its relation to the mental health and behavior of low-income school-age children. *Developmental Psychology, 35*, 246-257.

Blau, J. (1992). *The visible poor: Homelessness in the United States*. New York: Oxford University Press.

Bratt, R. G. (1989). *Rebuilding a low-income housing policy*. Philadelphia: Temple University Press.

Bratt, R. G. (1990). *Neighborhood-Reinvestment Corporation sponsored mutual housing associations: Experiences in Baltimore and New York*. Washington, DC: Neighborhood Reinvestment Corporation.

Bratt, R. G. (2002). Housing and family well-being. *Housing Studies, 17,* 13-26.

Bratt, R. G. (forthcoming). Housing and economic security. In R. G. Bratt, C. Hartman, & M. E. Stone (Eds.), *Housing: Foundation of a new social agenda*. Philadelphia: Temple University Press.

Bratt, R. G., & Keyes, L. C. (1997). *New perspectives on self-sufficiency: Strategies of nonprofit housing organizations* (prepared under contract to the Ford Foundation). Medford, MA: Tufts University.

Bratt, R. G., & Keyes, L. C. (1998). Challenges confronting nonprofit housing organizations' self-sufficiency programs. *Housing Policy Debate, 9,* 795-824.

Center for Community Change. (1999). *Comprehensive services in public housing: Lessons from the field*. Washington, DC: Author.

Cooper Marcus, C. (1995). *House as a mirror of self*. Berkeley, CA: Conari Press.

Council of State Community Development Agencies and the American Public Welfare Association. (1991). Linking housing and human services: Describing the context. Washington, DC: Author.

Currie, J. M. (1995). *Welfare and the well-being of children*. Chur, Switzerland: Harwood Academic.

Currie, J., & Yelowitz, A. (2000). Are public housing projects good for kids? *Journal of Public Economics, 75,* 99-124.

Daskal, J. (1998). *In search of shelter: The growing shortage of affordable rental housing*. Washington, DC: Center on Budget and Policy Priorities.

DeParle, J. (1996, October 20). Slamming the door. *New York Times Magazine,* pp. 52-57, 68, 94, 105.

Dolbeare, C. N. (2000). *Housing budget trends and 2000 advocate's guide to housing and community development policy* (National Low Income Housing Coalition/LIHIS). [Online]. Available: www.nlihc.org/advocates/06.htm

Downer, R. T. (1998). Children's psychological well-being as a function of housing status and process resources in low-income families. *Dissertation Abstracts International, 58*(11-B), 6256.

Dunn, J. R., & Hayes, M. V. (2000). Social inequality, population health, and housing: A study of two Vancouver neighborhoods. *Social Science and Medicine, 51,* 563-587.

Etzioni, A. (Ed.). (1995). *Rights and the common good* (A. Etzioni, Ed.). New York: St. Martin's.

Evans, G. W., Chan, H-Y. E., Wells, N. M., & Saltzman, H. (2000). Housing quality and mental health. *Journal of Consulting and Clinical Psychology, 68,* 526-530.

Fosburg, L. B., & Dennis, D. L. (Eds.). (1999). *Practical lessons: The 1998 National Symposium on Homelessness Research* (prepared for U.S. Department of Housing and Urban Development and U.S. Department of Health and Human Services). Washington, DC: U.S. Department of Housing and Urban Development.

Francescato, G., Weideman, S., Anderson, J. R., & Chenoweth, R. (1979). *Residents' satisfaction in HUD-assisted housing: Design and management factors* (report prepared for the U.S. Department of Housing and Urban Development and Office of Policy Development and Research). Washington, DC: U.S. Department of Housing and Urban Development.

Freeman, L. (1998). Interpreting the dynamics of public housing: Cultural and rational choice explanations. *Housing Policy Debate, 9,* 323-353.

Freeman, L., & Botein, H. (2002). Subsidized housing and neighborhood impacts: A theoretical discussion and review of the evidence. *Journal of Planning Literature, 16,* 359-378.

Friedman, J. (1992). *Empowerment: The politics of development*. Cambridge, MA: Blackwell.

Goering, J., Kraft, J., Feins, J., McInnis, D., Olin, M. J., & Elhassan, H. (1999). *Moving to Opportunity for Fair Housing demonstration*. Washington, DC: U.S. Department of Housing and Urban Development.

Goetz, E. G., Lam, H. K., & Heitlinger, A. (1996). *There goes the neighborhood? The impact of subsidized multi-family housing on urban neighborhoods*. Minneapolis: University of Minnesota, Center for Urban and Regional Affairs and Neighborhood Planning for Community Revitalization.

Harkness, J., & Newman, S. J. (2001). *The interaction of homeownership and neighborhood conditions: Effects on low-income children*. Unpublished manuscript, Institute for Policy Studies, Johns Hopkins University.

Hartman, C. (1998). The case for a right to housing. *Housing Policy Debate, 9*, 223-246.

Haveman, R., Wolfe, B., & Spaulding, J. (1991). Children events and circumstances influencing high school completion. *Demography, 28*, 133-157.

Hayden, D. (1984). *Redesigning the American Dream: The future of housing, work, and family life*. New York: Norton.

Hynes, H. P., Brugge, D., Watts, J., & Lally, J. (2000). Public health and the physical environment in Boston public housing: A community-based survey and action agenda. *Planning Practice and Research, 15*(1-2), 31-49.

Ihlanfeldt, K. R., & Sjoquist, D. L. (1998). The spatial mismatch hypothesis: A review of recent studies and their implications for welfare reform. *Housing Policy Debate, 9*, 849-892.

Institute for Policy Studies Working Group on Housing, with D. Cluster. (1989). *A progressive housing program for the United States*. Washington, DC: Institute for Policy Studies.

Joint Center for Housing Studies. (1998). *A decade of miracles: 1988-1998* (Christmas in April Tenth Year Anniversary Report and 1998 Housing Study). Cambridge, MA: Harvard University, Joint Center for Housing Studies.

Joint Center for Housing Studies. (1999). *The state of the nation's housing, 1999*. Cambridge, MA: Harvard University, Joint Center for Housing Studies.

Joint Center for Housing Studies. (2001). *The state of the nation's housing*. Cambridge, MA: Harvard University, Joint Center for Housing Studies.

Kain, J. F. (1992). The spatial mismatch hypothesis: Three decades later. *Housing Policy Debate, 3*, 371-460.

Kearns, A., Hiscock, R., Ellaway, A., & Macintyre, S. (2000). "Beyond four walls": The psycho-social benefits of home—Evidence from West Central Scotland. *Housing Studies, 15*, 387-410.

Kozol, J. (1988). *Rachel and her children*. New York: Fawcett Columbine.

Lassen, M. M. (1995). *Community-based family support in public housing*. Cambridge, MA: Harvard Family Research Project.

Law, B. (2000, September). Comments presented at a meeting discussing "A New Paradigm for Housing in Greater Boston," Chamber of Commerce, Boston.

Leavitt, J., & Loukaitou-Sideris, A. (1995). "A decent home and a suitable living environment": Dilemmas of public housing residents in Los Angeles. *Journal of Architectural and Planning Research, 12*, 221-239.

Lee, C.-M., Culhane, D. P., & Wachter, S. M. (1999). The differential impacts of federally assisted housing programs on nearby property values: A Philadelphia case study. *Housing Policy Debate, 10*, 75-93.

Leonard, P. A., Dolbeare, C. N., & Zigas, B. (1993). *Children and their housing needs*. Washington, DC: Center on Budget and Policy Priorities.

Li, X., Stanton, B., Black, M. M., Romer, D., Ricardo, I., & Kaljee, L. (1997). Risk behavior and perception among youths residing in urban public housing developments. *Bulletin of the New York Academy of Medicine, 71*, 252-266.

Ludwig, J., Ladd, H. F., & Duncan, G. J. (2000, November). *The effects of urban poverty on educational outcomes: Evidence from a randomized experiment.* Paper presented at the meeting of the Association of Public Policy and Management, Seattle, WA.

Marsh, A., Gordon, D., Heslop, P., & Pantazis, C. (2000). Housing deprivation and health: A longitudinal analysis. *Housing Studies, 15,* 411-428.

Matte, T. D., & Jacobs, D. E. (2000). Housing and health: Current issues and implications for research and programs. *Journal of Urban Health, 77,* 7-25.

Meehan, E. J. (1975). *Public housing policy: Myth versus reality.* New Brunswick, NJ: Rutgers University, Center for Urban Policy Research.

Meeks, C. B. (1980). *Housing.* Englewood Cliffs, NJ: Prentice Hall.

Meyers, A., Frank, D., Roos, N., Peterson, K., Casey, V., Cupples, A., & Levenson, S. (1993). Public housing subsidies may improve poor children's nutrition. *American Journal of Public Health, 83,* 1079-1084.

National Advisory Commission on Civil Disorders. (1968). *Report of the National Advisory Commission on Civil Disorders.* Washington, DC: Author.

National Association of Housing and Redevelopment Officials. (1990). *The many faces of public housing.* Washington, DC: Author.

National Coalition for the Homeless. (1999). *Homeless families with children* (NCH Fact Sheet No. 7). [Online]. Available: http://nch.ari.net/families.html.

National Housing Task Force. (1988). *A decent place to live.* Washington, DC: Author.

National Low Income Housing Coalition. (2000). *Out of reach.* Washington, DC: Author. Available: www.nlihc.org/oor2000/introduction.htm

National Low Income Housing Coalition. (2001). *Out of reach.* Washington, DC: Author. Available: http://www.nlihc.org/oor2001/introduction.htm

National Low Income Housing Coalition/LIHIS. (2000). *2000 advocate's guide to housing and community development.* Washington, DC: Author. Available: www.nlihc.org/advocates/00.htm

Nettleton, S., & Burrows, R. (1998). Mortgage debt, insecure home ownership, and health: An exploratory analysis. *Sociology of Health and Illness, 20,* 731-753.

Nettleton, S., & Burrows, R. (2000). When a capital investment becomes an emotional loss: The health consequences of the experience of mortgage possession in England. *Housing Studies, 15,* 463-479.

Newman, S. J. (Ed.). (1999). *The home front: Implications of welfare reform for housing policy.* Washington, DC: Urban Institute.

Newman, S. J., & Harkness, J. (2000). Assisted housing and the educational attainment of children. *Journal of Housing Economics, 9,* 40-63.

Newman, S. J., & Harkness, J. (2001). *The long-term effects of public housing on self-sufficiency.* Unpublished manuscript, Institute for Policy Studies, Johns Hopkins University.

Newman, S. J., & Schnare, A. B. (1992). *Beyond bricks and mortar: Reexamining the purpose and effects of housing assistance.* Washington, DC: Urban Institute.

Newman, S. J., & Schnare, A. B. (1993). Last in line: Housing assistance for households with children. *Housing Policy Debate, 4,* 417-455.

Newman, S. J., & Schnare, A. B. (1997). " And a suitable living environment": The failure of housing programs to deliver on neighborhood quality. *Housing Policy Debate, 8,* 703-741.

Ong, P. (1998). Subsidized housing and work among welfare recipients. *Housing Policy Debate, 9,* 775-794.

Peterman, W. (1996). The meanings of resident empowerment: Why just about everybody thinks it's a good idea and what it has to do with resident management. *Housing Policy Debate, 7,* 473-490.

Rabushka, A., & Weissert, W. G. (1977). *Caseworkers or police? How tenants see public housing.* Stanford, CA: Hoover Institution.

Rakoff, R. M. (1977). Ideology in everyday life: The meaning of the house. *Politics & Society, 7,* 85-104.

Reingold, D. A. (1997). Does inner city public housing exacerbate the employment problems of its tenants? *Journal of Urban Affairs, 19,* 469-486.

Ridgway, P., Simpson, A., Wittman, F. D., & Wheeler, G. (1994). Home making and community building: Notes on empowerment and place. *Journal of Mental Health Administration, 21,* 407-418.

Roessner, J. (2000). *A decent place to live: From Columbia Point to Harbor Point.* Boston: Northeastern University Press.

Rohe, W. M., & Kleit, R. G. (1997). From dependency to self-sufficiency: An appraisal of the Gateway Transitional Families Program. *Housing Policy Debate, 8,* 75-108.

Rohe, W. M., & Kleit, R. G. (1999). Housing, welfare reform, and self-sufficiency: An assessment of the Family Self-Sufficiency Program. *Housing Policy Debate, 10,* 333-369.

Roisman, F. W. (1990, May-June). Establishing a right to housing: An advocate's guide. *Housing Law Bulletin,* pp. 39-48.

Rosenbaum, J. E. (1995). Changing the geography of opportunity by expanding residential choice: Lessons from the Gautreaux program. *Housing Policy Debate, 6,* 231-269.

Sandel, M., Sharfstein, J., & Shaw, R. (1999). *There's no place like home: How America's housing crisis threatens our children.* San Francisco: Housing America.

Sard, B. (1998, June). *The role of housing providers in an era of welfare reform.* Paper prepared for the research roundtable, "Managing Affordable Housing Under Welfare Reform: Recognizing Competing Demands," sponsored by Fannie Mae Foundation and Center on Budget and Policy Priorities, Washington, DC.

Sard, B., & Lubell, J. (2000). *The increasing use of TANF and state matching funds to provide housing assistance to families moving from welfare to work.* Washington, DC: Center on Budget and Policy Priorities.

Schmitz, C. L., Wagner, J. D., & Menke, E. M. (1995). Homelessness as one component of housing instability and its impact on the development of children in poverty. *Journal of Social Distress and the Homeless, 4,* 301-317.

Schorr, A. L. (1966). *Slums and social insecurity* (prepared for the U.S. Department of Health, Education, and Welfare, Research Report No. 1). Washington, DC: Government Printing Office.

Schorr, L. B. (1997). *Common purpose: Strengthening families and neighborhoods to rebuild America.* Garden City, NY: Doubleday.

Shinn, M., Weitzman, B. C., Stojanovic, C., Knickman, J. R., Jimenez, L., Duchon, L., James, S., & Krantz, D. (1998). Predictors of homelessness among families in New York City: From shelter request to housing stability. *American Journal of Public Health, 88,* 1651-1657.

Shlay, A. B. (1993). Family self-sufficiency and housing. *Housing Policy Debate, 4,* 457-495.

Shlay, A. B. (1995). Housing in the broader context in the United States. *Housing Policy Debate, 6,* 695-719.

Skocpol, T. (2000). *The missing middle.* New York: Norton.

Smizik, F. I., & Stone, M. E. (1988). Single-parent families and a right to housing. In E. A. Mulroy (Ed.), *Women as single parents* (pp. 227-270). Dover, MA: Auburn House.

Sprague, J. F. (1991). *More than housing: Lifeboats for women and children.* Boston: Butterworth Architecture.

Stone, M. E. (1993). *Shelter poverty: New ideas on housing affordability.* Philadelphia: Temple University Press.

Stone, M. E. (forthcoming). Shelter poverty. In R. G. Bratt, C. Hartman, & M. E. Stone (Eds.), *Housing: Foundation of a new social agenda.* Philadelphia: Temple University Press.

Turner, M. A. (1998). Moving out of poverty: Expanding mobility and choice through tenant-based housing assistance. *Housing Policy Debate, 9,* 373-394.

U.S. Catholic Conference. (1975). *The right to a decent home: A pastoral response to the crisis in housing: A statement of the Catholic bishops of the United States.* Washington, DC: Author.

U.S. Department of Housing and Urban Development. (1995). *Reinvention blueprint.* Washington, DC: Author.

U.S. Department of Housing and Urban Development. (1999a). *Waiting in vain: An update on America's rental housing crisis.* Washington, DC: Author.

U.S. Department of Housing and Urban Development. (1999b). *The widening gap: New findings on housing affordability in America.* Washington, DC: Author.

U.S. Department of Housing and Urban Development. (2000a). *Rental housing assistance: The worsening crisis—A report to Congress on worst case housing needs.* Washington, DC: Author.

U.S. Department of Housing and Urban Development. (2000b). *A vision for change: The story of HUD's transformation.* Washington, DC: Author.

U.S. General Accounting Office. (1993). *Lead-based paint poisoning: Children not fully protected when federal agencies sell homes to public* (GAO/RCED-93-38). Washington, DC: Author.

U.S. General Accounting Office. (1994). *Elementary school children: Many change schools frequently, harming their education* (GAO/HEHS-94-45). Washington, DC: Author.

Vale, L. J. (1997). Empathological places: Residents' ambivalence toward remaining in public housing. *Journal of Planning Education and Research, 16,* 159-175.

White, A., & Saegert, S. (1997). Return from abandonment: The tenant interim lease program and the development of low-income cooperatives in New York City's most neglected neighborhoods. In W. Van Vliet— (Ed.), *Affordable housing and urban development in the United States* (pp. 158-180). Thousand Oaks, CA: Sage.

Whitehead, C. (1998). *The benefits of better homes: The case for good quality affordable housing.* London: Shelter, Paddington Churches Housing Association.

Williams, C., Scheier, L. M., Botvin, G. J., Baker, E., & Miller, N. (1997). Risk factors for alcohol use among inner-city minority youth: A comparative analysis of youth living in public and conventional housing. *Journal of Child & Adolescent Substance Abuse, 6*(1), 69-89.

Wright, J. D., Rubin, B. A., & Devine, J. A. (1998). *Beside the golden door: Policy, politics, and the homeless.* New York: Aldine de Gruyter.

CHAPTER 20

Philanthropy, Science, and Social Change

Corporate and Operating Foundations as Engines of Applied Developmental Science

LONNIE R. SHERROD

A cross the last century, philanthropy has become an important force influencing the development of children, families, and communities. It has been influential in the development of applied developmental science and in furthering the new view on developmental science that aims to promote positive development in children, youth, and families. This chapter describes how particular forms of philanthropy—corporate and operating foundations—contribute to applied developmental science and how they advance civil society. I begin with a brief history of philanthropy and then consider how corporate and operating foundations contribute to applied developmental science, including both university-community collaborations and views of positive development. I also consider how these forms of philanthropy contribute to civic engagement. In considering

what they have done, I also address how their efforts might be expanded.

First, I might explain why a professor of psychology would tackle such a topic. For 10 years, I was vice president of the William T. Grant Foundation. The Grant Foundation is a private, independent foundation, founded in the 1930s by Mr. Grant, who founded a chain of five-and-dime-type department stores. Because his jobs were entry level, many of his employees were young people, and he noticed that their development was compromised by a variety of problems relating to mental health, family functioning, and so forth. He therefore established this foundation to understand how to help youth live up to their full potential (Cahan, 1986). This mandate has always been interpreted as funding research on human development. In this regard, the Grant Foundation is a

AUTHOR'S NOTE: I wish to thank Barbara Bryan, Director of NYRAG, and volume editor Donald Wertlieb, Tufts University, for reading and usefully commenting on an earlier draft of this chapter.

very unusual foundation. However, as vice president of a foundation funding research, I sought to promote the importance of research within the field of philanthropy. Through this effort, I learned a great deal about the scope and diversity of foundations. I always considered that corporate and operating foundations had an untapped potential.

THREE TRADITIONS OF PHILANTHROPY

Philanthropy can be said to have originated early in the 20th century, and it has gone through three traditions (Wisely, 1998) and may now be in a fourth.

The Founding of Philanthropy

Around the turn of the century, a variety of charities existed. These charities, in fact, represent the first tradition of philanthropy, and their goal was to relieve the suffering of the poor, infirm, and otherwise unfortunate.

The industrialization of the early 20th century, however, generated a number of wealthy men who became determined to use their business sense and accumulated wealth to deal with some of society's problems. They viewed the existing charities as providing temporary relief through treating symptoms. These new philanthropists, such as Carnegie, Ford, and Rockefeller, wanted to "solve" social problems by identifying core causes and attending to them. Several of the currently largest private foundations arose early in the century: The Russell Sage Foundation in 1907, the Carnegie Corporation in 1911, the Rockefeller Foundation in 1913, and the Commonwealth Fund in 1918, for example. Government was not involved in social welfare to any appreciable degree, so the role for these new foundations was clear.

Religion had been important in furthering the previously existing charities. This good work arose in part because of the values inherent in people's religious beliefs. In fact, there had been a long history of volunteerism and citizens' organizations in this country and in Europe. But the new philanthropy was different; it had no formal connection to religion, but has, in fact, been referred to as "scientific philanthropy" (Gregorian, 2000). This new effort represents the second tradition of philanthropy and continued up through the 1960s.

Because of their interest in identifying core causes of social problems, these new philanthropists looked to science with its ability to separate causes and effects for the tools for their efforts. As general-purpose foundations, their objective was to advance public welfare, but science was seen as a means to that goal. Science with its clear distinction of cause and effect provided a strategy for approaching the "solution" of social problems by identifying core causes that could be addressed as opposed to alleviating symptoms or temporarily providing relief (Cahan, 1986; Katz & Katz, 1981). Although most of these new foundations did not fund very much science, the appreciation of science as a tool provided a funding context that fueled the growth of the social behavioral sciences and the universities in which they became housed (Prewitt, 1995; Sherrod, 1998). These new foundations were also different in that they were managed for the most part by boards of directors (Gregorian, 2000).

An Increasing Concern for Wider Social Change

What this approach to philanthropy meant was that foundations funded a lot of programs oriented to individual improvement, to giving individuals and families the wherewithal to improve their lives: educational programs, libraries, family support, and treatment of and cures for diseases. For example, the Russell Sage Foundation funded research on tuberculosis and provided for children's recreation; a Rosenwald Fund (from Sears Roebuck money) funded schools and scholarships for African Americans (Gregorian, 2000). Beginning in about the 1960s, at the same time as a variety of other social movements such as civil rights and the anti-Vietnam War effort, foundations began to question this past strategy. In fact, they had not been very successful at "solving" social problems or improving the overall status of human well-being. Although the success of their efforts can be debated at length, problems such as poverty did not disappear. Furthermore, as one problem was reduced, a new one arose. Hence, philanthropy came to believe that widespread social change was needed, and its efforts changed accordingly. It began to orient its efforts to systematic social reform (Wisely, 1998), to eliminating poverty and racism, and to promoting international cooperation, and in this shift, its relation to science was lost (Sherrod, 1998).

Government was also assuming an increasing role in addressing social problems, providing social services, and generally assuming some of the roles that philanthropy had undertaken. The passage of AFDC, Aid to Families with Dependent Children, in the 1930s is an early example. This program, criticized and abandoned in the 1990s because it allowed mothers with young children to stay home with the children, was, in fact, designed to allow mothers to stay home with their children. The 60-year change in attitude was due in large part to the fact that in the 1930s most recipients were widows, whereas in the 1990s, many recipients, not the majority, had become unwed teen mothers. At any rate, government's increasing role in the arena that philanthropy had dominated

may be another reason for the change in strategy.

This new focus on systematic social change that continues today represents the third tradition of philanthropy (Wisely, 1998). It is not clear if the connection to science was lost because science is less relevant to social than to individual change or that science, like past approaches, had just not been helpful. Government also began funding science in the 1950s, and this may have therefore been another factor.

A New Fourth Wave?

Some have now argued that the latest version of philanthropy represented by those who have made their money in the new technology industries and in a booming stock market constitutes a new fourth wave. In fact, the current social economic conditions are similar to those during the late 19th and early 20th centuries. There is a sizable population that is very poor, whereas there is an upper class that clearly constitutes an aristocracy. A large percentage of the poor are children. The cities provide very deprived environments for the poor. And there is increased immigration. Hence, it is not surprising that again there is a new surge of philanthropy.

However, the earlier philanthropists, such as Carnegie and Rockefeller, made their money working with people. The new philanthropists, such as Gates, Soros, and Turner, are much more into venture capitalism, quick returns, unstable markets, and globalization. Their style of making money is likely to influence their style of philanthropy, so that philanthropy comes to operate much more like business. In fact, this new philanthropy has been referred to as "venture philanthropy" to reflect the fact that it borrows its strategies from venture capitalism (Gregorian, 2000). Reflecting increasing globalization, these new foundations are also more likely to have a global agenda (Gregorian, 2000). Again there is little relationship to science, and government, despite devolution, continues to be a major force in the provision of human services. However, it is too early to determine if this new wave of philanthropy does represent a new fourth tradition; certainly it is too early to characterize this philanthropy in any detail. What is clear is that the financial investment is as significant as was true earlier in this century, so its influence will be fully as great.

The point is that our social strategy for using charity to attend to social problems has changed over the past century, and these changes have implications for the role of philanthropy in the society.

GROWTH IN PHILANTHROPY DURING THE LAST HALF OF THE CENTURY

At the same time that the nature of philanthropy was changing in this country, so, too, was its size and importance in the society. The last half of the 20th century has seen an accumulation of wealth in a limited portion of the population, as was true a century ago. This accumulation of wealth has led to a new wave of philanthropy as discussed earlier. However, the private foundations formed throughout the 20th century are now also part of the wealthy population that enjoys the advantages of growth due to ever-expanding bull markets.

The globalization of market economies, the emergence of new technologies in communication and information processing, and the resulting booming stock market have resulted in a substantial increase in the amount of money available through philanthropy. The tax laws in the United States also create an incentive both for the continuation of philanthropy and for its growth. Unlike private

individuals who make money on the stock market, philanthropies, being tax-exempt organizations, are not taxed. However, they are required by federal law to pay out 5% of their assets annually. So as foundation assets grow, so too does the amount of money available from philanthropy. However, few foundations actually pay out more than the required 5%, so when asset growth is in the double digits, as has been true during past decades, the absolute worth of the foundation grows, as does its spending.

Thus, both the number of foundations and their absolute worth has grown substantially during the last half century. Around the turn of the century, when philanthropy emerged in this country, it was estimated that there were more than 4,000 millionaires; in 1999, 7.2 million millionaires were estimated, and that was double the number from 5 years earlier (Gregorian, 2000). The number of private foundations has more than doubled since the 1970s; the total assets of these foundations have also doubled, even after controlling for inflation. The 1950s, 1980s, and 1990s were the decades of the greatest growth (Renz & Lawrence, 1993). Growth during the nineties has been unprecedented. It is estimated that the value of philanthropy has doubled since 1996; in 1996, the total amount of giving in this country from foundations was $26 billion (individual giving still remains highest, at about $150 billion). Between 1975 and 1998, foundation giving increased by 250% after controlling for inflation. About 1,000 new foundations are created each year; the total is now well over 50,000 (Gregorian, 2000).

THE DIVERSIFICATION OF PHILANTHROPY

In addition to growth in absolute numbers and asset value, foundations in this country have also become increasingly diverse. The foundations that originated early in this century are independent foundations. They are intended to be self-perpetuating, they have endowments, and the interest on the assets funds their programs and projects, according to the mandate established by their founder. Most are governed by a board of directors, whose responsibility is to uphold the mission of the founder, but they otherwise operate independent of any individuals or organization. The Carnegie Corporation, Ford Foundation, and Commonwealth Fund, currently large institutions formed early in the 20th century in the second tradition of philanthropy, are of this type. Chapter 19 addresses this category of foundation.

However, three other types of foundations have arisen. The one type that has grown the most in the past few decades is the community foundation. These foundations operate like private or independent foundations, except that their mandate is to serve a particular community, making them public charities; the New York Community Trust and the Chicago Community Trust are examples of this type of foundation. Chapter 20 deals with this category of philanthropy.

Three other types of foundations are family or corporate foundations and operating foundations. Family or corporate foundations function as direct arms of the family or corporation that founded them. Typically, family members constitute the major portion of the board for a family foundation, and the foundation is in effect a project of the founding family. The mission of the foundation, however, can be as diverse as independent foundations. In fact, most foundations began with a heavy involvement of the founding family member(s). Similarly, the CEO of the corporation may be the chairman of the board of the corporate foundation, but the mission of the corporate foundation is typically related to the goals of the corporation.

The Toshiba America Foundation, of the electronics giant, is appropriately focused on education. Corporate foundations also typically relate, at least initially, to the public relations or community outreach branch of the corporation. They represent the corporation's efforts at "giving back."

The financing of the corporate foundation may also differ from that of an independent foundation. In a few cases, the foundation does have an endowment, but in those cases, the endowment may disproportionately represent stock in the company. The W. K. Kellogg Foundation, for example, is an independent foundation but has approximately 75% of its assets in Kellogg stock; because the Foundation controls the majority of the corporation's stock, the Kellogg Company can never be taken over by another corporation. However, this means that the money available to the Foundation is directly related to how the corporation does financially. In corporate foundations, this relationship may be direct, in that the foundation may actually be set up to receive a percentage of the founding company's annual earnings.

The final type of foundation is the operating foundation. These foundations may be funded as any of the previous types, but rather than making grants to other institutions for their work—or in addition to making grants—these foundations actually design and run their own projects and thereby make grants to themselves. The Russell Sage Foundation is an operating foundation; one of its largest programs is an in-house fellowship program for visiting social scientists.

Categorizing foundations is a delicate matter. While at the Grant Foundation, I had the privilege of working for a while with Beatrice A. Hamburg as president, who had a favorite saying, "If you know one foundation, you know one foundation." Foundations are exceedingly diverse and thereby defy easy categorization. A resource organization on philanthropy, The Foundation Center, in New York City, publishes a directory, the introduction of which describes the various types of foundations. Nonetheless, the newer types of foundations have represented a substantial portion of the growth of philanthropy in the last decades, although they still represent a small percentage of philanthropy overall. But predictions are that local philanthropic activities, such as community foundations, may represent one intense area of future philanthropic activity (Hall, 1988; Nason, 1989).

A CONCERN FOR CHILDREN, YOUTH, AND FAMILIES

Children, youth, and families have been and continue to be a major concern of philanthropy. There is a special interest group of foundations concerned with children, youth, and families—Grantmakers for Children, Youth and Families. Based in Washington D.C., the organization has more than 300 members. It has an executive director and staff and holds an annual conference. Founded by Jane Dustan of the Foundation for Child Development and others, it began as an affinity group of the Council on Foundations, but became independent a few years ago. Most major foundations, including corporate ones, are members and attend the annual meeting, because most large foundations have some concern for children, youth, and families.

Grantmakers for Children, Youth and Families, or GCYF, as it is known to members, attempts to help members with professional development, covering topics such as how to make grants, insurance coverage for small organizations, and so forth. But more important, it covers program-relevant information. It has an annual 2- to 3-day meeting that brings in well-known speakers from academic, business, nonprofit, government, and other sectors. It organizes groups of members around topics to constitute learning circles. It publishes a newsletter. It is a professional organization for grantmakers concerned with children and youth as important as organizations such as the Society for Research in Child Development are to child development researchers.

There are also special interest groups concerned with relevant topics, education as well as families and neighborhoods, for example. In addition to the Council on Foundations, which is the major professional organization for philanthropy, comparable in many ways to the American Psychological Association, there are regional associations. The New York Regional Association, NYRAG, was very important to my work at the Grant Foundation. Although broader than children and youth, this topic constitutes a large portion of its work because of the interest within philanthropy. Hence, philanthropy is very relevant to this *Handbook*.

CORPORATE AND OPERATING FOUNDATIONS

Corporate and operating foundations in some ways offer the newest and most innovative approach to philanthropy. The remainder of this chapter is devoted to this form of philanthropy.

Corporate foundations provide a means for the private sector to exert its civic responsibility in the community. Their philanthropic work allows them to step out of their capitalist orientation and to act altruistically. Corporations, like charitable individuals, in fact receive sufficient tax benefit in this country that their giving can rarely be characterized as altruistic in terms of entailing some self-sacrifice. Nonetheless, it presents an image of civic engagement and altruism that is healthy for the society at large and buffers the overwhelming focus on the value of a dollar in a capitalist society. In this way, in my opinion, corporate foundations are valuable above and beyond the good work that they do. Andrew Carnegie, for example, viewed the rich as trustees of the public's wealth (Gregorian, 2000), and corporate foundations are, in some ways, explicit examples of this view.

Gregorian (2000) writes, "businesses are . . . discovering that giving is good for business and public relations as well as for making them part of the community of responsible citizens" (p. 15). The four companies that gave the most in 1998 were Bank of America, General Motors, Johnson & Johnson, and Phillip Morris; however, their giving is still only about 1% of their pretax income. When giving is calculated as percent of pretax income, rather than gross amount, a different set of companies emerge as most generous: Champion International, Humana, and Owens Corning. At any rate, business is discovering that social problems are economic problems (Gregorian, 2000), and its giving is increasing through corporate foundations as well as directly.

Operating foundations allow foundations to do the work they promote, rather than just funding grants. In this way, they become actual players in social change and, hence, true partners in the efforts. They provide a model for the use of private funding to impact society.

Both types of philanthropy are relevant to four themes that characterize this *Handbook* and that have figured prominently in my work across the past few years. Hence, in the remainder of this chapter, I discuss those themes and the contributions that can be made by these two types of philanthropy.

The four themes are the emergence of applied developmental science, the increasing popularity of university-community collaborations, the promotion of positive youth development, and recent attention to civic engagement.

APPLIED DEVELOPMENTAL SCIENCE

In recent years, a new perspective has emerged to guide developmental human science. This view recognizes the importance of context and culture, emphasizes developmental appropriateness, and focuses on continuity and change even in regard to prevention and intervention. Most important, it aims to bridge the gap between research and practice, bringing both to the table for collaborations (Fisher & Lerner, 1994). I have previously argued that this view has the potential to reestablish the connection between science and philanthropy that has been lost in recent decades (Sherrod, 1999b).

Three Important Contributions of Applied Developmental Science

Applied developmental science makes three particularly important and unique contributions. First, it blurs the distinction between applied and basic research. I have long believed this to be an artificial distinction. The two types of research are differentiated by the source of their question and the time frame for the relevance of the results, but both can be useful in our quest to improve the social good. Research on self-efficacy (Bandura, 1992) is an example of originally basic research that has proven extremely useful in the battle to prevent HIV infection (Sherrod, 1998). Because social problems arise more quickly than science can generate information to deal with them (Prewitt, 1980), we need some information on the shelves to pull off as new problems arise. The research on self-efficacy served this purpose in regard to the AIDS epidemic. Similarly, applied research is complex. Huston (2002) has differentiated two types of applied research: *policy relevant* research such as studies of the mechanisms by which poverty impacts child development and *policy analyses,* or studies of actual social programs and policies such as welfare reform. Psychologists have not typically been involved in the latter type of research, which is unfortunate because most programs and policies deal at some level with behavior change (Sherrod, 2002).

The second contribution of applied developmental science is the perspective on evaluations. Black box evaluations, based on clinical drug trials, are not necessarily appropriate for studies of social programs and policies. Although experimental designs with random assignment to control and program groups are desirable because they allow attribution of causality, social programs and policies are complex, multivariate endeavors that influence and are influenced by numerous micro and macro factors. They are not single-variable drugs. Hence, it is questionable how appropriate the experimental design may in fact be for evaluations of social programs and policies (Hollister & Hill, 1995). But more important, other approaches should be explored; something as simple as examining the relationship between program participation variables and outcome variables could be useful. I have previously argued that for disadvantaged children and youth, programs and policies are as important to their development as schools and families and so should be studied as contexts for development (Sherrod, 1997).

Third, perhaps the most important contribution of applied developmental science is its recognition that the communication between researchers and others must be bidirectional; both researchers and community participants, for example, have lessons to learn from each other (Sherrod, 1998). Nonacademicians can learn how to evaluate and critique information from scientists, and researchers can learn what information the community needs. Such communication serves not only to improve both endeavors but is also critical to maintaining a public commitment to science. In fact, one reason for the increasing separation of science and philanthropy may be that this type of communication has not occurred between these two constituencies.

Reconnecting to Science

Corporate and operating foundations have a particular contribution to make in regard to applied developmental science. Corporate foundations provide a means of connecting academia and the private sector. They can, thereby, influence both the development of this science as well as philanthropy by reestablishing its connection to science. We need to base what we do to improve human welfare in what we know, and we need to continue to learn as we work to improve the social good. Applied developmental science offers tools for both tasks. Applied developmental science is particularly appropriate to the work of corporate and operating foundations. And the merger of this scientific perspective with this type of philanthropy generates a new potential for accomplishing social change.

The private sector is an obvious collaborator with the academic community. Business is interested in results and practical applications. It therefore should be interested in using research to guide its actions to increase the odds that results will in fact occur. At the same time, it cannot determine if its efforts generate impact without research on the implemented program. Applied developmental science provides tools for assessing results and for guiding collaboration between researchers and practitioners.

Evaluation as Assessment of Return on Investment

Applied developmental science promotes attention to context and the diversity of the population and advocates the use of multiple methods. These are tools that could prove useful to corporate foundations interested in influencing the social good in a way that allows assessment of the impact. Return on investment is another idea popular in the private sector. Applied developmental science offers tools in evaluation research that allow attention to return on investment. Evaluation does not necessarily just mean determining if a program "works." Applied developmental science advocates that evaluation means learning attached to the program. For example, several years ago, businessman Eugene Lang mentioned to a group of high school students that if they graduated from high school, he would pay for their college. This led to the formation of a major philanthropic effort called "I Have a Dream" that began attending to the education of disadvantaged children as early as kindergarten and first grade. I do not know how much money Lang has put into this effort nor how many youth have received a college education with his funds; I also do not believe that there has ever been a formal experimental evaluation of the program. There has, however, been a great deal of learning associated with this effort in terms of small-scale exploratory studies and attention to the education of disadvantaged youth. Thus, whatever investment he has made, the returns have been great.

From this perspective, the program, hence, becomes another context in which to study development (Sherrod, 1997, 1998). For "I Have a Dream" one can, for example, ask what role hope and motivation play in the context of school quality and curriculum. Corporate programs do not carry the concern for public accountability that government

programs do. Hence, learning can be as important a return on investment as social impact. The learning then allows a better effort next time around—in the same way that a corporation may try one marketing scheme after another. Hence, even if Lang's efforts do not graduate many youth from college, hopefully in doing this, if appropriate mechanisms are applied using the tools of applied developmental science, we can learn something about what it takes to overcome the odds against educating disadvantaged youth. There have, in fact, been few cases where the appropriate learning effort was made; that was not the case, for example, with Lang's effort. Although it does offer numerous lessons for us, there was only a meager application of research. Corporate foundations have the wherewithal to do a better job in attaching learning to social change efforts.

Marketing and Dissemination

Corporations also know a lot about marketing. In fact, they possess a technology regarding marketing that is not typically tapped by the academic community. Dissemination of research to audiences other than academics is a newly recognized endeavor of importance, and dissemination efforts are increasing at universities and by philanthropy (Sherrod, 1999a). Applied developmental science promotes the importance of dissemination, of communication with multiple audiences. A collaboration between academia and the private sector, through corporate philanthropy, could contribute substantially to the development of the field of dissemination. Corporations have the marketing know-how; the research community has the ability to craft meaningful messages based on research.

Research on child and youth development and on families, both basic and applied, has much useful information to offer to the design as well as the evaluation of social programs and policies and to the efforts of all foundations, including corporate ones. Yet too often it is relegated to the shelves of libraries in academic journals. The scientific community is recognizing that it must take some responsibility for the dissemination of its work, and efforts are increasing (Sherrod, 1999a). The major research association of child developmentalists, the Society for Research in Child Development, is tackling dissemination as an important priority, through its Committee on Policy and Communication and its Washington, D.C.–based office. However, these efforts could benefit substantially from the expertise of the private sector.

Several years ago, in 1994 when the Congress was elected that began attending to welfare reform, the Society for Research in Child Development teamed with the other developmental research organizations (Division 7 of the American Psychological Association, Society for Research on Adolescence, and International Society for Infant Studies) to communicate to that Congress certain research information relevant to pending decisions. For example, Congress was considering eliminating the school lunch program, yet we know from research that even short bouts of malnutrition can have lasting effects on children's development. We hired a public relations firm to get the word out and through them learned a great deal about dissemination. For example, the media is interested in research only if it can be presented as new; relevance to pending policy decisions does not interest the media. The Center for Children in Poverty at Columbia University, under the directorship of Dr. Lawrence Aber, hired a Madison Avenue advertising firm to help them develop a campaign to raise awareness of child poverty in the public's consciousness.

The campaign was as elaborate as any other such campaign; regrettably, it was also very expensive. The point is that there is an expertise out there that academia needs to tap in its efforts to disseminate research. Corporate foundations provide a vehicle for bringing this expertise to the research world.

Hence, a collaboration between corporate foundations and applied developmental scientists could improve the work of each. Operating foundations then offer a means of testing some of the lessons learned through the collaboration.

UNIVERSITY-COMMUNITY COLLABORATIONS

Beginning with the land grant universities, schools of research and higher education across the country have begun to reach out to the communities in which they reside (Lerner & Simon, 1998). Universities are abandoning the ivy tower image, recognizing both that they have a great deal to contribute to communities and that they have a great deal to learn from their community partners. Numerous examples of university-community collaborations exist, each operating with somewhat different objectives and various approaches (Ralston, Lerner, Mullis, Simerly, & Murray, 1999). A special issue of a journal, *NHSA Dialog* (Vol. 5, No. 2, 2001), has recently appeared that covers this topic.

Business-Community Collaborations

The private sector offers another opportunity for developing collaborations with communities and with academia. In the previous section, I discussed how collaborations between corporate foundations and researchers could benefit each. Here I therefore emphasize collaboration between business and communities.

Already there are numerous examples where businesses have, for example, adopted schools or assumed some other role in the community. For example, in Warren, Ohio, General Motors developed a curriculum that uses real-world engineering problems to help middle schoolers work on math skills; an executive from Verizon chairs the board of a top-performing high school in Wilmington, Delaware (Gregorian, 2000). Corporations, like universities, have a great deal to contribute to communities, not just in financial resources but in expertise and know-how. Similarly, they may learn from communities.

At any rate, corporate foundations are obvious candidates to facilitate the development of business-community collaborations. Operating foundations, with their ability to pursue their own projects, could serve as catalysts for both private sector and university collaborations with the community.

Business Relevant Policy Issues

There are numerous examples of areas where government has not been especially effective in action. Child care and parental leave are two (Zigler, Kagan, & Hall, 1996). In both cases, these needs of families arise because of citizens' participation in the workforce. Hence, business also has some responsibility to assist.

We do not need more research to know the type of out-of-home care that young children need if they are to grow and thrive healthfully. Yet we cannot enact federal standards because of other unrelated political issues such as states' rights (Zigler & Hall, 2000). Here is an opportunity for the private sector, through corporate foundations, to step in and experiment with different strategies by which high-quality care can be provided in a cost-effective way.

Similarly, the United States is the only industrialized country without a well-developed

parental leave policy (Kammerman, 2000). The 1993 FMLA (Family and Medical Leave Act) represents only a token effort that does not benefit the majority of working citizens who become new parents (Zigler & Hall, 2000). One of the major obstacles to a good parental leave policy is the cost to employers, yet other countries have dealt with this issue (Kammerman, 2000). Here, therefore, is another example of an issue in which the private sector should become involved and experiment with different strategies, using the tools of applied developmental science to assess what works, when, for whom, and under what circumstances. Collaborations with community partners provide ideas for what exactly is needed, for community resources that might be developed or strengthened to meet the need, and for strategies that work for both the community and the business.

Perhaps the most obvious area where a collaboration of the private sector and communities is needed is in education, job training, provision of jobs, and management of the school to work transition. Some years ago, I participated in a Commission on the Workforce of the 21st Century established by Mayor David Dinkins of New York City. The message from the private sector was clear. We need a new three R's in education: reasoning, responsibility, and relationships (Hamburg, 1993). We need employees who can communicate, work in groups, work independently, and continue to learn across the life span, as jobs inevitably will change. With the exception of a few isolated reform efforts, education, including teacher training programs, have not yet gotten this message. The private sector should take some responsibility for molding public education to meet its needs.

Business has been somewhat effective at attending to education, job training, and the school-to-work transition for education and jobs at the high end. It needs now to attend equally to the disadvantaged members of our society. It needs to assume some responsibility for meeting the job needs of the population, as an increasing number of individuals are being transitioned from welfare to work, and for providing the training that they will inevitably need. The government cannot do this alone. One clear problem faced by this country is the increasing gap between the rich and the poor. Wilson (1987) dramatically documents the plight of the inner-city poor. Business, of course, is ultimately responsible for this situation through the mechanisms by which revenue is generated and work is rewarded. Perhaps as a result, it has a clear responsibility to use its corporate philanthropy to attend to the needs of the poor. It is by no means clear how to achieve this end at the same time that business must also worry about economic growth and the general economic climate, but it is essential that they do so. And it is much easier to attend when economic conditions are favorable.

Most of our antipoverty programs have been oriented to fixing individuals. A new experiment, New Hope in Milwaukee, Wisconsin, sought not to change poor individuals so that they themselves could improve their lives, but simply gave them the resources they needed to survive healthfully. Initial findings from this study show that it has much more positive impacts on children than the previous forms of antipoverty programs (Huston et al., 2001). This is a government-based social program, but the private sector has the means to launch and test other such experiments.

Hence, collaborations of communities and businesses, facilitated by corporate philanthropy, could provide another model, such as university-community collaborations, of mechanisms for achieving social change and for learning as we act.

PROMOTING POSITIVE YOUTH DEVELOPMENT

Across the past decades, a great deal of effort has been devoted to preventing problems in youth or to fixing problems once they occur. Delinquency and crime, high-risk sexual behavior, school failure, substance abuse, and teen pregnancy are among the problems tackled from this perspective. Efforts have met with mixed success. Recently a new approach has evolved. This new view aims to promote positive youth development (Larsen, 2000). The idea is that all youth have needs, which must be met if the youth are to develop successfully into productive, happy adults. Youth vary in the extent to which their needs are met by the resources naturally available to them (in terms of family, school, community) (Sherrod, 1997). This view reorients our approach to both research and policy. Rather than trying to fix kids or prevent individual problems, we assess environments and try to fix them. A number of efforts are already under way to identify the assets of youth and their environments (Benson, Leffert, Scales, & Blyth, 1998; Benson, Scales, Leffert, & Roehlkepartain, 1999).

Giving Youth Responsibility: Youth Philanthropy

One important aspect of this work is giving youth some significant type of adult responsibility. One form is youth philanthropy in which young people are provided or earn resources, which they then distribute philanthropically to projects improving their schools or communities. One example is a program initially based in New York City, CommonCents. Run by Teddy Gross, this project rallied youth to collect pennies throughout the city. Pennies are sufficiently worthless that most people discard them.

515

These New York City youth raised hundreds of thousands of dollars collecting pennies. The funds were allocated to small philanthropies run by the youth in their schools. Other students applied for funds for projects ranging from improving school property or organizing an activity to helping the homeless and hungry. Independent foundations, such as the Kellogg Foundation in Battle Creek, Michigan, have contributed to the development and growth of youth philanthropy in Michigan and throughout the country. Initial research shows that such efforts contribute both to youth development and to the improvement and smooth functioning of the organization (Topitzes, Camino, & Zeldin, 2001).

Keeping Policies Developmentally Appropriate

Corporate and operating foundations have a particular role to play in this new arena of promoting positive youth development. Too much of our attention to policies for children, youth, and families is driven by ideological factors, not by developmental needs. The growth of mass public schooling in this country is one example. The Carnegie Corporation report, *Turning Points* (1989), documents how middle schools, Grades 6 to 9, which arose due to the need to split up schools as a result of growth in size, conflict with the developmental needs of teens. Preadolescents must experience a school change at the same time that they face the multiple transformations of puberty. Change confounds change. Philanthropy can ensure that developmental needs guide policy formation for children and youth. The private sector and corporate foundations are less driven by ideology because they are not accountable to a public constituency. (Corporations are, of course, accountable to their shareholders, but this constituency is typically interested in economic issues—perhaps with

the exception of socially responsible investing.) Because they are not accountable to a public constituency with ideas about how things should be done, corporations are in a particularly strong position to make sure that what we do for children and youth is driven by this new developmentally informed perspective oriented to promoting positive development.

Relevance to Early Development

To date, this new developmental view oriented to promoting development rather than fixing problems has been focused on youth. One question is whether it is equally relevant to early development. Corporate foundations, through concerns for issues such as child care and parental leave, should be concerned with early development, as with youth. Hence, they would be perfect candidates to explore the relevance to early development. To some extent, the overarching concern in early development for maturation and brain growth lends itself to this new developmental orientation.

CIVIC ENGAGEMENT

We enjoy a renewed attention to civic engagement in this country, following a hiatus of almost two decades (Flanagan & Sherrod, 1998). This new attention is fueled in part by the writing of Robert Putnam (1996, 2000) arguing that we are now "bowling alone" in that we face a crisis in this country in terms of civic engagement—especially in regard to youth. There is a new thrust of research on the development of civic engagement; in recent years, there have appeared two special issues of journals on the topic (Flanagan & Sherrod, 1998; Neimi, 1999). Schools are once again attending to the topic; the American Political Science Association has formed a task force on civics education.

Corporate Philanthropy as Model of Civic Engagement

Corporate foundations are important to this effort because they represent models of civic engagement. Corporations, like individuals, have some responsibility to participate in the life of society above and beyond their provision of products and services and contributions to the economy. They are important players through lobbying and other such efforts in the policymaking process. And with increasing globalization, they become international citizens with responsibilities to multiple nation-states. The philanthropic side of business represents the most direct way in which corporations can step outside their business and act as citizens. Not only do they contribute directly to society through their philanthropic efforts, but their behavior can also serve as a model for other organizations and other sectors of society.

They can also contribute to the civic engagement of individuals by promoting and assisting with their civic behavior. Campaigns to encourage employees to vote, mentoring programs between employees and needy young people, training programs to assist youth with making the transition to work, and assisting employees with child care and parental responsibilities are just a few of the ways that corporations can contribute to the civic engagement of private citizens, their employees. Corporate foundations can assist by working directly with their corporation in establishing programs and by offering guidance to businesses that are not large enough to have a philanthropic side.

The Delay of Adulthood

One problem faced by youth that is particularly serious for civic engagement is the increasing delay between childhood and adult responsibilities. Children are maturing at earlier ages than ever before, and they are getting involved in some adult behaviors such as sexuality and substance use at younger ages. Yet the assumption of adult responsibilities such as parenthood (with the exception of the minority of teen parents), stable employment, and economic independence is occurring at older and older ages (Sherrod, 1996; Sherrod, Haggerty, & Featherman, 1993). It is interesting, therefore, that when asked what it means to be an adult, youth mention psychological characteristics such as the ability to experience intimacy rather than the traditional milestone events (Arnett, 2000). There are, however, opportunities for civic engagement at youthful ages. Youth can vote at 18, but an increasing number do not (McLeod, 2000). They can participate in political campaigns. They can work in their communities. There are numerous opportunities. In fact, one reason for the outcry about the lack of youth involvement is that they do not sufficiently take advantage of such opportunities. The private sector and corporate philanthropy can mobilize youth. They do not have an ax to grind regarding civic engagement, as do politicians. Hence, there is little reason for youth to be cynical about their efforts. They may, therefore, be able to reengage youth where other efforts have failed. Certainly businesses popular with youth—music, sports, entertainment, and clothing, for example—can at least capture their attention. Two good examples of this are work by MTV and Nickelodeon. MTV's project, Get Out and Vote, seems to have been noticed by youth. The impact on the youth vote is hard to ascertain because there was no research done on it. Similarly, Nickelodeon's child vote campaign was targeted to younger children. The Robert Wood Johnson Foundation funded a series of programs aired on MTV on ways to prevent STD infection; they were very widely watched programs. There is insufficient research on these efforts to make statements about impact, but it is clear that they captured the attention of children and youth because they were projects of corporations that already command youth attention.

Exercising Social Responsibility

Regardless of the approach it takes or the topic it chooses to address, businesses needs to demonstrate that they are responsible public citizens. There is really no reason that government must bear the sole responsibility of attending to social services and the social good. In fact, philanthropy continues to function in part because it recognizes that government alone cannot shoulder this burden. Business should display some civic responsibility by attending to this set of issues. One can argue that citizens contribute to business through their purchase of goods and loyalty to brands in the same way that they pay taxes. Hence, it is by no means unreasonable to argue that business has some social responsibility. Corporate philanthropy is the obvious manifestation of this civic responsibility.

The issue then arises whether government, philanthropy, and the private sector should assume different responsibilities for the social good. To some extent, philanthropy, because it has, despite its growth, less funds than government, sees its role as experimenting—testing

new models and new ideas. This is questionable but it is one view. Business might attend to those issues that directly affect it. Child care, parental leave, and education are three that I have previously discussed. My point here is that business has some social responsibility to attend to some set of such issues. Corporate philanthropy is one vehicle for doing so, but it need not be the only one.

IN CONCLUSION

In this chapter, I have argued that corporate and operating foundations, particularly corporate foundations through their representation of the private sector, have a particular contribution to make in regard to the promotion of the development of children, youth, families, and communities. Science, philanthropy, government, and the private sector need to join forces to pursue this aim—to create meaningful social change that improves the well-being of children, youth, and families. Children and youth truly are our future and, hence, should be treated as our most precious resource. Only through the concerted and conjoint efforts of all constituencies can we maximize the potential of this future.

REFERENCES

Arnett, J. (2000). Emerging adulthood: A theory of development from the late teens through the twenties. *American Psychologist, 55,* 469–480.

Bandura, A. (1992). A social cognitive approach to the exercise of control over AIDS infection. In R. J. DiClemente (Ed.), *Adolescents and AIDS: A generation in jeopardy.* Newbury Park, CA: Sage.

Benson, P., Leffert, N., Scales, P., & Blyth, D. (1998). Beyond the village rhetoric: Creating healthy communities for children and adolescents. *Applied Developmental Science, 2,* 138–159.

Benson, P., Scales, P., Leffert, N., & Roehlkepartain, E. (1999). *A fragile foundation: The state of developmental assets among American youth.* Minneapolis, MN: Search Institute.

Cahan, E. D. (1986). *William T. Grant Foundation: The first fifty years, 1936–1986*. New York: William T. Grant Foundation.

Carnegie Council on Adolescent Development. (1989). *Turning points: Preparing American youth for the 21st century*. New York: Carnegie Corporation of New York.

Fisher, C., & Lerner, R. (Eds.). (1994). *Applied developmental psychology*. New York: McGraw-Hill.

Flanagan, C., & Sherrod, L. R. (1998, Fall). Political development: Growing up in a global community. A special issue of the *Journal of Social Issues, 54*.

Gregorian, V. (2000). Some reflections on the historic roots, evolution, and future of American philanthropy. Report of the President. *Annual Report of the Carnegie Corporation of New York*. New York: Carnegie Corporation.

Hall, P. D. (1988). Private philanthropy and public policy: A historical appraisal. In R. Payton, M. Novak, B. O'Connell, & P. Hall (Eds.), *Philanthropy: Four views*. New Brunswick, NJ: Transaction Books.

Hamburg, B. A. (1993). President's Report: New Futures for the "Forgotten Half": Realizing Unused Potential for Learning and Productivity. *Annual Report of the William T. Grant Foundation*. New York: William T. Grant Foundation.

Hollister, R., & Hill, J. (1995). Problems in the evaluation of community-wide initiatives. In J. Connell, A. Kubisch, L. Schor, & C. Weiss (Eds.), *New approaches to evaluating community initiatives: Concepts, methods, contexts*. Washington, DC: The Aspen Institute.

Huston, A. (2002). My life as a policy researcher. In A. Higgins (Ed.), *Influential lives: New directions for child development*. San Francisco: Jossey-Bass.

Huston, A., Duncan, G., Granger, R., Bos, J. McLoyd, V., Mistry, R., et al. (2001). Work-based anti-poverty programs for parents can enhance the school performance and social behavior of children. *Child Development, 72*, 318–336.

Kammerman, S. (2000). Parental leave policies: An essential ingredient in early childhood education and care policies. *Social Policy Reports, 14* (2).

Katz, B., & Katz, S. (1981). The American private philanthropic foundation and the public sphere, 1890–1930. *Minerva, 19*, 236–269.

Larsen, R. (2000). Toward a psychology of positive youth development. *American Psychologist, 55*, 170–183.

Lerner, R., & Simon, L. (Eds.). (1998). *Creating the new outreach university for America's youth and families: Building university-community collaborations in the 21st century*. New York: Garland.

McLeod, J. (2000). Media and civic socialization of youth. *Journal of Adolescent Health, 27*, 45–51.

Nason, J. (1989). *Foundation trusteeship: Service in the public interest*. New York: The Foundation Center.

Neimi, R. (1999). Editor's introduction. *Political Psychology, 20*, 471–476.

Prewitt, K. (1980). The council and the usefulness of the social sciences. *Annual Report of the President, 1979–1980*. New York: Social Science Research Council.

Prewitt, K. (1995). *Social sciences and private philanthropy: The quest for social relevance* (Essays on Philanthropy, No. 15. Series on Foundations and Their Role in American Life). Indianapolis, IN: Indiana University Center on Philanthropy.

Putnam, R. (1996). The strange disappearance of civic America. *The American Prospect*, 34–48.

Putnam, R. (2000). *Bowling alone: The collapse and revival of American community*. New York: Simon and Schuster.

Ralston, P., Lerner, R., Mullis, A., Simerly, C., & Murray, J. (Eds.). (1999). *Social change, public policy, and community collaboration: Training human development professionals for the twenty first century.* Norwell, MA: Kluwer.

Renz, L., & Lawrence, S. (1993). *Foundation giving: Yearbook of facts and figures on private, corporate, and community foundations.* New York: The Foundation Center.

Sherrod, L. R. (1996). Leaving home: The role of individual and familial factors. In "Leaving Home," a special issue of *New Directions in Child Development, 71,* 111–119. San Francisco: Jossey-Bass.

Sherrod, L. (1997). Promoting youth development through research-based policies. *Applied Developmental Science, 1,* 17–27.

Sherrod, L. R. (1998). The common pursuits of modern philanthropy and the proposed outreach university: Enhancing research and education. In R. Lerner & L. Simon (Eds.), *Creating the new outreach university for America's youth and families: Building university-community collaborations for the 21st century.* New York: Garland.

Sherrod, L. R. (1999a). Giving child development knowledge away: Using university-community partnerships to disseminate research on children, youth and families. *Applied Developmental Science, 3,* 228–234.

Sherrod, L. R. (1999b). An historical overview of philanthropy: Funding opportunities for research in applied developmental science. In P. Ralston, R. Lerner, A. Mullis, C. Simerly, & J. Murray (Eds.), *Social change, public policy, and community collaboration: Training human development professionals in the twenty first century.* Norwell, MA: Kluwer.

Sherrod, L. R. (2002). The psychologist's role in setting a policy agenda for children. In A. Higgins (Ed.), *Influential lives: New directions for child development.* San Francisco: Jossey-Bass.

Sherrod, L. R., Haggerty, R. J., & Featherman, D. L. (1993). Late adolescence and the transition to adulthood: An introduction. *Journal of Research on Adolescence, 3*(3), 217–226.

Topitzes, D., Camino, L., & Zeldin, S. (2001). *A study of youth philanthropy and teen court programs in Jefferson County: Developmental processes and youth outcomes.* Madison: University of Wisconsin.

Wilson, W. J. (1987). *The truly disadvantaged.* Chicago: University of Chicago Press.

Wisely, S. (1998, Winter). The pursuit of a virtuous people. *Advancing Philanthropy,* 14–20.

Zigler, E., & Hall, N. (2000). *Child development and social policy.* New York: McGraw-Hill.

Zigler, E., Kagan, S., & Hall, N. (1996). *Children, families, and government: Preparing for the 21st century.* Cambridge, England: University of Cambridge Press.

Author Index

Martinez, E. A., 144
Martin Korpi, B., 449
Martinson, K., 259, 448, 449
Martland, N., 14
Mason, M. A., 461
Massachusetts Department of
    Education, 448
Masse, L., 438
Masten, A., 14, 203, 279
Maszk, P., 275
Matheson, P., 186
Mathieson, D. H., 425
Matte, T. D., 484
Mattis, J. S., 145
Matus-Grossman, L., 282, 283
Maurer, D., 46
Mayer, S. E., 274, 276
Maynard, R., 88
Maynard, R. A., 283, 284
McAdoo, H. P.,16, 142, 143, 144,
    145, 150, 190
McAlpin, J. P., 148
McBride, B. A., 190, 192
McBride, M. C., 36
McBride, R. J., 192
McCall, R. B., 4, 18
McCarthy, M. E., 181, 182
McCarton, C. M., 423
McClelland, G., 365
McClelland, P., 401
McCloud, B., 231
McCollum, J. A., 380
McConnell, M., 167
McConnell, S. K., 33, 35, 39
McConnochie, K. H., 423, 427
McCormick, M. C., 423
McCrary, C., 273
McCroskey, J., 461, 473
McCubbin, H. I., 381, 387
McCubbin, L., 3, 19, 113
McCullough, M. E., 64
McDevitt, 337
McDonald, D. S., 424
McFarlane, E. C., 295
McGillicuddy-De Lisi, A., 161,
    207, 208
McGourthy, T., 97
McGuigan, W., 102
McHale, J., 167
McHale, S. M., 383
McInnis, D., 488
McKinney, M. H., 10
McLanahan, S. S., 183, 184, 187,
    188, 190
McLaughlin, M., 388
McLeod, J., 516
McLeod, J. D., 275, 278
McLoyd, V. C., 3, 14, 203, 272,
    273, 276, 278,
    401, 430
McMahon, P., 259

McNeil, J. T., 422
McNeilly-Choque, M. K., 182
McPherson, M., 284
McQuiston, S., 181, 182
McRoy, R. G., 295
Meehan, E. J., 490
Meeks, C. B., 489
Meeks, L. F., 147
Meeks, W. A., 147
Meezan, W., 461
Mehler, J., 47, 98
Meinert, C. L., 423
Meisels, S. J., 379
Melamed, B. G., 162
Melaville, A., 230, 232,
    234, 240, 336
Melby, J. N., 278
Mellon, J., 63
Melnick, S., 238
Melton, D. A., 32
Melton, G. B., 115, 116, 118, 119
Menke, E. M., 485, 486
Meranze, M., 356
Merriam-Webster, 440, 441
Merzenich, M. M., 47
Meszaros, P. S., 4
Metcalf, K. K., 147
Metha, A. T., 64
MetLife Survey of the American
    Teacher, 231
Meyer, E. C., 385
Meyer, H. J., 186
Meyers, A., 483, 491
Meyers, K. A., 468
Meyers, M., 439
Meyers, M. K., 270, 280
Mezey, J., 261
Michael, R. T., 270, 271, 272
Michalopoulos, C., 276, 282,
    287, 430
Michel, A. E., 40
Micklewright, J., 273
Miech, R. A., 275
Mikulic, B., 273
Mikulich, S. K., 64
Miller, C., 285, 430
Miller, J., 167, 278
Miller, J. E., 274
Miller, J. F., 381
Miller, J. G., 202, 204, 205, 206,
    214, 215, 364, 366, 384, 390
Miller, J. R., 10, 12, 13, 18
Miller, L., 336
Miller, N., 491
Miller, P. C., 162, 278
Miller, P. J., 202, 205, 206, 214
Miller, S. L., 47
Miller-Johnson, S., 420
Miller-Loncar, C. L., 379
Milliken, G. W., 50
Mills, R. J., 273, 275

Minami, H., 386
Mink, I. T., 382
Minton, H., 382
Minuchin, P. P., 379, 382
Miringoff, M., 98
Mishkin, M., 49
Mistry, J., 213, 216, 218
Mistry, R., 276, 430
Mitchell, A., 440, 446, 448
Mitchell, S., 250
Mize, J., 182
Moen, P., 401
Moffitt, T. E., 275
Molliver, M. E., 41
Montgomery, I., 357
Montgomery, L. E., 149
Moore, K. A., 82, 89, 96, 97, 99,
    156, 157, 250
Moorehouse, M., 97
Mora, J. O., 290
Morelli, G., 209, 210, 385
Morenoff, J., 97
Morgan, G., 440, 449
Morison, P., 279
Morris, P., 96, 295, 430, 472
Morris, P. A., 4, 276, 287
Morrison, F. J., 12
Mortimer, A., 97
Morton, K. L., 118
Mosher-Williams, R., 332
Mosier, C., 213, 216
Mosley, J., 184
Mosteller, F., 150
Moynihan, D. P., 148
Mrazek, P. J., 64
Msall, M., 89
Mukamel, D. B., 291
Müller, F., 38
Mullin, C., 287
Mullis, A., 512
Mullis, N., 188
Mundfrom, D. J., 423
Mundfrom, D. M., 274
Munoz, R. F., 64, 65
Murphey, D., 99
Murphy, B. C., 275
Murphy, D., 192
Murphy, J. M., 273
Murphy, M., 66
Murray, C. J. L., 65
Murray, J., 512
Murray, J. P., 3, 7, 8, 11, 12, 13,
    18, 113, 114
Musselman, D. L., 64
Mussen, P. H., 8
Mustillo, S., 98
Mutter, J. D., 202

Nagarajan, S. S., 47
Nagel, R., 384
Naifeh, M., 146

Subject Index

Microcephaly, 44
Microencephaly, 34-35
Microgyria, 36
Millionaires, number of, 506
Million Mom March contact information, 347
Milwaukee New Hope project, 430
Minnesota Children's Report Card Web site, 109
Minnesota Family Independence Program, 430
Minnesota Family Investment Program, 285
Monitoring the Future, 91, 92, 102
    Web site, 109
Morella, Connie, 342
Mothers Against Drunk Driving contact
    information, 347
Mothers' pensions, 461
Motor and somatosensory systems, experience
    and,45, 49-51
Movement to Leave No Child Behind, 338-339
    mission, 339
Moving to Opportunity (MTO) demonstration
    project, 293, 487, 488
Multisystemic Therapy program (SC), 365

National Alliance for the Mentally Ill, 340
    contact information, 348
National Assessment of Educational Progress,
    86, 91, 92, 102
    Web site, 109
National Association for the Education of Young
    Children, 440, 447, 449
National Association of Child Advocates contact
    information, 348
National Association of Practitioners, 192
National Black Child Development Institute, 6
National Center for Children in Poverty, 287, 300
National Center for Education Statistics, 92
National Center for Strategic Nonprofit Planning
    and Community Leadership, 192
National Center on Families and Fathers, 192
National Child Abuse and Neglect Data System
    (NCANDS), 94
    Web site, 109
National Council on Family Relations, 6
National Crime Victimization Survey, 91
    Web site, 110
National Education Goals Report, 95
    Web site, 110
National Education Goals Panel, 82, 86, 95
National Education Goals 2000, 92
National Education Longitudinal Survey 1988, 100
    Web site, 110
National Governor's Association's Center for Best
    Practices, early care and education and, 450
National Health and Nutrition Examination
    Survey, 91
    Web site, 110
National Health Information Survey (NHIS), 90
National Health Interview Survey, 82, 99, 102
    Web site, 110

National Household Education Survey (NHES),
    91, 92, 101
    Web site, 110
National Household Survey of Drug Abuse, 91
    Web site, 110
National Immunization Survey (NIS), 93
    Web site, 110
National Institute for Drug Abuse (NIDA), 93
National Institute of Health, 18
National Institute of Mental Health, 62
National Juvenile Defender Center, 371
National Longitudinal Survey of Adolescent
    Health, 92, 100
    Web site, 110
National Longitudinal Survey of Youth 1997
    Cohort, 92, 99, 100, 277
    HOME inventory, 276, 277
    Web site, 110
National Neighborhood Indicators Project (NNIP),
    96, 103
    Web site, 110
National Partnership for Women and Children, 343
National Partnership for Women and Families, 346
    contact information, 348
National Resource Center for Youth Development
    contact information, 348
National Science Foundation, 121
National Surveys of Families and Households, 92
    Web site, 110
National Task Force on Applied Developmental
    Science, 6, 13
    definition of applied developmental science, 6-7
    goals, 6
National Youth Tobacco Survey (NYTS), 93
    Web site, 110
Nation at Risk, A, 227
Native Americans, 142, 143
    health care access, 150
    population figures, 143
Neural plasticity, 44-55
    anatomical change, 45
    developmental versus adult, 53-55
    experience-dependent system and, 45
    experience-expectant system and, 44-45
    metabolic change, 45
    neurobiological mechanisms underlying, 45-53
    neurochemical change, 45
    See also Brain injury, experience and; Learning
        and memory, experience and; Linguistic
        development, experience and; Motor and
        somatosensory systems, experience and;
        Visual development, experience and
Neural tube defects, 32
    folic acid deficiency and, 44
    See also specific neural tube defects
New Chance demonstration program, 283, 284-285,
    423-424, 426
    age at start of program, 409
    child outcomes, 418

About the Editors

Richard M. Lerner is Bergstrom Chair in Applied Developmental Science and Director of the Applied Developmental Science Institute in the Eliot-Pearson Department of Child Development at Tufts University. A developmental psychologist, he received a Ph.D. in 1971 from the City University of New York. He has been a fellow at the Center for Advanced Study in the Behavioral Sciences and is a fellow of the American Association for the Advancement of Science, the American Psychological Association, and the American Psychological Society. Prior to joining Tufts, he was on the faculty and held administrative posts at Michigan State University, Pennsylvania State University, and Boston College, where he was the Anita L. Brennan professor of education and the director of the Center for Child, Family, and Community Partnerships. During the 1994-1995 academic year, he held the Tyner eminent scholar chair in the human sciences at Florida State University. He is the author or editor of 59 books and more than 380 scholarly articles and chapters. He edited Volume 1, on *Theoretical Models of Human Development,* for the fifth edition of the *Handbook of Child Psychology.* He is the founding editor of the *Journal of Research on Adolescence* and of *Applied Developmental Science.* He is known for his theory of, and research about, relations between life span human development and contextual or ecological change. He has done foundational studies of adolescents' relations with their peer, family, school, and community contexts and is a leader in the study of public policies and community-based programs aimed at the promotion of positive youth development.

Francine Jacobs, Ed.D., is Associate Professor at Tufts University, with a joint appointment in the Eliot-Pearson Department of Child Development and the Department of Urban and Environmental Policy and Planning. Her research and teaching interests are primarily in the area of child and family policy—child welfare and protection, child care and early childhood education, family support, and community-based initiatives—and in program evaluation. During her time at Tufts, she has been the principal investigator for numerous grants, with projects ranging from coordinating an early childhood community planning process in Boston to developing an evaluation process for state family preservation programs. Her current project is a multiyear evaluation of a universal home visiting program for teen mothers, Healthy Families Massachusetts. In addition to her teaching and research, she has served on several advisory committees for child and family service organizations and research studies and was recently a member of the National Academy of Sciences' Committee on Family and Work Policies. She graduated from Brandeis University and received her master's and doctoral degrees from Harvard University. Prior to joining the Tufts faculty in 1986, she directed two early childhood programs and was the associate director and director of research at the Harvard Family Research Project. She also maintained an active program evaluation practice, consulting for numerous organizations on the planning and conduct of evaluation activities. She has lectured and written extensively about program evaluation and about child and family policy. Her two coedited volumes, *Evaluating Family Programs* and *More Than Kissing Babies: Current Child and Family Policy in the United States,* focus on these areas.

Donald Wertlieb, Ph.D., is Professor and former Chairman of the Eliot-Pearson Department of Child Development. He is an applied developmental scientist with a background in clinical-developmental and pediatric psychology. His major research interests are understanding the complex processes by which children and families cope with stressors such as marital separation and divorce and chronic illness. In addition to his basic research, he conducts program evaluations of community partnerships and other collaborations. He was recently funded by the National Cancer Institute to develop a multimedia interactive health education curriculum aimed at preventing drug, alcohol, and nicotine abuse by young people. He served on the steering group of the National Forum on the Future of Children and Families and was president of the Society of Pediatric Psychology (1996-1999), a professional membership organization of about 1,000 scholars and practitioners committed to the improvement of health care research and services for children and families. He has been interim chairman of the Department of Education at Tufts and a lecturer in the Department of Social Medicine and Health Policy at Harvard Medical School. His undergraduate education and first master's degree are from Tufts. He is a graduate of the Clinical and Community Psychology Program at Boston University. Prior to joining the Tufts faculty, he served on the faculty of the Judge Baker Guidance Center.

Contributors

J. Lawrence Aber
New York University

MaryLee Allen
Children's Defense Fund

William Blackwell
Massachusetts Department of Education

Martin J. Blank
Institute for Educational Leadership

Marc H. Bornstein
*National Institute of Child Health and
Human Development*

Rachel G. Bratt
Tufts University

Brett V. Brown
Child Trends

Natasha Cabrera
University of Maryland

Mary I. Campa-Muller
Cornell University

Jeffrey Capizzano
Urban Institute

Jana H. Chadhuri
Tufts University

Susan S. Chuang
*National Institute of Child Health and
Human Development*

Virginia Diez
Tufts University

John Eckenrode
Cornell University

Celia B. Fisher
Fordham University

Melissa Ganley
National PTA

Elizabeth Thompson Gershoff
University of Michigan

Jane E. Gillham
University of Pennsylvania

Penny Hauser-Cram
Boston College

Angela Howell
Boston College

Charles Izzo
Cornell University

Sheri DeBoe Johnson
Institute for Educational Leadership

Sharon Lynn Kagan
Columbia University

Alan Martin
Michigan State University

Susanne Martinez
Planned Parenthood Federation of America

Hariette P. McAdoo
Michigan State University

Jacquelyn McCroskey
University of Southern California

Jayanthi Mistry
Tufts University

Kristin Moore
Child Trends

Charles A. Nelson
University of Minnesota

Michelle J. Neuman
Columbia University

C. Cybele Raver
University of Chicago

Robert G. Schwartz
Juvenile Law Center

Martin E. P. Seligman
University of Pennsylvania

Bela Shah
National League of Cities

Andrew J. Shatté
University of Pennsylvania

Lonnie R. Sherrod
Fordham University

Matthew Stagner
Urban Institute